MW01044825

Sages of the Talmud

SAGES OF THE TALMUD

THE LIVES, SAYINGS, AND STORIES OF 400 RABBINIC MASTERS

MORDECHAI JUDOVITS

URIM PUBLICATIONS

Jerusalem • New York

Sages of the Talmud: The Lives, Sayings, and Stories of 400 Rabbinic Masters
By Mordechai Judovits
Copyright © 2009 Mordechai Judovits
All rights reserved. No part of this book may be used or reproduced in any manner whatsoever without written permission from the copyright owner, except in the case of brief quotations embodied in reviews and articles.
Printed in Israel. First Edition.
ISBN 13: 978-965-524-035-1
Urim Publications
P.O. Box 52287, Jerusalem 91521 Israel

Lambda Publishers Inc.
527 Empire Blvd., Brooklyn, New York 11225 U.S.A.
Tel: 718-972-5449 Fax: 718-972-6307, mh@ejudaica.com

www.UrimPublications.com

This Sefer "Sages of the Talmud" is being dedicated in honor of the Judovits Family

My אשת חיל
העגשא בת יוסף צבי
Helen Judovits

And to my son
שפרה and his wife שלמה
Robert Judovits & Shifra Judovits

And to my son
יוסף צבי and his wife חנה לאה
Lawrence Judovits & Nancy Judovits

And to my daughter
יהושע and her husband נחמה ריזל טובא
Joyce Israel & Ricky David Israel

And to my grandchildren:
שאול and her husband מיה יעל
Mayah Judovits Elkouss & Paul Elkouss

טליה רחל
Talya Rachel Judovits

עמית יפעת
Amete Yifat Judovits

שלמה
Benjamin Gregory Judovits

רבקה
Emily Rebecca Judovits

נח משה
Noah Alexander Israel

יונה אברהם
Jonah Oliver Israel

And to our great-grandson
מרדכי אריה
Mordechai Aryeh Elkouss

This Sefer "Sages of the Talmud" is being dedicated in loving memory
of the Judovits and Jakubovits Family

My Parents
ר' שלמה בן מרדכי   and   נחמה ריזל בת הרב משה
Who died in the Holocaust around June 1944, corresponding to around שבועות תש"ד

My Brothers and Sister
משה   מנחם מענדל   מאטל לאה
Who died in the Holocaust in the year 1944, corresponding to the year תש"ד

And to the loving memory of my wife's parents
ר' יוסף צבי בן משה וואלף   and   טובא בת יוסף משה
Who died in the Holocaust around June 1944, corresponding to around שבועות תש"ד

My wife's Brothers and Sister
מרדכי   יצחק   רחל יוטא
Who died in the Holocaust in the year 1944, corresponding to the year תש"ד

תנצבה

CONTENTS

FOREWORD

As a young student studying the Talmud I became familiar with the names of the Talmud's authors as they appeared on its pages. But even then, I often wondered about the lives of those sages. In what century did they live? What was the world like in their time?

On many of the Talmud's pages, the names of R. Hillel, R. Yohanan b. Zakkai, R. Akiva, R. Hiyya, Rav, Abbaye and R. Pappa appear in close proximity to each other. Did they all live at the same time? Certainly not – they have lived hundreds of years apart. Yet most students have no idea when they lived, where they lived or who their contemporaries were. The Talmud's text gives the contemporary student no clue as to whether a particular sage was the head of an academy or one of the many people who attended it.

This book is not a complicated Talmudic pilpul, which usually is true regarding books written about the Talmud. Rather, it is a simple recording of stories, anecdotes and sayings of the sages as recorded in the Talmud, its purpose is to make it easier for students to get to know the tannaim and the amoraim. All the quotations that appear in this book are fully cited. The anecdotes and stories appear in order to give the student an idea in what kind of social environment the sages lived. Similarly, I have included the contemporary history of the region – in other words, that of the Roman Empire and its early successors – so that the student may know the political climate of that time.

As a student of the Talmud, I always felt awe and admiration towards its authors. I have had the privilege of finishing the Talmud twice in my lifetime, in addition to many tractates, which I studied during my younger years in the yeshiva.

Therefore, it is with utmost humility and trepidation that I undertook to write this book. I did so because I felt that other students might have the same curiosity about the sages that I have.

On a more personal level: as a Holocaust survivor, I know something about persecution and what life is like under oppressive regimes. These giants of the Talmud labored under the harshest conditions, defying the authorities, risking all sorts of threats and dangers in order to preserve our heritage and to pass it on to us and our children. It is because of their dedication, sacrifices and even martyrdom that you and I are able to study the Talmud today. The least we can do is to know something about them.

Mordechai Judovits
May 8, 2008

INTRODUCTION

THE TALMUD has been a subject of study for over two thousand years. Jewish scholars have immersed themselves in the pages of the Talmud in every generation ever since it was created and compiled by the great rabbis in the land of Israel and in Babylonia.

It is not an easy subject to study. Students must have a keen mind and patience in order to master its intricacies. But once you have studied the Talmud for a while, you can't let go. It becomes addictive.

The Talmud encourages questioning. The text itself is full of questions – and questions upon questions – which the rabbis attempt to answer. If they are not satisfied with the answer they search for other answers until they find a satisfactory explanation.

The Talmud is usually studied with a partner or in a group. When one studies with a partner, the two are usually at an equal level of understanding the subject, though sometimes one of them is the teacher. In group study, there is always a seasoned teacher. During study sessions, the students ask questions about anything that might be puzzling to them, whether about the meaning of the text, the logic of the statement, or a contradiction.

Questioning is the way of the Gemara, as is illustrated in the following story (*Baba Metzia* 84a):

Rabbi Yohanan and Resh Lakish were close friends and regular study partners. When Resh Lakish died, R. Yohanan's grief was so profound that he became deeply depressed. The rabbis sent R. Eleazar b. Pedat to study with him and to comfort him.

As the two men studied together, R. Eleazar supported R. Yohanan's every statement with, "You are correct. There is a *baraita* that supports you."

"You are no replacement for Resh Lakish," Rabbi Yohanan complained. "When I stated a law, Resh Lakish raised twenty-four objections, to which I gave twenty-four answers. This led to a full understanding of the law. But you tell me that a baraita supports me. Don't I know myself that what I said is correct? I want more. I want to be challenged."

R. Yohanan rent his clothing and wept. "Where are you, Resh Lakish? Where are you, Resh Lakish?" he cried. Eventually, he died of grief.

Who is Rabbi Yehuda or Rabbi Shimon?

Let us examine the Talmud with our own questions, which need to be answered.

What is the Talmud?

Who are its authors?

Frequently, the Talmud refers to a tanna or an amora by his first name only – for example, "Rabbi Yehuda said," "Rabbi Yosi said," "Rabbi Shimon said." Since many rabbis mentioned in the Talmud were called Yehuda, Yosi and Shimon, which Rabbi Yehuda made the statement under discussion, and when did he and the others live?

In what time period did the great Rabbi Hillel live?

Where are the names of Avraham, Moshe, Aharon, David or Shlomo? Why are none of the rabbis of the Talmud named for biblical figures such as Avraham, Moshe, Aharon, David or Shlomo?

While we will address these questions in the next several pages of this introduction, first we must start explaining the workings of the Talmud from the beginning.

The Mishna and the Gemara

The sixty-three volumes of books that comprise the Talmud consist of two distinct parts, the Mishna and the Gemara.

The Mishna

The Mishna, which is written in Hebrew, was created mostly by the rabbis who were known as tannaim. Rabbi Yehuda ha-Nasi (second–third centuries C.E.) was the final redactor of the Mishna.

Yet not all the authors of the Mishna were tannaim. Its earlier authors were known as the Men of the Great Assembly (Anshei Keneseth ha-Gedola). Some of the early authors, who studied in pairs, are known as the *zugot* (pairs).

The Zugot

The following rabbis are known as the zugot of the Talmud:

Yosi ben Yoezer and Yosi ben Yohanan; Yehoshua ben Perachia and Nittai ha-Arbeli; Yehuda ben Tabbai and Shimon ben Shetah; Shemaya and Avtalyon; Hillel and Shammai.

The Gemara

The other component of the Talmud, which is called the Gemara, is written in Aramaic, mixed with Hebrew words. It was authored by the rabbis known as amoraim.

Ashi (fourth century C.E.) and R. Ravina (fourth and fifth centuries C.E.) were the final compilers and editors of the Gemara.

The Talmud is also known as Shas, an acronym for the two words *shisha sedarim* (Hebrew: "six orders"), because the Mishna is divided into six categories of topics. These are subdivided into several books on specific subjects, each of which is called a *masechet* (tractate). The tractates are divided into chapters called *perakim* (singular: *perek*) and then subdivided into smaller units, which are called *mishnayot* (singular: *mishna*).

Each mishna unit is accompanied by a Gemara text that sometimes dissects the mishna word by word and explains its meaning. At other times, when other sources might seem to contradict the mishna in question, the Gemara reconciles the other sources with it.

Who are the rabbis to whom the text refers only by their given names?

A little history is now necessary in order to show how the names of certain tannaim fit into the picture. It will also reveal to which rabbis the Talmud refers when it mentions only their first name.

In 132 C.E., Bar-Kochva led a revolution in Eretz Yisrael against the Roman occupation. Between 400,000 and 580,000 armed men joined him. They fought so successfully that Tinnius Rufus, the governor of Judea under Emperor Hadrian, had to give up fifty strongholds.

Hadrian sent his greatest general, Julius Severus, to Judea. After three years, the revolt faltered and the Romans destroyed 985 towns. Betar, where Bar Kochva made his last stand, fell in 135 C.E.

After the revolt was suppressed, Hadrian issued many harsh decrees in Judea, forbidding the practice of Judaism. Judea was completely defeated. The revolt claimed the lives of 580,000 men, in addition to thousands of women and children who died of starvation. Many others were sold as slaves.

The Sanhedrin was dissolved in 135 C.E. Rabbi Akiva, who had supported the revolution and disobeyed the edict against the teaching of Judaism, was jailed for three years and subsequently put to death.

Hadrian removed the Jewish population from Jerusalem, replacing it with Syrians and Phoenicians. In 136 C.E. he rebuilt Jerusalem, renaming it Aelia Capitolina.

Rabbis ordained at risk of death

When R. Yehuda ben Bava wanted to ordain his students in approximately 136 C.E., there was a decree against it. Tinnius Rufus enforced the ban cruelly, and R. Yehuda ben Bava was martyred during his attempt to defy it.

During the Hadrian persecution, the occupying authorities issued a decree that anyone who ordained a rabbi or received rabbinical ordination would be subject to the death penalty and the city where the ordination took place would be demolished and its boundary posts uprooted. In order to avoid causing the destruction of a city, Rabbi Yehuda b. Bava sat between two great mountains and between the two cities of Usha and Shefaram. Five prominent students sat before him: Rabbi Meir, Rabbi Yehuda, Rabbi Shimon, Rabbi Yosi and Rabbi Eleazar ben Shammua. The ceremony was held and he ordained them. Rabbi Avia adds the name of Rabbi Nehemia to the list of those ordained. As soon as the ceremony was completed, they noticed the Romans approaching. Rabbi Yehuda told his students to flee. "What will happen to you?" his students asked, urging him to flee together with them. "I would cause all of you to be captured," he said. "I am too old to run. I will lie before them like a stone." It was said that the Romans stabbed him three hundred times. It is noteworthy that four out of the five students were named only by their first name. They are the same names repeated later on in the Talmud without the addition of a father's name. (BT *Sanhedrin* 14a)

The following story appears in *Shabbat* 33b.

> Come and listen: When the rabbis entered the Kerem be-Yavne, Rabbi Yehuda, Rabbi Eleazar b. Yosi and Rabbi Shimon were among those persent and a question was raised before them. The speaker who speaks first on all occasions, which was R. Yehuda b. Illai, rose to answer the question.

The Talmud identifies here that R. Yehuda is actually R. Yehuda b. Illai. The Talmud discusses the subject at hand and asks later on why R. Yehuda is called the first speaker on all occasions. In answer, it cites the following story.

R. Yehuda, R. Yosi and R. Shimon were sitting together and a person by the name of Yehuda, a son of proselytes, was sitting next to them. Rabbi Yehuda was telling them how great the works of the Roman occupiers are. They have created roads; they have built bridges and established public baths. R. Yosi listened, but made no comment.

R. Shimon b. Yohai commented: Whatever the Romans have done, they have done for their own benefit. They built markets to have places for their prostitutes, they built bathhouses in order to indulge their bodies and they built bridges in order to levy tolls on them. Yehuda the son of proselytes repeated the discussion to friends and relatives. Eventually it reached the authorities. It was decreed that R. Yehuda, who spoke in praise of the Romans, should be rewarded; that R. Yosi, who was silent, should be held in his own community of Sepphoris, and R. Shimon was condemned to death.

R. Shimon and his son R. Eleazar ran away and hid in the bet midrash. His wife brought them bread and water, but this did not last, because they were worried that the Romans would discover them. They fled to a cave. Miraculously, a carob tree grew near the cave's opening and a well was shown to them. They shed their clothing, sitting naked in the sand up to their neck to keep their clothing from wearing out. They studied all day long and put on their clothes every day only for prayers. They hid in the cave twelve years. Eventually, Eliyahu came to the entrance and called out, "Who will inform the son of Yohai that the emperor is dead and the decrees have been annulled?" When they heard the good news, they emerged from the cave.

In the beginning of the story, Rabbi Shimon is called by his first name only, but later on, he is identified as Rabbi Shimon b. Yohai.

Although the Talmud refers to Rabbi Yosi by his first name only, it is obvious that it is referring to R. Yosi b. Halafta. In the story cited above, he is banished to Sepphoris, the hometown of R. Yosi b. Halafta and the home of his father and family.

These rabbis – Yehuda b. Illai, Shimon b. Yohai, Yosi b. Halafta, Eleazar ben Shammua and Meir – were colleagues and students of Rabbi Akiva and Rabbi Yehuda b. Bava. They emerged after the catastrophe of the failed Bar Kochva revolt in order to reestablish the religious life of a defeated nation. Their opinions and rulings were collected in the Mishna. When they quoted one another they did so using only first names because they were colleagues. When they quoted older sources or other rabbis, they used their full names. Therefore, we can establish the identity of rabbis whom the Talmud quotes according to the following table:

Name	Identity
Rabbi Yehuda	Rabbi Yehuda bar Illai
Rabbi Yosi	Rabbi Yosi ben Halafta
Rabbi Shimon	Rabbi Shimon bar Yohai

When Hadrian died in 138, Antoninus Pius became emperor. The following year, after the Hadrian persecution had subsided somewhat, the students of R. Akiva assembled at Usha to reestablish the halachic authorities and to reinstitute the Sanhedrin. Among those assembled were R. Meir, R. Yehuda b. Illai, R. Yosi b. Halafta and R. Shimon b. Yohai. At a subsequent meeting they elected R. Gamliel as president, R. Nathan as vice president and R. Meir as *hacham*.

When the name R. Eliezer is mentioned on its own, it refers to the tanna R. Eliezer b. Hyrcanus. When the name R. Yoshua is mentioned on its own, it refers to the tanna R. Yoshua b. Hanania. As a rule, when the Talmud mentions the name Eleazar on its own, without a patronymic, it refers to R. Eleazar b. Pedat, an amora of the third century C.E. and head of the academy in Tiberias. A colleague of R. Yohanan b. Nepaha, he should not be confused with the tanna R. Eleazar b. Shammua.

There were several amoraim by the name of Rabba, but when the Talmud mentions the name of Rabbah without a patronymic, it refers to Rabbah b. Nahmeni.

While Rav is the name of the famous leader of the Sura academy, it is also a title for a rabbi, as in "Rav Yehuda." In turn, Rav Yehuda is R. Yehuda b. Yehezkel, the founder and the leader of the academy in Pumbedita – and a student of Rav.

Names such as Avraham, Moshe, Aharon, David or Shlomo do not appear

Earlier, we asked why the tannaim and amoraim do not have traditional, biblical names such as the ones mentioned above.

In answering this question, we must consider the conditions under which they lived. During the entire talmudic period, the Jews endured constant persecution. The people of Israel feared not only the foreign occupiers but also their own leaders, such as the notoriously paranoid King Herod, and even some of the earlier Hasmonean kings, who were insecure regarding their position. Under Syrian and Roman occupation, circumcision was forbidden for many years.

Parents of newborn children had additional reason to fear the authorities. They were already risking a great deal by circumcising their sons. Giving the children traditional Hebrew names constituted an added risk. For example, the name Avraham is significant not only because it belonged to the founder of the Jewish faith, but also because of its association with circumcision. If a child was named Avraham, the authorities would know for certain that he had been circumcised. A child named after Moshe, the greatest Jewish leader, might be considered a threat to anyone who aspired to the kingship. The act of naming a child Aharon might be considered defiance against the high priests who were appointed by the foreign occupiers. To go so far as to name a son after an actual Jewish king, such as David or Shlomo, might be considered an act of outright rebellion.

The above answer is my own. While it is speculative, I believe that it is plausible.

In what time period did the various tannaim and amoraim live?

While the majority of the tannaim lived during the first and second centuries C.E., some of the tannaim who are mentioned in the Mishna lived earlier. The Anshei Keneset ha-Gedola, who preceded the tannaim, were active during the time of Ezra and Nehemia, in approximately the fifth century B.C.E.

The amoraic period, which started in the third century C.E. during Rav's time, lasted until the fifth century. Rav was probably the last of the tannaim and the first of the amoraim. According to the Talmud (*Ketubbot* 8a), Rav may differ because he is also a tanna, even though he is never quoted in the Mishna, where only the tannaim are quoted.

Rabbi Yosi ben Halafta was also very much interested in the time periods of our existence. The authorship of the book *Seder Olam,* a chronological history that begins with creation and ends with the Bar Kochva revolt, is attributed to Rabbi Halafta or to his son, R. Yosi b. Halafta (*Shabbat* 88a, *Yevamot* 82b, *Niddah* 46b): "Come and hear: it was taught in the book of *Seder Olam,*" and so on.

Rav Kahana said: When R. Yishmael b. R. Yosi b. Halafta became sick, the rabbis sent him a request: Tell us two or three things that you heard from your father.

He replied; "One hundred and eighty years before the Temple was destroyed, Eretz Yisrael was occupied by the wicked government. Eighty years before the Temple was destroyed, a rabbinical prohibition of ritual impurity was enacted against certain vessels and people. Forty years before the Temple was destroyed, the Sanhedrin went into exile and moved to the commercial zone of the Temple." (BT *Shabbat* 15a)

The Talmud further states that Hillel and his descendants Shimon, Gamliel and Shimon were the leaders of the Sanhedrin for one hundred years during the Temple's existence. Yosi b. Yoezer Ish Zereda and Yosi b. Yohanan were active much earlier.

Three Rabbis Named Hillel

Three prominent rabbis bore the name Hillel: Rabbi Hillel the Elder, Rabbi Hillel the amora, and Rabbi Hillel the Nasia.

Hillel ha-Zaken (Hillel the Elder, first centuries B.C.E. and C.E.), was the head of the Sanhedrin in Jerusalem. He and Shammai are referred to as one of the zugot of the Talmud.

While Hillel and Shammai had many disagreements about Halacha, they greatly respected each other. In most cases, the school of Shammai was more stringent. Yet tradition has it that both views are correct, and we follow Rabbi Hillel in the majority of halachot.

> Said Rabbi Abba in the name of Rabbi Shemuel: For three years there was a dispute between Bet Shammai and Bet Hillel, each one claiming that Halacha accords with their views. Then a *bat kol* [heavenly voice] was heard announcing that both are the words of the living God, but that Halacha accords with the rulings of Bet Hillel. **(*Eruvin* 13b)**

Hillel the Amora

Hillel the amora (Eretz Yisrael, third century C.E.) was the son of Rabbi Gamliel III and the grandson of Rabbi Yehuda ha-Nasi. He studied in his grandfather's academy (*Bava Batra* 83b) and asked him questions. Rashi comments (*Gittin* 37a) that this Rabbi Hillel was an amora.

Hillel Nasia

Hillel Nasia (Eretz Yisrael, fourth century C.E.), the son of R. Yehuda Nasia, was active as Nasi from approximately 330 to 365 C.E. During his time, the authorities issued harsh decrees against many forms of Jewish observance, including the intercalation of the Jewish months. The Jews had to inform each other in secret of the dates of new months and of Yom Kippur.

Rabbi Hillel came up with a solution. Using a complicated calculation, he created a perpetual Jewish calendar.

Rabbi Shimon b. Lakish said: In ancient times, when the Torah was forgotten in Eretz Yisrael, Ezra came up from Babylon and laid a new foundation for learning Torah. (*Sukkah* 20a)

When it was somewhat forgotten again, Hillel the Babylonian came and reestablished it. When more time passed and some of it was forgotten again, Rabbi Hiyya and his sons came up and established it once more.

The sacrifices that the sages made for Torah study

When we study the lives of the sages of the Talmud, we get only a glimpse of the sacrifices they made in order to study Torah. These giants of learning ignored their own suffering and poverty in order to pass on this heritage to us. With the help of excerpts from the Talmud, we will illustrate the conditions under which they lived.

Rabbi Yoshua b. Hananya

Although Rabbi Yoshua ben Hananya was one of the greatest scholars of his time, he lived in poverty.

Rabbi Gamliel once spoke harshly to him during a dispute on halachic matters. When Rabbi Gamliel realized how much respect R. Yoshua commanded, he went to visit him in order to apologize. When he saw the poor conditions in which Rabbi Yoshua lived, he told him: "From the black walls of your dwelling, it is apparent that you are a blacksmith."

To this R. Yoshua replied: "Woe to the generation of which you are the leader! You know nothing of the troubles that the scholars must endure in order to support themselves."

R. Gamliel apologized and asked forgiveness.

Elsewhere, the Talmud relates that as a young man, Rabbi Hillel used to work as a day-laborer in order to earn one tropek (an amount equivalent to a dinar). He split his earnings, giving half to the guard for admittance into the study hall and spending the other half on food and necessities. One day, when he had no money, the guard would not let him enter. He climbed up on the roof, which had a window above the lecture hall. There, he listened to the lectures of Rabbis Shemaya and Avtalyon.

This particular day, a Friday, happened to be the winter solstice. As the temperature dropped, Hillel lost consciousness, and overnight, he was covered by snow. On the following morning, which was Shabbat, Shemaya said to Avtalyon. "Every day at this time the room is bright with light, but today it is dark. Is it perhaps a cloudy day?"

They looked up and saw a human figure lying in the skylight. Climbing up, they discovered Hillel covered with three cubits of snow. They removed him from the roof, bathed and anointed him, and set him next to the fire.

They said to one another, "This man deserves that Shabbat be profaned on his account." From then on, Hillel gained permanent admittance to their school. (*Yoma* 35b)

Rabbi Akiva

R. Akiva was imprisoned for having disobeyed the Roman edict forbidding the teaching of Torah in public. R. Yoshua the Garsi, who attended Rabbi Akiva in prison, brought him a certain quantity of water every day. One day, the warden said to him, "Today you have too much water. Do you perhaps want to use it in order to dig beneath the prison?"

The warden spilled half the water and allowed R. Yoshua to take the remainder inside. When Rabbi Akiva saw how little water he had brought, he said to him. "Yoshua, don't you know that I am an old man and my life depends on you?" Rabbi Yoshua told him what happened.

Rabbi Akiva said to him. "Give me some water to wash my hands before I eat bread." The other hesitated. "It will not even suffice for drinking, let alone for washing hands." Rabbi Akiva answered him, "What can I do? Disobedience of the rabbis' rulings merits death."

He refused to taste any food until R. Yoshua had brought him water to wash his hands first.

Before the Romans killed R. Akiva, they tore his flesh with iron combs. He bore his suffering with fortitude. His students said to him, "Rabbi, even to this extent?"

Rabbi Akiva answered, "All my life I have been troubled by the biblical command *with all your soul.* I always wondered when I would have the opportunity to fulfill this commandment. Now that I have the opportunity, shall I not fulfill it?"

Another illustration of the hardship that the sages and their families endured for the sake of Jewish learning is the story of Rabbi Akiva's wife, Rachel. The daughter of Kalba Savua, the wealthiest man in Jerusalem, she incurred her father's anger by marrying Akiva, who was then his hired shepherd, without his permission. In response, her father disowned and disinherited her. Although they were later reconciled, for many years Rachel and Akiva were so poor that on one occasion Rachel sold her hair in order to buy food. (*Eruvin* 21b)

These great people ignored poverty, persecution and terrible hardship in order to leave us a legacy and a guide to a profound and unique tradition. This collection of biographies includes hundreds of similar accounts among the approximately two thousand anecdotes, quotations and stories that it contains.

SAGES

OF THE

TALMUD

SAGES OF THE TALMUD

אבא
Abba

(third–fourth centuries C.E.)
Amora, Eretz Yisrael

A student of Rabbi Huna and Rabbi Yehuda and a contemporary of Rabbi Ammi, Rabbi Assi and Rabbi Zeira, Rabbi Abba lived for a time in Tiberias, where he studied with Rabbi Eleazar and Resh Lakish.

The Talmud states: Whenever the phrase "our rabbis in Eretz Yisrael" occurs, it refers to Rabbi Abba. (*Sanhedrin* 17b)

Rabbi Abba was a businessman who dealt in silk. He became wealthy, which enabled him to honor Shabbat in a special way. (*Bava Kama* 117b)

R. Abba used to buy thirteen cuts of the finest meat from thirteen different butchers. He would then hand the meat over to his servants, urging them: Hurry, make haste and prepare for Shabbat. (*Shabbat* 119a)

When he gave charity to the poor, he did not want to embarrass them by facing them. Therefore, he would wear a scarf with money in it that he slung towards his back so that the poor could take what they needed without facing him. However, he kept an eye on would-be rogues. (*Ketubbot* 67b)

R. Abba said in the name of Resh Lakish: When two scholars listen to each other God listens to their voices. (*Shabbat* 63a)

R. Abba also said in the name of Resh Lakish: To lend money to a person in need is greater than giving charity. And to enable someone to go into business and then split the profits is greater than all charities. (*Shabbat* 63a)

Rabbi Abba avoided being in the presence of Rabbi Yehuda, his teacher, because he wanted to move to Eretz Yisrael in spite of Rabbi Yehuda's prohibition against doing so. Rabbi Yehuda had said: Whoever goes up from Babylonia to Eretz Yisrael violates a commandment. However, R. Abba wanted to hear his rabbi's lecture, so he decided to listen to it from the outside of the academy in order to avoid facing his rebbe. He left satisfied, saying: "Had I come only to learn only one thing what I heard today it was already worthwhile." (*Berachot* 24 b)

Rabbi Abba said in the name of Rabbi Shemuel: For three years there was a dispute between Bet Shammai and Bet Hillel, each one claiming that Halacha accords with their views. Then a bas kol (heavenly voice) was heard announcing that both are the words of the living God, but Halacha is in agreement with the rulings of Bet Hillel. (*Eruvin* 13b)

R. Abba said: On Shabbat, one is required to break bread over two loaves. R. Ashi said: I saw R. Kahana holding two loaves, but he broke only one of them. (*Shabbat* 117b)

R. Abba, who had a complaint against R. Yirmiyahu, felt that R. Yirmiyahu had insulted him. R. Yirmiyahu went to R. Abba's home to apologize and sat down just outside his door. As he was sitting there, the maid poured out some waste water, some of which fell upon R. Yermiyahu's head. He remarked, "They have made a dung heap of me." When R. Abba heard what had happened, he came outside in order to apologize. He said to R. Yirmiyahu: "Now I think that you are the injured

party and I must ask your forgiveness."
(*Yoma* 87a)

R. Abba traveled frequently to Babylonia, where he met with the Babylonian scholars.

When Rabbi Huna passed away and his body was brought to Eretz Yisrael for burial, Rabbi Abba eulogized him with these words: "Our master was worthy that the Shechina rest upon him, but it was prevented from doing so because he lived in Babylonia." (*Moed Katan* 25a)

For a glimpse of the world as it was in R. Abba's time, see the historical timeline from 250 to 350 C.E.

אבא
Abba

(third–fourth centuries C.E.)
Amora, Eretz Yisrael
Head of the academy in Acco

R. Abba, who was an intimate friend of Rabbi Abbahu, lived in Acco and was head of the yeshiva there.

Rabbi Abbahu said; "I used to think that I was humble, but when I saw Rabbi Abba of Acco offer one explanation and his interpreter offer a different explanation without him taking exception, I considered that I was not humble at all." (*Sotah* 40a)

The rabbis decided to appoint R. Abbahu as head of the academy in Acco, but when R. Abbahu saw that R. Abba of Acco had numerous creditors pressing him for payment, he told the rabbis: "There is a greater scholar more suitable for the office." (*Sotah* 40a)

For a glimpse of the world as it was in Rabbi Abba's time, see the historical timeline from 250 to 350 C.E.

אבא
Abba

(fourth–fiftn centuries C.E.)
Amora, Eretz Yisrael

R. Ashi said: "A scholar who is not as hard as iron is no scholar" [quoting a passage from Yirmiyahu 23:29]. R. Abba said to him: You learned it from that verse, but we learned it from another verse [Devarim 8: 9]. (*Taanit* 4a)

Rabbi Abba recited a case to Rabbi Ashi in the name of Rabbi Ulla that pertained to broken utensils: "In Eretz Yisrael the following is said in the name of Rabbi Ulla, and so on." (*Bava Kamma* 27b)

Rabbi Abba said to Rabbi Ashi: The Jordan River is called Yarden because it receives its water from Dan, a place formerly called Leshem [Yered Dan, Yehoshua 19:47]. R. Yitzhak said: Leshem is Pameas. (*Bechorot* 55a)

For a glimpse of the world as it was in Rabbi Abba's time, see the historical timeline from 350 to 450 C.E.

אבא בן אבא הכהן
Abba b. Abba ha-Kohen

(third century C.E.)
Amora of Babylonia

Rabbi Abba was a native of Nehardea. His son, Rabbi Shemuel, later became the head of the academy there.

When certain women captives came to Nehardea, R. Shmuel's father placed guards over them. Asked R. Shemuel his father: And who watched over them until now? His father answered him: If they were your daughters, would you speak so lightly of them? (*Ketubbot* 23a)

Later in his life, R. Abba moved briefly to Eretz Yisrael to study at the academy of Rabbi Yehuda ha-Nasi. He returned to Babylonia, where he worked as a silk trader. He also owned property. His charitable works supported many orphans, and he devoted a great deal of time and resources to redeem many Jewish captives.

R. Abba used to set the eruv for the whole town of Nehardea. (*Betzah* 16b)

It was said: the fathers of Shemuel and Levi were sitting in the Shaf Yativ synagogue in Nehardea. While they were in the synagogue they heard a sound of tumult. On perceiving that the Shechina had arrived, they rose from their seats and went out. Tradition has it that the synagogue in Nehardea was built during the first exile with stones that the exiles brought with them from Jerusalem. The name Shaf Yativ means "moved and settled." (*Megillah* 29a)

Rabbi Abba's colleagues and contemporaries were Rabbi Levi ben Sisi and Rav. (*Moed Katan* 26b, *Ketubbot* 51b)

When the rabbis in the Talmud were discussing eye medication on Shabbat, it was mentioned that R. Shemuel must have heard it from his father. (*Shabbat* 108b)

The Talmud relates that some money that belonged to orphans had been deposited for safekeeping with Rabbi Abba, Shemuel's father. However, since Shemuel was not in town when his father passed away, he never learned where his father kept the money. As a consequence, his deceased father was accused of having embezzled it. Distressed by this slight to his father's honor, Shemuel went to the cemetery where his father was buried in an attempt to find out where the money was hidden. He said to the spirits of the dead, "I wish to speak to my father." The spirits said, "He has gone up to learn in the heavenly academy." Shemuel noticed that the spirit of Rabbi Levi, who had passed away some time ago, was sitting outside. He asked him, "Why have you not gone up to the academy?" Rabbi Levi replied, "I was told that I would not be admitted to the heavenly academy for as many years as I did not attend the academy of Rabbi Afes and hurt his feelings." Meanwhile, Shmuel's father arrived. Shemuel saw that he was weeping and laughing. He asked him, "Why are you weeping?" His father

answered, "Because I am told that you will be coming to this world soon." "Why are you laughing?" his son asked. "Because they tell me that you are highly respected in the heavenly world," his father said. His son then said, "If I am so much respected, then as a favor to me, let Rabbi Levi be admitted to the heavenly academy."

Shortly after this, R. Levi was admitted to the heavenly academy. Shemuel then asked his father: "Where is the money that belongs to the orphans?"

His father told him: "The money is hidden in the wrap that covers the millstones. There are three bundles of money. The upper and lower ones belong to us and the middle one belongs to the orphans."

Shemuel asked his father: "Why did you store the money that way?"

Abba replied: "Because if thieves were to discover it, they would take mine, and if the earth were to destroy some of it, that would also be mine." (*Berachot* 18b)

For a glimpse of the world as it was in Rabbi Abba b. Abba's time, see the historical timeline from 200 to 300 C.E.

אבא בר אבינא
Abba bar Avina
(third century C.E.)
Amora, Eretz Yisrael

R. Abba, who was born in Babylonia and studied in the academy at Sura under Rav, later immigrated to Eretz Yisrael. His students were R. Abba bar Zavda and R. Berachia.

During a discussion about various sandals and shoes that may or may not be worn or not worn on Shabbat, Rabbi Abba b. Zavda asked R. Abba b. Avina a question about a sandal called *kalbus*. (*Shabbat* 60b)

For a glimpse of the world as it was in R. Abba bar Avina's time, see the historical timeline from 200 to 300 C.E.

אבא בר כהנא
Abba bar Kahana

(third century C.E.)
Amora from Eretz Yisrael

In the Talmud he is quoting Halachot in the name of Rabbi Hanina. (*Shabbat* 121b)

R. Abba b. Kahana had an interpretation of a passage in Kings 2:18 that differed from R. Hananel's. (*Kiddushin* 72a)

Rabbi Abba b. Kahana described an incident in which a snake entered the synagogue on Shabbat and a Nabatean Jew killed it. (*Shabbat* 121b)

R. Abba was a contemporary of Rabbi Levi.

R. Abba b. Kahana said. When king Ahashverosh removed his ring, it was a greater accomplishment than the accomplishments of forty-eight prophets and seven prophetesses. None of them was able to improve the lot of Israel as much as this one act. (*Megillah* 14a)

For a glimpse of the world as it was in Abba bar Kahana's time, see the historical timeline from 200 to 300 C.E.

אבא בר מרתא
Abba bar Marta

(third–fourth century C.E.)
Amora of Babylon

The Talmud relates the following stories about R. Abba b. Marta:

R. Abba's mother made for him a tube of gold for drinking. He had been bitten by a dog and it was suggested a gold tube for a cure. (*Yoma* 84a)

R. Abba was a contemporary of Rabbah and Abbaye from Pumbedita.

Abba b. Martha, who is one and same as Abba b. Minyumi, owed money to the house of the Resh Galuta. When he was brought before the Resh Galuta, he became aggravated. In exchanging words with him, the Resh Galuta realized that he was a scholar. He said to his officers: Let him go. He is a scholar. (*Shabbat* 121b)

R. Abba b. Marta owed money to Rabba, but was slow to make payment. When he finally came with the money, it was during a sabbatical year when, according to Halacha, all debts are cancelled.

He gave the money to Rabba, who said to R. Abba, 'It is cancelled'. So R. Abba took the money, put it in his pockets and left. Afterwards, Abbaye met Rabbah and found him to be in a bad mood. When he asked him why, Rabbah told Abbaye what had happened with R. Abba.

Abbaye went to R. Abba and asked him. "When you took the money to Rabba, what did you say to him?"

"I offered to pay him the money I owed him."

"And what did he say?"

He said. "It is cancelled."

"Did you say to him: 'Take it anyway'?"

"No, I did not."

Abbaye said to him. "If you had said to him, 'Take it anyway,' he would have taken it. Now go to him and offer him the money again, but make sure you say to him, 'Take it anyway.'"

Rabbah took the money from him and said, "This rabbinical student did have the sense to see this from the beginning." (*Gittin* 37b)

For a glimpse of the world as it was in Abba bar Marta's time, see the historical timeline from 250 to 350 C.E.

אבא בר ממל
Abba bar Memmel

(third–fourth century C.E.)
Amora, Eretz Yisrael

R. Abba was a contemporary of R. Ammi, R. Assi, R. Zeira and R. Eleazar ben Pedat.

Rabbi Abba bar Memmel disagreed with some of his contemporary rabbis with regards to the dead outside Israel; he firmly believed they would be resurrected, and he based it on Scripture. (*Ketubbot* 111a)

For a glimpse of the world as it was in R. Abba bar Memmel's time, see the historical timeline from 250 to 350 C.E.

אבא בר זבדא
Abba bar Zavda

(third century C.E.)
Amora, Eretz Yisrael

R. Abba bar Zavda studied in Babylonia in the Sura Academy under Rav and later under Huna in the same academy. One of the leading scholars in Tiberias, he was a contemporary of Rabbi Ammi and Rabbi Assi.

R. Abba bar Zavda said, Even if a Jew has sinned, he is still a Jew. Thus people say that even when a myrtle is mixed together with reeds, it is still a myrtle and is so called. (*Sanhedrin* 44a)

For a glimpse of the world as it was in R. Abba bar Zavda's time, see the historical timeline from 200 to 300 C.E.

אבא בנימין
Abba Binyamin (Abba Benjamin)
(first century C.E.)
Tanna of Jerusalem

Although the exact date of his activities is unknown, he flourished during the tannaitic period.

It has been taught that R. Abba Binyamin (who was also known as Binyamin the Tzadik) was the supervisor of the charity fund. One day a woman came to him during a year of terrible famine and asked for help. He said to her: "There is no money in the charity basket." She replied, "Rabbi, if you don't help me, then a mother and her seven children will die." When R. Abba Binyamin heard this, he took his own money and gave her what she needed.

Some time at a later period he became dangerously ill. The angels addressed the Holy One: "You have decreed that he who saves one soul of Israel is equal to saving a whole world. Benyamin the Tzadik saved a mother and her seven children. Is it right that he should die at such a young age?" His death sentence was immediately torn up, and he lived for another twenty-two years. (*Bava Batra* 11a)

One of his famous statements:

"If two people enter a synagogue to pray and one finishes first, he should wait for the other to finish. Otherwise, his prayers are for naught." (*Berachot* 5b)

He believed that only prayers uttered in the synagogue are heard. (*Berachot* 6a)

For a glimpse of the world as it was in R. Abba Binyamin's time, see the historical timeline from 1 to 100 C.E.

אבא חלקיה
Abba Hilkiah

(first century C.E.)
Tanna, Eretz Yisrael

Rabbi Abba Hilkiah was a grandson of Rabbi Honi ha-Maagel. (*Taanit* 23a)

People considered him to be a saintly person. Often they came to him in order to ask him to pray for rain.

Once, when there was an urgent need for rain, the rabbis sent two scholars to ask him to pray for rain. When they got to his house they didn't find him at home, they went after him to the fields where they found him hoeing the earth. They greeted him, but he took no notice. At the end of the day he gathered some wood and put it on his shoulder to go home. Throughout his journey he walked barefoot, but when he reached a stream he put on his shoes. When he reached the city, his wife, adorned with jewels, came out to meet him. He sat down to eat, but did not offer to share his meal with the scholars. He shared his meal with his children, giving the older child one portion and the younger two. When he finished his meal, he said to his wife, "I know the scholars have come on account of rain. Let's go up to the roof to pray." They went up to the roof, where he stood in one corner and she in another. At first, clouds appeared in the corner where she stood. When he came downstairs, he asked the scholars, "Why have you come to me?" They replied, "The rabbis sent us to ask you to pray for rain." He said to them, "Blessed be God that you are no longer dependent on me to pray for rain." They answered him, "We know that the rain has come on account of you. But tell us the meaning of your mysterious behavior. Why did you pretend not to notice us when we greeted you first?"

He answered. "I was a paid laborer; I could not steal my employer's time to greet you."

"Why did you walk barefoot on the road and put on your shoes when you entered the stream?"

"Because while I could see what was on the road, I could not see what was in the water."

"Why did your wife come out adorned with jewels to greet you?"

"She did it in order that I not set my eyes on any other woman."

"Why didn't you ask us to join you in the meal?"

"I could not ask you because there was not enough food to feed all of us."

"Why did you give only one portion to your older son and two portions to the younger?"

"I did that because one stays at home and the other is away in the synagogue."

"Why did the clouds appear first in the corner where your wife prayed?"

"My wife's prayers were answered first because she stays at home and feeds the poor, and they can enjoy the food immediately. I give them money, which they can't enjoy immediately." (*Taanit* 23b)

For a glimpse of the world as it was in R. Abba Hilkiah's time, see the historical timeline from 1–100 C.E.

אבא גוריון
Abba Gurion mi-Sidon

(second century C.E.)
Tanna, Eretz Yisrael

One of his famous statements was: "Abba Gurion of Tzedayan said in the name of Abba Guria: "One should not teach his son the occupation of an ass driver, camel driver, barber, sailor, shepherd or tavern keeper, because it is a trade of robbers." (*Kiddushin* 82a)

For a glimpse of the world as it was in R. Abba Gurion mi-Sidon's time, see the historical timeline from 100 to 200 C.E.

אבא כהן ברדלא
Abba Kohen Bardella

(second century C.E.)
Tanna, Eretz Yisrael

R. Abba Kohen Bardella is quoted by Rabbi Shimon ben Lakish as saying that a man's four cubits acquire property for him everywhere. (*Bava Metzia* 10a)

For a glimpse of the world as it was in R. Abba Kohen Bardella's time, see the historical timeline from 100 to 200 C.E.

אבא שאול
Abba Shaul (Abba Saul)

(second century C.E.)
Tanna, Eretz Yisrael

R. Shaul's occupation was a baker, but at times he also worked as a gravedigger.

It was taught: Abba Shaul stated, I was once a gravedigger and I made a practice of carefully observing the bones of the dead. The bones of one who drinks undiluted wine are burned, the bones of one who drinks wine excessively diluted are dry, and those who drink wine properly mixed are full of marrow. The bones of a person whose drinking exceeds his eating are burned, the bones of one whose eating exceeds his drinking are dry, and those who eat and drink in a proper manner are full of marrow. (*Niddah* 24b)

Abba Shaul stated: "I once worked as a gravedigger, and on one occasion a cave opened under me and I found myself in the eyeball of a corpse. I was told that it was the eye of Avshalom." (*Niddah* 24b)

His close associates were Rabbi Yehuda b. Illai and Rabbi Meir, and he studied in the yeshiva of Rabbi Akiva.

His father's name is unknown, but his mother's name was Miriam. (*Ketubbot* 87a)

One of his statements was that "One should strive to be gracious and merciful, as God is gracious and merciful." (*Shabbat* 133b)

For a glimpse of the world as it was in Abba Shaul's time, see the historical timeline from 100 to 200 C.E.

אבא שאול בן בטנית
Abba Shaul ben Batnit

(first century C.E.)
Tanna, Eretz Yisrael

Rabbi Abba Shaul was a businessman in Jerusalem. The Talmud states that he was a scrupulous and honest shopkeeper.

On the eve of a holiday, he would fill his measuring devices with his products and gave it to his customers. He did this in order to give his customers a full measure, to the last drop due them. (*Betzah* 29a)

The rabbis taught: He collected three hundred jugs of wine from the foam of the measures, and his friends collected three hundred jugs of oil from the drops of the measures wasted, and brought them to the treasurer of the Temple in Jerusalem.

Rabbi Shaul ben Batnit was very critical of the priests in the latter days of the Temple.

It was taught that Abba Shaul said: There were sycamore trees in Jericho, and strong-arm men seized them by force. Thereupon the owners of the trees consecrated them to Heaven. Of these kinds of deeds he used to say in the name of Abba Yoseph b. Hanin:

Woe is me because of the house of Boethus; woe is me because of their rods. Woe is me because of the house of Hanin; woe is me because of their whisperings. Woe is me because of the house of Kathros; woe is me because of their pens. Woe is me because of the house of Yishmael ben Phabi; woe is me because of their fists. For they are high priests and their sons are Temple treasurers, and their sons-in-law are trustees, and their servants beat the people with rods. (*Pesahim* 57a)

He was a contemporary and a colleague of R. Eliezer ben Tzadok.

The Talmud mentions that he and the father of Rabbi Tzadok measured out an opening in a barrel for halachic purposes. (*Shabbat* 24:5)

For a glimpse of the world as it was in R. Abba Shaul's time, see the historical timeline from 1 to 100 C.E.

אבא סקרא
Abba Sikra

(first century C.E.)
The leader of the Biryoni in Jerusalem

Abba Sikra was the son of Rabbi Yohanan ben Zakkai's sister. He was the head of the rebels fighting against the Romans in Jerusalem during the siege of the city. (*Gittin* 56a)

The Jewish people had two parties. One wanted peace and the other wanted to continue to resist the Romans. Rabbi Yohanan ben Zakkai sent word to his nephew, Abba Sikra, to come to visit him in secret. When Abba Sikra arrived, R. Yohanan asked him, "How long are you going to starve the people to death?"

He answered, "What can I do? If I say a word, they will kill me."

Rabbi Yohanan said to him, "Devise a plan so that I may escape from the city. Perhaps something can still be saved."

His nephew advised him, "Pretend to be ill so that people will come to visit you. Then put something with a terrible odor next to you so that people will say that you have died. Let your students carry you out in a coffin, but no one else, because people will notice you are lighter than a corpse." He listened to his advice and faked his death. His students carried the coffin, Rabbi Eliezer on one side and Rabbi Yehoshua on the other, and smuggled him out of Jerusalem. Abba Sikra himself also accompanied the coffin. When the gatekeepers wanted to pierce the coffin, Abba Sikra prevented them from doing so, saying, "Shall it be said that they pierced their own teacher?" Once Rabbi Yohanan had left Jerusalem, he met with Vespasian, who was the commander, and addressed him as Emperor. When Vespasian corrected him, Rabbi Yohanan told him that according to Scripture, only a king could conquer Jerusalem. Shortly afterward, a messenger arrived with news from Rome that the Emperor had died and that the Senate wished him to be the next Emperor of Rome.

As Rabbi Yohanan spoke with Vespasian, the latter realized that he was speaking to a very wise person. Finally, Vespasian told Rabbi Yohanan, "I must leave now, but make a request of me and I will grant it to you."

Rabbi Yohanan said, "Give me Yavne and its sages to be allowed to teach, allow the family chain of R. Gamliel to continue and send a physician to heal Rabbi Tzadok."

His wish was granted, and the academy at Yavne was established. (*Gittin* 56a)

For a glimpse of the world as it was in Abba Sikra's time, see the historical timeline from 1 to 100 C.E.

אבא יוסי בן חנן
Abba Yosi (Yose) ben Hanan (Hanin)

(first century C.E.)
Tanna, Eretz Yisrael

Abba Yosi b. Hanan, who was familiar with the Temple service, describes the various Temple gates and their functions. He said: Thirteen gates on the south faced the west; the upper gate, the gate of burning, the gate of the firstborn and the water gate. Through it they brought in the pitchers of water for libation on the festival." (Mishnah *Middot* 2:6)

R. Abba Yosi was a very outspoken person, especially about the Temple priests and their corrupt behavior.

For a glimpse of the world as it was in R. Abba Yosi's time, see the historical timeline from 1 to 100 C.E.

אבא יוסי בן דוסתאי
Abba Yosi ben Dostai

(second century C.E.)
Tanna, Eretz Yisrael

R. Abba Yosi ben Dostai was a contemporary of Rabbi Eliezer, Rabbi Yosi ha-Gelili and Rabbi Yosi ben Meshullam.

For a glimpse of the world as it was in R. Abba Yosi ben Dostai's time, see the historical timeline from 100 to 200 C.E.

אביי
Abbaye

(third–fourth centuries C.E.)
Amora, Babylonia
Head of the Academy in Pumbedita

According to some, R. Abbaye lived from 278 to 338 C.E.

His father died before he was born and his mother died giving birth to him. He was raised by Rabbah ben Nachmeni, his uncle, and a foster mother whom he called Mother. He studied first with his uncle, Rabbah b. Nachmeni, and then with Rabbi Yoseph, who succeeded Rabbah as head of the academy in Pumbedita.

The Talmud relates a similar story about R. Yohanan, whose father died before he was born and whose mother died on the day of his birth. But, asked someone, didn't Abbaye say "My mother told me"? He was referring to his foster-mother. (*Kiddushin* 31b)

Abbaye's wife's name was Huma. (*Ketubbot* 65a)

Abbaye and Rava were sitting before Rabbah when they were still young boys. Wishing to test them, Rabbah asked: "To whom do we say the benedictions?" They both answered: "To God."

"And where is God?" Rava pointed to the ceiling, while Abbaye went outside and pointed to the sky. Rabbah said to them: "Both of you will become rabbis."

This is why people say: Every pumpkin can be told from its stalk. (*Berachot* 48a)

When Abbaye was young he was poor. He had to work in the fields and watered them at night so that he could study during the daytime.

Once, R. Shimi ben Ashi came to Abbaye and asked him for lessons. Abbaye answered, "I have no time. I need my time for my own study."

The other said, "Then teach me at night."

Abbaye answered, "At night I am also busy, watering my fields."

R. Shimi offered to water his fields during the day and to receive lessons at night. Abbaye agreed.

However, one incident displeased Abbaye very much. R. Shimi went to the owners of the fields that were located above R. Abbaye's fields and told them that the owners of the fields below had the right to water their fields first. He then went to the owners of the fields below Abbaye's and told them that those who owned the fields above Abbaye's had the first right to water the fields. In the meantime, R. Shimi had all the water available for himself to irrigate Abbaye's fields. When Abbaye found out what R. Shimi had done, it displeased him so much that he refused to eat of that year's produce. (*Gittin* 60b)

When he was young, Abbaye used to juggle eight eggs (some say four eggs) in front of Rabbah. (*Sukkah* 53a)

When Rabbi Yoseph, died Rabbi Abbaye succeeded him as head of the academy in Pumbedita, a position that he held for the rest of his life. During Rabbi Yoseph's last years, Abbaye helped him recall many of the halachot that Rabbi Yoseph had forgotten due to illness.

Rav was meticulous about paying promptly for his purchases. He considered it a desecration to buy meat from the butcher without paying him immediately. Abbaye said, If the custom in the community is to collect afterwards, then it is permitted. Ravina said: Mata Mehasya is a place where they go out afterwards to collect.

Abbaye used to buy meat from two partners and pay each of them. Afterwards, he brought them together to square the account with both. (*Yoma* 86a)

Abbaye was a colleague of many amoraim, but the most prominent of them was Rava, with whom he had disagreements on many issues. Nevertheless, on some matters they agreed.

Halacha goes according to Rava except in six cases where, according to Abbaye, they are indicated by an acronym in Hebrew. (*Bava Metzia* 22b)

R. Abba b. Martha owed money to Rabbah. When Rabbah asked for payment, R. Abba stalled and he had to wait for a long time. Finally, one day, R. Abba came to Rabbah with the money to pay him, but it was during a sabbatical year, when all debts are usually cancelled.

Rabbah said to him, "I don't want it; it is cancelled."

So R. Abba took the money, put it in his pocket and left. Afterwards, Abbaye came to see Rabbah and he found him in a bad mood.

"Why are you in a bad mood?" he asked.

Rabbah told him what happened.

R. Abbaye went to R. Abba and asked him, "When you took the money to Rabba, what did you tell him?"

"I offered to pay him the money I owed him."

"And what did he say?"

"He said, 'It is cancelled.'"

"Did you say to him: 'Take it anyway'?"

"No, I did not."

Abbaye said to him, "If you had said, 'Take it anyway,' he would have taken it. Now go to him and offer him the money again, but make sure you say to him, 'Take it anyway.'"

He did as Abbaye advised him and Rabbah took it from him. After this, Rabbah commented:

"This rabbinical student did have the sense to see this from the beginning." (*Gittin* 37b)

R. Abbaye became a businessman and traded in wine.

Once, when Ravin and Abbaye were traveling together, Ravin's donkey went in front of Abbaye. When Ravin did not apologize, Abbaye became annoyed and thought to himself: *Since this student came up from Eretz Yisrael, he has become haughty.* When they arrived at the door of the synagogue, Ravin said to Abbaye, "Rabbi, would you please enter?" Abbaye answered, "And was I not your rabbi until now?" R. Ravin replied, "One gives honor only at a door where there is a mezuzah." (*Berachot* 47a)

Bar Hedya was an interpreter of dreams. If one paid him, he gave a favorable interpretation, while if one did not pay him, he gave an unfavorable interpretation. R. Abbaye came to him with a dream and paid him a zuz. For the fee, he interpreted the dream by saying, "Your business will prosper and you will not be able to eat from sheer joy."

Abbaye went to him many more times with dreams, and most of the time he received pleasant interpretations. (*Berachot* 56a)

R. Avin b. R. Adda quoted R. Menachem as saying: It once happened that a child was born to the same mother three months after the first one, and both of those students were sitting in our academy.

Who were these students? They were Rabbi Yehuda and Rabbi Hizkiyah, the sons of Rabbi Hiyya. But didn't we learn that a woman couldn't conceive twice during the same pregnancy? Abbaye replied: It was the same drop, which was split in two; the features of one were completed at the beginning of the seventh month, and the features of the other were completed at the end of the ninth month. (*Niddah* 27a)

After the destruction of the Temple, the rabbis wished the Jewish people to avoid ostentation. They ruled that during a lavish banquet, one item should be omitted. R. Pappa said that it should be the hors d'oeuvre.

R. Yitzhak said: At a wedding, ashes should be put on the bridegroom's head as a reminder of the destruction of the Temple. R. Pappa asked R. Abbaye: "Where on the head should the ashes be placed?" R. Abbaye answered, "On the spot where the tefilin are usually worn." (*Bava Batra* 60b)

Our rabbis taught: One should combine the study of Torah with a worldly occupation. This is the view of R. Yishmael. However, Rabbi Shimon b. Yohai says, "If you plow at the proper time and reap in the proper season, and so on, what will become of studying Torah?" (*Berachot* 35b)

R. Abbaye said. Many have followed the advice of R. Yishmael with good results, while others have followed R. Shimon b. Yohai and been less successful.

The Talmud states that when the majority of the rabbis left Rav's academy, twelve hundred students remained behind. When the students left R. Huna's academy, eight hundred students were left behind. (*Ketubbot* 106a)

When R. Huna delivered a lecture, thirteen interpreters assisted him.

When the students left the academy of Rabbah and R. Yoseph, four hundred students remained behind, and they described themselves as orphans.

When the students left R. Abbaye's academy – others say R. Pappa's and still others say R. Ashi's – there remained two hundred rabbis, and they described themselves as orphans of the orphans.

Abbaye asked Rabba, "It is known that the people of Pumbedita hate you because of your outspokenness. Now, that being a fact, which person might be willing to deliver the eulogy for you?" Rabbah replied; "You and Rabbah b. R. Hanan will do very well." (*Shabbat* 153a)

R. Rami b. Hama's sister was married to R. Avia, but her *ketubbah* was lost. They came to R. Yoseph for a ruling as to whether they could continue to live together nevertheless. He told them that it is a dispute between R. Meir and the sages. According to the sages; in such a case a man may live with his wife for two to three years without a *ketubbah*. When R. Abbaye objected, R. Yoseph told him; "In that case, go and write her a new *ketubbah*." (*Ketubbot* 56b–57a)

The Talmud relates that a certain man was traveling to redeem some captives when he was attacked by robbers. In order to save himself, he handed over the money intended for the redemption of the prisoners, and the robbers let him go. On his return, he was summoned before Rabba, who acquitted him of negligence. Abbaye said to Rabba: "Didn't this man save himself with another man's money?"

Rabbah replied: "There could hardly be a case of redeeming captives more urgent than this." (*Bava Kama* 117b)

A certain man pushed his donkey onto a ferryboat before the passengers had a chance to disembark. The boat was shaking and in danger of sinking. Another man who was on the boat came and pushed the donkey overboard, and the donkey drowned. When the case came before Rabba, he declared the man not guilty.

Abbaye said to Rabbah: "Didn't the man rescue himself with another man's money?"

Rabbah replied: "No. The donkey's owner was the pursuer from the beginning." (*Bava Kama* 117b)

R. Eliezer b. Yaakov had a disagreement with his colleagues about an *eruv* where Jews lived together with non-Jews in a single courtyard. R. Abbaye said to R. Yoseph, "We have a tradition that the teachings of R. Eliezer b. Yaakov are few in quantity but well sifted." (*Eruvin* 62b)

R. Abbaye quoted R. Shimon b. Gamliel, R. Shimon, R. Yishmael and R. Akiva, who maintained that all Israelites are princes. Abbaye quotes several pronouncements by the above-mentioned rabbis to prove his case. (*Bava Metzia* 113b)

Abbaye said, "When I was studying, I needed complete clarity and concentration. If my foster mother had told me, 'Bring me a dish of *kutcha*,' I would not have been able to study." (*Eruvin* 65a)

He also said: "At one time I used to study at home and pray in the synagogue, but when I noticed the words of David, I began to study in the synagogue as well." (*Megillah* 29a)

Abbaye composed the blessing known as *Asher yatzar,* thanking God for healthy body function, which Jews recite upon leaving the bathroom, after washing hands. (*Berachot* 60b)

He said: The *shin, dalet* and *yud* of *tefillin* are commanded through Moshe from Sinai. (*Shabbat* 62a)

Abbaye said: "In each generation the world must contain no fewer than thirty-six righteous men who merit the sight of the Shechina." (*Sanhedrin* 97b)

A favorite saying of R. Abbaye was that one should always be in fear of heaven and strive to be on the best terms with one's fellow human beings and relatives, and even with those of other faiths, in order to be beloved above and below and acceptable to one's fellow creatures. (*Berachot* 17a)

R. Shimon b. Yohai said: "Come and see how beloved Israel is in the sight of God; for in every place to which Israel was exiled, the Shechina accompanied them. When they were exiled to Egypt, the Shechina was with them, as it is written. When they were exiled to Babylonia, the Shechina was with them; as it is written. When they are redeemed in the future, the Shechina will be with them; as it is written. Abbaye said: In Babylonia, the Shechina is in the synagogue of Huzal and in the synagogue of Shaf Yativ, which is in Nehardea. But do not think it is in both places. Rather, it is sometimes in one and sometimes in the other. R. Abbaye always worshipped in that synagogue when he was in that town. (*Megillah* 29a)

Our rabbis taught: "Anyone who never saw the ceremony of the water-drawing at the Temple in Jerusalem has never seen rejoicing in his life. Anyone who never saw Jerusalem in its splendor has never seen a lovely city. Anyone who never saw the Temple in Jerusalem when it was fully rebuilt has never seen a beautiful building in his life." (*Sukkah* 51b)

The Talmud asks: Which Temple? R. Abbaye said – and some say R. Hisda said: This refers to the building that Herod built. The Talmud asks: What kind of material did he use to construct it? Rabbah answered: He built it of yellow and white marble. Some differ, saying that it was built of yellow, blue and white marble. The building was constructed in tiers, with one row projecting outward and one receding inward. His intention was to overlay the marble stones with gold, but the rabbis advised him to leave the marble as is because it had the appearance of the waves of the sea.

For a glimpse of the world as it was in R. Abbaye's time, see the historical timeline from 250 to 350 C.E.

אביי קשישא
Abbaye Kashisha

(second–third centuries C.E.)
Amora, Babylonia

Abbaye Kashisha was from the generation before that of the other, more famous Abbaye.

The later, better-known Abbaye quotes the former Abbaye in the Talmud. (*Ketubbot* 94a)

R. Abbaye Kashisha compared a particular ruling to a dying man who left his creditor two hundred zuz, with instructions to take the money if he wished in settlement for the debt or as a gift. (*Ketubbot* 96b)

Abbaye Kashisha spoke out against controversy and dissension, saying: "Strife is like planks in a wooden bridge. The longer you let them lie, the stronger they become." (*Sanhedrin* 7a)

For a glimpse of the world as it was in R. Abbaye Kashisha's time, see the historical timeline from 150 to 250 C.E.

אחא
Aha

(fourth century C.E.)
Amora, Eretz Yisrael

R. Aha, who was born in Lydda, was a student of Rabbi Yosi b. Hanina and of Rabbi Tanhum ben Hiyya.

R. Yonah and R. Yosi went to visit R. Aha, who was old and very ill. He lay in bed, still and silent. They followed the voices they heard. One woman was asking the other: "Is the light out?" The other replied: "Heaven forbid; the light of Israel is not out." (Talmud Yerushalmi *Shabbat* 6:9)

When R. Aha finished the mussaf service on Yom Kippur, he would urge the congregation with these words: "Those of you who have children, go out and feed them and give them to drink to avoid exposing them to danger." (*Yerushalmi Yoma* 6: 4)

He was quoted as saying: "The Divine Presence never departed from the Western Wall of the Temple."

For a glimpse of the world as it was in R. Aha's time, see the historical timeline from 300 to 400 C.E.

אחא אריכא
Aha Aricha (Aha b. Papa)
(third–fourth centuries C.E.)
Amora, Babylonia

R. Aha Aricha stated in the presence of Rav Hinena that reciting *Ha-mavdil* during the prayer service is more praiseworthy than reciting it over a cup of wine, and if one recited it on both occasions, blessings on his head. (*Berachot* 33a)

R. Aha discussed a remedy for toothache with R. Abbahu. (*Shabbat* 111a)

R. Aha engaged in a halachic discussion with R. Abba about tying a cow to the trough on Shabbat. (*Shabbat* 113a)

For a glimpse of the world as it was in R. Aha Aricha's time, see the historical timeline from 250 to 350 C.E.

אחא בר ביזנא
Aha b. Bizna

(third–fourth centuries C.E.)
Amora

Rabbi Aha bar Bizna said in the name of Rabbi Shimon Hasida: "A harp hung above David's bed, and at midnight a north wind would come and blow and play the harp in order to awaken him." (*Berachot* 3b) (*Sanhedrin* 16a)

For a glimpse of the world as it was in R. Aha b. Bizna's time, see the historical timeline from 250 to 350 C.E.

אחא בר חנינא
Aha b. Hanina

(third–fourth centuries C.E.)
Amora, Eretz Yisrael

In his youth, R. Aha lived in Lydda and studied with Rabbi Yoshua ben Levi. He moved to the Galilee and studied in Tiberias under Rabbi Assi, from whom he learned the traditions of Rabbi Yohanan. (*Sanhedrin* 42a)

Visiting the sick was very important to him. He said, "He who visits the sick removes one-sixtieth of their suffering." (*Nedarim* 39b)

R. Yehuda b. Hiyya said, "A Torah scholar who occupies himself studying Torah in poverty will have his prayers heard." Rabbi Aha b. Hanina added: "And neither will they draw the veil before him." (*Sotah* 49a)

R. Aha b. Hanina said in the name of R. Assi, in the name of R. Yohanan: "Blessing the new moon at the proper time is like being in the presence of the Shechina." (*Sanhedrin* 42a)

R. Aha b. Hanina said, "A slanderer has no remedy." (*Arachin* 15b)

R. Aha said, "The most acceptable time to pray is when the congregation prays." (*Berachot* 8a)

For a glimpse of the world as it was in R. Aha b. Hanina's time, see the historical timeline from 250 to 350 C.E.

אחא בר רב
Aha bar Rav

(fourth–fifth centuries C.E.)
Amora, Babylonia

R. Aha was a student of R. Ravina.

The Talmud quotes him several times discussing and disputing with the Amoraim. (*Hullin* 33a, *Sanhedrin* 76b)

In another case, R. Aha b. Rav said to R. Ravina: Amemar happened to come to our place and gave the following exposition: "A first born takes a double portion in a loan but not in its interest". (*Bava Batra* 124b)

For a glimpse of the world as it was in R. Aha bar Rav's time, see the historical timeline from 350 to 450 C.E.

אחא בר יעקב
Aha bar Yaakov (Aha b. Jacob)

(third–fourth centuries C.E.)
Amora, Babylonia

R. Aha, who was a student of Rabbi Huna, was also a contemporary of Abbaye and Rava.

His school was located in the city of Paphunia in Babylonia, near Pumbedita. (*Kiddushin* 35a)

R. Aha b. Yaakov sent his son, Yaakov, to study under R. Abbaye. When Yaakov returned, R. Aha realized that his own learning was dull. He said to his son: "Stay at home so that I may travel to R. Abbaye in order to study." When R. Abbaye heard that R. Aha was coming, he told the townspeople not to offer him hospitality so that he would be forced to sleep in the schoolhouse.

R. Abbaye's reason for doing this was that a demon was haunting the schoolhouse and injuring people when they entered. R. Abbaye believed that a miracle might occur on account of R.

Aha, who was known as a holy man. When R. Aha spent the night in the schoolhouse, the demon appeared to him as a seven-headed dragon. Each time R. Aha fell to his knees in prayer, one of the dragon's heads would fall off. The following day, R. Aha reproached the townspeople, saying: "If it had not been for a miracle, you would have endangered my life." (*Kiddushin* 29b)

The Talmud discusses the size of a Torah scroll. R. Aha wrote one on calfskin and hit it to the exact measurement. (*Bava Batra* 14a)

According to R. Aha b. Yaakov, the tribe of Levi is not called a "congregation." (*Horayot* 6b)

In a conversation with R. Nahman, Rava praised R. Aha b. Yaakov as a great man. He said to him: "When you meet him, bring him to me." When he came to see him, R. Nahman said to him, "You may ask me questions." They discussed several halachot. (*Bava Kama* 40a)

The Talmud relates a story in which Satan came to R. Aha in Paphunia and kissed his feet. (*Bava Batra* 16a)

Rava said: "The Paphunians know the reason for this halacha. Who is it? It is Rabbi Aha b. Yaakov." (*Kiddushin* 35a)

Rabbi Aha had Talmudic discussions and disputes with Rabbis Hisda, Rava and Abbaye. He also had discussions with Rabbi Nahman, whom he sometimes quotes as his source.

R. Aha b. Yaakov reared his daughter's son, R. Yaakov. (*Sotah* 49a)

For a glimpse of the world as it was in R. Aha b. Yaakov's time, see the historical timeline from 250 to 350 C.E.

אחי ברבי יאשיה
Ahai b. Yoshaya

(second century C.E.)
Tanna, Babylonia

R. Ahai established a yeshiva in the town of Huzal, where he settled, that was known as the School of Ahai.

The Talmud relates that there is a town in Babylonia called Birtha de-Satya. Once, a fishpond overflowed on Shabbat and the people went out to catch the fish. When Rabbi Ahai found out, he declared a ban against the people who had violated Shabbat. The people then renounced Judaism altogether. (*Kiddushin* 72a)

Rabbi Ahai ben Yoshaya left a silver cup in Nehardea by a certain person. He told R. Dostai b. Yannai and R. Yosi ben Kifar, who were traveling to Babylonia: "When you come back from Nehardea, bring me back my silver cup, which is at the home of So-and-so, who lives in Nehardea." When they reached Nehardea, the merchant gave them the cup, but asked for a bill of sale. They refused. The merchant then asked for the cup back. R. Dostai was willing, but R. Yosi refused. The men beat Rabbi Yosi and told R. Dostai: Do you see what your friend is doing? R. Dostai said to them: "Thrash him well." When they returned, Rabbi Yosi complained to Rabbi Ahai: "Not only didn't he help me, but he even told them to cause me more pain." Rabbi Dostai explained: "I had to do something. Those people are extremely tall and their hats are also tall. Their voices are loud and their names are very unusual, such as Arda and Arta and Pili Baris. If they had asked the authorities to have us arrested, we would have been arrested. If they had asked them to kill us, they would kill us. I had to appease them. Otherwise they would have killed us." Rabbi Ahai asked: "Do these people have influence with the authorities?" R. Dostai answered: "Yes. They have a whole retinue riding on horses and mules." "In that case," said R. Ahai, "you acted correctly." (*Gittin* 14a–b)

For a glimpse of the world as it was in R. Ahai b. Yoshaya's time, see the historical timeline from 100 to 200 C.E.

אדא בר אבא
Adda bar Abba

(fourth century C.E.)
Amora, Babylonia

It is related that R. Nahman, who was the regular lecturer on Shabbat, was about to deliver his lecture. However, it was his custom to run over his text with R. Adda b. Abba before delivering it, and only then would he deliver his lecture.

But this Shabbat, R. Papa and R. Huna b. Yehoshua approached R. Adda b. Abba and asked him to repeat for them the lecture that they had missed the day before, saying, "Tell us how Rabbah explained the law of tithing." He repeated the entire lecture for them.

In the meantime, R. Nahman was waiting for R. Adda to go over his lecture with him, and it was getting late. The rabbis told R. Nahman: "Come and lecture. It is late. Why are you still sitting?"

Angry over R. Adda's delay, he replied sarcastically, "I am waiting for R. Adda's coffin." But when R. Adda b. Abba passed away soon afterwards, R. Nahman blamed himself for his death. (*Bava Batra* 22a)

It is related that R. Dimi from Nehardea brought a load of figs in a boat to be sold on the market. The Exilarch said told Rava, "Go and see if he is a scholar. If he is, reserve the market for him."

The scholars had privileges. They could dispose of their merchandise before the rest of the merchants so that they could then go and study. Rava sent R. Adda b. Abba to test his scholarship. He put the following question to him: "If an elephant swallows a basket and then passes it out with excrement, is it still considered to be a basket, still subject to uncleanness?"

R. Dimi could not answer. He asked R. Adda, "Are you Rava?"

R. Adda answered: "Between Rova and me there is a great difference, but at any rate, I can be your teacher, and therefore Rava is the teacher of your teacher." Consequently they did not reserve the market for him, and his figs were a total loss. He appealed to Rabbi Yoseph, saying, "Do you see how they have treated me?"

Shortly afterwards, R. Adda died. R. Dimi became upset, saying, "It is because of me that he was punished, because he made me lose my figs."

R. Yoseph blamed himself for his death. Abbaye said: "It is because of me that he was punished, because he used to say to the students: Instead of gnawing bones in the school of Abbaye, eat meat in the school of Rava." (*Bava Batra* 22a)

For a glimpse of the world as it was in R. Adda bar Abba's time, see the historical timeline from 300 to 400 C.E.

אדא בר אהבה
Adda bar Ahava

(third century C.E.)
Amora, Babylonia

R. Adda was born on the day Rabbi Yehuda Hanasi died.

The Talmud relates that there is a place called Accra Deagama in Babylonia, in which a person by the name of Adda b. Ahava sits in Abraham's lap. It was also learned by an authority that on the day Rabbi Akiva died, Rebbe was born, and on the day Rebbe, died Rav Yehuda was born. When Rav Yehuda died, Rava was born, when Rava died, Rav Ashi was born. This is to teach us that when a righteous person leaves this world, another righteous person replaces him. (*Kiddushin* 72a)

R. Adda b. Ahava lived in the house of a proselyte who was running against R. Bibi for the position of town administrator. When they came before Rabbi Yoseph, R. Adda argued in favor of the proselyte. After listening to both sides, Rabbi Yoseph declared, "Let R. Bibi, who is a great man, devote his attention to heavenly matters such as distributing charity, and let the proselyte look after the affairs of the town." R. Abbaye remarked. "When one provides a scholar with housing, let him provide it for one like R. Adda b. Ahava, who is able to argue in his favor." (*Kiddushin* 76b)

Once, R. Huna suffered great financial loss when four hundred jars of his wine turned sour. Rav Yehuda, the brother of R. Sala Hasida, and the other rabbis visited him, though some say it was R. Adda b. Ahava and other rabbis who visited him. They said to him; "Master, you ought to examine your deeds."

He asked them, "Do you find me suspect?"

They answered him: "Is God to be suspected of punishing unjustly?"

He declared, "If somebody has heard that I am accused of any misdeed, let him speak."

They replied, "We heard that the master does not give his tenant his lawful share of vine twigs."

He replied, "Does he leave me any? He steals them all."

They said to him, "That is exactly what the proverb says. If you steal from a thief, a taste of his theft remains with you."

He said to the rabbis: "I take upon myself to give him his share in the future."

It was reported that after this visit, the vinegar became wine again. Others say that the price of vinegar increased so much that R. Huna sold the vinegar for the same price as wine. (*Berachot* 5b)

When Rav died, his students accompanied his bier. After they returned, they said; "Let us eat a meal at the river Danak."

After they finished eating, they discussed a question of Halacha about the blessing recited after a meal to which they did not know the answer. R. Adda b. Ahava stood up and tore his garment from front to back and tore it once more, saying, "Our teacher Rav is dead and we have not learned the rules for the blessing after the meal!" Finally, an elderly man solved their problem. (*Berachot* 42b)

In Nehardea there was a dilapidated wall. Rav and Shemuel avoided it for fear it might collapse, even though it had stood in the same position for thirteen years. One day, Rav and Shemuel were walking next to the wall, and R. Adda b. Ahava was with them. R. Shemuel said to Rav: "Let's walk around the wall." Rav replied, "That is not necessary because R. Adda b. Ahava is with us. His merit is so great that nothing bad will happen." (*Taanit* 20b)

The students once asked R. Adda b. Ahava: "To what do you attribute your longevity?" He replied, "I have never displayed my impatience at home, I have never walked in front of a man greater than myself, I have never had thoughts about Torah in a dirty place, I have never walked four cubits without thinking Torah thoughts, and I never fell asleep in the study hall. I never rejoiced at the embarrassment of my friends, and I never called my friends by a nickname." (*Taanit* 20b)

R. Adda b. Ahava said: If a person sinned and confesses but does not repent, that is comparable to holding a dead reptile in his hand. Though he immerse himself in all the waters in the world, his immersion is of no avail to him. If he throws it from his hand, then one immersion is effective. (*Taanit* 16a)

For a glimpse of the world as it was in R. Adda bar Ahava's time, see the historical timeline from 200 to 300 C.E.

אדמון
Admon b. Gadai

(first century C.E.)
Tanna, Eretz Yisrael

Admon was a judge in Jerusalem for criminal and civil cases.

The Talmud says, "Two judges of civil law were in Jerusalem, Admon and Hanan b. Avishalom." Elsewhere, the Talmud states that there were three judges, but the Talmud reconciles the discrepancy. Admon b. Gadai's decisions are quoted in the Talmud (*Shevuot* 6:3, *Ketubbot* 13:1, 3, 9.) Rabbi Gamliel is quoted as agreeing with Rabbi Admon. (*Shevuot* 6:3.)

For a glimpse of the world as it was in Admon b. Gadai's time, see the historical timeline from 1 to 100 C.E.

אפס
Afes

(third century C.E.)
Amora, Eretz Yisrael

When Rabbi Yehuda ha-Nasi died, he left instructions. One of them was that R. Hanina bar Hama should preside over the academy. However, when R. Hanina refused the position because R. Afes was two and a half years older, R. Afes became president of the academy.

R. Hanina did not study inside the academy, but remained outside in the company of Rabbi Levi. When Rabbi Afes passed away, R. Hanina bar Hama took over the presidency. As a consequence, Rabbi Levi, who now had no one to study with, moved to Babylonia. (*Ketubbot* 103b)

The Talmud relates that Rav was told: A very tall and lame man has come to Nehardea in order to lecture. Rav remarked: "It must be Rabbi Levi who has arrived, and it must be that Rabbi Afes died and Rabbi Hanina is now head of the academy." (*Shabbat* 59b)

The Talmud relates that some money that belonged to orphans had been deposited for safekeeping with Rabbi Abba, Shemuel's father. However, since Shemuel was not in town when his father passed away, he never learned where his father kept the money. As a consequence, his deceased father was accused of having embezzled it. Distressed by this slight to his father's honor, Shemuel went to the cemetery where his father was buried in an attempt to find out where the money was hidden. He said to the spirits of the dead, "I wish to speak to my father." The spirits said, "He has gone up to learn in the heavenly academy." Shemuel noticed that the spirit of Rabbi Levi, who had passed away some time ago, was sitting outside. He asked him, "Why have you not gone up to the academy?" Rabbi Levi replied, "I was told that I would not be admitted to the heavenly academy for as many years as I did not attend the academy of Rabbi Afes and hurt his feelings." Meanwhile, Shmuel's father arrived. Shemuel saw that he was weeping and laughing. He asked him, "Why are you weeping?" His father answered, "Because I am told that you will be coming to this world soon." "Why are you laughing?" his son asked.

"Because they tell me that you are highly respected in the heavenly world," his father said. His son then said, "If I am so much respected, then as a favor to me, let Rabbi Levi be admitted to the heavenly academy."

Shortly after this, R. Levi was admitted to the heavenly academy. Shemuel then asked his father: "Where is the money that belongs to the orphans?"

His father told him: "The money is hidden in the wrap that covers the millstones. There are three bundles of money. The upper and lower ones belong to us and the middle one belongs to the orphans."

Shemuel asked his father: "Why did you store the money that way?"

Abba replied: "Because if thieves were to discover it, they would take mine, and if the earth were to destroy some of it, that would also be mine." (*Berachot* 18b)

For a glimpse of the world as it was in Rabbi Afes's time, see the historical timeline from 200 to 300 C.E.

אייבו
Aibu, father of Rav (grandfather of Aibu 2)

(second–third centuries C.E.)
Amora/Tanna, Eretz Yisrael and Babylonia

R. Aibu, who was the father of the famous Rav, was the brother of Rabbi Hiyya. (*Pesahim* 4a)

Rav was a nephew of R. Hiyya. When Rav came to Eretz Yisrael from Babylonia, his uncle R. Hiyya asked him, "Is your father Aibu alive?"

He answered: "Ask me if my mother is alive."

He asked him: "Is your mother alive?"

He answered: "Ask me whether Aibu is alive."

When R. Hiyya heard all this, he knew that his brother and sister had died. He said to his servant, "Take off my shoes and afterwards bring my things to the bathhouse."

R. Hiyya wanted to teach his students Halacha. From this event, three things may be learned: a mourner is forbidden to wear shoes, one mourns for only one day for a death regarding which the news was received after thirty days, and part of the day is considered as an entire day. (*Pesahim* 4a)

A master said that Aibu, Hana, Shila, Martha and R. Hiyya were the sons of Abba b. Aha Karsela of Kafri. (*Sanhedrin* 5a)

Rav was also the son of R. Hiyya's sister.

R. Aibu was a follower of Rabbi Eleazar b. Tzadok. He quoted him as saying: One should not walk more than three parasangs on erev Shabbat because he might not reach his destination before Shabbat. (*Sukkah* 44b)

Aibu, the father of Rav, said, "I was next to Rabbi Eleazar ben Tzadok when a certain man came to ask him this question: 'I posses cities, vineyards and olive trees, and the inhabitants of the cities come and work the fields and eat the olives. Is this proper or improper during a sabbatical year?' He answered that it is improper. When the man left, Rabbi Eleazar remarked: 'I have now been living here for forty years, and never have I seen as righteous a man as he.' The man returned to ask, 'What should I do?' Rabbi Eleazar told him: 'Leave the olives for the poor and pay yourself for the labor.'" (*Sukkah* 44b)

For a glimpse of the world as it was in R. Aibu's time, see the historical timeline from 150 to 250 C.E.

אייבו
Aibu 2, son of Rav (grandson of Aibu 1)

(third century C.E.)
Amora, Babylonia

R. Aibu was the son of Rav. Rav said to his son Aibu: "I have worked hard to teach you knowledge, but without success. Therefore come and I will teach you worldly wisdom:

"Sell your merchandise while the sand is still upon your feet. Regarding everything you sell, you may have regrets, because you might have sold it for more – except wine, which might become sour if you keep it for a while. Pocket the money before you open your sack of merchandise. It is preferable to earn a smaller amount near your home than to earn a larger one far from your home. When you have harvested dates and they are in your bag, run to the brewery to make beer, before you eat them yourself." (*Pesahim* 113a)

For a glimpse of the world as it was in the time of R. Aibu, son of Rav, see the historical timeline from 200 to 300 C.E.

אייבו
Aibu 3

(third–fourth centuries C.E.)
Amora, Babylonia

R. Aibu was a grandson of Rav through his daughter. During one Sukkot festival, he and his brother Hizkiyah brought a willow branch to Rav, who shook it over and over again without reciting a blessing, for he was of the opinion that it was only a minhag of the Prophets. (*Sukkah* 44b)

For a glimpse of the world as it was in the time of R. Aibu, grandson of Rav, see the historical timeline from 250 to 350 C.E.

עקביא בן מהללאל
Akavia ben Mahalalel

(first century B.C.E.–first century C.E.)
Tanna, Eretz Yisrael

R. Akavia, who engaged in halachic disputes with Rabbi Hanina Segan ha-Kohanim and Rabbi Dosa ben Hyrcanus, was a member of the Sanhedrin.

He disagreed with his colleagues on several issues of Jewish law. When he was offered the position of head of the rabbinical court on condition that he change his position, he refused to do so. Some say that he was excommunicated for maintaining his position, while others say that he was not. (*Negaim* 1:4)

We have learned that R. Yehuda said: "Heaven forbid that we should think that R. Akavia was excommunicated. That was a mistake. The doors of the Temple hall did not hold any man in Israel who was the equal of Rabbi Akavia ben Mahalalel in wisdom, purity and fear of God. They actually excommunicated Eleazar ben Hanoch, who raised doubts about washing the hands. (*Berachot* 19a)

One of his famous sayings is: "Reflect upon three things: know whence you come from, where you are going, and before whom you will have to give account." (Tractate *Avot* 3:1)

For a glimpse of the world as it was in R. Akavia b. Mahalal's time, see the historical timeline from 50 B.C.E. to 50 C.E.

עקיבא
Akiva

(first–second centuries C.E.)
Tanna, Eretz Yisrael
Head of the Academy in Benei Berak

R. Akiva, who was born in Judea to parents of modest means, had no Torah or Talmudic education during his early years. Rabbi Shimon ben Gamliel was his contemporary.

Rabbi Akiva admitted, "When I was an *am ha-aretz*, I used to say: If I had a scholar before me, I would maul him like an ass." (*Pesahim* 49b)

R. Akiva was employed as a shepherd by Ben Kalba Savua, one of the wealthiest men in Jerusalem. His daughter, noticing how modestly and nobly Akiva conducted himself, said to him, "If I were betrothed to you, would you go to study in a Talmudic academy?" He replied in the affirmative, and they were betrothed secretly. When her father found out, he expelled her from his home, disowning and disinheriting her by oath. The young couple lived in poverty so extreme that at one point, Rachel had to sell her hair in order to buy food.

In the meantime R. Akiva left his job and went to study at the academy, where he remained for twelve years. (*Ketubbot* 62b)

The daughter of Kalba Savua, one of the wealthiest men in Jerusalem, betrothed herself to R. Akiva. When her father found out, he disinherited her. Nevertheless, she married him that winter. The couple was so poor that they had to sleep on straw. In the morning, as he picked the straw from her hair, he told her: "If I could only afford it, I would present you with a golden brooch carved with Jerusalem." Elijah came in disguise and called out at the door, "Give me some straw, for my wife is giving birth and I have nothing for her to lie on." R. Akiva said to his wife, "See, there is a man who lacks even straw." (*Nedarim* 50a)

Upon her insistence that he become a scholar, he left her and spent twelve years in Lydda in the yeshivas of Rabbi Eliezer ben Hyrcanus and Rabbi Yehoshua ben Hananya. Upon arriving home he overheard a wicked man telling Rachel, R. Akiva's wife, "Your father did the right thing because your husband is inferior to you and has abandoned you to a living widowhood." She replied; "If he would listen to me, he would spend another twelve years in the academy." He therefore departed again, spending another twelve years at the academy. When he finally returned, he was accompanied by twenty-four thousand students. Everyone came out to welcome him, and his wife also went out to meet him. When she approached him, his attendants tried to thrust her aside, but R. Akiva scolded them, saying: "Let her be! What you and I accomplished in learning actually belongs to her." (*Nedarim* 50a)

Her father, Kalba Savua on hearing that a great man and scholar came to town, said to himself, I shall go to him; perhaps he will annul my vow. When he came, R. Akiva asked him; if you had known that she was marrying a great scholar would you have made the vow? He replied; if I had known that he knows one chapter or even one Halacha I would not have made the vow. He annulled the vow and said to him, I am the man she married. Kalba Savua fell on his face and kissed the feet of R. Akiva. He also gave him half of his wealth. (*Ketubbot* 63a)

He later studied in the academy at Yavne, eventually establishing his own academy in Bene Berak. When he returned home, he was accompanied by twelve thousand students.

Ben Azzai was R. Akiva's son-in-law.

The Talmud says that the wife of Ben Azzai, who was the daughter of Rabbi Akiva, acted as her mother had, insisting that her husband go to study. He had a reputation as an outstanding scholar. (*Ketubbot* 63a)

The Talmud relates that Rabbi Akiva charged his son Yoshua with seven instructions:

Do not sit to study Torah at the highest point of the city.

Do not live in a town where the leaders of the town are scholars, because they will neglect the needs of the town.

Do not enter your house suddenly, and all the more so your neighbor's house.

Do not walk without shoes.

Arise early and eat; in the summer on account of the heat and in the winter on account of the cold.

Treat your Shabbat like a weekday rather than be dependent on others.

Be on good terms with the person on whom the hour smiles.

When Rabbi Akiva lost two sons, both of whom were bridegrooms, people came from all over Israel to mourn for them. Rabbi Akiva stood on a podium and addressed the people, saying, "Even though my two sons were bridegrooms, I am consoled on account of the honor you have done them." (*Moed Katan* 21b)

When Rabbi Akiva's daughter was about to be married, her father was concerned because astrologers had told him that on the day of her wedding, she would be bitten by a snake and die. Before retiring on her wedding night, she removed her golden brooch and stuck it into the wall. When she removed it the next morning, she found the pin stuck through the eye of a dead serpent. R. Akiva asked her, "Can you think of any good deed you did yesterday?"

She replied, "While everyone was busy with the wedding banquet, a poor man came to the door, but everyone ignored him. I took my portion from the banquet and gave it to him." Rabbi Akiva praised her and then delivered a sermon on the topic "Charity saves from death." (*Shabbat* 156b)

R. Akiva said: "A man whose wife performs good deeds is indeed a rich man." (*Shabbat* 25b)

Rabbi Akiva had thousands of students. Among the most outstanding of them were Rabbi Meir, Rabbi Shimon ben Yohai, Rabbi Yosi ben Halafta, Rabbi Eleazar ben Shammua, and Rabbi Nehemia (*Berachot* 22a). One of his very loyal and devoted students was Rabbi Yohanan ha-Sandlar.

When the Jewish community of Eretz Yisrael sent a delegation to Rome, Rabbi Akiva was one of its members. They met with the Emperor and asked him to rescind the decree forbidding the study of Torah.

Rabbi Akiva was also greatly concerned with the plight of the poor. He was appointed a supervisor of charitable funds, and made numerous trips to collect funds on their behalf. The Talmud called him "the hand of the poor." (*Kiddushin* 27a)

R. Akiva's riches came from six sources. The first was Kalba Savua, his father-in-law. The second was a ship's figurehead in the shape of a ram. Once, when the wooden figurehead was abandoned on the seashore, R. Akiva found it, with money hidden inside. The third source was from a treasure chest (or tree trunk). R. Akiva gave once four zuz to sailors to bring him back something from overseas, and they brought back the treasure chest or tree trunk. When he opened it, it turned out to be the treasure of a sunken ship

According to Rashi, another source was a Roman matron. At one point, when study hall needed a large sum of money, the community sent R. Akiva to borrow it from a wealthy Roman matron. When she gave R. Akiva the money, she asked: Who will guarantee its repayment? He asked her: Whom would you like to be the guarantor? Let God and the sea be the guarantors, she said. R. Akiva agreed. When the time for repayment became due, R. Akiva was ill and unable to bring her the money. She went out to the sea and declared: God of the Universe, it is well known to you that I entrusted the money to you and the sea. Soon afterwards, the emperor's daughter suffered a fit of madness, during which she seized a treasure chest and threw it into the sea. The matron who lived on the seashore found it. After R. Akiva recuperated, he brought her the money with apologies for being late. She refused to take it, saying that the sea had already repaid her, and gave it to him as a gift. (*Nedarim* 50a)

Another source of R. Akiva's wealth was from the wife of Tinnius Rufus, whom R. Akiva married after her conversion to Judaism.[1]

The other source of his wealth was from Ketia b. Shalom, who left his entire fortune to R. Akiva and his associates.

Rabbi Dosa ben Hyrcanus, who had a very high opinion of R. Akiva, is quoted as saying: "The name of Rabbi Akiva is known from one end of the world to the other." (*Yevamot* 16a)

Rabbi Akiva supported Bar Kochva's revolt in 132 against Rome and asked his students to support it as well.

A discussion once took place among the rabbis as to whether making a toast over wine is considered an imitation of non-Jewish customs, and therefore a transgression. It was related that during a party that Rabbi Akiva made for his son, he made a toast with these words: "Wine and life to the mouths of the rabbis; life and wine to the mouths of their students." (*Shabbat* 67b)

The Talmud relates during one Sukkot festival, when R. Gamliel, R. Yoshua, R. Eleazar b. Azaryah and R. Akiva were traveling together on a ship, the only one among them who owned a lulav was R. Gamliel, who had bought it for one thousand zuz. R. Gamliel performed the mitzvah of waving the lulav. When he finished, he gave the lulav to R. Yoshua as a gift. R. Yoshua performed the mitzva of waving it, and then gave it as a gift to R. Eleazar b. Azaryah, who did likewise and then gave it as a gift to R. Akiva. R. Akiva performed the mitzvah and then returned the lulav to R. Gamliel. (*Sukkah* 41b)

During R. Akiva's time, the Roman authorities issued a decree forbidding Jews to study the Torah or observe its commandments.

The Talmud relates that during this time, a Jew by the name of Pappus b. Judah approached Rabbi Akiva and found him teaching Torah in a public gathering. He said to him, "Aren't you afraid of the government?"

R. Akiva replied, "Let me explain it to you with a parable. A fox was once walking on the riverbank, and he saw fish swimming away from the bank. 'From what are you fleeing?' asked the fox. The fish replied, 'We are fleeing from the nets that people cast into the water to catch us.'

"He said to them, 'Come up to the dry land and live with me in safety.' They said to him, 'Are you the one they call the cleverest of all the animals? You are not clever but foolish. If we are afraid in the element in which we live, how much more endangered shall we be in the element that is strange to us?

"So it is with us Jews. If such is our condition when we study Torah, which is our natural environment, how much

---

[1] Rachel had most likely passed away by this time (author's opinion).

worse off we shall be if we neglect the Torah?"

Soon afterward, Rabbi Akiva was imprisoned for teaching Torah openly in defiance of the decree. The Romans also arrested Pappus b. Judah and held him in the same prison. Rabbi Akiva asked Pappus: "Why were you imprisoned?"

Pappus replied, "Fortunate are you, Akiva, that you were arrested for teaching Torah. Alas for Pappus, who was arrested for things of no importance."

When Rabbi Akiva was arrested, he was already an old man. The Romans, who had no consideration for his old age, condemned him to death.

When R. Akiva was led to execution, it was the time for the recital of the shema. As his executioners tore his flesh with iron combs, he accepted upon himself the kingship of Heaven. His students asked him: "Rabbi, even now?" He answered, "All my life I have been troubled by a verse in the Torah that says, 'With all your soul.' I wondered when I would have the opportunity to fulfill that commandment. Now that I have the opportunity, shall I not fulfill it?" (*Berachot* 61b)

Rabbi Yoshua ha-Garsi was a student of Rabbi Akiva and a very devoted and loyal friend. (*Eruvin* 21b)

He attended R. Akiva in prison, and every day he brought him a certain quantity of water. One day the warden said to him, "Today you have far too much water. Perhaps you want to use it in order to dig beneath the prison?"

The warden spilled half the water and allowed R. Yoshua to take the rest inside. When Rabbi Akiva saw how little water he had brought, he said, "Yoshua, don't you know that I am an old man and my life depends on you?"

Rabbi Yoshua told him what the warden had done. Rabbi Akiva said to

him, "Give me some water to wash my hands." The other hesitated and said, "There is not enough water here for drinking, let alone for washing hands."

Rabbi Akiva answered him, "What can I do, seeing that those who disobey the words of the rabbis deserve to die?" He refused to taste any food until R. Yoshua brought him water to wash his hands first.

It is stated Rabbi Akiva had twelve thousand pairs of students from Gabbath to Antipharas, all of whom died at the same time because they did not treat each other with respect. A tanna taught that all of them died between Pesah and Shavuot. These were the remaining students of Rabbi Akiva who revived the Torah at that time: Rabbi Meir, Rabbi Yehuda bar Illai, Rabbi Yosi ben Halafta, Rabbi Shimon bar Yohai and Rabbi Eleazar ben Shammua. (*Yevamot* 62b)

(*Menachot* 29b) The Talmud tells us: R. Yehuda said in the name of Rav: "When Moshe ascended to Heaven in order to receive the Torah, he found the Almighty engaged with placing coronets over the letters of the Torah. Moshe said to the Lord of the Universe, "Is not the Torah perfect as it is? Is anything missing from the Torah that additions are needed?"

God answered him: "In future years there will be a man by the name of Akiva ben Yoseph who will expound on this subject and will derive something from each point or elevation. Moshe said. "Lord of the Universe, permit me to see this person." He replied. "Turn around!"

Moshe turned around and found himself in the yeshiva of Rabbi Akiva. He went and sat down in the eighth row, where Rabbi Akiva's students were sitting. Although he listened to the discussion, he could not follow what the students were arguing about. He felt ill at ease, but then a student asked, "Where do we know this from?" Rabbi Akiva replied. "This is the law according to Moshe, which was given to him on Mount Sinai." When Moshe heard this, he was comforted. He then addressed God: "How is it that even though you have such a great man as Rabbi Akiva, you chose to give the Torah through me?"

He replied. "Be silent. Do not question me. Such is my decree."

Turnus Rufus, the Roman governor, asked Rabbi Akiva, "If God loves the poor, why does He not support them?"

Rabbi Akiva replied. "God gave us the commandment of giving charity in order to save us from the punishment of Gehinnom."

"On the contrary," countered Rufus. "It is this deed of giving food to the poor that condemns you to Gehinnom. I will give you an illustration. Suppose a king was angry with his servant and sent him to prison with orders that no food be given to him, and someone gave him food. Would the king not be angry with this man? Would he not punish him?"

Rabbi Akiva retorted, "Suppose the king became angry with his son and put him in prison with orders not to feed him, and someone gave him food. Would the king not be grateful to this man and even send him a gift?" (*Bava Batra* 10a)

The River Sambatyon is often mentioned in Jewish literature. According to some, the ten lost tribes have vanished beyond that river. Every day of the week, the river is in turmoil, with strong currents carrying rocks with tremendous force. It is impassable except on Shabbat. On that day, the river rests and all is quiet.

Tinnius Rufus or Turnus Rufus, the governor of Judea, asked R. Akiva: "In what way is the Jewish Sabbath different

from any other day of the week"? R. Akiva asked in turn. "In what way is one man different from any other man – you, for example?"

Rufus answered, "I am different because the Emperor wishes it so."

R. Akiva rejoined: "The Sabbath day is different because the Master of the World wishes it so." Rufus asked; "How do you know for certain which day is the Sabbath? Perhaps you are mistaken and another day of the week is the actual Sabbath."

R. Akiva answered: "The River Sambatyon is proof." Rashi comments that this river of stones is turbulent and impassable every day of the week except for Shabbat, when it rests. (*Sanhedrin* 65b)

R. Gamliel and R. Akiva disagreed about building a sukkah on a ship. Once they were on a journey on a ship during the Sukkot festival. R. Akiva erected a sukkah on the deck. The next day, a wind tore the sukkah down and blew it away. R. Gamliel asked R. Akiva: "Akiva, where is your sukkah?" (*Sukkah* 23a)

Rabbi Gamliel and the Elders disagreed about the blessing to be said over fruit. Once, R. Gamliel and the Elders were sitting in an upper chamber in Jericho and they were served dates. R. Gamliel gave R. Akiva permission to recite the blessings. R. Akiva recited one blessing that included three. R. Gamliel said to him in disapproval, "How long will you stick your head into quarrels that go against me?"

R. Akiva replied, "My teacher, you rule one way and the rabbis rule differently. You have taught us that when an individual takes issue with the majority, the Halacha is decided according to the majority. (*Berachot* 37a)

R. Bizna b. Zavda said in the name of R. Akiva, who had it from R. Panda, who had it from R. Nachum, who had it from R. Birim, who said it in the name of an Elder by the name of R. Banah: "There were twenty-four interpreters of dreams in Jerusalem. R. Banah once had a dream and he went to all twenty-four. Each gave him a different interpretation, and all were fulfilled." (*Berachot* 55b)

R. Huna said in the name of Rav, who learned it from R. Meir, who learned it from R. Akiva, "One should always say: 'Whatever God does is for the good.' By way of illustration, once, when R. Akiva was traveling, he arrived at a certain town. He was traveling with a rooster, a donkey and a lamp. He looked around in the town for lodging, but none was available. Saying to himself, 'Whatever God does is for the good,' he slept in an open field. A strong wind came and blew out the lamp, a wild cat came and ate the rooster, and a lion came and ate the donkey. He said again, 'Whatever God does is for the good.' That night, a band of raiders came, captured all the inhabitants of the town and carried them away. He said: 'Did I not say that whatever God does is for the good?'"

He must have learned it from R. Nachum Ish Gam Zu, who was R. Akiva's teacher for many years. (*Berachot* 60b)

R. Yaakov and R. Zerika said, "Whenever R. Akiva and one of his colleagues are in disagreement, Halacha accords with R. Akiva. When R. Yosi is in disagreement with his colleagues, Halacha accords with R. Yosi. Between R. Yehuda ha-Nasi and one of his colleagues, Halacha accords with Rebbe."

"What practical difference does it make?"

R. Assi said: "The general practice of law."

R. Hiyya b. Abba said, "The difference is that we tend in their favor."

R. Yosi b. Hanina said, "They are seen as acceptable views." (*Eruvin* 46b)

The Talmud says: When Rabbi Akiva died, the glory of the Law came to an end. (*Sotah* 49a)

R. Abbaye said: R. Shimon b. Gamliel, R. Shimon, R. Yishmael and R. Akiva all maintain that all Israelites are princes. We have learned that if one was a debtor for a thousand zuz and he wore a robe costing a hundred maneh, he is stripped of that robe and dressed in a less expensive one. That was the opinion of the rabbis, but R. Yishmael and R. Akiva disagreed because all Israel is worthy of that robe. (*Bava Metzia* 113b)

R. Yehuda said: We were once sitting in the presence of R. Akiva; and that day was the ninth of the month of Av, which occurred on a Friday. They brought him a lightly roasted egg and he ate it without salt. He did this not because he had an appetite for it, but to demonstrate the halacha to the students. (*Eruvin* 41a)

Rabbi Yoshua ben Levi said: "Whenever you find the following statement in the Talmud: 'A student said it in the name of Rabbi Yishmael before Rabbi Akiva,' this refers to Rabbi Meir, who was an attendant of both Rabbi Akiva and Rabbi Yishmael."

It was taught that Rabbi Meir said, "When I was with Rabbi Yishmael, I used to put a chemical called kankantum into the ink, and he did not object. But when I was with Rabbi Akiva and I tried to do the same thing, he forbade it." (*Eruvin* 13a)

Our rabbis taught: when R. Eliezer fell ill, four sages went to visit him: R. Tarfon, R. Yoshua, R. Eleazar b. Azaryah and R. Akiva.

R. Tarfon said to him: "You are more valuable to Israel than rain, for rain is precious in this world, but you are precious in this world and the next."

R. Yoshua said: "You are more valuable to Israel than the disc of the sun, for the sun's disc is only in this world, while you are for this and the next world."

R. Eleazar b. Azaryah said: "You are better to Israel than a father and mother, they are only for this world, but you are for this and the next world."

But R. Akiva remarked: "Suffering is precious." R. Eliezer liked R. Akiva's remark best. (*Sanhedrin* 101a)

The Talmud states: The day R. Akiva died, Rebbe was born. When Rebbe died, Rav Yehuda was born. When Rav Yehuda, died Rava was born. When Rava died, R. Ashi was born. (*Kiddushin* 72b)

For a glimpse of the world as it was in R. Akiva's time, see the historical timeline from 50 to 150 C.E.

אמימר

Amemar

(fourth–fifth centuries C.E.)
Amora, Babylonia
Head of the academy in Mehoza

R. Amemar, a dayyan, lived in Nehardea. (*Baba Batra* 31a)

Amemar said, "I am a Nehardean, and I hold that pleas may be retracted or altered."

Later on, he became the head of the yeshiva in Mehoza. R. Mar Zutra and R. Ashi were some of his students. One of his close friends was Rabbi Chuna ben Nathan.

Amemar was so much esteemed by his students that they carried him to his synagogue of Mechuza on their shoulders. (*Betzah* 25b)

Amemar, as a judge, was in the middle of a trial when a bird flew down and landed on his head. A man approached and removed the bird. "What is your business here?" asked Amemar. "I have a lawsuit pending,"

replied the man. "In that case," said Amemar, "I am disqualified as a judge." (*Ketubbot* 105b)

The Talmud states that R. Ashi said: R, Huna b. Nathan told me that Amemar has issued a law in Mehoza that a Persian document signed by Israelite witnesses is sufficient for recovering even mortgaged property.

It is related in the Talmud that R. Ameimar, Mar Zutra and Rabbi Ashi were sitting at the gate of the Persian king Yezdegerd, when the king's table-steward passed them by.

When R. Ashi observed that Mar Zutra turned pale he dipped his finger into the dish the steward was carrying and put it in the mouth of Mar Zutra.

The king's officers said, "You have spoiled the King's meal. Why have you done this? You have rendered the meal unsuitable for the king."

R. Ashi answered them: "I noticed a piece of contaminated meat in the dish." They examined the dish, but found nothing contaminated. He pointed with his finger to a part of the dish, and asked. "Did you examine this part?" They examined that part and found it contaminated.

The rabbis asked him, "Why did you rely on a miracle?"

He answered them, "I saw a sickness hovering over Mar Zutra." (*Ketubbot* 61a–b)

Amemar, Mar Zutra and R. Ashi were once sitting together. They said: "Let each one of us say something that the others did not hear before." One of them said: "If one had a dream and does not understand what he dreamt, he should stand before the Kohanim when they spread their hands to bless the congregation, and he should recite the prayer for dreams, which starts with the phrase "Ribbono shel Olam." (*Berachot* 55b)

Amemar, Mar Zutra and R. Ashi were sitting together when raw vegetables were set before them before the fourth hour. Amemar and R. Ashi ate, but Mar Zutra would not eat. They asked him, "Why do you not eat?" He answered, "Because R. Yitzhak said that if one eats vegetables before the fourth hour, his breath will smell." (*Berachot* 44b)

Amemar, Mar Zutra and R. Ashi were dining together and they were served dates and pomegranates. Mar Zutra took some and threw them in front of R. Ashi as his portion to eat. Said R. Ashi to Mar Zutra, "Does not your honor agree with what was taught – that food is not to be thrown?" (*Berachot* 50b)

Amemar said: "A wise man is superior even to a prophet." (*Bava Batra* 12a)

For a glimpse of the world as it was in R. Amemar's time, see the historical timeline from 350 to 450 C.E.

אמי בר נתן
Ammi b. Nathan

(third–fourth century C.E.)
Amora, Eretz Yisrael
Head of the academy in Tiberias

R. Ammi studied in Rav's yeshiva in Babylonia and under Rabbi Oshaya and Rabbi Hanina in Eretz Yisrael. However, his main teacher was Rabbi Yohanan, under whom he and his colleague, Rabbi Assi, studied in the yeshiva of Tiberias. (*Nedarim* 40b, *Shabbat* 119a)

Rabbi Ammi and Rabbi Assi, both of whom were kohanim, are frequently mentioned together. (*Megillah* 22a, *Gittin* 59b)

When they were ordained together, a special song was sung in their honor: "Ordain us only men like these, only men like these." (*Ketubbot* 17a, *Sanhedrin* 14a)

Both were spoken of as the *dayyanim* of Eretz Yisrael. (*Sanhedrin* 17b)

R. Hisda spoke of R. Ammi as a great man. (*Yevamot* 21b)

R. Ammi and R. Assi used to set the eruv for the whole city of Tiberias. They later became the heads of the academy there. (*Betzah* 16b)

On the day R. Eleazar b. Pedat was to be married, R. Ammi and R. Assi decorated his bridal canopy. He said to them: While you are busy decorating, I will go to the *bet midrash* to learn something there. (*Berachot* 16a)

After Rabbi Eleazar ben Pedat passed away, Rabbi Ammi was appointed head of the academy in Tiberias with Rabbi Assi as his assistant.

R. Ammi and R. Assi sat and studied between the pillars of the synagogue in Tiberias. Every now and then they knocked on the side of the door and announced: If anyone has a lawsuit, let him come forward. (*Shabbat* 10a)

Although Rabbi Ammi and Rabbi Assi had thirteen synagogues in Tiberias, they prayed only in the synagogue where they studied. (*Berachot* 8a)

It was stated: When R. Dimi came, he related that it was R. Bibi's turn to wait on the students that Shabbat. R. Ammi and R. Assi happened to be there. He placed a whole basket of fruit before them. I do not know whether he did it out of generosity or for some other reason. (*Shabbat* 74a)

Rabbi Avira, one of their students, transmitted many of the sayings of Rabbi Ammi and Rabbi Assi. (*Berachot* 20b)

R. Ammi once sent out a decree in Israel with these words: I, Ammi son of Nathan, issue a Torah decree to all of Israel regarding a law about slaves. (*Gittin* 44a)

When R. Huna passed away, his body was brought to Eretz Yisrael for burial. People told R. Ammi and R. Assi that R. Huna had come. They remarked: When we were in Babylonia, he was so great that we could not lift up our heads on account of him, and now that we are here, he has come after us? They were then informed that it was his coffin that had arrived. When they heard the sad news, R. Ammi and R. Assi went out to pay their last respects to him. (*Moed Katan* 25a)

When Rabbi Yohanan passed away, Rabbi Ammi sat *shiva* and observed *sheloshim* for him. (*Moed Katan* 25b)

R. Avira was quoted as saying the following, sometimes in the name of Rabbis Ammi and sometimes in the name of R. Assi: "A man should always eat and drink less than he can afford, clothe himself in accordance with his means, and honor his wife and children more than he can afford, because they are dependent on him, and he depends on the Creator." (*Hullin* 84b)

A man once deposited seven pearls wrapped in a cloth with R. Miasha, the grandson of R. Yoshua b. Levi. When R. Miasha died without a will, they came before R. Ammi to claim the pearls. R. Ammi said to them: I know that R. Miasha was not a wealthy man, and secondly, the man did give recognizable clues. (*Ketubbot* 85b)

R. Avira quoted R. Ammi and R. Assi at various times: The angels said to God, "Master of the Universe, it is written in Your Torah: 'He neither engages in favoritism nor takes bribes,' but You favor the Jewish people." God answered the angels: "How could I not favor them? I wrote in my Torah: Eat, be satisfied and bless your God, and they are so meticulous that they bless God even over a quantity as small as that of an olive or an egg." (*Berachot* 20b)

As R. Yohanan was ascending a staircase with R. Ammi and R. Assi supported him, the staircase collapsed beneath them. R. Yohanan rose and carried both R. Ammi and R. Assi to the top. The rabbis asked him: "Since your strength is fully present, why do you need to be supported?" He answered, "If I use up my strength, what shall I keep for my old age?" (*Ketubbot* 62a)

The Talmud relates that when R. Ammi and R. Assi sat before R. Yitzhak Nepaha, one of them asked him, "Would you please teach us some halacha?" The other requested, "Would you please relate some agadata?"

When he began speaking on agadata, one of them was unhappy, and when he started instruction on halacha, the other was unhappy. Noticing this, he stopped and said. "I will tell you a story. A man had two wives, one younger and one older. The younger one used to pluck out his white hair, while the older one used to pluck out his black hair. At the end he was left completely bald. Therefore I will tell you something that will be of interest to both of you." (*Bava Kamma* 60b)

Rabbi Zerika said in the names of Rabbi Ammi and Rabbi Yehoshua ben Levi: When in the presence of one deceased, speak of nothing but him. (*Berachot* 3b)

For a glimpse of the world as it was in Rabbi Ammi's time, see the historical timeline from 250 to 350 C.E.

עמרם
Amram
(third century C.E.)
Amora, Babylonia

R. Amram's favorite quotes were from Rabbi Assi and Rav.

Once R. Rammi b. Yechezkel sent a request to Rabbi Amram for some of the excellent sayings of Rabbi Assi, and he obliged him. (*Eruvin* 102a)

R. Amram quoted Rav about Kiddush and Havdala. (*Pesahim* 105a)

R. Amram quoted Rav regarding a vow. (*Nedarim* 28a)

R. Amram and Rabbah were having a heated discussion about two different issues. (*Bava Metzia* 20b)

R. Amram said in the name of Rav: Three transgressions daily are hard to avoid: sinful thoughts, insincere prayers, and slander or shades of slander. (*Bava Batra* 164b)

Rabbi Amram said in the name of Rav: Happy is the one who repents while still in full vigor. (*Avoda Zara* 19a)

For a glimpse of the world as it was in Rabbi Amram's time, see the historical timeline from 200 to 300 C.E.

עמרם
Amram

(fourth century C.E.)
Amora, Babylonia

R. Amram was a student of Rabbi Sheshet in Nehardea and in Mehoza.

Once it happened that R. Sheshet decided a matter in Nehardea by referring to a baraita, and R. Amram argued against it. Said R. Sheshet to him, "Perhaps you are from Pumbedita, where they draw an elephant through the eye of a needle." He engaged in debates with Rabbah and with R. Yoseph. (*Bava Metzia* 38b)

Amram quotes R. Nahman on a halachic issue: whether one must repeat a blessing if he omitted an important part of it. (*Berachot* 49b)

R. Amram quoted R. Sheshet about a woman who is forbidden to marry a Kohen. (*Yevamot* 35a)

R. Amram had a halachic discussion with R. Sheshet about utensils. (*Avoda Zara* 76a)

R. Amram quoted R. Sheshet regarding a *sotah* who has witnesses overseas. (*Sotah* 6a)

For a glimpse of the world as it was in R. Amram's time, see the historical timeline from 300 to 400 C.E.

ענן
Anan

(third century C.E.)
Amora, Babylonia

R. Anan was a student of R. Shemuel. (*Kiddushin* 39a)

He was a *dayyan* and a judge in Nehardea.

A man once brought R. Anan a load of fish. R. Anan asked him: "What is your business here?" The man answered, "I have a lawsuit before you." R. Anan did not accept the gift, telling him, "I am now disqualified from hearing your case." The man said to R. Anan, "I do not expect you to be the judge in my case, but I would like you to accept my gift as a substitute for my first-fruits offering."

R. Anan replied, "I had no intention of accepting the gift, but since you have given me your reason, I will accept." He sent him to R. Nahman, who was also a judge, with a message: "Please hear this case because I am not qualified to be his judge." After reading the message, R. Nahman thought that the man was his relative. R. Nahman postponed another case – a lawsuit of orphans – to take this one, and showed great consideration to this man. The man, for his part, was astonished at the consideration he was shown.

Until this incident, Eliyahu was a frequent visitor to R. Anan, whom he was teaching the Seder Eliyahu. After this incident Eliyahu stopped his visits. R. Anan spent his time in fasting and prayer. Eventually, Eliyahu came to him again, but a fear came over R. Anan when Eliyahu appeared. In order not to be frightened, he made himself a box and he sat inside it until he finished the Seder Eliyahu. This is the reason there is a Seder Eliyahu Rabbah and a Seder

Eliyahu Zuta; one part is before this incident and one after. (*Ketubbot* 105b)

R. Anan said in R. Shmuel's name: "Orphans' money may be lent out at interest." R. Nachman objected. (*Bava Metzia* 70a)

(Kesuvos 111 a) R. Anan said: "Whoever is buried in the land of Israel is considered to be buried under the altar."

(Kesuvos 69 a) R. Anan sent a message to R. Huna with regards to a woman's inheritance. When the message arrived to R. Huna R. Sheishes was present. R. Huna told R. Sheishes to deliver a message to R. Anan, in which he addressed him "Anan, Anan"

When R. Sheishes delivered the message to R. Anan he was offended by the tone of the letter. Mar Ukva, the Exilarch got involved to smooth things out.

For a glimpse of the world as it was in R. Anan's time, see the historical timeline from 200 to 300 C.E.

אנטיגנוס איש סוכו
Antigonus Ish Socho

(second century B.C.E.)
Tanna, Eretz Yisrael

R. Antigonus was one of the earliest tannaim, who were called sofrim.

He used to quote in the name of Shimon ha-Zaddik: be not like servants who serve for an expected reward, but be like servants who do not expect rewards. (*Pirke Avos* 1:3)

For a glimpse of the world as it was in R. Antigonus's time, see the historical timeline from 200 to 100 B.C.E.

אשי
Ashi

(fourth–fifth centuries C.E.)
Amora, Babylonia
Head of the academy in Sura

R. Ashi was appointed the head of the Sura academy after Rabbi Papa passed away. He occupied the position for almost sixty years.

Some of his great teachers were Rava, R. Papa, and R. Rammi b. Abba, who was his father-in-law. (*Hullin* 111a)

He lived in Mata Mehasya, a small community near Sura.

Rabbi Ashi is credited with the redaction of the Babylonian Talmud. The Talmud states: Rebbe and Rabbi Nathan completed the Mishna, and Rav Ashi and R. Ravina completed the Talmud. Later on, Ravina b. Huna edited it to its final completion. (*Bava Metzia* 86a)

Rabbi Ashi was also wealthy and influential. Even the Exilarch, R. Huna b. Nathan, accepted his halachic authority. He was the spokesman and the leader of his generation. Most likely, he had connections in the Persian palace. (*Gittin* 59a)

It is related in the Talmud that R. Ameimar, Mar Zutra and Rabbi Ashi were sitting at the gate of the Persian king Yezdegerd, when the king's table-steward passed them by.

When R. Ashi observed that Mar Zutra turned pale he dipped his finger into the dish the steward was carrying and put it in the mouth of Mar Zutra.

The king's officers said, "You have spoiled the King's meal. Why have you done this? You have rendered the meal unsuitable for the king."

R. Ashi answered them: "I noticed a piece of contaminated meat in the dish." They examined the dish, but found nothing contaminated. He pointed with his finger to a part of the dish, and asked. "Did you examine this part?" They examined that part and found it contaminated.

The rabbis asked him, "Why did you rely on a miracle?"

He answered them, "I saw a sickness hovering over Mar Zutra." (*Ketubbot* 61a–b)

Amemar, Mar Zutra and R. Ashi were once sitting together. They said: "Let each one of us say something that the others did not hear before." One of them said: "If one had a dream and does not understand what he dreamt, he should stand before the Kohanim when they spread their hands to bless the congregation, and he should recite the prayer for dreams, which starts with the phrase "Ribbono shel Olam." (*Berachot* 55b)

The Talmud states that when the majority of the rabbis left Rav's academy, twelve hundred students remained behind. When the students left R. Huna's academy, eight hundred students were left behind. (*Ketubbot* 106a)

When R. Huna delivered a lecture, thirteen interpreters assisted him.

When the students left the academy of Rabbah and R. Yoseph, four hundred students remained behind, and they described themselves as orphans.

When the students left R. Abbaye's academy – others say R. Pappa's and still others say R. Ashi's – there remained two hundred rabbis, and they described themselves as orphans of the orphans.

Rabbi Ashi had two sons; Mar b. Rav Ashi and Sama. He also had a daughter, who is mentioned in the Talmud.

Come and hear: R. Ravina allowed the daughter of R. Ashi to collect her inheritance from her brother Mar without an oath. He gave her permission to choose from his medium-grade properties. But from her brother Sama he allowed her to collect property only with an oath, and a lower-grade property. (*Ketubbot* 69a)

Once it happened that Ravina examined a slaughterer's knife in Babylonia. R. Ashi, who was the halachic authority in the area, was offended and said to him: "Why are you acting in this manner?"

Ravina answered: "Did not R. Hamnuna decide legal matters at Harta di Argiz during the lifetime of R. Hisda? Just as in their case, I am also your colleague and your student." (*Eruvin* 63a)

When Rabbi Ashi's daughter suffered from a stomach ailment, Rabin of Naresh cured her with herbal medicines. (*Gittin* 69b)

R. Ashi had a forest in Shelania. He went to chop down some branches on hol ha-mo'ed. R. Sheila from Shelania asked him: On whom are you relying in order to do this? Is it on R. Hananel, who said in the name of Rav that one may chop down branches from a palm tree on hol ha-mo'ed? But Abbaye denounced it vehemently. R. Ashi answered, I do not agree with Abbaye. Later on, when he was chopping some branches, the hatchet slipped and almost cut off his leg. He stopped working and continued some other time. (*Moed Katan* 12b)

Amemar, Mar Zutra and R. Ashi were dining together and they were served dates and pomegranates. Mar Zutra took some and threw them in front of R. Ashi as his portion to eat. Said R. Ashi to Mar Zutra, "Does not your honor agree with what was taught – that food is not to be thrown?" (*Berachot* 50b)

When R. Assi attended the wedding feast of Mar, the son of R. Ashi. he recited six benedictions. (*Ketubbot* 8a)

R. Ashi attended the wedding feast of R. Kahana. On the first day he recited all the benedictions, but the following days he recited them all only if there were new guests at the table. (*Ketubbot* 8a)

Among his statements are the following: "Anyone who is haughty will in the end be degraded." (*Sotah* 5a)

"A scholar who is not as hard as iron is no scholar." (*Taanit* 4a)

R. Abba said: On Shabbat it is one's duty to break bread over two loaves. R. Ashi said: I saw R. Kahana holding two loaves, but he broke only one of them. (*Shabbat* 117b)

R. Adda b. Ahava said: From Rebbe's time to R. Ashi's, we do not find learning and high office combined in the same person. (*Sanhedrin* 36a)

It was recorded in R. Levi's notebook that one who is born on a Sunday will be either completely virtuous or completely wicked. R. Ashi said: I and Dimi b. Kakuzta were born on a Sunday; I am a head of the academy and he is captain of thieves. (*Shabbat* 156a)

The Talmud states: "The day R. Akiva died, Rebbe was born. When Rebbe died, Rav Yehuda was born. When Rav Yehuda died, Rava was born, and when Rava died, R. Ashi was born." (*Kiddushin* 72b)

For a glimpse of the world as it was in R. Ashi's time, see the historical timeline from 350 to 400 C.E.

אסי

Assi

(third century C.E.)
Amora, Babylonia

R. Assi was a resident of Huzal, a community near Nehardea.

A wealthy person, he inspected his property daily. The Talmud relates that one day, as Rabbi Assi was inspecting his property, he noticed that a pipe had burst and was flooding his property. He took off his coat, rolled it up and plugged the leak with it. He then called aloud, and people came to help him repair the damage. R. Assi was a contemporary of Rav and Shemuel, with whom he had halachic engagements. A highly-respected authority in all of Babylonia, he often differed with Rav and Shemuel. (*Hullin* 105a)

Rabbi Assi read the Megillah in Huzal on both the fourteenth and the fifteenth of Adar because he was in doubt whether his town had been walled in the time of Yehoshua. According to another report, R. Assi said: Huzal of the house of Binyamin was walled in the days of Yehoshua Bin Nun. (*Megillah* 5b)

When Rav visited a certain place, he refrained from doing something that he had ruled permissible on other occasions out of respect for Rabbi Kahana and Rabbi Assi. (*Shabbat* 146b)

Rav and Shemuel and R. Assi once met at a circumcision ceremony, though some say it was at a ceremony of the redemption of the first-born. Rav did not want to enter before Shemuel, and Shemuel did not want to enter before R. Assi. Finally, it was decided that Rav and R. Assi would enter together first and Shemuel would enter last. (*Bava Kamma* 80a)

Sheila b. Avina decided a matter according to Rav. When Rav was on his deathbed, he said to R. Assi: Go and restrain him, and if he does not listen try to convince him. After Rav passed away, R. Assi asked him to retract, because Rav had retracted his ruling.

R. Sheila said, "If Rav had retracted, he would have told me," and refused to retract. R. Assi put him under the ban.

R. Sheila asked him: "Are you not afraid of the fire?"

He answered: "I am Issi b. Yehuda, who is Issi b. Gur-aryeh, who is Issi b.

Gamliel, who is Issi b. Mahalalel, a cooper mortar, which does not rust."

The other retorted: "I am Sheila b. Avina, an iron mallet that breaks the cooper mortar."

Soon after this incident, R. Assi became very sick and died. R. Sheila told his wife: "Prepare my burial clothes because I do not want him to have the opportunity to tell Rav things about me." When R. Sheila died, people saw a myrtle fly from one grave to the other. We may conclude that the rabbis made peace. (*Niddah* 36b)

For a glimpse of the world as it was in R. Assi's time, see the historical timeline from 200 to 300 C.E.

אסי

Assi

(third–fourth centuries C.E.)
Amora, Eretz Yisrael
Head of the academy in Tiberias

Rabbi Assi and his friend and colleague, Rabbi Ammi, studied together in the academy of Rabbi Shemuel in Nehardea and also under Rabbi Huna in Sura. They are frequently mentioned in the Talmud. Both were *kohanim*. (*Megillah* 22a)

When they were ordained together, a special song was sung in their honor: "Ordain us only men like these, only men like these." (*Ketubbot* 17a, *Sanhedrin* 14a)

Both were spoken of as the *dayyanim* of Eretz Yisrael. (*Sanhedrin* 17b)

R. Ammi and R. Assi used to set the eruv for the whole city of Tiberias. They later became the heads of the academy there. (*Betzah* 16b)

In Eretz Yisrael, R. Assi went to study under Rabbi Yoshua ben Levi and Rabbi Hanina. He eventually settled in Tiberias, where he studied with Rabbi Yohanan Nepaha.

Once, R. Assi's elderly mother asked him for ornaments, and he bought them for her. She said to him: "I want a husband." He told her: "I will take care of you." When she told him: "I want a husband as handsome as you," he left and moved to Eretz Yisrael. When he heard that she was following him to Eretz Yisrael, he went to R. Yohanan and asked him: "May I leave Eretz Yisrael to go abroad?" He answered that it was forbidden.

He then asked, "May I leave to meet my mother?" R. Yohanan said, "I do not know." He waited a while and asked him again, and this time, R. Yohanan answered, "Assi, I see that you are determined to go. May God bring you back in peace."

He went to R. Eleazar and said to him. "Perhaps, God forbid, he was angry?" R. Eleazar replied: Had he been angry, he would have not blessed you. In the meantime, R. Assi found out that his mother died on the way to Eretz Yisrael. (*Kiddushin* 31b)

On the day R. Eleazar b. Pedat was to be married, R. Ammi and R. Assi decorated his bridal canopy. He said to them: While you are busy decorating, I will go to the *bet midrash* to learn something there. (*Berachot* 16a)

After Rabbi Eleazar ben Pedat passed away, Rabbi Ammi was appointed head of the academy in Tiberias with Rabbi Assi as his assistant.

R. Ammi and R. Assi sat and studied between the pillars of the synagogue in Tiberias. Every now and then they knocked on the side of the door and announced: If anyone has a lawsuit, let him come forward. (*Shabbat* 10a)

Although Rabbi Ammi and Rabbi Assi had thirteen synagogues in Tiberias, they prayed only in the synagogue where they studied. (*Berachot* 8a)

It was stated: When R. Dimi came, he related that it was R. Bibi's turn to wait on the students that Shabbat. R. Ammi and R. Assi happened to be there. He placed a whole basket of fruit before them. I do not know whether he did it out of generosity or for some other reason. (*Shabbat* 74a)

Rabbi Avira, one of their students, transmitted many of the sayings of Rabbi Ammi and Rabbi Assi. (*Berachot* 20b)

When R. Huna passed away, his body was brought to Eretz Yisrael for burial. People told R. Ammi and R. Assi that R. Huna had come. They remarked: When we were in Babylonia, he was so great that we could not lift up our heads on account of him, and now that we are here, he has come after us? They were then informed that it was his coffin that had arrived. When they heard the sad news, R. Ammi and R. Assi went out to pay their last respects to him. (*Moed Katan* 25a)

R. Avira was quoted as saying the following, sometimes in the name of Rabbis Ammi and sometimes in the name of R. Assi: "A man should always eat and drink less than he can afford, clothe himself in accordance with his means, and honor his wife and children more than he can afford, because they are dependent on him, and he depends on the Creator." (*Hullin* 84b)

R. Avira quoted R. Ammi and R. Assi at various times: The angels said to God, "Master of the Universe, it is written in Your Torah: 'He neither engages in favoritism nor takes bribes,' but You favor the Jewish people." God answered the angels: "How could I not favor them? I wrote in my Torah: Eat, be satisfied and bless your God, and they are so meticulous that they bless God even over a quantity as small as that of an olive or an egg." (*Berachot* 20b)

As R. Yohanan was ascending a staircase with R. Ammi and R. Assi supported him, the staircase collapsed beneath them. R. Yohanan rose and carried both R. Ammi and R. Assi to the top. The rabbis asked him: "Since your strength is fully present, why do you need to be supported?" He answered, "If I use up my strength, what shall I keep for my old age?" (*Ketubbot* 62a)

The Talmud relates that when R. Ammi and R. Assi sat before R. Yitzhak Nepaha, one of them asked him, "Would you please teach us some halacha?" The other requested, "Would you please relate some agadata?"

When he began speaking on agadata, one of them was unhappy, and when he started instruction on halacha, the other was unhappy. Noticing this, he stopped and said. "I will tell you a story. A man had two wives, one younger and one older. The younger one used to pluck out his white hair, while the older one used to pluck out his black hair. At the end he was left completely bald. Therefore I will tell you something that will be of interest to both of you." (*Bava Kamma* 60b)

When the Talmud does not refer to a rabbi by name, but instead uses a reference term, the following rule applies: The phrase "The judges of Eretz Yisrael" refers to Rabbi Ammi and Rabbi Assi. (*Sanhedrin* 17b)

R. Yaakov and R. Zerika said: Whenever R. Akiva and one of his colleagues disagree, Halacha goes according to R. Akiva. When R. Yosi disagrees with his colleagues, Halacha goes according to R. Yosi.

In a dispute between R. Yehuda ha-Nasi and one of his colleagues, Halacha goes according to Rebbe. What practical difference does it make? R. Assi said: The general practice of law. R. Hiyya b. Abba said: The practical difference is that we tend in their favor. R. Yosi b. Hanina said: they are seen as acceptable views.

R. Yaakov b. Idi said in the name of R. Yohanan: Whenever there is a dispute between R. Meir and R. Yehuda, Halacha goes according to R. Yehuda. In a dispute between R. Yehuda and R. Yosi, Halacha goes according to R. Yosi. Needless to say, in a dispute between R. Meir and R. Yosi, Halacha goes according to R. Yosi.

R. Assi said: I also learn that a dispute between R. Yosi and R. Shimon, Halacha goes according to R. Yosi.

R. Abba said in the name of R. Yohanan: In a dispute between R. Yehuda and R. Shimon, Halacha goes according to R. Yehuda. A dispute between R. Meir and R. Shimon is left unresolved. (*Eruvin* 46b)

R. Yehuda b. Shila said in the name of R. Assi in the name of R Yohanan: "There are six good deeds from which one may derive benefit in this world and still be rewarded for it in the world to come: hospitality to guests, visiting the sick, concentration during prayer, rising early for prayer, bringing up a son with Torah study and judging everyone as being upright." (*Shabbat* 127a)

R. Assi said: At first, the evil inclination is as weak as the thread of a spider web, but ultimately it becomes as strong as the ropes of a wagon. (*Sukkah* 52a)

For a glimpse of the world as it was in R. Assi's time, see the historical timeline from 250 to 350 C.E.

אבידן
Avidan (Avdan)
(second–third centuries C.E.)
Amora, Eretz Yisrael

R. Avidan, who lived in a time of transition between the periods of the tannaim and the amoraim, attended the academy of Rabbi Yehuda ha-Nasi.

It is related that R. Avidan and the students of Rabbi Yehuda ha-Nasi's academy were discussing a halachic matter. As they talked with each other, Rebbe entered. They all hurried to their seats except R. Yishmael ben Yosi; who, because of his corpulent body, could not reach his seat in time. He climbed over the seats of other students to get to his seat.

R. Avidan asked: "Who is this man who climbs over the heads of the holy people?" R. Yishmael replied, "I am Yishmael, son of Rabbi Yosi. I have come to learn Torah from Rebbe."

R. Avidan asked him, "Are you fit to learn Torah from Rebbe?"

"Was Moses fit to learn Torah from God?"

"Are you Moses?" he retorted.

"Is your teacher God?" asked R. Yishmael.

In the meantime, Rebbe sent Avdan to take care of some other matter at hand. While he was out, R. Yishmael quoted his father on the matter. Avdan was called back because the matter had been settled.

When Avdan returned, he had to climb over other students. Yishmael called out: "The person for whom the holy people have a need may climb over their heads, but you, for whom the holy people have no need – how dare you climb over?" (*Yevamot* 105b)

(Berachos 27 b) Avdan said, once on a Shabbas the sky became very cloudy and the congregation thought that it was nighttime. But after they had recited the prayers for the termination of Shabbat, and the clouds scattered and the sun came out. They came to ask Rebbe what to do, and he told them. Once they prayed; they prayed, because a congregation is different; we try to avoid too much trouble for a whole congregation.

For a glimpse of the world as it was in R. Avdan's time, see the historical timeline from 150 to 250 C.E.

אבדימי בר חמא
Avdimi bar Hama

(third–fourth centuries C.E.)
Amora, Babylonia

The Talmud says: R. Avdimi b. Hama b. Hasa said that when the Jewish people stood at Mount Sinai, God uprooted the mountain and held it over their heads, telling them: "If you accept the Torah, well and good. If not, this will be your burial place." (*Shabbat* 88a)

R. Avdimi b. Hama said: A person who occupies himself with the study of Torah will have his wishes granted by God. (*Avoda Zara* 19a)

For a glimpse of the world as it was in R. Avdimi b. Hama's time, see the historical timeline from 250 to 350 C.E.

אבדימי דמן חיפא
Avdimi de-man Haifa

(fourth–fifth centuries C.E.)
Amora from Eretz Yisrael

R. Avdimi was a student of Rabbi Levi ben Sisi and Rabbi Shimon b. Lakish. He is quoted as saying "Since the day the Temple was destroyed, prophecy has been taken from the prophets and given to the wise." (*Bava Batra* 12a)

R. Hizkiya stated: R. Hanina b. R Abbahu said it to me in the name of R. Avdimi of Haifa that when a scholar passes, one should rise before him within four cubits. When the president of the court walks in, one should rise while he is in sight. When the president of the Sanhedrin walks in one should rise when he is in sight and be seated only after he is seated. (*Kiddushin* 33b)

R. Avdimi is buried in Haifa.

For a glimpse of the world as it was in R. Avdimi's time, see the historical timeline from 350 to 450 C.E.

אויא
Avia

(fourth century C.E.)
Amora from Babylonia

R. Avia was a student of Rabbi Yoseph ben Hiyya in the Pumbedita academy. (*Berachot* 28b)

When R. Avia was ill and did not come to the academy of Rabbi Yoseph; R. Abbaye asked him; "Why didn't you come to the academy yesterday?" "I felt weak and was not able to come," he answered. "You should have taken some food and come," was the reply. The conversation continued, discussing halachic issues.

Later in his life, R. Avia settled in Eretz Yisrael and studied under Rabbi Ammi in Caesarea. (*Hullin* 50a)

One of his associates was Rabbah ben Rav Hanan, and he married the sister of Rammi ben Hama. He and his wife had three sons: R. Adda, R. Aha and R. Hilkiah. (*Kiddushin* 39a)

The sister of R. Rami b. Hama was married to R. Avia, but her ketubbah was lost. The couple came before R. Yoseph to obtain a ruling as to whether they could continue to live together without a ketubbah. He told them that the matter is a dispute between R. Meir and the sages. According to the sages, in such a case, a man may live with his wife for two to three years without a ketubbah. When R. Abbaye objected, R. Yoseph told him: In that case, go and write her a new ketubbah. (*Ketubbot* 56b–57a)

R. Avia once visited Nehardea and noticed that a man was tying the gate with a reed. He remarked that most likely, the gate did not need to be locked for Shabbat. (*Eruvin* 102a)

R. Avia visited Rabba, but his boots were soiled with mud and he sat down on a bed. Wishing to show his annoyance at this, Rabbah asked him difficult halachic questions. (*Shabbat* 46a)

For a glimpse of the world as it was in R. Avia's time, see the historical timeline from 300 to 400 C.E.

אבימי
Avimi

(third century C.E.)
Amora from Babylonia

Rabbi Hisda was the outstanding student of Rabbi Avimi.

The Talmud relates that at one time, Rabbi Avimi forgot some of his learning. R. Zeira said that R. Avimi was studying Tractate Menachot under R. Hisda.

But was it not the reverse? Was it not R. Hisda who studied under R. Avimi? And did not R. Hisda say: I received many beatings from R. Avimi?

The answer is that he had forgotten this tractate and went to his student, Rabbi Hisda, in order to refresh his memory. Why did he not send for him to come to him? He thought by going to him he would get more out of it. (*Arachin* 22a, *Menuhot* 7a)

Rabbi Hisda transmitted a tradition in the name of Rabbi Avimi: The Tent of Meeting that Moshe constructed during the wanderings in the wilderness, including its boards, hooks, bars, pillars and sockets, were stored away after the first Temple was erected by King Solomon. Where was it stored? R. Hisda said in the name of R. Avimi: they stored them beneath the crypts of the Temple. (*Sotah* 9a)

For a glimpse of the world as it was in Avimi's time, see the historical timeline from 200 to 300 C.E.

אבימי בר אבהו
Avimi bar Abbahu

(fourth century C.E.)
Amora from Eretz Yisrael

The Talmud relates that Rabbi Avimi had some commercial transactions with Babylonia. Once he sent money to Hozai, in Babylonia, with Rabbi Hama b. Rabbah b. Abbahu as payment for a debt. After he gave them the money and asked for a receipt, the people claimed that the payment was for another debt. Rabbi Hama went to complain to Rabbi Abbahu, who asked him: "Do you have witnesses that you paid him?" R. Hama said that he did not. In that case, they could plead that you didn't pay at all. Therefore, we must believe them that it is for another debt. (*Ketubbot* 85a)

Respect for parents was a very important teaching of his, which he stressed and practiced.

His father, R. Abbahu, said: "One may feed his father pheasants and yet not fulfill the mitzvah of honoring his father, while another may set him to grind in a mill and yet fulfill the mitzvah, because he does it with respect. A good example is my son Avimi, who has fulfilled the commandment to honor one's father. Every time when R. Abbahu visited his son Avimi; he himself ran to the door to open it, and while running he would call out: Yes, yes, until he reached the door, even though R. Avimi had five sons who were already ordained rabbis in his father's lifetime. (*Kiddushin* 31a–b)

One day his father asked him for a glass of water. While he went to bring him the water, he fell asleep. He stood there in place with the glass of water in his hand until his father awoke.

R. Avimi b. Abbahu stated: The days of Israel's Mashiach shall be seven thousand years. (*Sanhedrin* 99a)

For a glimpse of the world as it was in R. Avimi b. Abbahu's time, see the historical timeline from 300 to 400 C.E.

אבין
Avin

(third–fourth centuries C.E.)
Amora, Babylonia

R. Avin, who was originally from Babylonia, immigrated to Eretz Yisrael. A colleague of Rabbi Yohanan and of Rabbi Shimon ben Lakish, he studied under Rabbi Abbahu in Caesarea, Rabbi Zeira and Rabbi Illai. In later life, he returned to Babylonia and settled in Pumbedita. Rabbi Abbaye, who was the head of the academy in Pumbedita, was a close associate of his.

R. Avin said in the name of R. Illai: Whenever it is written in the Torah the words *hishamer, pen*, and *al,* this denotes a negative precept.

When Ravin came from Eretz Yisrael to Babylonia, he stated: "There was a city that belonged to King Yannai, on the King's mountain, where they were chopping down fig trees." (*Eruvin* 96a) They needed a great amount of salted fish to feed the workers. He also stated: King Yannai had a tree on the king's mountain from which they used to take down every month forty young pigeons from three broods. (*Berachot* 44a)

Once, when Ravin and Abbaye were traveling together, Ravin's donkey went in front of Abbaye. When Ravin did not apologize, Abbaye became annoyed and thought to himself: *Since this student came up from Eretz Yisrael, he has become haughty.* When they arrived at the door of the synagogue, Ravin said to Abbaye, "Rabbi, would you please enter?" Abbaye answered, "And was I not your rabbi until now?" R. Avin replied, "One gives honor only at a door where there is a mezuzah." (*Berachot* 47a)

For a glimpse of the world as it was in R. Avin's time, see the historical timeline from 250 to 350 C.E.

אבין בר אדא
Avin b. Rav Adda

(third century C.E.)
Amora, Babylonia

R. Avin b. Rav Adda said in the name of R. Yitzchak: the reason why there are no fruits called Ginossar in Jerusalem, because it should not be said that the pilgrims went to Jerusalem during the festivals solely to eat from the fruit of Ginossar. (*Pesahim* 8b)

R. Avin b. Rav Adda said in the name of R. Yitzhak: how do we know that God puts on tefilin? We know it from a passage in Yeshaya 62:8. (*Berachot* 6a)

R. Avin b. Rav Ahava said in the name of R. Yitzchak: "if a man is accustomed to attend the synagogue daily and does not attend one day, God asks for him." (*Berachot* 6b)

R. Avin b. R. Adda quoted R. Menahem Ish Kefar Shearim (or Bet Shearim) as saying: It once happened that a child was born to the same mother three months after the first one, and both of those students sat in our academy. Who are these students? They are Rabbi Yehuda and Rabbi Hizkiya, the sons of Rabbi Hiyya. But didn't we learn that a woman couldn't conceive twice during one pregnancy? Rabbi Abbaye replied. It was the same drop, which was split in two; the features of one were completed at the beginning of the seventh month, and the features of the other were completed at the end of the ninth month. (*Niddah* 27a)

For a glimpse of the world as it was in Avin's time, see the historical timeline from 200 to 300 C.E.

אבינא
Avina

(third–fourth centuries C.E.)
Amora, Babylonia

At some time in his life R. Avina immigrated to Eretz Yisrael, where he became a colleague of Rabbi Zeira and Rabbi Yaakov ben Aha and a close friend of Rabbi Geniva.

The Talmud relates that his friend, R. Geniva, was sentenced to death. When the sentence was about to be carried out, he instructed the people to give Rabbi Avina four hundred zuz from his wine estate. (*Gittin* 65b)

A non-believer engaged Rabbi Avina into an argument about the Jewish people. Rabbi Avina answered him with a quotation from the Torah. (*Sanhedrin* 39a–b)

R. Eleazar said in the name of Rabbi Avina: Whoever recites Ashrei and Tehillah le-David three times a day is sure to inherit the World to Come. (*Berachot* 4b)

For a glimpse of the world as it was in R. Avina's time, see the historical timeline from 250 to 350 C.E.

עוירא
Avira

(third–fourth centuries C.E.)
Amora, Eretz Yisrael

Rabbi Avira was a close associate of Rabbi Chelbo and Rabbi Yosi ben Hanina.

(*Hullin* 51a) The Talmud relates that Rabbi Safra asked Rabbi Abbaye, "Did you meet the scholar from Eretz Yisrael by the name of Avira? He supposedly brought an important ruling from Eretz Yisrael." Abbaye went to see him, but Avira was on the roof. Abbaye asked him to come down, but he refused.

Abbaye went up on the roof to speak to him. He asked him about the ruling he brought from Eretz Yisrael. When Rabbi Avira told him what it was, Abbaye said to him. "You caused me a lot of trouble for nothing. This is already well known to us. It is a specific mishna that addresses this issue."

Rabbi Avira was quoted as saying the following, sometimes in the name of Rabbi Ammi and sometimes in the name of R. Assi. "A man should always eat and drink less than he can afford, clothe himself according to his means, honor his wife and children more than he can afford, because they are dependent on him, and he depends on the Creator." (*Hullin* 84b)

R. Avira quoted R. Ammi and R. Assi at various times: The angels said to God, "Master of the Universe, it is written in Your Torah: 'He neither engages in favoritism nor takes bribes,' but You favor the Jewish people." God answered the angels: "How could I not favor them? I wrote in my Torah: Eat, be satisfied and bless your God, and they are so meticulous that they bless God even over a quantity as small as that of an olive or an egg." (*Berachot* 20b)

For a glimpse of the world as it was in Avira's time, see the historical timeline from 250 to 350 C.E.

עוירא
Avira

(fourth century C.E.)
Amora, Babylonia

Rabbi Avira transmitted tradition in the name of Rova. (*Hullin* 55a)

The famous Rabbi Aha was his son. (Berachot 44a)

R. Avira had halachic disagreements with R. Ravina about a man who came to them with a dispute with another man. (*Ketubbot* 103a)

He also debated halachic issues with Rabbi Ravina. (*Pesahim* 73a)

For a glimpse of the world as it was in R. Avira's time, see the historical timeline from 300 to 400 C.E.

אבהו
Abbahu
(third–fourth centuries C.E.)
Amora, Eretz Yisrael
Head of academy in Caesarea

R. Abbahu's residence was in Caesarea, which was at that time the seat of the Roman government. R. Abbahu was a student of Rabbi Yohanan, R. Shimon b. Lakish and of Rabbi Eleazar b. Pedat. His scholarship went beyond Jewish subjects. He was learned in mathematics, Greek and rhetoric. He also taught his daughters Greek and mathematics. In spite of his wealth and scholarship, he was modest.

On Friday before Shabbat, R. Abbahu would sit on an ivory chair and fan the fire for Shabbat. (*Shabbat* 119a)

Rabbi Abbahu represented the people to the Roman governor. (*Ketubbot* 17a)

R. Abbahu said, "I used to think that I was humble, but when I saw R. Abba from Acco offer one explanation and his interpreter another and he did not object, I figured that I was not humble at all." (*Sotah* 40a)

The rabbis decided to appoint R. Abbahu as head of the academy, but when R. Abbahu saw that R. Abba of Acco had numerous creditors asking for payment, he said to the rabbis, "There is a greater scholar more suitable for the office than I."

When R. Abbahu came from his academy to the palace of the emperor in Caesarea; the ladies of the palace went out to receive him and sang for him:

"Great man of your people, leader of your nation, lantern of light, may your coming be blessed with peace." (*Sanhedrin* 14a)

R. Abbahu praised R. Safra to the *minim* as a great scholar, and consequently they exempted him from paying taxes for thirteen years. One day they encountered him and they asked him to explain a passage in the bible. He could not give them an answer. They took a scarf and wound it around his neck in order to torture him. When R. Abbahu came and found him being tortured in this way, he asked, "Why do you torture him?" They answered: "Have you not told us that he is a great scholar? He cannot even explain the meaning of a verse in the Bible."

He replied, "I might have told you that he is a great scholar, which he is, but what I meant was that he is a scholar in tannaitic learning, not in Scripture. But how is it that you do know Scripture?"

"The rabbis and I, who are with you frequently, make it our business to study it thoroughly, but others do not." (*Avoda Zara* 4a)

Once his interpreter's wife said to R. Abbahu's wife: "My husband has no need for instructions from your husband, and when he bows down to your husband he is merely being courteous."

When his wife told R. Abbahu what she had said, he replied, "Why should we worry about it? All that matters is that through the two of us, God is praised." (*Sotah* 40a)

R. Abbahu and R. Hiyya b. Abba traveled to a place to deliver lectures. R. Hiyya lectured on legal matters while R. Abbahu lectured on aggadah. The people left the hall where R. Hiyya was lecturing in order to listen to R. Abbahu.

When R. Hiyya became upset, R. Abbahu said to him, "I will tell you a parable. Two salesmen are selling merchandise. One sells precious jewels while the other sells small knick-knacks of various kinds. To whom do the people flock? Is it not to the one who sells the knick-knacks?"

R. Hiyya used to accompany R. Abbahu every day to his lodging, but on this day R. Abbahu accompanied R. Hiyya to his lodging. He tried to make him feel better, but R. Hiyya was still upset. (*Sotah* 40a)

His better-known students were R. Yirmiyahu, R. Yonah and R. Yosi.

R. Safra said: R. Abbahu used to tell this story: When R. Hananya b. Ahi Yoshua left for Babylonia, he began to intercalate the years and to fix the new months outside Israel. The bet din of Israel sent two scholars to stop him from doing so: R. Yosi b. Kippar and the grandson of R. Zechariah b. Kavutal. When R. Hananya saw them, he asked them, "Why have you come?" They answered, "We have come to learn Torah from you." When he heard that, he proclaimed to the community: These men are the great scholars of our generation. They and their ancestors have served in the Temple. As we have learned, Zechariah b. Kavutal said: Many times have I read from the book of Daniel.

Shortly afterwards, they issued rulings against his declarations. Everything that he said was impure they declared pure, and permitted what he had forbidden. R. Hananya became upset and announced to the community: "These men are false and worthless."

They said to him, "You have already built our reputation and you cannot destroy it. You have already made fences and you cannot break them down." He asked them, "Why do you declare pure that which I declared to be impure?"

They answered him, "Because you intercalate years and fix the new moon outside Israel." He retorted, "Did not R. Akiva b. Yoseph intercalate years and fix the new month outside of Israel?" They

answered him; "Do not cite R. Akiva, who had no equal in Israel." He retorted; "I also left no equal in the land of Israel." They said to him, "The kids that you left behind in Israel have become goats with horns, and they sent us to speak to you in their name. If you listen, well and good, but if you do not, you will be excommunicated. They also empowered us to tell the community here in Babylonia: If you heed us, well and good. But if you do not, then let them go up the mountain, let Ahia build an altar, and Hananya play the harp. All of you will become deniers and will have no portion in the God of Israel." When the community heard this, they started to weep and declared: Heaven forbid. (*Berachot* 63a)

The rabbis were discussing how to recite the words *Baruch shem*. R. Abbahu said that they should be recited aloud because if they were said quietly, then the heretics might accuse the worshippers of cursing them in secret. But since there were no heretics in Nehardea, they recited the phrase in a low voice. (*Pesahim* 56a)

R. Abbahu said: "In the place where the baalei teshuva stand even the wholly righteous cannot stand." (*Berachot* 34b)

One of his famous sayings was: "Be among the persecuted rather than persecutors." (*Bava Kamma* 93a)

R. Abbahu said: A man should never impose too much fear upon his household. (*Gittin* 7a)

R. Abbahu said: The deceased knows what is said in his presence until the top stone closes the grave. (*Shabbat* 152b)

R. Abbahu said: The world exists on account of people who are humble. (*Hullin* 89a)

Rabbi Abbahu stated in the name of Rabbi Yohanan: Rabbi Meir had a student by the name of Sumchos who was able to supply forty-eight reasons to support every rule of ritual impurity. (*Eruvin* 13b)

It is related that after Rabbi Meir passed away, Rabbi Yehuda told his students, "Do not allow the students of Rabbi Meir to enter our academy because they come only for disputations and to overwhelm me with citations from traditions, but not to learn Torah." Rabbi Sumchos forced his way into the academy. He quoted Rabbi Meir on an important halachic issue. Rabbi Yehuda became very angry and told his students: "Didn't I instruct you not to admit any of Rabbi Meir's students?" Rabbi Yosi responded, "People will say that Rabbi Meir is dead, Rabbi Yehuda is angry and Rabbi Yosi is silent." (*Nazir* 49b)

When R. Zeira was ill, R. Abbahu went to visit him. R. Abbahu made a vow, saying: "If the little one with burned legs recovers, I will make a Yom Tov meal for the rabbis." R. Zeira recovered and R. Abbahu made a feast in his honor. When the time came to begin the meal, R. Abbahu said to R. Zeira, "Would you please make the blessing and begin?"

But R. Zeira said to him: "Don't you accept R. Yohanan's ruling that the host begins the meal?" R. Abbahu began the meal with the blessing. When it came to reciting the blessings after the meal, R. Abbahu said to R. Zeira: "Would you lead us in the blessings?"

R. Zeira said to him: "Don't you accept the ruling of R. Huna from Babylon that the person who recites the blessings before the meal also recites the blessing after the meal?" (*Berachot* 46a)

In Caesarea R. Abbahu prescribed a certain order for blowing the shofar. (*Rosh ha-Shannah* 34a)

For a glimpse of the world as it was in R. Abbahu's time, see the historical timeline from 250 to 350 C.E.

אבטליון
Avtalyon

(first century B.C.E.)
Tanna, Eretz Yisrael

Rabbi Avtalyon and his colleague, Rabbi Shemaya, comprised one of the zugot.

Tradition has it that both of these rabbis are descendents of proselytes. According to some, he was a descendant of Sennacherib. (*Gittin* 57b, *Sanhedrin* 96b)

Rabbi Avtalyon was the Av Beit Din while Shemaya was the Nasi.

Having received his tradition from Shimon ben Shetah and from Yehuda ben Tabbai, he became one of the most influential and beloved scholars of his time.

Rabbi Hillel was a student of Shemaya and Avtalyon. (*Pesahim* 66a)

Elsewhere, the Talmud relates that as a young man, Rabbi Hillel used to work as a day-laborer in order to earn one tropek (an amount equivalent to a dinar). He split his earnings, giving half to the guard for admittance into the study hall and spending the other half on food and necessities. One day, when he had no money, the guard would not let him enter. He climbed up on the roof, which had a window above the lecture hall. There, he listened to the lectures of Rabbis Shemaya and Avtalyon.

This particular day, a Friday, happened to be the winter solstice. As the temperature dropped, Hillel lost consciousness, and overnight, he was covered by snow. On the following morning, which was Shabbat, Shemaya said to Avtalyon. "Every day at this time the room is bright with light, but today it is dark. Is it perhaps a cloudy day?"

They looked up and saw a human figure lying in the skylight. Climbing up, they discovered Hillel covered with three cubits of snow. They removed him from the roof, bathed and anointed him, and set him next to the fire.

They said to one another, "This man deserves that Shabbat be profaned on his account." From then on, Hillel gained permanent admittance to their school. (*Yoma* 35b)

When Jerusalem was besieged in 37 B.C.E., Avtalyon advised the people to open the gates of Jerusalem and to receive Herod. Later on, Herod favored him and did not kill him, as he did to some of the other scholars.

One of his sayings was: "Scholars, be careful with your words, lest you incur the penalty of exile into a place of evil waters, and the disciples who follow you drink of them and die." (*Avot* 1:11)

Our rabbis taught: It happened that the High Priest came out from the Sanctuary and the people followed him, but when they saw Shemaya and Avtalyon, they turned away from the High Priest and followed them. Shemaya and Avtalyon went to greet the High Priest, and they exchanged words. (*Yoma* 71b)

For a glimpse of the world as it was in Avtalyon's time, see the historical timeline from 100 to 1 B.C.E.

אבטולמוס
Avtolemus

(second century C.E.)
Tanna, Eretz Yisrael

Rabbi Yosi b. Halafta was a student of R. Avtolemus. (*Eruvin* 3:4)

For a glimpse of the world as it was in R. Avtolemus's time, see the historical timeline from 100 to 200 C.E.

עזריה
Azaryah

(first century C.E.)
Tanna, Eretz Yisrael

Rabbi Azaryah was a wealthy businessman and a close friend of Rabbi Dosa ben Hyrcanus. His brother Rabbi Shimon, who was also a Tanna and the Talmud calls him the brother of Azaryah, was supported by him in order that he could devote all his time to study. (*Sotah* 21a, *Zevahim* 2a)

Rabbi Eleazar ben Azaryah was his son. (*Yevamot* 16a)

For a glimpse of the world as it was in R. Azaryah's time, see the historical timeline from 1 to 100 C.E.

בר קפרא
Bar Kappara

(second–third centuries C.E.)
Tanna-Amora, Eretz Yisrael

R. Bar Kappara was a student of Rabbi Yehuda ha-Nasi. R. Shimon the son of Rebbe was studying with Bar Kappara. When they encountered a difficult passage in the text, Rabbi Shimon said to him, "This requires an explanation by my father." Bar Kappara replied, "And what could your father say about it?" Rabbi Shimon repeated this to his father. The next time Bar Kappara met Rabbi Yehuda, the Master said to him, "I do not know you."

Realizing that Rebbe was hurt, Bar Kappara undertook a thirty-day withdrawal.

The Talmud states Rabbi Shimon ben Lakish asked Rabbi Yohanan about the teachings of the Mishna of Bar Kappara. (*Bava Batra* 154b)

His academy must have been in a community called Parud, because when Rabbi Yohanan was in Parud he inquired if there was a Mishna manuscript that had been written by Bar Kappara. Rabbi

Tanhum, a local resident, quoted him a certain mishna. (*Avodah Zarah* 31a)

R. Shimon ben Pazzi said in the name of Rabbi Yoshua ben Levi in the name of Bar Kappara: "If one knows how to calculate the cycles of the planetary courses and does not do it, then that person has no regard for God's work." (*Shabbat* 75a)

R. Bar Kappara stated: When the merchandise is cheap, hurry to buy. In a place where there is no leader, you be the leader. One should always teach one's offspring a clean and easy trade. (*Berachot* 63a)

It is taught that Bar Kappara says: "Once every sixty or seventy years, the accumulated incense leftovers were enough for half a year's supply for the Temple."

R. Hoshaya visited Bar Kappara frequently in order to study with him, but after a while he left him and joined R. Hiyya. One day, he met Bar Kappara and asked him a halachic question. Bar Kappara asked him, "And what does R. Hiyya have to say about this matter?" (*Keritot* 8a)

For a glimpse of the world as it was in R. Bar Kappara's time, see the historical timeline from 150 to 250 C.E.

בר פדא
Bar Pada (Yehuda b. Pedaya)

(third century C.E.)
Amora, Eretz Yisrael

R. Ilfa was a student of Bar Pada. (*Zevahim* 13b)

Bar Pada said: If one consecrates saplings as an offering and then redeems them, they revert to their sanctity again and again until they are cut down. (*Nedarim* 28b)

For a glimpse of the world as it was in R. Bar Pada's time, see the historical timeline from 200 to 300 C.E.

בן עזאי
Ben Azzai

(second century C.E.)
Tanna, Eretz Yisrael

A resident of Tiberias, his full name was Rabbi Shimon ben Azzai. Ben Azzai was a student of Rabbi Yoshua ben Hananya and transmitted halachic rulings in his name. He was also a disciple and colleague of Rabbi Akiva, whose daughter he married.

Rabbi Simlai said: Rabbi Akiva was both a colleague and the teacher of Ben Azzai. (*Bava Batra* 158b)

He is quoted as saying anyone who does not procreate is considered as though he had shed blood. They asked Ben Azzai: "Some preach well and act well, while others act well but do not preach well. You, however, preach well but do not act well." Ben Azzai replied: "But what can I do? My soul desires the Torah. The world will have to be carried on by others." (*Yevamot* 63b)

The Talmud says that the wife of Ben Azzai, who was the daughter of Rabbi Akiva, acted in a similar manner as her mother, insisting that he go to study. He had a reputation as an outstanding scholar. (*Ketubbot* 63a)

Rava said, "Today I feel as sharp as Ben Azzai in the market of Tiberias, where Ben Azzai used to give lectures." (*Eruvin* 29a)

Abbaye said: I feel as sharp as Ben Azzai in the market of Tiberias. (*Kiddushin* 20a)

Ben Azzai used to say: "Do not despise any person and do not disparage anything. For there is not a person who does not have his hour and there is not an object that does not have its place." (Avot 4:3)

The Talmud states that when ben Azzai died there were no more industrious scholars. (*Sotah* 49a)

The Talmud does not always refer to a rabbi by name, but sometimes uses a reference term instead. The following rules apply:

When the Talmud states: "It was discussed before the rabbis," this refers to R. Shimon ben Azzai, Rabbi Shimon ben Zoma, Rabbi Hanan ha-Mitzri and R. Hanania ben Hachinai. (*Sanhedrin* 17b)

The rabbis taught: Four went into the Pardes: Ben Azzai, Ben Zoma, Aher [R. Elisha ben Avuya] and R. Akiva. R. Akiva said to them, "When you reach the pure marble stones, do not say, "Water, water." (Hagiga 14b)

The story continues that Ben Azzai glanced and died, Ben Zoma looked and became stricken, Aher became an apostate and R. Akiva emerged unharmed.

The rabbis taught: If one sees Ben Azzai in a dream, he will aspire to be pious. (*Berachot* 57b)

For a glimpse of the world as it was in R. Ben Azzai's time, see the historical timeline from 100 to 200 C.E.

בן בג בג
Ben Bag Bag

(first century C.E.)
Tanna, Eretz Yisrael

Rabbi Ben Bag Bag is quoted as saying: "Turn it over again and again, because everything is within the Torah." (*Avot* 5:22) Regarding private property he had this to say. "Do not enter your neighbor's property without his knowledge even to retrieve something that belongs to you, because he may think you are a thief." (*Bava Kamma* 27b)

Ben Bag Bag is quoted in a ruling with regards to sacrifices. (*Eruvin* 27b)

For a glimpse of the world as it was in R. Ben Bag Bag's time, see the historical timeline from 1 to 100 C.E.

בן בוכרי
Ben Buchri

(first century C.E.)
Tanna, Jerusalem

R. Ben Buchri is quoted in the Talmud about contributions. He was a contemporary of Rabbi Yohanan ben Zakkai. (*Shekalim* 1:4)

For a glimpse of the world as it was in R. Ben Buchri's time, see the historical timeline from 1 to 100 C.E.

בן הא הא
Ben He He

(first century C.E.)
Tanna, Eretz Yisrael

It is said that his name originated from the additional letter heh added to Abraham and Sarah's name, meaning he was the son of Abraham and Sarah, as are all proselytes.

He declared, "According to the effort is the reward." (*Avot* 5:23)

The Talmud mentions that Eliyahu spoke to Ben Heh Heh. (*Hagigah* 9b)

For a glimpse of the world as it was in R. Ben Heh Heh's time, see the historical timeline from 1 to 100 C.E.

בן זומא
Ben Zoma

(second century C.E.)
Tanna, Eretz Yisrael

Rabbi Shimon ben Zoma was a contemporary of Rabbi Akiva and a student of Rabbi Yoshua ben Hananya (*Hagigah* 15a). Once, when Rabbi Yoshua was standing on the Temple Mount, Ben Zoma saw him but did not rise before him. Rabbi Yoshua asked him: "What are you thinking about?" He replied: "I was gazing between the upper and the lower waters, and there is barely three fingers'-breadth between them." Thereupon, R. Yoshua said to his disciples: "Ben Zoma is still outside."

He used to say: "Who is wise? One who learns from everyone. Who is strong? One who subdues his passions. Who is rich? One who is happy with his lot. Who is honored? One who honors his fellow human beings." (*Avot* 4:1)

The Talmud states that when ben Zoma died, there were no more explainers. (*Sotah* 49a)

It was stated: the Talmud does not always refer to a rabbi by name, but instead it uses a reference term. The following rules apply. (*Sanhedrin* 17b)

When the Talmud states: "It was discussed before the rabbis," this refers to R. Shimon ben Azzai, Rabbi Shimon ben Zoma, Rabbi Hanan ha-Mitzri and R. Hanania ben Hachinai. (*Sanhedrin* 17b)

The rabbis taught: Four went into the Pardes: Ben Azzai, Ben Zoma, Aher [R. Elisha ben Avuya] and R. Akiva. R. Akiva said to them, "When you reach the pure marble stones, do not say, "Water, water." (*Hagigah* 14b)

The story continues that Ben Azzai glanced and died, Ben Zoma looked and became stricken, Aher became an apostate and R. Akiva emerged unharmed.

The rabbis taught: If one sees Ben Zoma in a dream, he may hope for wisdom. (*Berachot* 57b)

For a glimpse of the world as it was in R. Ben Zoma's time, see the historical timeline from 100 to 200 C.E.

בני בתירא
Bene Betera
(Bene Betheira, Bathyra)
(first century B.C.E.–second century C.E.)

The family known as Bene Betera (literally, "the sons of Betera") flourished in Eretz Yisrael from the first century B.C.E. to the second century C.E.

A well-known family, they were known for the great influence they had

in Jerusalem and for the many scholars among them, who include, among many others, Rabbi Shimon, Rabbi Yehuda and Rabbi Yehoshua.

It is stated: The rabbis of the Bene Betera family were the heads of the Sanhedrin and this halacha was hidden from them. On one occasion, when the fourteenth of Nisan fell on a Shabbat, they did not remember whether the slaughter of the paschal lamb overrides Shabbat. They inquired: is there anyone who knows this halacha? They were told: "There is a man by the name of Hillel from Babylonia, who studied under Shemaya and Avtalyon, the two greatest man of our time."

They summoned Hillel and asked him. He told the Sanhedrin: Surely we have more than two hundred paschal lambs during the year, which override Shabbat. He quoted sentences from the Torah and used logic to prove to them that the slaughter of the paschal lamb overrides Shabbat. After this incident, which took place in 30 B.C.E., the president of the Sanhedrin resigned and Hillel was elected president. (*Pesahim* 66a)

The Talmud quotes Rabbi Yehuda ha-Nasi as saying: "Three prime examples of humble people are these: my father, the Bene Betera and Yonatan, the son of King Saul." The Bene Betera were the presidents of the Sanhedrin during Herod's reign. (*Bava Metzia* 85a)

For a glimpse of the world as it was in the time of the Bene Betera, see the historical timeline from 100 B.C.E. to 200 C.E.

בנימין בר יפת
Binyamin ben Yafet
Amora, Eretz Yisrael
Lived in the 3rd century CE

R. Binyamin was a student of R. Yohanan.

R. Binyamin b. Yafet said, "In Sidon, R. Yosi asked R. Yohanan a question about making Havdala. Some say that it was R. Shimon b. Yaakov from Tyre who asked the question." (*Berachot* 33a)

R. Binyamin b. Yafet said in the name of R. Eleazar: "The Torah says that Joseph's brothers fell down before him. This bears out the popular saying: A fox in its hour – bow down to it." (*Megillah* 16b)

R. Binyamin b. Yafet also said in the name of R. Eleazar: "The Torah says that Joseph comforted his brothers. This tells us that he made statements that reassured them greatly, such as: If ten lights cannot put out one light, how can one light put out ten?"

R. Hiyya b. Abba said in the name of R. Yohanan: "The blessing over boiled vegetables is *peri adama*." However, R. Binyamin b. Yafet said in the name of R. Yohanan: "The blessing over boiled vegetables is *she-ha-kol*." R. Nahman b. Yitzhak said: "Ulla made an error in accepting the word of R. Benyamin b. Yafet."

R. Zeira expressed astonishment. "How can you compare R. Binyamin b. Yafet to R. Hiyya b. Abba? R. Hiyya b. Abba was very particular to get the exact teachings of R. Yohanan, while R. Binyamin b. Yafet was not so careful. Furthermore, R. Hiyya b. Abba used to go over his learning with R. Yohanan every thirty days, while R. Binyamin did not." (*Berachot* 38b)

When R. Zeira came to Eretz Yisrael, he found R. Binyamin b. Yafet teaching a halacha about Shabbat in R. Yohanan's name. He said to him, "Well spoken, and the same was taught by Arioch in Babylonia." Who is Arioch? Arioch is R. Shemuel. (*Shabbat* 53a)

For a glimpse of the world as it was in R. Binyamin b. Yafet's time, see the historical timeline from 200 to 300 C.E.

ברכיה
Berachia (Berechiah)

(fourth century C.E.)
Amora, Eretz Yisrael

His father's name was R. Hiyya.

Although he appears mostly in the Jerusalem Talmud, he is also mentioned in the Babylonian Talmud.

R. Berachia said, "Even though the Congregation of Israel made thoughtless requests of God, God granted Israel's requests nevertheless." R. Berachia was a student of Rabbi Helbo. (*Taanit* 4a)

For a glimpse of the world as it was in R. Berachia's time, see the historical timeline from 300 to 400 C.E.

ברוקא חוזאה
Beroka of Hozeah (Beroka b. Hozeah)

(second century C.E.)

R. Beroka may be the father of R. Yohanan.

R. Beroka used to frequent the market in Be-lapat, where he frequently met with Eliyahu. Once he asked Eliyahu, "Is anyone in this market who merits the World to Come?" Eliyahu replied, "No."

In the meantime he saw a man wearing black shoes, but no tzitzit. Pointing him out, Eliyahu said, "That man has a share in the World to Come."

R. Beroka ran after him and asked him, "What is your occupation?"

The man replied, "Go away and come back tomorrow."

The next day he asked him again: "What is your occupation?"

The man replied, "I am a jailer. I keep the men and women separated, and place my own bed between them. When I see non-Jewish men casting their eye upon a Jewish woman, I risk my life to save her from them. Once, when we had a betrothed Jewish woman and the gentiles cast their eyes on her, I stained her skirt with red wine and told the men that she was menstruating."

R. Beroka asked further, "Why don't you wear tzitzit, and why do you wear black shoes?"

The jailer replied, "I move constantly among gentiles, and I don't want them to know that I am Jewish. This way I can find out whether there are any harsh decrees against the Jews and I can inform the rabbis, who pray to have the decrees annulled."

R. Beroka continued: "Why did you ask me to come back the next day?"

The jailer answered, "Because I had just found out that a harsh decree had been issued and I wanted to inform the rabbis immediately."

Another time, as R. Beroka and Eliyahu walked together in the marketplace, two men passed by. Eliyahu said to R. Beroka: "These two men have a share in the World to Come."

R. Beroka ran after them and asked them, "What is your occupation?"

They replied: "We are jesters. When we see people who are sad, we cheer them up. When we see two people quarreling, we try to make peace between them." (*Taanit* 22a)

For a glimpse of the world as it was in R. Beroka's time, see the historical timeline from 100 to 200 C.E.

ברונא
Berona
(third century C.E.)
Amora, Babylonia

R. Berona was a student of R. Shemuel.

He was sitting in his academy and quoting R. Shemuel when a student by the name of R. Eleazar asked him, "Did R. Shemuel really say that?" R. Berona replied, "Yes." The student asked, "Would you show me where he lives?"

He showed him. He approached R. Shemuel and asked him, "Did the master make this statement?" "Yes," replied R. Shemuel. "But didn't you make a contradictory ruling in another case?" The debate continued. (*Eruvin* 74a)

R. Berona said in the name of Rav, "One who washed his hands for bread should not make Kiddush over wine." R. Yitzhak b. Shemuel b. Mata said to them: "Rav has barely died, and have we already forgotten his ruling? I stood before Rav many times. Sometimes he chose bread and made Kiddush over bread, while at other times he preferred wine and made Kiddush over wine." (*Pesahim* 106a)

For a glimpse of the world as it was in R. Berona's time, see the historical timeline from 200 to 300 C.E.

ביבי בר אביי
Bibi bar Abbaye (Bibai)
(fourth century C.E.)
Amora, Babylonia
Head of the Academy in Pumbedita

Rabbi Bibi was the son of the famous R. Abbaye, the director of the Pumbedita academy.

R. Bibi, who served as a dayyan in his community, succeeded his father as the director of the academy in Pumbedita after his death. (*Ketubbot* 85a) (*Yevamot* 75b)

A contemporary of Rabbi Papi, R. Bibi was wealthy. He did some farming and owned farms. (*Bava Metzia* 109a)

R. Bibi b. Abbaye leased a field and surrounded it with a ridge. When his lease expired, he said to the owner: "Reimburse me for the improvements I made." But R. Papi said to him: "You come from Mamla, where they might be reimbursed, but here it is not done. Even R. Papa claimed reimbursement only for losses, but what losses did you suffer?"

The Talmud relates that when they discussed the wall of a mansion that collapsed and Rabbi Bibi was about to rule one way, Rabbi Papi remarked, "Since you are a descendant of short lived people, you speak frail words." He was referring to the fact that R. Bibi was a descendent of Eli the High Priest at Shiloh, who lived during the time of Samuel the Prophet. (*Eruvin* 25b)

A certain woman owned a palm tree on R. Bibi's property. Whenever she went to prune it, he showed annoyance. She transferred ownership to him during his lifetime with the stipulation that after his death, it would revert to her. However he, in turn, transferred ownership to his young son. (*Bava Batra* 137b)

The Angel of Death used to visit R. Bibi b. Abbaye frequently and have conversations with him. (*Hagigah* 4b)

For a glimpse of the world as it was in R. Bibi b. Abbaye's time, see the historical timeline from 300 to 400 C.E.

ביבי
Bibi (Bebai)

(third century C.E.)
Amora, Eretz Yisrael

A student of Rabbi Yohanan, R. Bibi also studied with Resh Lakish, R. Eleazar b. Pedat and R. Yoshua b. Levi. He also interacted with Rabbi Ammi and Rabbi Assi, who were his contemporaries. (*Bava Kama* 61a)

It was stated: When R. Dimi came, he related that it was R. Bibi's turn to wait on the students that Shabbat, and R. Ammi and R. Assi happened to be there. He placed a whole basket of fruit before them. I do not know whether he did it because he was just generous or for some other reason. (*Shabbat* 74a)

R. Bibi said in the name of R. Yoshua b. Levi: Anyone who spits on the Temple Mount these days is considered as if he had spat in the pupil of His eye. (*Berachot* 62b)

For a glimpse of the world as it was in R. Bibi's time, see the historical timeline from 200 to 300 C.E.

ביבי
Bibi (Bebai)

(fourth century C.E.)
Amora, Babylonia

R. Bibi was a student of Rabbi Nachman. (*Bava Metzia* 23b, *Bava Batra* 36b)

R. Adda b. Ahava lived in the house of a proselyte who was running against R. Bibi for the position of town administrator. When they came before Rabbi Yoseph, R. Adda argued in favor of the proselyte. After listening to both sides, Rabbi Yoseph declared, "Let R. Bibi, who is a great man, devote his attention to heavenly matters such as distributing charity, and let the proselyte look after the affairs of the town." R. Abbaye remarked. "When one provides a scholar with housing, let him provide it for one like R. Adda b. Ahava, who is able to argue in his favor." (*Kiddushin* 76b)

R. Bibi held the opposite view from the other rabbis. Rabbi Yoseph said, "Adopt R. Bibi's view." (*Megillah* 18b)

Resh Galuta Yitzhak, the son of R. Bibi's sister, traveled from Cordova to Spain and died there. A message came from there as follows: Resh Galuta Yitzhak, son of R. Bibi's sister, traveled from Cordova to Spain and died there. There was a question that it might have been another man by the same name. (*Yevamot* 115b)

R. Papa once sat behind R. Bibi in the presence of R. Hamnuna as they engaged in a discussion about ritual impurity. (*Niddah* 27a)

For a glimpse of the world as it was in R. Bibi's time, see the historical timeline from 300 to 400 C.E.

בּיזנא בר זבדא
Bizna b. Zavda
(second–third centuries C.E.)

Most likely he was one of the students of R. Akiva.

R. Bizna b. Zavda said in the name of R. Akiva, who had it from R. Panda, who had it from R. Nahum, who had it from R. Birim, who said it in the name of an elder by the name of R. Banah: "There were twenty-four interpreters of dreams in Jerusalem. When R. Banah once had a dream, he went to all twenty-four, each of whom gave him a different interpretation. All were fulfilled." (*Berachot* 55b)

For a glimpse of the world as it was in Bizna b. Zavda's time, see the historical timeline from 150 to 250 C.E.

בבא בן בוטא
Bava ben Buta
(first century B.C.E.)
Tanna, Eretz Yisrael

R. Bava, a contemporary of King Herod, was a judge in Jerusalem.

Although he was a disciple of Shammai, he supported a ruling of Bet Hillel. On that day they got the upper hand and established Halacha according to Bet Hillel, and no one disputed it. (*Betzah* 20a)

Rabbi Bava ben Buta was very thorough in his investigations.

Once a man wanted to divorce his wife without paying her the settlement stipulated in her *ketubbah*. He invited his friends to a feast and got them drunk, and then he put them all in one bed. Then he brought egg whites and scattered them among the men, and brought witnesses to see it. He then went to court in order to claim that he was not obligated to pay his wife her settlement on the grounds of her infidelity. Rabbi Bava said that he had

learned from Rabbi Shammai that egg white contracts when brought near the fire, while semen becomes faint from fire. They tested the egg whites and found that it was so. They brought the man to court, flogged him and made him pay his wife her marriage settlement. (*Gittin* 57a)

The Talmud relates that Rabbi Bava ben Buta used to offer a provisional guilt-offering every day except the day after Yom Kippur. (*Keritot* 25a)

Once, a woman broke two candles on his head. When he asked her why she did it, she answered, "My husband ordered me to do it." Unwilling to cause trouble between her and her husband, he blessed her. (*Nedarim* 66b)

King Herod wiped out the entire Hasmonean family except one girl whom he wished to marry, but who was unwilling to become his wife. She went up onto the roof and called out, "Whoever claims to be from the Hasmonean family is a slave, since I alone am left from that family and I am throwing myself down from the roof." After her death, Herod preserved her body in honey for seven years. (*Baba Batra* 3b–4a)

Herod heard rumors that people were saying that a king of Judea must be Jewish. He asked his advisers: "Who are they who teach that a king can be chosen 'only from thy brethren'?"

They told him, "It is the rabbis." He therefore killed all the rabbis except R. Bava b. Buta, whom he blinded. One day Herod, pretending to be a commoner, sat before R. Bava b. Buta and complained, saying, "This former slave, Herod, does wicked things."

"What do you want me to do to him?" asked R. Bava b. Buta.

"I want you to curse him," said Herod.

"It is written in Scripture that you should not curse a king even in thought," replied R. Bava b. Buta.

Herod tested him with more suggestions, but R. Bava did not fall into his trap. Finally, Herod revealed himself, saying, "Had I known that the rabbis were so circumspect, I would not have killed them."

Herod asked Rabbi Bava ben Buta: "What can I do to make amends for my sin in having killed all the scholars?"

R. Bava answered: "Since you have extinguished the light of the world by killing the rabbis, you should attend to the other light of the world, the Temple."

Herod told him, "I am afraid of the government in Rome."

Bava b. Buta advised him, "Send an envoy to Rome to ask permission. Let him take a year to get there, stay in Rome for a year and take another year to return. In the meantime, rebuild the Temple."

Herod followed his advice and received the following reply from Rome: "If you have not yet pulled down the old one, do not do so. If you have pulled it down, do not rebuild it. If you have pulled it down and already rebuilt it, then you are one of those bad servants who act first and ask permission afterwards." (*Baba Batra* 4a)

It used to be said: He who has not seen the Temple of Herod has never seen a beautiful building. Rabbah said, "It was built of yellow and white marble. Some say that it was blue, yellow and white. He originally intended to cover it with gold, but the rabbis advised him to leave it alone because it was more beautiful as it was. It looked like the waves of the sea." (*Baba Batra* 4a)

For a glimpse of the world as it was in R. Bava ben Buta's time, see the historical timeline from 100 to 1 B.C.E.

חגי
Haggai
(third–fourth centuries C.E.)
Amora, Eretz Yisrael

Originally R. Haggai was from Babylonia, but moved to Eretz Yisrael, and settled in Tiberias.

His teacher in Tiberias was Rabbi Zeira, but he also quotes R. Yosi. (*Bava Batra* 19b, *Bava Metzia* 113b) R. Haggai also had halachic discussions with Rava and Abbaye. Rabbi Manna was a close friend and student of R. Haggai. His son Eleazar studied under Rabbi Manna in Sepphoris.

In his later years, Rabbi Haggai moved back to Babylonia.

R. Haggai had discussions with R. Ulla. (*Avodah Zarah* 68a)

For a glimpse of the world as it was in R. Haggai's time, see the historical timeline from 250 to 350 C.E.

חלפתא
Halafta
(first–second centuries C.E.)
Tanna, Eretz Yisrael

R. Halafta's activities in the Gemara took place in approximately 120–140 C.E. Also known as Abba Halafta, he lived in Sepphoris, where he was a community leader. Some of his close associates were Rabbi Yohanan ben Nuri, Rabbi Akiva, Rabbi Eleazar ben Azaryah and R. Hananya ben Teradion.

His son, Rabbi Yosi ben Halafta, mentions that when his father went to study under Rabbi Yohanan ben Nuri, they were discussing the subject of renting the land in order to use the fruit that the land produces. (*Bava Batra* 56b)

Another time, Rabbi Yosi said, "It happened that my father Halafta visited R. Gamliel Berabbi in Tiberias. He sat at the table of Yohanan b. Nizuf, and they reminisced about his grandfather, R. Gamliel." (*Shabbat* 115a)

"The authorship of the book *Seder Olam* is attributed to Rabbi Halafta or to his son R. Yosi b. Halafta. It was taught in the book *Seder Olam,* and so on. The book is a history in chronological order; it begins with creation and ends with the Bar Kochva revolt." (*Shabbat* 88a, *Yevamot* 82b, *Niddah* 46b)

The Talmud relates that in the town of Sepphoris, in the days of Rabbi Halafta and Rabbi Hananya ben Teradion, special prayers were recited and the shofar was blown on fast days. (*Taanit* 15b)

For a glimpse of the world as it was in R. Halafta's time, see the historical timeline from 50 to 150 C.E.

חלפתא בן דוסא
Halafta b. Dosa, Ish Kefar Hananya

(second century C.E.)
Tanna, Eretz Yisrael

A student of Rabbi Meir, R. Halafta is quoted saying: "If a group of people sit and study Torah, the Shechina is present among them." (*Avot* 3:6)

For a glimpse of the world as it was in R. Halafta b. Dosa's time, see the historical timeline from 100 to 200 C.E.

חלפתא בן שאול
Halafta ben Shaul

(third century C.E.)
Amora, Eretz Yisrael

R. Halafta is being quoted as giving a ruling in a halachic matter. (*Zevahim* 93b) The question was asked: what is the significance of the seven blessings recited on Shabbat? To what do they correspond? R. Halafta b. Shaul answered: To the seven sounds of voices that King David mentions in Psalm 29. (*Berachot* 29a)

For a glimpse of the world as it was in R. Halafta's time, see the historical timeline from 200 to 300 C.E.

חמא
Hama

(fourth century C.E.)
Amora, Babylonia
Director of the Academy in Pumbedita

R. Hama was originally from Nehardea, but became the head of the academy in Pumbedita; he succeeded Rabbi Nahman ben Yitzhak.

Some orphans inherited a bond from their father against which a receipt was produced by the borrower that it had been paid. R. Hama ruled that we neither enforce payment on the strength of the bond nor tear it up, because when the orphans grow up, they may find more conclusive evidence. (*Bava Batra* 7b)

R. Hama was a businessman who speculated on price differentials from one market to another at his own risk. (*Bava Metzia* 65a)

R. Hama used to hire out his money for a small amount per day. As a result, his money evaporated. (*Bava Metzia* 69b)

King Shapur of Persia interacted and had discussions with Rabbi Hama. (*Sanhedrin* 46b)

The Talmud does not always refer to a rabbi by name, but instead uses a reference term. When the Talmud states, "The Amoraim from Nehardea," it is referring to Rabbi Hama. (*Sanhedrin* 17b)

For a glimpse of the world as it was in R. Hama's time, see the historical timeline from 300 to 400 C.E.

חמא בר ביסא
Hama bar Bisa

(second–third centuries C.E.)
Tanna, Eretz Yisrael

R. Hama was a judge and a contemporary of Rabbi Yehuda ha-Nasi.

Rami b. Hama said the following: "A three-fold cord is not easily broken." This is exemplified by R. Oshaya, who is the son of R. Hama, the son of R. Bisa. (*Bava Batra* 59a)

The Talmud tells us that Rabbi Hama left his home and spent twelve years studying Torah in the academy. When he returned home, he stopped at the local academy before going home. A young man entered the academy and sat down next to him and asked him a question on the subject of study. When R. Hama saw the great knowledge this young man possessed he became depressed. He was thinking, "Had I been here, I also could have had such a son." After he went home, the young man followed him and knocked on the door. Believing that he had come to ask him another question, he rose before him as he entered the house. His wife broke out in laughter. "What kind of father stands up before his son?" The young man that followed him happened to be Rabbi Oshaya, his son. It was said of them: A threefold cord is not quickly broken. (*Ketubbot* 62b)

Rebbe was praising R. Hama b. Bisa to R. Yishmael b. Yosi as a great man. He said to him: "When you see him, bring him to me." When they finally met, he encouraged him to ask him halachic questions. (*Niddah* 14b)

For a glimpse of the world as it was in R. Hama b. Bisa's time, see the historical timeline from 150 to 250 C.E.

חמא בר חנינא
Hama b. Hanina

(third century C.E.)
Amora, Eretz Yisrael

According to some sources, R. Hama, who was a wealthy man, built a synagogue in Sepphoris. One of his close associates was Rabbi Oshaya.

As he discussed a halacha with his colleagues, he related a story that Rabbi Nesiah and he were guests at a place where they were served boiled eggs. (Shabbat 38a)

R. Hama b. Hanina said if one sees that his prayers are not answered, he should pray again. (*Berachot* 32b)

He has several explanations about the mystery of R. Moshe's burial place. (*Sotah* 14a)

He also said: great is penitence, because it brings healing to the world. (*Yoma* 86a)

Another saying of his was: what is the remedy for slanderers? If he is a scholar, he should engage in learning Torah, but if he is an ignorant person, he should become a humble person. (*Arachin* 15b)

For a glimpse of the world as it was in R. Hama ben Hanina's time, see the historical timeline from 200 to 300 C.E.

חמא בר גוריא
Hama b. Gurya

(third–fourth centuries C.E.)
Amora, Babylonia

Rava b. Mehasya said in the name of R. Hama b. Gurya in Rav's name: A man should never show preference for one son over the others because our ancestor Yaakov preferred Yoseph over his brothers and they became jealous. Consequently, our ancestors wound up in Egypt as slaves. (*Shabbat* 10b)

Rava b. Mehasya said in the name of R. Hama b. Gurya in Rav's name: A man should always prefer to live in a city that was recently established because it is less sinful. (*Shabbat* 10b)

For a glimpse of the world as it was in R. Hama b. Gurya's time, see the historical timeline from 250 to 350 C.E.

חנן בן אבישלום
Hanan ben Avishalom (Hanan b. Avshalom)

(first century C.E.)
Tanna, Eretz Yisrael

R. Hanan, who was a colleague of R. Admon and a contemporary of Rabbi Yohanan ben Zakkai, was one of the civil judges in Yerushalayim.

The Talmud states that there were two judges of civil law in Jerusalem: Admon and Hanan ben Avishalom. (*Ketubbot* 104b)

The Talmud also relates that in certain cases Rabbi Yohanan ben Zakkai agreed with Rabbi Hanan. (*Ketubbot* 107b)

For a glimpse of the world as it was in the time of R. Hanan ben Avishalom, see the historical timeline from 1 to 100 C.E.

חנן בר רבא
Hanan b. Rava

(third–fourth centuries C.E.)
Amora, Babylonia

Rav Yehuda, R. Yirmiyahu b. Abba and R. Hanan b. Rava visited the home of Avin de-man Neshikya. The host ordered seats for the guests but not for R. Hanan b. Rava, which annoyed him very much. The host was busy teaching his son some halachic laws with which R. Hanan disagreed. He remarked, "Avin the fool teaches his son nonsense." (*Shabbat* 121 a–b)

חנן המצרי
Hanan ha-Mitzri (Hanan the Egyptian)

(second century C.E.)
Tanna, Alexandria

A judge, he heard cases involving robbery in the city of Jerusalem. (*Ketubbot* 105a)

The Talmud does not always refer to a rabbi by name, but instead it uses a reference term. When the Talmud states: "It was discussed before the rabbis," it is referring to R. Shimon ben Azzai, Rabbi Shimon ben Zoma, Rabbi Hanan ha-Mitzri and R. Hanania ben Hachinai. (*Sanhedrin* 17b)

For a glimpse of the world as it was in the time of R. Hanan ha-Mitzri, see the historical timeline from 100 to 200 C.E.

חנניא בן אחי רבי יהושע
Hananya ben Ahi Yehoshua

(first–second centuries C.E.)
Tanna, Eretz Yisrael

A leading scholar of his generation, R. Hananya studied under his uncle, Rabbi Yoshua ben Hananya. He lived in Eretz Yisrael in his younger years and then moved to Babylonia. He later returned briefly to Eretz Yisrael but moved back to Babylonia, where he remained until his death. This turbulent time was marked by Hadrian's persecutions and the Bar Kochva revolt. The Jews in Babylonia followed R. Hananya's lead in halachic matters.

The Talmud relates that R. Hanina was asked to rule in case of an aborted malformed baby. When R. Gamliel heard the ruling, he sent word to R. Yoshua, saying, "Seize your nephew and bring him to me!" R. Yoshua sent the following message to R. Gamliel: "Hanina issued his ruling on my authority." (*Niddah* 24b)

R. Safra said: R. Abbahu used to tell this story: When R. Hananya b. Ahi Yoshua left for Babylonia, he began to intercalate the years and to fix the new months outside Israel. The bet din of Israel sent two scholars to stop him from doing so: R. Yosi b. Kippar and the grandson of R. Zechariah b. Kavutal. When R. Hananya saw them, he asked them, "Why have you come?" They answered, "We have come to learn Torah from you." When he heard that, he proclaimed to the community: These men are the great scholars of our generation. They and their ancestors have served in the Temple. As we have learned, Zechariah b. Kavutal said: Many times have I read from the book of Daniel.

Shortly afterwards, they issued rulings against his declarations. Everything that he said was impure they declared pure, and permitted what he had forbidden. R. Hananya became upset and announced to the community: "These men are false and worthless."

They said to him, "You have already built our reputation and you cannot destroy it. You have already made fences and you cannot break them down." He asked them, "Why do you declare pure that which I declared to be impure?"

They answered him, "Because you intercalate years and fix the new moon outside Israel." He retorted, "Did not R. Akiva b. Yoseph intercalate years and fix the new month outside of Israel?" They answered him; "Do not cite R. Akiva, who had no equal in Israel." He retorted; "I also left no equal in the land of Israel." They said to him, "The kids that you left behind in Israel have become goats with horns, and they sent us to speak to you in their name. If you listen, well and good, but if you do not, you will be excommunicated. They also empowered us to tell the community here in Babylonia: If you heed us, well and good. But if you do not, then let them go up the mountain, let Ahia build an altar, and Hananya play the harp. All of you will become deniers and will have no portion in the God of Israel." When the community heard this, they started to weep and declared: Heaven forbid. (*Berachot* 63a)

R. Hanina was highly respected. Once, when he was ill, R. Nathan and all the great men of that generation came to visit him. (*Hullin* 47b)

R. Hanina stated: "When I traveled to Babylonia I met an old man who told me that a reed may be used as an upper covering for the sukkah. When I returned, I spoke about it to my uncle, R. Yoshua, and he agreed." (*Sukkah* 20b)

It was taught that R. Hanania said: One must examine his garment pockets on Friday before Shabbat. R. Yoseph observed: This is an important Shabbat law. (*Shabbat* 12a)

For a glimpse of the world as it was in R. Hananya b. Ahi Yehoshua's time, see the historical timeline from 50 to 150 C.E.

חנניא בן עקשיא
Hananya ben Akashia
(second century C.E.)
Tanna, Eretz Yisrael

R. Hananya was a contemporary of Rabbi Yehuda ha-Nasi and Rabbi Yosi. One of his well-known sayings is, "God was pleased to confer favors on Israel. Therefore he multiplied his commandments for them, for which they will be rewarded." This passage is usually recited at the end of a learning session. (*Makkot* 23b)

For a glimpse of the world as it was in R. Hananya b. Akashia's time, see the historical timeline from 100 to 200 C.E.

חנניא בן עקביא
Hananya ben Akavia
(second century C.E.)
Tanna, Eretz Yisrael

A contemporary of Rabbi Yehuda ha-Nasi, R. Hananya had his own academy in Tiberias.

R. Hananya discussed the inheritance of a woman. (*Ketubbot* 78a)

R. Hananya discussed valuations. (*Arachin* 6b)

For a glimpse of the world as it was in Hananya b. Akavia's time, see the historical timeline from 100 to 200 C.E.

חנניא בן חזקיה בן גוריון
Hananya ben Hizkiya b. Guryon

(first century C.E.)
Tanna, Eretz Yisrael

R. Hananya was a slightly younger contemporary of Hillel and Shammai.

The Mishna relates that when Rabbi Hananya was ill, the rabbis went to visit him. "These are the rulings that they issued in the upper chamber of Hanania ben Hizkiya ben Gurion when they went up to visit him. They voted, the school of Shammai outnumbered those of the school of Hillel and they decided on eighteen matters that day." (*Shabbat* 13b)

For a glimpse of the world as it was in R. Hananya b. Hizkiya b. Guryon's time, see the historical timeline from 1 to 100 C.E.

חנניא בן תרדיון
Hananya ben Teradion (Hananiah, or Hanina, b. Teradyon)

(second century C.E.)
Tanna, Eretz Yisrael
Head of the academy in Sichnin

Rabbi Hananya ben Teradion was the head of the academy in Sichnin in the Galilee, and the overseer of charity in his community. His daughter, Berurya, was the wife of Rabbi Meir.

Our rabbis taught: "Follow the scholars to their academies: R. Eliezer to Lydda, R. Yohanan b. Zakkai to Beror Hayil, R. Yoshua to Peki'in, R. Gamliel to Yavneh, R. Akiva to Bene Berak, R. Matya to Rome, R. Hananya b. Teradyon to Sichnin, R. Yosi b. Halafta to Sepphoris, R. Yehuda b. Betera to Nisibis, R. Hanina b. Ahi Yoshua to exile, Rebbe to Bet Shearim and the

Sages to the Chamber of Hewn Stone. (*Sanhedrin* 32b)

Our rabbis taught: When Rabbi Yosi b. Kisma was ill, R. Hananya b. Teradion went to visit him. R. Yosi said to him: "Don't you know that Heaven ordained that the Romans would destroy our Temple and rule over us? I heard that you are defying them and teach Torah in public."

R. Hananya answered: "Heaven will show mercy."

R. Yosi said to him, "I am telling you plain facts and you say, 'Heaven will show mercy'? I would not be surprised if they burned you and the Torah scroll together with you in one fire."

R. Hananya asked R. Yosi: "How do I stand in the future world?"

R. Yosi replied, "Is there any particular act that you are concerned about?"

"Yes," R. Hananya replied. "Once I mistakenly mixed up the Purim money with the ordinary charity."

Rabbi Yosi replied, "I wish that my lot were like yours."

R. Yosi b. Kisma died several days afterwards, and all the great men of Rome came to his funeral and eulogized him. On their return, they came upon R. Hanania b. Teradion sitting and teaching Torah in public. They seized him and his Torah scroll, wrapped the scroll around his body, placed bundles of wood around him and set them on fire. They soaked woolen cloths in water and placed them over his heart in order to prolong his agony. When his daughter saw him, she exclaimed. "Father, woe is me to see you thus!"

He told her, "If it were only myself it would be hard to bear, but to be burned together with the Torah is more comforting."

His students asked him, "Rabbi, what do you see?"

He answered, "I see the parchment burning, but the letters are soaring high."

The executioner, moved by R. Hananya's firm faith during his sufferings, asked him: "Rabbi, if I remove the wool from your heart, will you take me with you to heaven?"

He replied, "Yes." The executioner removed the wool and fed the fire, allowing R. Hananya to die quickly. The executioner then threw himself into the flames.

When R. Yehuda ha-Nasi heard the news, he wept, saying: One may acquire the World to Come in a single hour, others after many years.

Rabbi Hananya ben Teradion became one of the Ten Martyrs. (*Avodah Zarah* 18a)

The Talmud relates that one of Rabbi Hanania b. Teradion's daughters was condemned to serve in a brothel. Her sister, Berurya, told her husband, R. Meir: I am ashamed to have my sister in a brothel. Can you do something to get her out of there? He took a bag full of dinars and set out to ransom her, saying to himself: If she has kept herself pure, then a miracle will happen. He disguised himself as a knight and came to the place where she was imprisoned. He told her, "Prepare yourself for me." She replied, "I am menstruating." He answered, "I am willing to wait." She replied, "But there are many women here who are more beautiful than I am." R. Meir determined that she probably used these excuses with everyone. He offered the money to the watchman, who released her. When the government found out what R. Meir had done and wished to arrest him, he had to flee Eretz Yisrael for Babylonia. (*Avodah Zarah* 18a)

R. Hananya said: two people who sit together and discuss Torah, the Shechina is present with them. (*Avot* 3: 2)

For a glimpse of the world as it was in R. Hananya b. Teradion's time, see the historical timeline from 100 to 200 C.E.

חיינא

Hanina

(third–fourth centuries C.E.)
Amora, Eretz Yisrael

Originally from Babylonia, R. Hanina moved to Eretz Yisrael and was a student of Rabbi Yohanan. (*Menahot* 79b, *Yevamot* 58b)

At one time, R. Hanina lived in Sepphoris, where he served as that community's av bet din.

It is related in the Talmud that Rabbi Yohanan was very anxious to ordain Rabbi Hanina and Rabbi Hoshia, but somehow it never materialized, because he could not get a quorum of three qualified rabbis to do it. When Rabbi Hanina saw that Rabbi Yohanan was distressed on account of it, he said to him, "Master, do not grieve, for we the descendants of Eli are destined not to be ordained."

Although they were kohanim and descendants of Eli the High Priest, Rabbi Hanina and Rabbi Oshaya earned their living as sandal-makers. (*Sanhedrin* 14a)

R. Yohanan said, "Three kinds of people earn special approval from God: a bachelor who lives in a large city and does not sin, a poor man who returns lost property to its owner, and a wealthy man who tithes his produce in secret." (*Pesahim* 113 a–b)

When R. Safra, who was a bachelor living in a large city, heard this statement, his face lit up. Rava told him, "Rabbi Yohanan did not have someone like you in mind, but rather persons like R. Hanina and R. Hoshia. They are sandal makers in Eretz Yisrael who live in a neighborhood of prostitutes. They make sandals for them, and when they deal with them they do not lift their eyes to look at them. When the prostitutes take an oath, they do so 'by the life of the holy rabbis of Eretz Yisrael.'"

Rabbi Hanina used to dress up in his finest garments on Friday evening and call out, "Let us go out to welcome the Shabbat Queen." (*Shabbat* 119a)

When R. Yohanan fell ill, R. Hanina went to visit him. He asked him: "Are your sufferings welcome to you?" He answered, "No, I desire neither the suffering nor its reward." R. Hanina then said to him: "Give me your hand." He gave him his hand and he cured him. (*Berachot* 5b)

If R. Yohanan cured others, why could he not cure himself? The rabbis replied: A prisoner cannot set himself free.

R. Hanina said: everything is in the hands of heaven except the fear of heaven. (*Megillah* 25a)

R. Hanina said: Moshe received the measurements of all the vessels of the *mishkan* that he prepared from the Torah – their length, width and height. (*Sukkah* 5a)

For a glimpse of the world as it was in R. Hanina's time, see the historical timeline from 250 to 350 C.E.

חנינא בן אנטיגנוס
Hanina ben Antigonus

(second century C.E.)
Tanna, Eretz Yisrael

In his younger years, Rabbi Hanina lived in Jerusalem, and was there when the Temple was destroyed.

He had great knowledge about the Temple and its vessels and was an expert on the blemishes of animal sacrifices. (*Bechorot* 6:3, 4, 10, 38b)

Regarding an eruv, R. Hanina b. Antigonus ruled that the two thousand cubits are figured for a circular area rather than a square area. (*Eruvin* 49b)

For a glimpse of the world as it was in the time of R. Hanina b. Antigonus, see the historical timeline from 100 to 200 C.E.

חנינא בר אבהו
Hanina b. Abbahu

(third–fourth century C.E.)
Amora, Eretz Yisrael

The son of the famous Rabbi Abbahu of Caesarea, R. Hanina studied at his father's academy.

(*Kiddushin* 33b) He is quoted as saying in the name of his father Abbahu and in the name of R. Avdimi Deman Haifa: "When a scholar passes by, one should rise for him from a distance of four cubits. When the head of a beit din enters the room, one should rise as soon as he is seen and be seated when he has passed four cubits. When the *nasi* enters the room, one rises when he is seen and sits down only after he is seated."

R. Hanina also studied in Tiberias. Later on he lived in Caesarea, where he served as a dayyan.

For a glimpse of the world as it was in the time of R. Hanina b. Abbahu, see the historical timeline from 250 to 350 C.E.

חנינא בר חמא
Hanina bar Hama

(third century C.E.)
Head of the academy of Sepphoris

Hanina bar Hama, a native of Babylonia, lived during the transitional period when the tannaitic period ended and the amoraic period began. After studying briefly in Babylonia, he moved to Sepphoris in Eretz Yisrael, where he studied in the academy of Rabbi Yehuda ha-Nasi. Among his close associates were Rabbi Yishmael b. Yosi, R. Bar Kappara, Rabbi Hiyya, Rav, R. Yonathan and R. Yoshua b. Levi.

Among his distinguished students were Rabbi Yohanan, Rabbi Shimon b. Lakish and Rabbi Eleazar.

A businessman who traded in honey, R. Hanina bar Hama was also familiar with medicines. (*Yoma* 49a)

Before Rabbi Yehuda ha-Nasi died, he left instructions that R. Hanina bar Hama preside over the academy. However, R. Hanina would not accept the position because R. Afes was two and a half years older. Therefore, R. Afes took the position. During his tenure, R. Hanina did not attend studies inside the academy, but instead studied outside together with Rabbi Levi. When Rabbi Afes passed away, R. Hanina bar Hama took over the presidency. His study partner gone, Rabbi Levi moved to Babylonia. (*Ketubbot* 103b)

When Rebbe was about to expire, he said, "I would like to have my sons present." When they came, he instructed them: "Take care to show respect to your mother. The light shall continue to burn in its usual place, the table shall be set in its usual place and my bed shall be made up in its usual place. Yoseph of Haifa and Shimon of Efrat, who attended on me in my lifetime, shall attend on me when I am dead." (*Ketubbot* 103a)

Rebbe then said, "I would like to speak to the sages of Israel." When they entered, he said to them: "Do not lament for me in the smaller towns, and reassemble the academy after thirty days. My son Shimon is to be the Hacham, my son Gamliel shall be the Nasi and Hanina b. Hama is to be Rosh Yeshiva." (*Ketubbot* 103b)

On the day Rebbe died, a *bat kol* was heard announcing: Whoever was present at the death of Rebbe is destined to enjoy the life of the World to Come.

Rebbe said: "I would like to speak to my younger son." When R. Shimon entered, Rebbe instructed him in the rules and regulations of being a Hacham.

Rebbe then said, "I would like to see my elder son." When R. Gamliel entered, he instructed him in the traditions and regulations of the patriarchate. He said, "My son, conduct your patriarchate with high-caliber men and keep strong discipline among your students."

On the day Rebbe died the Rabbis decreed a public fast-day. (*Ketubbot* 104a)

The Talmud relates that Rav, who was the head of the academy in Sura, Babylonia, was told that a great tall and lame man has come to Nehardea to lecture. Rav remarked, "It must be Rabbi Levi, and it must be that R. Afes died and R. Hanina is now the head of the academy. Rabbi Levi used to study with R. Hanina ben Hama, and he must have left because he lost his study partner." Rabbi Yehuda ha-Nasi had left specific instructions that when he died, R. Hanina ben Hama should direct the academy. But R. Hanina yielded to R. Afes because he was two and a half years older. (*Shabbat* 59b)

It was said of Rabbi Hanina that at the age of eighty he could stand on one foot and put his shoe on the other foot. He credited the warm bath and the oil with which his mother anointed him in his youth with having given him this agility. (*Hullin* 24b)

Rabbi Eleazar transmitted in the name of Rabbi Hanina the famous saying, "Torah scholars increase peace in the world." (*Berachot* 64a)

It was recorded in R. Yehoshua b. Levi's notebook that the day of the week on which a person was born determines his fate. When R. Hanina heard this, he said to his people, "Go and tell the son of Levi." (*Shabbat* 156a)

"It is not the *mazal* [astrological influence] of the day that influences one's fate, but the *mazal* of the hour."

"A person born under the influence of the sun will be distinguished. He will eat and drink from his own provisions and his secrets shall be revealed. If he becomes a thief, he will not be successful.

"A person who is born under Venus will be wealthy and immoral.

"A person born under Mercury will have a retentive memory and will be wise.

"A person born under the moon will suffer. He will construct and demolish, he will eat and drink that which is not his own, his secrets will remain hidden, and if he chooses to be a thief he will be successful. A person born under Saturn will have his plans frustrated."

R. Hanina states that one who lifted a hand to strike another is called a sinner even if he did not actually strike him. (*Sanhedrin* 58b)

R. Eleazar said in the name of R. Hanina: "The blessing of a common man should not be taken lightly." (*Megillah* 15a)

R. Hanina said; one should always set his table after the departure of Shabbat, even if he needs to eat an amount of food the size of an olive. (*Shabbat* 119b)

R. Hanina also said, Jerusalem was destroyed because they did not rebuke each other.

R. Hanina said. Everything is in the hand of heaven except fear of heaven. (*Berachot* 33b)

R. Eleazar said further in the name of R. Hanina: The death of a righteous person is a great loss to his generation, but he is not really lost because his legacy remains. It is like when one loses a precious pearl. It is a loss only to the owner, but the pearl remains a pearl wherever it is. (*Megillah* 15a)

Resh Lakish marked the burial caves of the rabbis in order to prevent the priests from becoming defiled. But when he could not locate the grave of R.

Hiyya, he felt humiliated and called out, Sovereign of the Universe; did I not debate on the Torah like R. Hiyya did? A heavenly voice responded: You did indeed debate like he did, but you did not spread the Torah as he did. Whenever R. Hanina and R. Hiyya were in dispute; R. Hanina would say to R. Hiyya: "Would you argue with me if the Torah, God forbid, were to be forgotten? I would restore the Torah in Israel by my debating powers." R. Hiyya would reply: "Would you argue with one who restored the Torah in Israel?" How did R. Hiyya do this? He went out and sowed flax, from which he made nets to trap deer. He gave the venison to orphans, and from the skins he prepared scrolls upon which he wrote the five books of Moshe. Then he went to a town that had no teachers and taught to five children the five books of Moshe and to six children the six orders of the Mishna. When he left, he told the children, "Until I return, I want you to teach each other what I have taught you." Thus he kept the Torah from being forgotten by the Jewish people. (*Bava Metzia* 85b)

This is what Rebbe meant when he said: "How great are the works of R. Hiyya!" "Are they greater than yours?" asked R. Yishmael b. R. Yosi. "Yes," replied Rebbe.

R. Eleazar said in the name of R. Chanina: If one quotes a saying in the name of its originator; that person brings deliverance to this world. (*Megillah* 15a)

For a glimpse of the world as it was in R. Hanina's time, see the historical timeline from 200 to 300 C.E.

חנינא בן דוסא
Hanina ben Dosa
(first century C.E.)
Tanna, Eretz Yisrael

Rabbi Hanina was a colleague and disciple of Rabbi Yohanan ben Zakkai. (*Berachot* 5:5, 34b) The Talmud relates that when he prayed for the healing of sick people, he could tell in advance who would recover and who would not. He was asked how he knew. He replied: If my prayers are uttered fluently, then it is a positive sign.

Rav Yehuda said in the name of Rav: Every day a heavenly voice went forth from Mount Horev and proclaimed, "The whole world is being fed for the sake of My son Hanina – and yet My son Hanina is satisfied with a small measure of carobs from one Friday to the next Friday." (*Berachot* 17b)

The Talmud declares that when Rabbi Hanina ben Dosa died, men of great deeds ceased to exist. (*Sotah* 9:15, 49a)

Rabbi Hanina used to say: "He whose deeds exceed his wisdom, his wisdom will endure, but he whose wisdom exceeds his deeds, his wisdom will not endure." (*Avot* 3:9)

He also used to say: "A person who is pleasing to humankind is also pleasing to God, but a person who is disliked by humankind is not pleasing to God." (*Avot* 3:10)

In a certain place, a lizard was injuring people. They came to tell R. Hanina b. Dosa. He said to them: Show me its hole. When they did, he put his heel over it. The lizard came out and bit him – and the lizard died. R. Hanina put the dead lizard on his shoulder and brought it to the bet midrash, where he said to those assembled there: "See, my sons, it is not the lizard that kills. It is

sins that kill." They then said, "Woe to the man who meets up with a lizard, but woe to the lizard that meets up with R. Hanina b. Dosa!" (*Berachot* 33a)

Rav said: the world was created only for Ahav ben Omri and for R. Hanina b. Dosa; this world for Ahav b. Omri, and the future world for R. Hanina b. Dosa. (*Berachot* 61b)

When R. Gamliel's son became ill, R. Gamliel sent two scholars to R. Hanina b. Dosa to ask him to pray.

R. Hanina went up to the upper chamber and prayed. When he came down, he told them, "Go home. The fever has left him." They asked him, "Are you a prophet?" He replied, "I am neither a prophet nor the son of a prophet, but I have learned this from experience. If I utter my prayers smoothly, I know that my prayers are accepted, but if I do not utter the prayers smoothly, then I know that they have not been accepted." (*Berachot* 34b)

On another occasion, the son of R. Yohanan ben Zakkai became ill. R. Yohanan said to R. Hanina, who was his student, "Hanina, my son, pray for my son that he may live." R. Hanina put his head between his knees and prayed. R. Yohanan ben Zakkai later remarked, "If Ben Zakkai had stuck his head between his knees all day long, no one would have noticed." His wife said to him, "Is Hanina greater than you are?" He replied, "No, but he is like a servant before a king, while I am like a nobleman before a king." (*Berachot* 34b)

On a Friday, R. Hanina b. Dosa noticed that his daughter was sad, and he asked her why. She replied, "My container of oil was mixed up with the vinegar, and I used the vinegar for the Shabbat candles by mistake." He told her, "Do not let it bother you. He who commanded oil to burn will also command vinegar to burn." It was learned that the candles lasted until Havdalah. (*Taanit* 25a)

Once a woman, a neighbor of R. Hanina b. Dosa, was building a house, but the beams were not long enough to reach the walls. She came to him with her problem. When he asked her for her name, she replied, "Aiku." He told her, "Aiku, may your beams reach your walls."

A tanna taught that the beams projected one cubit on either side. Polemu says: "I saw that house. Its beams projected one cubit on either side, and people told me: This is the house that was covered with beams by the prayers of R. Hanina b. Dosa." (*Taanit* 25a)

It once happened that the daughter of Nehunya the well-digger fell into a deep cistern. The people came to R. Hanina b. Dosa for help. In the first hour, he said to them, "All is well." In the second hour he said to them, "All is well." In the third hour, he told them, "She is saved." They asked her, "Who brought you out?" She replied: "A ram with an old man leading it came to my aid." They asked R. Hanina b. Dosa: "Are you a prophet?" He replied, "I am neither a prophet nor the son of a prophet." (*Yevamot* 121b)

For a glimpse of the world as it was in the time of R. Hanina b. Dosa, see the historical timeline from 1 to 100 C.E.

חנינא בן גמליאל
Hanina ben Gamliel
(second century C.E.)
Tanna, Eretz Yisrael

A student of Rabbi Tarfon, Rabbi Hanina had halachic disputes with Rabbi Akiva and Rabbi Yosi ha-Gelili. Rabban Gamliel the Nasi of the Yavne academy was his father, and Rabbi Shimon ben Gamliel was his younger brother. Rabbi Hanina died at a young age.

He clarifies the usage of certain frying pans in the Temple. (*Menahos* 5:8, 63a)

It was said of R. Hanina b. Gamliel that he would recite Halacha and Aggadah in a house of mourning. (*Moed Katan* 23a)

For a glimpse of the world as it was in the time of R. Hanina b. Gamliel, see the historical timeline from 100 to 200 C.E.

חנניא בן הכינאי
Hanania (Hanina) ben Hachinai
(second century C.E.)
Tanna, Eretz Yisrael

Rabbi Hanania, who was one of the outstanding students of Rabbi Akiva, lived briefly in Sidon. The youngest of the great rabbis who attended the academy in Yavne, he spoke many foreign languages.

It is related that at the conclusion of R. Shimon b. Yohai's wedding, R. Hanania b. Hachinai was about to leave for the academy in Bene Berak. He said to him, "Wait for me until I can join you." However, he did not wait for him spent twelve years there. By the time R. Hanania returned home, the streets of the town had changed so much that he could not find his way home. When he decided to go to the riverbank in order to find his way home, he heard people addressing a young girl, "Daughter of Hachinai, fill up your pitcher and let us go." (*Ketubbot* 62b)

Although he did not recognize her, he followed her and found his home. When he arrived, his wife was sifting flour. When she turned around and saw her husband, she was so overcome with joy that she fainted.

One of his quotations is "One who is awake at night, or walks alone and directs his thoughts to frivolous matters, is liable for his life." (*Avot* 3:4)

He was one of the ten martyrs.

When the Talmud states: "It was discussed before the rabbis," it is referring to R. Shimon ben Azzai, Rabbi Shimon ben Zoma, Rabbi Hanan ha-Mitzri and R. Hanania ben Hachinai. (*Sanhedrin* 17b)

R. Chananya once met R. Shimon b. Yohai in Sidon and told him: "When you see R. Akiva, ask him a question for me about the Halacha regarding a young girl." (*Niddah* 52b)

For a glimpse of the world as it was in the time of R. Hanania b. Hachinai, see the historical timeline from 100 to 200 C.E.

חנינא בר פפא
Hanina bar Papa

(third–fourth centuries C.E.)
Amora, Eretz Yisrael

R. Hanina bar Papa's colleagues considered him a righteous and holy man, and his community respected him greatly. (*Kiddushin* 81a)

It is related that a woman once tried to seduce R. Hanina b. Papi. He pronounced a magic formula that made his body full of scabs so that he would be undesirable, but she pronounced a magic formula and his scabs were removed. He fled to a bathhouse. In those days it was not safe to enter a bathhouse alone. They asked him, "Perhaps you were guarded because you resisted an immoral act? As it is written; miracles befall people who resist immoral acts." (*Kiddushin* 39b)

It is related that when Rabbi Hanina bar Papi was about to die, the angel of death was sent to his house with orders to carry out any wish of his. Rabbi Hanina said to the angel, "Allow me thirty days in order to revise my studies." He was granted the wish. It is said that when he died, a pillar of fire formed a partition between him and the world. We have it as a tradition that such a partition by a pillar of fire is granted only to a person who is unique in his generation. (*Ketubbot* 77b)

For a glimpse of the world as it was in the time of R. Hanania b. Hachinai, see the historical timeline from 250 to 350 C.E.

חנינא סגן הכהנים
Hanina Segan ha-Kohanim

(first century C.E.)
Tanna, Eretz Yisrael

Rabbi Hanina, who served as deputy high priest while the Temple was still in existence, survived the destruction of the Temple.

Having been in that exalted office, R. Hanina was able to transmit many details of the Temple service and customs that were prevalent during the Temple period. (*Pesahim* 1:6)

The Talmud relates that Rabbi Hanina explained the reason why the deputy stands on the right side of the high priest. If the high priest should suddenly become disqualified from serving, the deputy steps in and officiates in his stead. (*Yoma* 39a)

He said. "Pray for the welfare of the government, for without the fear of it, men would swallow each other alive." (*Avot* 3:2)

For a glimpse of the world as it was in the time of Rabbi Hanina Segan ha-Kohanim, see the historical timeline from 1 to 100 C.E.

חביבא
Haviva

(third–fourth centuries C.E.)
Amora, Babylonia

R. Haviva was a student of R. Yehuda and a contemporary of Rava and Abbaye.

He said: the elders of Pumbedita issued an additional ruling. While Rava had said that they ruled on two matters, R. Haviva added one more because Rav Yehuda said in R. Shmuel's name that it is permitted to light a fire on Shabbas for a woman in childbirth. (*Eruvin* 79b)

For a glimpse of the world as it was in R. Haviva's time, see the historical timeline from 250 to 350 C.E.

חלבו

Helbo

(third–fourth centuries C.E.)
Amora, Babylonia

R. Helbo studied in Babylonia and in Eretz Yisrael.

In Babylon he studied at Rabbi Huna. He quoted his rabbi several times. R. Chelbo said in the name of R. Huna: "A person who has a fixed place when he prays has the God of Avraham as his helper." (*Berachot* 6b)

He also studied under Rabbi Hama ben Gurya. R. Helbo spoke in the names of R. Hama b. Gurya and of Rav regarding the laws of Shabbat. (*Shabbat* 37a)

A colleague of R. Ulla of Birah, he quoted him regarding the reading of the Megillah on Purim. (*Megillah* 4a)

In Eretz Yisrael, Rabbi Ammi and Rabbi Yitzhak Nepaha were his associates. He also studied with Rabbi Shemuel ben Nahman.

Rabbi Helbo said that the wines of Perugitha and the water of Diomsith caused the ten tribes of Israel to be cut off from their brethren. R. Eleazar b. Arach, who visited there, liked it and decided to remain. As a result, he forgot his learning. When he returned to his former home he tried to read from the Torah but did not remember and read incorrectly. When the rabbis who had been his colleagues prayed for him, his memory returned. R. Nehorai said, "If you have to move to another location, be sure that you move to a place of Torah. Do not say that Torah will follow you, and do not rely on your own understanding of the Torah." Some say

that his name was not Nehorai but R. Nehemia, while others say that his name was Eleazar b. Arach. Why was he called Nehorai? Because he enlightened the eyes of the sages with his knowledge of the law. (*Shabbat* 147b)

R. Helbo said in the name of R. Huna: "If one knows that his friend is used to greet him, strive to greet him first." (*Berachot* 6b)

R. Helbo said, "When a man leaves the synagogue he should not be in a hurry." (*Berachot* 6b)

"A person should always be extra careful to recite the afternoon prayer because Eliyahu ha-Navi prayed in the afternoon and was answered favorably."

"At a wedding, one should partake of the wedding meal and bring joy to the newlyweds."

The Galileans asked R. Helbo about the proper order of calling people to the Torah. He put the question to R. Yitzhak Nepaha. (*Gittin* 59b–60a)

He used to preach: "One must always give high honor to his wife because all the blessings in one's home are on account of his wife." (*Bava Metzia* 59a)

When R. Helbo became ill, R. Kahana announced it publicly, yet no one came to visit him. He said to them: It happened that a student of R. Akiva became sick and none of the students visited him. R. Akiva was upset and he himself went to visit, and because they swept and sprinkled the ground before him he recovered. He said to R. Akiva: "My rebbe, you have revived me." Thereupon, R. Akiva lectured: "He who does not visit the sick is considered as though he had shed blood." (*Nedarim* 39b–40a)

For a glimpse of the world as it was in R. Helbo's time, see the historical timeline from 250 to 350 C.E.

חזקיה
Hizkiya (Hezekiah)

(fourth century C.E.)
Amora, Eretz Yisrael

A student of Rabbi Yirmiyahu and a colleague of Rav Huna, R. Hizkiya resided in Caesarea. (*Zevahim* 75b)

R. Hizkiya said in the name of R. Hanina b. R Abbahu and in the name of R. Avdimi from Haifa that when a scholar passes by, one should rise before him within four cubits. When the head of the court walks in, one should remain standing as long as he is in sight. When the president of the Sanhedrin walks in, one should rise as soon as he sees him and sit only after he is seated. (*Kiddushin* 33b)

For a glimpse of the world as it was in R. Hizkiya's time, see the historical timeline from 300 to 400 C.E.

חזקיה בר חייא
Hizkiya bar Hiyya (Hezekiah b. Hiyya)

(third century C.E.)
Amora, Eretz Yisrael

Although R. Hizkiya and his father, Rabbi Hiyya, originally came from Babylonia, R. Hizkiya lived in Tiberias. He was the twin brother of Rabbi Yehuda ben Hiyya. (*Megillah* 5b)

R. Avin b. R. Adda quoted R. Menachem as saying: It once happened that a child was born to the same mother three months after the first one, and both of those students studied in our academy. Who are these students? They are Rabbi Yehuda and Rabbi Hizkiya, the sons of Rabbi Hiyya. But didn't we learn that a woman couldn't conceive twice during one pregnancy? Rabbi Abbaye explained: it was semen that split in two. After it split, the features of one were completed at the beginning of the seventh month, and the features of the

other were completed at the end of the ninth month. (*Niddah* 27a)

Rabbi Shimon ben Lakish said that in ancient times, when the Torah was forgotten, Ezra came up from Babylon and reestablished it. When it was forgotten again, Hillel the Babylonian came up and reestablished it. Yet again some of it was forgotten, and Rabbi Hiyya and his sons came up from Babylonia and established it again. (*Berachot* 18b) Rabbi Hizkiya earned his living from agriculture, as did his brother. (*Sukkah* 20a)

Rabbi Hizkiya is the author of the work *Debei Hizkiya* (it was taught in the school of Hizkiya). (*Sanhedrin* 37b)

R. Yehuda and R. Hizkiya, the sons of R. Hiyya, were having dinner with Rebbe. Their father, R. Hiyya, was also present. When the sons did not utter a word during the meal, Rebbe said, "Give the young men plenty of strong wine so that they will open up and say something."

As the wine took effect, they started talking and said, "The son of David cannot come until the two ruling houses of Israel come to an end." To support this assertion, they quoted a passage from scripture. Rebbe became annoyed and exclaimed, "My children, you are throwing thorns in my eyes." R. Hiyya intervened, saying, "Rebbe, please do not be angry. The numerical value of the Hebrew letters for the word 'wine' is the same as for the word 'secret.' When wine goes in, secrets come out." (*Sanhedrin* 38a)

When R. Huna passed away, his coffin was brought to Tiberias and buried next to R. Hiyya and his two sons, R. Yehuda and R. Hizkiya. (*Moed Katan* 25a)

For a glimpse of the world as it was in the time of R. Hizkiya bar Hiyya, see the historical timeline from 200 to 300 C.E.

חידקא
Hidka

(second century C.E.)
Tanna, Eretz Yisrael

Rabbi Hidka is mentioned several times in the Talmud. He said: R. Shimon ha-Shikmoni was my friend among the students of R. Akiva, and this is what he said: "Moses knew that the daughters of Zelofhad were entitled to an inheritance, but was not sure whether the eldest was entitled to the birthright." (*Bava Batra* 119a)

According to Rabbi Hidka, one is obligated to have four meals on Shabbat. (*Shabbat* 117b)

For a glimpse of the world as it was in R. Hidka's time, see the historical timeline from 100 to 200 C.E.

חיננא
Hinena

(fourth century C.E.)
Amora, Babylonia

R. Aha Aricha stated in the presence of Rav Hinena that one who recites "ha-mavdil" in the prayer service is more praiseworthy than one who says it over a cup of wine. If he said it in both, blessings on his head. (*Berachot* 33a)

For a glimpse of the world as it was in R. Hinena's time, see the historical timeline from 300 to 400 C.E.

חסדא
Hisda

Amora, Babylonia
Head of the academy at Sura

Rabbi Hisda (c. 217–309 C.E.) was poor in his youth.

It is related that whenever R. Hisda walked in his farm among the thorns, he would lift up his garment, saying: If my body should be injured, nature will heal it, but if my garments should be torn, there is no cure. In time, he established a brewery and became very wealthy. (*Bava Kama* 91b)

R. Hisda said, "If I were not a brewer, I would not have become wealthy." He was known for his charitable behavior. An example of his generosity is the large sum of money he contributed to have the academy in Sura rebuilt when it became run down and neglected. (*Pesahim* 113a)

R. Hisda said. The reason that I have an advantage over my colleagues is that I was married at sixteen years of age. He and his wife had seven sons and two daughters.

Rabbi Hisda also studied under Rabbi Huna and Rav. When he studied under Rabbi Huna, he once asked him: "What of a student whose teacher needs him more?" Rabbi Hisda had traditions from other rabbis that Rabbi Huna did not know. R. Huna took offense and relations between them were chilly for forty years. On account of this Rabbi Hisda kept forty fast days because he felt he insulted his rabbi. Rabbi Huna also fasted forty days because in his thoughts he had suspected Hisda of arrogance. Eventually, they reconciled. (*Bava Metzia* 33a)

R. Rami b. Hama was married to the daughter of R. Hisda.

The Talmud relates when R. Yitzhak came from Eretz Yisrael to Babylonia, he said: There was a town in Eretz Yisrael by the name of Gofnit where eighty pairs of brothers, all priests, married eighty pairs of sisters, all from priestly families. The rabbis searched from Sura to Nehardea and could not find a similar case except for the daughters of R. Hisda, who were married, respectively, to Rami b. Hama and to Mar Ukva b. Hama, who were brothers. While the daughters of R. Hisda were the daughters of kohanim – Rabbi Hisda was a kohen – their husbands were not kohanim. Originally, Rabbi Hisda came from Kofri, a town south of Sura in Babylonia, and returned to Kofri to live there for a while. (*Berachot* 44a)

After Rabbi Huna passed away, Rabbi Hisda became the head of the yeshiva in Sura, serving there for the last ten years of his life.

He attached great importance to human dignity. He conducted himself in a humble way and went out of his way to greet everyone first in the marketplace, Jews and gentiles alike. (*Gittin* 62a)

Rabbi Huna asked his son Rabbah, "Why do you not attend Rabbi Hisda's lectures, which are so sharp and enlightening?"

"Why should I? He talks about profane matters most of the time. He speaks about how one should behave in the toilet – not to sit down abruptly or to strain the rectum, because the glands might become dislocated."

R. Huna became annoyed with his son and said to him: "He is discussing matters that pertain to health, and you call them profane? All the more reason to attend his lectures!" (*Shabbat* 82a)

R. Hisda advised his daughters: "Act modestly in your home, do not eat bread before your husband, do not eat greens at night, do not eat dates or drink beer at night, do not use the same toilet as your husband, and when someone knocks on the door, do not ask who he is, but who *she* is." (*Shabbat* 140b)

R. Hisda would hold in his closed hands two objects, a pearl in one hand and a seed grain in the other. He would show the pearl, but would not show the seed until people became very curious.

R. Hisda said: "Whoever contends against his rebbe's ruling is as though he contends against the Shechina." (*Sanhedrin* 110a)

R. Hisda lived to the age of ninety-two. Sixty wedding feasts were held in his home. (*Moed Katan* 28a)

R. Hisda was praising R. Hamnuna to R. Huna, saying, "He is a great man." R. Huna said to him: "When he comes to you, bring him to me." (*Kiddushin* 29b)

When he arrived, he did not wear the cap customarily worn by married men. When he was asked, "Why are you not wearing a cap?"

He answered, "I am not wearing a cap because I am not married."

R. Huna turned his face away from him and said, "See to it that you do not come before me before you are married."

As a student of Rabbi Avimi, he helped him with his studies, because at one time Rabbi Avimi forgot some of his learning, as is mentioned in the Talmud. (*Menahot* 7a) R. Zeira said that R. Avimi was studying Tractate *Menahot* under R. Hisda. But, the Talmud asks, wasn't it the reverse? R. Hisda studied under R. Avimi. And did not R. Hisda say: I received many beatings from R. Avimi? The answer is that he had forgotten this tractate and went to his student, Rabbi Hisda, to refresh his memory.

Why didn't he send for his student to come to him? He thought that by going to him, he would get more out of it.

Rabbi Hisda transmitted a tradition in the name of Rabbi Avimi: "The Tent of Meeting built by Moshe was stored away after the first Temple was erected by King Solomon, including its boards, hooks, bars, pillars and sockets."

"Where were they stored?"

R. Hisda said in the name of R. Avimi: "They stored them beneath the crypts of the Temple." (*Sotah* 9a)

As Rabbi Ulla and Rabbi Hisda were walking, they passed the house of R. Hana b. Hanilai. R. Hisda sighed. R. Ulla asked him, "Why are you sighing?" He answered him. "How can I refrain from sighing? He used to have sixty cooks to cook and bake for the poor. He always had his purse ready to give charity. In time of scarcity he put grain and barley outside at nighttime for anyone to take because he did not want people to have to come inside and be embarrassed. Now that it is all in ruins, shall I not sigh?" (*Berachot* 58b)

Whenever R. Hisda and R. Sheshet met, they trembled in admiration of each other. R. Hisda admired R. Sheshet's extensive knowledge of Mishna. R. Sheshet admired R. Hisda for his deep and penetrating mind in pilpul. (*Eruvin* 67a)

Rava said: "Length of life, the ability to have children, and whether one will have sustenance does not depend on merit, but rather on one's fortune. Take, for example; Rabbah and R. Hisda. Both were rabbis and tzadikim. R. Hisda lived to the age of ninety-two, while Rabbah lived only to the age of forty. In the house of R. Hisda they celebrated sixty weddings, while in the house of Rabbah they had sixty bereavements. In the house of R. Hisda they fed the dogs with the finest food, while in the house of Rabbah there was barely enough food for humans." (*Moed Katan* 28a)

R. Zerika said to R. Safra: Come and see the difference in approach between the good men of Eretz Yisrael and the pious men of Babylonia. When the world was in need of rain, the pious men of Babylonia, R. Huna and R. Hisda, would come forward and say: "Let us pray. Perhaps the Almighty will be propitiated and send us rain. But the great men of Eretz Yisrael, such as R. Yonah the father of R. Mani, would stand in a low spot dressed in sackcloth and pray for rain." (*Taanit* 23b)

During one of the festivals, a deer was served at the Exilarch's table. This was on the second day of the festival, but the deer was caught by a non-Jew on the first day and slaughtered on the second day. Among the guests at the table were R. Nahman, R. Hisda and R. Sheshet. R. Nahman and R. Hisda partook of the venison, but R. Sheshet would not. "What can I do with R. Sheshet, who does not want to eat any of this venison?"

"How can I," retorted R. Sheshet, "in view of what R. Issi quoted in R. Yosi's name?" (*Eruvin* 39b)

When the daughter of R. Hisda asked her father to take a nap, he answered her, "Soon the days in the grave shall be long and short, and I shall have plenty of time to sleep long." (*Eruvin* 65a)

R. Hisda said, "A synagogue should not be demolished before another has been built to take its place." (*Bava Batra* 3b)

He said, "The letters *mem* and *samech,* which were in the Tablets, were miraculously suspended, and the writing on the Tablets could be read from within and without or from both sides." (*Shabbat* 104a)

After the destruction of the Temple, the rabbis felt that one should not have a house that is too ornate. Therefore, they declared that while a house may be plastered, one should leave a small area bare. How large should that area be? R. Yoseph said that it should be a cubit square. R. Hisda said that it should be near the entrance. (*Bava Batra* 60b)

One of R. Hisda's sayings was, "Leave the drunkard alone. He will fall on his own." (*Shabbat* 32a)

Whenever the Talmud states "the elders of Sura," it is referring to Rabbi Huna and Rabbi Hisda. (*Sanhedrin* 17b)

Rav Hisda, kohen, held two priestly gifts from an ox in his hand and declared: If someone comes and tells me a new dictum in the name of Rav, I will give him these gifts. Rava b. Mehasya said to him, Rav said the following: 'If one gives a gift to a neighbor, he must inform him first.' Upon this, R. Hisda gave him the gifts.

Rava asked him: "Are Rav's statements so dear to you?"

"Yes," R. Hisda replied. Rava said, "This illustrates what Rav said: 'A garment is precious to its wearer.' "Did Rav really say that, too?" asked Hisda. "I like this saying even better than the first. If I had another gift, I would give it to you as well." (*Shabbat* 10b)

When R. Hisda and R. Hamnuna were eating a meal together, they were served dates and pomegranates. R. Hamnuna said a blessing over the dates, but R. Hisda asked him: "Don't you agree with R. Yoseph or R. Yitzhak, who stated that the blessing should be recited over whichever fruit is mentioned first?"

He replied; "The dates are second after the word land and the pomegranates are fifth." R. Hisda complimented him, saying, "I wish we had feet of iron to be able to run and listen to you." (*Berachot* 41b)

R. Zeira said to R. Hisda, "Teach us about the blessings after the meal." (*Berachot* 49a)

R. Hisda replied, "I do not know the blessings after the meal myself. How could I teach them to others?"

"What do you mean?" asked R. Zeira.

"I was once in the house of the Resh Galuta, and when I recited the blessings after the meal, R. Sheshet stretched out his neck at me like a serpent because I left out some passages."

R. Hisda and Rabbah b. Huna slept on the riverbank of Sura when they visited the Exilarch during the festival of Sukkot. By way of explanation, they said, "We are engaged in a religious errand and therefore we are exempt from the mitzvah of sleeping in the sukkah." (*Sukkah* 26a)

Our rabbis taught: Anyone who never saw the Festival of the Water-Drawing at the Temple in Jerusalem never saw rejoicing in his life. Anyone who never saw Jerusalem in its splendor has never seen a lovely city. Anyone who has not seen the Temple in Jerusalem when it was fully rebuilt has never seen a beautiful building in his life. The Talmud asks: Which Temple? R. Abbaye said, and some say R. Hisda, said, This refers to the building Herod built. The Talmud asks: What kind of material did he use to build it? Rabbah answered: He built it of yellow and white marble. Some differ and say that it was built of yellow, blue and white marble. The building was constructed in tiers; one row was projecting out and one row was receding inward. His intention was to overlay the marble stones with gold, but the rabbis advised him to leave the marble as is, because it had the appearance of the waves of the sea. (*Sukkah* 51b)

(*Shevuot* 48 b) R. Nahman was visiting in the town of Sura. R. Hisda and Rabbah b. R. Huna went to see him; they asked him to abrogate a certain ruling by Rav and Shemuel.

He replied to them: "Do you think I have traveled this long distance to come here to annul a ruling of Rav and Shemuel?"

(*Bava Metzia* 39b) A man came to Mari b. Isaac from Behozai claiming that he was his own brother and that he wanted a share in their father's estate.

"I do not know you," said R. Mari. The case came before R. Hisda.

R. Hisda said to the man: "He speaks the truth," but R. Hisda also said to the brother, 'Go and produce witnesses that you are his brother.' I have witnesses, but they are afraid to testify because he is a powerful man."

R. Hisda then said to R. Mari: "Go and bring witnesses who will testify that you are not his brother."

"Is that justice?" exclaimed R. Mari. "The burden of proof lies on the plaintiff." "This is the way I judge in your case and in the cases of powerful men like you," was R. Hisda's reply. Subsequently, witnesses came to testify that he was his brother.

R. Huna used to say: "One who lights his house well will have scholarly sons. A person who is observant in placing a mezuza on the door of his house will merit a beautiful home. A person who is observant in wearing tzitzit will merit a beautiful garment. A person who is observant in making Kiddush will merit full barrels of wine." (*Shabbat* 23b)

R. Hisda used to pass frequently the house of R. Shizbi's father. Upon noting that the house was always well lit, he remarked: "A great man and scholar will be born to this couple."

When the time came for R. Hisda to die, he was sitting and studying in the academy. The Angel of Death could not take his life because he was studying Torah. In order to interrupt his studies, the Angel of Death leaned on a cedar tree next to the academy. The tree cracked and the sound interrupted R. Hisda's studies, allowing the Angel of Death to take him. (*Makkot* 10a)

For a glimpse of the world as it was in R. Hisda's time, see the historical timeline from 250 to 350 C.E.

חייא
Hiyya

(second century C.E.)
Tanna, Eretz Yisrael

Rabbi Hiyya bar Abba, who was born in Kafri, a community near Sura in Babylonia, left Babylonia and moved to Eretz Yisrael. (*Ketubbot* 5a)

Since he lived in a transitional generation, he can be considered both a tanna and an amora. (*Bava Metzia* 5a)

R. Hiyya was a tall man. His nephew, Rav, who was also considered to be tall, came up to his shoulder. (*Niddah* 24b)

He and his wife, Yehudit, had twin sons, Yehuda and Hizkiya. (*Yevamot* 65b)

They also had twin daughters, Pazi and Tavi. Rabbinai was Rabbi Hiyya's brother. (*Berachot* 21b)

R. Avin b. R. Adda quoted R. Menahem as saying: It once happened that a child was born to the same mother three months after the first one, and both of those students were sitting in our academy. Who are these students? They are Rabbi Yehuda and Rabbi Hizkiya, the sons of Rabbi Hiyya. But didn't we learn that a woman cannot conceive twice during one pregnancy? Rabbi Abbaye replied: It was the same drop, which split in two. The features of one were completed at the beginning of the seventh month, while the features of the other were completed at the end of the ninth month. (*Niddah* 27a)

R. Hiyya's parents stayed in Babylonia.

While living in Eretz Yisrael, he was informed that his father had passed away. (*Pesahim* 4a)

A colleague and student of Rabbi Yehuda ha-Nasi, R. Hiyya was probably the most outstanding student of his yeshiva. He was particularly known for the Talmudic teachings called *baraitot,* which he and his students compiled. Although he had interactions constantly with Rabbi Yehuda ha-Nasi and they quoted each other, Rabbi Hiyya had his own bet midrash.

R. Hiyya is the author of the Baraita, which he taught in his own academy. As the Talmud says, "Abbaye says that our Mishna is in accordance with R. Safra, who learned it in R. Hiyya's academy, on the subject of charging interest." (*Bava Metzia* 62b–65b)

Rav said: I found a secret scroll of the school of R. Hiyya in which he discusses the thirty-nine principal forms of labor that are forbidden on Shabbat. (*Shabbat* 6b)

R. Hiyya taught: "There are twenty four kinds of principal damages." (*Bava Kama* 4b)

In one instance, Rabbi Zeira asked Rabbi Yehuda ha-Nasi a question, upon which he received a ruling that differed from Rabbi Hiyya's. When he told Rebbe that Rabbi Hiyya has a different opinion, he answered, "Ignore my reply and adopt Rabbi Hiyya's." (*Avodah Zarah* 36b)

In monetary matters, R. Hiyya decided cases by himself and gave judgment on his own, as a single judge. (*Sanhedrin* 5a)

Rabbi Hiyya was also a contemporary of Rabbi Yishmael ben Yosi, Rabbi Yannai, Rabbi Shimon ben Rebbe, and Bar Kappara.

Rabbi Hiyya's most outstanding student was Rav, who was also his nephew. It was with R. Hiyya's encouragement and initiative that Rav founded the yeshiva in Sura. He spoke to Rabbi Yehuda ha-Nasi on his behalf.

When Rabbah b. Hana was leaving for Babylonia, R. Hiyya said to Rebbe, "My brother's son is going to Babylonia. May he rule on monetary cases?"

"He may," Rebbe answered.

"May he issue rulings regarding first-born animals?"

"He may," Rebbe answered.

When Rav left for Babylonia, R. Hiyya said to Rebbe: "My sister's son is going to Babylonia. May he rule on matters of ritual law?"

"He may," Rebbe answered.

"May he rule on monetary cases?"

"He may," answered Rebbe.

"May he issue rulings regarding first born animals?"

"He may not," answered Rebbe. (*Sanhedrin* 5a)

On one occasion when Rav was still very young, he and R. Hiyya were having dinner at Rabbi Yehuda ha-Nasi's table. Rebbe said to Rav, "Get up and wash your hands." When R. Hiyya saw that Rav was trembling, he said to him, "Son of princes, he is telling you to prepare yourself to lead the blessings after the meal." (*Berachot* 43a)

Although R. Hiyya was Rav's uncle, he was humble, as illustrated by the fact that he followed Halacha according to Rav. (*Pesahim* 8b)

Once, when Rabbi Yehuda was delivering a lecture, he noticed a smell of garlic in the room. He told his students, "Let the person who ate garlic leave the room." R. Hiyya rose and left the room, and then all the students left the room. The next morning, R. Hiyya was asked by R. Shimon, the son of Rabbi Yehuda, "Was it you who caused annoyance to my father? Heaven forbid that such a thing should happen in Israel!" (*Sanhedrin* 11a)

From whom did R. Hiyya learn such conduct? He learned it from Rabbi Meir. The story is told that a woman appeared in the Rabbi Meir's academy and declared: "One of you rabbis has taken me as a wife by cohabitation." Rabbi Meir rose and gave her a bill of divorce.

Thereupon all the students stood up and did likewise.

Other outstanding students of R. Hiyya were Rabbah bar Hana, who was his nephew, R. Zeira, and R. Judah ben Kenosa.

R. Hiyya once saw the old moon in the sky on the morning of the twenty-ninth of the month. He said to the moon, "Tonight we want to sanctify you, and you are still here? Go and hide yourself." Rebbe said to him: "Go to Ein Tov and sanctify the month and send me the watchword, 'David King of Israel is alive and enduring.'" (Rosh ha-Shanah 25a)

R. Hiyya and R. Yonatan were visiting a cemetery when R. Hiyya noticed that R. Yonatan's blue fringes were trailing upon the ground. R. Hiyya said to him, "Lift your fringes so that the deceased should not say: Tomorrow they are coming to join us and today they insult us." (Berachot 18a)

When Rav, R. Hiyya's nephew, came to Eretz Yisrael from Babylonia, his uncle asked him, "Is your father Aibu alive?"

He answered, "Ask me if my mother is alive." R. Hiyya asked, "Is your mother alive?" He answered, "Ask me if Aibu is alive." When R. Hiyya heard all this, he realized that his brother and sister had died. Thereupon he said to his servant, "Take off my shoes, and afterwards bring my things to the bathhouse." R. Hiyya wanted to teach his students Halacha. From this, three things can be learned: a mourner may not wear shoes, one mourns only for one day on a death found out after thirty days, and part of the day is considered like a whole day. (Pesahim 4a)

Rabbi Hiyya, who loved teaching best, was a great and devoted teacher, spreading Torah much of the time. He was very concerned about orphans and

was very scrupulous not to offend anyone. He made a living as a businessman and traded in silks.

A Talmudic saying is attributed to him: "This is the punishment of a liar: even when he tells the truth, no one believes him." (Sanhedrin 89b)

It is stated that Rabbi Shimon ben Lakish said, "In ancient times, when the Torah was forgotten, Ezra came up from Babylon and established it. When it was forgotten again, Hillel came up from Babylon and established it. When it was forgotten again, Rabbi Hiyya and his sons came up and established it." (Sukkah 20a)

R. Hiyya and Bar Kappara were debating an issue and it was quite intense. R. Hiyya jumped up several times in order to make a point. (Yevamot 32b)

Rabbah quoted R. Hiyya as saying: R. Yehuda ha-Nasi once went to a certain place to teach there on Shabbat, but because the place was too small, he went outside to the field. When they came to the field it was full of sheaves and not suitable for an assembly. He removed the sheaves to clear the area. R. Yoseph related a similar story about R. Hiyya, and told it in the name of R. Oshaya. (Shabbat 127a)

Resh Lakish marked the burial caves of the rabbis in order to prevent the priests from becoming defiled. But when he could not locate the grave of R. Hiyya, he felt humiliated and called out, Sovereign of the Universe; did I not debate on the Torah like R. Hiyya did? A heavenly voice responded: You did indeed debate like he did, but you did not spread the Torah as he did. Whenever R. Hanina and R. Hiyya were in dispute; R. Hanina would say to R. Hiyya: "Would you argue with me if the Torah, God forbid, were to be forgotten? I would restore the Torah in

Israel by my debating powers." R. Hiyya would reply: "Would you argue with one who restored the Torah in Israel?" How did R. Hiyya do this? He went out and sowed flax, from which he made nets to trap deer. He gave the venison to orphans, and from the skins he prepared scrolls upon which he wrote the five books of Moshe. Then he went to a town that had no teachers and taught to five children the five books of Moshe and to six children the six orders of the Mishna. When he left, he told the children, "Until I return, I want you to teach each other what I have taught you." Thus he kept the Torah from being forgotten by the Jewish people. (*Bava Metzia* 85b)

This is what Rebbe meant when he said: "How great are the works of R. Hiyya!" "Are they greater than yours?" asked R. Yishmael b. R. Yosi. "Yes," replied Rebbe.

R. Yehuda and R. Hizkiya, the sons of R. Hiyya, were having dinner with Rebbe. Their father, R. Hiyya, was also present. When the sons did not utter a word during the meal, Rebbe said, "Give the young men plenty of strong wine so that they will open up and say something." (*Sanhedrin* 38a)

As the wine took effect, they started talking and said, "The son of David cannot come until the two ruling houses of Israel come to an end." To support this assertion, they quoted a passage from scripture. Rebbe became annoyed and exclaimed, "My children, you are throwing thorns in my eyes." R. Hiyya intervened, saying, "Rebbe, please do not be angry. The numerical value of the Hebrew letters for the word 'wine' is the same as for the word 'secret'. When wine goes in, secrets come out."

When R. Huna passed away, his coffin was brought to Tiberias and buried next to R. Hiyya and his two sons, R. Yehuda and R. Hizkiya. (*Moed Katan* 25a)

R. Hiyya said: "Anyone who can keep a clear mind under the influence of wine has the characteristics of the seventy elders. The numerical value of the word *yayin* [wine] is seventy." (*Eruvin* 65a)

Rebbe and R. Hiyya were once walking on the road. They turned off the main road and walked on private property to avoid the pegs on the road. This is according to Halacha established during the time of Yehoshua. But R. Yehuda b. Kenosa stayed on the main road. Rebbe asked R. Hiyya: "Who is that man in front of us, showing off?" R. Hiyya answered, "I think it is R. Yehuda b. Kenosa, who is a student of mine, who does everything out of piety." When they caught up with him, R. Hiyya said to him, "If you were not Yehuda b. Kenosa, I would have cut your joints off with an iron saw." (*Bava Kamma* 81b)

(*Kesuvos* 103 b) There are different opinions concerning whether Rebbe or R. Hiyya died first.

For a glimpse of the world as it was in R. Hiyya's time, see the historical timeline from 100 to 200 C.E.

חייא בר אבא
Hiyya bar Abba
(third–fourth centuries C.E.)
Amora, Eretz Yisrael

R. Hiyya was born in Babylonia but moved to Eretz Yisrael, where he studied under Rabbi Yohanan. R. Hiyya b. Abba asked R. Yohanan a question, and when R. Yohanan answered it, R. Yohanan called him "Babylonian." (*Shabbat* 105b)

He was a meticulous student. Rabbi Zeira said, "Rabbi Hiyya b. Abba was very particular to get the exact teachings of Rabbi Yohanan, his teacher. He would go over what he learned every thirty days with his teacher, Rabbi Yohanan." He traveled a great deal in Eretz Yisrael to many localities, where he addressed the concerns of the various communities. (*Berachot* 38b)

R. Hiyya b. Abba said in the name of R. Yohanan: It is a mitzvah to pray with the first and last appearance of the sun. (*Berachot* 29b)

R. Hiyya b. Abba said in the name of R. Yohanan, "The blessing over boiled vegetables is *peri ha-adama.*" However, R. Benyamin b. Yafet said in the name of R. Yohanan: "The blessing over boiled vegetables is *she-ha-kol.*" (*Berachot* 38b)

R. Nahman b. Yitzhak said: Ulla made an error in accepting the word of R. Binyamin b. Yafet. R. Zeira expressed astonishment. How can you compare R. Binyamin b. Yafet with R. Hiyya b. Abba? R. Hiyya b. Abba was very particular to get the exact teachings of R. Yohanan, while R. Binyamin b. Yafet was not so careful. Furthermore, R. Hiyya b. Abba used to go over his learning with R. Yohanan every thirty days, while R. Binyamin did not.

R. Hiyya b. Abba related a story: "I was once a guest in a house in Lodokia where they served the host on a golden table which was carried by sixteen men who wore sixteen silver chains. On the table were plates, goblets, pitchers and bottles. In those utensils were all kinds of delicious foods and spices. I said to him, 'What did you do to merit all this?' He replied, I was a butcher, and every time I came across a fine piece of meat, I put it aside for Shabbat." (*Shabbat* 119a)

R. Abbahu and R. Hiyya b. Abba traveled to a place to deliver lectures. R. Hiyya lectured on legal matters while R. Abbahu lectured on aggadah. The people left the hall where R. Hiyya was lecturing in order to listen to R. Abbahu.

When R. Hiyya became upset, R. Abbahu said to him, "I will tell you a parable. Two salesmen are selling merchandise. One sells precious jewels while the other sells small knick-knacks of various kinds. To whom do the people flock? Is it not to the one who sells the knick-knacks?"

R. Hiyya used to accompany R. Abbahu every day to his lodging, but on this day R. Abbahu accompanied R. Hiyya to his lodging. He tried to make him feel better, but R. Hiyya was still upset. (*Sotah* 40a)

When R. Hiyya b. Abba fell ill, R. Yohanan went to visit him. He asked him, "Are your sufferings welcome to you?" He answered him, "Neither the sufferings nor their reward are welcome to me. R. Yohanan said to him, "Give me your hand," and he did. After that he felt cured. (*Berachot* 5b)

Rabbi Hiyya traveled to Babylonia and to Rome in order to meet with the leaders of the Jewish community. He had discussions with the greatest scholars of his generation, including Rabbi Hanina, Rabbi Yoshua ben Levi and Rabbi Eleazar.

He had many sons, who included Rabbi Abba, Rabbi Yirmiyahu, Rabbi Kahana, and Rabbi Nehemia. (*Berachot* 5a)

His brother's name was Benai. (*Ketubbot* 50b)

It has been taught, Sumchos says: "Whoever prolongs the word *ehad* will have his days prolonged." R. Abba b. Yaakov said that the stress is on the dalet. R. Yirmiyahu was once sitting before R. Hiyya b. Abba, and when R. Hiyya noticed that R. Yirmiyahu was prolonging the word *ehad* a great deal, he explained to him how long to prolong it. (*Berachot* 13b)

R. Yirmiyahu said, though some say that it was R. Hiyya b. Abba who spoke as follows: "The Targum on the Torah was authored by Onkelos the proselyte under the guidance of R. Eliezer and R. Yoshua." (*Megillah* 3a)

R. Hiyya b. Abba said: "It is improper for a scholar to walk in patched shoes. (*Berachot* 43b)

R. Hiyya b. Abba said: a person should always try to pray in a house with windows. (*Berachot* 31a)

When R. Hiyya b. Abba once visited Gabla, he found that women were married to proselytes whose conversion was only by circumcision, without immersion in a mikveh. He also noticed that non-Jews were serving Jewish wine to Jews and they were eating a non-kosher animal. R. Hiyya said nothing to them at first because he wanted to consult first with his rabbi, R. Yohanan. After they spoke together, R. Yohanan instructed him to tell them that their children are considered bastards, that their wine is *nesech* and forbidden and the meat that they were eating was not kosher. (*Yevamot* 46a)

For a glimpse of the world as it was in the time of R. Hiyya b. Abba, see the historical timeline from 250 to 350 C.E.

חייא בר אמי
Hiyya b. Ammi

(third–fourth centuries C.E.)
Amora, Eretz Yisrael

R. Hiyya b. Ammi said in the name of R. Ulla, "One who lives from the labor of one's hands is greater than one who fears God." (*Berachot* 8a)

R. Hiyya also said in the name of R. Ulla, "One should always live in the same town as one's teacher."

R. Hiyya b. Ammi said in the name of Ulla, "Since the Temple was destroyed, the most precious thing to God in this world are the four cubits of space where they learn Halacha." (*Berachot* 8a)

For a glimpse of the world as it was in the time of R. Hiyya b. Ammi, see the historical timeline from 250 to 350 C.E.

חייא בר אבין
Hiyya bar Avin

(fourth century C.E.)
Amora, Babylonia

R. Hiyya, a student of Rabbi Huna, was a son of Rabbi Avin the carpenter. In his later years he moved to Eretz Yisrael, where he studied under Rabbi Eleazar in Tiberias. He was a contemporary of Rabbi Zeira and Rabbi Assi, with whom he had halachic discussions. (*Kiddushin* 58a)

R. Zeira once rode on a donkey and R. Hiyya b. Avin followed him on foot as they discussed a quotation by R. Yohanan. (*Shabbat* 111b)

When Rava was discussing a particular halacha with his colleagues, he said, "I and the lion of the company explained it." Who is the lion among us? It is R. Hiyya b. Avin. (*Berachot* 33b)

The great scholar Rabbi Nahman ben Yitzhak asked Rabbi Hiyya b. Avin to explain a question that bothered him: What is inscribed on God's tefillin? R. Avin replied: The tefillin of the Ruler of the Universe are inscribed with these words "And who is like your people Israel?" (*Berachot* 6a)

R. Huna used to say: One who lights his house well will have scholarly sons. R. Huna used to pass the house of R. Avin the carpenter frequently. He noticed that many lights were always lit in the house. He remarked, "Two great men will be born to him," and so it was: his sons were R. Idi b. Avin and R. Hiyya b. Avin. (*Shabbat* 23b)

For a glimpse of the world as it was in the time of R. Hiyya b. Avin, see the historical timeline from 300 to 400 C.E.

חייא בר רב
Hiyya bar Rav
(third century C.E.)
Amora, Babylonia

R. Hiyya was the son of the famous Rav, who was the head of the academy in Sura.

The Talmud relates that Rav advised his son Hiyya: "Do not take drugs, do not leap in high jumps, do not have your teeth extracted, do not provoke serpents and do not provoke a Syrian woman." (*Pesahim* 113a)

For a glimpse of the world as it was in the time of R. Hiyya bar Rav, see the historical timeline from 200 to 300 C.E.

חנא בר ביזנא
Hana bar Bizna
(third–fourth century C.E.)
Amora, Babylonia

R. Hana, who served as a judge in Pumbedita, also lived in Nehardea.

He is quoted as saying in the name of Rabbi Shimon Hasida: "The Torah hints that God showed Moses the knots on the tefillin." (*Berachot* 7a)

R. Zutra b. Toviya said in the name of Rav – and according to others, R. Hana b. Bizna said it in the name of R. Shimon Hasida, and others say it was said by R. Yohanan in the name of R. Shimon b. Yohai: "It is better that one leap into a fiery furnace than shame another in public." (*Berachot* 43b, *Bava Metzia* 59a)

R. Hana b. Bizna said in the name of R. Shimon Hasida: "Who are the four craftsmen referred to in Yehezkel?" He answered: "They are Mashiah b. David, Moshiah b. Yoseph, Eliyahu and the Kohen Tzedek." R. Sheshet objected, saying: "It does not fit." To this R. Hana replied: "Read the end of the verse." R. Sheshet conceded, saying: "Who am I to argue with R. Hana regarding *aggadata*?" (*Sukkah* 52b)

R. Hana b. Bizna once entered a sukkah. All the town's notables were with him. It was the eighth day of Sukkot or perhaps the seventh. They sat in the sukkah but did not recite the benediction for the holiday of Sukkot. (*Sukkah* 47a)

When R. Hana b. Bizna was on the road to Nehardea, he stopped at a barbershop to have his hair cut. The barber was an idol-worshipper, and R. Meir had said that a Jew should not have his hair cut by an idol-worshipper. The barber remarked to R. Hana: "Hana, Hana, your throat is very attractive to the scissors." R. Hana said, "I deserved this because I violated R. Meir's prohibition." (*Avodah Zarah* 29a)

For a glimpse of the world as it was in the time of R. Hana bar Bizna, see the historical timeline from 250 to 350 C.E.

חנא בר חנילאי
Hana bar Hanilai
(third century C.E.)
Amora, Babylonia

R. Hana was a wealthy man whose charitable acts were well known.

As Rabbi Ulla and Rabbi Hisda were walking, they passed the house of R. Hana b. Hanilai. R. Hisda sighed.

R. Ulla asked, "Why do you sigh?"

He answered, "How can I refrain from sighing? He used to have sixty cooks by day and sixty cooks by night who cooked for everyone in need. He always had his purse ready to give charity. The house had four doors, one on each side. Whoever went in hungry came out full. In times of scarcity, he placed wheat and barley outside at night for anyone to take since he did not want people to have to come inside to be embarrassed. Now that all is in ruins, shall I not sigh?" (*Berachot* 58b)

He was a great follower of Rabbi Huna. Whenever he saw Rabbi Huna carrying his tools on his shoulder, he would take the tools from him and carry them himself. (*Megillah* 28a)

For a glimpse of the world as it was in the time of R. Hana bar Hanilai, see the historical timeline from 200 to 300 C.E.

חנה בר ציפוראה
Hana bar Tzipori (Sepphoris)

(third–fourth centuries C.E.)
Amora, Eretz Yisrael

R. Hana was a student of Rabbi Yohanan (*Rosh ha-Shanah* 34b).

For a glimpse of the world as it was in the time of Hana bar Tzipori, see the historical timeline from 250 to 350 C.E.

חנן בר רבא
Hanan bar Rava

(third–fourth centuries C.E.)
Amora, Babylonia

R. Hanan was a student of Rav.

R. Hanan b. Rava said in the name of Rav: "Elimelech, Salmon, Peloni Almoni and Naomi's father were all the sons of Nachshon ben Amminadav." (*Bava Batra* 91a)

R. Hanan b. Rava also stated in Rav's name: "The name of Avraham's mother was Amatlai, and her father's name was Karnevo.

"The name of Haman's mother was Amatlai, and she was the daughter of Orabti. The name of David's mother was Nitzevet, and she was the daughter of Adael.

"The mother of Shimshon was Tzelalponit, and his sister's name was Nashyan."

R. Hanan b. Rava also said in the name of Rav: "Abraham was imprisoned for ten years – three in Kutha and seven in Kardu."

For a glimpse of the world as it was in the time of R. Hanan bar Rava, see the historical timeline from 250 to 350 C.E.

חוני המעגל
Honi ha-Me'aggel

(first century B.C.E.)
Tanna, Eretz Yisrael

Rabbi Honi ha-Me'aggel, who lived during the second Temple period, was also known as Onias the miracle-worker and the circle-maker. There are legends about him, particularly about his prayers for rain, which were always answered.

Rabbi Shimon ben Shetah sent this message to Honi ha-Me'aggel: "You deserve to be excommunicated for the things you do, and if you weren't Honi ha-Meaggel I would pronounce you excommunicated. But what can I do, seeing that you are a favorite of God? He accedes to your wishes, and you are like a son who is favored by his father." (*Berachot* 19a)

It once happened that the greater part of the month of Adar passed by without rain, and the people were concerned that there would be no grain to harvest. They sent word to R. Honi to pray for rain. He did so, and no rain fell. He drew a circle around himself on the ground where he stood and exclaimed to God: "Master of the Universe, Your children have turned to me because they are under the impression that I am a member of Your household. I swear by Your great name that I will not move from here until You have mercy upon them."

A light rain began to fall, but the people said to him: "All that this rain can do is release you from your oath. We look to you to save us from death."

Honi continued his prayer, saying, "This is not what I prayed for. I prayed for rain that would fill the cisterns, ditches and caves."

A forceful rain now fell, and the people were concerned there would be flooding. Honi said, "Master of the Universe, this is not what I prayed for, but for rain of benevolence and blessing." After his prayer, the rain fell normally, but kept falling until and the people had to go up to the Temple Mount to escape it. The people said to Honi, "Please pray for the rain to cease, just as you prayed for it to fall."

He answered, "I have it as a tradition that we may not pray for an excess of good." (*Taanit* 23a)

There are various legends about Honi's death. According to Josephus, he died in 65 B.C.E. during the war between the two Hasmonean brothers, Aristobulus II and Hyrcanus II. Hyrcanus's men ordered him to pray for their side to win the battle. Rabbi Honi prayed for both sides, and for this he was stoned to death. However, the story in the Talmud is different.

One day, as R. Honi ha-Ma'agel was traveling on the road, he encountered a man planting a carob tree. He asked the man, "How long does it take for the tree to bear fruit?"

The man replied, "It takes seventy years for the tree to bear fruit."

He asked him, "Are you certain you will live another seventy years?"

The man replied, "When I came upon this land, I found a grown carob tree that my ancestors had planted for me. I am doing the same by planting this tree for my descendants."

R. Honi ha-Me'aggel fell asleep in a cave, waking up only after seventy years. When he awoke, he saw a man gathering the fruit of the carob tree. He asked him, "Are you the man who planted the tree?" The man replied, "I am his grandson." He reached the conclusion that he had slept for seventy years.

When he returned home, he asked, "Is the son of Honi ha-Ma'agel still alive?" The people told him that his son had died, but that his grandson was alive. He said, "I am Honi ha-Me'aggel," but no one believed him.

He went to the study hall, where he overheard the rabbis saying, "The Halacha is as clear as in the days of Honi ha-Me'aggel, which he made very clear to us. When Honi ha-Me'aggel came to the study hall, he would settle every difficulty that the rabbis had." When Honi heard this, he said to the rabbis, "I am Honi," but the rabbis did not believe him, and they did not give him the honor due to him. Terribly hurt, Honi prayed for death, and he died. (*Taanit* 23a)

For a glimpse of the world as it was in the time of Honi ha-Me'aggel, see the historical timeline from 100 to 1 B.C.E.

חוצפית (המתורגמן)
Hutzpit (ha-Meturgeman)

(first century C.E.)
Tanna, Eretz Yisrael

R. Hutzpit was the official interpreter in the academy of Yavne during the time when Rabbi Gamliel II was the Nasi. He was one of the ten martyrs.

It is related that a certain student asked Rabbi Yehoshua a question as to whether the evening prayer was compulsory or optional. Rabbi Yehoshua replied that it was optional. When the same student asked Rabbi Gamliel, he replied that it is compulsory.

The student replied, "Rabbi Yehoshua told me it is optional."

Rabbi Gamliel told the student to wait until the beginning of the session. When the question was asked, Rabbi Gamliel said that it was compulsory. He then asked the Sages, "Does anyone here disagree?"

"No," replied Rabbi Yehoshua.

"Did they not report to me that you said it is optional? Rise now, and let them testify against you."

Rabbi Yehoshua stood up, while Rabbi Gamliel remained sitting and expounding for a long time. Rabbi Yehoshua was still standing until all the scholars in the assembly began to shout at Hutzpit the interpreter, "Stop!"

The interpreter stopped. They said, "How long will Rabbi Gamliel go on insulting R. Yehoshua? Last Rosh ha-Shanah he insulted him, in the matter of R. Tzadok regarding the first-born he insulted him, and now he insults him again. Come, let us depose Rabbi Gamliel."

"Whom shall we appoint in his place? We can hardly appoint R. Yehoshua, because he is a party to the dispute."

"Let us appoint Rabbi Eleazar ben Azaryah, who is wise, wealthy and a descendant of Ezra. He is wise, for he gives the proper answer to a question. Since he is wealthy, he can pay if money is needed to appease the government. As a descendant of Ezra, he has great ancestral merit."

They asked him, "Would you honor us by becoming the head of the academy?"

He replied, "I will consult the members of my family."

When he consulted his wife, she said, "Maybe they will also depose you."

He answered: "Let one use a cup of honor for one day, even if it be broken on the morrow." She said to him, "You have no white hair." He was eighteen years old that day, and a miracle occurred: eighteen rows of his hair turned white. That is why R. Eleazar b. Azaryah said: I am like a seventy-year-old man. He accepted the position.

It was learned that on that day the doors were opened for all the disciples to enter the assembly. Rabbi Gamliel had previously issued an injunction to the assembly that those students whose interior did not match their exterior appearance were not permitted entrance.

During R. Eleazar's presidency, the doors of the yeshiva were opened for everyone who wished to study. They added hundreds of benches to accommodate the students. This had not been the case under R. Gamliel.

It was taught that testimonies were formulated on that day, and whenever the phrase "on that day" is mentioned, it refers to this particular day.

Rabbi Gamliel also did not absent himself from the assembly, even for one hour, after he was deposed. (*Berachot* 27b)

R. Yoseph said: "Had Aher (Elisha b. Avuyah) not seen the fate of Hutzpit, he would not have sinned." When he saw the tongue of Hutzpit being dragged upon the ground by a swine, he exclaimed, "The mouth that uttered pearls licks the dust!" This had such an effect on him that he became a changed man. (*Kiddushin* 39b)

For a glimpse of the world as it was in R. Hutzpit's time, see the historical timeline from 1 to 100 C.E.

דימי
Dimi
(fourth century C.E.)
Amora, Babylonia

R. Dimi traveled frequently between Eretz Yisrael and Babylonia, visiting the academies in both countries, and exchanging halachic ideas and teachings, in particular the Academies of Tiberias and Pumbedita.

He was very familiar with the geography of Israel. When R. Dimi came to Babylonia he stated that no one had ever drowned in the Dead Sea. (*Shabbat* 108b)

He also told his colleagues that the custom at weddings in Eretz Yisrael is to sing a song before the bride with the words, "Without powder, paint or braided hair, she is still a beautiful gazelle." (*Ketubbot* 17a)

R. Abbaye asked R. Dimi, "What do people in Eretz Yisrael try to avoid the most?" He answered, "Putting another person to shame." (*Bava Metzia* 58b)

It was stated that when R. Dimi arrived, he related that it was R. Bibi's turn to wait on the students that Shabbat, and R. Ammi and R. Assi happened to be there. He placed a whole basket of fruit before them. I do not know whether he did it because he was just generous or for some other reason. (*Shabbat* 74a)

R. Dimi quoted R. Yohanan regarding a halacha about woven material. Later on, when he came to Nehardea, he sent the following message: "The things I told you were mistaken," and he sent them the correct statement by R. Yohanan. (*Shabbat* 63b)

When R. Dimi came from Eretz Yisrael to Babylonia, he said that King Yannai had a city in the royal mountain where, from Friday to Friday, they would feed sixty huge vessels of salted fish to the men who were cutting down the fig trees. (*Berachot* 44a)

R. Dimi was a brother of R. Safra.

A man once deposited a silk cloth with R. Dimi, the brother of R. Safra. When R. Dimi died without a will, they came before R. Abba, claiming the silk cloth. R. Abba said to them, "In the first place, I know that R. Dimi was not a wealthy man. Secondly, the man is giving us recognizable clues." (*Ketubbot* 85b)

When R. Dimi came to Babylon, he said, "A word is worth the monetary value of a *sela,* and silence is worth two *sela'im.*" (*Megillah* 18a)

R. Dimi b. Hama said, "God suspended the mountain over Israel like a roof and told them: 'If you accept the Torah, it will be well with you, but if not, here will be your graves.'" (*Avodah Zarah* 2b)

For a glimpse of the world as it was in R. Dimi's time, see the historical timeline from 300 to 400 C.E.

דימי מנהרדעא
Dimi of Nehardea
(fourth century C.E.)
Amora, Babylonia
Head of the academy in Pumbedita

As a young man, R. Dimi was a fruit merchant, but in his later years he became the director of the academy in Pumbedita.

It is related that R. Dimi of Nehardea brought a load of figs in a boat. The Exilarch said to Rava, "Go and see if he is a scholar. If so, reserve the market for him." The scholars, who had privileges, could dispose of their merchandise ahead of the rest of the merchants so that they could then go and study. Rava sent R. Adda b. Abba to test R. Dimi's scholarship. He put the following question to him: "If an elephant swallows a basket and then passes it out with excrement, is it still considered a basket?" R. Dimi could not give an answer. He asked R. Adda, "Are you Rava?"

R. Adda answered, "Between Rova and me there is a great difference, but at any rate, I can be your teacher, and therefore Rava is the teacher of your teacher." Consequently they did not reserve the market for him, and his figs were a total loss. He appealed to Rabbi Yoseph, by saying. "See how they have treated me?" R. Adda died shortly afterward. Terribly upset, R. Dimi blamed himself, saying, "It is because of me that he was punished, because he made me lose my figs." (*Bava Batra* 22a)

R. Dimi disagreed with Abbaye on halachic matters. (*Menahot* 35a)

R. Dimi said it is better to appoint a teacher who teaches slowly, but makes no mistakes; because once a mistake is implanted in a child it is difficult to erase it. (*Bava Batra* 21a)

R. Dimi said: "Hospitality to guests is a greater mitzvah than the mitzvah of arriving early at the bet midrash." (*Shabbat* 127a)

For a glimpse of the world as it was in the time of R. Dimi of Nehardea, see the historical timeline from 300 to 400 C.E.

דוסא בן הרכינס
Dosa ben Hyrcanus (Harkinas)

(first–second centuries C.E.)
Tanna, Eretz Yisrael

R. Dosa, who was born during the second Temple period, engaged in halachic disputes with Akavia ben Mahalalel and with Hanina Segan ha-Kohanim. A wealthy and influential man, he survived the destruction of the Temple. As a member of the Sanhedrin, he often disagreed with Rabbi Gamliel.

On one occasion, he and Rabbi Yoshua ben Hananya had a halachic dispute with Rabbi Gamliel regarding on which day to fix the new month. As president of the academy, Rabbi Gamliel ordered Rabbi Yoshua to appear before him with his staff and money on the day that Rabbi Yoshua had determined, according to his calculation, to be Yom Kippur. Although Rabbi Dosa ben Hyrcanus agreed with Rabbi Yoshua, Rabbi Gamliel took no action against him.

When Rabbi Yoshua went to Rabbi Dosa to talk to him about the matter, Rabbi Dosa told him, "You may be correct in your calculation, but if we want to argue against the court of Rabbi Gamliel, then we could argue against every court that has arisen from the days of Moses until now." Rabbi Yoshua did as Rabbi Gamliel ordered, taking his staff and money and traveling to Yavne on the day that was Yom Kippur according to his calculations. When he arrived, Rabbi Gamliel rose and kissed him on his head, saying to him: "Come in peace, my teacher and my disciple – my teacher in wisdom and my disciple because you have accepted my decision." (*Rosh ha-Shanah* 2:9 and 25a)

One of Rabbi Dosa's sayings was: "Morning sleep, midday wine, children's talk and sitting in company of the ignorant remove a man from this world." (*Avot* 3:10)

R. Dosa said that on Rosh ha-Shanah, one should mention the holiday of Rosh Hodesh during the Amida. (*Eruvin* 39a)

When R. Dosa b. Hyrcanus grew old, his eyes dimmed and he was unable to come to the academy. His colleagues, who needed to discuss an important ruling with him, decided among themselves as to who should go to visit him, because he was a great scholar. R. Yoshua said: "I will go." They asked, "Who will go with him?" In the end they decided that R. Eleazar b. Azaryah would go with him. They asked further, "Who else will go with them?" They decided upon R. Akiva. The three scholars went and stood by the door. The maid announced them to R. Dosa, and when they entered he received them with great respect. (*Yevamot* 16a)

For a glimpse of the world as it was in the time of R. Dosa b. Hyrcanus, see the historical timeline from 50 to 150 C.E.

דוסתאי בן ינאי
Dostai ben Yannai

(second century C.E.)
Tanna, Eretz Yisrael

A student of Rabbi Meir, R. Dostai was a contemporary of Rabbi Yehuda ha-Nasi.

Rabbi Ahai ben Yoshaya left a silver cup in Nehardea by a certain person. He told R. Dostai b. Yannai and R. Yosi ben Kifar, who were traveling to Babylonia: "When you come back from Nehardea, bring me back my silver cup, which is at the home of So-and-so, who lives in Nehardea." When they reached Nehardea, the merchant gave them the cup, but asked for a bill of sale. They refused. The merchant then asked for the cup back. R. Dostai was willing, but R. Yosi refused. The men beat Rabbi Yosi and told R. Dostai: Do you see what your friend is doing? R. Dostai said to them: "Thrash him well." When they returned, Rabbi Yosi complained to Rabbi Ahai: "Not only didn't he help me, but he even told them to cause me more pain." Rabbi Dostai explained: "I had to do something. Those people are extremely tall and their hats are also tall. Their voices are loud and their names are very unusual, such as Arda and Arta and Pili Baris. If they had asked the authorities to have us arrested, we would have been arrested. If they had asked them to kill us, they would kill us. I had to appease them. Otherwise they would have killed us." Rabbi Ahai asked: "Do these people have influence with the authorities?" R. Dostai answered: "Yes. They have a whole retinue riding on horses and mules." "In that case," said R. Ahai, "you acted correctly." (Gittin 14a–b)

R. Dostai taught that if one gives even a small amount of charity, one is deemed worthy to be received by the Divine Presence. (Bava Batra 10a)

R. Dostai b. Yannai said: "Why are there no hot springs in Jerusalem? So that it should not be said of the festival pilgrims that the only reason they came to Jerusalem was to bathe in the hot springs." (Pesahim 8b)

For a glimpse of the world as it was in the time of R. Dostai b. Yannai, see the historical timeline from 100 to 200 C.E.

אלעזר בן ערך
Eleazar ben Arach (Arakh)

(first century C.E.)
Tanna, Eretz Yisrael

R. Eleazar lived around 80–120. He was a student of Rabbi Yohanan ben Zakkai, and the most outstanding of the five disciples. Rabbi Eleazar engaged in mystical speculation of the Divine Chariot. He followed his wife's advice to move to Emmaus, where he established a school, instead of following Rabbi Yohanan to Yavne.

He is quoted as saying: "The best character trait that one can have is a good heart." When Rabbi Eleazar grew older he had a problem with his memory that caused him to forget his learning. (Avot 2:9)

Rabbi Helbo said: "The wines of Perugitha and the water of Diomsit caused the ten tribes of Israel to be cut off from their brethren. When R. Eleazar b. Arach visited that place, he was attracted and stayed there. Consequently, he forgot his learning. When he returned to his former home he tried to read from the Torah but did not remember and read incorrectly. The rabbis who were his colleagues prayed for him and his memory returned." (Shabbat 147b)

According to R. Nehorai, we have learned: "If you must move to another location, be sure you move to a place of Torah. Do not say that Torah will follow you, and do not rely on your own understanding of the Torah."

Some say that his name was not Nehorai but R. Eleazar b. Arach. Why was he called Nehorai? He enlightened the eyes of the sages with his knowledge of the law.

R. Yohanan b. Zakkai had five outstanding students. He said to them, "Go and discern the proper path that a person should follow."

R. Eliezer said, "A good eye."

R. Yoshua said, "A good friend."

R. Yosi said, "A good neighbor."

R. Shimon said, "One who considers the outcome of his actions."

R. Eleazar said, "A good heart."

R. Yohanan b. Zakkai remarked, "I prefer the words of R. Eleazar b. Arach, because all your words are included in his words." (*Avot* 2:13)

R. Eleazar said: "Be diligent in the study of Torah, and know what to answer a non-believer. Know before Whom you toil, and be aware that your Employer can be relied upon to pay your earned wages." (*Avot* 2:19)

For a glimpse of the world as it was in the time of R. Eleazar b. Arach, see the historical timeline from 1 to 100 C.E.

אלעזר בר אבינא
Eleazar b. Avina

(third–fourth centuries C.E.)
Amora, Babylonia

R. Eleazar said in the name of Rabbi Avina: Whoever recites Tehillah le-David [Psalm 145] – which is preceded by the sentence Ashrei – three times a day is assured of the World to Come. (*Berachot* 4b)

For a glimpse of the world as it was in Eleazar b. Avina's time, see the historical timeline from 250 to 350 C.E.

אלעזר בן עזריה
Eleazar ben Azaryah (Azariah)

(first–second centuries C.E.)
Tanna, Eretz Yisrael
Head of the Sanhedrin in Yavne

A kohen, Rabbi Eleazar could trace his ancestry to Ezra ha-Sofer. When Rabban Gamliel II was deposed as president of the Sanhedrin, Rabbi Eleazar was chosen to replace him at the young age of eighteen.

On one occasion, Rabbi Yoshua ben Hananya had a halachic dispute with Rabbi Gamliel regarding the day on which to fix the new month. As head of the academy, Rabbi Gamliel ordered Rabbi Yoshua to appear before him with his staff and money on the day that Rabbi Yoshua had determined, according to his calculation, to be Yom Kippur. Although Rabbi Dosa ben Hyrcanus agreed with Rabbi Yoshua, Rabbi Gamliel took no action against him.

When Rabbi Yoshua went to Rabbi Dosa to talk to him about the matter, Rabbi Dosa told him, "You may be correct in your calculation, but if we want to argue against the court of Rabbi Gamliel, then we could argue against every court that has arisen from the days of Moses until now." Rabbi Yoshua did as Rabbi Gamliel ordered, taking his staff and money and traveling to Yavne on the day that was Yom Kippur according to his calculations. When he arrived, Rabbi Gamliel rose and kissed him on his head, saying to him: "Come in peace, my teacher and my disciple – my teacher in wisdom and my disciple because you have accepted my decision." (*Rosh ha-Shanah* 2:9 and 25a)

It is related that a certain student asked Rabbi Yehoshua a question as to whether the evening prayer was compulsory or optional. Rabbi Yehoshua replied that it was optional. When the same student asked Rabbi Gamliel, he replied that it is compulsory.

The student replied, "Rabbi Yehoshua told me it is optional."

Rabbi Gamliel told the student to wait until the beginning of the session. When the question was asked, Rabbi Gamliel said that it was compulsory. He then asked the Sages, "Does anyone here disagree?"

"No," replied Rabbi Yehoshua.

"Did they not report to me that you said it is optional? Rise now, and let them testify against you."

Rabbi Yehoshua stood up, while Rabbi Gamliel remained sitting and expounding for a long time. Rabbi Yehoshua was still standing until all the scholars in the assembly began to shout at Hutzpit the interpreter, "Stop!"

The interpreter stopped. They said, "How long will Rabbi Gamliel go on insulting R. Yehoshua? Last Rosh ha-Shanah he insulted him, in the matter of R. Tzadok regarding the first-born he insulted him, and now he insults him again. Come, let us depose Rabbi Gamliel."

"Whom shall we appoint in his place? We can hardly appoint R. Yehoshua, because he is a party to the dispute. Nor can we appoint R. Akiva because he has no ancestral merit."

"Let us appoint Rabbi Eleazar ben Azaryah, who is wise, wealthy and a descendant of Ezra. He is wise, for he gives the proper answer to a question. Since he is wealthy, he can pay if money is needed to appease the government. As a descendant of Ezra, he has great ancestral merit."

They asked him, "Would you honor us by becoming the head of the academy?"

He replied, "I will consult the members of my family."

When he consulted his wife, she said, "Maybe they will also depose you."

He answered: "Let one use a cup of honor for one day, even if it be broken on the morrow." She said to him, "You have no white hair." He was eighteen years old that day, and a miracle occurred: eighteen rows of his hair turned white. That is why R. Eleazar b. Azaryah said: I am like a seventy-year-old man. He accepted the position.

It was learned that on that day the doors were opened for all the disciples to enter the assembly. Rabbi Gamliel had previously issued an injunction to the assembly that those students whose interior did not match their exterior appearance were not permitted entrance.

During R. Eleazar's presidency, the doors of the yeshiva were opened for everyone who wished to study. They added hundreds of benches to accommodate the students. This had not been the case under R. Gamliel.

It was taught that testimonies were formulated on that day, and whenever the phrase "on that day" is mentioned, it refers to this particular day.

Rabbi Gamliel also did not absent himself from the assembly, even for one hour, after he was deposed. (*Berachot* 28a)

There was another halachic dispute between Rabbi Gamliel and Rabbi Yehoshua. It concerned whether Ammonites may be accepted into the Jewish community. Rabbi Yehoshua was in favor and Rabbi Gamliel was opposed. The Sanhedrin sided with Rabbi Yehoshua. When Rabbi Gamliel saw the great respect that the Sanhedrin accorded to Rabbi Yehoshua, he decided to go to him to apologize. When he reached his house he saw that the walls were black with charcoal. He said to him,

"I can tell by your walls that you are a blacksmith."

Rabbi Yehoshua replied, "Woe to the generation of which you are the leader, since you know nothing of the problems, struggles and difficulties that the scholars must undergo in order to sustain themselves."

He said to him, "I apologize. Forgive me." But Rabbi Yehoshua ignored him. Then he persisted, saying, "Do it out of respect for my father." Rabbi Yehoshua agreed and they became reconciled.

Later, Rabbi Gamliel was restored to his office, and the presidency was rotated between him and Rabbi Eleazar ben Azaryah. R. Gamliel preached there for three Shabbatot and R. Eleazar one Shabbat per month.

Rabbi Eleazar and Rabban Gamliel journeyed together to Rome, where they met with the Emperor, the Roman authorities and the Jewish leaders.

The rabbis taught: If one dreams of R. Eleazar b. Azaryah, he may hope to become wealthy. (*Berachot* 57b)

Our rabbis taught: when R. Eliezer fell sick four sages went to visit him: R. Tarfon, R. Yoshua, R. Eleazar b. Azaryah and R. Akiva.

R. Tarfon said to him: "You are more valuable to Israel than rain."

R. Yoshua said: "You are more valuable to Israel than the sun."

R. Eleazar b. Azaryah said: "You are better to Israel than a father and mother." But R. Akiva said to him, "Suffering is precious." R. Eliezer liked R. Akiva's remark best. (*Sanhedrin* 101a)

One of R. Eleazar's sayings is: "On Yom Kippur, God forgives transgressions on matters between human beings and God, but transgressions between people are not forgiven until one has placated one's fellow human beings."

Another statement of his is: "A Sanhedrin that puts one person to death in seventy years is termed a tyrannical court." (*Makkot* 1:10)

The Talmud relates that R. Gamliel, R. Yoshua, R. Eleazar b. Azaryah and R. Akiva were traveling together on a ship. Only R. Gamliel owned a lulav, which he had bought for one thousand zuz. R. Gamliel performed the mitzvah of waving the lulav. When he finished he gave it as a gift to R. Yoshua. R. Yoshua did likewise and then gave it as a gift to R. Eleazar b. Azaryah. He, in turn, performed the mitzvah, and when he finished he gave it as a gift to R. Akiva. R. Akiva performed the mitzvah and returned it to R. Gamliel. (*Sukkah* 41b)

R. Sheshet said in the name of R. Eleazar b. Azaryah: "I could justify the exemption from judgment for all Jews for all the sins they committed from the day the Temple was destroyed and for all the generations since to the present day." (*Eruvin* 65a)

R. Eleazar b. Azaryah said: "Where there is no Torah, there is no proper conduct. Where proper conduct is absent, there is no Torah. If there is no wisdom, there is no fear of God. If there is no fear of God, there is no wisdom. Where there is no knowledge, there is no understanding. Where there is no understanding, there is no knowledge. If there is no bread, there is no Torah. If there is no Torah, there is no bread."

He also said, "Anyone whose wisdom exceeds his deeds is like a tree whose branches are many but whose roots are few. When the wind comes and blows against such a tree, it, will be uprooted. However, anyone whose deeds exceed his wisdom is compared to a tree whose branches are few but whose roots are many. Even if all the winds of the world come and blow against it, the tree will not be uprooted." (*Avot* 3:21, 22)

When R. Eleazar b. Azaryah died, the crowns of wisdom ceased. (*Sotah* 49b)

For a glimpse of the world as it was in the time of R. Eleazar b. Azaryah, see the historical timeline from 50 to 150 C.E.

אלעזר בן חנניה בן חזקיה
Eleazar ben Hananya ben Hizkiya
Tanna, Eretz Yisrael
(first century C.E.)

Rabbi Eleazar was a student of the school of Rabbi Shammai.

(*Shabbat* 1:4, 13b) His father, Rabbi Hananya ben Hizkiya ben Gurion, is mentioned as one who participated in ruling on the eighteen decrees of Halacha. During that time, he was ill and the rabbis came to visit him.

R. Eleazar b. Hananya said, Do not take the blessing of an ordinary man lightly, for two great men received blessings from ordinary men and they were fulfilled. They were David and Daniel. (Perhaps this saying is by R. Eleazar b. Pedat in the name of R. Hanina.) (*Megillah* 15a)

For a glimpse of the world as it was in the time of R. Eleazar b. Hananya b. Hizkiya, see the historical timeline from 1 to 100 C.E.

אלעזר בן חסמא
Eleazar ben Hisma
(second century C.E.)
Tanna, Eretz Yisrael

Rabbi Eleazar, who was a student of Rabbi Yoshua ben Hananya, was active in the yeshiva of Yavne circa 120–140. In addition to being a great talmudic scholar, he was also an expert in astronomy and mathematics. Nevertheless, he felt that these fields were secondary in importance to the study of Torah.

Rabbi Gamliel and Rabbi Yehoshua once traveled on board a ship. Rabbi Gamliel's food supply ran out and he had to rely on the food that Rabbi Yehoshua had brought with him. "Did you know that we would be delayed so long that you brought additional food with you?" asked Rabbi Gamliel.

"I calculated that a certain star that appears every seventy years is due to appear," answered Rabbi Yehoshua. "It leads sailors to miscalculate their position."

"You posses so much knowledge," Rabbi Gamliel told him, "and yet you travel on board a ship."

"Don't marvel at me. Rather be surprised at two of your students who live on land, Rabbi Eleazar b. Hisma and Rabbi Yohanan ben Gudgeda (perhaps it was R. Yohanan b. Nuri), who can calculate how many drops of water there are in the sea, and yet they have neither bread to eat nor clothes to wear."

Rabbi Gamliel decided to appoint them as supervisors, and when he landed he sent for them to offer them those positions. Reluctant to accept the positions on account of their humility, they did not show up, but Rabbi Gamliel sent for them again, saying, "Do you imagine that I offer you rulership? It is servitude that I offer you." (*Horayot* 10a)

In the Mishna, Rabbi Eliezer ben Hisma says, "Bird offerings and the onset of menstruation are principal ordinances, while calculations and geometry are trivia compared to the laws of Torah." (*Avot* 3:18)

Throughout most of his life, he was very poor.

For a glimpse of the world as it was in the time of Eleazar b. Hisma, see the historical timeline from 100 to 200 C.E.

אלעזר בן דמא
Eleazar ben Damma

(second century C.E.)
Tanna, Eretz Yisrael

Rabbi Eleazar ben Damma was the son of Rabbi Yishmael's sister.

He once asked his uncle, R. Yishmael: "I dreamt that both my jaws fell out; what could it mean?" He replied, "Two Roman counselors have plotted against you, but they have died." (*Berachot* 56b)

On another occasion, he asked R. Yishmael, "May a person such as I, who has studied the whole Torah, study Greek wisdom?" His answer was: "If you can find a time that is neither day nor night, then you may study Greek." (*Menahot* 99b)

Ben Damma died of snakebite. (*Avodah Zarah* 27b)

For a glimpse of the world as it was in the time of Eleazar ben Damma, see the historical timeline from 100 to 200 C.E.

אלעזר בן דולעאי
Eleazar ben Dolai

(second century C.E.)
Tanna, Eretz Yisrael

R. Eleazar was a contemporary of the following scholars: Rabbi Meir, R. Yehuda b. Illai, R. Shimon bar Yohai, R. Yosi and R. Eleazar ben Shammua. He is quoted in *Mikvaot* 2:10.

For a glimpse of the world as it was in the time of Eleazar b. Dolai, see the historical timeline from 100 to 200 C.E.

אלעזר בן פרטע
Eleazar ben Parta

(second century C.E.)
Lived in the 2nd century CE)

Rabbi Eleazar lived in the town of Sepphoris in his younger years. The Romans arrested him for violating the Hadrian's decree against teaching Torah. Rabbi Hananya ben Teradion was imprisoned together with him for the same offense.

Our rabbis taught: When Rabbi Eleazar ben Parta and Rabbi Hananya ben Teradion were arrested, R. Eleazar said to R. Hananya: "You are fortunate that they arrested you only on one charge, but woe to me, for I have been arrested on five charges."

Rabbi Hananya replied. "You are fortunate that they have brought five charges against you for learning Torah and for acts of benevolence! You will be rescued, but woe to me, since I was arrested on one charge only: learning Torah." Rabbi Eleazar was miraculously saved from execution. (*Avodah Zarah* 17b)

Three statements were made by Rabbi Eleazar ben Parta before the sages, who upheld them. (*Gittin* 3:4, 28b)

Even though the Torah was not given through Ezra, its writing was changed through him. It has been taught that Rebbe said, "The Torah was originally given to Israel in Assyrian script [*ketav Ashurit*]. When the Israelites sinned, it was changed into Roetz writing. When they repented, the former writing was reintroduced. Why was it called Ashurit – because its script was upright?" R. Shimon b. Eleazar said in the name of R. Eliezer b. Parta, who said in the name of R. Eleazar ha-Moda'i: "The style of the Torah writing was never changed." (*Sanhedrin* 21b, 22a)

For a glimpse of the world as it was in the time of R. Eliezer ben Parta, see the historical timeline from 100 to 200 C.E.

אלעזר בן פדת
Eleazar ben Pedat

(third century C.E.)
Amora, Babylonia
Head of the academy in Tiberias

R. Eleazar, who was born in Babylonia to a priestly family, studied there under Rabbi Shemuel and under Rav. (*Hullin* 111b, *Moed Katan* 28a, *Eruvin* 66a)

He was still single when he moved to Eretz Yisrael, where he married. The Talmud mentions Rabbi Ammi and Rabbi Assi as decorating the huppah for his wedding. (*Berachot* 16a)

As a rule; when the Talmud mentions the name Eleazar without mentioning his father's name, it refers to R. Eleazar b. Pedat.

In Eretz Yisrael, R. Eleazar b. Pedat studied under Rabbi Hanina in Sepphoris. (*Berachot* 27b)

He also studied under Rabbi Oshaya.

The Talmud describes Rabbi Eleazar as the student of Rabbi Yohanan. (*Bava Batra* 135b)

However, elsewhere the Talmud refers to him as being the equal of Rabbi Yohanan. Rabbi Eleazar was appointed to be Rabbi Yohanan's study partner after Rabbi Shimon ben Lakish passed away. (*Yoma* 9b)

Although R. Eleazar had children, all but one died in his lifetime. The name of his surviving son was R. Pedat, who served as interpreter for R. Assi.

(*Hagigah* 13a) Once, R. Yohanan said to R. Eleazar: "Come, and I will teach you the mysteries of the Chariots."

"I am not old enough," he answered.

However, when he was old enough, R. Yohanan died.

R. Assi said to R. Eleazar: "Come and I will teach you the mysteries of the Chariots." R. Eleazar replied, "Had I

been worthy, I would have learned it from R. Yohanan, your master."

Although Rabbi Eleazar was very poor, he refused to accept gifts. (*Taanit* 25a)

When R. Yehuda ha-Nasi sent a present to R. Eleazar he would not accept it, and when he was invited to his home, he would not go. He quoted a passage in Scripture as his reason. (*Megillah* 28a)

On the other hand, when he acquired some money, he helped support the needy scholars in secret in order to avoid embarrassing them.

R. Ulla once visited Pumbedita and they brought some blood for him to examine, but he refused to see it. The town was under the jurisdiction of R. Yehuda. He explained. "If R. Eleazar, who was the supreme authority in the land of Israel, refused to examine blood when he visited the town of R. Yehuda, how could I do so?" (*Niddah* 20b)

Why was he described as the supreme authority in the land of Israel? Because a woman once brought to R. Eleazar some blood to be examined while R. Ammi was present. R. Eleazar smelled it and declared. "This is blood of desire." After she left, R. Ammi followed the woman to question her, and she admitted, "My husband was away on a trip, and I desired him." (*Niddah* 20b)

Rabbi Yohanan and Resh Lakish were close friends and regular study partners. When Resh Lakish died, R. Yohanan's grief was so profound that he became deeply depressed. The rabbis sent R. Eleazar b. Pedat to study with him and to comfort him.

As the two men studied together, R. Eleazar supported R. Yohanan's every statement with, "You are correct. There is a *baraita* that supports you."

"You are no replacement for Resh Lakish," Rabbi Yohanan complained.

"When I stated a law, Resh Lakish raised twenty-four objections, to which I gave twenty-four answers. This led to a full understanding of the law. But you tell me that a baraita supports me. Don't I know myself that what I said is correct?" (*Bava Metzia* 84a)

R. Ulla, who was in the habit of visiting the land of Israel frequently, passed away outside the land of Israel. His body was brought to Israel for burial. When R. Eleazar was informed that his coffin had arrived, he remarked, "Receiving a man in his lifetime is not the same as receiving him after his death." (*Ketubbot* 111a)

It was said of R. Eleazar b. Pedat that he studied Torah in the lower market of Sepphoris, but left his coat in the town's upper market. R. Yitzhak b. Eleazar told a story: "A man once wanted to take the coat for himself and found a poisonous snake inside it." (*Eruvin* 54b)

R. Benyamin b. Yafet said in the name of R. Eleazar: "The Torah says that Yoseph's brothers fell down before him. This bears out the popular saying. 'A fox in its hour – bow down to it.'" (*Megillah* 16b)

R. Benyamin b. Yafet also said in the name of R. Eleazar: "The Torah says that Yoseph comforted his brothers. This tells us that he spoke to them words that greatly reassured them, such as: If ten lights cannot put out one light, how can one light put out ten?"

R. Eleazar said in the name of R. Hanina: "Whoever quotes another person by name brings deliverance to the world." (*Megillah* 15a)

R. Eleazar further said in the name of R. Hanina, "The death of a righteous person is a loss only to his generation, but his legacy remains. It is like when one loses a precious pearl. It is a loss only to the owner, but the pearl remains a pearl wherever it is."

R. Eleazar stated: "The performance of charity is greater than offering all the sacrifices." (*Sukkah* 49b)

R. Eleazar further stated: "The act of *gemilat hasadim* is greater than charity."

He also stated: "The reward of charity is dependent on the kindness inherent it."

R. Yohanan and R. Eleazar stated: "Even if a sharp sword rests on one's neck, one should not desist from praying." (*Berachot* 10a)

R. Eleazar said: "A man who has no wife is not a complete man." (*Yevamot* 63a)

"Any man who does not own land is not a proper man."

"There will come a time when all craftsmen will take up agriculture."

R. Eleazar said: "Whoever lives in Eretz Yisrael lives without sin." (*Ketubbot* 111a)

R. Eleazar said: "Why are prayers of a righteous person compared to a pitchfork? In order to teach us that just as a pitchfork turns over the corn in the barn, so do the prayers of the righteous turn the mind of God from harsh decrees into decrees of mercy." (*Sukkah* 14a)

When R. Eleazar went up to Israel, he met R. Zeiri and he asked him: "Is there a tanna here who was taught the laws of measurement by Rav? He introduced him to R. Yitzhak b. Avdimi. R. Yitzhak asked him, "What is your difficulty?" (*Bava Batra* 87a)

Once, R. Eleazar was sick and R. Yohanan went to visit him. He saw R. Eleazar crying. He asked him, "Why are you crying? Are you crying because you have no children?" R. Yohanan took a bone from his pocket, showed it to him and said, "This tooth is from my tenth son, who died." (*Berachot* 5b)

For a glimpse of the world as it was in the time of Eleazar b. Pedat, see the historical timeline from 200 to 300 C.E.

אלעזר בן שמוע
Eleazar ben Shammua

(second century C.E.)
Tanna, Eretz Yisrael

Rabbi Eleazar, a student of Rabbi Akiva, survived the Bar Kochva revolt. Later on, he was ordained by Rabbi Yehuda ben Bava.

His teacher, Rabbi Yehuda ben Bava, became a martyr when he disobeyed the decree of the Roman authorities banning rabbinical ordination. During the Hadrianic persecutions, the authorities issued a decree that anyone who ordained a rabbi or received ordination would be liable to the death penalty, the city where the ordination took place would be demolished, and the boundaries around the city uprooted.

In order to avoid the destruction of a city, Rabbi Yehuda b. Bava sat between two great mountains and between the two cities of Usha and Shefaram. Five prominent students sat before him: Rabbi Meir, Rabbi Yehuda bar Illai, Rabbi Shimon, Rabbi Yosi, and Rabbi Eleazar ben Shammua. The ceremony was held and he ordained them. Rabbi Avia adds the name of Rabbi Nehemia. As soon as the ceremony ended, they noticed the Romans approaching from a distance. Rabbi Yehuda told his students to flee. They wanted to take him with them, but he urged them to flee without him, saying, "I would cause all of you to be captured. I am too old to run. I will lie before them like a stone." It was said that the Romans stabbed him three hundred times. (*Sanhedrin* 14a)

It is stated that Rabbi Akiva had twelve thousand pairs of students, all of whom died in the same period because they did not treat one another with respect. A tanna taught that they died between Pesah and Shavuot. The remaining students of Rabbi Akiva who revived the Torah at that time were Rabbi Meir, Rabbi Yehuda, Rabbi Yosi, Rabbi Shimon and Rabbi Eleazar ben Shammua.

After the revolt, Rabbi Eleazar b. Shammua and Rabbi Yohanan ha-Sandlar left Eretz Yisrael for Nisibis in order to study under Rabbi Yehuda ben Betera. However, they missed Eretz Yisrael and did not stay very long. Rabbi Eleazar, who was a kohen, lived to a very old age. (*Yevamot* 62b)

When asked by his students to what he attributed his longevity, his answer was, "I have never taken a shortcut through a synagogue, I never stepped over the heads of the holy people, and I never lifted my hands to perform the priestly benedictions without first reciting a blessing." Rabbi Eleazar is mentioned among the ten Martyrs during the Hadrianic persecutions. (*Sotah* 39a, *Megillah* 27b)

R. Yohanan said: The hearts and intellectual capacity of the ancients were like the door of the *ulam*. Those of the last generations were like the door of the *hechal,* and our generation's capacity is like the eye of a needle. R. Akiva is classified among the ancients and R. Eleazar b. Shammua among the last generation. (*Eruvin* 53a)

Rabbi Yehuda ha-Nasi was one of his students. (*Menachot* 18a)

R. Eleazar b. Shammua said, "Let the honor of your student be as precious as your own, the honor of your colleague be as that of your teacher, and the honor of your teacher as the honor of God." (*Avot* 4:12)

R. Eleazar said: "A messenger on his way to perform a mitzvah will not suffer harm either going or returning." (*Pesahim* 8b)

For a glimpse of the world as it was in the time of R. Eleazar b. Shammua, see the historical timeline from 100 to 200 C.E.

אלעזר בן שמעון בן יוחאי
Eleazar ben Shimon bar Yohai
(Eleazar b. Simeon)

(second century C.E.)
Tanna, Eretz Yisrael

Rabbi Eleazar and his father, R. Shimon bar Yohai, lived during very difficult times, barely escaping capture by the Romans.

They had to hide in a cave for thirteen years because on one occasion Rabbi Yehuda, Rabbi Shimon and Rabbi Yosi were making remarks to an audience. Rabbi Yehuda b. Illai remarked on how fine the works of the Romans were, citing their markets, bridges and bathhouses. Rabbi Yosi ben Halafta was silent, but Rabbi Shimon ben Yohai commented, "Whatever they built, they did for themselves. They built markets to place prostitutes in them, bridges to levy tolls on them, and bathhouses to indulge their bodies." Someone carried his words to the Romans. They decreed that Rabbi Yehuda should be rewarded, Rabbi Yosi exiled to Sepphoris and Rabbi Shimon executed. Rabbi Shimon and his son Rabbi Eleazar went and hid in a cave. Miraculously, a carob tree grew nearby and they found a well in the cave. To conserve wear and tear on their clothing, they sat in the sand during the day as they studied Torah. Twelve years later, when the emperor Hadrian died, they left the cave, but due to some circumstances they returned for one more year. (*Shabbat* 33b, *Taanit* 20a)

Rabbi Eleazar was a contemporary of Rabbi Yehuda ha-Nasi, Rabbi Yosi and Rabbi Meir.

Under compulsion, he accepted an official position from the Romans to be in charge of apprehending thieves and robbers. This came about from a chance meeting between R. Eleazar and a Roman officer who was sent to arrest thieves. R. Eleazar asked him, "How can you tell who the thief is? Perhaps you are arresting the innocent while the guilty go free." The officer replied, "What can I do? I am commanded by the emperor." R. Eleazar advised the officer to go to the tavern and talk to the people there, taking care to learn their occupations. He explained that if they had no trade and could not give a satisfactory answer as to how they made a living, then they were thieves. When the report of this conversation was brought to the authorities, they issued an order: "Let the advisor become the enforcer." They sent for R. Eleazar b. Shimon and ordered him to go out and arrest the thieves, an order which he had to obey. R. Yoshua b. Korha sent him a reproof, saying, "Vinegar, son of wine, how long will you deliver the people of our God to slaughter?" R. Eleazar sent a reply: "I weed out thorns from the vineyard." R. Yoshua retorted, "Let the owner of the vineyard come and weed out the thorns." (*Bava Metzia* 83b)

R. Eleazar was married to the daughter of Rabbi Shimon ben Yosi ben Lakonia.

When R. Shimon b. Gamliel and R. Yoshua b. Korha were learning in the academy they sat on couches, while R. Eleazar b. Shimon and Rebbe sat in front of them on the ground asking questions and raising objections. When the other students objected, they said: "We are drinking from their water, but they are sitting on the ground. Let seats be placed for them."

They placed seats for them. R. Shimon b. Gamliel objected: "I have a pigeon amongst you and you want to destroy it?" So Rebbe was put down again. R. Yoshua b. Korha was displeased and said, "Shall he who has a father live, while he who has no father dies?" Thereupon R. Eleazar was also put on the ground. R. Eleazar was hurt and expressed himself by saying: "You have made him equal to me."

Until this incident, whenever Rebbe made a statement R. Eleazar supported him, but after this day when Rebbe spoke, R. Eleazar said, "Your statement lacks substance." Humiliated, Rebbe complained to R. Shimon b. Gamliel, his father, who replied, "Let it not bother you. He is a lion and the son of a lion, whereas you are a lion and the son of a fox." (*Bava Metzia* 84b)

R. Eleazar b. Shimon was coming home from the house of his teacher in Migdal Gedor. He was riding on his donkey in a leisurely manner by the riverside, and he was feeling happy and elated because he studied a great deal of Torah. A man of ugly appearance passed by and greeted him, saying, "Peace shall be upon you." R. Eleazar did not return the greeting. Instead, he said to him: "Raca, how ugly you are! Are all your townspeople as ugly as you?"

"I do not know," answered the man, "but go and tell the craftsman who made me."

When R. Eleazar realized that he had done wrong, he dismounted from his donkey, bowed down before the stranger and said to him. "I am in your debt. Please forgive me."

The man said: "I will not forgive you until you go to the craftsman who made me and tell him, 'How ugly is the vessel that you have made!'"

They started walking, with R. Eleazar walking behind him until they reached the city where R. Eleazar lived. The townspeople came out, greeting him with the words, "Peace be upon you, master and teacher!"

The man asked, "Whom are you addressing with those words?"

The townspeople replied, "We are addressing the man walking behind you."

The man exclaimed: "If this man is a teacher, may there be no more like him in Israel!"

The people asked him, "Why?"

He replied, "He did such and such to me." They asked the man to forgive R. Eleazar for the sake of his Torah scholarship.

The man replied, "For your sake I forgive him, but only on condition that he never act in this manner again." Soon afterwards, R. Eleazar entered the bet midrash and delivered a speech on the subject, saying, "A man should always be gentle as a reed, never unyielding as the cedar." (*Taanit* 20a)

R. Eleazar b. Shimon said: "Every individual person has the opportunity to affect the whole world for good or evil because the world is judged by its majority of good people and not so good, while an individual is judged by the majority of his deeds, good or bad." (*Kiddushin* 40b)

When R. Eleazar was about to die, he said to his wife, "I know that the rabbis, who are angry with me, will not attend to me properly. Please let me lie in a room on the upper floor, and do not be afraid of me." R. Shemuel b. Nachmeni said, "R. Yonatan's mother told me that she was told by the wife of R. Eleazar that she kept him in the upper floor from eighteen to twenty-two years. She would walk up to examine his hair, and not a single hair had fallen out. One day, when she saw a worm crawl out of his ear, she was very upset, but he appeared to her in a dream and told her that it was nothing. It happened because he once heard an insult to a scholar and did not protest." While his body lay upstairs, people used to come to the house with disputes between them. They stood near the door, each stating his case, and a voice would issue from the upper chamber proclaiming: So-and-so is liable, and So-and-so is not. One day, R. Eleazar's wife was quarreling with a neighbor and the other woman told her, "You deserve to be like your husband, unworthy of burial!" It was said that R. Shimon b. Yohai appeared to the rabbis of the town in a dream and complained, "I have a pigeon amongst you and you refuse to bring it to me." Then the rabbis decided to attend to R. Eleazar's burial, but the people of Akavaria refused to let him be taken away because during the years that R. Eleazar was kept in the upper floor of his house, no bad thing happened to the town. One day on Erev Yom Kippur, as the people were busy preparing for Yom Kippur, the rabbis took his bier and carried it to his father's tomb. (*Bava Metzia* 84b)

R. Yehuda ha-Nasi visited the town of R. Eleazar b. Shimon. He inquired, "Did that tzadik leave a son?" "Yes," they replied, "and every harlot whose hire is two zuz is willing to hire him for herself for eight zuz." R. Yehuda summoned him, ordained him as a rabbi in order to bestow respect on him, and entrusted him to be educated by R. Shimon b. Issi b. Lakonia, his maternal uncle. Every day, the young man would say, "I am going back to my town." The teacher would reply, "They made you a sage, spread a gold-trimmed cape on you and call you rabbi, and in spite of it you say, 'I am going back to my town'?" The young man replied, "I swear that I am cured, that my desires have been abandoned." Some years later, when he became a great scholar, he went to Rebbe's academy and participated in the discussions. On hearing his voice, Rebbe observed: "This voice is similar to the voice of R. Eleazar b. Shimon."

"He is the son of R. Eleazar," said the students of the academy. Very pleased, Rebbe cited a verse from scripture in praise. He also complimented R. Shimon b. Issi b. Lakonia for accomplishing his mission. When R. Eleazar's son died, they buried him next to his father. (*Bava Metzia* 85a)

For a glimpse of the world as it was in R. Eleazar b. Shimon bar Yohai's time, see the historical timeline from 100 to 200 C.E.

אלעזר בן צדוק
Eleazar ben Tzadok (Zadok) (1)
(first–second centuries C.E.)
Tanna, Eretz Yisrael

R. Eleazar was the son of R. Tzadok, who fasted for many years and to whom R. Yohanan b. Zakkai asked Vespasian to send a physician.

R. Eleazar told the sages how things were done in Yavneh. (*Niddah* 48b)

R. Eleazar b. Tzadok said: "Do good deeds for the sake of your Maker. Do not make a crown for yourself from your Torah learning, or a spade to dig with. (*Nedarim* 62a)

For a glimpse of the world as it was in the time of R. Eleazar b. Tzadok, see the historical timeline from 50 to 150 C.E.

אלעזר בן צדוק
Eleazar ben Tzadok (Zadok) (2)
(second century C.E.)
Tanna, Eretz Yisrael

Rabbi Eleazar was a student of Rabbi Meir and Rabbi Shimon ben Gamliel. Rabbi Yehuda b. Illai and Rabbi Yosi b. Halafta were his contemporaries, and Rabbi Yehuda ha-Nasi was a close friend of his.

(Suka 44 b) Aibu, the father of Rav, stated. I was next to Rabbi Eleazar ben Tzadok when a certain man came to ask him this question: "I possess cities, vineyards and olive trees, and the inhabitants of the cities come and work the fields and eat the olives. Is this proper or improper to do during a sabbatical year?" He replied that it is improper. When the man left, Rabbi Eleazar remarked, "I have lived here for forty years, and never have I seen a man as righteous as this one. The man returned to ask. "What should I do?" Rabbi Eleazar told him, "Abandon the olives to the poor and pay yourself for the labor."

Elsewhere in the Talmud there is a statement. The rabbis relied upon the words of R. Shimon ben Gamliel and R. Eleazar b. Tzadok, who said, "No law may be imposed upon the public unless a majority can endure it." (*Horayot* 3b)

For a glimpse of the world as it was in the time of Eleazar b. Tzadok, see the historical timeline from 100 to 200 C.E.

אלעזר בן יוסי
Eleazar ben Yosi

(second century C.E.)
Tanna, Eretz Yisrael

Rabbi Eleazar, whose family lived in Sepphoris for several generations, was the second son of Rabbi Yosi ben Halafta. When Rabbi Shimon ben Yohai traveled to Rome in an attempt to persuade the emperor to rescind the edicts forbidding Jewish religious practices, R. Eleazar went with him (*Meilah* 17a–b)

According to the story in the Talmud, at one point the Roman authorities prohibited the observance of the Sabbath, the performance of circumcision and the observance of the mitzvah of family purity. When the edict was issued, a Jew named Reuben b. Istroboli, who lived in Rome, disguised himself as a Roman and mingled among the Romans. When he convinced the authorities that carrying out these restrictions would be detrimental to the

Romans, they annulled the laws on his advice. When it was learned that Reuben was a Jew, the authorities reinstituted the decrees. The Jews in Judea then decided to send a delegation to Rome to find a way to have the law repealed, and R. Shimon bar Yohai and R. Eleazar b. Yosi were chosen to travel to Rome.

On the way, they were met by a demon whose name was Ben Temalion. Rabbi Shimon wept, saying, "My ancestor Abraham's maid, Hagar, was worthy to meet angels three times, and I don't deserve to meet an angel even once!" But R. Shimon continued to pray that a miracle occur no matter who its agent might be.

Ben Temalion advanced ahead of them and entered into the body of the emperor's daughter. When R. Shimon arrived at the palace, there was a great commotion, and the emperor's daughter repeatedly called out the name of R. Shimon. When the palace guards learned that the man who had arrived was in fact Rabbi Shimon, they brought him to the palace and R. Shimon called out: "Ben Temalion, depart from her! Ben Temalion, depart from her!"

The demon departed from the body of the emperor's daughter. The grateful emperor told them to ask for whatever they wished. The boon that they requested was that the decree be annulled, and so it was.

While Rabbi Eleazar was in Rome, he saw the vessels plundered from the Temple. He also saw the splattered blood of the sacrifices on the curtain that had hung before the Holy of Holies.

He also states that in Rome, he saw the *tzitz* (the high priest's head plate) with the inscription "Holy to God," which was engraved on a single line. (There had been a disagreement as to whether the phrase was engraved on one or two lines.) (*Sukkah* 5a)

It has been taught: R. Eleazar b. Yosi said, "I refuted the books of the Samaritans, who maintained that resurrection cannot be deduced from the Torah. "You have falsified your Torah, yet it availed you nothing." (*Sanhedrin* 90b)

He was one of the scholars in the Academy of Yavne. It is told that when the rabbis entered Kerem be-Yavne, Rabbi Yehuda, R. Eleazar b. Yosi and R. Shimon were present, and they were asked a question about a particular halacha. (*Shabbat* 33b)

It has been taught: R. Eleazar b. Yosi said: "All the charity and deeds of kindness performed by the Jewish people in this world promotes peace and brings them closer to their father in heaven. (*Bava Batra* 10a)

For a glimpse of the world as it was in the time of R. Eleazar b. Yosi, see the historical timeline from 100 to 200 C.E.

אלעזר המודעי
Eleazar ha-Modai

(first–second centuries C.E.)
Tanna, Eretz Yisrael

Rabbi Eleazar was born and lived in Modiin, the well-known city where the Hasmoneans began the revolt against Antiochus.

About 260 years later, during the revolt against the Romans, his nephew, Bar Kochva, had him executed on charges of treachery that turned out to be false.

Rabbi Gamliel said of him, we still need the interpretations of the Modiinite. (*Shabbat* 55b, *Bava Batra* 10b)

It happened once that R. Tarfon, R. Yishmael and the sages were sitting and discussing the Torah portion that mentions the manna. R. Eleazar of Modiin, who was seated among them, commented that the manna that came down was sixty cubits high. R. Tarfon said to him, "Modiinite! How long will you take words and stack them up against us?" He answered, "I am only expounding on the scriptural text." (*Yoma* 76a)

He used to say, "Anyone who embarrasses another person in public will have no portion in the World to Come." (*Avot* 3:11)

In a condemnation he made of those who hide their Jewish origin, he was probably referring to those who had an operation to reverse their circumcision.

R. Shimon b. Eleazar said in the name of R. Eliezer b. Parta, who said in the name of R. Eleazar ha-Modai: "The writing of the Torah script was never changed." (*Sanhedrin* 22a)

For a glimpse of the world as it was in the time of Eleazar ha-Modai, see the historical timeline from 50 to 150 C.E.

אליעזר בן דגלאי
Eliezer ben Diglai

(first–second centuries C.E.)
Tanna, Eretz Yisrael

The Talmud mentions that Rabbi Eliezer talked about the use of incense in the Temple. He stressed the fact that the incense had a strong fragrance. Even though the Temple was a long distance away from his father's house; the goats that his father kept on Mount Michvar would sneeze every time the incense was ground in the Temple. (*Tamid* 3:8)

For a glimpse of the world as it was in the time of Eliezer ben Diglai, see the historical timeline from 50 to 150 C.E.

אליעזר בן הורקנוס
Eliezer ben Hyrcanus

(first–second centuries C.E.)
Tanna, Eretz Yisrael

R. Eliezer ben Hyrcanus, who came from a wealthy family, worked on his father's estate until he was close to thirty years of age. At that point, he decided to devote his life to the study of Torah. He entered the school of Rabbi Yohanan ben Zakkai in Jerusalem, where he studied hard and became one of the school's most distinguished students. R. Eliezer's father, displeased that his son was spending his time at the school, was about to disinherit him, but when he visited Jerusalem and discovered that his son had become a prominent scholar, he changed his mind. Rabbi Yohanan ben Zakkai had a very high opinion of him. (*Avot* 2:8) He said, "If all the scholars of Israel were to be put in one side of the scale and Rabbi Eliezer in the other, he would outweigh them all."

R. Eliezer, who was stringent in his halachic rulings, was considered a Shamuti (follower of Shammai). (*Shabbat* 130b)

On the other hand, he permitted carrying weapons on Shabbat because he considered that an adornment. (*Gittin* 56a) Rabbi Eliezer was one of the students who smuggled Rabbi Yohanan ben Zakkai out of Jerusalem in a coffin during the siege. (*Shabbat* 6:4, 63a)

The Talmud relates that Abba Sikra, the head of the Jewish guards, was a nephew of Rabbi Yohanan ben Zakkai, who summoned him for a secret visit. Jerusalem was under siege by the army of Vespasian, and the people were suffering from starvation.

Rabbi Yohanan, who was a member of the peace party, asked him: "How long can the people endure this suffering?"

He answered, "If I say a word they will kill me."

Rabbi Yohanan told him to devise a plan that would enable him to escape in order to meet with Vespasian, the Roman general. Abba Sikra suggested that his students smuggle him out in a coffin. He agreed, and the two students

who smuggled him out were Rabbi Eliezer ben Hyrcanus and Rabbi Yoshua ben Hananya. When he reached the Roman camp, he met with Vespasian.

Rabbi Yohanan addressed Vespasian as emperor. When Vespasian corrected him, Rabbi Yohanan replied, "You are destined to become emperor." Shortly afterward, a messenger arrived to inform Vespasian that the Senate had chosen him to succeed the former emperor, who had died. Vespasian told Rabbi Yohanan, "I must leave now, but make a request of me and I will grant it to you."

Rabbi Yohanan said: "Give me Yavne and its sages, and a physician to heal Rabbi Tzadok." The wish was granted, and the yeshiva in Yavne was spared. (*Gittin* 56a)

After the Temple was destroyed Rabbi Eliezer was one of the leading scholars at the academy of Yavne. He was a member of the delegation who traveled to Rome to intercede on behalf of the Jewish people. Later on, he established a school in Lydda. Among his prominent students were Rabbi Akiva, Rabbi Illai, Rabbi Yosi ben Dormaskos, Rabbi Abba Hanan and Aquila the proselyte. (*Sanhedrin* 17b)

The overseer for King Agrippas II asked R. Eliezer: "One like myself, who eats only one meal a day – may I eat one meal in the sukkah and be exempt from the rest?"

He also asked R. Eliezer: "One like myself who has two wives, one in Tiberias and one in Sepphoris – may I go from sukkah to sukkah?" (*Sukkah* 27a)

It happened that while R. Eliezer spent a Shabbat in the Upper Galilee, he was asked thirty questions on the halachot of Sukkot. (*Sukkah* 28a)

His answer was: "I heard the answer to twelve of the questions from my teacher, but I did not hear the answer to eighteen of the questions from my teachers."

R. Yosi b. Yehuda said: "Reverse the words "I heard the answer to eighteen questions, but I did not hear the answer to twelve questions."

They asked him: "Do you answer only according to what you heard from your teachers?"

He replied, "You are trying to make me say something I did not hear from my teachers. Throughout my life, no one ever preceded me to the bet midrash. I never slept or dozed off in the bet midrash. Never did I go out and leave anyone behind me in the bet midrash. I never used profane language, and I never said anything that I did not hear from my teachers."

R. Yirmiyahu said – some say that R. Hiyya b. Abba said – "The Targum on the Torah was written by Onkelos the proselyte under the guidance of R. Eliezer and R. Yoshua." (*Megillah* 3a)

Rabbi Eliezer had halachic differences with the rabbis. Although he brought forth every argument to prove his point, the rabbis refused to accept them. He declared: "If Halacha agrees with me, let this carob tree prove it." The carob tree uprooted itself. The rabbis retorted: "The carob tree cannot prove the argument."

He then said to them: "If I am right, then let the stream of water prove it." Thereupon the stream of water started flowing in the opposite direction. The rabbis retorted: "The stream of water couldn't prove anything in this matter." Rabbi Eliezer then said: "If I am right, then let the walls of this school prove it." Thereupon the walls began to incline. Rabbi Yehoshua spoke up and rebuked the walls. "When scholars are disputing sacred matters, what business do the walls have to interfere?" The walls

stopped to incline, but did not straighten out either.

Rabbi Eliezer said: "If I am right, let the heavens prove it." Thereupon a heavenly voice came forth, saying, "The halacha goes according to Rabbi Eliezer." Rabbi Yoshua spoke up and said: "The Torah is not in heaven." Rabbi Yirmiyahu arose and declared: "The Torah was already given on Mount Sinai. It belongs here on earth, and we do not pay attention to heavenly voices." He added, "It has been written in the Torah that the majority decides."

Later on, Rabbi Natan encountered Elijah the Prophet and asked him, "What did God do during that time?" Elijah answered, "He rejoiced, laughing, 'My sons have defeated me! My sons have defeated me!'"

On that day, all the objects that R. Eliezer had declared ritually pure were brought forth and burned. The rabbis then took a vote and excommunicated him. Afterwards, they said, "Who will go and inform him of the excommunication?"

"I will go," said R. Akiva. He donned black garments and sat at a distance of four cubits from R. Eliezer.

"Akiva," said R. Eliezer, "what has happened today?" R. Akiva replied, "Master, it appears to me that your companions are keeping a distance from you."

R. Eliezer rent his garments, removed his shoes, gave up his seat and sat on the floor as tears flowed from his eyes. It was later learned that a great calamity almost happened on that day. Rabbi Gamliel was traveling in a ship when a huge wave arose to drown him. Rabbi Gamliel thought to himself, "It appears to me that this is on account of Rabbi Eliezer ben Hyrcanus." Thereupon he arose and exclaimed: "Sovereign of the Universe, You know full well that I did not act for my own honor or for the honor of my paternal house, but for Your honor, so that strife not multiply in Israel." At that, the raging sea subsided.

Imma Shalom, the wife of Rabbi Eliezer, was the sister of Rabbi Gamliel. After this incident took place, she would not allow him to fall on his face in order to recite Tahanun because she feared that her husband's hurt feelings might cause him to pray, and her brother, R. Gamliel, would die. However, one day a poor man came to the door and she gave him food. When she returned, she found her husband fallen on his face. "Arise," she cried to him. "You have slain my brother!" Soon afterward, R. Gamliel's household announced his death. (Bava Metzia 59b)

One of Rabbi Eliezer's famous sayings was, "Let the honor of your fellow-man be as precious as your own, be not easily provoked to anger, repent one day before you die, warm yourself at the fire of the sages, but beware of their glowing coals." (Avot 2:15)

In Imma Shalom's vicinity there lived a sectarian judge who had a reputation for never accepting bribes. In order to expose him, Imma Shalom brought him a golden lamp and said to him, "My father left an estate, and I want my share of the inheritance."

The judge ordered the estate divided so that she would receive her share. R. Gamliel argued that according to Torah law, daughters do not inherit if there are sons. The judge replied, "Since the day you were exiled from your land, the law of the Torah has been superseded by other laws that give daughters an equal inheritance." The next day, R. Gamliel brought a Libyan donkey before the judge. At this, the judge reversed his own ruling by declaring, "I have found at the end of the book that it is written, 'I came

neither to destroy the Law of Moshe nor to add to it.' And it is written therein that a daughter does not inherit where there is a son."

Imma Shalom said to the judge, "Let your light shine forth like a lamp." R. Gamliel said to him, "A donkey came and knocked the lamp over." (Sotah 49a–b) Shabbat 116a)

R. Eliezer the Great said, "From the day the Temple was destroyed the sages began to be like schoolteachers, schoolteachers like synagogue attendants, synagogue attendants like common people, and the common people became more debased. There was none to ask, none to inquire. Upon whom can we rely? We can rely only upon our Father in Heaven." (Sotah 49a, b)

"Just before the arrival of the Messiah, insolence will increase and honor will be scarce. The vine will yield its fruit abundantly, but wine will be dear. The government will adopt a new religion and no one will disapprove.

"The meeting places will be used for immorality, Galilee will be destroyed, Gablan desolated, and the dwellers on the frontier will go begging from place to place without no one to take pity on them.

"The wisdom of the scholars will degenerate, fearers of sin will be despised and truth will be lacking. Youth will put old men to shame, the old will stand up in the presence of the young, a son will revile his father, a daughter will rebel against her mother, and a daughter-in-law against her mother-in-law.

"The members of one's household will be the household's own enemies.

"That generation will have a face of a dog. A son will not be ashamed before his father. Therefore, upon whom can we rely? We can rely only upon our Father in Heaven."

Once a student who led the prayer service in the presence of R. Eliezer drew it out, so that it lasted much longer than usual. The other students said to R. Eliezer, "Rabbi, this student is taking an extremely long time." He replied to them, "He is taking no longer than Moshe was when he was on the mountain for forty days and nights." Another time, a student led the prayer service in R. Eliezer's presence, and he cut the prayers very short. The students complained to R. Eliezer, "This student's praying is extremely brief." He replied to them, "His prayer is no shorter than that of Moshe when he prayed for Miriam with only a few words."(*Berachot* 34a)

Once R. Eliezer entered a synagogue and did not find ten people inside. His Jewish slave was with him. He therefore freed his slave in order to complete the minyan. (*Berachot* 47b)

R. Yohanan b. Zakkai had five outstanding students. He said to them, "Go and discern the proper way to which a person should adhere."

R. Eliezer said, "A good eye."

R. Yoshua said, "A good friend."

R. Yosi said, "A good neighbor."

R. Shimon said, "One who considers the outcome of his actions."

R. Eleazar said, "A good heart."

R. Yohanan b. Zakkai remarked, "I prefer the words of R. Eleazar b. Arach, because all your words are included in his words." (*Avot* 2:13)

Our rabbis taught: when R. Eliezer fell ill, four sages went to visit him: R. Tarfon, R. Yoshua, R. Eleazar b. Azaryah and R. Akiva.

R. Tarfon said to him, "You are more valuable to Israel than rain, for rain is precious in this world, but you are precious in this world and the next."

R. Yoshua said, "You are more valuable to Israel than the disc of the sun, for the sun's disc is only in this

world, while you are for this and the next world."

R. Eleazar b. Azaryah said, "You are better to Israel than a father and mother, they are only for this world, but you are for this and the next world."

But R. Akiva remarked, "Suffering is precious." R. Eliezer liked R. Akiva's remark best. (*Sanhedrin* 101a)

During R. Eliezer's illness, his students came to visit him. They said to him: "Teach us the way of life so that we may merit the future world." He advised them: "Give honor to your colleagues, keep your children from nonsense, and place them between the knees of scholars. When you pray, know before Whom you stand. In this way, you will merit the future world." (*Berachot* 28b)

For a glimpse of the world as it was in the time of R. Eliezer b. Hyrcanus, see the historical timeline from 50 to 150 C.E.

אליעזר בן מתיא
Eliezer ben Mathya (Eleazar b. Matya)

(second century C.E.)
Tanna, Eretz Yisrael

R. Eliezer ben Mathya, who was one of the most important students of Yavne, was a pupil of Rabbi Tarfon.

It was taught: A Sanhedrin that contains two members who can speak seventy languages while the rest of the Sanhedrin can understand those languages is a fit Sanhedrin. If there are three who can speak the seventy languages, that body is a middling Sanhedrin. If there are four who can speak the seventy languages, that body is a wise Sanhedrin. In Yavneh there were four: Ben Azzai, Ben Zoma, Ben Hachinai and R. Eleazar b. Mathya. It was related that he, Rabbi Halafta and Rabbi Hanina Hachinai climbed upon the twelve stones that had been taken from the Jordan and erected by Joshua at Gilgal. (JT *Shekalim* 5:1)

He is quoted as saying: "If my father should order me, 'Give me a drink of water' while I have a mitzvah to perform, I disregard my father and perform the mitzvah, because both my father and I are obligated to fulfill the mitzvah." (*Kiddushin* 32a)

For a glimpse of the world as it was in the time of Eliezer ben Mathya, see the historical timeline from 100 to 200 C.E.

אליעזר בן יעקב
Eliezer ben Yaakov

(first century C.E.)
Tanna, Eretz Yisrael

R. Eliezer, who was a young man when the second Temple was still standing, was intimately familiar with its structure and customs. R. Huna said, "Who is the authority for the measurements in the Temple? R. Eliezer b. Yaakov is the authority on measurements for the Temple." (*Yoma* 16a)

The Talmud states that Rabbi Shimon ben Azzai said, "I found a roll of genealogical records in Jerusalem with a halacha written inside. In addition, it said that the teachings of R. Eliezer b. Yaakov are small in quantity, but thoroughly sifted." (*Yevamot* 49b)

His recollections are mentioned several times in the Mishna discussing the arrangements in the Temple. Several times, he admits that he forgot what it was used for. (*Middot* 1:9 and 2:6, etc.)

For a glimpse of the world as it was in the time of Eliezer ben Yaakov, see the historical timeline from 1 to 100 C.E.

אליעזר בן יעקב
Eliezer ben Yaakov

(second century C.E.)
Tanna, Eretz Yisrael

R. Eliezer is quoted as disagreeing with his colleagues Rabbi Yehuda, Rabbi Shimon and others regarding leprosy. (*Negaim* 10:4)

It is stated: Rabbi Yosi, son of Rabbi Hanina, said in the name of Rabbi Eliezer ben Yaakov: "If a man is hosting a scholar in his home and lets him use his possessions, he is comparable to one who has offered the daily sacrifices." He also said: "A man should not stand on a high platform when he prays." (*Berachot* 10b)

R. Yosi also said in the name of R. Eliezer b. Yaakov: "One should not eat before praying first." (*Berachot* 10b)

He also said in the name of R. Eliezer b. Yaakov: "One should pray with feet next to each other, and erect."

R. Eliezer b. Yaakov was in disagreement with his colleagues with regards to an eruv where Jews live with non-Jews in one courtyard. Further on in the same tractate (62 b) Abbaye said to R. Yoseph: "We have a tradition that the teachings of R. Eliezer b. Yaakov are few in quantity but well sifted." Also Rav Yehuda said in the name of R. Shemuel that the Halacha is in agreement with R. Eliezer b. Yaakov. (*Eruvin* 61b)

(Perhaps this statement refers to the other R. Eliezer b. Yaakov, who lived in the first century.)

For a glimpse of the world as it was in the time of Eliezer ben Yaakov, see the historical timeline from 100 to 200 C.E.

אליעזר הקפר
Eliezer ha-Kafar (Eleazar ha-Kappar)

(second century C.E.)
Tanna, Eretz Yisrael

R. Eliezer lived and taught in Lydda. Rabbi Yehoshua ben Levi was one of his students. He used to say, "Envy, greed and chasing after honors take a person out of this world." (*Avot* 4:21)

He said that in Messianic times, the synagogues and houses of learning that are located in Babylon will be transported to Eretz Yisrael. (*Megillah* 29a)

Both Rabbi Eliezer and his father are quoted discussing halachic matters in the same tractate. (*Hullin* 28a, *Hullin* 27b)

R. Eliezer ha-Kapar said, "The newborn are destined to die, the dead will live again and the living will be judged. Know that everything goes according to the reckoning. Let not your evil inclination mislead you into believing that your grave will be an escape for you. You were created against your will, you were born against your will; against your will you live, against your will you will die and against your will you are destined to give an account before the King of kings." (*Avot* 4:22)

For a glimpse of the world as it was in the time of R. Eliezer ha-Kapar, see the historical timeline from 100 to 200 C.E.

אלישע בן אבויה
Elisha ben Avuyah

(second century C.E.)
Tanna, Eretz Yisrael

R. Elisha ben Avuyah was born in Jerusalem. In his younger years he was one of the great scholars of his time. His father was a prominent member of the community. In his later years, he turned away from Jewish observance and was denounced by his associates. None of his colleagues wanted to have any association with him except his student, Rabbi Meir.

There are several explanations for his abandonment of Torah and Jewish tradition. One version has it that the Bar Kochva revolt, its failure, and the resulting persecutions and suffering caused him to question his faith.

Rabbi Yoseph said: Had Aher interpreted the Torah verse as Rabbi Yaakov, his daughter's son, he would not have sinned. Others say that he saw the tongue of Hutzpit the interpreter being dragged along by a swine and exclaimed, "The mouth that uttered pearls now licks the dust! Is this the Torah and is this its reward?"

He went away and sinned. After he turned away from Judaism, the rabbis did not refer to him by name, but called him Aher ("the other"). (*Kiddushin* 39b)

One of his famous sayings was: "Learning while young is like writing on fresh paper, but learning in old age is like writing on blotted paper." (*Avot* 4:20)

Rabbi Meir, who continued to discuss Torah with him, tried to bring him back to Jewish observance.

Our rabbis taught: Once Aher was riding on a horse on the Shabbat, and Rabbi Meir was walking behind him in order to learn Torah from him. When they had gone a certain distance, Aher said to R. Meir, "Turn back, because by my measurement we have gone already to the limit of distance that may be traveled on Shabbat."

Rabbi Meir answered, "You turn back, too."

Aher replied, "Have I not told you that I have heard from behind the Heavenly Curtain that there is a way back to Judaism for everyone except for Aher?"

Rabbi Meir prevailed upon him and took him to a schoolhouse. Aher stopped one of the pupils and said, "Recite for me the verse you learned today." The child recited a verse from the Prophet Yeshaya: "There is no peace for the wicked, says the Lord."

They went to another school and Aher asked a child to recite his verse. The child recited another verse which was similar in rebuke to the wicked. They went to a total of thirteen schoolhouses, where all the children quoted verses in a similar vein. The last child stuttered, and the word he used sounded like "Elisha." Aher, whose given name was Elisha, became angry and said: "If a knife had been in my hand, I would have cut him up." (Hagigah 15a)

For a glimpse of the world as it was in the time of Elisha ben Avuyah, see the historical timeline from 100 to 200 C.E.

גמליאל בן שמעון דיבנה
Gamliel ben Shimon de-Yavne

(first–second centuries C.E.)
Tanna, Eretz Yisrael
Head of the academy in Yavne

R. Gamliel, the grandson of Rabban Gamliel I, was a descendant of Rabbi Hillel. When Rabbi Yohanan ben Zakkai passed away, he was appointed Nasi of the Sanhedrin at Yavne. He went on several missions to Rome on behalf of his people.

His dictatorial approach, particularly the fact that he humiliated Rabbi Yoshua ben Hanania three times, caused unhappiness in the Sanhedrin. His colleagues deposed him and appointed Rabbi Eleazar ben Azaryah in his place.

Regarding observance of the mitzvot, he was lenient with others but strict with himself. (Berachot 2:5, 16a)

He also conducted philosophical debates with the Roman philosophers. (Avodah Zarah 44b, Rosh ha-Shannah 25a)

Rav Yehuda said in the name of Shemuel in the name of Rabbi Shimon ben Gamliel: "There were a thousand students in my father's house. Five hundred studied Torah and five hundred studied Greek wisdom. (Sotah 49b)

When R. Gamliel's son became ill, R. Gamliel sent two scholars to R. Hanina b. Dosa to ask him to pray.

R. Hanina went up to the upper chamber and prayed. When he came down, he told them, "Go home. The fever has left him." They asked him, "Are you a prophet?" He replied, "I am neither a prophet nor the son of a prophet, but I have learned this from experience. If I utter my prayer smoothly, I know that it has been accepted, but if I do not utter it smoothly, then I know that it has not been accepted." The rabbis made a note of the exact time when he said that the fever had left R. Gamliel's son. When they returned to R. Gamliel's house, he confirmed to them that the child's fever had broken at that exact moment. (Berachot 34b)

The story in the Talmud is that Rabbi Yoshua disagreed with Rabbi Gamliel on which day to fix the calendar for the new month. Rabbi Gamliel, as head of the academy, fixed the date and ordered Rabbi Yoshua to appear before him with his staff and money on the day that he had calculated to be Yom Kippur. Rabbi Yoshua did as he was ordered. (Rosh ha-Shannah 25a)

It is related that a certain student asked Rabbi Yehoshua a question as to whether the evening prayer was compulsory or optional. Rabbi Yehoshua replied that it was optional. When the same student asked Rabbi Gamliel, he replied that it is compulsory.

The student replied, "Rabbi Yehoshua told me it is optional."

Rabbi Gamliel told the student to wait until the beginning of the session. When the question was asked, Rabbi Gamliel said that it was compulsory. He then asked the sages, "Does anyone here disagree?"

"No," replied Rabbi Yehoshua.

"Did they not report to me that you said it is optional? Rise now, and let them testify against you."

Rabbi Yehoshua stood up, while Rabbi Gamliel remained sitting and expounding for a long time. Rabbi Yehoshua was still standing until all the scholars in the assembly began to shout at Hutzpit the interpreter, "Stop!"

The interpreter stopped. They said, "How long will Rabbi Gamliel go on insulting R. Yehoshua? Last Rosh ha-Shanah he insulted him, in the matter of R. Tzadok regarding the first-born he insulted him, and now he insults him again. Come, let us depose Rabbi Gamliel."

"Whom shall we appoint in his place? We can hardly appoint R. Yehoshua, because he is a party to the dispute."

"Let us appoint Rabbi Eleazar ben Azaryah, who is wise, wealthy and a descendant of Ezra. He is wise, for he gives the proper answer to a question. Since he is wealthy, he can pay if money is needed to appease the government. As a descendant of Ezra, he has great ancestral merit."

They asked him, "Would you honor us by becoming the head of the academy?"

He replied, "I will consult the members of my family."

When he consulted his wife, she said, "Maybe they will also depose you."

He answered: "Let one use a cup of honor for one day, even if it be broken on the morrow." She said to him, "You have no white hair." He was eighteen years old that day, and a miracle occurred: eighteen rows of his hair turned white. That is why R. Eleazar b. Azaryah said: I am like a seventy-year-old man. He accepted the position.

It was learned that on that day the doors were opened for all the disciples to enter the assembly. Rabbi Gamliel had previously issued an injunction to the assembly that those students whose interior did not match their exterior appearance were not permitted entrance.

During R. Eleazar's presidency, the doors of the yeshiva were opened for everyone who wished to study. They added hundreds of benches to accommodate the students. This had not been the case under R. Gamliel.

It was taught that testimonies were formulated on that day, and whenever the phrase "on that day" is mentioned, it refers to this particular day.

Rabbi Gamliel also did not absent himself from the assembly, even for one hour, after he was deposed. (*Berachot* 27b, 28a)

Another halachic dispute between Rabbi Gamliel and Rabbi Yehoshua concerned whether Ammonites may be accepted into the Jewish community. Rabbi Yehoshua was in favor and Rabbi Gamliel was opposed. The Sanhedrin sided with Rabbi Yehoshua. When Rabbi Gamliel saw the great respect that the Sanhedrin accorded to Rabbi Yehoshua, he decided to go to him to apologize. When he reached his house, he saw that the walls were black from charcoal. He said to him, "I can tell by your walls that you are a blacksmith."

Rabbi Yehoshua replied, "Woe to the generation of which you are the leader, since you know nothing of the problems, struggles and difficulties that the scholars must undergo in order to sustain themselves."

He said to him: "I apologize. Forgive me." But Rabbi Yehoshua ignored him. Then Rabbi Gamliel said, "Do it out of respect for my father." Rabbi Yehoshua agreed and they became reconciled. (*Berachot* 28a)

On seeing Rabbi Yoshua after the Yom Kippur incident, Rabbi Gamliel rose from his seat, kissed him on his head and addressed him as "my teacher and my student." (*Rosh ha-Shannah* 2:9, 25a)

When Rabbi Gamliel was later restored to his office, the presidency rotated between him and Rabbi Eleazar ben Azaryah.

Rabbi Gamliel and Rabbi Yehoshua once traveled by ship. Rabbi Gamliel's food supply ran out and he had to rely on the food that Rabbi Yehoshua had brought with him. "Did you know that we would be delayed so long that you brought additional food with you?" asked Rabbi Gamliel.

"I calculated that a certain star that appears every seventy years was due to appear," answered Rabbi Yehoshua. "It leads sailors to miscalculate their position."

"You possess so much knowledge," said Rabbi Gamliel, "and yet you travel by ship."

"Don't marvel at me," Rabbi Yoshua replied. "Rather be surprised at two of your students who live on land, Rabbi Eleazar Hisma and Rabbi Yohanan ben Gudgeda (perhaps it was R. Yohanan b. Nuri), who can calculate how many drops of water there are in the sea, and yet they have neither bread to eat nor clothes to wear."

Rabbi Gamliel decided to appoint them as supervisors. When he landed, he sent for them to offer them the positions. Reluctant to accept them on account of their humility, they did not show up. Rabbi Gamliel sent for them again, saying, "Do you imagine that I am offering you authority? It is servitude that I offer you." (*Horayot* 10a)

R. Gamliel and R. Akiva were on a journey by ship during the festival of Sukkot. R. Akiva erected a sukkah on the deck. The next day, a wind tore it down and blew it away. R. Gamliel asked his colleague, "Akiva, where is your sukkah?" (*Sukkah* 23a)

Rabbi Gamliel's sister, Imma Shalom, was the wife of Rabbi Eliezer ben Hyrcanus.

The Talmud relates during one Sukkot festival, when R. Gamliel, R. Yoshua, R. Eleazar b. Azaryah and R. Akiva were traveling together on a ship, the only one among them who owned a lulav was R. Gamliel, who had bought it for one thousand zuz. R. Gamliel performed the mitzvah of waving the lulav. When he finished, he gave the lulav to R. Yoshua as a gift. R. Yoshua performed the mitzva of waving it, and then gave it as a gift to R. Eleazar b. Azaryah, who did likewise and then gave it as a gift to R. Akiva. R. Akiva performed the mitzvah and then returned the lulav to R. Gamliel. (*Sukkah* 41b)

Rabbi Eliezer had halachic differences with the rabbis. Although he brought forth every argument to prove his point, the rabbis refused to accept them. He declared: "If Halacha agrees with me, let this carob tree prove it." The carob tree uprooted itself. The rabbis retorted: "The carob tree cannot prove the argument."

He then said to them: "If I am right, then let the stream of water prove it." Thereupon the stream of water started flowing in the opposite direction. The rabbis retorted: "The stream of water couldn't prove anything in this matter."

Rabbi Eliezer then said: "If I am right, then let the walls of this school prove it." Thereupon the walls began to incline. Rabbi Yehoshua spoke up and rebuked the walls. "When scholars are disputing sacred matters, what business do the walls have to interfere?" The walls stopped to incline, but did not straighten out either.

Rabbi Eliezer said: "If I am right, let the heavens prove it." Thereupon a heavenly voice came forth, saying, "The halacha goes according to Rabbi Eliezer." Rabbi Yoshua spoke up and said: "The Torah is not in heaven." Rabbi Yirmiyahu arose and declared: "The Torah was already given on Mount Sinai. It belongs here on earth, and we do not pay attention to heavenly voices." He added, "It has been written in the Torah that the majority decides."

Later on, Rabbi Natan encountered Elijah the Prophet and asked him, "What did God do during that time?" Elijah answered, "He rejoiced, laughing, 'My sons have defeated me! My sons have defeated me!'"

On that day, all the objects that R. Eliezer had declared ritually pure were brought forth and burned. The rabbis then took a vote and excommunicated him. Afterwards, they said, "Who will go and inform him of the excommunication?"

"I will go," said R. Akiva. He donned black garments and sat at a distance of four cubits from R. Eliezer.

"Akiva," said R. Eliezer, "what has happened today?" R. Akiva replied, "Master, it appears to me that your companions are keeping a distance from you."

R. Eliezer rent his garments, removed his shoes, gave up his seat and sat on the floor as tears flowed from his eyes. It was later learned that a great calamity almost happened on that day.

Rabbi Gamliel was traveling in a ship when a huge wave arose to drown him. Rabbi Gamliel thought to himself, "It appears to me that this is on account of Rabbi Eliezer ben Hyrcanus." Thereupon he arose and exclaimed: "Sovereign of the Universe, You know full well that I did not act for my own honor or for the honor of my paternal house, but for Your honor, so that strife not multiply in Israel." At that, the raging sea subsided. (*Bava Metzia* 59b)

R. Gamliel used to say: "Whoever does not mention these three things on Pesah is not fulfilling the mitzvah of Pesah: the paschal lamb, matzah and maror." (*Pesahim* 116a)

Once, as R. Gamliel and the elders sat in an upper chamber in Jericho, they were served dates. R. Gamliel gave R. Akiva permission to recite the blessings. R. Akiva recited one blessing that included three. R. Gamliel disapproved and asked him, "How long will you stick your head into quarrels that go against me?"

R. Akiva replied, "My teacher, you rule one way and the rabbis rule differently. You have taught us that when an individual takes issue with the majority, Halacha is decided according to the majority." (*Berachot* 37a)

R. Shemuel was a very humble person. The Talmud relates that once, Rabbi Gamliel asked his assistant to summon certain seven rabbis to a meeting in the upper chamber. When Rabbi Gamliel arrived, he found eight rabbis there. He declared, "Let the one who was not invited leave." Rabbi Shemuel stood up and declared, "I am the one who came uninvited, but I did not come to take part in the decision-making. I came only to learn how to intercalate the month." Rabbi Gamliel answered, "Sit down, my son, sit down. You are worthy to intercalate all the months of the year, but it was the decision of the rabbis to have only those present who were specially invited for this purpose."

Yet it was not Rabbi Shemuel who was uninvited. It was another rabbi, but wishing to spare him humiliation, Rabbi Shemuel told the others that he himself was the uninvited one. (*Sanhedrin* 11a)

Rabbi Gamliel was one of the rabbis responsible for the adoption of the final version of the *Eighteen Benedictions,* also known as the Amida.

It has been taught: Shimon ha-Pakuli formulated in the proper order the eighteen blessings of the Amida in the presence of R. Gamliel in Yavne. (*Megillah* 17b, *Berachot* 28b)

R. Gamliel used a telescope in order to observe the stars and planets. He had copies of shapes of the moon in its various phases hung on the wall of his office for the examination of witnesses. (*Eruvin* 43b)

The rabbis taught: A year may be intercalated only with the approval of the Nasi. It once happened that R. Gamliel was away in Syria to meet with the governor, and his return was delayed. The year was intercalated without him, but subject to his approval. When R. Gamliel returned, he gave his approval, and the fixed calendar held good. (*Sanhedrin* 11a)

Rabbi Gamliel was asked by a sectarian: "How do we know that the dead will be resurrected?" He replied: "We know it from the Torah, from the Prophets and from the Hagiographa. In book of Devarim (31:16), it is written: "You shall die and rise." (*Sanhedrin* 90b)

The Talmud relates that R. Gamliel was riding on a donkey immediately after Pesah, from Acco to Kheziv. R. Illai was following him. R. Gamliel saw an expensive loaf of bread on the ground and said to R. Illai, "Please pick up the loaf of bread." Further along the road, they met a non-Jew by the name of Mavgai.

R. Gamliel called Mavgai by name and told him to take the loaf of bread. R. Illai approached the stranger and asked him, "Where are you from?"

"I am an attendant at the station-house," the man answered.

"And what is your name?"

"My name is Mavgai."

"Did you ever meet R. Gamliel?"

"No," answered Mavgai.

From this experience we became aware that R. Gamliel had *ruah ha-kodesh.* We also learned three things: One may not leave eatables on the road; we may assume that the food was left on the road by the majority of the travelers, who are non-Jews, and that one may derive benefit from leavened bread that belongs to a non-Jew after Pesah. (*Eruvin* 64b)

In Imma Shalom's vicinity there lived a sectarian judge who had a reputation for never accepting bribes. In order to expose him, Imma Shalom brought him a golden lamp and said to him, "My father left an estate, and I want my share of the inheritance."

The judge ordered the estate divided so that she would receive her share. R. Gamliel argued that according to Torah law, daughters do not inherit if there are sons. The judge replied, "Since the day you were exiled from your land, the law of the Torah has been superseded by other laws that give daughters an equal inheritance." The next day, R. Gamliel brought a Libyan donkey before the judge. At this, the judge reversed his own ruling by declaring, "I have found at the end of the book that it is written, 'I came neither to destroy the Law of Moshe nor to add to it.' And it is written therein that a daughter does not inherit where there is a son."

Imma Shalom said to the judge, "Let your light shine forth like a lamp." R. Gamliel said to him, "A donkey came and knocked the lamp over." (*Shabbat* 116a)

For a glimpse of the world as it was in R. Gamliel's time, see the historical timeline from 50 to 150 C.E.

גמליאל בן יהודה הנשיא
Gamliel ben Yehuda ha-Nasi
(third century C.E.)
Amora, Eretz Yisrael

Rabbi Gamliel, the son of Rabbi Yehuda ha-Nasi, had many outstanding students, some of whom became great scholars and amoraim. Among them were Rabbi Shemuel, Rabbi Hanina, Rabbi Hoshia and Rabbi Yohanan.

Our rabbis taught: When Rebbe was about to die, he said; "I would like to have my sons present." When they came, he instructed them: "Take care to show respect to your mother. The light shall continue to burn in its usual place, the table shall be set in its usual place and my bed shall be made up in its usual place. Yoseph of Haifa and Shimon of Efrat, who attended to me in my lifetime, shall attend on me when I am dead." (*Ketubbot* 103a)

Rebbe then said, "I would like to speak to the sages of Israel." When they entered, he said to them: "Do not lament for me in the smaller towns, and reassemble the academy after thirty days. My son Shimon is to be the Hacham, my son Gamliel shall be the Nasi and Hanina b. Hama is to be Rosh Yeshiva." (*Ketubbot* 103b)

On the day Rebbe died, a *bat kol* was heard announcing: Whoever was present at the death of Rebbe is destined to enjoy the life of the World to Come.

He designated R. Hanina to be rosh yeshiva, but R. Hanina did not accept

because R. Afes was two and a half years his senior, so R. Afes presided.

R. Hanina sat and studied outside the academy and R. Levi joined him. When R. Afes passed away, R. Hanina took over the presidency and R. Levi moved to Babylonia.

Rebbe said: "I would like to speak to my younger son." When R. Shimon entered, Rebbe instructed him in the rules and regulations of being a Hacham.

Rebbe then said, "I would like to see my elder son." When R. Gamliel entered, he instructed him in the traditions and regulations of the patriarchate. He said, "My son, conduct your patriarchate with high-caliber men and keep strong discipline among your students." (*Ketubbot* 103b)

On the day Rebbe died, the rabbis decreed a public fast day. (*Ketubbot* 104a)

R. Gamliel said: "Torah study combined with an occupation is excellent. All Torah study that is not in combination with work is for naught. All who occupy themselves with the community's needs should do so for the sake of heaven." (*Avot* 2:2)

R. Gamliel said: "Beware of the authorities, for they befriend people only for their own benefit. They act friendly when it benefits them, but are not there when one needs them." (*Avot* 2:3)

R. Gamliel said: Make His will your will so that He will treat your will as if it were His will." (*Avot* 2:4)

For a glimpse of the world as it was in the time of R. Gamliel b. Yehuda ha-Nasi, see the historical timeline from 200 to 300 C.E.

גמליאל הזקן
Gamliel ha-Zaken (Gamliel the Elder)

(first century C.E.)
Tanna, Eretz Yisrael

Rabbi Gamliel was a grandson of Rabbi Hillel and president of the Sanhedrin. Many of the great Talmudic scholars, including Shimon of Mitzpeh, Yoezer of Ha-Bira and Nehemia of Beit Dali, were his students.

It once happened that R. Gamliel was sitting on a step on the Temple Mount, and Yohanan, the well-known scribe, was before him, prepared with three sheets of parchment. R. Gamliel said to him: Take one sheet and write instructions to our brethren in Upper Galilee and to those in Lower Galilee, saying: 'Peace be upon you! We are pleased to inform you that the time has arrived for the taking of tithes from the olive heaps.'

"Take another sheet and write to our brethren in the south: 'Peace be upon you! We are pleased to inform you that the time has arrived for the taking of tithes from the corn sheaves.'

"Take another sheet and write to our brethren, the exiles in Babylonia and in Media, and to all the other exiled children of Israel, saying: 'Peace be upon you forever! We are pleased to inform you that the doves are still tender and the lambs still too young and the crops not yet ripe. It seems advisable to me and in the opinion of my colleagues to add thirty days to this year." (*Sanhedrin* 11b)

It once happened that the king and queen instructed their servants to slaughter the Passover offering on their behalf. There was some question as to whether it had been done properly. The king and queen sent the servants to ask

Rabban Gamliel. On another occasion, a lizard was found in the Temple area. Once more, the king and queen sent the servants to Rabban Gamliel to inquire what to do. (*Pesahim* 88b)

R. Gamliel said: Provide yourself a teacher and you will avoid making mistakes. Train yourself to be accurate and not to estimate. (*Avot* 1:16)

R. Kahana said: When R. Yishmael ben R. Yosi b. Halafta became ill, the rabbis sent him the following message: "Tell us two or three things that you heard from your father." He replied: "My father said: 'One hundred and eighty years before the destruction of the Temple, the wicked kingdom of Rome occupied Eretz Yisrael. Eighty years before the destruction of the Temple, the rabbis imposed a state of ritual impurity on certain things. Forty years before the destruction of the Temple, the Sanhedrin went into exile and took its seat in the Temple's commercial area.'" His son Rabbi Shimon ben Gamliel succeeded him as Nasi. His daughter was married to Rabbi Shimon ben Nathanel ha-Kohen. (*Shabbat* 15a)

The Talmud states that when Rabban Gamliel the Elder died, the glory of the Law ceased. (*Sotah* 9:15)

For a glimpse of the world as it was in the time of Rabban Gamliel the Elder, see the historical timeline from 1 to 100 C.E.

גניבא
Geniva

(third–fourth centuries C.E.)

R. Geniva was a close friend of R. Avina.

The Talmud relates that as Geniva, who had been condemned to death, was being led to execution, he instructed the people to give Rabbi Avina four hundred zuz from his wine estate. (*Gittin* 65b)

For a glimpse of the world as it was in R. Geniva's time, see the historical timeline from 250 to 350 C.E.

גביהא דבי כתיל
Geviha of Be-Katil

(fourth–fifth centuries C.E.)

Amora, Babylonia

R. Geviha was a contemporary of R. Ashi and Amemar. R. Geviha confirmed to R. Ashi what R. Abbaye said, and at another time R. Geviha confirmed to R. Ashi, "An interpreter once quoted this statement before Abbaye in just the opposite way." (*Meilah* 10a, *Hullin* 64b)

R. Geviha corrected a statement about Rava: "The report of Rava having blushed is incorrect. It never happened." (*Avodah Zarah* 22a)

For a glimpse of the world as it was in R. Geviha's time, see the historical timeline from 350 to 450 C.E.

גביהא בן פסיסא
Geviha ben Pesisa

(fourth century B.C.E.)

Pre-tannaitic personality

The rabbis taught: The children of the Africans (Phoenicians) came before Alexander the Macedonian in order to make a claim against Israel. They argued that Canaan and its coast belonged to them. Geviha ben Pesisa came before the rabbis and said, "Authorize me to plead against them before Alexander. Should they defeat me, you can claim that they defeated an unlearned person. However, if I defeat them, you can claim that the Torah defeated them." The rabbis gave him authority to argue before Alexander.

Geviha asked the Phoenicians to bring proof for their claim. They said, "It is written in the Torah: 'Canaan with its coastline,' and we are descendants of Canaan." Geviha answered them, "I will also bring proof from the Torah. The Torah says, 'Cursed be Canaan; a servant of servants shall he be to his brethren.' Now the law is that if a slave acquires property it belongs to his master.

Therefore, as a slave of ours your property belongs to us. Furthermore, you have not served us for many years."

Alexander ordered the Phoenicians to respond. They asked for three days to prepare an answer, but when they could not find an answer they fled, leaving their planted fields and vineyards behind. That year happened to be a sabbatical year.

On another occasion, the Egyptians came to Alexander to make a claim against the Israelites. They said: "It is written in the Torah, 'God gave the people favor in the eyes of the Egyptians, and they lent them gold and silver.' Now we want you to repay us for all that gold and silver."

When Geviha ben Pesisa asked the rabbis' permission to go before Alexander and argue against the Egyptians, he received it. Geviha asked the Egyptians to bring proof of their claim. They gave him proof from the Torah, where it says that the Egyptians lent the Israelites gold and silver. Geviha answered, "I will also bring proof from the Torah that Israel does not owe anything to the Egyptians. The Torah says that the Israelites were slaves in Egypt for four hundred and ten years. Now pay us the wages for the labor of six hundred thousand men for four hundred and ten years."

Unable to respond, the Egyptians fled, leaving behind their planted fields and vineyards.

On another occasion the children of Ishmael and the children of Ketura came before Alexander with a claim against the children of Israel. They claimed that the land belonged to them just as much as it did to the Israelites because they are also the children of Abraham. Geviha, who was given authority to argue before Alexander, said to them: "You bring your proof from the Torah, and I will bring proof from the Torah that you are wrong. The Torah says: "'Avraham gave all that he possessed to Yitzhak, and to the children of his concubines he gave gifts and he sent them away.'" (*Sanhedrin* 91a)

For a glimpse of the world as it was in the time of Geviha ben Pesisa, see the historical timeline from 400 to 300 B.C.E.

גידל
Giddal

(third century C.E.)
Amora, Babylonia

R. Giddal, who was a brilliant student of Rav, transmitted many of his teacher's sayings. When Rav passed away, R. Giddal studied in Sura at the academy of R. Huna, who succeeded Rav as head of the academy. He became a close associate of Rabbi Zeira.

It is related that Rabbi Zeira was once sitting behind R. Giddal facing R. Huna during a discussion of a halachic matter about Shabbat. (*Berachot* 49a)

On another occasion, Rabbi Giddal was negotiating for a certain field, but R. Abba bought it in the meantime. R. Giddal was unhappy and complained to R. Zeira, who in turn took the complaint to R. Yitzhak Nepaha, who lived in another town.

R. Zeira told R. Giddal, "Wait until he comes for the festival." When R. Yitzhak came, he asked R. Abba, "If a poor man wants to buy a cake and he is examining it, but in the meantime another man comes and takes it away from him and buys it, what then?"

"He is called a wicked man," replied R. Abba.

"Then why did you buy the field that R. Giddal wanted to buy?"

"I did not know that he was negotiating for it."

R. Yitzchak suggested that now that he knew, he should let R. Giddal have the field. R. Abba replied, "I cannot sell it to him because it is the first field I have ever bought and it is not a good omen to sell it. But if he wants it as a gift, he may have it."

But R. Giddal refused to accept the field as a gift. R. Abba no longer wanted it because R. Giddal had negotiated for it. And so no one took possession of the field, and it was called the rabbis' field. (*Kiddushin* 59a)

R. Giddal said in the name of Rav: "If someone from Naresh gives you a kiss, count your teeth. If a man from Nahar Pakod accompanies you, it is because of the fine garments you wear. If a man from Pumbedita accompanies you, change your address." (*Hullin* 127a)

R. Yehuda permitted R. Giddal to buy wheat from a Bedouin on the day of his holiday. (*Avodah Zarah* 11b)

For a glimpse of the world as it was in R. Giddal's time, see the historical timeline from 200 to 300 C.E.

גידל בר מניומי
Giddal b. Minyumi

(third–fourth centuries C.E.)
Amora, Babylonia

When R. Giddal b. Minyumi was dining with R. Nahman and the latter made a mistake in the blessings after the meal, he went back and recited the blessings once more from the beginning. (*Berachot* 49b)

For a glimpse of the world as it was in the time of R. Giddal b. Minyumi, see the historical timeline from 250 to 350 C.E.

המנונא
Hamnuna

(third century C.E.)
Amora, Babylonia

R. Hamnuna the elder was a student of Rav. (*Bava Kamma* 106a, *Eruvin* 16b)

Rav said to R. Hamnuna: "My son, do good to yourself according to your ability, for there is no enjoyment in the grave and death is not far away." "Children are like the grass in the field. Some blossom and some fade." (*Eruvin* 54a)

R. Hisda and R. Hamnuna were dining together. The attendants set dates and pomegranates before them. R. Hamnuna took some dates and recited a blessing over them. R. Hisda asked him whether he agreed with the rabbis who say one should recite the blessing on the fruit that is mentioned first in the Torah. He replied that the date is mentioned second and the pomegranates fifth. Rabbi Hisda remarked, "If only we had feet of iron so that we could always run and listen to you!" (*Berachot* 41b)

R. Hamnuna said: "Jerusalem was destroyed because the education of children was neglected." (*Shabbat* 119b)

He also stated that Moses brought six hundred thirteen commandments down from Mount Sinai. The numeric value of the word Torah is six hundred and eleven. The two missing commandments are the first two, which the people heard from God himself. (*Makkot* 23b, 24a)

R. Hamnuna said: "The beginning of judgment for a person's deeds is the study of Torah." (*Kiddushin* 40b)

The Talmud does not always refer to a rabbi by name, but instead uses a reference term. When the Talmud states, "They said in the school of Rav," it is referring to Rabbi Hamnuna. (*Sanhedrin* 17b)

For a glimpse of the world as it was in R. Hamnuna's time, see the historical timeline from 200 to 300 C.E.

המנונא
Hamnuna

(fourth century C.E.)
Amora, Babylonia

R. Hamnuna originally was born and raised in Harpania, Babylonia. (*Yevamot* 17a)

R. Hamnuna was sitting before Ulla as they discussed Halacha. R. Ulla made a remark about R. Hamnuna: "What a man! If he had not come from Harpania, he would have been even greater." Seeing that R. Hamnuna was embarrassed, he added a question: "Where do you pay poll taxes?" "I pay poll taxes to Pum Nahara," R. Hamnuna replied. "In that case," said R. Ulla, "you belong to Pum Nahara."

He was a student of Rav Yehuda. (*Shavuot* 34a)

During the lifetime of Rabbi Hisda he was a dayyan, deciding legal cases in Harta de-Argaz; he also taught there in his yeshiva. (*Eruvin* 63a)

R. Hisda was praising R. Hamnuna to R. Huna, saying that he was a great man. R. Huna said, "When he comes to you; bring him to me." When R. Hamnuna arrived, he was not wearing the cap that was customarily worn by married men. R. Huna asked him, "Why aren't you wearing a cap?"

R. Hamnuna answered, "I'm not wearing a cap because I am not married." R. Huna turned his face away from him, saying, "See that you do not come before me before you are married." (*Kiddushin* 29b)

For a glimpse of the world as it was in R. Hamnuna's time, see the historical timeline from 300 to 400 C.E.

המנונא זוטא
Hamnuna Zuta

(fourth century C.E.)
Amora, Babylonia

R. Hamnuna must have had a good singing voice, because the Talmud relates that at the wedding of Mar, Rabbi Ravina's son, they asked Rabbi Hamnuna Zuta to sing a song, and he obliged them. (*Berachot* 31a)

The confession of R. Hamnuna Zuta on Yom Kippur is given in *Berachot* 17a.

For a glimpse of the world as it was in R. Hamnuna Zuta's time, see the historical timeline from 300 to 400 C.E.

הלל
Hillel

(third century C.E.)
Amora, Eretz Yisrael

R. Hillel, the son of Rabbi Gamliel III, was the grandson of Rabbi Yehuda ha-Nasi.

He studied in the academy of his grandfather, Rabbi Yehuda ha-Nasi, and asked him questions. (*Bava Batra* 83b)

It once happened that Yehuda and Hillel, the sons of R. Gamliel, went to bathe in Kabul, and the community criticized them. On another occasion, Yehuda and Hillel the sons of R. Gamliel went out weaing slippers in Biri, in the Galilee, and the community criticized them. (*Pesahim* 51a)

Rabbi Hillel is quoted teaching that a prosbul has to be prepared in a certain manner. Rashi comments (on the same page) that this Rabbi Hillel was an amora. (*Gittin* 37a)

For a glimpse of the world as it was in Rabbi Hillel's time, see the historical timeline from 200 to 300 C.E.

הלל
Hillel

(fourth century C.E.)
Nasi of Sanhedrin, Eretz Yisrael

R. Hillel was active as Nasi in Tiberias from approximately 330 to 365 C.E. The son of R. Yehuda Nesia, he was a grandson of Gamliel IV. During his time, the authorities forbade the observance of the Jewish religion, in particular the intercalation of the Hebrew months. The Jews had to inform each other in secret when the new month was fixed or when Yom Kippur was to be observed.

In order to solve the problem, Rabbi Hillel set the Jewish calendar for all time by means of a complicated calculation.

For a glimpse of the world as it was in Rabbi Hillel's time, see the historical timeline from 300 to 400 C.E.

הלל הזקן
Hillel ha-Zaken

(first century B.C.E.–first century C.E.)
Tanna, Eretz Yisrael
Head of the Sanhedrin in Jerusalem

A native of Babylonia, R. Hillel moved to Jerusalem at the approximate age of forty. Tradition has it that he is a descendant of King David and that he lived to the age of 120.

Elsewhere, the Talmud relates that as a young man, Rabbi Hillel used to work as a day-laborer in order to earn one tropek (an amount equivalent to a dinar). He split his earnings, giving half to the guard for admittance into the study hall and spending the other half on food and necessities. One day, when he had no money, the guard would not let him enter. He climbed up on the roof, which had a window above the lecture hall. There, he listened to the lectures of Rabbis Shemaya and Avtalyon.

This particular day, a Friday, happened to be the winter solstice. As the temperature dropped, Hillel lost consciousness, and overnight, he was covered by snow. On the following morning, which was Shabbat, Shemaya said to Avtalyon. "Every day at this time the room is bright with light, but today it is dark. Is it perhaps a cloudy day?"

They looked up and saw a human figure lying in the skylight. Climbing up, they discovered Hillel covered with three cubits of snow. They removed him from the roof, bathed and anointed him, and set him next to the fire. They said to one another, "This man deserves that Shabbat be profaned on his account." From then on, Hillel gained permanent admittance to their school. (*Yoma* 35b)

Hillel kept on working, earning a slender living by manual labor, but was assisted by his brother Shebna while he studied under Shemaya and Avtalyon.

Later on, during Herod's reign, he was appointed Nasi of the Sanhedrin. It happened because of the following incident:

It is stated: The rabbis of the Bene Betera family were the heads of the Sanhedrin and this halacha was hidden from them. On one occasion, when the fourteenth of Nisan fell on a Shabbat, they did not remember whether the slaughter of the paschal lamb overrides Shabbat. They inquired: Is there anyone who knows this halacha? They were told: "There is a man by the name of Hillel from Babylonia, who studied under Shemaya and Avtalyon, the two greatest men of our time."

They summoned Hillel and asked him. He told the Sanhedrin: Surely we have more than two hundred paschal lambs during the year, which override Shabbat. He quoted verses from the Torah and used logic to prove to them that the slaughter of the paschal lamb

overrides Shabbat. After this incident, which took place in 30 B.C.E., the president of the Sanhedrin resigned and Hillel was elected president. (*Pesahim* 66a)

Hillel and Shammai were one of the zugot (pairs of study partners) mentioned in the Talmud.

Rav Kahana said: When R. Yishmael b. R. Yosi b. Halafta became sick, the rabbis sent him a request: Tell us two or three things that you heard from your father.

He replied; "One hundred and eighty years before the Temple was destroyed, Eretz Yisrael was occupied by the wicked government. Eighty years before the Temple was destroyed, a rabbinical prohibition of ritual impurity was enacted against certain vessels and people. Forty years before the Temple was destroyed, the Sanhedrin went into exile and moved to the commercial zone of the Temple."

During this period, the heads of the Sanhedrin were R. Yosi b. Yoezer, R. Yosi b. Yohanan, R. Hillel, R. Shimon, R. Gamliel and R. Shimon. The Talmud further states that Hillel and his descendants Shimon, Gamliel and Shimon were the leaders of the Sanhedrin for one hundred years during the Temple's existence. (BT *Shabbat* 15a)

R. Hillel, who was the author of the seven rules for the interpretation of the Written Law, was the head of the school known as Beit Hillel.

The prosbul, a halachic device that facilitates the lending of money to the poor, is one of Hillel's innovations. The biblical law canceling all debts in the seventh year became a hardship because the rich refused to lend money to the poor for fear that the money would never be returned. Hillel created the prosbul, whereby the debt was paid to the court, which had the authority to collect it. (*Gittin* 34b and 36a)

Although Hillel and Shammai had many halachic disagreements, they greatly respected each other. In most cases, the school of Shammai was more stringent. Nevertheless, tradition has it that both views are correct, and we follow Rabbi Hillel in the majority of Halachot.

Rabbi Abba said in the name of Rabbi Shemuel: "For three years there was a dispute between Beit Shammai and Beit Hillel, each one claiming that Halacha is in agreement with their views. Then a bat kol (heavenly voice) was heard announcing that while both are the words of the living God, Halacha is in agreement with the rulings of Beit Hillel." The Talmud asks: If both are correct, then how was Beit Hillel found worthy to have Halacha fixed according to them? It answers: Because the members of that school were kind and modest. The Beit Hillel school studied both the rulings of Beit Shammai and their own, and even mentioned Beit Shammai first. (*Eruvin* 13b)

(*Hagiga* 2:2, 16a) At first, Rabbi Hillel's study partner was Rabbi Menahem, but Rabbi Menahem left and Rabbi Shammai took his place. According to some, R. Menahem went into the service of King Herod, while others say that he withdrew into seclusion.

Many great Talmud scholars, including Rabbi Yonatan ben Uzziel and Rabbi Yohanan ben Zakkai, were the students of R. Hillel.

Many stories illustrate the patience of Rabbi Hillel. One such story is that a non-Jew came before Shammai and asked him to convert him to Judaism – and to teach him the Torah while he stands on one leg. Shammai chased him away with a builder's ruler. When the man approached Hillel with the same request, Hillel replied, "I will convert you – and this is what the Torah and Judaism are all about: What is hateful to you, do not impose on your neighbor. That is the whole Torah. The rest is commentary. Now go and study." (*Shabbat* 31a)

A non-Jew approached Shammai and asked him, "How many Torahs do you have?" Shammai answered, "We have two: the Written Torah and the Oral Torah." The non-Jew said to Shammai, "I accept the Written Torah, but not the Oral Torah. Make me a Jew on condition that you teach me only the Written Torah." R. Shammai became angry and chased him out of his house.

The same man came to Hillel with the same request, and Hillel accepted him. On the first day he taught him the letters aleph, beit, gimmel, and dalet, but the following day he taught him the reverse: dalet, gimmel, beit, aleph. The non-Jew complained to Hillel, saying, "Yesterday you taught me differently." Hillel replied, "You must rely on me – not only on what is written, but also on what I tell you. It is the same with the Torah. You must rely not only on the Written Torah, but also on the Oral Torah." (*Shabbat* 31a)

Once there was a person of good family who became impoverished. Hillel obligated himself to provide him with a horse to ride upon and a slave to run before him. On one occasion he could not find a slave to run before him, so he himself ran before him for three miles. (*Ketubbot* 67b)

These are the sayings of Rabbi Hillel: "He that does not add to his knowledge decreases it. He who does not study deserves to die. He who uses the crown of Torah for unworthy purposes shall waste away." (*Avot* 1:13)

"If I am not for myself, who will be for me? Yet if I am for myself only, what am I? And if not now, when?" (*Avot* 1:14)

"Do not separate yourself from the community, do not believe you know it all, and do not judge your friend until you have been put in his position." (*Avot* 2:4)

"Where there is no one able to lead, strive to be a competent leader." (*Avot* 2:5)

"The more flesh, the more worms; the more possessions, the more anxiety." (*Avot* 2:7)

"The more Torah, the more life; the more thought, the more wisdom; the more counsel, the more understanding; the more righteousness, the more peace." (*Avot* 2:8)

Rabbi Shimon ben Lakish said: "In ancient times, when the Torah was forgotten, Ezra came up from Babylon and reestablished it. When it was forgotten again, Hillel came up from Babylon and reestablished it. When it was forgotten again, Rabbi Hiyya and his sons came up and reestablished it." (*Sukkah* 20a)

It was taught: When R. Hillel the Elder rejoiced at the Water Drawing ceremony, he would say, "If I am here, everyone is here, but if I am not here, who is here?" (*Sukkah* 53a)

Our rabbis taught: When Haggai, Zecharyah and Malachi died, *ruah ha-kodesh* departed from Israel. Nevertheless they still had the bat kol to make use of. On one occasion, when the rabbis were sitting in the upper chamber of Gurya's house in Jericho, a bat kol from heaven was heard saying: "Among you is a man who deserves that the Shechina should rest upon him, but his generation is unworthy of it." (*Sotah* 48b)

For a glimpse of the world as it was in R. Hillel's time, see the historical timeline from 50 B.C.E. to 50 C.E.

הושעיא
Hoshia (Hoshaiah)
(third–fourth centuries C.E.)
Amora, Babylonia

R. Hoshia was a student of Rav Yehuda b. Yechezkel and of Rabbi Huna. (*Gittin* 25a, *Bechorot* 37b)

Although at one time he lived in Nehardea and in Pumbedita, later on he moved to Eretz Yisrael and stayed briefly in Caesarea, where he had discussions with Rabbi Ammi, a student of Rabbi Yohanan. (*Shabbat* 19b, *Hullin* 124a)

It is related that Rabbi Yohanan was very anxious to ordain R. Chanina and R. Hoshia, but his hope could not be realized because the presence of three qualified rabbis is required in order to confer ordination, and the opportunity never arrived. This bothered him very much.

They told him, "Master, you need not grieve, for we are descendants of the house of Eli, and it is written that none of the house of Eli is destined to be ordained." (*Sanhedrin* 14a)

R. Yohanan said: "Three kinds of people earn special approval from God: a bachelor who lives in a large city and does not sin, a poor man who returns lost property to its owner, and a rich man who tithes his produce in secret." R. Safra was a bachelor living in a large city. When he heard this quotation, his face lit up. R. Rava said to him, "This does not refer to someone like you, but to people like R. Hanina and R. Hoshia. They are sandal makers in Eretz Yisrael and they live in a neighborhood of prostitutes. They make sandals for them, and when they deal with them they do not lift their eyes to look at them. When the prostitutes take an oath, they do so 'by the life of the holy rabbis of Eretz Yisrael.'" (*Pesahim* 113b)

For a glimpse of the world as it was in R. Hoshia's time, see the historical timeline from 250 to 350 C.E.

הונא
Huna

(third century C.E.)
Amora, Babylonia
Head of the academy in Sura

R. Huna is mentioned hundreds of times in the Talmud.

Although he was poor as a young man, in his later years he became wealthy. (*Megillah* 27b)

One day, R. Huna entered the academy of Rav with a string tied around his waist. Rav asked him, "What is the meaning of this?" He explained that he had no wine for Kiddush and had to pledge his girdle in order to buy wine. Rav blessed him as follows: "May it be the will of God that one day you shall have enough silk robes to be smothered in them."

On the wedding day of R. Huna's son, Rabbah, R. Huna, who was a short man, was lying on a couch, his daughters and daughters-in-law were choosing clothes for themselves. Without noticing R. Huna, they threw silk dresses on the couch until he was smothered in them. When Rav heard of this, he remarked: "When I blessed you, why did you not say, 'The same to you, Sir?'"

He was one of the outstanding students of Rav; he also studied at Rabbi Shemuel and he was a close colleague of Rabbi Hisda. (*Shabbat* 128a, *Sukkah* 32b, *Arachin* 16b)

R. Huna had one son, Rabbah b. Huna.

R. Huna owned sheep that needed the shade during the day and open air at night. On weekdays, a mat would be spread over the area and removed for the night, but on Shabbat, R. Huna was concerned this might be an act of construction, which is forbidden on that day. He asked his teacher, Rav, what to do. Rav advised him to roll up the mat on Friday evening before Shabbat but to leave a handbreadth unrolled, so that the next morning when the mat was unrolled, R. Huna would only be adding to an existing temporary tent.

Once, R. Huna suffered great financial loss when four hundred jars of his wine turned sour. Rav Yehuda, the brother of R. Sala Hasida, and the other rabbis visited him, though some say it was R. Adda b. Ahava and other rabbis who visited him. They said to him; "Master, you ought to examine your deeds."

He asked them, "Do you find me suspect?"

They answered him: "Is God to be suspected of punishing unjustly?"

He declared, "If somebody has heard that I am accused of any misdeed, let him speak."

They replied, "We heard that the master does not give his tenant his lawful share of vine twigs."

He replied, "Does he leave me any? He steals them all."

They said to him, "That is exactly what the proverb says. If you steal from a thief, a taste of his theft remains with you."

He said to the rabbis: "I take upon myself to give him his share in the future."

It was reported that after this visit, the vinegar became wine again. Others say that the price of vinegar increased so much that R. Huna sold the vinegar for the same price as wine. (*Taanit* 20b)

The Talmud relates that Rabbah said to Rafram b. Papa: "Tell me some of the good deeds Rabbi Huna has done." He replied: "On cloudy days they used to drive him in his golden carriage to survey every part of the city of Sura. When he saw walls that were unsafe he would order them to be demolished, and if the owner could not afford to rebuild them he would rebuild them at his own expense.

On Friday afternoons he would send messengers to the market and buy all the leftover vegetables.

Whenever he discovered a new medicine, he would suspend it above his door with a jug of water next to it, and would place a notice with it that stated that anyone in need of it should come and take it.

Whenever he ate a meal, he would open his doors wide open and announce, "Whoever is in need of a meal, come and eat."

He came from Babylonia from a town called Drukeret. Once, when a fire broke out there, it did not spread to the neighborhood where R. Huna lived. People thought that it was in the merit of R. Huna, but in a dream it was made clear that it was far too small a matter to need R. Huna's great merit. Rather, it was in the merit of a woman who heated her house on Friday nights and let her neighbors make use of it.

He was appointed head of the Sura academy, where he served for forty years. (*Taanit* 21b)

R. Huna had many litigants who asked him to hear their lawsuits. He would tell them: "Find me a man who will draw water for me so that I will have the time to be your judge." (*Ketubbot* 105a)

R. Huna said in the name of Rav, who learned it from R. Meir, who learned it from R. Akiva: "A person should always say: 'Whatever happens, God has done it for a good purpose.'" As the following story illustrates:

R. Huna said in the name of Rav, who learned it from R. Meir, who learned it from R. Akiva, "One should always say: 'Whatever God does is for

the good.' By way of illustration, once, when R. Akiva was traveling, he arrived at a certain town. He was traveling with a rooster, a donkey and a lamp. He looked around in the town for lodging, but none was available. Saying to himself, 'Whatever God does is for the good,' he slept in an open field. A strong wind came and blew out the lamp, a wild cat came and ate the rooster, and a lion came and ate the donkey. He said again, 'Whatever God does is for the good.' During the same night, a band of raiders came and captured all the inhabitants of the town and carried them away. He said: 'Did I not say that whatever God does is for the good?'"

He must have learned it from R. Nachum Ish Gam Zu, who was the teacher of R. Akiva for many years. (*Berachot* 60b)

Rabbi Huna asked his son Rabbah, "Why do you not attend Rabbi Hisda's lectures, which are so sharp and enlightening?"

"Why should I? He talks about profane matters most of the time. He speaks about how one should behave in the toilet – not to sit down abruptly or to strain the rectum, because the glands might become dislocated."

R. Huna became annoyed with his son and said to him: "He is discussing matters that pertain to health, and you call them profane? All the more reason to attend his lectures!" (*Shabbat* 82a)

R. Zerika said to R. Safra: "Come and see the difference in style between the good men of Eretz Yisrael and the pious men of Babylonia. When the world was in need of rain, the pious men of Babylonia, R. Huna and R. Hisda said, 'Let us pray. Perhaps the Almighty might be reconciled and send us rain.' But the great men of Eretz Yisrael, such as R. Yonah the father of R. Mani, would go and stand in a low spot dressed in sackcloth and pray for rain." (*Taanit* 23b)

The Talmud states that when the majority of the rabbis departed from the academy of Rav in Sura there still remained behind twelve hundred students. When the students left the academy of R. Huna in Sura there remained behind eight hundred students. (*Ketubbot* 106a)

When R. Huna delivered a lecture, thirteen interpreters assisted him.

When the students left the academy of Rabbah and R. Yoseph in Pumbedita there remained four hundred students, who described themselves as orphans.

When the students left the academy of R. Abbaye – others say the academy of R. Pappa and still others say from the academy of R. Ashi – two hundred rabbis remained, who described themselves as orphans of the orphans.

R. Huna said in Rav's name, others say R. Huna said in Rav's name, which he heard from R. Meir: "One should always teach his student to use concise language and refined speech." (*Pesahim* 3b)

R. Helbo said in the name of Rav Huna: "If one knows that his friend is used to greet him; do not wait for him to greet you, greet him first instead." (*Shabbat* 23b)

R. Helbo attributed the following sayings to R. Huna: "If one has a fixed place when he prays in the synagogue, then the God of Avraham comes to his aid."

"When a man leaves the synagogue he should not be in a hurry."

"One should always be particularly careful about the afternoon prayers. Eliyahu ha-Navi prayed in the afternoon and was answered favorably."

"A person should partake of the wedding meal and make the newlyweds merry." (*Berachot* 6b)

R. Huna used to say: "One who lights his house well will have scholarly sons. One who is careful to place a mezuza on the doorpost of his house will merit a beautiful home. One who is observant in wearing tzitzit will merit a beautiful garment. One who is observant in making Kiddush will merit full barrels of wine." (*Shabbat* 23b)

R. Huna used to pass the house of R. Avin the carpenter frequently. Upon noticing that many lights were always lit inside, he remarked, "Two great men will be born to him," and so it was. R. Avin's sons were R. Idi b. Avin and R. Hiyya b. Avin. (*Berachot* 6b)

When the Talmud mentions "the elders of Sura," it is referring to Rabbi Huna and Rabbi Hisda. (*Sanhedrin* 17b)

According to the Talmud, R. Huna was at least eighty years old when he died. (*Moed Katan* 28a)

When R. Huna died suddenly, the rabbis of the academy were surprised that he died in such a way. Zoga of Adiabene said, "When one dies at the age of strength, which is eighty, a sudden death is tantamount to dying by the Divine Kiss."

When R. Huna passed away, they brought him to Eretz Yisrael for burial. People told R. Ammi and R. Assi that R. Huna had come. They said, "When we were in Babylonia, he was so great that we could not raise our heads on account of him, and now that we are here, he has come after us?" They were told that it was his coffin that had arrived. R. Ammi and R. Assi went out to pay him their last respects. (*Moed Katan* 25a)

When the people wanted to place a sefer Torah on the bier, Rabbi Hisda stopped them because Rabbi Huna would not have approved. (*Moed Katan* 25a)

He was buried next to R. Hiyya in the cave of Tiberias.

For a glimpse of the world as it was in Rav Huna's time, see the historical timeline from 200 to 300 C.E.

הונא
Huna

(second century C.E.)
Amora, Babylonia
Resh Galuta (Exilarch)

Tradition has it that when he died he was taken to Eretz Yisrael and buried in Beit Shearim. He was a contemporary of R. Yehuda ha-Nasi.

R. Huna said: strife is similar to an opening made by a rush of water that widens as the water pushes through the opening. (*Sanhedrin* 7a)

Rabbah said in the name of R. Sechora in the name of R. Huna: "If a person studies too much at a time, his learning decreases, but if he studies a little at a time, his knowledge increases." Rabbah remarked, "The rabbis were aware of this advice, but disregarded it." R. Nahman b. Yitzhak said, "I acted on this advice and it benefited me greatly." (*Eruvin* 54b)

For a glimpse of the world as it was in R. Huna's time, see the historical timeline from 100 to 200 C.E.

הונא בר נתן
Huna bar Natan

(fourth–fifth centuries C.E.)
Amora, Babylonia
Resh Galuta

In addition to being a great scholar, R. Huna was also Exilarch of the Jewish people in Babylonia and a friend of Izgedar I, the king of Persia.

Rabbi Ashi said, Rabbi Huna once told me. "I was standing next to Izgedar, the king of Persia, and my girdle (the insignia of the Exilarch) was pushed high up. He reached over and pulled my girdle down, observing to me. "It is written of you: You shall be unto me a kingdom of priests and a holy nation."

R. Huna was a contemporary of R. Ashi, R. Nahman b. Yitzhak, R. Papa and R. Amemar, with whom he had halachic discussions. (*Zevahim* 19a)

R. Huna was also a humble person, as can be seen from this discussion.

"The bride turns her face away:" (*Pesahim* 86b) What is the reason? R. Hiyya b. Abba said in R. Yohanan's name: It shows modesty.

R. Huna b. Natan visited the home of R. Nahman b. Yitzhak. They asked him: "What is your name?"

He replied, "Rav Huna."

"Would you sit down?" He sat down. They offered him a cup to drink and he accepted it without hesitation, but drank from it twice. They asked him: "What is the reason you called yourself Rav Huna?"

"That is my name."

"What is the reason you sat down when asked?"

"Whatever the host asks, one should do."

"What is the reason you accepted the drink on the first offering?"

"One must not show reluctance to a great man."

"Why did you drink twice?"

"He who drinks his cup in one gulp is considered to be a glutton. Two gulps show good breeding. Three gulps show arrogance."

"Why did you not turn your face away?"

"Only a bride turns her face away."

Amemar permitted R. Huna b. Nathan to take a wife from Khuzestan, even though it is not within the boundaries of Babylon as defined by the rabbis. R. Ashi questioned R. Ameimar on this. He answered that this is the view of R. Meir. (*Kiddushin* 72b)

R. Pappa was once visiting R. Huna b. Natan. After they finished their meal, they brought some additional food to the table. R. Pappa took some food and ate. They said to him: "Don't you hold that after the meal is concluded it is forbidden to eat?"

He replied, "The proper term is 'when the food is removed.'" (*Berachot* 42a)

Rabbi Aha, the son of Rava, said: "Between Rabbi Yehuda ha-Nasi and Rabbi Ashi there was no one who was supreme in Torah and in worldly affairs." He was asked: "Is that really so? What about Rabbi Huna ben Natan?" He answered, "That is different because Rabbi Huna deferred to Rabbi Ashi." (*Gittin* 59a)

For a glimpse of the world as it was in the time of R. Huna bar Natan, see the historical timeline from 350 to 450 C.E.

הונא בר יהושע
Huna b. Yoshua

(fourth century C.E.)
Amora, Babylonia

Rabbi Huna, who was a student of Rabbi Abbaye, was a close friend of Rabbi Papa. He was also a student of R. Idi b. Avin.

He became the deputy for Rabbi Papa in the Naresh academy.

Rabbi Papa and Rabbi Huna both had dreams that they walked into a lake, but Rabbi Papa dreamt that he was carrying a drum as he did so. On the other hand, R. Huna dreamt that he only walked into a lake. Rabbi Papa became the head of the academy and Rabbi Huna became his deputy. (*Berachot* 57a)

R. Abbaye was walking along with R. Papa on his right and R. Huna b. Yoshua on his left. When R. Abbaye noticed some demons approaching, he transferred R. Papa to his left and R. Huna to his right. R. Papa asked R. Abbaye, "What is different about me that you were not afraid on my behalf?"

R. Abbaye answered, "The time is in your favor." (*Pesahim* 111b)

R. Papa and R Huna b. Yoshua sat before R. Idi b. Avin studying, while R. Idi dozed off. The two students were going back and forth with arguments, but could not come up with an answer. In the meantime, R. Idi woke up and gave them the answer without asking what they were arguing about. (*Pesahim* 35a)

Rava was serving drinks at his son's wedding. When he offered drinks to R. Papa and to R. Huna b. Yoshua, they stood up before him out of respect. (*Kiddushin* 32b)

R. Huna b. Yoshua said: May I be rewarded for never having walked four cubits bareheaded. (*Shabbat* 118b)

Once R. Huna was very ill, and R. Papa went to visit him. When he saw that he was very sick, he told the people, "Make ready for his trip to heaven."

When R. Huna recovered, R. Papa was embarrassed for having thought that it was the end. He asked him: "What did you see?"

He answered him. "You were right. It was indeed my end, but the Almighty said to the angels: 'He deserves to live longer because he has never insisted on his rights and is a forgiving person.'" (*Rosh ha-Shannah* 17a)

R. Papa and R. Huna bought sesame seeds on the bank of Nahar Malka. They hired a boatman to bring the merchandise across the river, with a guarantee against any accident that might happen. However, the canal was blocked and they could not deliver the merchandise. They told the boatman to hire donkeys and make the delivery because he had guaranteed it. The boatman appealed to Rava, who ruled against R. Papa and R. Huna, saying, "White ducks that strip men of their clothing – this is an exceptional kind of situation." (*Gittin* 73a)

A man who had bought a boatload of wine was looking for a place to store it. A certain woman had a storage room, but she was not willing to rent it to him. He decided to marry her and was able to use her storage room for his wine. Soon after the marriage, he wrote her a bill of divorce and sent it to her. She hired porters, paid them the proceeds from having sold some of the man's wine, and had the wine put out on the street. The matter came before R. Huna b. Yoshua, who said: "As he did, so let it be done to him. She can say to him: 'I am willing to rent the place to anyone but you, because you are like a lion in ambush.'" (*Bava Metzia* 101b)

Rava instructed R. Papa and R. Huna b. Yoshua: "When a written legal decision of mine comes before you and you find an objection to it, do not tear it up before you speak to me. If I have valid reasons for my decision, I will tell them to you, and if not, I will withdraw my ruling. After my death, you shall neither tear it up nor draw any conclusions from it. Do not tear it up because had I been there I might have given you my reasons, and do not draw any conclusions, because a judge must be guided by what his own eyes see." (*Bava Batra* 130b)

It is related R. Nahman, who was the regular lecturer on Shabbat, was about to deliver his lecture. However, it was his custom to run over his text with R. Adda b. Abba before delivering it, and only then would he deliver his lecture.

But this Shabbas R. Papa and R. Huna b. Yehoshua approached R. Adda b. Abba and asked him to recite the lecture that they had missed the day before. They asked, "Tell us how Rava explained the law of tithing." He repeated the entire lecture for them. In the meantime, R. Nahman was waiting for R. Adda to go over his lecture with him, and it was getting late. The rabbis told R. Nachman: "Come to lecture. It is late. Why are you still sitting?" (*Bava Batra* 22a)

When R. Papa and R. Huna b. Yoshua once came before Rava, he asked them, "Have you learned this particular tractate and the other tractate?" They replied in the affirmative. "Are you a little richer?" "Yes," they replied, "because we bought some land." Rava exclaimed with joy, "Happy are the righteous who are rewarded in this world also!" (*Horayot* 10b)

One of the rabbis was discussing the subject of Mount Sinai and why it is called Sinai with R. Kahana. Then he asked him: "Why don't you attend the lectures of R. Papa and R. Huna b. Yoshua, who delve deep into *aggadata*?" (*Shabbat* 89a)

For a glimpse of the world as it was in the time of R. Huna b. Yoshua, see the historical timeline from 300 to 400 C.E.

הונה ציפוראה
Huna of Sepphoris

(third–fourth centuries C.E.)
Amora, Eretz Yisrael

R. Huna, a student of R. Yohanan, quoted his teacher frequently. (*Rosh ha-Shannah* 34b)

R. Pinhas said in the name of R. Huna of Sepphoris: "The spring that comes out of the Holy of Holies resembles the horns of locusts, and farther on, when it reaches the entrance to the Temple court, it becomes as large as the mouth of a small bottle." (*Yoma* 77b)

For a glimpse of the world as it was in the time of R. Huna of Sepphoris, see the historical timeline from 250 to 350 C.E.

אידי בר אבין
Idi bar Avin
(fourth century C.E.)
Amora, Babylonia

R. Idi, a student of Rabbi Hisda, discussed halachic matters with Abbaye and Rava. (*Pesahim* 101b, *Bava Metzia* 35b)

Among his students were Rabbi Papa and Rabbi Huna b. Yoshua. They sat before R. Idi b. Avin studying while R. Idi dozed off. The two students argued back and forth, but could not come up with an answer. In the meantime, R. Idi awoke and, without asking them what they had been discussing, gave them the answer. His sons, Rabbi Sheshet and Rabbi Yoshua, were outstanding scholars. (*Pesahim* 35a)

Although R. Idi was not a Kohen, he ate the priestly portion on behalf of his wife, who was the daughter of a Kohen. (*Hullin* 132a)

R. Idi said: A person who is suspected of selling non-kosher meat cannot be rehabilitated unless he moves to a place where he is unknown and finds an opportunity to return a lost article of considerable value, or to take a heavy loss when a piece of meat belonging to him becomes unfit to eat. (*Sanhedrin*)

R. Huna used to say, "One who lights his house well will have scholarly sons. R. Huna used to pass the house of R. Avin the carpenter frequently. Upon noticing that many lights were always lit inside the house, he remarked, "Two great men will be born to him," and so it was. R. Idi b. Avin and R. Hiyya b. Avin were born to him. (*Shabbat* 23b)

For a glimpse of the world as it was in the time of Idi bar Avin, see the historical timeline from 300 to 400 C.E.

איקא בר אמי
Ika b. R. Ammi
(third–fourth centuries C.E.)
Amora, Babylonia

The proselyte Issur had twelve thousand zuz deposited for safekeeping with Rava, but the question arose as to whether Issur's son Mari was entitled to the money. The problem was that when Mari was conceived Issur was not yet Jewish, but became Jewish before Mari was born. R. Ika b. R. Ammi suggested that Issur should declare that the money belongs to R. Mari. That is how the matter was solved: Issur declared that the money belonged to his son, Mari. (*Bava Batra* 149a)

For a glimpse of the world as it was in the time of R. Ika b. R. Ammi, see the historical timeline from 250 to 350 C.E.

אילפא
Ilfa
(third century C.E.)
Amora, Eretz Yisrael

R. Ilfa, a student of Rabbi Yehuda ha-Nasi, also studied under Rabbi Yehuda bar Hiyya and Bar Pada. (*Zevahim* 13b)

Rabbi Ilfa and Rabbi Yohanan studied together, but had no income. Although they spoke to each other about going into business, Rabbi Yohanan had a dream warning not to do so and therefore continued to study. Rabbi Ilfa decided to seek employment. Years later, when Rabbi Ilfa returned to the community, Rabbi Yohanan presided over his academy. The scholars teased him by telling him, "If you had remained here to study, you might have presided over the academy." In order to prove to the scholars that he had indeed studied, Ilfa suspended himself from the mast of a ship and shouted, "Let anyone ask me a question from a baraita of Rabbi Hiyya and Rabbi Oshaya. If I do not know the subject, then I will throw myself into the water to drown!" An old man came forward and asked a question, and Rabbi Ilfa provided the correct answer. (*Taanit* 21a)

Once, during a drought, Rabbi Yehuda ha-Nasi ordained a fast, but no rain fell. R. Ilfa went before the ark and recited the prayers for rain, and rain fell.

Rebbe asked him, "What is your special merit?"

He answered, "I live in a remote and poverty-stricken neighborhood where wine for kiddush and havdalah is hard to come by. I make sure that I have wine, and in this way I help others to fulfill the mitzvah of kiddush." (*Taanit* 24a)

For a glimpse of the world as it was in R. Ilfa's time, see the historical timeline from 200 to 300 C.E.

אלעי
Illai

(first–second centuries C.E.)
Tanna, Eretz Yisrael

Rabbi Illai studied with Rabbi Eliezer ben Hyrcanus, Rabbi Yehoshua, Rabbi Eleazar ben Azaryah, and Rabbi Yishmael.

One of his well-known sayings is the following: "A man's character can be determined by three things: his cup, his purse and his anger. Some say also by his laughter."

The Talmud relates that R. Gamliel was riding on a donkey immediately after Pesah, from Acco to Kheziv. R. Illai was following him. R. Gamliel saw an expensive loaf of bread on the ground and said to R. Illai, "Please pick up the loaf of bread." Further along the road, they met a non-Jew by the name of Mavgai.

R. Gamliel called Mavgai by name and told him to take the loaf of bread. R.

Illai approached the stranger and asked him, "Where are you from?"

"I am an attendant at the station-house," the man answered.

"And what is your name?"

"My name is Mavgai."

"Did you ever meet R. Gamliel?"

"No," answered Mavgai.

From this experience we became aware that R. Gamliel had *ruah ha-kodesh*. We also learned three things: One may not leave eatables on the road; we may assume that the food was left on the road by the majority of the travelers, who are non-Jews, and that one may derive benefit from leavened bread that belongs to a non-Jew after Pesah. (*Eruvin* 64b)

He quotes Rabbi Eliezer with regards to the rules of carrying on Shabbat. (*Eruvin* 2:6, 23a)

R. Illai said: If one has a great urge to sin and one cannot overcome his urges; rather than sin publicly one should go to a place where no one knows him, put on black garments and do as his heart desires, but let him not profane the Name of heaven publicly. (*Hagigah* 16a)

For a glimpse of the world as it was in R. Illai's time, see the historical timeline from 50 to 150 C.E.

אלעי
Illai

(third–fourth centuries C.E.)
Amora, Eretz Yisrael

R. Illai, who was a student of Rabbi Yohanan and of Rabbi Shimon ben Lakish, was a colleague of Rabbi Zeira, Rabbi Ammi and Rabbi Assi. (*Shabbat* 5a)

He quotes Rabbi Shimon ben Lakish as saying in the name of Rabbi Meir: "The *tahash*, which is mentioned in the Torah, was a separate species particular to those days. It had a single horn on its forehead and it came to Moses providentially, just for that occasion. Moshe made the Tabernacle cover from its skin." After that period, the *tahash* disappeared. (*Shabbat* 28b)

R. Illai stated; "They ordained in Usha that a man should not give more than a fifth of his assets to charity." (*Ketubbot* 50a)

R. Avin said in the name of R. Illai: "Whenever the words *hishamer, pen*, and *al* appear in the Torah, they denote a negative precept." (*Eruvin* 96a)

R. Illai and R. Abbahu used enigmatic speech. When he was asked, "Show us where R. Abbahu is hiding," he answered with an enigma. (*Eruvin* 53b)

For a glimpse of the world as it was in R. Illai's time, see the historical timeline from 250 to 350 C.E.

איו
Iyo
(second century C.E.)
Tanna, Eretz Yisrael

R. Iyo was a student of R. Yehuda b. Illai.

R. Iyo was quoting R. Yehuda about making two conditions simultaneously. As the Talmud continues to debate the issue, it quotes R. Iyo again in subsequent pages. (*Eruvin* 36b)

For a glimpse of the world as it was in R. Iyo's time, see the historical timeline from 100 to 200 C.E.

כהנא
Kahana I
(second–third centuries C.E.)
Amora, Babylonia

R. Kahana was a close associate of Rabbi Assi. Both men studied with Rav, who held them in high esteem, in the academy at Sura. (*Sanhedrin* 36b, *Nazir* 19a, *Betzah* 6a, 37b)

One time, when Rav visited a certain place, he did not act according to his own rulings out of respect for the local

rabbis. Who were they? R. Kahana and R. Assi. (*Shabbat* 146b)

Later on, when R. Kahana lived in Eretz Yisrael, he studied with the rabbis, who were considered tannaim, such as Rabbi Shimon, the son of Rabbi Yehuda ha-Nasi, Rabbi Yehuda and Rabbi Hizkiya, the sons of Rabbi Hiyya. He also studied with Rabbi Yohanan and Resh Lakish. Among his students were Rabbi Zeiri and Rabbi Eleazar ben Pedat.

When Rabbi Kahana had a hard time making a living; Rav advised him: "Flay carcasses in the marketplace, but earn a living. Do not say, 'I am a kohen and a great man, and this type of work is beneath my dignity." (*Pesahim* 113a)

When a person who had once hosted Rav came before him in a lawsuit against another man, he said to Rav, "Were you not once a guest in my house?"

"Yes," said Rav. "What can I do for you?"

"I have a case before you."

"If so, I must recuse myself as your judge."

Rav turned to R. Kahana and said, "You be the judge for this case." When R. Kahana noticed that the man was relying too much on his acquaintance with Rav, he told the man, "If I am to be your judge, you must put Rav out of your mind." (*Sanhedrin* 7b, 8a)

Rav Kahana said: When R. Yishmael b. R. Yosi b. Halafta became sick, the rabbis sent him a request: Tell us two or three things that you heard from your father.

He replied; "One hundred and eighty years before the Temple was destroyed, Eretz Yisrael was occupied by the wicked government. Eighty years before the Temple was destroyed, a rabbinical prohibition of ritual impurity was enacted against certain vessels and people. Forty years before the Temple was destroyed, the Sanhedrin went into exile and moved to the commercial zone of the Temple." During this period, the heads of the Sanhedrin were R. Yosi b. Yoezer, R. Yosi b. Yohanan, R. Hillel, R. Shimon, R. Gamliel and R. Shimon. (BT *Shabbat* 15a)

R. Kahana said: If the Sanhedrin voted unanimously to convict the defendant, the verdict is annulled and the defendant acquitted. (*Sanhedrin* 17a)

For a glimpse of the world as it was in the time of Kahana I, see the historical timeline from 150 to 250 C.E.

כהנא
Kahana II

(third century C.E.)
Amora, Babylonia

R. Kahana, who was a student of Rav in Babylonia, was also associated with Rabbi Shemuel.

Rabbi Kahana had to flee Babylonia because of the following incident. A man who planned to denounce another Jew to the Persian authorities and show them where he was hiding his straw was brought before Rav. Rav ordered the man not to do so, but the man insisted. "I will." Rabbi Kahana, who was present during this incident, became enraged that the man was defying Rav, and during the argument he struck him, killing him accidentally. Rav advised Rabbi Kahana to move to Eretz Yisrael and to study under Rabbi Yohanan, but made him promise that for seven years he would not give Rabbi Yohanan a hard time with his sharp questions.

When Kahana arrived, he found Resh Lakish going over the lecture with the young rabbis. When he sat down to listen, he pointed out the difficult points in the lecture and also provided some of the answers.

Resh Lakish went to R. Yohanan and told him, "A lion has come up from Babylonia. Be well prepared for tomorrow's lecture." The next day, R. Kahana was seated in the first row because Resh Lakish thought him a scholar. But he kept quiet for a long while, as he had promised Rav. Consequently, the scholars of the academy demoted him, seating him in the seventh row.

R. Yohanan said to Resh Lakish, "It looks like the lion is a fox."

Rabbi Kahana prayed that the humiliation that he had suffered in having been demoted to the seventh row be considered equivalent to the seven years during which he had promised Rav not to ask R. Yohanan difficult questions. The next day, when Rabbi Yohanan lectured, he threw out one question after another, quoting sources in contradiction. After this, the academy's scholars seated him in the first row once more. (*Bava Kamma* 117a)

R. Kahana said, "Had I not married a priest's daughter, I would not have gone into exile." The rabbis said to him, "But you were exiled to a place of learning." He retorted, "I was not exiled as people are normally exiled." (*Pesahim* 49a)

For a glimpse of the world as it was in Kahana II's time, see the historical timeline from 200 to 300 C.E.

כהנא
Kahana III

(third century C.E.)
Amora, Babylonia

Rabbi Kahana studied under Rabbi Huna in the Sura academy and under Rabbi Yehuda b. Yehezkel in the Pumbedita academy. (*Moed Katan* 13b, *Hullin* 19b)

The land of R. Kahana was flooded by a dam, which was breached. He built a fence around the dam on the property of another man. They took the case to R. Yehuda and they brought witnesses. One witness said that R. Kahana encroached on two rows of the other man's land, and the other witness said he encroached on three rows. R. Yehuda told R. Kahana to compensate the man for two rows. (*Bava Batra* 41a, b)

R. Kahana discusses King Cyrus, contending that his demeanor has not changed. (*Rosh ha-Shannah* 3a, b)

R. Yoseph sat behind R. Kahana, who sat before R. Yehuda. He said the following: "Israel will hold a festival when Tarmod is destroyed." (*Yevamot* 17a)

For a glimpse of the world as it was in the time of Kahana III, see the historical timeline from 200 to 300 C.E.

כהנא
Kahana IV

(fourth century C.E.)
Amora, Babylonia

R. Kahana was a student of Rabbah b. Nachmeini in the Pumbedita academy. (*Sanhedrin* 41b)

He had already studied the entire Talmud by the time he was eighteen. His close associates were Rabbi Aha b. Huna, Rabbi Rama b. Hama and Rabbi Safra. (*Shabbat* 63a)

Rabbi Kahana joined Rabbi Safra on a trip abroad and remained with him for a while. He earned a living by selling baskets to the people in his town.

The Talmud relates that when he came to the house of a Roman woman to sell the baskets she tried to seduce him; he excused himself to clean up first. He went to the roof and jumped. The Angel Elijah flew towards him and caught him in mid-air, rescuing him from certain death. Elijah then complained to him. "You caused me to have to fly four hundred parasangs to save you." "What

caused me to end up in this kind of situation?" he asked. "Is it not my poverty?" Thereupon Elijah gave him a shifa full of dinari. (*Kiddushin* 40a)

For a glimpse of the world as it was in the time of Kahana IV, see the historical timeline from 300 to 400 C.E.

כהנא
Kahana V

(fourth century C.E.)
Amora, Babylonia
Head of the academy in Pum Nahara

One of his prominent students was Rabbi Ashi, the redactor of the Babylonian Talmud. (*Berachot* 39a)

Rabbi Kahana was the head of the yeshiva at Pum Nahara. (*Hullin* 95b)

R. Ashi stated: When we were at the academy of R. Kahana we authorized the collection of money that was due to a daughter. (*Ketubbot* 69a)

Rabbi Hanan of Nehardea was a close associate of R. Kahana.

Rabbi Kahana's son was very wealthy. R. Zevid told R. Kahana that his daughter-in-law threw gold around as if it were worthless. (*Meilah* 19a)

R. Kahana escorted R. Shimi b. Ashi from Pum Nahara to Beit Zenitha in Babylonia. When they arrived, he asked him: "Do people really say that these palm trees date all the way back to Adam?"

He answered, "Your question reminds me of a saying by R. Yosi b. Hanina: 'Any land that was decreed by Adam to be inhabited became inhabited, and any land that Adam decreed to be uninhabited is still uninhabited.'" (*Berachot* 31a)

R. Abba said, "On Shabbat, one must break bread over two loaves." R. Ashi said, "I saw R. Kahana holding two loaves, but he broke only one of them." (*Shabbat* 117b)

When certain merchants came to Pum Nahara to sell their merchandise, the town's people tried to stop them from selling. They appealed to R. Kahana, who told them, "The townspeople have a right to stop you." They argued, "The people in this town owe us money." R. Kahana told them, "You may sell enough to sustain you until you collect your debt, but after that you must leave." (*Bava Batra* 22a)

For a glimpse of the world as it was in the time of Kahana V, see the historical timeline from 300 to 400 C.E.

קרנא
Karna

(third century C.E.)
Amora, Babylonia

Shemuel and Karna were sitting by the bank of the Nahar Malka. They saw the water rising and becoming discolored. Shemuel said to Karna: "A great man is arriving from Eretz Yisrael who suffers from stomach trouble. Go and smell his bottle." (*Shabbat* 108a)

The man who arrived was Rav. Karna went and asked him several tricky questions in order to test his knowledge. Subsequently Shemuel took him into his house and gave him barley bread, fish and strong liquor, but did not show him where the outhouse was. Rav was annoyed with him because of it.

There was a disagreement between R. Shemuel and Karna regarding the divorce of a minor. It was sent to the court of Mar Ukva in the town of Kafri, where a decision was made, but it was then sent to Rav for his ruling. (*Kiddushin* 44b)

Karna, who was a judge, used to take a fixed fee from both parties before he informed them of his decision. (*Ketubbot* 105a)

Karna received compensation for loss of work that could be proved, for he was occupied regularly as a wine smeller and taster for which he was paid a fee.

The Talmud asks whether this is against a prohibition of the Torah. The Talmud explains that Karna received compensation for loss of work time. Since Karna was regularly employed in a wine shop, when he took time out to act as a judge, he incurred a loss of time and money. This is similar to the case of R. Huna who, when a lawsuit was brought before him, would tell the litigants, "Find me a man who will draw the water for my fields and I will serve as your judge."

For a glimpse of the world as it was in Karna's time, see the historical timeline from 200 to 300 C.E.

כרוספדאי
Keruspedai

(third century C.E.)
Amora, Eretz Yisrael

R. Keruspedai was a student of Rabbi Yohanan.

R. Keruspedai said in the name of R. Yohanan: "Three books are opened in heaven on Rosh ha-Shannah: one for the completely wicked, one for the completely righteous and one for those in between. The completely righteous are immediately inscribed for life, the completely wicked are immediately inscribed for death and the fate of those in between is suspended from Rosh ha-Shannah till Yom Kippur. If they are worthy, they are inscribed for life. If not, they are inscribed for death. (*Rosh ha-Shannah* 16b)

R. Keruspedai said in the name of R. Yohanan: If an ox was condemned to be stoned and the witnesses proved to be false, whoever takes possession of the ox is the legal owner. (*Keritot* 24a)

For a glimpse of the world as it was in the time of R. Keruspedai, see the historical timeline from 200 to 300 C.E.

לוי

Levi

(second–third centuries C.E.)
Amora, Eretz Yisrael and Babylonia

R. Levi was a student and colleague of Rabbi Yehuda ha-Nasi. (*Berachot* 49a)

When Rabbi Yehuda ha-Nasi died, he left instructions. One was that R. Hanina bar Hama preside at the academy. However, R. Hanina did not accept the position because R. Afes was two and a half years older. Therefore, R. Afes became president of the academy. (*Ketubbot* 103b)

R. Hanina did not attend the studies inside the academy, but instead studied outside in the company of Rabbi Levi. When Rabbi Afes passed away and R. Hanina bar Hama took over the presidency, R. Levi was left without a study partner. As a result, he moved to Babylonia.

The Talmud relates that Rav was told, "A great man who is tall and lame has come to Nehardea to lecture." Rav remarked, "It must be Rabbi Levi, and it must be that Rabbi Afes died and Rabbi Hanina is now head of the academy. For Rabbi Levi used to study with Rabbi Hanina ben Hama, and it must be that he lost his study partner." (*Shabbat* 59b)

The Talmud relates that some money that belonged to orphans had been deposited for safekeeping with Rabbi Abba, Shemuel's father. However, since Shemuel was not in town when his father passed away, he never learned where his father kept the money. As a consequence, his deceased father was accused of having embezzled it. Distressed by this slight to his father's honor, Shemuel went to the cemetery where his father was buried in an attempt to find out where the money was hidden. He said to the spirits of the dead, "I wish to speak to my father."

The spirits said, "He has gone up to learn in the heavenly academy." Shemuel noticed that the spirit of Rabbi Levi, who had passed away some time ago, was sitting outside. He asked him, "Why have you not gone up to the academy?" Rabbi Levi replied, "I was told that I would not be admitted to the heavenly academy for as many years as I did not attend the academy of Rabbi Afes and hurt his feelings." Meanwhile, Shmuel's father arrived. Shemuel saw that he was weeping and laughing. He asked him, "Why are you weeping?" His father answered, "Because I am told that you will be coming to this world soon." "Why are you laughing?" his son asked. "Because they tell me that you are highly respected in the heavenly world," his father said. His son then said, "If I am so much respected, then as a favor to me, let Rabbi Levi be admitted to the heavenly academy." (*Berachot* 18b)

Shortly after this, R. Levi was admitted to the heavenly academy. Shemuel then asked his father: "Where is the money that belongs to the orphans?"

His father told him: "The money is hidden in the wrap that covers the millstones. There are three bundles of money. The upper and lower ones belong to us and the middle one belongs to the orphans."

Shemuel asked his father: "Why did you store the money that way?"

Abba replied: "Because if thieves were to discover it, they would take mine, and if the earth were to destroy some of it, that would also be mine."

Levi traveled frequently to Babylonia, and in his later years he joined Rav's academy there.

Later on, Levi settled in Nehardea and was frequently in the company of Abba b. Abba, who was Rabbi Shmuel's father. As is mentioned, "The father of Shemuel and Levi sat in the Shaf Yativ synagogue, which was located in Nehardea." (*Megillah* 29a)

When R. Shemuel's father and R. Levi were leaving for a journey, they prayed before sunrise. (*Berachot* 30a)

Rabbi Levi was a judge in the court of Mar Ukva, the Exilarch. His students were some of the great Amoraim: Rabbi Mattna, Rabbi Assi, Rabbi Hiyya b. Abba and Rabbi Zeira. (*Pesahim* 76b)

R. Levi attended the wedding feast of R. Shimon, the son of Rebbe, and recited five benedictions. (*Ketubbot* 8a)

Rabbi Levi, who was often a guest at the home of Rabbi Yehuda ha-Nasi, he used to entertain his guests with acrobatic feats. (*Sukkah* 53a)

It is related that he used to juggle eight knives in front of Rabbi Yehuda ha-Nasi. At one point, he dislocated his hip during a performance, which resulted in a permanent limp.

Once, when there had been no rain for a long time and R. Levi ordained a fast, no rain fell. He prayed and said, Master of the Universe, have You no mercy on Your children? Rain fell, but R. Levi became lame. The Talmud asks: Wasn't it another cause for his lameness? (*Taanit* 25a)

R. Shemuel used to juggle eight glasses of wine before King Shapur.

R. Abbaye used to juggle eight eggs before Rabbah, but some say four.

When the Talmud states: "It was argued before the rabbis," it refers to R. Levi arguing before Rebbe. (*Sanhedrin* 17b)

R. Levi wanted to introduce a solution in agreement with a baraita, but Rav told him that his uncle, R. Hiyya, who was the author of the baraita, told him that the law is not in agreement with that baraita. (*Ketubbot* 52a)

Rav said: One should never absent himself from the beit ha-midrash even for a single hour. Levi and I attended the

academy of Rebbe together. In the evening, he would teach a Halacha, but in the morning he would retract it. (*Betzah* 24b)

Rebbe said to Levi after he returned from Babylonia, "What are the Persians like? They are like the armies of the house of David. What are the Guebers fire-worshippers like? They are like the destroying angels. What are the Ishmaelites like? They are like the demons of the outhouse. What are the scholars of Babylon like? They are like the ministering angels. (*Kiddushin* 72a)

For a glimpse of the world as it was in R. Levy's time, see the historical timeline from 150 to 250 C.E.

לוי
Levi

(third–fourth centuries C.E.)
Amora, Eretz Yisrael

R. Levi was a contemporary of R. Zeira, R. Abba b. Kahana and R. Hama b. Ukva.

R. Levi stated: The punishment for false weights and measures is harsher than the punishment for marrying forbidden relatives. (*Bava Batra* 88b)

R. Levi also stated, "To rob a human is worse than the theft of sacred items."

For a glimpse of the world as it was in R. Levi's time, see the historical timeline from 250 to 350 C.E.

לויטס איש יבנה
Levitas Ish Yavne

(second century C.E.)
Tanna, Eretz Yisrael

R. Levitas is quoted as saying, "Be exceedingly humble, because in the end we all must die." He was a contemporary of Rabbi Yohanan ben Beroka and Rabbi Akiva. (*Avot* 4:4)

For a glimpse of the world as it was in the time of Levitas Ish Yavne, see the historical timeline from 100 to 200 C.E.

מני
Mani

(fourth century C.E.)
Amora, Eretz Yisrael
Head of the academy in Sepphoris

Mani's father, Rabbi Yonah, was also his teacher. He also studied with Rabbi Yosi and Rabbi Hizkiya. As a young man he lived in Tiberias, where he succeeded his father as leader of the Tiberias community.

When Rabbi Hanina retired as head of the academy in Sepphoris, he became the head of that academy and remained there until he passed away.

When there was a drought in the land of Israel, R. Yonah, the father of R. Mani, would go into his house and tell his family, "Bring me my sacks so that I can go and buy grain for a zuz." He was so humble that he did not want his family to know that he was the person who prayed for rain. He then went to a low area, put on sackcloth and prayed for rain, and rain came. When he returned home, his family asked him: "Have you brought grain?" He would answer, "Now that rain has come, the world will feel relieved." (*Taanit* 23b)

The members of the Nasi household annoyed R. Mani. He went to his father's grave and cried, "Father, Father, these people are persecuting me."

Something happened and they stopped persecuting him.

At another point, when he attended the lectures of R. Yitzhak b. Elishav, he complained, "My father-in-law's wealthy relatives are annoying me." (*Taanit* 23b)

He used to say, "He who recites the shema at its proper time is greater than one who studies Torah." (*Berachot* 10b)

Rabbi Mani also had an explanation as to why King Saul did not kill all the Amalekites. King Saul reasoned that since the children were innocent, they should be spared. (*Yoma* 22b)

For a glimpse of the world as it was in R. Mani's time, see the historical timeline from 300 to 400 C.E.

מר בר רב אשי
Mar b. R. Ashi

(fifth century C.E.)
Amora, Babylonia
Head of academy in Sura

The given name of Mar bar Rav Ashi was Tavyomi. The son of the well-known Rabbi Ashi who compiled the Babylonian Talmud, he participated in that enormous undertaking.

The Talmud relates that Rabbi Yohanan said: "Since the Temple was destroyed, prophecy was taken from prophets and given to fools and children."

One day Mar b. R. Ashi was present in a certain place in Mechuza, when he overheard a well-known town-idiot exclaim: "The man who signs his name Tavyomi is to be elected as head of the academy in Matha Mehasya."

Rabbi Mar said to himself, "It must be that my time has come." He rushed to Matha Mehasya. When he arrived he found that the rabbis of the academy had voted to appoint Rabbi Aha mi-Difti as head of the academy. When they heard of his arrival, they sent a delegation of rabbis to consult with him about the appointment of R. Aha. He detained them in a discussion and the rabbis sent another delegation. He detained the second delegation and a third delegation until they numbered ten rabbis present. Having ten rabbis present he began to discourse and expound on the Oral Law They changed their mind and elected him as head of the academy. (*Bava Batra* 12b)

His contemporaries included Rabbi Ravina, Rabbi Yehuda b. Meremar and

Rabbi Aha mi-Difti. As a young man he studied under his father, Rabbi Ashi. (*Berachot* 36a)

Rabbi Mar b. R. Ashi is quoted often in the Talmud.

Ravina allowed R. Ashi's daughter to collect her inheritance from her father from the property of R. Mar b. Ashi without an oath. (*Ketubbot* 69a)

Mar b. R. Ashi said: "I was once standing next to my father when they brought a bird to be examined in order to see whether it was kosher. He found only fifteen tendons where there should have been sixteen. On further examination, he found that one tendon had a different appearance, so he split it and found that it consisted of two tendons." (*Hullin* 76b)

Mar b. R. Ashi was making a garland for his daughter. Ravina asked him: "Don't you obey the prohibition against garlands?" He answered, "It applies only to men who wish to imitate the High Priest." (*Gittin* 7a)

Yehuda b. Meremar, Mar b. R. Ashi and R. Aha mi-Difti used to dine together. (*Berachot* 45b)

The Talmud relates that certain people who were carrying a barrel of wine and put it under a drainpipe to take a rest. Demons caused the barrel to burst. The people came to R. Mar b. Ashi. He brought trumpets and exorcised the demons, which now stood before him. "Why did you break the barrel?" he asked them.

A demon replied: "What else could I do? They placed the barrel on my ear."

R. Mar asked them: "What business do you have in a public place? You are in the wrong and you must pay for the damage."

The demon asked for time to pay. A day was fixed for the payment to be made, but the demon did not keep his promise. His excuse was that he could

acquire only items that are not tied, sealed or measured or counted, and he could not find other items. (*Hullin* 105b)

King Yezdegerd III, who was a Jew-hater, ruled the region during Mar b. R. Ashi's lifetime.

Mar b. R. Ashi said, "I am unqualified to be a judge when one litigant is a Torah scholar, because he is as dear to me as I am to myself." (*Shabbat* 119a)

For a glimpse of the world as it was in the time of Mar bar Rav Ashi, see the historical timeline from 400 to 500 C.E.

מר בר רבינא
Mar bar Ravina
(fourth century C.E.)
Amora, Babylonia

The Talmud says: Mar b. Ravina, who was very pious, used to fast often, except on holidays. He did not believe that one should be very merry. (*Pesahim* 68b)

During the wedding feast that he made for his son, when he saw that the rabbis became very merry, he took a cup worth four hundred zuz and shattered it in front of them. This shocked them and they became serious. (*Berachot* 30b, 31a)

He used to finish the Amida with a special prayer: "O God, keep my tongue from evil and my lips from speaking falsehood. May I be silent to those who curse me, and may I be like dust before all. Open my heart to Your Torah and let my spirit pursue your commandments," etc. Most congregations have adopted this prayer and recite it at the conclusion of the Amida. (*Berachot* 17a)

Mar b. Ravina's mother prepared seven clean garments for him every week so that his mind would be clear for studying. (*Eruvin* 65a)

It is preferable to make the blessing over a whole loaf of bread. Mar b. Ravina used to put the broken piece under the whole loaf, then break it and recite the blessing. (*Berachot* 39b)

As Mar b. Ravina went through a valley called Aravot, he became dehydrated. Miraculously, a well was created and he drank. At another time, as he walked through a famous building in Mehoza, a wild camel was about to attack him. Just at that moment, one of the walls fell in and he was able to escape from the camel. Thereafter, whenever he passed these places he would recite a blessing of thanksgiving for the miracles that had saved his life.

For a glimpse of the world as it was in the time of Mar b. Ravina, see the historical timeline from 300 to 400 C.E.

מרי בר איסק
Mari b. Isaac

(third–fourth centuries C.E.)
Amora, Babylonia

A man came to Mari b. Isaac from Be-Hozai who claimed to be his brother, and he wanted to share in the inheritance of their father.

"I do not know you," said R. Mari. The case came before R. Hisda.

R. Hisda said to the man: "He speaks the truth," but R. Hisda also said to the brother, "Go and produce witnesses that you are his brother." "I have witnesses," he said, "but they are afraid to testify because he is a powerful man."

R. Hisda then said to R. Mari, "Go and bring witnesses who will testify that you are not his brother."

"Is that justice?" exclaimed R. Mari. "The onus of proof lies on the claimant." "This is the way I judge in your case and in the cases of powerful men like you," R. Hisda replied. Subsequently, witnesses came to testify that he was his brother. (*Bava Metzia* 39b, *Ketubbot* 27b)

For a glimpse of the world as it was in the time of R. Mari bar Isaac, see the historical timeline from 250 to 350 C.E.

מרי בר איסור
Mari bar Issur

(fourth century C.E.)
Amora, Babylonia

R. Mari's father, Issur, was a convert to Judaism.

The proselyte Issur had twelve thousand zuz deposited for safekeeping with Rava, but the question arose whether Issur's son Mari was entitled to it. The problem was that when Mari was conceived, Issur was still not Jewish, but became Jewish before Mari was born. R. Ika b. R. Ammi suggested that Issur should declare that the money belonged to R. Mari. Thus the matter was solved: Issur declared that the money belonged to his son.

According to Rashi, Mari's mother was Rachel, the daughter of Rabbi Shemuel. She was taken captive by bandits while she was still single.

Issur, after his conversion, became friendly with Rabbi Safra and Rava. (*Bava Batra* 149a)

He struck up a business partnership with Rabbi Safra. (*Bava Metzia* 31b)

The Talmud mentions two sons of Rabbi Mari: Mar Zutra and Rabbi Adda Saba. (*Kiddushin* 65b)

R. Mari, the son of the daughter of R. Shemuel pointed out to Rava a contradiction regarding prayer, but he gave him no answer. Later, he said to him, "Did you hear any statement on this subject?" He answered, "Yes. I heard R. Sheshet clarify this contradiction." (*Berachot* 16a)

For a glimpse of the world as it was in the time of Rabbi bar Issur, see the historical timeline from 300 to 400 C.E.

מתנא
Mathna

(third century C.E.)
Amora, Babylonia

R. Mathna was a student of Rabbi Shemuel and he was also a student of Rav. At one time he was a teacher in Papuna (a town in Babylonia between Baghdad and Pumbedita) (*Eruvin* 6b, *Shabbat* 24a)

Rabbi Mathna said, "The fourth blessing after meals was instituted in Yavne with reference to those who were slain in Yavne." He said further, "On the day that permission was given to bury those slain, they ordained that the blessing *Ha-tov ve-ha-metiv* (Who is good and Who bestows good) should be said." (*Berachot* 48b, *Bava Batra* 121b, *Taanit* 31a)

Rabbi Mathna's sons were Rabbi Ahadbai, Rabbi Tobi and Rabbi Hiyya. (*Bava Batra* 151a)

For a glimpse of the world as it was in Rabbi Mathna's time, see the historical timeline from 200 to 300 C.E.

מתנא
Mathna II

(fourth century C.E.)
Amora, Babylonia

R. Mathna, who was a close associate of Rabbi Abbaye, was a student of Rabbi Hisda. (*Ketubbot* 35b, *Kiddushin* 32a)

For a glimpse of the world as it was in the time of Mathna II, see the historical timeline from 300 to 400 C.E.

מתיא בן חרש
Matya ben Heresh

(second century C.E.)
Tanna, Eretz Yisrael and Rome

R. Matya, who was born in Eretz Yisrael, was a student of Rabbi Yohanan ben Zakkai. In his later years, he established a great academy in Rome. (*Sanhedrin* 32b)

When Rabbi Shimon bar Yohai visited Rome, Rabbi Matya consulted him on an important halachic issue. (*Meilah* 17a)

He also asked him about the Holy Ark of the Temple. (*Yoma* 53b)

He used to say, "Be the first to extend greetings to all people. Be rather a tail to lions than a head to foxes." (*Avot* 4:15)

For a glimpse of the world as it was in the time of R. Matya ben Heresh, see the historical timeline from 100 to 200 C.E.

מאיר
Meir

(second century C.E.)
Tanna, Eretz Yisrael

R. Meir was married to Berurya, the daughter of Rabbi Hananya ben Teradion. Their two sons died in their lifetime. Late in life, Rabbi Meir retired to Tiberias, where he founded the well-known academy there. When he was a young man, he was a scribe by profession. Although Rabbi Akiva and Rabbi Yishmael were his teachers, he was also a pupil of Rabbi Elisha ben Avuyah, with whom he kept a close relationship even after the latter became an apostate.

The Talmud relates that Rabbi Yohanan said, "The following instructions were issued in the days when Rabbi Shimon ben Gamliel was president of the Sanhedrin. Whenever the president of the Sanhedrin enters the room, everyone should rise, but when the Hacham or the president of the court enters, only a small number of the assembly should rise. Rabbi Meir was the Hacham and Rabbi Nathan was the president of the court. Rabbi Meir and Rabbi Nathan were not present when the instructions were issued. The next day, when Rabbi Meir and Rabbi Nathan entered the hall of the Sanhedrin, they noticed the lack of respect accorded to them. When they asked the reason for the change, they were told that those were the instructions of Rabbi Shimon.

Rabbi Meir and Rabbi Nathan decided to engage in a discourse in which Rabbi Shimon was not familiar. When Rabbi Yaakov ben Korshai found out what was planned, he feared that this might lead to a disgrace to the presidency of the Sanhedrin. He therefore started to study the subject just outside Rabbi Shimon's chamber, repeating it loudly, over and over. When R. Shimon heard him, he perceived that something was happening in the Sanhedrin. He concentrated on the subject and familiarized himself with it.

The next day, his two opponents approached him in order to discuss the subject. He agreed and he was able to hold his ground. When they finished, he said to them, "Had I not familiarized myself with the subject, you would have disgraced me." He issued an order to have them removed from the Sanhedrin. When they were on the outside they wrote down difficult scholastic questions on slips of paper, which they threw inside. Many of the questions could not be answered inside, and they were sent back outside unanswered. They wrote down the answer and sent it back inside. Rabbi Yosi said to the assembly, "The Torah is outside and we are sitting inside." Rabbi Shimon changed his mind and said, "We shall readmit them, but impose on them this penalty: no traditional statement shall be quoted in their names." They decided that the phrase "others say" would refer to Rabbi Meir, while the phrase "some say" would refer to Rabbi Nathan.

At one time during the persecutions Rabbi Meir was compelled to flee from Eretz Yisrael, but returned after the danger abated. He was among the sages who assembled in the valley of Kidron to intercalate the year.

At the convention in Usha, he was one of the leaders who enacted far-reaching legislation. The seat of the Sanhedrin and the great academy were located briefly in Usha.

He was one of the foremost leaders after the Bar Kochva revolt.

The Talmud poses a rhetorical question. From whom did Rabbi Hiyya learn his humble conduct? From Rabbi Meir.

Rabbi Meir's contribution to the Mishna is considerable. The final edition, which was completed by Rabbi Yehuda ha-Nasi, was based on much of what Rabbi Meir had compiled. Most scholars agree that the Mishna was edited by Rabbi Yehuda ha-Nasi based on the arrangements of the style and form taught by Rabbi Meir, who had learned it from his teacher, Rabbi Akiva. (*Sanhedrin* 86a)

Rabbi Abba b. Hanina said: "In the generation of Rabbi Meir there was none equal to him. Why, then, was not the Halacha fixed in agreement with his views? Because his colleagues could not fathom the depth of his mind."

Rabbi Meir was one of five students who received ordination from Rabbi Yehuda ben Bava at great peril. They all risked their lives in defying the authorities receiving ordination. (*Eruvin* 13b)

During the Hadrian persecution, the occupying authorities issued a decree that anyone who ordained a rabbi or received rabbinical ordination would be subject to the death penalty and the city where the ordination took place would be demolished and its boundary posts uprooted. In order to avoid causing the destruction of a city, Rabbi Yehuda b.

Bava sat between two great mountains and between the two cities of Usha and Shefaram. Five prominent students sat before him: Rabbi Meir, Rabbi Yehuda, Rabbi Shimon, Rabbi Yosi and Rabbi Eleazar ben Shammua. The ceremony was held and he ordained them. Rabbi Avia adds the name of Rabbi Nehemia to the list of those ordained. As soon as the ceremony was completed, they noticed the Romans approaching. Rabbi Yehuda told his students to flee. "What will happen to you?" his students asked, urging him to flee together with them. "I would cause all of you to be captured," he said. "I am too old to run. I will lie before them like a stone." It was said that the Romans stabbed him three hundred times.

The students fled their separate ways, meeting again only after Hadrian's death. Seven of the students assembled in the valley of Rimmon to intercalate the year. They were: Rabbi Meir, Rabbi Yehuda, Rabbi Yosi, Rabbi Shimon, Rabbi Nehemia, Rabbi Eliezer ben Yaakov and Rabbi Yohanan ha-Sandlar.

Later on, Rabbi Shimon ben Gamliel was appointed Nasi and Rabbi Meir was appointed Hacham. At that time, the title of Hacham carried a great deal of prestige since it was one rank below the Nasi.

In his older years, when Rabbi Elisha turned away from observing Judaism, all of his colleagues, except for Rabbi Meir, dissociated themselves from him. There are several explanations for his having abandoned Jewish practice. One version has it that the Bar Kochva revolt, its failure, and the resulting persecutions and suffering caused him to question his faith. (*Sanhedrin* 14a)

Rabbi Yoseph said: "Aher would not have sinned if he had interpreted the Torah verse as did Rabbi Yaakov, his daughter's son." Others say that he witnessed the tongue of Hutzpit, the translator, being dragged by a swine and exclaimed, "The mouth that uttered pearls licks the dust! Is this the Torah and its reward?" He went away and sinned. Once he left Jewish observance, the rabbis did not refer to him by his name, but called him Aher (the other). Only Rabbi Meir continued to discuss Torah with him and tried to bring him back to Judaism. (*Kiddushin* 39b)

Our rabbis taught: Once Aher was riding on a horse on the Shabbat, and Rabbi Meir was walking behind him in order to learn Torah from him. When they had gone a certain distance, Aher said to R. Meir, "Turn back, because by my measurement we have gone already to the limit of distance that may be traveled on Shabbat."

Rabbi Meir answered, "You turn back, too."

Aher replied, "Have I not told you that I have heard from behind the Heavenly Curtain that there is a way back to Judaism for everyone except for Aher?"

Rabbi Meir prevailed upon him and took him to a schoolhouse. Aher stopped one of the pupils and said. "Recite for me the verse you learned today." The child recited a verse from the Prophet Yeshaya: "There is no peace for the wicked, says the Lord."

They went to another school and Aher asked a child to recite his verse. The child recited another verse which was similar in rebuke to the wicked. They went to a total of thirteen schoolhouses, where all the children quoted verses in a similar vein. The last child stuttered, and the word he used sounded like "Elisha." Aher, whose given name was Elisha, became angry and left. (*Hagigah* 15a)

It is said Rabbi Akiva had twelve thousand pairs of students. All of them died at the same time because they did not treat each other with respect. A tanna taught that all of them died between Pesah and Shavuot. These were the remaining students of Rabbi Akiva who revived the Torah at that time: Rabbi Meir, Rabbi Yehuda bar Illai, Rabbi Yosi ben Halafta, Rabbi Shimon bar Yohai and Rabbi Eleazar ben Shammua. (*Yevamot* 62b)

One story relates that a woman appeared in the academy of Rabbi Meir and said, "One of you rabbis has taken me as a wife by cohabitation." Rabbi Meir rose and gave her a bill of divorce. Thereupon all the students stood up and did likewise. (*Sanhedrin* 11a)

Rabbi Abbahu stated in the name of Rabbi Yohanan: "Rabbi Meir had a student by the name of Sumchos who could supply forty-eight reasons to support every rule of ritual impurity." (*Eruvin* 13b)

It is related that after Rabbi Meir passed away, Rabbi Yehuda told his students, "Do not allow the students of Rabbi Meir to enter our academy. They come only for disputations and to overwhelm me with citations from traditions, but not to learn Torah." Rabbi Sumchos forced his way into the academy and quoted Rabbi Meir on an important halachic issue. Rabbi Yehuda became very angry and told his students. "Didn't I instruct you not to admit any of Rabbi Meir's students?" Rabbi Yosi responded: "People will say, Rabbi Meir is dead, Rabbi Yehuda is angry and Rabbi Yosi is silent." (*Nazir* 49b)

Once there were some hoodlums in R. Meir's neighborhood who caused him a great deal of aggravation. When R. Meir wanted to pray for their deaths, his wife Berurya said, "That is not a good idea. Pray instead that they should repent." He prayed and they repented. (*Berachot* 10a)

R. Elau said in the name of Resh Lakish that Rabbi Meir stated the animal that the Torah calls the *tahash* was a distinct species that existed only in the time of Moses. The rabbis could not decide whether it was wild or domestic. It had a single horn in its forehead. It was provided to Moshe providentially so that its skin would be used as a cover for the Holy Tabernacle. It disappeared afterwards. (*Shabbat* 28b)

Rabbi Yoshua ben Levi said: "Whenever the Talmud says, 'A student said it in the name of Rabbi Yishmael in front of Rabbi Akiva, it refers to Rabbi Meir, who was an attendant to both Rabbi Akiva and Rabbi Yishmael." (*Eruvin* 13a)

It was taught that Rabbi Meir said: "When I was with Rabbi Yishmael I used to put a chemical called kankantum into the ink, and he never told me not to do it. But when I was with Rabbi Akiva and tried to do the same thing, he forbade it."

Rav Yehuda related a similar story in the name of Rabbi Shemuel in the name of Rabbi Meir. "When I studied under Rabbi Akiva, I used to put kankantum into the ink and he never told me not to do it. But when I came to study under Rabbi Yishmael, he asked me, "What is your profession?" I answered, "I am a scribe." Rabbi Yishmael then said, "Be meticulous in your work, because your work is sacred to Heaven. Should you omit a single letter or add a single letter, you could cause a situation where a world is destroyed." (Rashi comments that by adding one letter to a word, one can change that word from singular to plural, and when speaking of God, that would be blasphemous.)

"I told him I put kankantum in the ink, which makes the ink permanent immediately."

Rabbi Yehuda ha-Nasi declared, "The reason why I am keener than my colleagues is because I saw the back of Rabbi Meir, but if I had seen a front view of him, I would have been keener still." According to Rashi, Rabbi Yehuda studied at the academy of Rabbi Meir, and his seat was in a row from which he could see Rabbi Meir from the back.

R. Shimon b. Eleazar, who accompanied R. Meir on his journeys, was able to pass down many Halachot under special circumstances.

R. Shimon b. Eleazar said in the name of Rabbi Meir that on Shabbat, one could mix oil and wine as a remedy. Once, when Rabbi Meir was suffering internally and his students wanted to mix wine and oil for him, he would not allow it. They said to him, "Your words shall be nullified in your own lifetime."

He replied to them: "Even though I ruled that it is permissible, my colleagues ruled otherwise. I have never presumed to disregard the words of my colleagues."

He was stringent in respect to himself, but for all others he ruled that it is permissible. (*Shabbat* 134a)

Rabbi Yohanan said: "When Rabbi Meir delivered his public discourses; they consisted of one third Halacha, one-third *aggadata* and one third parables."

R. Meir also had three hundred parables about foxes, but we have only three left. (*Sanhedrin* 38b)

Rabbi Yohanan also said: "The author of an anonymous Mishna is Rabbi Meir; of an anonymous Tosefta, Rabbi Nehemia; of an anonymous Sifra, Rabbi Yehuda; of an anonymous Sifri, Rabbi Shimon, and all are taught according to the views of Rabbi Akiva." (*Sanhedrin* 86a)

What did Yehuda, the son of Jacob, do in order to merit a special blessing from Yaakov?

We have learned that R. Meir used to say: "When the Israelites stood at the Red Sea, the tribes argued about who would jump in first. Men from the tribe of Benjamin jumped in first, and the princes of Yehuda hurled stones at them because they wanted to be first.

R. Yehuda said to R. Meir: "That is not the story I heard, but this is what happened. The tribes were unwilling to jump into the sea, but Nahshon ben Amminadav, who was a prince from the tribe of Yehuda, came forward and jumped in first."

At that time, Moshe was busy praying to God, who said to him, "My children are drowning and you are uttering a long prayer?"

"What should I do?" asked Moshe. God answered him, "Lift up your staff, stretch it over the sea and go forward."

As they marched into the water, the sea split. For this reason, the kings of Israel belong to the tribe of Yehuda. (*Sotah* 36b)

R. Huna said in Rav's name, others say R. Huna said in Rav's name, which he heard from R. Meir: "One should always teach his student to use concise language and refined speech." (*Pesahim* 3b)

Rabbi Meir said: "A man should always teach his son a clean trade." (*Kiddushin* 4:14)

Rabbi Meir also used to say: "He who studies Torah but does not teach it to others puts the words of the Torah to shame." (*Sanhedrin* 99a)

Rabbi Meir also stated: "A non-Jew who occupies himself with the study of Torah can achieve the status of the high priest." (*Bava Kamma* 38a)

The Talmud relates that the sister of Berurya, the wife of Rabbi Meir and the daughter of Rabbi Hanania b. Teradion, was captured and condemned to serve in a brothel. Berurya told her husband, "I am ashamed to have my sister in a brothel. Can you do something to get her out of there?" He took a bag full of dinars and set out to ransom her, saying to himself: If she has kept herself pure, then a miracle will happen. He disguised himself as a knight and came to the place where she was imprisoned. He told her, "Prepare yourself for me." She replied, "I am menstruating." He answered, "I am willing to wait." She replied, "But there are many women here who are more beautiful than I am." R. Meir determined that she probably used these excuses with everyone. He offered the money to the watchman, who released her. When the government found out what R. Meir had done and wished to arrest him, he had to flee Eretz Yisrael for Babylonia. (*Avodah Zarah* 18a)

R. Huna said in the name of Rav, who learned it from R. Meir, who learned it from R. Akiva, "One should always say: 'Whatever God does is for the good.' By way of illustration, once, when R. Akiva was traveling, he arrived at a certain town. He was traveling with a rooster, a donkey and a lamp. He looked around in the town for lodging, but none was available. Saying to himself, 'Whatever God does is for the good,' he slept in an open field. A strong wind came and blew out the lamp, a wild cat came and ate the rooster, and a lion came and ate the donkey. He said again, 'Whatever God does is for the good.' That night, a band of raiders came, captured all the inhabitants of the town and carried them away. He said: 'Did I not say that whatever God does is for the good?'"

He must have learned it from R. Nachum Ish Gam Zu, who was R. Akiva's teacher for many years. (*Berachot* 60b)

When Rabbi Meir died, composers of parables ceased to exist. (*Sotah* 9:15, 49a)

R. Meir said: "Do not judge wine by the jug it is in, but by its contents." (*Avot* 4:20)

R. Meir said: "Do a little less work and use that time to study Torah. Be humble before everyone." (*Avot* 4:10)

R. Yaakov and R. Zerika said, "Whenever R. Akiva disagrees with one of his colleagues, Halacha accords with R. Akiva. When R. Yosi is in disagreement with his colleagues, Halacha accords with R. Yosi. If there is a disagreement between R. Yehuda ha-Nasi and one of his colleagues, Halacha goes according to Rebbe. What practical difference does it make? R. Assi said: General practice. R. Hiyya b. Abba said: We tend in their favor. R. Yosi b. Hanina said: They are seen as acceptable views."

R. Yaakov b. Idi said in the name of R. Yohanan: In a dispute between R. Meir and R. Yehuda, Halacha goes according to R. Yehuda. In a dispute between R. Yehuda and R. Yosi, Halacha is like R. Yosi, and, needless to say, in a dispute between R. Meir and R. Yosi, Halacha goes according to R. Yosi.

R. Assi said: I also learned that in a dispute between R. Yosi and R. Shimon, Halacha goes according to R. Yosi.

R. Abba said in the name of R. Yohanan: In a dispute between R. Yehuda and R. Shimon, Halacha goes according to R. Yehuda. Disputes between R. Meir and R. Shimon are left unresolved. (*Eruvin* 46b)

R. Yosi ha-Gelili was once traveling when he met Berurya, the wife of Rabbi Meir. He asked her: "Which road should one take to reach Lydda?" She replied: "Foolish Galilean, didn't the rabbis teach that you should not engage in much conversation with a woman? You should

have asked, 'Which way to Lydda?'"
(*Eruvin* 53b)

For a glimpse of the world as it was in R. Meir's time,
see the historical timeline from 100 to 200 C.E.

מנחם
Menahem

(first century B.C.E.)
Tanna, Eretz Yisrael

R. Menahem was a contemporary of
Hillel and Shammai.

In a dispute over the laying of hands
on offerings during festivals, Menahem
sided with Hillel. At one time, Rabbi
Menahem served as the head of the
Sanhedrin together with Hillel, but he
withdrew and Shammai was chosen to
replace him. R. Menahem joined King
Herod's service at a later date. (*Hagiga*
2:2, 16a)

For a glimpse of the world as it was in R. Menahem's
time, see the historical timeline from 1 to 100 C.E.

מנחם בן יוסי בן חלפתא
Menahem ben Yosi b. Halafta

(first century B.C.E.)
Tanna, Eretz Yisrael

Menahem ben Yosi b. Halafta is
quoted in *Yoma* 4:4.

For a glimpse of the world as it was in the time of
Menahem ben Yosi b. Halafta, see the historical
timeline from 100 to 1 B.C.E.

מנשיא בר תחליפא
Menashye b. Tahlifa

(third century C.E.)
Amora, Babylonia

R. Menashye was a student of Rav.

R. Menashye b. Tahlifa said in Rav's
name: "The subject we discussed above
is proof that there is no chronological
order in the Torah." R. Papa observed:
"This was said only of two different
subjects, but if it is about the same
subject what is written first is earlier, and
what is written second is later. Otherwise

the principle of 'If a general proposition
is followed by a specific proposition the
general proposition applies only to what
is contained in the specific' could not be
sustained." (*Pesahim* 6b)

One Shabbat, when R. Ulla visited R.
Menashye, he heard a knock on the
door. "Who is knocking on the door on
Shabbat? It is a desecration of Shabbat."
Rabbah told him that only a musical
sound is prohibited. (*Eruvin* 104a)

Rami b. Hama did not want to
include R. Menashye b. Tahlifa in the
zimmun of three even though he could
recite Sifra, Sifri and Halacha. When
Rami b. Hama died, Rava said, "Rami b.
Hama died because he would not include
R. Menashye b. Tahlifa in the zimmun."
(*Berachot* 47b)

R. Giddal b. Minyumi was dining
with R. Nahman, who made a mistake in
the blessings after the meal and started
all over again. R. Menashye b. Tahlifa
said in the name of Rav that one starts
all over again if one has begun another
blessing. (*Berachot* 49 a–b)

For a glimpse of the world as it was in the time of R.
Menashye b. Tahlifa, see the historical timeline from
200 to 300 C.E.

מרימר
Meremar

(fourth–fifth centuries C.E.)
Amora, Babylonia
Head of the academy in Sura

R. Meremar, who was a student of
Rabbi Ravina, was a colleague of Rabbi
Ashi and Mar Zutra. (*Yevamot* 75b)

Meremar and Mar Zutra used to ask
ten people to join them for prayers on
Shabbat before a holiday, and then they
delivered the lecture. R. Ashi did it
differently. They asked him, "Why don't
you do as Meremar and Mar Zutra do?"
He answered, "It is too troublesome."
(*Berachot* 30a)

Meremar became head of the academy in Sura after Rabbi Ashi. His students were Rabbi Aha mi-Difti and Rabbi Ravina the younger. (*Shabbat* 81b)

R. Meremar had one son R. Yehuda, who was a colleague of Mar b. Rav Ashi and Rabbi Aha. (*Berachot* 45b)

For a glimpse of the world as it was in R. Meremar's time, see the historical timeline from 350 to 450 C.E.

משרשיא
Mesharshia

(fourth century C.E.)
Amora, Babylonia

R. Mesharshia was a contemporary of Rava and Pappa. They had halachic discussions.

When the son of R. Mesharshia was going to visit R. Pappa, R. Mesharshia told him to ask R. Pappa the following question about measurements: "When the rabbis established measurements, did they have the same standard measurement for everyone, or are the measurements determined by the size of each individual? Does a large person have a different measurement from a small person?" (*Eruvin* 48a)

In another case, R. Mesharshia engaged in a long debate with his colleagues about interpreting the meaning of the tannaim concerning an eruv. (*Eruvin* 46a, b)

For a glimpse of the world as it was in R. Mesharshia's time, see the historical timeline from 300 to 400 C.E.

מיאשא
Miasha

(third–fourth century C.E.)
Amora, Eretz Yisrael

R. Miasha was a grandson of R. Yoshua b. Levi. A man once deposited seven pearls wrapped in a sheet with him. When he died without having made a will, the owner came before R. Ammi

to claim the pearls. R. Ammi said to them, "I know that R. Miasha was not a wealthy man. Furthermore, does not the man indicate the marks?" (*Ketubbot* 85b)

For a glimpse of the world as it was in R. Miasha's time, see the historical timeline from 250 to 350 C.E.

מרדכי
Mordechai

(third–fourth centuries C.E.)
Amora, Babylonia

R. Mordechai was a student of Rabbah. (*Shabbat* 99b).

For a glimpse of the world as it was in R. Mordechai's time, see the historical timeline from 250 to 350 C.E.

נחמן בר יעקב
Nahman bar Yaakov

(third–fourth centuries C.E.)
Amora, Babylonia

R. Nahman was born in Nehardea to parents who were followers of Rabbi Shemuel. According to some sources, he died in 320 C.E.

The Talmud relates, "Rabbi Nachman said, 'My father was a scribe for the court of Rabbi Shemuel. I remember that when I was about six or seven years old, they would make an announcement in public that any deed found on the street should be returned to its owners." (*Bava Metzia* 16b)

His main teacher was Rabbah b. Abbahu. (*Yevamot* 80b)

Rabbi Nahman, who is frequently mentioned in the Talmud, became a judge in his community, and was very highly regarded by his contemporary colleagues.

He married Yalta, the daughter of the Exilarch. (*Hullin* 124a)

His contemporaries included Rabbi Yehuda b. Yehezkel, Rabbi Ammi, Rabbi Assi, Rabbi Hiyya b. Abba and Rabbi Yitzhak. Among his outstanding students were Rabbi Zeira, Rabbah, Rabbi Yoseph and Rava.

Four of his sons – Rabbah, Hon, Mar Zutra, and Hiyya – are mentioned in the Talmud. (*Shabbat* 119, *Yevamot* 34b, *Bava Batra* 7a, 46a

He also had two daughters. (*Gittin* 45a)

The Talmud relates a story in which a woman died and left a child who needed to be nursed. When her husband could not afford to pay for a wet-nurse, a miracle occurred: his breasts began to produce milk. Rabbi Yoseph commented, "How great this man must be that such a miracle befell him."

Rabbi Nahman observed, "The proof is that miracles occur frequently, while food is rarely created miraculously." (*Shabbat* 53b)

Rabbi Yitzhak was a guest of Rabbi Nahman. When he was about to leave, R. Nahman asked, "Please bless me."

Rabbi Yitzhak replied: "Let me tell you to what your request may be compared. A traveler crossing the desert was hungry, weary and thirsty, but he had no more food and he longed for a little shade. All of a sudden, he came upon a fruit tree. He ate from the fruit, which was sweet. He rested in its shade and drank from the stream of water flowing beneath the tree. When he was about to continue on his journey, he said: "O tree, with what should I bless you? Your fruit is sweet, your shade is already pleasant and the stream of water is already flowing beneath you. Therefore I bless you with this: May it be God's will that all the shoots taken from you should also be like you." The same is with you. Shall I bless you with Torah knowledge? You are already blessed with Torah knowledge. Shall I bless you with riches? You have riches already. Shall I bless you with children? You have children already. Therefore, may it be

God's will that your offspring be like you." (*Taanit* 5b)

An army stationed in Nehardea took over the living quarters of the local population. Rabbi Nahman told his students to go out to the swamp and prepare a place for Shabbat by covering the area with reeds so that they could sit there and study. (*Eruvin* 34b)

R. Ulla once visited R. Nahman and they dined together. When they finished, R. Ulla recited the grace after meals over a cup of wine. R. Ulla passed the cup of wine to R. Nahman, who said to him, "Please pass the cup to my wife Yalta." R. Ulla and R. Nahman then had an exchange which was uncomplimentary to women. When Yalta heard about it, she got up in a rage, went to the wine cellar and smashed four hundred jars of wine. R. Nahman said to R. Ulla, "Please send her another cup of wine." R. Ulla sent her a cup with the following message: "All that wine can be counted as a blessing." Yalta replied, "Peddlers spread gossip and rags produce vermin." (*Berachot* 51b)

R. Nahman was visiting in the town of Sura. When R. Hisda and Rabbah b. R. Huna went to see him, they asked him to abrogate a certain ruling by Rav and Shemuel. He replied to them, "Do you think I have traveled all the way here in order to annul a ruling of Rav and Shemuel?" (*Shevuot* 48b)

The mother of Rami b. Hama gave her property in writing to Rami b. Hama in the morning, but in the evening she gave it in writing to Mar Ukva b. Hama. Rami b. Hama came to R. Sheshet, who confirmed his inheritance. Mar Ukva then went to R. Nahman, who confirmed Mar Ukva in his inheritance.

R. Sheshet thereupon went to R. Nahman and said to him: "What is the reason that you acted as you did in this matter?"

R. Nahman replied: "And what is the reason that you acted in this matter as you did?"

R. Sheshet answered, "Because the will of R. Rami was written first."

R. Nahman replied; "Do we live in Jerusalem, where the hours are recorded? We live in Babylonia, where the hours are not recorded."

R. Sheshet asked: "And why did you act the way you did?"

"I treated it as a case to be decided at the discretion of the judges," replied R. Nahman.

R. Sheshes retorted, "I also treated it as a case to be decided at the discretion of the judges."

But R. Nahman replied: "I am a judge and you are not. Furthermore, you did not say at first that you treated it as a case to be decided by a judge." (*Ketubbot* 94b)

During one of the festivals, a deer was served at the Exilarch's table. This was on the second day of the festival, but the deer was caught by a non-Jew on the first day and slaughtered on the second day. Among the guests at the table were R. Nahman, R. Hisda and R. Sheshet. R. Nahman and R. Hisda partook of the venison, but R. Sheshet would not. "What can I do with R. Sheshet, who does not want to eat any of this venison?"

"How can I," retorted R. Sheshet, "in view of what R. Issi quoted in R. Yosi's name?" (*Eruvin* 39b)

R. Nahman said: R. Yehuda ben Bava testified about five things: that they instruct an orphan girl below the age of majority to refuse marriage, a woman may remarry based on the testimony of one witness, a rooster was stoned in Jerusalem because it had killed a human being, that wine forty days old was poured as an offering on the altar, and that the daily offering was brought in the

fourth hour of the morning. (*Berachot* 27a)

R. Giddal b. Minyumi was dining with R. Nahman, who made a mistake in the blessings after the meal; therefore he started all over again. R. Menashye b. Tahlifa said in the name of Rav that if one began another blessing, one must start again from the beginning. (*Berachot* 49a, b)

For a glimpse of the world as it was in the time of Nahman bar Yaakov, see the historical timeline from 250 to 350 C.E.

נחמן בר יצחק
Nahman bar Yitzhak

(third–fourth centuries C.E.)
Amora, Babylonia

R. Nahman, who died in 356 according to some sources, was the son of the sister of R. Aha b. Yoseph. (*Shabbat* 140a)

R. Nahman studied under his uncle, Rabbi Aha, and took him around when he needed to go out, since because of his advanced age he had to lean on his shoulder.

When R. Nahman b. Yitzhak was seated among the ordinary people, R. Nahman b. Hisda said to him: "Would you please come and sit closer to us?" R. Nahman b. Yitzhak replied: "We have learned that R. Yosi says: 'It is not the place that honors the man, but the man who honors the place.'" (*Taanit* 21b)

When a corpse lay in Drukeret, R. Nahman b. Yitzchak permitted it to be carried out into the karmelit on Shabbat. (*Shabbat* 94b)

When R. Aha b. Yoseph walked with R. Nahman on his way to R. Safra; he had to lean on R. Nahman's shoulders because he was old and feeble. He said, "When we reach the house, please lead me inside." R. Nahman complied. Once they were inside, they discussed several halachic questions. (*Shabbat* 140a)

R. Nahman was the *resh kalla* at Rava's yeshiva in Mehoza.

It is related that R. Nahman, who was the regular lecturer on Shabbat, was about to deliver his lecture. However, it was his custom to run over his text with R. Adda b. Abba before delivering it, and only then would he deliver his lecture.

But this Shabbat, R. Papa and R. Huna b. Yehoshua approached R. Adda b. Abba and asked him to repeat for them the lecture that they had missed the day before, saying, "Tell us how Rava explained the law of tithing." He repeated the entire lecture for them.

In the meantime, R. Nahman was waiting for R. Adda to go over his lecture with him, and it was getting late. The rabbis told R. Nahman: "Come and lecture. It is late. Why are you still sitting?"

Angry over R. Adda's delay, he replied sarcastically, "I am waiting for R. Adda's coffin." But when R. Adda b. Abba passed away soon afterwards, R. Nahman blamed himself for his death. (*Bava Batra* 22a)

R. Nahman b. Yitzhak took great care to quote rabbis properly. When one of the rabbis quoted R. Giddal Deman Naresh, R. Nahman b. Yitzhak said, "I call him neither Giddal b. Menashye nor Giddal b. Minyoni, but simply Giddal." (*Pesahim* 107a)

R. Hiyya b. Abba said in the name of R. Yohanan: "The blessing over boiled vegetables is *peri ha-adama*." However, R. Benyamin b. Yafeth said in the name of R. Yohanan: "The blessing over boiled vegetables is *she-ha-kol*." R. Nahman b. Yitzhak said, "Ulla made an error in accepting the word of R. Benyamin b. Yafeth." R. Zeira expressed astonishment, saying, "How can you compare R. Benyamin b. Yafeth with R. Hiyya b. Abba? R. Hiyya b. Abba was very particular to get the exact teachings

of R. Yohanan, while R. Benyamin b. Yafeth was not so careful. Furthermore, R. Hiyya b. Abba used to go over his learning with R. Yohanan every thirty days, while R. Benyamin did not." (*Berachot* 38b)

Rabbah said in the name of R. Sehora, who said in the name of R. Huna: "If a person studies too much at a time his learning decreases, but if he studies little at a time, his knowledge increases." Rabbah remarked, "The rabbis were aware of this advice, but disregarded it." R. Nahman b. Yitzhak said, "I acted on this advice and it benefited me greatly." (*Eruvin* 54b)

Astrologers told the mother of R. Nahman bar Yitzhak that her son would be a thief. Therefore, she told her son to wear a head covering all the time so that the fear of God would be on him and keep him from temptation. One day, as he studied under a palm tree that did not belong to him and an urge came upon him, he climbed up and bit off a cluster of dates. (*Shabbat* 156b)

Once, R. Nahman b. Yitzhak asked R. Hiyya b. Avin: "What is written on the tefillin worn by the Ruler of the Universe?"

He replied, "'Who is like your people Israel?'" (*Berachot* 6a)

For a glimpse of the world as it was in the time of R. Nahman bar Yitzhak, see the historical timeline from 250 to 350 C.E.

נחום המדי
Nahum ha-Madai (Nahum the Mede)

(first century C.E.)
Tanna, Eretz Yisrael

R. Nahum, a resident of Jerusalem, lived through the period of the destruction of the Temple. According to Rabbi Nathan, Rabbi Nahum was one of the judges of civil law in Jerusalem. (*Ketubbot* 105a)

He is in dispute with the rabbis about lighting material for Shabbat. (*Shabbat* 2:1, 20b)

He disagrees with the rabbis concerning the vows of a Nazirite. (*Nazir* 5:4, 32b)

He also disagrees with the rabbis regarding the sale of a donkey. (*Bava Batra* 5:2, 78a)

For a glimpse of the world as it was in the time of R. Nahum ha-Madai, see the historical timeline from 1 to 100 C.E.

נחום איש גם זו
Nahum Ish Gam Zu

(first–second centuries C.E.)
Tanna, Eretz Yisrael

R. Nahum's most distinguished student was Rabbi Akiva. (*Berachot* 22a)

(*Hagiga* 12a) It is related that Rabbi Yishmael questioned Rabbi Akiva when they were traveling together on a trip. "You have served Rabbi Nahum Ish Gam Zu for twenty-two years. How did he explain heaven and earth to you?"

The Talmud explains the reason why he was called Nachum Ish Gam Zu, because whatever befell him he would always say, "This also is for the best."

Once, the Jewish people of Eretz Yisrael wanted to send a gift to the Emperor. After debating who should take the gift, they chose Rabbi Nahum. The gift they sent was a bag full of precious stones and pearls. Rabbi Nahum stayed overnight in an inn, but while he slept, thieves emptied his bag and filled it with earth. In the morning, when he discovered that he had been robbed, he declared, "This is also for the best."

When he arrived at the Emperor's palace and the officers opened his bag, they found the bag was full of earth. The Emperor became furious. "The Jews are mocking me," he declared, and wanted to kill the entire delegation. The prophet Elijah appeared in the guise of one of the king's ministers and said, "Could this be some of that legendary earth from their ancestor Abraham? When he threw earth at his enemies, it turned into swords."

The Emperor ordered it tested, and it turned out to be a potent weapon. They bestowed honors on Rabbi Nahum and filled his bag with precious stones and pearls. On his return trip he slept again in the same inn. The people asked him, "What did you take to the Emperor that he honored you so greatly?" He replied, "I took him what was in my bag."

Thereupon the innkeepers rushed to the same spot from where they had dug up the earth. They dug up more earth and filled several bags. They came before the Emperor, explaining that this was the same earth that Rabbi Nahum had brought. When they tested the earth and they found it ineffective, the Emperor condemned the innkeeper to death. (*Taanit* 21a)

R. Bizna b. Zavda said in the name of R. Akiva, who had it from R. Panda, who had it from R. Nahum, who had it from R. Birim, who said it in the name of an elder by the name of R. Banah: There were twenty-four interpreters of dreams in Jerusalem. R. Banah once had a dream and went to all twenty-four. Each of them gave him a different interpretation, and all were fulfilled. (*Berachot* 55b)

Rabbi Yohanan said, "Rabbi Yishmael expounded the Torah on the principle of generalization and specification, just as his teacher Rabbi Nehunya b. Hakoneh did. Rabbi Akiva expounded the Torah on the principle of amplification and limitation, as his teacher Rabbi Nahum Ish Gam Zu taught him. (*Shevuot* 26a)

For a glimpse of the world as it was in Rabbi Nahum Ish Gam Zu's time, see the historical timeline from 50 to 150 C.E.

נתן
Nathan

(fourth century C.E.)
Amora, Eretz Yisrael

R. Nathan, the father of R. Huna visited R. Pappa. When he recited the Kiddush in accordance with the minhag in Pumbedita, R. Pappa praised him. His son, R. Huna, was the Exilarch of Babylonia. (*Pesahim* 117b)

For a glimpse of the world as it was in R. Nathan's time, see the historical timeline from 300 to 400 C.E.

נתן הבבלי
Nathan ha-Bavli

(second century C.E.)
Tanna, Eretz Yisrael and Babylonia

Rabbi Nathan was born in Babylonia, where his father was an important community leader. (*Bava Metzia* 50b)

He immigrated to the Land of Israel and studied under Rabbi Yishmael ben Elisha and Rabbi Eliezer ben Hyrcanus. (*Shabbat* 12b, *Pesahim* 48a)

Rabbi Nathan and Rabbi Meir were involved in a dispute with Rabbi Shimon ben Gamliel at the academy in Usha. Rabbi Nathan was the Av Beis Din in the Sanhedrin when R. Shimon b. Gamliel was the Nasi.

The Talmud relates that Rabbi Yohanan said, "The following instructions were issued in the days when Rabbi Shimon ben Gamliel was president of the Sanhedrin. Whenever the president of the Sanhedrin enters the room, everyone should rise, but when the Hacham or the president of the court enters, only a small number of the assembly should rise." Rabbi Meir was the Hacham and Rabbi Nathan was the president of the court. Rabbi Meir and Rabbi Nathan were not present when the instructions were issued. The next day, when Rabbi Meir and Rabbi Nathan entered the hall of the Sanhedrin, they noticed the lack of respect accorded to them. When they asked the reason for the change, they were told that those were the instructions of Rabbi Shimon.

Rabbi Meir and Rabbi Nathan decided to engage in a discourse in which Rabbi Shimon was not familiar. When Rabbi Yaakov ben Korshai found out what was planned, he feared that this might lead to a disgrace to the presidency of the Sanhedrin. He therefore started to study the subject just outside Rabbi Shimon's chamber, repeating it loudly, over and over. When R. Shimon heard him, he perceived that something was happening in the Sanhedrin. He concentrated on the subject and familiarized himself with it.

The next day, his two opponents approached him in order to discuss the subject. He agreed and he was able to hold his ground. When they finished, he said to them, "Had I not familiarized myself with the subject, you would have disgraced me." He issued an order to have them removed from the Sanhedrin. When they were on the outside they wrote down difficult scholastic questions on slips of paper, which they threw inside. Many of the questions could not be answered inside, and they were sent back outside unanswered. They wrote down the answer and sent it back inside. Rabbi Yosi said to the assembly, "The Torah is outside and we are sitting inside." Rabbi Shimon changed his mind and said, "We shall readmit them, but impose on them this penalty: no traditional statement shall be quoted in their names." They decided that the phrase "others say" would refer to Rabbi Meir, while the phrase "some say" would refer to Rabbi Nathan.

Rabbi Nathan was eventually reinstated. One of his famous quotations is "Do not mock your neighbor for a blemish that you yourself have." (*Horayot* 13b)

Rabbi Nathan said: Once, when I arrived in a coastal town, I was approached there by a woman whose first two sons had died after being circumcised. She brought her third son to me. When I saw that the child was red, I said to her, "My daughter; wait until the blood becomes absorbed in him." She waited accordingly. Thereafter, the child was circumcised and he lived. They named the child Nathan the Babylonian after me.

"On another occasion, when I traveled to Cappadocia, I was approached by a woman whose first two sons had died after being circumcised. She brought her third son to me. When I saw that the child had a greenish color; I examined him and found him to be anemic. I said to her: 'My daughter, wait until the blood circulates more freely.' She waited accordingly and thereafter the child was circumcised and lived. They named the baby Nathan ha-Bavli." (*Hullin* 47b, *Shabbat* 134a)

When partners who owned a dilapidated two-story house had no money to rebuild it, Rabbi Nathan ruled that the owner of the lower floor should receive two-thirds of the land and the owner of the upper should receive one third. Others ruled differently. Rabbah said, "Hold fast to Rabbi Nathan's ruling because he is a judge and has penetrated to the depths of civil law." (*Bava Metzia* 117b)

There is another famous story in which Rabbi Nathan was involved. Rabbi Eliezer had halachic differences with the rabbis. Although he brought forth every argument to prove his point, the rabbis refused to accept them. He declared: "If Halacha agrees with me, let this carob tree prove it." The carob tree uprooted itself. The rabbis retorted: "The carob tree cannot prove the argument."

He then said to them: "If I am right, then let the stream of water prove it." Thereupon the stream of water started flowing in the opposite direction. The rabbis retorted: "The stream of water couldn't prove anything in this matter." Rabbi Eliezer then said: "If I am right, then let the walls of this school prove it." Thereupon the walls began to incline. Rabbi Yehoshua spoke up and rebuked the walls. "When scholars are disputing sacred matters, what business do the walls have to interfere?" The walls stopped to incline, but did not straighten out either.

Rabbi Eliezer said: "If I am right, let the heavens prove it." Thereupon a heavenly voice came forth, saying, "The halacha goes according to Rabbi Eliezer." Rabbi Yoshua spoke up and said: "The Torah is not in heaven." Rabbi Yirmiyahu arose and declared: "The Torah was already given on Mount Sinai. It belongs here on earth, and we do not pay attention to heavenly voices." He added, "It has been written in the Torah that the majority decides."

Later on, Rabbi Natan encountered Elijah the Prophet and asked him, "What did God do during that time?" Elijah answered, "He rejoiced, laughing, 'My sons have defeated me! My sons have defeated me!'" (*Bava Metzia* 59b)

It is stated Rebbe and Rabbi Nathan were the ones to conclude the Mishna, and Rav Ashi and Ravina concluded the Horaah. (*Bava Metzia* 86a)

Rabbi Illai said in the name of Rabbi Eleazar ben Shimon: "One may modify a statement in the interest of peace." Rabbi Nathan said: "It is a commandment." (*Yevamot* 65b)

For a glimpse of the world as it was in the time of Nathan ha-Bavli, see the historical timeline from 100 to 200 C.E.

נחמיה
Nehemia

(second century C.E.)
Tanna, Eretz Yisrael

R. Nehemia, a student of Rabbi Akiva, was a survivor of the Bar Kochva revolt.

(Kesuvos 67 b) Rabbi Nehemia was a poor person; his diet consisted of lentils most of the time.

Rabbi Nehemia was one of the students ordained by Rabbi Yehuda ben Bava at the cost of his life.

During the Hadrian persecution, the occupying authorities issued a decree that anyone who ordained a rabbi or received rabbinical ordination would be subject to the death penalty and the city where the ordination took place would be demolished and its boundary posts uprooted. In order to avoid causing the destruction of a city, Rabbi Yehuda b. Bava sat between two great mountains and between the two cities of Usha and Shefaram. Five prominent students sat before him: Rabbi Meir, Rabbi Yehuda, Rabbi Shimon, Rabbi Yosi and Rabbi Eleazar ben Shammua. The ceremony was held and he ordained them. Rabbi Avia adds the name of Rabbi Nehemia to the list of those ordained. As soon as the ceremony was completed, they noticed the Romans approaching. Rabbi Yehuda told his students to flee. "What will happen to you?" his students asked, urging him to flee together with them. "I would cause all of you to be captured," he said. "I am too old to run. I will lie before them like a stone." It was said

that the Romans stabbed him three hundred times.

The students fled, meeting again only after Hadrian's death. Seven of the students assembled in the valley of Rimmon to intercalate the year. They were Rabbi Meir, Rabbi Yehuda, Rabbi Yosi, Rabbi Shimon, Rabbi Nehemia, Rabbi Eliezer ben Yaakov and Rabbi Yohanan ha-Sandlar. (*Sanhedrin* 14a)

It is stated that when the rabbis entered the vineyard of Yavne, among them were Rabbi Yehuda, Rabbi Yosi, Rabbi Nehemia and Rabbi Eliezer ben Yosi ha-Gelili. They all spoke in honor of hospitality and expounded on the texts of the Torah. When Rabbi Nehemia's turn came, he also praised hospitality and cited texts from the Torah and Samuel. (*Berakhot* 63b)

Rabbi Yohanan said, "The author of an anonymous Mishna is Rabbi Meir, of an anonymous Tosefta, Rabbi Nehemia, of an anonymous Sifra, Rabbi Yehuda, of an anonymous Sifri, Rabbi Shimon, and all are taught according to the views of Rabbi Akiva. (*Sanhedrin* 86a)

For a glimpse of the world as it was in R. Nehemia's time, see the historical timeline from 100 to 200 C.E.

נחמיה איש בית דלי
Nehemia Ish Beit Deli

(second century C.E.)
Tanna, Babylonia

R. Nehemia, a student of Rabban Gamliel the Elder, was a contemporary of Rabbi Akiva.

The Talmud relates that Rabbi Akiva said, "When I visited Nehardea in Babylonia in order to declare a leap year, I met with Rabbi Nehemia Ish Beit Deli. He told me I heard that in Eretz Yisrael they do not permit a woman to remarry on testimony of one witness. He went on to say that he learned otherwise from Rabban Gamliel. (*Yevamot* 16:7, 122a)

For a glimpse of the world as it was in the time of R. Nehemia Ish Beit Deli, see the historical timeline from 100 to 200 C.E.

נחוניה בן הקנה
Nehunya ben Hakoneh

(first century C.E.)
Tanna, Eretz Yisrael

Rabbi Nechunya was a native of Emmaus in Judea and a student of Rabbi Yohanan ben Zakkai.

His students once asked him: "By what merit did you reach such old age?"

He replied, "Never in my life did I try to elevate myself by degrading others, never did I go to sleep with a curse against my fellowmen on my lips, and I have been generous with my money." (*Megillah* 28a)

Rabbi Yohanan said: "Rabbi Yishmael who served Rabbi Nehunya b. Hakoneh," his teacher, expounded the Torah on the principle of generalization and specification, just as his teacher did. Rabbi Akiva, who served Rabbi Nahum Ish Gam Zu, his teacher, expounded the Torah on the principle of amplification and limitation, as his teacher taught him. (*Shevuot* 26a)

One of his famous sayings was, "one who takes upon himself the yoke of the Torah will have the yoke of worldly pressures removed from him." (*Avot* 3:5)

For a glimpse of the world as it was in the time of Nehunya b. Hakoneh, see the historical timeline from 1 to 100 C.E.

נחוניה איש בקעת בית חורתן
Nehunya Ish Bikat Beit Hortan

(third century C.E.)
Amora, Eretz Yisrael

R. Nechunya is sometimes referred to as Hunya, or Hanina.

Rabbi Assi said in the name of Rabbi Yohanan who had it from R. Nechunya Ish Bikas Chorton: The laws of the ten plants, the willow branch and the Nisuch Hamayim were given to Moshe on Mount Sinai. (*Sukkah* 44a)

For a glimpse of the world as it was in the time of Nehunya Ish Bikat Beit Hortan, see the historical timeline from 200 to 300 C.E.

נהוראי
Nehorai

(second century C.E.)
Tanna, Eretz Yisrael

A tanna taught: His name was not R. Nehorai but Nehemia, while others say his name was R. Eleazar ben Arach. Why did they call him Nehorai? He enlightened the eyes of the sages in Halacha. This Nehorai is not the same as Rabbi Meir, whose name was also Nehorai. Quotes from these sages appear adjacent to each other in *Pirkei Avot*. (*Shabbat* 147b)

One of Rabbi Nehorai's sayings was: "If you must move, move to a place of Torah, and do not expect the Torah to follow you. Make sure you have a colleague with whom to discuss it, because that way it will be fixed in your mind. Do not depend entirely on your own knowledge." (*Avot* 4:14)

It has been taught: "Rabbi Nehorai said: In the generation just before the Messiah arrives, young men will insult the old, old men will rise before the young, daughters will rebel against their mothers, and daughters-in-law against their mothers-in-law. The people's faces will resemble faces of dogs, and a son will not be embarrassed in his father's presence." (*Sanhedrin* 97a)

It is stated that on one occasion, Rabbi Nehorai accompanied a witness to Usha to testify. (*Rosh ha-Shannah* 22b)

For a glimpse of the world as it was in Nehorai's time, see the historical timeline from 100 to 200 C.E.

נתאי הארבלי
Nittai ha-Arbeli

(second century B.C.E.)
Tanna, Eretz Yisrael

R. Nittai was one of the zugot. His colleague was Rabbi Yoshua ben Perahia.

He was a student of Rabbi Yosi ben Yoezer and of Rabbi Yosi ben Yohanan Ish Yerushalayim. (*Avot* 1:6)

Rabbi Nittai was the head of the court. (*Hagiga* 2:2)

He is known for the saying: "Keep your distance from an evil neighbor, do not associate yourself with wicked people and do not think that there is no retribution." (*Avot* 1:7)

For a glimpse of the world as it was in R. Nittai's time, see the historical timeline from 200 to 100 B.C.E.

אונקלוס
Onkelos

(first–second centuries C.E.)
Tanna, Eretz Yisrael

Rabbi Onkelos was the son of Kalonikus and the son of the sister of Titus, the Roman emperor. Wishing to convert to Judaism, he went to a medium who raised the spirit of Titus and asked him, "Who is most honored in the heavenly world?"

Titus answered, "It is Israel, but its observances are burdensome and you will not be able to perform them."

Undeterred, Onkelos converted to Judaism after coming into contact with Rabbi Yehoshua ben Hananya and Rabbi Eliezer ben Hyrcanus, whose student he was for many years. His conversion angered the Roman emperor. (*Gittin* 56b)

The Talmud relates that the emperor sent a contingent of Roman soldiers to arrest him, but he convinced the soldiers to convert. The emperor sent two more contingents and he was able to convince them not to arrest him. He showed the soldiers the mezuzah on the door post and asked them, "What is this?" They replied, "You tell us." He told them, "According to universal custom, a mortal king dwells inside his palace and the soldiers guard his palace outside. But in this case, the servants are inside the house and God guards them from outside." The guards did not arrest him, and the emperor sent no more soldiers. (*Avodah Zarah* 11a)

His translation of the Torah has been so well accepted that all biblical scholars read his Aramaic translation of the Torah to this day.

He was a contemporary of Rabbi Gamliel from Yavne and had a close relationship with him.

Onkelos states that the faces of the Cherubim in the Temple were turned sideways similar to a student who takes leave of his master. (*Bava Batra* 99a)

R. Yirmiyahu – some say R. Hiyya b. Abba – said, "The Targum on the Torah was authored by Onkelos the proselyte under the guidance of R. Eliezer and R. Yoshua." (*Megillah* 3a)

For a glimpse of the world as it was in Onkelos's time, see the historical timeline from 50 to 150 C.E.

פפי
Papi I

(fourth century C.E.)
Amora, Babylonia

R. Papi was the son-in-law of Rabbi Yitzhak Nepaha. (*Hullin* 110a)

R. Papi was a wealthy landowner with many employees. On Friday evening, he would recite the kiddush early for his family and then repeat it later, when his employees came in from the fields. (*Rosh ha-Shannah* 29b)

He established an academy that many students, including Rabbi Ashi, attended. (*Hullin* 77a)

Rav Papi visited the Exilarch Mar Samuel. They served him a dish that he refused to eat. (*Betzah* 14b)

There was a case of a person by the name of Bar Hama who was accused of murder. Two witnesses testified against him. However, two other witnesses came forward to disqualify one of the former witnesses. Rabbi Papi defended Bar Hama and was able to have him acquitted. Thereupon, Bar Hama kissed his feet and undertook to pay his taxes for the rest of his life. (*Sanhedrin* 27a, b)

For a glimpse of the world as it was in R. Papi's time, see the historical timeline from 300 to 400 C.E.

פפי
Papi
(fourth century C.E.)
Amora, Eretz Yisrael

R. Papi, who studied under Rabbi Yehoshua de-Sichni, is mentioned several times in the Talmud.

A contemporary of Rabbi Papa, he was well-to-do. He engaged in agriculture and owned farms. (*Bava Metzia* 109a)

R. Bibi b. Abbaye leased a field and surrounded it with a ridge. When his lease expired, he said to the owner: "Reimburse me for the improvements that I made." But R. Papi said to him, "You come from Mamla, where you might be reimbursed, but here it is not done. Even R. Papa claimed reimbursement only for losses, but what losses did you suffer?"

R. Papi said in the name of R. Yehoshua de-Sichni, "In the future, Jerusalem will be three times its present size, and each building will contain thirty dwellings, one over the other." (*Bava Batra* 75b)

For a glimpse of the world as it was in R. Papi's time, see the historical timeline from 300 to 400 C.E.

פפייס
Papiyas
(first–second centuries C.E.)
Tanna, Eretz Yisrael

R. Papiyas was a contemporary of Rabbi Yehoshua. He is mentioned several times in the Talmud. At one point, he testified before the rabbis concerning a heifer that was offered as a peace offering. (*Eduyot* 7:6)

For a glimpse of the world as it was in R. Papiyas's time, see the historical timeline from 50 to 150 C.E.

פפא
Pappa
(fourth century C.E.)
Amora, Babylonia
Head of the academy in Naresh

R. Pappa was a student of Rava and Abbaye. After Abbaye passed away, Pappa founded the yeshiva in Naresh, a town near Sura, and headed it for nineteen years until his death. His yeshiva attracted hundreds of students. (*Berachot* 20a, *Eruvin* 51a)

R. Pappa was born into a wealthy family and became even wealthier on his own. He was a brewer of date beer and a poppy-seed merchant.

R. Pappa said: if I were not a brewer, I would not have become wealthy. (*Pesahim* 113a)

The rabbis have taught if one dreams of walking into a lake, he will become the head of the academy. Rabbi Papa and Rabbi Huna b. Yoshua both dreamed that they walked into a lake, but Rabbi Papa dreamed that he was carrying a drum as he did so. R. Huna dreamed that he only walked into a lake. Rabbi Papa became the head of the academy and Rabbi Huna became his deputy. (*Berachot* 57a)

As R. Abbaye was walking together with R. Papa on his right and R. Huna b. Yoshua on his left, he noticed some demons approaching. He transferred R. Papa to his left and R. Huna to his right. R. Papa asked R. Abbaye, "What is different about me that you were not afraid on my behalf?" R. Abbaye answered, "The time is in your favor." (*Pesahim* 111b)

R. Papa and R Huna b. Yoshua sat before R. Idi b. Avin studying as R. Idi dozed off. The two students argued going back and forth but could not come up with an answer. In the meantime R. Idi awoke and gave them the answer without asking what they been arguing about. (*Pesahim* 35a)

Rava was serving drinks at his son's wedding. When he offered drinks to R. Papa and to R. Huna b. Yoshua, they rose before him out of respect. (*Kiddushin* 32b)

Once R. Huna b. Yoshua was very ill, and R. Papa went to visit him. When he saw how ill he was, he said to the people, "Make ready for his trip to heaven."

R. Huna recovered and R. Papa was embarrassed for having thought that it was the end. He asked him: "What did you see?"

He answered him, "You were right, it was indeed my end, but the Almighty said to the angels, 'He deserves to live longer because he never insisted on his rights and is a forgiving person.'" (*Rosh ha-Shannah* 17a)

R. Pappa and R. Huna b. Yoshua bought sesame seeds on the bank of Nahar Malka. They hired a boatman to bring the merchandise across the river with a guarantee against any accident that might happen. However, the canal was blocked and they could not deliver the merchandise. They told the boatman to hire donkeys and deliver it because he

guaranteed it. The boatmen appealed to Rava, who ruled against R. Papa and R. Huna b. Yoshua. He said, "White ducks that strip men of their clothing – this is an exceptional kind of situation." (*Gittin* 73a)

Rova instructed R. Papa and R. Huna b. Yoshua: "When a written legal decision of mine comes before you and you have an objection to it, do not tear it up before you speak to me. If I have valid reasons for my decision, I will share them with you, and if not, I will withdraw my decision. After my death, do not tear it up or draw any conclusions from it. Do not tear it up because had I been there I might have given you my reasons, and do not draw any conclusions because a judge must be guided by what he sees with his own eyes." (*Bava Batra* 130b)

It is related that R. Nahman, who was the regular lecturer on Shabbat, was about to deliver his lecture. However, it was his custom to run over his text with R. Adda b. Abba beforehand, and only then would he deliver his lecture.

But this Shabbat, R. Papa and R. Huna b. Yehoshua approached R. Adda b. Abba first and asked him to repeat the lecture they missed the day before. "Tell us how Rava explained the law of tithing," they said. He repeated the entire lecture for them. In the meantime, R. Nahman was waiting for R. Adda to go over his lecture with him, and it was getting late. The rabbis told R. Nahman: "Come to lecture, it is late, and why are you still sitting?" (*Bava Batra* 22a)

R. Papa and R. Huna b. Yoshua once came before Rava, who asked them, "Have you learned this particular tractate and the other tractate?" They replied in the affirmative. "Are you a little more wealthy?" "Yes," they replied, "because we bought some land." Rava exclaimed joyfully, "Happy are the righteous who are rewarded also in this world!" (*Horayot* 10b)

One of the rabbis was discussing with R. Kahana the subject of why Mount Sinai has that particular name. Then he asked him: "Why don't you attend the lectures of R. Papa and R. Huna b. Yoshua, who delve deeply into aggadeta?" (*Shabbat* 89a)

Come and hear: There was a man who sold a plot of land to R. Pappa; he needed the money to buy some oxen. Eventually he didn't need to buy the oxen. When R. Pappa found out he returned the land to the man. (*Ketubbot* 97a)

He made it his practice to visit the local rabbi when he visited a town.

Once, when R. Pappa was giving a lecture to his students, he raised some questions and asked the students for an answer. R. Huna b. Nahman gave him the answer. R. Pappa went over to his student, kissed him on the head and offered him his daughter in marriage. (*Horayot* 12b)

R. Pappa's second wife was the daughter of R. Abba of Sura. (*Sanhedrin* 14b, *Ketubbot* 39b)

The Talmud states that when the majority of the rabbis departed from the academy of Rav in Sura there still remained behind twelve hundred students. When the students left the academy of R. Huna in Sura there remained behind eight hundred students. (*Ketubbot* 106a)

When R. Huna delivered a lecture, thirteen interpreters assisted him.

When the students left the academy of Rabbah and R. Yoseph in Pumbedita, the four hundred students who remained described themselves as orphans.

When the students left the academy of R. Abbaye in Pumbedita (others say from the academy of R. Pappa and still others say from the academy of R. Ashi), there remained two hundred rabbis, who described themselves as orphans of the orphans.

R. Pappa was once visiting R. Huna b. Nathan. After they finished their meal, they brought some additional food to the table. R. Pappa took some food and ate. They said to him: "Don't you hold that after the meal is concluded it is forbidden to eat?" He replied: "The proper term is 'when the food is removed.'" (*Berachot* 42a)

R. Menashye b. Tahlifa said in Rav's name, "What we learned in our studies proves that there is no chronological order in the Torah." R. Pappa observed, "This holds true only if we are talking about two different subjects, but if it is about the same subject, then what is written first is earlier, and what is written second is later. Otherwise, the principle of 'If a general proposition is followed by a specific proposition the general proposition applies only to what is contained in the specific' could not be sustained." (*Pesahim* 6b)

When the son of R. Mesharshia was going to visit R. Pappa, his father asked him to ask R. Pappa the following question about measurements: "When the rabbis speak about measurements, is there a standard measurement or is it determined by the size of each individual. Is a large person's measurement different from a small person?" (*Eruvin* 48a)

After the destruction of the Temple, the rabbis wished the Jewish people to avoid ostentation. They ruled that during a lavish banquet, one item should be omitted. R. Pappa said that it should be the hors d'oeuvre.

R. Yitzhak said: At a wedding, ashes should be put on the bridegroom's head as a reminder of the destruction of the Temple. R. Pappa asked R. Abbaye: "Where on the head should the ashes be placed?" R. Abbaye answered, "On the spot where the tefilin are usually worn." (*Bava Batra* 60b)

Rabbi Papa advised people to be considerate of their wives, saying, "If your wife is short, bend down to listen to her." (*Bava Metzia* 59a)

Rabbi Pappa was sitting behind Rabbi Bibi in the presence of Rabbi Hamnuna as they discussed a halachic subject. When Rabbi Pappa asked them a question, they laughed at it. He remarked, "A student should always ask his teacher even such a question, which you consider laughable, because even a foolish question elevates a person." (*Niddah* 27a)

R. Pappa had a saying: "If you hear that your neighbor died, believe it. If you hear that your neighbor became wealthy, do not believe it." (*Gittin* 30b)

R. Pappa said, "At the gates of shops there are many brothers and friends, but at the gates of loss there are neither brothers nor friends." (*Shabbat* 32a)

When the Talmud mentions "the judges of Pumbedita," it refers to Rabbi Pappa b. Shemuel. (*Sanhedrin* 17b)

For a glimpse of the world as it was in R. Pappa's time, see the historical timeline from 300 to 400 C.E.

פפוס בן יהודה
Pappus ben Yehuda

(first–second centuries C.E.)
Tanna, Eretz Yisrael

R. Pappus, a contemporary of Rabbi Akiva, was imprisoned together with him during the Hadrianic persecutions.

During R. Akiva's time, the Roman authorities issued a decree forbidding Jews to study the Torah or observe its commandments.

The Talmud relates that during this time, a Jew by the name of Pappus b. Judah approached Rabbi Akiva and found him teaching Torah in a public

gathering. He said to him, "Aren't you afraid of the government?"

R. Akiva replied, "Let me explain it to you with a parable. A fox was once walking on the riverbank, and he saw fish swimming away from the bank. 'From what are you fleeing?' asked the fox. The fish replied, 'We are fleeing from the nets that people cast into the water to catch us.'

"He said to them, 'Come up to the dry land and live with me in safety.' They said to him, 'Are you the one they call the cleverest of all the animals? You are not clever but foolish. If we are afraid in the element in which we live, how much more endangered shall we be in the element that is strange to us?

"So it is with us Jews. If such is our condition when we study Torah, which is our natural environment, how much worse off we shall be if we neglect the Torah?"

Soon afterward, Rabbi Akiva was imprisoned for teaching Torah openly in defiance of the decree. The Romans also arrested Pappus b. Judah and held him in the same prison. Rabbi Akiva asked Pappus: "Why were you imprisoned?"

Pappus replied, "Fortunate are you, Akiva, that you were arrested for teaching Torah. Alas for Pappus, who was arrested for things of no importance." (*Berachot* 61b)

For a glimpse of the world as it was in R. Pappus ben Yehuda's time, see the historical timeline from 50 to 150 C.E.

פנחס בן חמא הכהן
Pinhas ben Hama ha-Kohen

(fourth century C.E.)
Amora, Eretz Yisrael

R. Pinhas was a student of Rabbi Yirmiyahu.

He states that if one leaves behind a son who follows in his ways, then that person is considered as having gone to sleep when he dies. However, a person who does not leave behind a son who follows in his ways can be considered dead when he dies. (*Bava Batra* 116a)

He also said that poverty in a man's house is worse than fifty plagues. R. Pinhas b. Hama also said: When there is a sick person in the house they should go to a sage who is also a saintly person who will pray for mercy.

For a glimpse of the world as it was in the time of Pinhas ben Hama ha-Kohen, see the historical timeline from 300 to 400 C.E.

פנחס בן יאיר
Pinhas ben Yair

(second century C.E.)
Tanna, Eretz Yisrael

Rabbi Pinchas was a son-in-law of Rabbi Shimon ben Yohai and his student for many years. He lived in southern Israel, not far from Ashkelon, and was active in the mitzvah of redeeming prisoners.

(*Hullin* 7a) Once, R. Pinhas ben Yair was on his way to redeem captives. When he arrived at the river Ginnai, he said, "O river, divide your waters so that I may pass." The river replied, "You are about to do the commandments of God, and I too am doing the will of God. While you may or may not succeed in accomplishing your purpose, I am sure of accomplishing mine." Rabbi Pinhas replied, "If you will not divide yourself, I will decree that no water shall ever flow again in your bed." Thereupon the river parted. In another case, there was a certain man who was carrying wheat for Passover. R. Pinhas asked the river to divide itself for the man because he was engaged in performing a mitzvah, and the river obeyed. When an Arab joined them on the journey, R. Pinhas asked the river to part again so that the non-Jew would not say, "This is how Jews treat a fellow traveler." The river parted. In

another case, R. Pinhas arrived at an inn, where they put food before his donkey, but the donkey would not eat. When they asked R. Pinhas why his donkey would not eat, he answered, "Perhaps the grain was not tithed." They immediately tithed the grain and the donkey ate it.

It is said of Rabbi Pinhas that never in his life did he eat bread that was not his own, and from the day he reached maturity he derived no benefit from his father's table.

He once declined to dine at the home of Rabbi Yehuda ha-Nasi. He told him "Presently I am engaged in a mitzvah of redeeming prisoners." Not even flooding rivers kept him from performing his good deeds. He was a close friend of Rabbi Hanina ben Dosa. (*Hullin* 7a, b)

When Rabbi Shimon ben Yohai had to flee from the Roman authorities, he hid in a cave for thirteen years. When he emerged from the cave, his son-in-law, Rabbi Pinhas ben Yair, went to meet him. He took him into the bath and massaged his body. Seeing the lumps on his body, he wept, and as the tears trickled from his eyes, he said, "Woe is me that I see you in such condition."

"No," he replied, "happy are you that you see me thus. Before the cave experience, Rabbi Shimon would ask a question and Rabbi Pinhas would have thirteen answers, but now when Rabbi Pinhas raised a question, Rabbi Shimon had twenty-four answers."

R. Pinhas said it in the name of R. Huna from Sepphoris: "The spring that emerges from the Holy of Holies resembles the horns of locusts, and further on, when it reaches the entrance to the Temple court, it becomes as large as the mouth of a small bottle." (*Yoma* 77b)

R. Pinhas lamented: "Since the Temple was destroyed, scholars and noblemen have been put to shame, and they cover their faces. Men of accomplishment are disregarded, while pushy and loudmouthed men gained the upper hand. There is no one to rely upon except our Father in Heaven." (*Sotah* 49a)

R. Pinhas b. Yair said, "Zeal leads to cleanliness, and cleanliness leads to purity. Purity leads to self-restraint, and self-restraint leads to sanctity. Sanctity leads to humility, and humility leads to fear of sin. Fear of sin leads to piety, and piety leads to divine intuition. Divine intuition leads to the resurrection of the dead, and the resurrection of the dead shall come through Eliyahu ha-Navi of blessed memory. (*Sotah* 9:15)

For a glimpse of the world as it was in the time of R. Pinhas ben Yair, see the historical timeline from 100 to 200 C.E.

רבה בר אבוה
Rabbah bar Avuha

(third century C.E.)
Amora, Babylonia
Head of the academy in Mehoza

A student of Rav, Rabbah ben Avuha also studied under Rabbi Shemuel in Nehardea. (*Shabbat* 129b)

At a later date Rabbah moved to Mehoza because Nehardea was destroyed by the Palmyras. He became head of the academy in Mehoza and was appointed a judge. (*Shabbat* 59b and *Yevamot* 115b)

Rabbah b. Avuha met Elijah standing in a non-Jewish cemetery. He started a conversation with him and they discussed halachic matters, but Elijah was in a hurry, saying, "I am pressed for time." He led him through paradise and offered him to collect some of the leaves and take them with him in his robe. He

gathered them and took them away. As he was coming out, he heard voices.

"Who would consume his portion of the World to Come in this world?" Therefore he scattered the leaves and threw them away. But the fine fragrance remained and was absorbed in his robe. Someone bought it from him for twelve thousand dinarii, which he distributed among his sons-in-law.

He had a son by the name of Chama, and his foremost student was Rabbi Nachman ben Yaakov. (*Eruvin* 3a, *Yevamot* 80b)

For a glimpse of the world as it was in the time of Rabbah bar Avuha, see the historical timeline from 200 to 300 C.E.

רבה בר בר חנה
Rabbah bar b. Hana

(third century C.E.)
Amora from Babylonia

Although Rabbah was born in Babylonia, he went to Eretz Yisrael to study at the academy of Rabbi Yohanan. He returned to Babylonia where he taught many students successfully and transmitted many teachings of Rabbi Yohanan in various academies.

He had intentions to return to Eretz Yisrael and he suffered persecution in Babylonia at the hands of the Persians. (*Pesahim* 51a)

On one occasion R. Yehuda and Rabbah went to visit Rabbah Bar b. Hana at his home while he was sick. They were having a nice visit and a discussion on a halachic matter when some fanatical fire worshipping Persian gangs invaded his house. The gangs caused havoc and confiscated the lamps from the house. When Rabbah bar b. Hana was praying for relief he was mentioning that it is hard to believe that the Persians are worse than the Romans. Rabbah achieved great fame with his legendary stories. Many of his stories were exaggerations and he was criticized by some of his colleagues for it, but others saw in the stories allegories and a hint to matters beyond our comprehension. (*Gittin* 16b, 17a)

Rabbah said in the name of Rabbi Yohanan. In the future, God will spread a banquet for the righteous, and will serve them the flesh of the Leviathan. (*Bava Batra* 74a–b, 75a)

Rabbah Bar b. Hana had a death in the family and he thought he should abstain from giving his lecture. But R. Hanina told him that if the public had a need for him, then he did not need to refrain. He then wished to use an interpreter, but Rav told him not to do so. (*Mo'ed Katan* 21a)

Rabbah bar b. Hana said: "I was traveling on the road when I met up with an Arab. He said to me: Come and I will show you the place where the people of Korach were swallowed up. I went and saw smoke coming out from two cracks in the earth. The Arab took a piece of cut wool, soaked it in water and put it on the tip of his spear and then passed it over the opening of the earth. The wool was immediately singed. He said to me: Listen to the voices, and I heard voices calling out. Moshe and his Torah are true, and we are liars." (*Sanhedrin* 110a, b)

Rabbah bar b. Hana said in the name of R. Yohanan, "To pair a couple for marriage is as difficult as splitting the Red Sea." (*Sanhedrin* 22a)

Rabbah bar b. Hana said: "What is the meaning of the passage, 'Fear of God prolongs one's life, but the years of the wicked shall be shortened'? The first part refers to the first Temple, which lasted four hundred and ten years, and was served by only eighteen high priests. The second part refers to the second Temple, which lasted for four hundred and twenty years, but was served by more than three hundred priests. Deduct

from the four hundred and twenty years of the Temple's existence the forty years served by Shimon ha-Tzaddik. Deduct also eighty years served by Yohanan and ten years served by Yishmael b. Phabi. Some say, eleven years served by Eleazar b. Harsum. After the deductions, you will reach the conclusion that the rest of the high priests did not complete a full year in service. (*Yoma* 9a)

For a glimpse of the world as it was in the time of Rabbah Bar b. Hana, see the historical timeline from 200 to 300 C.E.

רבה בר חנה
Rabbah bar Hana

(third century C.E.)
Amora, Babylonia

Rabbah bar Hana's early teacher was his uncle, Rabbi Hiyya.

When Rabbah was about to move to Babylonia, his uncle, Rabbi Hiyya, spoke to Rabbi Yehuda Hanasi on his behalf.

When Rabbah b. Hana was leaving for Babylonia, R. Hiyya said to Rebbe, "My brother's son is going to Babylonia. May he rule on monetary cases?"

"He may," Rebbe answered.

"May he issue rulings regarding first-born animals?"

"He may," Rebbe answered.

When Rav left for Babylonia, R. Hiyya said to Rebbe: "My sister's son is going to Babylonia. May he rule on matters of ritual law?"

"He may," Rebbe answered.

"May he rule on monetary cases?"

"He may," answered Rebbe.

"May he issue rulings regarding first born animals?"

"He may not," answered Rebbe. (*Sanhedrin* 5a)

In addition to being a great scholar he was also a wine merchant and a businessman. (*Bava Metzia* 83a)

When the wife of Rabbah b. Hana, who died before her husband, was on her deathbed, she said, "Those precious stones belong to Martha and to his daughter's family." Martha was the brother of Rabbi Hiyya. (*Bava Batra* 52a)

Rabbah was sitting with R. Zera and Rabbah b. R. Hanan having a halachic discussion. R. Abbaye was sitting beside them. R. Zera and R. Abbaye disagreed with each other, and each brought proof to make his point. Then Rabbah b. Hanan also argued with R. Abbaye. In the meantime Rava, who was not present, heard about the argument and sent word to them with R. Shemaya b. Zeira, giving them his opinion. It was a lively debate. (*Eruvin* 92a, b, and 93a)

Rabbah quoted R. Hiyya as follows: "R. Yehuda ha-Nasi once went to a certain place to teach there on Shabbat, but the place was too small. He therefore went out to the field to lecture there. However, the field was not suitable. It was full of sheaves, so he removed the sheaves to make room in the field. R. Yoseph related a similar story about R. Hiyya in the name of R. Oshaya." (*Shabbat* 127a)

For a glimpse of the world as it was in the time of Rabbah bar Hana, see the historical timeline from 200 to 300 C.E.

רבה בר הונא
Rabbah bar Huna

(third–fourth centuries C.E.)
Amora, Babylonia
Head of academy in Sura

Rabbah Bar Huna was a student of Rav and also of Shemuel. However, his first taste of real learning came from his father, who was the head of the academy at Sura. Later in his life he developed a close relationship with Rabbi Chisda; he and Rabbi Chisda also served together as judges. (*Bava Batra* 136b, *Eruvin* 49a)

When Rabbi Hisda passed away Rabbah was appointed as head of the Sura Academy.

R. Hisda and Rabbah b. Huna sat all day long engaged in judgment, but their hearts grew faint. R. Hiyya b. Rav recited for them a passage from the Torah. (*Shabbat* 10a)

The Talmud relates that R. Levi b. R. Huna b. Hiyya and Rabbah b. R. Huna were traveling together on a road, when R. Levi's donkey went ahead of Rabbah. Afterwards R. Levi noticed that Rabbah seemed to feel insulted. In order to pacify him, R. Levi asked him a question. Can a donkey with bad manners like mine be taken out on Shabbat wearing a halter?" (*Shabbat* 51b)

Rabbi Huna asked his son Rabbah, "Why do you not attend the lectures of Rabbi Hisda, whose talks are so sharp and enlightening?" (*Shabbat* 82a)

"Why should I attend? He talks most of the time about mundane matters. He speaks about how one should behave in the toilet – that one should not sit down abruptly or strain the rectum because the glands might become dislocated."

R. Huna became annoyed with his son and said to him, "He is discussing health matters and you call them mundane! All the more reason why you should attend his lectures."

Rabbah b. Huna wanted to institute the practice of saying the Ten Commandments during the prayer service, but R. Hisda told him that the practice had long been abolished on account of the *minim,* who spoke against the Torah. (*Berachot* 12a)

Rabbah b. Huna made a halachic statement that R. Hisda questioned. After the correction, Rabbah b. Huna said through an interpreter, "A man does not fully understand the words of the Torah until he has been made to stumble over them." (*Gittin* 43a)

Our rabbis taught day and night travelers are free from the obligation of the sukkah. R. Hisda and Rabbah b.

Huna slept on the river bank of Sura when they were visiting the Exilarch during the sukkah holiday, saying: "We are engaged in a religious errand and therefore are exempt from the mitzvah of sleeping in the sukkah." (*Sukkah* 26a)

Once on Shabbat, Rabbah b. R. Huna visited the home of Rabbah b. Nahman and was offered three special cakes.

He asked, "Did you know that I was coming?"

He answered him with a question: "Do you think that you are more important to us than Shabbat is?" (*Shabbat* 119a)

R. Nahman was visiting in the town of Sura. When R. Hisda and Rabbah b. R. Huna went to see him, they asked him to abrogate a certain ruling by Rav and Shemuel. He replied to them: "Do you think I traveled all the way here in order to annul a ruling of Rav and Shemuel?" (*Shevuot* 48b)

Rabbah was a frequent visitor to the home of the Exilarch. (*Shabbat* 157b)

One time Rabbah was having a disagreement with the officers of the Exilarch. He told them, "I do not derive my authority from your office. I hold it from my father, who received it from Rav, who received it from R. Hiyya, who received it from R. Yehuda ha-Nasi." (*Sanhedrin* 5a)

Although Rabbah died in Babylonia, his remains were taken to Eretz Yisrael. When Rabbah b. Huna and R. Hamnuna died, they took their remains to Israel. As they arrived at a bridge, the camels stopped. An Arab who was there (probably a bridge attendant) asked those carrying the coffins: "What is this?" They answered, "The two rabbis are paying honor to one another, as if to say: 'You proceed first,' and the other is saying, 'You proceed first.' The Arab gave his opinion, saying, "A notable

person like Rabbah b. Huna should take precedence." Therefore the camel bearing the coffin of Rabbah went first. The Arab's teeth fell out. (*Moed Katan* 25b)

For a glimpse of the world as it was in the time of Rabbah bar Huna, see the historical timeline from 250 to 350 C.E.

רבה
Rabbah
(third–fourth centuries C.E.)
Amora, Babylonia
Head of academy in Pumbedita

According to the Talmud, Rabbah bar Nahmeni was a descendent of Eli ha-Kohen. (*Rosh ha-Shannah* 18a)

He studied with Rabbi Huna in the academy of Sura, and also with Rabbi Yehuda b. Yehezkel in Pumbedita. (*Eruvin* 17a)

His brothers in Eretz Yisrael sent a message to him: "Although you are a great scholar, you must admit that studying alone does not equal studying with a master. And in case you think there is no one here with whom you could study, there is Rabbi Yohanan.

"However, if you are not coming up to Eretz Yisrael, then we give you the following advice: Do not sit too long, because sitting for a long time leads to abdominal troubles. Do not stand for a long time, because long standing is injurious to the heart. Do not walk too much, because excessive walking is harmful to the eyes. Rather divide your time by one third of the time sitting, one third standing and one third walking."

When Rabbi Yehuda b. Yehezkel, the head of the Pumbedita academy passed away, Rabbah became head of the academy. (*Ketubbot* 111a)

The Talmud relates that the scholars were about to choose a leader for the yeshiva in Pumbedita. The choice was between Rabbah and Rabbi Yoseph. The elders of Pumbedita sent a query to Eretz Yisrael asking which one to choose. One is Sinai, which is R Yoseph, and the other is an up-rooter of mountains, which is Rabbah. The answer came from Eretz Yisrael that Sinai is preferred, because everyone is in need of the knowledge of Sinai. However, R. Yoseph declined, because the astrologers told him that he would serve as head of the yeshiva for only two years. Rabbah took the position and he served for twenty-two years. After that R. Yoseph served for two and a half years. During Rabbah's entire term as head of the academy, R. Yoseph did not summon anyone to his house, but went to the person himself. (*Berachot* 64a)

Before beginning his lecture in the academy, Rabbah would say something humorous. Thus the students were cheerful, and afterwards they sat in awe and studied. (*Shabbat* 30b)

R. Abba b. Marta owed money to Rabba, but was slow to make payment. When he finally came with the money, it was during a sabbatical year when, according to Halacha, all debts are cancelled.

He gave the money to Rabba, who said to R. Abba, 'It is cancelled'. So R. Abba took the money, put it in his pockets and left. Afterwards, Abbaye met Rabbah and found him to be in a bad mood. When he asked him why, Rabbah told Abbaye what had happened with R. Abba.

Abbaye went to R. Abba and asked him. "When you took the money to Rabba, what did you say to him?"

"I offered to pay him the money I owed him."

"And what did he say?"

He said. "It is cancelled."

"Did you say to him: 'Take it anyway'?"

"No, I did not."

Abbaye said to him. "If you had said to him, 'Take it anyway,' he would have taken it. Now go to him and offer him the money again, but make sure you say to him, 'Take it anyway.'"

Rabbah took the money from him and said, "This rabbinical student did have the sense to see this from the beginning." (*Gittin* 37b)

Rabbah said in the name of R. Yohanan, "In the future, God will make a banquet for the righteous and they will be served the flesh of the Leviathan." (*Bava Batra* 75a)

Rabbah also said in the name of R. Yohanan: "In the future, God will make a tabernacle for the righteous from the skin of the Leviathan."

Rabbah said, "If one dies at the age between fifty to sixty years, that is death by *karet*."(*Moed Katan* 28a)

Rova said: "How long one is given to live, the gift of having children, and the gift of sustenance do not depend on merit, but rather on one's fortune."

For example; Rabbah and R. Hisda both were rabbis and tzaddikim. R. Hisda lived to the age of ninety-two, while Rabbah lived only to the age of forty (some say sixty). In the house of R. Hisda they celebrated sixty weddings, while in the house of Rabbah they had sixty bereavements. In the house of R. Hisda they fed the dogs with the finest food, while in the house of Rabbah there was barely enough food for human beings.

R. Abbaye, being an orphan, grew up in the house of Rabbah.

Abbaye and Rava were sitting before Rabbah when they were still young boys. Wishing to test them, Rabbah asked them, "To whom do we say the benedictions?"

Both answered, "To God."

"And where is God?"

Rava pointed to the roof, while Abbaye went outside and pointed to the sky.

Rabbah said to them, "Both of you will become rabbis." (*Berachot* 48a)

Rabbah said: It is a mitzvah for each individual to write a Torah scroll, even if one inherits a Torah from one's parents, as it is written in Devarim 31:19. (*Sanhedrin* 21b)

It used to be said: He who has not seen the Temple of Herod has never seen a beautiful building. (*Shabbat* 119a)

Rabbah said: "It was built of yellow and white marble. Herod originally intended to cover it with gold, but the rabbis advised him to leave it as is, because it was more beautiful as it was; it looked like the waves of the sea." (*Bava Batra* 4a)

Once, on Shabbat, Rabbah b. R. Huna visited the home of Rabbah b. Nahmeni and was offered three special cakes.

He asked, "Did you know that I was coming?"

He was answered with a question, "Do you think you are more important to us than Shabbat is?"

Rabbah used to prepare for Shabbat by chopping wood in honor of the day. (*Shabbat* 119a)

The Talmud relates that a certain man was traveling in order to redeem some captives. He had a purse of money with him, which was the ransom money, but when he was attacked by robbers, he handed the money over, as they demanded, and they let him go. Upon his return, he was summoned before Rabbah for having used the money to redeem himself, but Rabbah acquitted him of negligence.

Abbaye said to Rabbah: "Didn't this man rescue himself with another man's money?"

Rabbah replied: "There could hardly be a case of redeeming captives more urgent than this." (*Bava Kamma* 117b)

A certain man pushed his donkey onto a ferry boat before the passengers had a chance to disembark. The boat started to shake and was about to capsize. Another man who was on the boat came and pushed the donkey overboard, saving the boat, but the donkey drowned. When the case came before Rabbah, he declared the man not guilty.

Abbaye said to Rabbah: "Didn't the man rescue himself with another man's money?"

Rabbah replied: "No. The owner of the donkey was the pursuer from the beginning." (*Bava Kamma* 117b)

Our rabbis taught: Anyone who never saw the ceremony of the water-drawing at the Temple in Jerusalem never saw rejoicing in his life. Anyone who has not seen Jerusalem in its splendor has never seen a lovely city. Anyone who has not seen the temple in Jerusalem when it was fully rebuilt has never seen a beautiful building in his life. The Talmud asks: "Which Temple?" R. Abbaye said, and some say R. Hisda said: This refers to the building that Herod built." The Talmud asks: "What kind of material did he use to build it?" Rabbah answered, "He built it of yellow and white marble. Some differ and say that it was built of yellow, blue and white marble. The building was constructed in tiers; one row was projecting out and one row was receding inward. His intention was to overlay the marble stones with gold, but the rabbis advised him to leave the marble as is, because it had the appearance of the waves of the sea." (*Sukkah* 51b)

When Rabbah and R. Zera visited the Exilarch, they were served a nice meal. After the trays were removed, a basket of fruit, a gift from the Exilarch, was brought to them. Rabbah ate of the fruit, but R. Zera did not. R. Zera asked Rabbah: "Don't you hold that if the food has been removed it is forbidden to eat?"

Rabbah replied: "We can rely on the Exilarch that he usually sends a gift."

Rabbah sat with R. Zera and Rabbah b. R. Hanan, having a halachic discussion, and Abbaye was sitting beside them; R. Zera and R. Abbaye disagreed with each other and each brought proof to make his point. Then Rabbah b. Hanan also argued with R. Abbaye. In the meantime, Rava, who was not present, heard about the argument and sent word to them with R. Shemaya b. Zeira giving his opinion. It was a lively debate. (*Eruvin* 92a, b and 93a)

Rabbah said in the name of R. Sehora in the name of R. Huna: "If a person studies too much at a time, his learning decreases, but if he studies little at a time, his knowledge increases." Rabbah remarked, "The rabbis were aware of this advice, but disregarded it. R. Nahman b. Yitzchak said, I acted on this advice and it benefited me greatly." (*Eruvin* 54b)

Rabbah and R. Yoseph were traveling together on a Friday evening, but it was getting close to Shabbat. Rabbah said to R. Yoseph: "Let our Shabbat resting place be under that particular palm tree, which is leaning on another tree."

"I do not know that tree," said R. Yoseph. "Rely on me and make me your messenger, and I will declare our Shabbat resting place." (*Eruvin* 51a)

On one occasion R. Yehuda and Rabbah went to visit Rabbah bar b. Hana at his home while he was sick. They were having a pleasant visit, discussing a halachic matter, when some fanatical fire-worshipping Persian gangs

invaded his home. The gangs caused havoc and removed the lamps from the house. When Rabbah bar b. Hana prayed for relief, he mentioned that it was hard to believe that the Persians were worse than the Romans. (*Gittin* 16b, 17a)

The Talmud states that when the majority of the rabbis departed from the Rav's academy in Sura, twelve hundred students remained. When the students left the academy of R. Huna, eight hundred students remained.

When R. Huna delivered a lecture, thirteen interpreters assisted him.

When the students left the academy of Rabbah and R. Yoseph at Pumbedita, there remained four hundred students, who described themselves as orphans.

When the students left the academy of R. Abbaye (others say the academy of R. Pappa and still others say the academy of R. Ashi), two hundred rabbis remained who described themselves as orphans of the orphans. (*Ketubbot* 106a)

For a glimpse of the world as it was in Rabbah's time, see the historical timeline from 250 to 350 C.E.

רבה בר שילא
Rabbah bar Shila

(third–fourth centuries C.E.)
Amora, Babylonia

Rabbah b. Shila was a student of Rabbi Hisda. (*Shabbat* 81a)

He was so scrupulous about bribery that he would not permit a judge to try a case involving neighbors from whom he might have borrowed. (*Ketubbot* 105b)

The Talmud relates that when Rabbah ben Shila met Elijah, he asked him what the Almighty was doing. He answered. "He is reciting traditions taught by the rabbis and mentions their names, except that of Rabbi Meir."

"Why?"

"The reason is that he learned the traditions from Aher (Elisha ben Avuyah)."

Said Rabbah to Elijah, "Why punish him? R. Meir found a pomegranate. He ate the fruit and threw the peel away." At a later meeting Elijah said to him, "Now that you pleaded his case, the Almighty says, 'Meir, my son.'" (*Hagigah* 15b)

For a glimpse of the world as it was in the time of Rabbah bar Shila, see the historical timeline from 250 to 350 C.E.

רפרם בר פפא
Rafram b. Papa

(fourth–fifth centuries C.E.)
Amora, Babylonia
Head of the academy in Pumbedita

The Exilarch once came to Hagronia and stayed with R. Nathan. Rafram and all the rabbis came to listen to his lecture, but Ravina did not. The next day, Rafram wanted to be able to tell the Exilarch that Ravina had not intended to slight him. He therefore asked Ravina, "Why didn't you come to the lecture?" He answered that his foot hurt him. (*Yoma* 78a)

For a glimpse of the world as it was in the time of Rafram b. Papa, see the historical timeline from 350 to 450 C.E.

רמי בר חמא
Rami b. Hama

(fourth century C.E.)
Amora, Babylonia

The sister of R. Rami b. Hama was married to R. Avia, but her *ketubbah* was lost. They came to R. Yoseph to obtain a ruling as to whether they might continue to live together without one. He told them that it is a dispute between R. Meir and the sages. According to the sages, in such a case, a man may live with his wife for two to three years without a *ketubbah*. R. Abbaye objected and R. Yoseph told

him; in that case go and write her a new *ketubba*. (*Ketubbot* 56b, 57a)

R. Rami b. Hama was married to the daughter of R. Hisda. The Talmud relates that when R. Yitzhak came from Eretz Yisrael to Babylonia, he said, "There was a town in Eretz Yisrael by the name of Gofnit where eighty pairs of brothers, all priests, married eighty pairs of sisters, all from priestly families. The rabbis searched from Sura to Nehardea and could not find a similar case except the daughters of R. Hisda, who were married to Rami b. Hama and to Mar Ukva b. Hama. While the daughters of R. Hisda were daughters of kohanim, their husbands were not kohanim." (*Berakhot* 44a)

The mother of Rami b. Hama gave her property in writing to Rami b. Hama in the morning, but in the evening she gave it in writing to Mar Ukva b. Hama. Rami b. Hama came to R. Sheshet, who confirmed his inheritance. Mar Ukva then went to R. Nahman, who confirmed Mar Ukva in his inheritance.

R. Sheshet thereupon went to R. Nahman and said to him: "What is the reason you acted this way in this matter?"

R. Nahman replied: "And what is the reason you acted in this matter this way?"

R. Sheshet answered: "The will of R. Rami was written first."

R. Nahman replied: "Are we living in Jerusalem, where the hours are recorded? We live in Babylonia, where the hours are not recorded."

R. Sheshet asked: "And why did you act the way you did?"

"I treated it as a case to be decided at the discretion of the judges, replied R. Nahman."

R. Sheshet then retorted, "I also treated it as a case to be decided at the discretion of the judges."

R. Nahman replied, "But I am a judge and you are not, and furthermore, you did not at first say that you were treating it as a case to be decided by a judge." (*Ketubbot* 94b)

For a glimpse of the world as it was in the time of Rami b. Hama, see the historical timeline from 300 to 400 C.E.

רב

Rav

(third century C.E.)
Amora, Babylonia
Founder, head of the Academy in Sura

Rav, whose full name was Abba ben Aibu, was also known as Abba Aricha because he was very tall. Other sources have it that he was born about 175 C.E. in Kofri in southern Babylonia and that he died in approximately 247.

When Rabbah b. Hana was leaving for Babylonia, R. Hiyya said to Rebbe, "My brother's son is going to Babylonia. May he rule on monetary cases?"

"He may," Rebbe answered.

"May he issue rulings regarding first-born animals?"

"He may," Rebbe answered.

When Rav left for Babylonia, R. Hiyya said to Rebbe: "My sister's son is going to Babylonia. May he rule on matters of ritual law?"

"He may," Rebbe answered.

"May he rule on monetary cases?"

"He may," answered Rebbe.

"May he issue rulings regarding first-born animals?"

"He may not," answered Rebbe. (*Sanhedrin* 5a)

Eventually, Rabbi Yehuda ha-Nasi ordained him and authorized him to issue rulings in ritual law and in civil cases. Rabbi Huna was one of Rav's outstanding students.

Rav was a descendant of a very distinguished family and could trace his ancestry all the way back to King David.

Rabbi Hiyya, who was his uncle and also his teacher, brought him to the academy of Rabbi Yehuda in Eretz Yisrael, where he studied as a young man.

The Talmud states that R. Hiyya went out to teach the sons of his two brothers in the open market place. They were Rav and Rabbah b. Hana. (*Moed Katan* 16b)

Once, R. Hiyya and Rav were dining together with R. Yehuda ha-Nasi. At the time, Rav was still very young. At the end of the meal, Rebbe said to Rav, "Rise and wash your hands." (*Berachot* 46b)

When R. Hiyya saw that Rav was trembling, he said to him, "Son, he is telling you to get ready for the Grace after Meals."

Rav was one of the first rabbis they called amora, but he was also considered to be a tanna. Some say he was the last of the tannaim.

(*Ketubbot* 8a) The Talmud said that Rav had a right to differ because he was a tanna.

Samuel and Karna were sitting by the bank of the Nahar Malka. They saw the water rising and becoming discolored.

When R. Shemuel saw the water, he said to Karna: "I can tell by the water rising that a great man is arriving from Eretz Yisrael who suffers from stomach trouble. Go and smell his bottle" (i.e., find out how much learning he has). It was Rav, who had arrived in Babylonia. Karna went to Rav and asked him several tricky Talmudic questions in order to test his knowledge. Subsequently Shemuel took him into his house and gave him barley bread, fish and strong liquor, but did not show him where the outhouse was. Rav was suffering from stomach trouble and he was annoyed with Shemuel because of it. (*Shabbat* 108a)

As a young man, Rav came to the place where R. Shila was teaching. When no interpreter was available one day, Rav offered his services. When he interpreted the words *keriat ha-gever* as "the call of man," R. Shila said to him, "Would you change that to 'the call of the rooster'?"

Rav replied: "'A flute is a nice musical instrument for the educated, but give it to weavers and they will not accept it.' When I interpreted this word before R. Hiyya as meaning a man, he did not object." R. Shila asked Rav to sit down. (*Yoma* 20b)

Rav was the founder of the academy in Sura, Babylonia, which a minimum of twelve hundred students attended. He settled in Sura when he was visiting Tatelfush, a nearby community, and overheard a woman asking her neighbor, "How much milk is required to cook a certain piece of meat?" Rav thought to himself, *Do they not know that it is forbidden to mix meat and milk?*

He decided to stay there and declared to the community that mixtures of meat and milk are forbidden. (*Hullin* 110a)

The people addressed him as Rav.

The Talmud states that when the majority of the rabbis left Rav's academy in Sura, twelve hundred students remained behind. When the students left R. Huna's academy in Sura, eight hundred students remained behind.

When the students left the academy of Rabbah and R. Yoseph in Pumbedita, four hundred students remained, and they described themselves as orphans.

When the students left the academy of R. Abbaye in Pumbedita (others say from the academy of R. Pappa and still others say from the academy of R. Ashi), two hundred rabbis remained, and they described themselves as orphans of the orphans. (*Ketubbot* 106a)

When Rav lived in Nehardea, the Exilarch appointed him as market commissioner, but he resigned because his duties clashed with his religious beliefs. He moved to Sura, where he established his academy. Rav was independently wealthy. He owned land and had an income from the manufacture and sale of beer.

Rav was a nephew of R. Hiyya. Once, when he came from Babylonia for a visit to Eretz Yisrael, his uncle R. Hiyya asked him, "Is your father Aibu alive?"

He answered, "Ask me if my mother is alive."

R. Hiyya asked, "Is your mother alive?"

He answered, "Ask me if Aibu is alive."

When R. Hiyya heard all this, he knew that his brother and sister died. He said to his servant: "Take off my shoes, and afterwards bring my things to the bathhouse." R. Hiyya wanted to teach his students the Halacha.

We may learn three things from his action: a mourner is forbidden to wear shoes, one mourns only one day if one hears about a death thirty days after it occurred, and that part of the day is considered like a whole day.

Rabbah b. Bar Hana gave money to Rav with instructions to buy him a certain property, but he bought the property for himself. The Talmud asks: Did we not learn that this is the behavior of a cheat? The explanation is that it was a stretch of land adjacent to some land that belonged to lawless men. Rav could maintain his property because they would show respect for him, but they would not show respect to Rabbah b. Bar Hana. Nevertheless, should he have not informed him of the situation? He feared that another person might buy it in the meantime. (*Kiddushin* 59a)

R. Huna owned sheep that needed the shade during the day and open air at night. On weekdays, this was arranged by spreading a mat over the area and removing it for the night, but on Shabbat he was concerned this might be considered building, a forbidden activity on that day. He went to his teacher Rav and asked him what to do. Rav advised him to roll up the mat in the evening but to leave a handbreadth unrolled, so that the next morning, when the mat was unrolled, he would only be adding to an existing temporary tent.

A former host of Rav came before him in a lawsuit against another man, and said to Rav, "Were you not once a guest in my house?"

"Yes," replied Rav. "What can I do for you?"

"I have a case before you," said the man.

Rav replied, "In that case, I must recuse myself as your judge."

Rav turned to R. Kahana and said, "You be the judge of this case." When R. Kahana noticed that the man was relying too much on his acquaintance with Rav, he told him, "If I am to be your judge, you must put Rav out of your mind." (*Sanhedrin* 7b, 8a)

Rav and Rabbi Shemuel are the two scholars most often quoted in the Babylonian Talmud.

R. Huna said in the name of Rav, who learned it from R. Meir, who learned it from R. Akiva: "A person should always say; whatever happens, God is doing it for a good purpose." As the following story illustrates:

R. Huna said in the name of Rav, who learned it from R. Meir, who learned it from R. Akiva, "One should always say: 'Whatever God does is for the good.' By way of illustration, once,

when R. Akiva was traveling, he arrived at a certain town. He was traveling with a rooster, a donkey and a lamp. He looked around in the town for lodging, but none was available. Saying to himself, 'Whatever God does is for the good,' he slept in an open field. A strong wind came and blew out the lamp, a wild cat came and ate the rooster, and a lion came and ate the donkey. He said again, 'Whatever God does is for the good.' During the same night, a band of raiders came and captured all the inhabitants of the town and carried them away. He said: 'Did I not say that whatever God does is for the good?'" (*Berachot* 60b)

He is quoted as saying, "It is more important to study Torah than to build the Temple." (*Megillah* 16b)

Rav cautioned his students against listening to slander, warning them of its grave consequences. (*Shabbat* 56b)

Rav also declared that withholding knowledge from a student is tantamount to robbing him of his ancestral heritage. (*Sanhedrin* 91b)

R. Menashye b. Tahlifa said in Rav's name, "What we have learned in our studies proves that there is no chronological order in the Torah."

R. Papa observed, "This was said only of two different subjects, but if it is about the same subject, then what is written first occurred earlier, and what is written second occurred later. Otherwise the principle of "if a general proposition is followed by a specific proposition, the general proposition applies only to what is contained in the specific" cannot be sustained. (*Pesahim* 6b)

The Talmud tells us that R. Yehuda said in the name of Rav, "When Moshe ascended on high to receive the Torah, he found the Almighty busy placing coronets over the letters of the Torah. Moshe said to the Lord of the Universe, "What is hindering you? Is anything missing from the Torah that additions are necessary?"

God answered, "In the future, a man by the name of Akiva ben Yoseph will expound on this and derive something from each point or elevation."

Moshe said, "Lord of the Universe, allow me to see this man."

God replied, "Turn around!"

When Moshe turned around, he found himself in the academy of Rabbi Akiva. He sat down in the eighth row where the students were sitting and listened to the discussion that was going on, but could not follow what they were arguing about. He felt ill at ease, but when they came to a certain subject and a student asked, "How do we know all this?" Rabbi Akiva replied, "It is the law given to Moshe on Mount Sinai."

When Moshe heard the answer, he was comforted. He went back and addressed the Lord of the Universe, "You have such a great man there, and you give the Torah through me?"

God replied, "Be silent. Do not question me, for that is my decree." (*Menahot* 29b)

Rav Yehuda said in the name of Rav: "Every day a bat kol goes forth from Mount Horev and proclaims, 'The whole world is fed thanks to the merits of my son Hanina, and yet my son Hanina is satisfied with a small measure of carobs from one Friday to the next.'" (*Berachot* 17b)

Rav Yehuda related a story in the name of Rav: The daughter-in-law of R. Yoshaya went to the bathhouse on a Friday, but was delayed. Before she could go home, dusk fell and Shabbat began. She was in a place outside the limit beyond which one may travel on Shabbat. Her mother-in-law solved the problem by preparing an eruv for her. (*Eruvin* 80a)

Rav Yehuda related in the name of Rav: "When the husband of the daughter of Nakdimon b. Gurion died, the rabbis granted her an allowance of four hundred gold coins for her perfume basket. She said to them, 'May you grant such allowances for your own daughters.' They answered her, 'Amen.'" (*Ketubbot* 66b)

Rav said that the dead whom the prophet Yehezkel revived were the Ephraimites, who had left Egypt prematurely. They had miscalculated the four hundred years that had been prophesied to Abraham because they counted them from a different starting point. The Egyptians intercepted and killed them. (*Sanhedrin* 92b)

Rava b. Mechasya said in the name of R. Hama b. Gurya in Rav's name: "A man should never show preference for one son over the others because our ancestor Yaakov preferred Yoseph over his brothers and they became jealous. As a consequence, our ancestors wound up in Egypt as slaves." (*Shabbat* 10b)

Rava b. Mechasya said in the name of R. Hama b. Gurya in Rav's name: "A man should always choose to live in a city that was recently established because it is less sinful." (*Shabbat* 10b)

Rav Yehuda said in Rav's name, "Once, Queen Shlomzion [Salome Alexandra] made a banquet for her son, and all her utensils became defiled. She ordered [probably on the advice of her brother R. Shimon b. Shetah] all her golden dishes melted down and new ones made of the molten gold." (*Shabbat* 16b)

R. Yehuda said in Rav's name, "This was the practice of Rabbi Yehuda bar Illai. On Friday afternoon, they placed a basin of water before him. He washed his face, hands and feet and wrapped himself in a fringed linen robe, and he looked like an angel of God." (*Shabbat* 25b)

R. Yitzchak b. Shemuel said in the name of Rav: "The night has three watches, and at each watch, the Holy One sits and roars like a lion, lamenting: 'Woe to my children! On account of their sins I have destroyed My house and burnt My Temple, and exiled them among the nations of the world.'" (*Berachot* 3a)

R. Hanan b. Rava said in the name of Rav: "Elimelech, Salmon, Peloni Almoni and Naomi's father were all the sons of Nahshon ben Amminadav."

R. Hanan b. Rava also stated in Rav's name: "The name of Avraham's mother was Amathlai, and her father's name was Karnevo.

"The name of David's mother was Nitzevet, and she was the daughter of Adael.

"The mother of Shamshon was Tzelalfonith, and his sister's name was Nashyan." (*Bava Batra* 91a)

Whenever the Talmud states, "Our rabbis in Babylon," it refers to Rav and Shemuel. (*Sanhedrin* 17b)

R. Yehuda said in the name of Rav: "One may not eat before feeding one's animals." (*Berachot* 40a)

R. Zutra b. Toveya said in the name of Rav: "It is better to be thrown into a fiery furnace than to shame one's fellow in public." (*Berachot* 43b)

R. Huna said in Rav's name, though others say R. Huna said in Rav's name, which he heard from R. Meir: "One should always teach his student to use concise language and refined speech." (*Pesahim* 3b)

Two students were sitting before Rav discussing a difficult subject. One of them said, "This discussion has exhausted me like a swine." The other said, "This discussion made me as tired as a baby goat." Upon hearing this, Rav

would not speak to the one who used vulgar language. (*Pesahim* 3b)

It was asked, how far does Babylon extend as far as family purity is concerned? Rav said, "It extends as far as the river Azak."

Shemuel said, "It extends as far as the river Yoani."

"How far does it extend on the upper Tigris?"

Rav said, "It extends as far as Bagda and Awana."

Shemuel said, "It extends as far as Moscani."

"How far does it extend on the lower reaches of the Tigris?"

Shemuel said, "It extends as far as the lower Apamea."

"How far does it extend on the upper reaches of the Euphrates?"

Rav said, "It extends to Tulbakene."

Shemuel said, "It extends to the bridge of Be-Pherat." (*Kiddushin* 71b)

Rav and Shemuel were dining together, and R. Shimi b. Hiyya joined them a while later. He began to eat very quickly, and Rav said to him: "Are you trying to join us for the blessing after the meal? We have finished already." Shemuel interjected, "If they were to bring me some mushrooms, and if they were to bring you, Abba, some pigeons, would we not continue eating?" (*Berachot* 47a)

R. Yehuda said in the name of Rav: "Forty days before the embryo is formed, a heavenly voice calls out, 'The daughter of So-and-so shall be the wife of So-and-so.'" (*Sanhedrin* 22a)

Rav was very meticulous about paying promptly for his purchases. He considered it a desecration to buy meat from the butcher and not pay him right away.

Abbaye said that if local custom was to go to the customers afterwards to collect payment, then it was permitted.

Ravina said: "Mata Mehasya is a place where they go out afterwards to collect." Abbaye used to buy meat from two partners and pay each of them. Afterwards he would bring them together in order to settle the account with both of them. (*Yoma* 86a)

When Rav died, his students accompanied his bier. After they returned, they said, "Let us eat a meal at the river Danak." After they finished eating, they discussed a matter of Halacha regarding which they did not know the answer.

R. Adda b. Ahava stood up and tore his garment from front to back, then tore it once more and said, "Our teacher Rav is dead, and we have not learned the rules for the blessings after the meal!" Finally, an old man solved their problem. (*Berachot* 42b)

When they informed Shemuel that Rav has passed away, he rent thirteen garments on account of him and declared, "Gone is the man before whom I trembled." (*Moed Katan* 24a)

Sura, which is located south of Baghdad, is situated on the banks of the Euphrates River, where the river divides into two. It was an important Torah center for several centuries. It was also an important agricultural area, where the rabbis of the Talmud engaged in farming, planting vineyards, producing wine, raising cattle and engaging in commerce. Sura became a famous Torah center when Rav moved there in 219 and established his famous academy, which attracted hundreds of students and scholars. When Rav passed away in 247, the academy lost its preeminence to Nehardea for seven years. However, when Rabbi Shemuel of Nehardea passed away in 254, Sura regained its prominence under the leadership of Rabbi Huna.

Once, when there was a plague in the town of Sura, it did not affect the neighborhood where Rav lived. Although at first people attributed it to Rav's merit, it was made clear to them in a dream that the neighborhood had been spared on account of a man who made it a practice to lend shovels and spades for burials. (*Taanit* 21b)

For a glimpse of the world as it was in Rav's time, see the historical timeline from 200 to 300 C.E.

רב בר שבא
Rav b. Sheva
(fourth century C.E.)
Amora, Babylonia

Rav was a student of R. Pappa. It is stated that while R. Pappa sat and taught a law about the eruv, Rav b. Sheva asked him a puzzling question. (*Eruvin* 33b)

For a glimpse of the world as it was in the time of Rav b. Sheva, see the historical timeline from 300 to 400 C.E.

רבינא
Ravina I
(fourth–fifth centuries C.E.)
Amora, Babylonia

Ravina, who studied in Rava's academy in Mehoza, had halachic discussions with R. Ashi, R. Nahman ben Yitzhak, R. Papa and R. Huna ben Yehoshua. According to some, he died in 422. (*Berachot* 20b)

Once it happened that Ravina examined the slaughterer's knife in Babylonia, but R. Ashi, who was the halachic authority in the area, was offended and said to him: "Why are you doing this?" Ravina answered: "Did not R. Hamnuna decide legal matters at Harta di-Argiz during the lifetime of R. Hisda? Just as in their case, I am your colleague and also your student." (*Eruvin* 63a)

A certain man leased a field in order to plant a sesame crop, but planted wheat instead. Although the price of sesame was usually higher, in this particular year the price of wheat was higher than that of sesame. When Ravina wanted to rule in favor of the tenant, R. Abba mi-Difti pointed out to him that the earth was also a contributor to the higher value of the product. (*Bava Metzia* 104b)

The Exilarch once came to Hagronia and stayed with R. Nathan. Rafram and all the rabbis came to listen to his lecture, but Ravina did not. The next day, Rafram wanted to be able to tell the Exilarch that Ravina had not intended to slight him. He therefore asked Ravina, "Why didn't you come to the lecture?" He answered him that his foot hurt him. (*Yoma* 78a)

Rav was very meticulous about paying promptly for his purchases. He considered it a desecration to buy meat from the butcher and not pay him right away. Abbaye said that if local custom was to go to the customers afterwards in order to collect, then it was permitted.

Ravina said, "Mata Mehasya is a place where they go out afterwards to collect."

Abbaye used to buy meat from two partners and pay each of them. Afterwards, he brought them together in order to settle the account with both. (*Yoma* 86a)

R. Ashi sent a message to Ravina asking for the loan of ten zuz so that he could buy a small parcel of land. His reply was: "Bring witnesses and we will draw up a contract."

Rabbi Ashi was surprised. "I am one of your best friends, and even from me you want a written contract?"

Ravina answered: "It is especially from you that I want a contract. You are so immersed in Torah study that you are bound to forget and thereby cause me to sin and bring a curse upon me."

Ravina had a son. The Talmud relates that he was engaged in preparations for his son's wedding at the house of R. Hanina. (*Niddah* 66a)

He also had a daughter, as mentioned in the Talmud. Ravina was writing a large amount of dowry for his daughter. (*Bava Metzia* 104b)

R. Yehuda ha-Nasi and R. Nathan concluded the Mishna. R. Ashi and Ravina concluded the Horaah (Gemara). Rashi notes that prior to them, there was no particular order to the teachings of the Mishna. (*Bava Metzia* 86a)

For a glimpse of the world as it was in the time of Ravina I, see the historical timeline from 350 to 450 C.E.

רבינא
Ravina II
(fifth century C.E.)
Amora, Babylonia
Head of the academy in Sura

Ravina II's father, whose name was Huna, died while Ravina was still very young. (*Berachot* 39b) He often quoted his mother about matters of the past. According to some, R. Ravina died in 499.

His main teacher was Meremar. (*Shabbat* 81b)

Ravina became the head of the academy at Sura in the fifth century C.E.

Ravina served as judge in a case where Rabbi Ashi's daughter made a claim. "Come and hear: Ravina ruled that the daughter of R. Ashi may collect her inheritance from Mar, the son of R. Ashi, and choose from his medium-grade land. She may also collect from the lowest grade of fields belonging to R. Ashi's other son, R. Sama." (*Ketubbot* 69a)

For a glimpse of the world as it was in the time of Ravina II, see the historical timeline from 400 to 500 C.E.

רחומי
Rehumei I

(fourth century C.E.)
Amora, Babylonia

R. Rehumei was a student of Abbaye and Rava. He died on Yom Kippur while in Mehoza, at Rava's academy, while still a young man. (*Pesahim* 39a)

R. Rehumei was studying on the roof of Rava's academy in Mehoza when the roof suddenly collapsed, killing him. (*Ketubbot* 62b)

For a glimpse of the world as it was in the time of Rehumei I, see the historical timeline from 300 to 400 C.E.

רחומי
Rehumei II

(fifth century C.E.)
Amora, Babylonia
Head of the academy in Pumbedita

R. Rehumei was a student of Rabbi Ravina, whose teachings he transmitted. He said that he saw Ravina cross a body of water in his sandals. He became the head of the academy at Pumbedita and held that position for thirteen years. During his lifetime, King Yezdegerd II persecuted the Jews harshly. (*Yoma* 78a)

For a glimpse of the world as it was in the time of Rehumei II, see the historical timeline from 400 to 500 C.E.

רבא
Rava

(third–fourth centuries C.E.)
Amora, Babylonia
Founder and head of the academy at Mehoza

Rava's full name was R. Abba b. Yoseph b. Chama. Some sources have it that he died in 352 C.E.

Abbaye and Rava were sitting before Rabbah when they were still young boys. Wishing to test them, Rabbah asked, "To whom do we say the benedictions?"

Both children answered, "To God."

"And where is God?" Rava pointed to the roof, while Abbaye went outside and pointed to the sky. Rabbah said to them: "Both of you will become rabbis." (*Berachot* 48a)

Rava, who lived in Mehoza, studied with Rabbi Hisda in the academy in Sura. He also studied under Rabbi Nahman b. Yaakov and Rabbi Yoseph in the academy in Pumbedita.

His debating partner was Rabbi Abbaye, with whom he had disagreements on many halachic issues. After Rabbi Yoseph passed away, he wished to become the head of the yeshiva in Pumbedita, but the authorities chose his colleague Rabbi Abbaye. Rava moved back to Mehoza, where he established his own yeshiva.

The academy in Mehoza became prominent, and many students flocked to it. (*Bava Batra* 22a)

When he delivered his lectures in Mehoza on Shabbat, a large crowd would come to the synagogue in order to hear them. (*Eruvin* 44b)

Rava became wealthy. He owned fields and vineyards, and traded in wine. (*Bava Metzia* 73a)

Rava said: I made three requests of Heaven. Two were granted and one was not. I prayed for the scholarship of R. Huna and the wealth of R. Hisda, which were granted to me, but the modesty of Rabbah b. Huna was not granted to me. (*Moed Katan* 28a)

Rava married the daughter of R. Hisda. (*Bava Batra* 12b)

R. Hisda's daughter was sitting on her father's lap as R. Hisda's two students, Rava and Rami b. Hama, sat before him. R. Hisda asked the little child, "Which one do you like?" She replied, "I like both of them." To this Rava replied, "Let me be the second."

R. Yoseph had a grievance against Rava b. Yoseph b. Hama and felt insulted. The day before Yom Kippur, Rava went to R. Yoseph, who had become blind in his later years, in order to apologize. He found R. Yoseph's attendant mixing him a cup of wine. Rava said to the attendant, "Give it to me. I will mix it." When R. Yoseph tasted the wine, he said, "This wine tastes the way Rava used to mix it." (*Eruvin* 54a)

"I am here," Rava said.

R. Yoseph said to him: "Do not sit down until you interpret a Scriptural passage for me."

Ifra Hormuz, the mother of King Shapur II of Persia,thought very highly of Rava. The Talmud recounts that Ifra Hormuz sent four hundred dinars to R. Ammi, but he would not accept them. She sent the money to Rava and he accepted it. When R. Ammi heard about it, he was angry and quoted a passage from Isaiah. But Rava defended his action on the grounds that one should not offend the government.

Was R. Ammi not concerned not to offend the government? He did not want to distribute the money to the non-Jewish poor. But Rava distributed the money both to the Jewish and non-Jewish poor alike. R. Ammi was angry because he was not fully informed. (*Bava Batra* 10b)

Ifra Hormuz once sent some blood to Rava to be examined while R. Ovadiah was present. He smelled it and declared, "This blood is the result of lust." When she heard what Rava said, she said to her son the king, "See how wise the Jews are."

The king replied, "He is guessing." She sent him sixty blood samples and Rava identified all of them except one, which was lice blood. However, he sent her a comb for removing lice. She exclaimed, "You Jews – you seem to know one's inner heart!" (*Niddah* 20b)

Rava had to bribe the Persian court on several occasions for various reasons.

Rava said to the rabbis, "Do you have an idea how much I send secretly to the court of King Shapur?" Nevertheless, the king sent men to seize some of his property. (*Hagigah* 5b)

Bar Heyda was an interpreter of dreams. If one paid him well, he gave a good interpretation. Otherwise he did not. Rava came to him with his dreams but did not pay him, and Bar Heyda always gave him bad news. Finally, Rava decided to give Bar Heyda a fee, and from then on he received good interpretations. (*Berachot* 56a)

He was a frequent visitor to the Exilarch. Rava said, "When we eat together at the Exilarch's, we recite the Grace after Meals in groups of three." He was asked, "Why not eat in groups of ten?" He replied, "Because the Exilarch might hear them finish without waiting for him and be angry." (*Berachot* 50a)

Rava and R. Zera visited the Exilarch and were served a lavish meal. After the servants removed the trays, they brought in a basket of fruit, a gift from the Exilarch. Rava ate some of the fruit, but R. Zera did not. R. Zera asked Rava: "Don't you hold that if the food has been removed it is forbidden to eat?"

Rava replied, "We can rely on the Exilarch that he usually sends a gift."

When the government placed troops in the town of Mehoza, the Jews had to quarter them in their homes. (*Berachot* 42a)

Rava told the people of Mehoza: "Remove from your homes the leavened bread that belongs to the troops because it is in your possession. If it were lost or stolen, you would be held responsible. Therefore, it is considered to be your property and your hametz." (*Pesahim* 5b)

Rava and R. Nahman b. Yitzhak were once sitting together outside when R. Nahman b. Yaakov, the Exilarch's son-in-law, passed by in a gilded carriage, wearing a purple robe. Rava went over to meet him, but R. Nahman b. Yitzhak did not. (*Gittin* 31b)

R. Mari, the son of R. Shemuel's daughter, showed Rava a contradiction regarding prayer, but Rava gave him no answer. Later, he said to him: "Did you hear any statement on this subject?"

He answered: "Yes. I heard R. Sheshet clarify this contradiction." (*Berachot* 16a)

The proselyte Issur had twelve thousand zuz deposited for safekeeping with Rava, but the question arose as to whether Issur's son Mari was entitled to it. The problem was that when Mari was conceived, Issur had not yet converted, though he became Jewish before Mari was born. R. Ika b. R. Ammi suggested that Issur declare that the money belonged to R. Mari. That is how the matter was solved: Issur declared that the money belonged to his son, Mari. (*Bava Batra* 149a)

Once a Sadducee saw Rava engrossed in his studies. Rava was completely unaware that his finger was under his foot, bleeding.

"You are irrational people," said the Sadducee. "You gave your consent at Mount Sinai before you heard what was expected of you."

Rava answered him: "We are a people of integrity, and we trusted that God would not ask us to do the impossible." (*Shabbat* 88a)

The Talmud states: "The day R. Akiva died, Rebbe was born. When Rebbe died, Rav Yehuda was born. When Rav Yehuda died, Rava was born,

and when Rava died, R. Ashi was born." (*Kiddushin* 72b)

Rava said: "The gift of life span that is given to humankind, or the gift of having children, or how much sustenance one earns, does not depend on merit, but rather on one's fortune. For example, both Rabbah and R. Hisda were rabbis and tzadikim. R. Hisda lived to the age of ninety-two while Rabbah lived only to the age of forty (some say sixty). In the house of R. Hisda they celebrated sixty weddings, while in the house of Rabbah they had sixty bereavements. In the house of R. Hisda, they fed the dogs with the finest food, while in the house of Rabbah there was barely enough food for human beings." (*Moed Katan* 28a)

It is related that R. Dimi of Nehardea brought a load of figs in a boat. The Exilarch said to Rava, "Go and see if he is a scholar. If so, reserve the market for him." The scholars had the privilege of being allowed to dispose of their merchandise before of the rest of the merchants so that they could go and study. Rava sent R. Adda b. Abba to test R. Dimi's scholarship. He put to him the following question. "If an elephant swallows a basket and then passes it out with excrement, is it still considered to be a basket?" R. Dimi could not give an answer. He asked R. Adda: "Are you Rava?"

R. Adda answered: "Between Rava and me there is a great difference, but at any rate, I can be your teacher, and therefore Rava is the teacher of your teacher." Consequently they did not reserve the market for him, and his figs were a total loss. He appealed to Rabbi Yoseph, by saying. "See how they have treated me!" When R. Adda died shortly afterwards, R. Dimi afflicted himself, saying, "It is because of me that he was punished, because he made me lose my figs."

Abbaye blamed himself for his death because R. Adda used to say to the students, "Instead of chewing on bones in the school of Abbaye, come and eat fat meat in the school of Rava." (*Bava Batra* 22a)

R. Shemuel b. Nahmeni said in the name of R. Yonathan: "A man is shown in a dream only that which is suggested by his own thoughts." (*Berachot* 55b)

Rava said: "This is proven by the fact that no one dreams of a golden palm tree or an elephant going through the eye of a needle."

Rava used to tell the men brought before him for refusing to support their young children, "Would it please you to have your children supported from the charity fund?" (*Ketubbot* 49b)

A man once came to Rava and asked for community support.

Rava asked him: "What do your meals consist of?"

"They consist of fat chicken and old wine," the man answered

"Did you consider the burden of the community?" asked Rava.

"Am I eating what belongs to them?" asked the man. "I am eating the food of God, Who provides for every individual according to his habits."

In the meantime, Rava's sister, whom he had not seen in thirteen years, arrived with a basket of fat chicken and old wine.

"What a remarkable incident," said Rava. "I apologize. Come and eat." (*Ketubbot* 67b)

Rava remarked, "At first I thought that all the people of Mehoza love me. When I was appointed a judge, I thought that some people would hate me and some would love me. But I observe that a litigant may lose today and win tomorrow. Therefore, my conclusion is

that if I am loved, they all love me, and if I am hated, they must all hate me." (*Ketubbot* 105b)

Rava said: "Everyone is obligated to mellow himself with wine on Purim until he cannot tell the difference between the phrases 'cursed be Haman' and 'blessed be Mordechai.'" (*Megillah* 7b)

Once a message was sent to Rava, saying: "Several scholars have arrived from Rakkath (Tiberias). They had been captured by an eagle (Roman troops). They were in possession of articles manufactured in Luz, such as purple (tzitzis). Through divine mercy they escaped. The offspring of Nahshon (the Nasi) wished to establish a Neziv (month), but the Edomites would not permit it. However, the assembly met and established a Neziv in the month (Adar) in which Aaron the Priest died." (*Sanhedrin* 12a)

The wife of Rava was the daughter of R. Hisda. (*Ketubbot* 39b)

A man asked his friend to buy him four hundred barrels of wine. When he brought him the wine, it turned out to be sour. The man came to Rava to claim that his friend bought him sour wine. Rava said to the man who bought the wine, "If you can bring proof that the wine was good when you bought it, you will be free of any liability." (*Bava Metzia* 83a)

Rava said, "When a man dies and goes up to heaven he is asked: "Did you deal honestly and in good faith with your fellow-men?"

"Did you set a regular time for learning Torah?"

"Did you engage in procreation?"

"Did you hope for redemption?"

"Did you participate in intellectual discussions?"

"Were you able to deduce one thing from another?" (*Shabbat* 31a)

Rava had a brother by the name of Rav Seorim. It is stated that while Rav Seorim sat at Rava's deathbed and saw that he was about to die; he bent toward him in order to listen to what he had to say. Rava said to his brother, "Please tell the Angel of Death not to torment me."

"Are you not his intimate friend?" asked Rav Seorim.

Rava answered: "Since my fate has been turned over to him, he pays no attention to me."

Rav Seorim then said to his brother, "After you are gone, please show yourself to me in a dream."

Rava did so. Rav Seorim asked him then, "Was it painful?"

"I felt as though I were being pricked by needles," Rava said. (*Moed Katan* 28a)

Rava instructed R. Papa and R. Huna b. Yoshua as follows: "When a written legal decision of mine comes before you and you object to it, do not tear it up before you speak to me. If I have valid reasons for my decision, I will share them with you, and if not, I will withdraw it. After my death, do not tear up my decision or draw any conclusions from it. Do not tear it up because if I had been there, I might have given you my reasons, and do not draw any conclusions because a judge must be guided by what he sees with his own eyes." (*Bava Batra* 130b)

Mehoza, a town on the banks of the Tigris River, is located next to the Malka canal, which connects the Euphrates with the Tigris.

In Talmudic times, Mehoza was located on a central trading route, through which many caravans passed. The town became a place of learning when the Nehardea academy was destroyed in 259 C.E. by Papa b. Nasser, the commander in chief of Palmyra. It gained prominence after Abbaye passed

away. Rava lived in Mehoza and headed its academy for fourteen years. Mehoza's large Jewish community constituted a majority of the town's population. (*Berachot* 59b)

Abbaye was surprised that there was no mezuzah on the town's gates. (*Yoma* 11a)

For a glimpse of the world as it was in Rava's time, see the historical timeline from 250 to 350 C.E.

רבא בר מתנא
Rava bar Mathna

(third–fourth century C.E.)
Amora, Babylonia

Rava bar Mathna was a student of Rabbah and R. Sheshet. Abbaye bar Avin and Rabbi Hanania b. Avin were his colleagues. (*Pesahim* 34a)

Abbaye b. Avin and R. Hanania b. Avin studied Tractate Terumot at Rabbah's academy. Rava b. Mathna came to meet them and asked, "What have you studied in the academy about *terumot*?" (*Pesahim* 34a)

For a glimpse of the world as it was in the time of Rava bar Mathna, see the historical timeline from 250 to 350 C.E.

רבא בר מחסיא
Rava b. Mehasya

(third–fourth centuries C.E.)
Amora, Babylonia

Rava b. Mehasya said in the name of R. Hama b. Gurya in Rav's name: "A man should never show preference for one son over the others, because our ancestor Yaakov preferred Yoseph over his brothers and they became jealous. Consequently, our ancestors wound up in Egypt as slaves. (*Shabbat* 10b)

Rava b. Mehasya said in the name of R. Hama b. Gurya in Rav's name: "A man should always choose to live in a city that was recently established because it is less sinful." (*Shabbat* 10b)

Rav Hisda held two pigeons in his hand and said, "If someone comes and tells me a new dictum in the name of Rav, I will give him these pigeons." Rava b. Mehasya said to him, "Rav said the following: 'If one gives a gift to a neighbor, he must inform him first.'" Upon this, R. Hisda gave him the pigeons.

Rava asked him, "Are Rav's dicta so dear to you?"

"Yes," he replied. (*Shabbat* 10b)

For a glimpse of the world as it was in the time of Rava b. Mehasya, see the historical timeline from 250 to 350 C.E.

רבא בר זימונא
Rava b. Zimuna (Abba bar Zemina)
(fourth century C.E.)
Amora, Eretz Yisrael

At one time, R. Rava b. Zimuna lived in Rome, where he worked as a tailor. It is told that while he was in Rome, his employer offered him some meat as a gift, which he declined. His employer told him, "If you refused to eat my meat I would kill you." He still declined because the animal from which the meat had come had not been slaughtered properly. After the incident his employer told him, "I would have killed you if you had eaten the meat and not the other way around, because if you are a Jew, then be a Jew."

After he left Rome, he moved to Eretz Yisrael, and studied with Rabbi Zeira.

R. Zera said in the name of Rava b. Zimuna: "If the earlier scholars were the children of angels, then we are children of humans, and if the earlier scholars were children of humans, then we are like children of donkeys. Not like the donkeys of R. Hanina b. Dosa or R. Pinhas b. Yair, but like common donkeys." (*Shabbat* 112 b)

Once, R. Pinhas ben Yair arrived at an inn where they put grain before his donkey, but the donkey would not eat. When they asked R. Pinhas why, he answered, "Perhaps its food was not tithed." They tithed the grain immediately and the donkey ate. (*Hullin* 7a)

For a glimpse of the world as it was in the time of Rava b. Zimuna, see the historical timeline from 300 to 400 C.E.

רבא מברניש
Rava me-Barnish
(fourth–fifth centuries)
Amora, Babylonia

Rava was a contemporary of Rabbi Ashi and engaged with him in a halachic dispute about the defilement of animal skins. (*Shabbat* 28a)

For a glimpse of the world as it was in the time of Rava me-Barnish, see the historical timeline from 350 to 450 C.E.

ספרא
Safra
(fourth century C.E.)
Amora, Babylonia

R. Safra, a student of Rabbi Abba, was a close friend of Rabbi Abbahu. (*Pesahim* 51b, *Avodah Zarah* 4a)

Other colleagues of his were Rabbi Hanina b. Papa, R. Huna b. Hanina and R. Aha b. Huna. (*Shabbat* 124a)

The father of R. Safra left a large sum of money. R. Safra took it and invested it in business. His brothers took him before Rava's court and demanded a share in the profits. Rava told them that since R. Safra was a great scholar, he could not be expected to leave his studies in order to make a profit for others. (*Bava Batra* 144a)

Rabbi Safra went into partnership with Issur, but then he divided the stock in front of two witnesses, without Issur's knowledge. They came before R. Rabbah b. Huna to settle the matter. (*Bava Metzia* 31b)

R. Safra's honesty was legendary. A story is told that a person who wanted to buy his donkey once approached him and made him an offer. Rabbi Safra did not answer him because he was in the midst of prayers. Thinking that his first offer had not been satisfactory, the person offered R. Safra a higher price, and raised it further. Finally, when R. Safra completed his prayers, he insisted on selling the donkey for the first price that had been offered.

Rabbi Safra married, but his wife died soon after their marriage, and he never married again. (Rashi on *Makkot* 24a)

R. Zerika said to R. Safra, "Come and see the difference in approach between the good men of Eretz Yisrael and the pious men of Babylonia. When the world was in need of rain, the pious men of Babylonia, R. Huna and R. Hisda, said, "Let us assemble and pray. Perhaps the Almighty will be appeased and send us rain." But the great men of Eretz Yisrael, such as R. Yonah the father of R. Mani, would go and stand in a low spot dressed in sackcloth and pray for rain. (*Taanit* 23b)

R. Yohanan said: "Three kinds of people earn special approval from God: a bachelor who lives in a large city and does not sin, a poor man who returns lost property to its owner, and a rich man who tithes his produce in secret."

R. Safra, a bachelor living in a large city, was in the company of Rava when he heard this quotation, and his face lit up. Rava said to him, "This does not apply to someone like you, but to people like R. Hanina and R. Hoshia. They are sandal-makers in Eretz Yisrael and they live in a neighborhood of prostitutes, where they make sandals for them.

When they deal with them, they do not lift their eyes to look at them. When the prostitutes take an oath, they swear 'by the life of the holy rabbis of Eretz Yisrael.'" (*Pesahim* 113 a–b)

R. Safra said: R. Abbahu used to tell this story: When R. Hananya b. Ahi Yoshua left for Babylonia, he began to intercalate the years and to fix the new months outside Israel. The bet din of Israel sent two scholars to stop him from doing so: R. Yosi b. Kippar and the grandson of R. Zechariah b. Kavutal. When R. Hananya saw them, he asked them, "Why have you come?" They answered, "We have come to learn Torah from you." When he heard that, he proclaimed to the community: These men are the great scholars of our generation. They and their ancestors have served in the Temple. As we have learned, Zechariah b. Kavutal said: Many times have I read from the book of Daniel.

Shortly afterwards, they issued rulings against his declarations. Everything that he said was impure they declared pure, and permitted what he had forbidden. R. Hananya became upset and announced to the community: "These men are false and worthless."

They said to him, "You have already built our reputation and you cannot destroy it. You have already made fences and you cannot break them down." He asked them, "Why do you declare pure that which I declared to be impure?"

They answered him, "Because you intercalate years and fix the new moon outside Israel." He retorted, "Did not R. Akiva b. Yoseph intercalate years and fix the new month outside of Israel?" They answered him; "Do not cite R. Akiva, who had no equal in Israel." He retorted; "I also left no equal in the land of Israel." They said to him, "The kids that you left behind in Israel have become goats with horns, and they sent us to speak to you in their name. If you listen, well and good, but if you do not, you will be excommunicated. They also empowered us to tell the community here in Babylonia: If you heed us, well and good. But if you do not, then let them go up the mountain, let Ahia build an altar, and Hananya play the harp. All of you will become deniers and will have no portion in the God of Israel." When the community heard this, they started to weep and declared: Heaven forbid. (*Berachot* 63a)

R. Abbahu praised R. Safra to the *minim* as a great scholar, and consequently they exempted him from paying taxes for thirteen years. One day they encountered him and they asked him to explain a passage in the bible. He could not give them an answer. They took a scarf and wound it around his neck and tortured him. When R. Abbahu came and found him being tortured, he asked. "Why do you torture him?"

They answered: "Have you not told us that he is a great scholar? He cannot even explain the meaning of a biblical verse."

He replied: "I might have told you that he is a great scholar, and he is, but what I meant was that he is a scholar in tannaitic learning, but not in Scripture."

"But how is it that you know Scripture?" they asked.

He replied: "The rabbis and I who are frequently with you make it our business to study it thoroughly, but others do not." (*Avodah Zarah* 4a)

As R. Aha b. Yoseph was walking to R. Safra's home, he had to lean on the shoulders of R. Nahman, his sister's son, because he was old and feeble. R. Aha said, "When we reach the house, please lead me in." R. Nahman complied. Once inside, they discussed several halachic questions. (*Shabbat* 140a)

When Rabbi Safra died, Rabbi Abbaye's students did not rend their clothing because he was not their teacher. Nevertheless, Rabbi Abbaye instructed them to accord him the highest honors. (*Moed Katan* 25a)

For a glimpse of the world as it was in the time of Rabbi Safra, see the historical timeline from 300 to 400 C.E.

סחורה
Sehora

(third–fourth centuries C.E.)
Amora, Babylonia

Rabbah said in the name of R. Sehora in the name of R. Huna: "If a person studies too much at a time his learning decreases, but if he studies little at a time, his knowledge increases." Rabbah remarked, "The rabbis were aware of this advice, but disregarded it." R. Nahman b. Yitzhak said, "I acted on this advice and it benefited me greatly. My learning stayed with me." (*Eruvin* 54b)

For a glimpse of the world as it was in R. Sehora's time, see the historical timeline from 250 to 350 C.E.

שמאי
Shammai

(first century B.C.E.–first century C.E.)
Tanna, Eretz Yisrael

Shammai and his colleague, Hillel, were one of the zugot, or pairs of study partners, mentioned in the Talmud.

At first Rabbi Hillel's partner was Rabbi Menahem, but Rabbi Menahem left and Rabbi Shammai took his place. According to some, R. Menahem went into the service of King Herod, while others say that he withdrew into seclusion.

When Rabbi Menahem retired from the Sanhedrin, Rabbi Shammai was appointed to succeed him as *av beit din* of the Sanhedrin. He established a school known as Beit Shammai. His school and Rabbi Hillel's disagreed on many of the Halachot. (*Hagiga* 2:2, 16a, b)

There are many stories that illustrate the difference between Rabbi Shammai and Rabbi Hillel. One is that a non-Jew came before Shammai and asked him to convert him to Judaism, and to teach him the Torah while he stood on one foot. Enraged, Shammai chased him away with a builder's ruler. The man came to Hillel with the same request. Rabbi Hillel told him: "Yes, I will convert you to Judaism, and this is what the Torah teaches: 'What is hateful to you, do not impose on your neighbor.' That is the whole Torah. The rest is commentary. Now go and study." (*Shabbat* 31a)

The Talmud hints that Rabbi Shammai was a builder. (*Shabbat* 31a)

A story is told that Rabbi Shammai's daughter-in-law gave birth to a boy, and Rabbi Shammai wanted the boy to be under a sukkah. Therefore he removed the ceiling plaster and replaced it with sukkah coverings for the sake of the child. (*Sukkah* 2:8, 28a)

He used to say, "Make the study of Torah a steady habit, say little and do much, and receive every person cheerfully." (*Avot* 1:15)

Although Rabbi Hillel and Rabbi Shammai had many disagreements about Halacha, they greatly respected each other. In most cases, the school of Shammai was more stringent. Nevertheless, tradition has it that both views are correct, and we follow Rabbi Hillel in the majority of Halachot.

Rabbi Abba said in the name of Rabbi Shemuel: "For three years there was a dispute between the schools of Beit Shammai and Beit Hillel, each one claiming that Halacha accords with their views." Then a bat kol was heard announcing that both are the words of the living God, but the Halacha is in agreement with the rulings of Beit Hillel. (*Eruvin* 13b)

For a glimpse of the world as it was in R. Shammai's time, see the historical timeline from 50 B.C.E. to 50 C.E.

שילא
Shila

(third century C.E.)
Amora Babylonia

R. Shila was a contemporary of Rav and Shemuel.

As a young man, Rav came to the place where R. Shila was teaching. One day there was no interpreter available and Rav offered to be one. Rav interpreted the words *keriat ha-gever* as "the call of man." R. Shila said, "Would you change that to 'the call of the rooster'?"

Rav replied, "A flute is a nice musical instrument for the educated, but give it to weavers and they will not accept it. When I interpreted this word as meaning a man before R. Hiyya, he did not object."

R. Shila asked Rav to sit down. (*Yoma* 20b)

On another occasion, Rav disapproved of R. Shila's ruling. It happened that a man was said to have drowned in the swamps, but there were no witnesses. Rabbi Shila permitted his wife to marry again. Rav said to Rabbi Shemuel. "Let us place him in *herem*." Shemuel told Rav, "First let us ask him for an explanation." When they discussed the merits of the case, Rabbi Shila admitted that he made a mistake. (*Yevamot* 121a)

Rabbi Hisda referred to Rabbi Shila as a great man. (*Ketubbot* 75a)

Shila b. Avina decided a matter according to Rav. When Rav was on his deathbed, he said to R. Assi: "Go and restrain him, and if he does not listen try to convince him." After Rav passed away, R. Assi asked R. Shila to retract because Rav had retracted his ruling.

R. Shila said, "If Rav had retracted, he would have told me." When he persisted in his refusal, R. Assi put him under the ban.

R. Shila asked him, "Are you not afraid of the fire?"

He answered, "I am Issi b. Yehuda, who is Issi b. Gur-aryeh, who is Issi b. Gamliel, who is Issi b. Mahalalel, a cooper mortar that does not rust." The other retorted, "I am Shila b. Avina, an iron mallet that breaks the cooper mortar."

Soon after this incident, R. Assi fell ill and died. R. Shila told his wife, "Prepare my shrouds, because I don't want him to have the opportunity to tell Rav things about me." When R. Sheila died, people saw a myrtle fly from one grave to the other. We may conclude that the rabbis have made peace. (*Niddah* 36b)

R. Sheila ordered a man flogged for having had sexual intercourse with an Egyptian woman. The man went to the authorities and told them, "There is a man among the Jews who acts like a judge without the government's permission. An official was sent to investigate. When he arrived, he asked R. Shila: "Why did you flog that man?" He answered, "Because he had sexual intercourse with a female donkey."

"Do you have witnesses?"

"I have."

Elijah came in the guise of a man and gave evidence. The investigator said to R. Shila, "In that case, he deserves the death penalty."

R. Shila answered, "Since our exile, we have no authority to impose the death penalty."

While the official was considering the case, R. Shila praised God in Hebrew. When he was asked what he had said, he replied, "I said, 'Bessed is the All-Merciful Who invested royalty on earth with love of justice.'" For this they handed him a staff and gave him permission to act as a judge. (*Berachot* 58a)

For a glimpse of the world as it was in R. Shila's time, see the historical timeline from 200 to 300 C.E.

שׁשׁת
Sheshet

(third–fourth centuries C.E.)
Amora, Babylonia

R. Sheshet lived in Shilhi, a community on the Tigris River in Babylonia, where he established a yeshiva. His colleagues were Rabbi Hisda and Rabbi Nahman b. Yaakov.

Whenever R. Hisda and R. Sheshet met each other, they trembled in mutual admiration. R. Hisda admired R. Sheshet's extensive knowledge of Mishna, while R. Sheshet admired R. Hisda for his deep, penetrating mind in pilpul. (*Eruvin* 67a)

Rava spoke of R. Sheshet as a scholar who was as hard as iron. (*Menahot* 95b)

R. Sheshet taught in the academy at Nehardea and in Mehoza.

Rabbi Sheshet was blind and physically frail. Once the king came to town and all the people went out to see him. R. Sheshet, who also went to see him met a Sadduccee on the way who poked fun at him.

He said: "The pitchers that are whole go to the river, but where do the broken ones go?" R. Sheshet replied, "I can show you that even blind, I know more than you do." The first contingent of troops passed by and a loud shout could be heard. "The king is coming," said the Sadducee. "He is not coming yet," replied R. Sheshet. A second contingent of troops passed by and a loud shout could be heard. "Now the king is coming," said the Sadduccee. "The king is not coming yet," replied R. Sheshet. A third contingent of troops passed by and there was silence. "Now," said R. Sheshet, "here comes the king." When the king passed by, R. Sheshet recited a blessing over him. (*Berachot* 58a)

There was a question as to whether the next of kin of people being held captive were permitted to enter their estate.

Now this happened in Nehardea, and R. Sheshet decided the matter by reference to a baraita. R. Amram said to him, "Perhaps that baraita is about a case where they want to sell the estate?"

R. Sheishes answered: "Perhaps you are from Pumbedita, where they draw an elephant through the eye of a needle." (*Bava Metzia* 38b)

Some people in Mehoza owed money to R. Sheshet for items that he had sold them. R. Yoseph b. Hama was traveling to Mehoza, and R. Sheshet asked him to collect the money for him. They gave him the money and asked him for a receipt. At first he agreed, but then changed his mind. When he returned, R. Sheshet said to him, "You acted correctly in refusing to assume responsibility. 'A borrower is the slave of the lender.'" (*Gittin* 14a)

During one of the festivals, a deer was served at the Exilarch's table. This was on the second day of the festival, but the deer was caught by a non-Jew on the first day and slaughtered on the second day. Among the guests at the table were R. Nahman, R. Hisda and R. Sheshet. R. Nahman and R. Hisda partook of the venison, but R. Sheshet would not. "What can I do with R. Sheshet, who does not want to eat any of this venison?"

"How can I," retorted R. Sheshet, "in view of what R. Issi quoted in R. Yosi's name?" (*Eruvin* 39b)

The Exilarch said to R. Sheshet, "Even though you are a respected rabbi, the Persians have mastered a better etiquette at mealtime." (*Berachot* 46b)

R. Zera said to R. Hisda, "Teach us about the blessings after the meal." R. Hisda replied: "I do not know the blessings myself. How can I teach them to others?"

"What do you mean?" asked R. Zera.

"Once, when I recited the blessings after the meal in the house of the Resh Gelutha, R. Sheshet stretched out his neck at me like a serpent because I left out some passages." (*Berachot* 49a)

The mother of Rami b. Hama gave her property in writing to Rami b. Hama in the morning, but in the evening she gave it in writing to Mar Ukva b. Hama. Rami b. Hama came to R. Sheshet, who confirmed his inheritance. Mar Ukva then went to R. Nahman, who confirmed Mar Ukva in his inheritance.

R. Sheshet thereupon went to R. Nahman and asked him, "Why did you act this way in this matter?"

R. Nahman replied, "Why did you?"

R. Sheshet answered, "R. Rami's will was written first."

R. Nachman replied, "Are we living in Jerusalem, where the hours are recorded? We live in Babylonia, where the hours are not recorded."

R. Sheshet asked, "And why did you act as you did?"

"I treated it as a case to be decided at the discretion of the judges," replied R. Nahman.

R. Sheishes replied, "I also treated it as a case to be decided at the discretion of the judges."

R. Nahman replied, "I am a judge and you are not. Furthermore, you did not say at first that you treated it as a case to be decided by a judge." (*Ketubbot* 94b)

R. Sheshet said in the name of R. Eleazar b. Azaryah, "I could justify the exemption from judgment of all the generations of all the Jews who lived from the day of the Temple's destruction to the present day." (*Eruvin* 65a)

For a glimpse of the world as it was in R. Sheshet's time, see the historical timeline from 250 to 350 C.E.

שמעיה
Shemaya

(first century B.C.E.)
Tanna, Eretz Yisrael

R. Shemaya, together with his colleague, Avtalyon, constituted one of the zugot, or pairs of study partners, mentioned in the Talmud.

Both taught in the same academy during Herod's rule. (*Yoma* 35b)

Shemaya and his colleague Avtalyon were descendants of Sennacherib after he became a convert. (*Gittin* 57b)

He became one of the greatest scholars in Judaism, and Rabbi Hillel was one of his students.

Elsewhere, the Talmud relates that as a young man, Rabbi Hillel used to work as a day-laborer in order to earn one tropek (an amount equivalent to a dinar). He split his earnings, giving half to the guard for admittance into the study hall and spending the other half on food and necessities. One day, when he had no money, the guard would not let him enter. He climbed up on the roof, which had a window above the lecture hall. There, he listened to the lectures of Rabbis Shemaya and Avtalyon.

This particular day, a Friday, happened to be the winter solstice. As the temperature dropped, Hillel lost consciousness, and overnight, he was covered by snow. On the following

morning, which was Shabbat, Shemaya said to Avtalyon. "Every day at this time the room is bright with light, but today it is dark. Is it perhaps a cloudy day?"

They looked up and saw a human figure lying in the skylight. Climbing up, they discovered Hillel covered with three cubits of snow. They removed him from the roof, bathed and anointed him, and set him next to the fire.

They said to one another, "This man deserves that Shabbat be profaned on his account." From then on, Hillel gained permanent admittance to their school. (*Yoma* 35b)

Rabbi Shemaya is mentioned in the Talmud giving an opinion to his colleagues. (*Hagigah* 2:2, 16a)

He used to say, "Love work, hate mastery over others, and avoid familiarity with the authorities." (*Avot* 1:10)

For a glimpse of the world as it was in Shemaya's time, see the historical timeline from 100 to 1 B.C.E.

שמואל
Shemuel

(third century C.E.)
Amora, Babylonia
Head of the academy in Nehardea

R. Shemuel was born in Nehardea, where he studied under his father, whose name was R. Abba b. Abba ha-Kohen. (*Shabbat* 108b)

They also refer to him as Mar Shemuel, or as Shemuel ben Abba ha-Kohen.

R. Shemuel had a brother named Pinhas. They married two sisters. (*Sanhedrin* 28b)

He also studied with Rabbi Levi b. Sisi.

R. Shemuel became the head of the academy in Nehardea, which was a prestigious and important institution. He was considered the outstanding authority on halachic matters.

His concern for poor orphans was so great that he allowed the money of orphans to be lent at interest to Jews in spite of the prohibition against lending money at interest. (*Bava Metzia* 70a)

R. Shemuel believed that even words can be considered a bribe.

It happened that Shemuel was crossing a river on a ferry and a man offered him his hand to get off the ferry. R. Shemuel asked him, "What is your business here?"

"I have a lawsuit in which you are to be the judge," the man answered.

R. Shemuel told him, "I am now disqualified to act as judge in your case." (*Ketubbot* 105b)

R. Shmuel's father used to sell his fruit immediately after the harvest, when prices were low. On the other hand, R. Shemuel kept the fruit until later when prices were higher, but he sold them at the low prices of the season. Word was sent from Israel to Babylonia that the father's practice was preferable because when prices are reduced, they remain so. (*Bava Batra* 90b)

Shemuel was wealthy. His father left him fields and vineyards.

Shemuel said, "In the matter of industry, compared to my father I am like vinegar compared to wine. My father used to inspect his properties twice a day, but I do it only once a day." (*Hullin* 105a)

His maxim was, "He who inspects his property daily will find a silver coin."

A field worker once brought Shemuel some dates from his property. When Shemuel bit into the date it had a winy taste. When he asked why this was so, his worker told him that the date trees were located next to the vines. He instructed his worker to cut out the roots

of the dates because they were weakening the vines. (*Bava Kamma* 92a)

It is related that certain women captives were brought to Nehardea and Shmuel's father placed guards over them.

Shemuel said to his father, "And who guarded them until now?"

His father retorted, "If they were your daughters, would you still speak of them so lightly?" (*Ketubbot* 23a)

Later on, the daughters of Rabbi Shemuel were taken captive in Babylonia and taken to Eretz Yisrael. When their captors brought them to Rabbi Hanina, both daughters told him that they had not been violated. Rabbi Hanina said to R. Shimon b. Abba, "Go and take care of your kinswomen."

Another daughter of Shemuel who was taken captive became pregnant by her captor. Later on, he converted and married her, after which they had a son, R. Mari. (See also Rashi there). (*Berachot* 16a, *Bava Batra* 149a)

R. Shemuel told the merchants, "Sell the Hadassah (myrtle) during Sukkot at normal prices. Otherwise, I will issue a ruling that a lower quality is acceptable, like R. Tarfon, who was lenient regarding myrtle." (*Sukkah* 34b)

Once, R. Berona, a student of R. Shemuel, sat in his academy and quoted R. Shemuel when a student named R. Eleazar asked him, "Did R. Shemuel really say so?" R. Berona replied, "Yes." The student asked: "Would you show me where he lives?" He did, and the man came to R. Shemuel and asked him: "Did the master make this statement?"

"Yes," replied R. Shemuel.

"But didn't you issue a ruling in another case that contradicts this statement?" he persisted. The debate continued. (*Eruvin* 74a)

Rabbi Abba said in the name of Rabbi Shemuel: "For three years there was a dispute between Beit Shammai and

Beit Hillel, each one claiming that Halacha accorded with their views. Then a bat kol was heard announcing that while both are the words of the living God, Halacha accords with the rulings of Beit Hillel." (*Eruvin* 13b)

Rabbi Shemuel, who had great knowledge of medicine, invented an eye medication that was called Killurin de-Mar Shemuel.

The Talmud states: "Shemuel Yarchina was the physician of R. Yehuda ha-Nasi. Rebbe suffered from an eye ailment. Shemuel suggested treating it with a certain lotion, but Rebbe said, 'I couldn't bear it.'"

When Shemuel suggested using an ointment, Rebbe said, "I cannot tolerate that, either." Shemuel came up with another idea: he placed a chemical under Rebbe's pillow and he was healed. (*Bava Metzia* 85b)

Rebbe was most anxious to ordain R. Shemuel, but the opportunity never came. R. Shemuel said to Rebbe, "Do not be upset. I have seen the book of Adam ha-Rishon in which it is written, 'Shemuel Yarchina will be called a sage, but not a rabbi, and Rebbe's healing will come through him.'"

He was ahead of his time regarding awareness of hygiene. He was called Yarchina because he was knowledgeable in astronomy, which helped him in halachic matters.

What is *zikkin*? R. Shemuel said, "It is a comet." R. Shemuel also said, "I am as familiar with the paths of heaven as with the streets of Nehardea." (*Berachot* 58b)

Samuel and Karna were sitting by the bank of the Nahar Malka when they saw the water rising and becoming discolored. Shemuel said to Karna: "A great man is arriving from Eretz Yisrael who suffers from stomach trouble. Go and smell his bottle (investigate how

learned he is)." Karna went and asked him several difficult questions in order to test his knowledge. The newcomer turned out to be Rav. Subsequently, Shemuel took him into his house and gave him barley bread, fish and strong liquor, but did not show him where the outhouse was. Rav was annoyed with him because of it. (*Shabbat* 108a)

Whenever the Talmud states, "Our rabbis in Babylon," it refers to Rav and Shemuel. (*Sanhedrin* 17b)

Rava declared that two rulings had been issued by the elders of Pumbedita. R. Haviva observed, "The elders of Pumbedita issued an additional ruling, which is this: Rav Yehuda said in R. Shmuel's name that one may light a fire on Shabbat for a woman in childbirth." (*Eruvin* 79b)

R. Shemuel says that Israel is immune from planetary influences. (*Shabbat* 156b)

R. Shemuel and his Persian friend Avlat were having a conversation near a meadow. Some people were walking to the meadows and they were passing by them. Avlat pointed to a man and said, "That man is going to the meadows, but he will not return, because a snake will bite him and he will die."

R. Shemuel replied: "If he is an Israelite, he will go and return."

They were still talking when the man returned from the field. Surprised, Avlat approached the man, took his carrying case, opened it and found inside a snake cut in two. R. Shemuel asked the man, "Is there anything that you have done to merit this?"

The man answered, "Every day, all of us in the group pooled and shared our food equally. However, today the man next to me had no food to share, and he was embarrassed. I told the group that I was going to collect the food from everyone. When I came to him I pretended to take food from him so that he would not be embarrassed."

Once, when Avlat found Shemuel sleeping in the sun, he said to him, "My Jewish sage, can something that is injurious possibly be beneficial?" Shemuel answered, "It is the day of bloodletting." (*Shabbat* 129a)

R. Shemuel was on friendly terms with King Shapur I of Persia. He used to juggle eight glasses of wine before him. (*Sukkah* 53a)

R. Levi used to juggle before R. Yehuda ha-Nasi with eight knives during the celebration of the water-drawing.

R. Abbaye used to juggle eight eggs – some say four eggs – before Rabbah.

King Shapur I asked R. Shemuel: "Can you tell me what I will dream about?"

R. Shemuel answered him: "You will see the Romans taking you captive and making you grind date pits in a golden mill."

He thought about it all day, and at night that was what he dreamt. (*Berachot* 56a)

R. Shemuel was the head of the academy and Mar Ukva was the Exilarch. When they were sitting together in the academy, Mar Ukva sat four cubits in front of R. Shemuel. When they sat together at a court session, R. Shemuel sat four cubits in front of Mar Ukva. The place where Mar Ukva sat was dug out and lined with matting.

Every day, Mar Ukva would accompany R. Shemuel to his house. One day, he was preoccupied with a case and walked ahead of R. Shemuel. When they reached R. Shemuel's house, R. Shemuel said to Mar Ukva, "You have been preoccupied with your case for a long time. Now pay attention to my case." Realizing that he had hurt R. Shemuel's feelings, Mar Ukva apologized. (*Moed Katan* 16b)

Once, when Rav and Shemuel dined together, R. Shimi b. Hiyya joined them a while later. He began to eat very quickly, and Rav said to him, "Are you trying to join us for the blessing after the meal? We have already finished."

But Shemuel interjected: "If they were to bring me some mushrooms, and if they were to bring you, Abba some pigeons, would we not continue eating?" (*Berachot* 47a)

The Talmud relates that some money that belonged to orphans had been deposited for safekeeping with Rabbi Abba, Shemuel's father. However, since Shemuel was not in town when his father passed away, he never learned where his father kept the money. As a consequence, his deceased father was accused of having embezzled it. Distressed by this slight to his father's honor, Shemuel went to the cemetery where his father was buried in an attempt to find out where the money was hidden. He said to the spirits of the dead, "I wish to speak to my father." The spirits said, "He has gone up to learn in the heavenly academy." Shemuel noticed that the spirit of Rabbi Levi, who had passed away some time ago, was sitting outside. He asked him, "Why have you not gone up to the academy?" Rabbi Levi replied, "I was told that I would not be admitted to the heavenly academy for as many years as I did not attend the academy of Rabbi Afes and hurt his feelings." Meanwhile, Shmuel's father arrived. Shemuel saw that he was weeping and laughing. He asked him, "Why are you weeping?" His father answered, "Because I am told that you will be coming to this world soon." "Why are you laughing?" his son asked. "Because they tell me that you are highly respected in the heavenly world," his father said. His son then said, "If I am so much respected, then as a favor to me, let Rabbi Levi be admitted to the heavenly academy."

Shortly after this, R. Levi was admitted to the heavenly academy. Shemuel then asked his father: "Where is the money that belongs to the orphans?"

His father told him: "The money is hidden in the wrap that covers the millstones. There are three bundles of money. The upper and lower ones belong to us and the middle one belongs to the orphans."

Shemuel asked his father: "Why did you store the money that way?"

Abba replied: "Because if thieves were to discover it, they would take mine, and if the earth were to destroy some of it, that would also be mine." (*Berachot* 18b)

Rav Yehuda said in the name of Rabbi Shemuel, quoting Rabbi Shimon ben Gamliel, "There were a thousand students in my father's house. Five hundred of them studied Torah, while the other five hundred studied Greek wisdom. Of these, only I was left, together with my uncle's son in Assia." (*Sotah* 49b)

The Talmud states, Rav Yehuda said in the name Shemuel "Sumchos ruled that money claimed by two parties whose ownership is in doubt must be shared by both parties. However, the rabbis say that it is a fundamental principle that if one has the money and the other makes a claim, the claimant must bring proof." (*Bava Kama* 46a)

R. Shemuel said: "The only difference between this world and the world of Mashiah is servitude to foreign powers." (*Shabbat* 63a, *Berachot* 34b, 151b)

R. Zera said in the name of R. Yirmiyahu b. Abba: "'In the time just before Mashiah, the generation's scholars will be persecuted.' When I repeated this statement in front of R.

Shemuel he exclaimed, 'There will also be test after test.' (*Ketubbot* 112b)

There was a man who used to say, "Happy is a person who hears abuse of himself and ignores it, for hundreds of evils pass him by." On this, R. Shemuel remarked to R. Yehuda, "This is hinted at in a verse in Scripture." (*Sanhedrin* 7a)

R. Yehuda stated in the name of R. Shemuel: When King Solomon ordained the laws of preparing an eruv and washing hands before eating bread, a heavenly voice proclaimed, "My son, if your heart be wise, my heart, even mine, will be glad." (*Eruvin* 21b, *Shabbat* 14b)

R. Eliezer b. Yaakov was in disagreement with his colleagues regarding an eruv in a case where Jews and non-Jews live in same courtyard. Abbaye said to R. Yoseph, "We have a tradition that the teachings of R. Eliezer b. Yaakov are few in quantity but well sifted." (*Eruvin* 62b)

Also Rav Yehuda said in the name of R. Shemuel: "Halacha accords with R. Eliezer b. Yaakov."

Rav Yehuda related the following story in the name of Rabbi Shemuel in the name of Rabbi Meir: "When I was a student of Rabbi Akiva, I used to put kankantum into the ink and he did not tell me not to do it. But when I came to study with Rabbi Yishmael, he asked me, 'What is your profession?' I answered him, 'I am a scribe.' Upon this Rabbi Yishmael said to me, 'Be meticulous in your work, because your work is sacred to Heaven. Should you omit one letter or add one letter, you could cause a situation where a world is destroyed.' (Rashi comments that by adding one letter to a word, one might change that word from singular to plural, which would be blasphemy when speaking of God.) I told him I put kankantum in the ink, which makes the ink permanent immediately. (*Eruvin* 13a)

R. Yannai sent word to Mar Ukva: "Send me some of Mar Shmuel's eye medication." He sent him the medicine with instructions. This is what Shemuel recommends: "A drop of cold water in the morning, and bathing the hands and feet in hot water in the evening is better than all the eye medicines in the world." (*Shabbat* 108b)

R. Yehuda says in the name of R. Shemuel: "Scholars are obligated to have marital relations every Friday night." (*Ketubbot* 62b)

He believed in enjoying the wonderful things that God created in this world. R. Shemuel said to Rav Yehuda: "Hurry to eat and drink, because the world from which we must depart is like a wedding feast." (*Eruvin* 54a)

It was asked, how far does Babylon extend as far as family purity is concerned? Rav said, "It extends as far as the river Azak."

Shemuel said, "It extends as far as the river Yoani."

"How far does it extend on the upper Tigris?"

Rav said, "It extends as far as Bagda and Awana."

Shemuel said, "It extends as far as Moscani."

"How far does it extend on the lower reaches of the Tigris?"

Shemuel said, "It extends as far as the lower Apamea."

"How far does it extend on the upper reaches of the Euphrates?"

Rav said, "It extends to Tulbakene."

Shemuel said, "It extends to the bridge of Be-Pherat." (*Kiddushin* 71b)

R. Shemuel said: "It is forbidden to deceive non-Jews as well as Jews." (*Hullin* 94a)

He established the important halachic principle that: "The law of the land is the law." (*Bava Kamma* 113a)

When the town of Nehardea and its academy were destroyed in the year 259 C.E. by Papa b. Nasser, the commander-in-chief of Palmyra, the scholars fled and started a new academy in Pumbedita.

For a glimpse of the world as it was in R. Shemuel's time, see the historical timeline from 200 to 300 C.E.

שמואל בר נחמני
Shemuel bar Nahmeni

(third–fourth centuries C.E.)
Amora, Eretz Yisrael

Rabbi Shemuel bar Nahmeni studied under Rabbi Yoshua ben Levi and Rabbi Yonathan ben Eleazar. He visited Babylonia twice on official business. On one of these visits, he presented a petition to the Empress Zenobia to pardon an orphaned youth who had committed a political offense.

R. Shemuel b. Nahmeni said, "Whoever accepts his sufferings as the will of God will have his provisions fly to him like a bird." (*Berachot* 63a)

R. Shemuel b. Nahmeni said that when R. Yonatan read a certain passage from Scripture, he was moved to tears. (*Yoma* 9b)

R. Shemuel b. Nachmeni said in the name of R. Yonatan: "A man is shown in a dream only what is suggested by his own thoughts."

Rava said: "This is proven by the fact that no one dreams of a golden palm tree or an elephant going through the eye of a needle." (*Berachot* 55b)

R. Shemuel b. Nahmeni said in the name of R. Yonathan: "When one teaches Torah to the son of his neighbor, it is as if he had given him birth." (*Sanhedrin* 19b)

For a glimpse of the world as it was in the time of R. Shemuel bar Nahmeni, see the historical timeline from 250 to 350 C.E.

שמואל הקטן
Shemuel ha-Katan

(first–second centuries C.E.)
Tanna, Eretz Yisrael

R. Shemuel was a contemporary of Rabbi Gamliel of Yavne.

Rabbi Gamliel asked for a volunteer to compose a prayer reflecting Jewish opposition to the sectarians and non-believers. Rabbi Shemuel volunteered and composed the prayer that begins "Ve-la-malshinim," which was added to the other eighteen blessings of the Amida. (*Berachot* 28b)

R. Shemuel was a very humble person. The Talmud relates, Rabbi Gamliel asked his assistant to call certain seven rabbis to a meeting in the upper chamber. When Rabbi Gamliel arrived, he found eight rabbis present.

He said, "The one who was not invited should leave."

Rabbi Shemuel stood up and said, "I am the one who came uninvited, but I did not come to take part in the decision-making. I came only to learn how to intercalate the month."

Rabbi Gamliel answered, "Sit down, my son, sit down. You are worthy to intercalate all the months of the year, but it was the rabbis' decision to have only those present who were specially invited for this purpose."

In reality, Rabbi Shemuel was not the uninvited party. It was another rabbi, but because Rabbi Shemuel wished to spare him humiliation, he told them it was he who had come uninvited. (*Sanhedrin* 11a)

He prophesied the persecutions that were to follow. Unfortunately, they all came true. When he died, he was eulogized by the leading rabbis of his time, including Rabbi Gamliel. (*Sanhedrin* 11a)

At one time when the Sanhedrin met in the upper chamber, a bat kol was heard to say, "There is one among you who is worthy that the Shechina should rest on him, but his generation does not merit it." The sages present directed their gaze at R. Shemuel ha-Katan. (*Sanhedrin* 11a)

R. Shemuel ha-Katan used to say, "Control your emotions. Do not rejoice over your enemy's misfortune." (*Avot* 4:19)

For a glimpse of the world as it was in the time of R. Shemuel ha-Katan, see the historical timeline from 50 to 150 C.E.

שימי בר אשי
Shimi b. Ashi

(fourth–fifth centuries C.E.)
Amora, Babylonia

R. Shimi was a student of R. Pappa and of his father, R. Ashi.

R. Kahana escorted R. Shimi b. Ashi from Pum Nahara to Bet Zenitha in Babylonia. (*Berachot* 31a)

When they arrived, he asked him: "Do people really say that these palm trees date back to Adam's time?"

He answered: "Your question reminds me of a saying by R. Yosi b. Hanina, who used to day, 'Any land that was decreed by Adam to be inhabited became inhabited, and any land that Adam decreed to be uninhabited is still uninhabited.'"

For a glimpse of the world as it was in the time of Shimi b. Ashi, see the historical timeline from 350 to 450 C.E.

שימי בר חייא
Shimi b. Hiyya

(third century C.E.)
Amora, Babylonia

(Berachot 47a) Rav and Shemuel were dining together and R. Shimi b. Hiyya joined them a while later. When he began to eat very quickly, Rav said to him: "Are you trying to join us for the blessing after the meal? We finished already." But Shemuel interjected, "If they were to bring me some mushrooms, and if they were to bring you, Abba, some pigeons, would we not continue eating?"

For a glimpse of the world as it was in the time of Shimi b. Hiyya, see the historical timeline from 200 to 300 C.E.

שמעון אחי עזריה
Shimon Ahi Azaryah

(first–second centuries C.E.)
Tanna, Eretz Yisrael

R. Shimon, who was a contemporary of Rabbi Eliezer and Rabbi Yehoshua, is mentioned in the Mishna (*Zevahim* 1:2, 2a and *Taharot* 8:7).

For a glimpse of the world as it was in the time of R. Shimon Ahi Azaryah, see the historical timeline from 50 to 150 C.E.

שמן בר אבא
Shimon bar Abba

(third century C.E.)
Amora, Babylonia

R. Shimon was a student of Rabbi Shemuel, to whom he was related. He was also considered an Amora from Eretz Yisrael.

It happened that the daughters of Rabbi Shemuel were taken captive in Babylonia and taken to Eretz Yisrael. When their captors brought them to Rabbi Hanina, they told him that they had not been violated. Rabbi Hanina said to R. Shimon b. Abba, "Go and take care of your kinswomen." (*Ketubbot* 23a)

R. Shimon was a descendant of a distinguished priestly family in whose path he followed. He also studied under Rabbi Hanina and Rabbi Yehoshua ben Levi. But his principal teacher was Rabbi Yohanan, whose customs and sayings he

transmitted. He married the daughter of Rabbi Shemuel, but she died soon afterwards. After her death he married her sister, who also died during his lifetime.

For a glimpse of the world as it was in the time of R. Shimon bar Abba, see the historical timeline from 200 to 300 C.E.

שמעון בן עקשיה
Shimon ben Akashia

(second century C.E.)
Tanna, Eretz Yisrael

R. Shimon used to say: "The older Torah scholars get, the wiser they become." (*Kinnim* 3:6)

For a glimpse of the world as it was in the time of Shimon ben Akashia, see the historical timeline from 100 to 200 C.E.

שמעון בן חלפתא
Shimon ben Halafta

(second century C.E.)
Tanna, Eretz Yisrael

R. Shimon ben Halafta lived in Ein Teena, a small community in Israel between Tiberias and Sepphoris. He was a student of Rabbi Meir, and his colleagues were Rabbi Hiyya and Rabbi Shimon ben Yehuda ha-Nasi.

Once, when Rabbi Shimon left Rebbe's house, Rebbe told his son to go after him in order to get a blessing from him. He blessed him as follows: "May God grant you his grace so that you are never put to shame or feel ashamed yourself."

When he came back to his father, the latter asked him, "What did he say to you?" He replied: "He made some common remarks to me," quoting the blessing. Said Rebbe to his son, "He blessed you with the blessing with which God blessed Israel twice." (*Moed Katan* 9b)

R. Shimon made a living from farming. He had leased a field from Rabbi Hiyya. In his younger years, Rabbi Yehuda ha-Nasi helped him financially, but did so discreetly so as not to cause him embarrassment.

It is said of Rabbi Shimon ben Halafta that he was an experimenter in all things. Once he had a hen that had no down at all. He put the hen into the oven, having first wrapped it in a warm blanket. When the hen came out it grew feathers even larger than the original one. Why was he called an experimenter with flora and fauna? R. Mesharshia said because he personally experimented with all sorts of insects and plants. Once he went out to find out whether it is true that ants have no king. First he put a blanket over an anthill during the summer solstice to create a shade over the anthill. Next he removed the blanket and the sun beat down on the anthill. He kept watch over the ants during the experiment to come to a conclusion. (*Hullin* 57b)

Once, when Rabbi Shimon ben Halafta was on the road, he encountered roaring lions. He quoted a passage from Psalms 104 and two lumps of meat descended from heaven. The lions ate one and left the other. He brought the other lump of meat to the academy and asked whether it was pure or not. The scholars answered, "Nothing impure descends from heaven." (*Sanhedrin* 59b)

Rabbi Yehuda ha-Nasi asked R. Shimon b. Halafta: "Why do we not have the pleasure of receiving you during the festivals, as my ancestors used to receive your ancestors?"

R. Shimon answered, "The rocks have grown tall, the near has become distant, two have become three and the peacemaker of my home is gone." (*Shabbat* 152a)

For a glimpse of the world as it was in the time of R. Shimon ben Halafta, see the historical timeline from 100 to 200 C.E.

שמעון בן אלעזר
Shimon ben Eleazar

(second century C.E.)
Tanna, Eretz Yisrael

Rabbi Shimon, a contemporary of Rabbi Yehuda ha-Nasi, was a student of Rabbi Meir in the yeshiva in Tiberias, where he lived. When Rabbi Meir traveled, Rabbi Shimon accompanied him and was able to pass down many halachot under special circumstances.

Rabbi Shimon said in the name of Rabbi Meir that it was permissible to mix oil and wine on Shabbat for use as a remedy. Once, when Rabbi Meir was suffering internally and his students wanted to mix wine and oil for him, he would not allow them to do so.

They told him, "Your words shall be nullified in your own lifetime."

He replied, "Even though I ruled that it is permissible, my colleagues ruled otherwise. I have never presumed to disregard the words of my colleagues." (*Shabbat* 134a)

While he ruled strictly for himself, he was lenient with others.

It was taught, "Four general rules were stated by Rabbi Shimon ben Eleazar to apply to the laws of torts." The rules are listed in the Talmud. (*Bava Kamma* 14a)

Rabbi Shimon ben Eleazar said: "Every precept for which Israel was willing to die during the time of royal decrees and persecution are still held firmly in the minds of Jews." (*Shabbat* 130a)

He is quoted as saying, "Have you ever seen a wild beast or bird have a profession? Yet they sustain themselves without care." (*Kiddushin* 4:14, 82a)

He is also quoted as saying, "Do not try to placate a person when he is angry, and do not comfort him when his dead lies before him." (*Avot* 4:18)

R. Shimon and R. Eleazar were sitting together, while others say that Rebbe and R. Shimon b. Eleazar were together, when R. Yaakov ben Aha walked by.

One said to the other, "Let us rise before him because he is a man who fears sin."

The other said, "Let us rise before him because he is a man of learning."

The other retorted, "I tell you that he fears sin, and you tell me that he is a man of learning?" (*Shabbat* 31b)

R. Shimon b. Eleazar said in the name of R. Eliezer b. Parta, who said it in the name of R. Eleazar ha-Modai: "The writing of the Torah script was never changed." (*Sanhedrin* 22a)

For a glimpse of the world as it was in the time of Shimon ben Elazar, see the historical timeline from 100 to 200 C.E.

שמעון בן גמליאל
Shimon ben Gamliel

(first century C.E.)
Tanna, Eretz Yisrael

Rabbi Shimon ben Gamliel, the Nasi of the Sanhedrin, was described as a man of great intelligence and judgment. Tradition includes him in the list of the ten martyrs who were put to death by the Roman authorities.

The Talmud describes him in a colorful way. "When Rabbi Shimon ben Gamliel rejoiced at the Water-drawing festivities, he used to take eight lighted torches, throw them up in the air and catch them one after another, and they did not touch one another. When he prostrated himself, he would dig his two thumbs into the ground, bend down, kiss the ground, and draw himself up again, a feat that no one else could duplicate." (*Sukkah* 53a)

(*Avot* 1:17) Rabbi Shimon ben Gamliel is quoted "I was brought up all my life amongst the Sages and I have found nothing as essential as silence. Also, the study is not the important thing, but the deeds. Anyone who talks too much brings on sin."

Halacha requires women to bring pigeons to the Temple altar after they have given birth. It once happened in Jerusalem that the price of a pair of pigeons became inflated to a golden dinar. Rabban Shimon b. Gamliel declared, "I will not rest this night until the price drops to a silver dinar." He was terribly upset with the merchants for charging such a high price. He issued a decree reducing the number of pigeons required, and the price dropped that very same day. (*Keritot* 1:7, 8a)

The Midrash relates that R. Shimon b. Gamliel once sent his servant, Tavi, to buy the best food that he could find. When Tavi returned, he brought a tongue. Later, R. Shimon sent Tavi to buy the worst food that he could find. Tavi returned once again with a tongue. R. Shimon asked him to explain how the same food could be both good and bad. Tavi explained that when the tongue speaks well, there is nothing better, but when the tongue speaks evil, there is nothing worse.

R. Kahana said: When R. Yishmael ben R. Yosi b. Halafta became ill, the rabbis sent him the following message: "Tell us two or three things that you heard from your father." He replied; "One hundred and eighty years before the Temple was destroyed, Eretz Yisrael was occupied by the wicked government. Eighty years before the Temple was destroyed, a rabbinical prohibition of ritual impurity was enacted against certain vessels and people. Forty years before the Temple was destroyed, the Sanhedrin went into exile and moved to the commercial zone of the Temple." During this period the heads of the Sanhedrin were R. Yosi b. Yoezer, R. Yosi b. Yohanan, R. Hillel, R. Shimon, R. Gamliel and R. Shimon. (*Shabbat* 15a)

For a glimpse of the world as it was in the time of R. Shimon ben Gamliel, see the historical timeline from 1 to 100 C.E.

שמעון בן גמליאל
Shimon ben Gamliel

(second century C.E.)
Tanna, Eretz Yisrael

This R. Shimon was a grandson of the first R. Shimon b. Gamliel. After the destruction of Bethar and the failure of the Bar Kochva revolt Rabbi Shimon was in hiding for a long time.

It has been taught: When the wicked Turnus Rufus destroyed the Temple, Rabbi Gamliel was condemned to death. (According to some, this refers to Rabbi Shimon b. Gamliel, his son.) A high-ranking officer who came for him arose in the beit ha-midrash and called out, "The nose man is wanted! The nose man is wanted!" When R. Gamliel heard this, he went into hiding. The officer went to him in secret and asked him, "If I save you, will you bring me into the World to Come?" Rabbi Gamliel promised him that he would.

The officer then threw himself from the roof and died. In the Roman Empire, there was a tradition that when a Roman officer died while enforcing a decree, that decree was annulled. A voice from heaven was heard declaring, "The officer is destined to enter the World to Come." (*Taanit* 29a)

Rabbi (Shimon) ben Gamliel survived in hiding. Rabbi Yehuda ha-Nasi was his son.

The seat of the presidency was briefly vacant due to the Roman

persecutions, but at a meeting of the sages in Usha, R. Shimon was appointed Nasi of the Sanhedrin. When he took office, he tried to strengthen the prestige of the Presidency and decreed a certain protocol. This decree aroused great opposition to him in the assembly, but in the end they accepted his decision.

The Talmud relates that Rabbi Yohanan said, "The following instructions were issued in the days when Rabbi Shimon ben Gamliel was president of the Sanhedrin. Whenever the president of the Sanhedrin enters the room, everyone should rise, but when the Hacham or the president of the court enters, only a small number of the assembly should rise. Rabbi Meir was the Hacham and Rabbi Nathan was the president of the court. Rabbi Meir and Rabbi Nathan were not present when the instructions were issued. The next day, when Rabbi Meir and Rabbi Nathan entered the hall of the Sanhedrin, they noticed the lack of respect accorded to them. When they asked the reason for the change, they were told that those were the instructions of Rabbi Shimon.

Rabbi Meir and Rabbi Nathan decided to engage in a discourse in which Rabbi Shimon was not familiar. When Rabbi Yaakov ben Korshai found out what was planned, he feared that this might lead to a disgrace to the presidency of the Sanhedrin. He therefore started to study the subject just outside Rabbi Shimon's chamber, repeating it loudly, over and over. When R. Shimon heard him, he perceived that something was happening in the Sanhedrin. He concentrated on the subject and familiarized himself with it.

The next day, his two opponents approached him in order to discuss the subject. He agreed and he was able to hold his ground. When they finished, he said to them, "Had I not familiarized myself with the subject, you would have disgraced me." He issued an order to have them removed from the Sanhedrin. When they were on the outside they wrote down difficult scholastic questions on slips of paper, which they threw inside. Many of the questions could not be answered inside, and they were sent back outside unanswered. They wrote down the answer and sent it back inside. Rabbi Yosi said to the assembly, "The Torah is outside and we are sitting inside." Rabbi Shimon changed his mind and said, "We shall readmit them, but impose on them this penalty: no traditional statement shall be quoted in their names." They decided that the phrase "others say" would refer to Rabbi Meir, while the phrase "some say" would refer to Rabbi Nathan. (*Horayot* 13b)

In spite of his strictness in the assembly he was known for his humility, and his son Rabbi Yehuda ha-Nasi describes it. Hundreds of halachot are mentioned in his name in the Talmud. (*Bava Metzia* 84b)

Rav Yehuda said in the name of Rabbi Shemuel, quoting Rabbi Shimon ben Gamliel, "There were a thousand students in my father's house. Five hundred of them studied Torah and five hundred studied Greek wisdom. Of these, only I and the son of my uncle in Assia were left." (*Sotah* 49b)

When R. Shimon b. Gamliel and R. Yoshua b. Korha were learning in the academy they sat on couches, while R. Eleazar b. Shimon b. Yohai and Rebbe sat in front of them on the ground asking questions and raising objections. R. Yehuda (called Rebbe later on) was R. Shimon's son. The students objected, saying, "We are drinking from their water, but they are sitting on the ground. Let seats be placed for them." They placed seats for them, but R. Shimon b. Gamliel objected, saying, "I have a

pigeon amongst you and you want to destroy it?"

So Rebbe was put down again. R. Yoshua b. Korha was not happy and he said, "Shall he who has a father live, while he who has no father dies?"

Thereupon R. Eleazar was also made to sit on the ground. R. Eleazar was hurt and said, "You have made him equal to me."

Until this incident, whenever Rebbe made a statement R. Eleazar supported him, but after this day, whenever Rebbe spoke, R. Eleazar said, "Your statement has no substance." Humiliated, Rebbe complained to R. Shimon b. Gamliel, his father.

"Do not let it bother you," his father told him. "He is a lion and the son of a lion, whereas you are a lion and the son of a fox." R. Eleazar was the son of R. Shimon ben Yohai. Rebbe later on became Rabbi Yehuda ha-Nasi. (*Bava Metzia* 84b)

Rabbi Shimon ben Gamliel said: "There was a fine custom in Jerusalem: if one entrusted the preparation of a banquet to a caterer and he spoiled it, the caterer had to indemnify the host for the insult to him and to his guests. There was another fine custom in Jerusalem: when there was a party in a home, they spread a cloth over the doorway. As long as the cloth was spread over the doorway, guests could enter. When the cloth was removed, no guests could enter. (*Bava Batra* 93b)

In another Mishna Rabbi Shimon ben Gamliel says: "There were no happier days for Israel than the fifteenth of Av and Yom Kippur. On those two days, the daughters of Jerusalem would go out dressed in white garments that were borrowed in order not to shame those who had none. They would dance in the vineyards and call out, "Young man, lift your eyes and choose for yourself. Do not consider only beauty, but family too." (*Taanit* 4:8, 26b)

R. Abbaye said, "R. Shimon b. Gamliel, R. Shimon, R. Yishmael and R. Akiva all maintain that all Israelites are princes. We have learned that if one was a debtor for a thousand zuz and he wore a robe costing a hundred maneh, he is stripped of that robe and dressed in a less expensive one. R. Yishmael and R. Akiva disagreed because all Israel are worthy of that robe." (*Bava Metzia* 113b)

R. Shimon ben Gamliel said: "Shabbat may be desecrated for a living day-old infant, but it may not be desecrated for King David if he is dead." (*Shabbat* 151b)

R. Shimon b. Gamliel said, "All my life I was raised among scholars, and I found nothing better than silence." (*Avot* 1:17)

He also said, "The world rests on three foundations: truth, justice and peace." (*Avot* 1:18)

For a glimpse of the world as it was in the time of R. Shimon ben Gamliel, see the historical timeline from 100 to 200 C.E.

שמעון בן הסגן
Shimon ben ha-Segan

(first–second centuries C.E.)
Tanna, Eretz Yisrael

R. Shimon is quoted by Rabbi Shimon ben Gamliel that if one claims to be a Kohen one witness is sufficient to accept him as such. (*Ketubbot* 2:8, 23b)

Also in another case Rabbi Shimon ben Gamliel quotes him again. (*Menahot* 11:9)

For a glimpse of the world as it was in the time of Shimon ben ha-Segan, see the historical timeline from 50 to 150 C.E.

שמעון בן לקיש
Shimon ben Lakish

(third century C.E.)
Amora, Eretz Yisrael

R. Shimon ben Lakish is also known by the abbreviated name Resh Lakish. Not much is known about his younger years except that he was physically strong and that he participated in gladiatorial contests. He also earned a living by guarding plantations.

One day, when Rabbi Yohanan was bathing in the Jordan River, Resh Lakish also happened to be there. When he jumped into the river next to R. Yohanan, the latter told him, "Your strength should be used for learning Torah."

Resh Lakish returned the compliment by saying, "Your good looks should be reserved for women."

Rabbi Yohanan replied. "I have a sister who is more beautiful than I am. If you repent, I will give you my sister in marriage."

Resh Lakish agreed to repent. Rabbi Yohanan taught him the Torah and Mishna, and after years of study, Resh Lakish became a great scholar. (*Bava Metzia* 84a)

A diligent student, he prepared himself well before studying with Rabbi Yohanan. He systematically went over the text forty times, corresponding to the forty days that Moshe spent on Mount Sinai to receive the Torah, and only then did he attend the lecture. (*Taanit* 8a)

He married Rabbi Yohanan's sister, and they had a son who also became a great scholar. (*Taanit* 9a)

Resh Lakish had halachic disagreements with Rabbi Yohanan and with other scholars. (*Ketubbot* 84b)

Once, Rabbi Yohanan inadvertently insulted Resh Lakish when he referred to the latter's past during a discussion about the ritual purity of a sword, saying, "A robber knows his trade." One word led to another and they hurt one another's feelings.

Shortly afterwards, Resh Lakish fell ill. His wife came to her brother, R. Yohanan, and pleaded, "Forgive my husband for the sake of my son." (*Bava Metzia* 84a)

Resh Lakish died, and R. Yohanan was plunged into a deep depression. The rabbis sent R. Eleazar b. Pedat to comfort him. He went and sat before him and they learned together. R. Eleazar supported R. Yohanan's every dictum by saying, "There is a baraita that supports you."

"You are no replacement for Resh Lakish," R. Yohanan complained. "When I stated a law, Resh Lakish raised twenty-four objections, to which I gave twenty-four answers. This led to a fuller understanding of the law. You tell me that a baraita supports me. Do I not know myself that what I said is correct?"

R. Yohanan rent his garments and wept, "Where are you, Resh Lakish? Where are you, Resh Lakish?" Shortly afterwards, he died of grief. (*Bava Metzia* 84a)

R. Ulla said: One who saw Resh Lakish in the beit ha-midrash engaged in debate would get a picture of him uprooting mountains and grinding them together. (*Sanhedrin* 24a)

Relatives of R. Yohanan seized a cow that belonged to orphans. They were brought before R. Yohanan, who ruled the seizure lawful, but when they appealed to Resh Lakish, he ruled that they must return the cow. They appealed again to R. Yohanan, who told them, "What can I do when one of equal authority differs from me?" (*Ketubbot* 84b)

R. Yirmiyahu said in the name of Resh Lakish, "When two scholars are agreeable to each other, God listens to them." (*Shabbat* 63a)

R. Abba said in the name of Resh Lakish, "When two scholars listen to each other God listens to their voice." (*Shabbat* 63a)

R. Abba also said in the name of Resh Lakish: "To lend money to a person who needs it is greater than giving charity. And to give money to someone who wants to go into business and then split the profits is greater than anything."

Resh Lakish said in the name of R. Yehuda Nesia: "Children may not be deprived of their studies even for the building of the Temple." (*Shabbat* 119b)

Resh Lakish also said to R. Yehuda Nesia: "I have it from the tradition of our fathers that any town that has no school where children can study will be destroyed."

Rabbi Kahana had to flee Babylonia because of the following incident. A man who planned to denounce another Jew to the Persian authorities and show them where he was hiding his straw was brought before Rav. Rav ordered the man not to do so, but the man insisted. "I will." Rabbi Kahana, who was present during this incident, became enraged that the man was defying Rav, and during the argument he struck him, killing him accidentally. Rav advised Rabbi Kahana to move to Eretz Yisrael and to study under Rabbi Yohanan, but made him promise that for seven years he would not give Rabbi Yohanan a hard time with his sharp questions.

When Kahana arrived, he found Resh Lakish going over the lecture with the young rabbis. When he sat down to listen, he pointed out the difficult points in the lecture and also provided some of the answers.

Resh Lakish went to R. Yohanan and told him, "A lion has come up from Babylonia. Be well prepared for tomorrow's lecture." The next day, R. Kahana was seated in the first row because Resh Lakish thought him a scholar. But he kept quiet for a long while, as he had promised Rav. Consequently, the scholars of the academy demoted him, seating him in the seventh row.

R. Yohanan said to Resh Lakish, "It looks like the lion is a fox."

Rabbi Kahana prayed that the humiliation that he had suffered in having been demoted to the seventh row be considered equivalent to the seven years during which he had promised Rav not to ask R. Yohanan difficult questions. The next day, when Rabbi Yohanan lectured, he threw out one question after another, quoting sources in contradiction. After this, the academy's scholars seated him in the first row once more. (Bava Kamma 117a)

R. Hiyya b. Zarnuki and R. Shimon b. Yehotzedek were on their way to Assia to intercalate the year. Resh Lakish, who joined them, told them he wished to see the procedure. (Sanhedrin 26a)

Rabbi Illai quotes Rabbi Shimon ben Lakish as saying in the name of Rabbi Meir: "The tahash, which is mentioned in the Torah, was a separate species particular to those days. It had a single horn on its forehead and it came to Moses providentially, just for that occasion. Moshe made the Tabernacle cover from its skin." After that period, the tahash disappeared. (Shabbat 28b)

The Talmud relates that Resh Lakish said, "In ancient times when the Torah was forgotten, Ezra came up from Babylon and established it. When it happened again, Rabbi Hillel came up from Babylon and established it. When

some of it was forgotten again, R. Hiyya and his sons came up and established it." (Sukkah 20a)

As Resh Lakish was marking the burial caves of the rabbis in order to prevent the priests from becoming defiled, he could not locate the grave of R. Hiyya. Feeling humiliated, he called out, "Sovereign of the Universe; did I not debate on the Torah like R. Hiyya did?" A heavenly voice responded, "You did indeed debate like he did, but you did not spread the Torah as he did."

R. Hiyya prepared scrolls upon which he wrote the Five Books of Moses. Then he went to a town where there were no teachers and taught the five books to five children, and the six orders of the Mishna to six children. He told them, "Until I return, teach each other what I taught you." In this way, he kept the Torah from being forgotten.

This is what Rebbe meant when he said, "How great are the works of R. Hiyya!" "Are they greater than yours?" asked R. Yishmael b. R. Yosi. "Yes," replied Rebbe. (Bava Metzia 85b)

R. Yehuda b. Nachmeni was the interpreter for Rabbi Shimon ben Lakish. It happened once that the office of the Nasi appointed an unqualified person to lecture at the academy. They asked Rabbi Yehuda to stand near him and interpret. Rabbi Yehuda bent down to listen what the lecturer had to say, but made no attempt to say anything. Thereupon Rabbi Yehuda delivered his own lecture. He said, "Woe to him who talks to wood or to a dumb stone. Though it be overlaid with gold and silver, there is no breath in it." (Sanhedrin 7b)

For a glimpse of the world as it was in the time of Shimon ben Lakish, see the historical timeline from 200 to 300 C.E.

שמעון בן מנסיא
Shimon ben Menasye

(second–third centuries C.E.)
Tanna, Eretz Yisrael

Rabbi Shimon was a contemporary of Rabbi Yehuda ha-Nasi and a student of Rabbi Meir. He and Rabbi Yosi Meshullam were close colleagues. It was said of them that they divided the waking hours of the day into three parts, using a third for Torah study, a third for prayer and a third for work.

He said: "In order to save a life one may violate Shabbat, because it is better to profane one Shabbat so that one may keep many Shabbatot." (*Yoma* 85b)

He disagreed with Rabbi Yehuda ha-Nasi in halachic matters. (*Betzah* 26a)

For a glimpse of the world as it was in the time of Shimon ben Menasye, see the historical timeline from 150 to 250 C.E.

שמעון בן ננס
Shimon ben Nanas

(second century C.E.)
Tanna, Eretz Yisrael

Rabbi Shimon, a contemporary and a colleague of Rabbi Akiva and Rabbi Yishmael, is mentioned several times in the Talmud.

Rabbi Yishmael said, He who wishes to become wise should study property law because it is like a welling spring, and the best place to study it is to become a student of Rabbi Shimon ben Nanas. (*Bava Batra* 10:8, 175b)

For a glimpse of the world as it was in the time of R. Shimon ben Nanas, see the historical timeline from 100 to 200 C.E.

שמעון בן נתנאל
Shimon ben Nathanel

(first century C.E.)
Tanna, Eretz Yisrael

R. Shimon was a student of Rabbi Yohanan ben Zakkai, who called him a sin-fearing person.

A kohen, he married the daughter of Rabbi Gamliel the Elder.

Rabbi Shimon used to say, "Do not recite your prayers mechanically, but offer them as an appeal for mercy to the Almighty." (*Avot* 2:13)

Another saying of his was, "Before you act, be sure to consider the consequences." (*Avot* 2:9)

He also said: "It is evil to borrow and not to repay, whether borrowing from man or from God." (*Avot* 2:9)

For a glimpse of the world as it was in the time of Shimon ben Nathanel, see the historical timeline from 1 to 100 C.E.

שמעון בן פזי
Shimon ben Pazi

(third century C.E.)
Amora, Eretz Yisrael

R. Shimon, who studied under Rabbi Yoshua ben Levi, transmitted many of his sayings.

He is quoted as saying, "Woe to me because of my creator, if I do not follow him, and woe to me because of my evil inclination." (*Berachot* 61a)

R. Shimon ben Pazi said in the name of Rabbi Yoshua ben Levi in the name of Bar Kappara, "If one knows how to calculate the cycles of the planetary courses and does not do it, then that person has no regard for God's work." (*Shabbat* 75a)

R. Shimon b. Pazi once introduced the Book of Chronicles as follows: "All Your words are one, and we know how to find their inner meanings." (*Megillah* 13a)

R. Shimon b. Pazi was saying: "One is permitted to flatter the wicked in this world." (*Sotah* 41b)

For a glimpse of the world as it was in the time of Shimon ben Pazi, see the historical timeline from 200 to 300 C.E.

שמעון בן שטח
Shimon ben Shetah

(first century B.C.E.)
Tanna, Eretz Yisrael

Rabbi Shimon ben Shetah and his colleague, Rabbi Yehuda ben Tabbai, constituted one of the pairs of study partners mentioned in the Talmud. (*Avot* 1:8)

At this time in history, Alexander Yannai was both king and high priest, and Salome Alexandra was his queen. Rabbi Shimon b. Shetah was the queen's brother. (*Berachot* 48a)

King Yannai, who was not well disposed towards the Pharisees, persecuted them for a long time and had many put to death. Many rabbis fled the country, but after some time Rabbi Shimon was able to effect a reconciliation between the rabbis and the king. Rabbi Shimon restored the Torah to its former glory.

After King Yannai died, his widow, Queen Salome Alexandra, acceded to the throne. Through the influence of Rabbi Shimon ben Shetah, the Pharisees were victorious over the Sadducees. (*Kiddushin* 66a)

It is stated Yohanan the High Priest officiated for eighty years and in the end became a Sadducee. Rabbi Abbaye said, "Yohanan is the same as Yannai the king." (*Berachot* 29a)

Rabbi Shimon had many disagreements with King Yannai.

On one occasion, a slave of king Yannai killed a man. As head of the Sanhedrin, Rabbi Shimon told the members of the Sanhedrin, "Set your eyes boldly upon him and let us judge him."

They sent a messenger to summon the king. The king sent the slave to the Sanhedrin. They sent another messenger to summon him also. King Yannai came and sat down. Shimon ben Shetah told the king, "Stand on your feet so that the witness may testify against you as the law requires."

King Yannai answered: "I shall not do as you tell me, but I want to hear what your colleagues have to say."

The king looked first to the right and then to the left, but they all looked to the ground for fear of the king. Rabbi Shimon ben Shetah asked the Sanhedrin: "What are your thoughts? Let the Master of thoughts call you to account."

It was there and then that a new decree was enacted: a king may neither judge nor be judged, testify, nor be testified against. (*Sanhedrin* 19a, b)

Rav Yehuda said in Rav's name, "Once Queen Shel Zion (Alexandra) made a banquet for her son and all her utensils became defiled. She ordered (probably on the advice of her brother R. Shimon b. Shetah) all her golden dishes melted down and new ones made of the molten gold." (*Shabbat* 16b)

King Yannai and his queen were sitting at the table having a meal together. There was no one to say a blessing for them because he had killed the rabbis. He expressed a wish to his queen to have someone give a blessing. She said to him: "Swear to me that if I bring you a rabbi, you will not harm him."

He swore, and she brought her brother, Rabbi Shimon ben Shetah, to the palace and seated him between herself and the king. She said to him, "See what honor I pay you?"

He replied, "It is not you who honor me, but the Torah that honors me." The king said to her: "You see, he still does not recognize authority." (*Berachot* 48a)

R. Shimon b. Shetah said: "May I never witness the consolation of Zion if I did not see a man running after another man into a ruin. I ran after him and found him with a sword in his hand and blood dripping from it, while the other man lay in his death-throes.

"I said to him: 'Wicked one, who killed this man? It was either me or you, but what can I do? I do not have two witnesses, but God will exact retribution from you.'"

It was told that they had not yet left the place when a serpent bit the man and he died. (*Shevuot* 34a)

Rabbi Shimon ben Shetah sent the following message to Honi ha-Maagel: "You deserve to be excommunicated for the things you do, and if you weren't Honi ha-Maagel, I would pronounce you excommunicated. But what can I do, since you are a favorite of God? He accedes to your wishes, and you are like a son who is favored by his father." (*Berachot* 19a)

On another occasion Rabbi Shimon ben Shetah took drastic action to eradicate sorcery. In Ashkelon, he ordered eighty sorceresses hanged. (*Sanhedrin* 6:4, 45b)

Shimon ben Shetah said: "Question witnesses thoroughly, and do not lead them to false testimony." (*Avot* 1:9)

For a glimpse of the world as it was in the time of R. Shimon ben Shetah, see the historical timeline from 100 to 1 B.C.E.

שמעון בן יהוצדק
Shimon b. Yehotzedek

(second–third centuries C.E.)
Tanna, Eretz Yisrael

R. Shimon was an eminent scholar and the teacher of Rabbi Yohanan.

In several tractates, he is quoted as being involved in a discussion about the four species. Rabbi Yohanan transmitted some halachic rulings in his name. (*Sukkah* 11b)

R. Yohanan said in the name of R. Shimon b. Yehotzedek, "A community should not appoint an administrator over its affairs unless he carries a basket of reptiles on his back. If he becomes arrogant the community can tell him, 'Turn around.'" (*Yoma* 22b)

R. Hiyya b. Zarnuki and R. Shimon b. Yehotzedek were on their way to Assia to intercalate the year. Resh Lakish, who joined them, told them he wanted to see the procedure. (*Sanhedrin* 26a)

For a glimpse of the world as it was in the time of Shimon ben Yehotzedek, see the historical timeline from 150 to 250 C.E.

שמעון בן יהודה הנשיא
Shimon ben Yehuda ha-Nasi

(second–third century C.E.)
Tanna, Eretz Yisrael

Rabbi Shimon was the younger son of Rabbi Yehuda ha-Nasi. He and his brother, Rabbi Gamliel, took part in arranging and completing the Mishna, the task that had been undertaken by their father. He was a contemporary of outstanding scholars such as Rabbi Hiyya, Rabbi Levi and Rabbi Bar Kappara.

R. Shimon was appointed by his father to be the Hacham of the yeshiva, while his older brother, Gamliel, was appointed Nasi. (*Ketubbot* 103b)

Our Rabbis taught that when Rebbe was about to die, he said, "I would like to have my sons present." When they arrived, he instructed them: "Take care to show respect to your mother. The light shall continue to burn in its usual place, the table shall be set in its usual place and my bed shall be made up in its usual place. Yoseph of Haifa and Shimon of Efrat, who attended me in my lifetime, shall attend me when I am dead." (*Ketubbot* 103a)

Rebbe then said: "I would like to speak to the Sages of Israel." When they entered, he said to them: "Do not lament for me in the smaller towns, and reassemble the academy after thirty days. My son Shimon is to be the Hacham, my son Gamliel shall be the Nasi and Hanina b. Hama is to be Rosh Yeshiva."

Rebbe said, "I would like to speak to my younger son." R. Shimon came in, and Rebbe instructed him in the rules of being a Hacham.

Rebbe then said: "I would like to see my elder son." R. Gamliel entered, and he instructed him in the traditions and regulations of the Patriarchate. "My son," he said, "fill your patriarchate with high-caliber men and keep strong discipline among your students."

On the day Rebbe died, a bat kol was heard announcing, "Whoever was present at the death of Rebbe is destined to enjoy the life of the World to Come."

Although he designated R. Hanina as Rosh Yeshiva, R. Hanina did not accept the position because R. Afes was two and a half years older, and so R. Afes presided.

R. Hanina sat and studied outside the academy, where R. Levi joined him. When R. Afes passed away, R. Hanina took over the presidency and R. Levi moved to Babylonia. (*Ketubbot* 103b)

On the day Rebbe died the Rabbis decreed a public fast-day. (*Ketubbot* 104a)

It is related that Rabbi Hiyya was sitting in a bathhouse when Rabbi Shimon entered, and he did not rise before him. Rabbi Shimon was offended because he had taught him two-fifths of the Book of Psalms, and he felt that Rabbi Hiyya should have risen before him. (*Kiddushin* 33a)

Rabbi Yehuda taught his son Shimon that gold may acquire silver, and the son pointed out to his father that he had taught differently at another time. (*Bava Metzia* 44a)

In a year of scarcity, Rabbi Yehuda ha-Nasi opened his storehouse and proclaimed, "Let those who have studied Scripture, Mishna and Halacha enter to receive food for free. But the ignorant shall not be admitted."

R. Yonathan b. Amram entered and asked for food. They asked him, "Have you learned the Torah?"

He answered, "No."

"Have you learned Mishna?"

He answered, "No."

He was refused food.

"Feed me as a dog or as a raven," he said. Thereupon, he was given some food. After he left, Rebbe was upset and regretted that he had fed a man who did not take the time or trouble to learn. When Rebbe's son Shimon saw his father so distressed, he told him, "Don't be upset. That man was your student, Rabbi Yonathan, who has made it his principle not to derive benefit from his Torah study."

After this incident, Rebbe changed his rules and declared, "Everyone may enter and receive food without payment." (*Bava Batra* 8a)

For a glimpse of the world as it was in the time of Shimon ben Yehuda ha-Nasi, see the historical timeline from 150 to 250 C.E.

שמעון בן יוחאי
Shimon bar Yohai

(second century C.E.)
Tanna, Eretz Yisrael

Rabbi Shimon bar Yohai, who was a student of Rabbi Akiva, was one of the five prominent students who survived the Bar Kochva revolt. For thirteen years, he and Rabbi Hanina b. Hachinai studied under Rabbi Akiva in Benai

Berak, and even after Rabbi Akiva was imprisoned for teaching Torah in public, Rabbi Shimon attended to his needs and studied with him. He received his ordination from Rabbi Akiva, but later he also received ordination from Rabbi Yehuda ben Bava.

Rabbi Yehuda ben Bava became a martyr when he disobeyed the Romans' decree banning rabbinical ordination. This decree, which was issued by the authorities during the persecutions of Hadrian, stipulated that anyone who ordained a rabbi would be subject to the death penalty, anyone who received ordination would also be put to death, the city where the ordination took place would be demolished, and the boundaries around the city would be uprooted. In order to avoid the destruction of a city, Rabbi Yehuda b. Bava sat between two large mountains and between the two cities of Usha and Shefaram. Five prominent students sat before him: Rabbi Meir, Rabbi Yehuda bar Illai, Rabbi Shimon Bar Yohai, Rabbi Yosi, and Rabbi Eleazar ben Shammua. The ceremony was held and he ordained them. Rabbi Avia adds Rabbi Nehemia to the list.

As soon as the ceremony was finished, they saw the Romans approaching. Rabbi Yehuda told his students to flee. They wanted to take him along, but he urged them to go without him. "I would cause all of you to be captured," he said. "I am too old to run. I will lie before them like a stone." It was said that the Romans stabbed him three hundred times. (*Sanhedrin* 14a)

Rabbi Shimon bar Yohai, who was very vocal in his denunciation of the Roman authorities, was condemned to death for it.

R. Shimon b. Yohai commented: Whatever the Romans have done, they have done for their own benefit. They built markets to have places for their prostitutes, they built bathhouses in order to indulge their bodies and they built bridges in order to levy tolls on them. Yehuda the son of proselytes repeated the discussion to friends and relatives. Eventually it reached the authorities. It was decreed that R. Yehuda, who spoke in praise of the Romans, should be rewarded; that R. Yosi, who was silent, should be held in his own community of Sepphoris, and R. Shimon was condemned to death.

R. Shimon and his son R. Eleazar ran away and hid in the bet midrash. His wife brought them bread and water, but this did not last, because they were worried that the Romans would discover them. They fled to a cave. Miraculously, a carob tree grew near the cave's opening and a well was shown to them. They shed their clothing, sitting naked in the sand up to their neck to keep their clothing from wearing out. They studied all day long and put on their clothes every day only for prayers. They hid in the cave twelve years. Eventually Eliyahu came to the entrance and called out: Who will inform the son of Yohai that the emperor is dead and the decrees have been annulled. When they heard the good news, they came out of the cave. (*Shabbat* 33b)

(Shabbas 33 b) When Rabbi Shimon ben Yohai emerged from the cave, his son-in-law, Rabbi Pinhas ben Yair, went to meet him. He took him into the bathhouse and massaged his body. Seeing the lumps in his body, he cried with tears streaming from his eyes, "Woe to me that I see you in such condition!"

"No," he replied, "happy are you that you see me thus. Before the cave experience, Rabbi Shimon would ask a question and Rabbi Pinhas would have thirteen answers, but now when Rabbi

Pinhas raises a question, Rabbi Shimon has twenty-four answers."

It is stated Rabbi Akiva had twelve thousand pairs of students. All of them died at the same time because they did not treat each other with respect. A tanna taught that all of them died between Pesach and Shavuot. These were the remaining students of Rabbi Akiva who revived the Torah at that time: Rabbi Meir, Rabbi Yehuda bar Illai, Rabbi Yosi ben Halafta, Rabbi Shimon ben Yohai and Rabbi Eleazar ben Shammua. (*Yevamot* 62b)

After he emerged from the cave, he was recognized as one of the greatest leaders of his generation. The Sanhedrin sent him to Rome as an emissary in order to plead for the abolition of the anti-Jewish decrees. On this trip, Rabbi Eleazar b. Yosi accompanied him to Rome.

The Talmud relates that at one point, the Roman authorities issued a decree forbidding the Jewish religious practices of Shabbat, circumcision and family purity. When the edict was issued, a Jew living in Rome by the name of Reuben b. Istroboli disguised himself as a Roman and mingled among the Romans. In his disguise, he succeeded in convincing the authorities that to enact these restrictions would be detrimental to the Romans. On his advice, they repealed the decrees. However, when it was learned that Reuben was Jewish, the Romans re-instituted them.

In desperation, the Jews in Judea decided to send a delegation to Rome in order to try to reverse the edict. They chose R. Shimon ben Yohai and R. Eleazar b. Yosi. On the way to Rome they were met by a demon named Ben Temalion. He asked: "Would you like me to accompany you?" Rabbi Shimon wept, saying, "My ancestor Avraham's maid, Hagar, was worthy to be met three times by angels, yet I do not deserve to be met by an angel even once!" Nevertheless, R. Shimon continued to pray that a miracle might occur, no matter who its agent might be.

The demon Ben Temalion advanced ahead of them and entered into the body of the emperor's daughter. When R. Shimon arrived at the palace, there was great anguish and no one knew what to do. The emperor's daughter called out the name of R. Shimon repeatedly. When the palace officials were told who R. Shimon was, they asked him to enter the palace because the princess was calling him by name. R. Shimon entered and called out, "Ben Temalion, depart from her! Ben Temalion, depart from her!"

The demon left her body. The grateful emperor told the delegation, "Ask for anything you desire."

They were led into a treasure chamber and were told to choose anything they desired. Among the treasure, they found the anti-Jewish decree and tore it to pieces. (*Meilah* 17b)

Rabbi Eleazar, who accompanied Rabbi Shimon to Rome, described what he saw there: the vessels that had been plundered from the Temple, the sacrificial blood splattered on the veil and the High Priest's engraved golden headpiece.

The authorship of the Zohar is attributed to Rabbi Shimon ben Yohai.

Rabbi Shimon lived for a while in Sidon, but he also lived in Pagi and in the Galilee. He established a yeshiva in Tekoa, a community near Jerusalem. Some of his outstanding students were Rabbi Yehuda ha-Nasi, his son Eleazar and his son-in-law, Rabbi Pinhas ben Yair.

Rabbi Yehuda ha-Nasi related: "When we studied under Rabbi Shimon in Tekoa, we used to carry oil and a towel from roof to roof, from the roof to a courtyard, from that courtyard to a *karpaf* and from that *karpaf* into another *karpaf* until we arrived at the well where we bathed." (*Eruvin* 91a)

Rabbi Yohanan said in the name of Rabbi Shimon ben Yohai, "If Israel were to keep two Shabbatot according to the laws, they would be redeemed immediately." (*Shabbat* 118b)

Another saying of his was, "One should rather throw himself in a burning furnace than to shame someone in public." (*Berachot* 43b)

R. Yohanan said in the name of R. Shimon b. Yohai, "Where do we find in Scripture that God will resurrect the dead? (Deut. 31:16) 'Behold, you shall sleep with your fathers and rise again.'" (*Sanhedrin* 90b)

R. Shimon's tomb is located in Meron, Israel, and the anniversary of his death is the eighteenth day of the Hebrew months of Iyyar, the thirty-third day of the *omer* period, which is the festival of Lag ba-Omer. Thousands of people flock to his grave on that day.

R. Yaakov and R. Zerika said: Whenever R. Akiva and one of his colleagues are in disagreement, Halacha goes according to R. Akiva. When R. Yosi is in disagreement with his colleagues, Halacha goes according to R. Yosi.

In a dispute between R. Yehuda ha-Nasi and one of his colleagues, Halacha goes according to Rebbe.

What practical difference does it make? R. Assi said, "General practice." R. Hiyya b. Abba said, "We tend in their favor." R. Yosi b. Hanina said, "They are seen as acceptable views."

R. Yaakov b. Idi said in the name of R. Yohanan, "In a dispute between R. Meir and R. Yehuda, Halacha goes according to R. Yehuda. In a dispute between R. Yehuda and R. Yosi, Halacha

goes according to R. Yosi. Needless to say, in a dispute between R. Meir and R. Yosi, Halacha goes according to R. Yosi."

R. Assi said: I also learn that a dispute between R. Yosi and R. Shimon, Halacha is decided according to R. Yosi.

R. Abba said in the name of R. Yohanan, "In a dispute between R. Yehuda and R. Shimon, Halacha goes according to R. Yehuda."

A dispute between R. Meir and R. Shimon is left unresolved. (*Eruvin* 46b)

For a glimpse of the world as it was in the time of R. Shimon bar Yohai, see the historical timeline from 100 to 200 C.E.

שמעון הפקולי
Shimon ha-Pakuli

(first–second centuries C.E.)
Tanna, Eretz Yisrael

R. Shimon ha-Pakuli was a member of the Yavne academy.

It is stated: at Rabbi Gamliel's request, Rabbi Shimon arranged the eighteen blessings of the Amida in their proper order in Yavne. (*Berachot* 28b)

It has been taught: Shimon ha-Pakuli formulated the eighteen blessings of the Amida in their proper order in R. Gamliel's presence in Yavne. (*Megillah* 17b)

For a glimpse of the world as it was in the time of Shimon ha-Pakuli, see the historical timeline from 50 to 150 C.E.

שמעון התמני
Shimon ha-Tameni

(second century C.E.)
Tanna, Eretz Yisrael

A great scholar, Rabbi Shimon spoke seventy languages.

Rav Yehuda said in Rav's name. A Sanhedrin may not be established in a city, which does not have at least two persons who can speak seventy languages and one who understands them. In the city of Bethar there were three and in Yavne there were four: Rabbi Eliezer, Rabbi Yehoshua, Rabbi Akiva and Shimon ha-Timni. (*Sanhedrin* 17b)

R. Shimon ha-Tameni used to sit on the floor, study Torah and engage in discussions. He also engaged in halachic disputes and discussions with some of the greatest rabbis of his time, such as Rabbi Akiva and Rabbi Yehoshua.

It is stated: R. Shimon ha-Timni disagreed with Rabbi Akiva as to who is a *mamzer*. He was a member of the academy at Yavne when Rabbi Gamliel was the Nasi. (*Yevamot* 4:13, 49a)

When the Talmud states, "It was discussed before the rabbis," it refers to R. Shimon ben Azzai, Rabbi Shimon ben Zoma, Rabbi Hanan ha-Mitzri and R. Hanania ben Hachinai. Rabbi Nahman b. Yitzhak taught that there were five. He also included Rabbi Shimon ha-Timni. (*Sanhedrin* 17b)

For a glimpse of the world as it was in R. Shimon ha-Timni time, see the historical timeline from 100 to 200 C.E.

שמעון הצדיק
Shimon ha-Tzadik

(third century B.C.E.)
Before the tannaitic period

The Talmud refers to him as one of the last survivors of the Great Assembly. (*Avot* 1:2)

The Talmud relates: It was taught that on the twenty-fifth of Tevet, known as the day of Mount Gerizim, no mourning is permitted. On that day, the Samaritans asked Alexander the Macedonian for permission to destroy the Temple, and he granted their request. Messengers came and informed Shimon ha-Tzadik of the decree. Putting on his priestly garments, he went out and took the noblemen of Israel with him. All of them carried lit torches and walked all night, some on one side of the road and some on the other side. When Alexander saw the lit torches in the night from a distance, he asked the Samaritans. "Who are those people walking?"

They told him, "Those are the Jews who rebelled against you." The two camps met at Antipatris. When Alexander saw Shimon ha-Tzadik, he descended from his carriage and bowed down before him. They said to him, "Should a great king like you bow down to a Jew?"

He answered, "It is his image that I see when I win all my battles."

He asked them, "Why have you come to see me?"

They said to him, "Is it possible that you would listen to the advice of star-worshippers to destroy the Temple in which we pray for your welfare and that of your kingdom, that it never be destroyed?"

"Who are those star-worshippers?"

"They are the Samaritans who stand before you."

He answered, "They are delivered into your hands."

That day was made into a festive day. (*Yoma* 69a)

R. Shimon stated: "The world is based on three things: the Torah, Divine service and charity." (*Avot* 1:2)

Antigonus Ish Socho said in the name of Shimon ha-Tzadik: "Do not be like servants who serve for the sake of a reward. Be rather like servants who expect no rewards." (*Avot* 1:3)

It is stated: "In the year in which Shimon ha-Tzadik died, he foretold that he would die. When asked how he knew, he replied, 'On every Yom Kippur when I entered the Holy of Holies I would see a vision of an old man dressed in white entering and leaving with me, but today I saw an old man dressed in black who

entered with me, but did not leave.'"
(*Yoma* 39b)

For a glimpse of the world as it was in the time of R. Shimon ha-Tzadik, see the historical timeline from 300 to 200 B.C.E.

שמעון איש המצפה
Shimon Ish ha-Mizpah

(first century C.E.)
Tanna, Eretz Yisrael

Rabbi Shimon was from the town of Mizpah in Judea. The Temple was still in existence when he was still a young man.

There is a dispute as to the order of the Temple services. According to Rabbi Shimon, it is different from what others have taught. (*Yoma* 14b)

The Talmud relates a story that when Rabbi Shimon planted his field with two kinds of grain, he came before Rabbi Gamliel to ask if he must leave two corners for the poor. (*Peah* 2:6)

For a glimpse of the world as it was in the time of R. Shimon Ish ha-Mizpah, see the historical timeline from 1 to 100 C.E.

שמעון שזורי
Shimon Shezuri

(second century C.E.)
Tanna, Eretz Yisrael

R. Shimon Shezuri, who was a student of Rabbi Tarfon, was a contemporary of Rabbi Meir and Rabbi Yosi b. Halafta.

He often engaged in halachic disputes with Rabbi Meir and Rabbi Yosi. (*Demai* 4:1, *Hullin* 4:5, 74b)

For a glimpse of the world as it was in R. Shimon Shezuri's time, see the historical timeline from 100 to 200 C.E.

שיזבי
Shizbi

(third–fourth centuries C.E.)
Amora, Babylonia

R. Shizbi, who was a student of R. Hisda, quoted R. Hisda about participating in the preparation of an eruv. (*Eruvin* 80b)

R. Huna used to say: One who lights his house well will have scholarly sons. R. Hisda used to pass by the house of R. Shizbi's father frequently. On noticing that the house was always well lit, he remarked, "A great man and scholar will be born to this couple." (*Shabbat* 23b)

For a glimpse of the world as it was in R. Shizbi's time, see the historical timeline from 250 to 350 C.E.

שמלאי
Simlai

(third century C.E.)
Amora, Babylonia

Although Simlai himself was a great scholar, he worked as Rabbi Yannai's assistant.

Once, when Rabbi Yannai was walking on the street, leaning on the shoulder of Rabbi Simlai, Rabbi Yehuda Nasia came to meet them. R. Yannai said, "The man who comes towards us is a special person and his garment is special" (R. Yannai had poor eyesight). When R. Yehuda Nasia approached, R. Yannai touched his garment and made a halachic remark about it. (*Bava Batra* 111a)

Rabbi Yehuda Nasia was once walking and leaning on the shoulder of R. Simlai, and during the conversation he remarked, "You were not present yesterday in the house of study. You missed an important session, during which we made an important ruling." The two were close friends. (*Avodah Zarah* 37a)

Although he was born in Babylonia, moved to Eretz Yisrael and lived in Lod. (*Avodah Zarah* 36a)

Rabbi Simlai declared that six hundred and thirteen commandments were given to Moshe: three hundred sixty-five prohibitions, corresponding to the number of solar days, and two hundred forty-eight positive precepts, corresponding to the number of organs in the human body. Rav Hamnuna remarked that the numerical value of the word Torah adds up to six hundred eleven, and the first two commandments were spoken directly by God. (*Makkot* 23b)

For a glimpse of the world as it was in R. Simlai's time, see the historical timeline from 200 to 300 C.E.

סומכוס
Sumchos ben Yoseph

(second–third centuries C.E.)
Tanna, Eretz Yisrael

Rabbi Sumchos was a student of Rabbi Meir at the yeshiva in Tiberias. (*Bava Metzia* 6:5, 80a)

He spoke many languages, was fluent in Greek and lived a very long life. (*Nazir* 8b)

He was an authority on halachic matters. The Talmud records that both Rabbi Nathan and Rabbi Abba asked him for rulings. (*Ketubbot* 52a, 81a)

The Talmud quotes Rabbi Sumchos as saying: "When one prolongs the word *ehad* in the shema, his days and years are prolonged." (*Berachot* 13b)

The Talmud states that Rav Yehuda said in the name of Shemuel: "It is a ruling by Sumchos that money claimed by two parties whose ownership is in doubt must be shared by both. However, the rabbis say that it is a fundamental principle that if one has the money and the other makes a claim, the claimant must bring proof." (*Bava Kamma* 46a)

Rabbi Abbahu stated in the name of Rabbi Yohanan: "Rabbi Meir had a student by the name of Sumchos who could provide forty-eight reasons to support every ruling of ritual impurity." (*Eruvin* 13b)

It is related that after Rabbi Meir passed away, Rabbi Yehuda told his students, "Do not allow the students of Rabbi Meir to enter our academy. They come only for disputations and to overwhelm me with citations from traditions, but not to learn Torah." Rabbi Sumchos forced his way into the academy and quoted Rabbi Meir on an important halachic issue. Rabbi Yehuda became angry and told his students. "Didn't I tell you not to admit any of Rabbi Meir's students?" Rabbi Yosi responded: "People will say, 'Rabbi Meir is dead, Rabbi Yehuda is angry and Rabbi Yosi is silent.'" (*Nazir* 49b)

For a glimpse of the world as it was in the time of R. Sumchos b. Yoseph, see the historical timeline from 150 to 250 C.E.

תנחום בר אבא
Tanhum bar Abba

(fourth century C.E.)
Amora, Eretz Yisrael

According to the Talmud, the Emperor made the following suggestion to Rabbi Tanhum: "Come; let us all be one people." (*Sanhedrin* 39a)

"Very well," Rabbi Tanhum answered, "but since we are all circumcised, we cannot become like you. Therefore, the only way we can become all alike is if you are circumcised." The Emperor replied, "You have spoken well. Nevertheless, anyone who bests the Emperor in debate must be thrown to the lions." So it was done, but Rabbi Tanhum emerged alive. A heretic remarked, "The reason he was not eaten was because the lions were not hungry." Wishing to test the truth of the heretic's statement, they threw him to the lions, who devoured him.

For a glimpse of the world as it was in the time of R. Tanhum bar Abba, see the historical timeline from 300 to 400 C.E.

תנחום בר חנילאי
Tanhum bar Hanilai

(third century C.E.)
Amora, Eretz Yisrael

R. Tanhum was a student of Rabbi Yoshua ben Levi. (*Bava Kamma* 55a)

He said the following in the name of Rabbi Hanilai, who was his father: "Any man who has no wife lives without joy, without blessing, and without goodness." (*Yevamot* 62b)

R. Tanhum said: "One should divide his time of study in three: one third Tanach, one third Mishna and one third in Talmud." (*Avodah Zarah* 19b)

For a glimpse of the world as it was in Tanhum bar Hanilai's time, see the historical timeline from 200 to 300 C.E.

תנחום בר חייא
Tanhum bar Hiyya

(third–fourth centuries C.E.)
Ish Kefar Acco
Amora, Eretz Yisrael

R. Tanhum was a student of R. Yaakov and R. Huna. Several amoraim were close associates of his, among them R. Yehoshua ben Levi, Rabbi Yohanan and others. He was a wealthy man and very charitable. (*Moed Katan* 16b)

Once he redeemed with the assistance of Rabbi Aha, Jewish captives for a great sum of money. These captives were brought to Tiberias from Armenia. (*Yevamot* 45a)

It is related that whenever his mother bought meat for his household, she bought an equal amount of meat to be distributed to the poor.

For a glimpse of the world as it was in the time of R. Tanhum bar Hiyya, see the historical timeline from 250 to 300 C.E.

טרפון
Tarfon

(first century C.E.)
Tanna, Eretz Yisrael

Rabbi Tarfon was still a young man when the Temple was destroyed. A kohen, he remembered many things from when the Temple was still standing. Among the students in the Yavne academy he was a leading scholar, as well as a contemporary of Rabbi Yohanan ben Zakkai and of Rabbi Akiva, with whom he spent one seder night in Benai Berak. They were friends and held each other in very high esteem.

There is a disagreement among the rabbis whether Rabbi Tarfon was the teacher of Rabbi Akiva or that they were only colleagues. (*Ketubbot* 84b)

It once happened that Rabbi Tarfon ordered a cow whose womb had been removed to be fed to the dogs. When the matter was brought before the sages in Yavne, they permitted the cow's flesh for human consumption because a prominent physician, Theodos, stated that no cow was allowed to leave Alexandria unless her womb had been cut out, to prevent her from having offspring. Thereupon, Rabbi Tarfon said, "There goes my donkey," meaning that he would have to compensate the owner of the cow.

But Rabbi Akiva said to him, "You are not bound to make compensation because you are publicly recognized as an expert in these matters." (*Sanhedrin* 33a)

Rabbi Tarfon was an expert in monetary matters and the laws pertaining to them. He established a yeshiva in Lydda, where he lived. (*Bava Metzia* 49b)

The Talmud states, "Long ago it happened that Rabbi Tarfon, Rabbi Yishmael and the Elders were learning Torah. Rabbi Eleazar Modin, who was among them, stated that the manna was sixty cubits high. R. Tarfon said to him, "How long will you make up words and throw them at us?" Rabbi Eleazar answered, "My teacher, I am only expounding on the Torah." Among his outstanding students were Rabbi Yehuda b. Illai, Rabbi Yosi ha-Gelili, Rabbi Shimon b. Yohai, Rabbi Yishmael and Rabbi Eliezer Modin. (*Yoma* 76a)

He was a wealthy person, and very charitable. Once, he made a wedding for three hundred needy brides because it was a year of severe drought. (*Nedarim* 62a)

He took extreme care to honor his mother. When she wished to mount her bed, he would lie down on the floor so that she could step on his back in order to reach it. (*Kiddushin* 31b)

Rabbi Tarfon and the elders were once reclining in the upper floor of a house in Lydda. They were asked, "Which is greater, study or practice?"

R. Tarfon said, "Practice is greater," while Rabbi Akiva said, "Study is greater." Then they all agreed that study is greater because it leads to action. (*Kiddushin* 40b)

Our rabbis taught: when R. Eliezer fell ill, four sages went to visit him: R. Tarfon, R. Yoshua, R. Eleazar b. Azaryah and R. Akiva.

R. Tarfon said to him: "You are more valuable to Israel than rain, for rain is precious in this world, but you are precious in this world and the next."

R. Yoshua said: "You are more valuable to Israel than the disc of the sun, for the sun's disc is only in this world, while you are for this and the next world."

R. Eleazar b. Azaryah said: "You are better to Israel than a father and mother, they are only for this world, but you are for this and the next world."

But R. Akiva remarked: "Suffering is precious." R. Eliezer liked R. Akiva's remark best. (*Sanhedrin* 101a)

One of his sayings was: "The day is short, the task is great, the laborers are lazy, the reward is plentiful and the master is pressing urgently." (*Avot* 2:15)

Another saying of his is: "It is not your obligation to complete the task, but neither are you at liberty to be idle. If you studied much Torah you will have great reward because your Employer is faithful, and you should know that the righteous will be rewarded in the time to come." (*Avot* 2:16)

Unfortunately, he did not have much luck with his children. When R. Yehuda ha-Nasi visited R. Tarfon's town, he inquired: "Has the Tzadik who used to swear by the life of his children left a son?" They answered, "He left no son, but a daughter's son survives." (*Bava Metzia* 85a)

For a glimpse of the world as it was in Rabbi Tarfon's time, see the historical timeline from 1 to 100 C.E.

מר עוקבא
Mar Ukva

(third century C.E.)
Amora, Babylonia
Exilarch

The title Mar was usually added to the Exilarch family. Some sources say that Mar Ukva succeeded R. Huna as Exilarch.

He completed most of his studies under Rabbi Shemuel, who was his teacher. (*Eruvin* 81a)

Mar Ukva was the head of the rabbinical court in the town of Kafri. (*Kiddushin* 44b)

His father-in-law, R. Hisda, who also lived in Kafri, quotes Mar Ukva sometimes. (*Berachot* 10b)

Mar Ukva had two sons, Mari and Nathan. (*Hullin* 43b, *Berachot* 13b)

When they sat together in the academy, Mar Ukva would sit in front of R. Shemuel at a distance of four cubits because he was the head of the academy. When they sat together at a court session, R. Shemuel would sit in front of Mar Ukva at a distance of four cubits because Mar Ukva was the Exilarch. The place where Mar Ukva sat was dug out and lined with matting.

Every day, Mar Ukva would accompany R. Shemuel to his house. One day, he was preoccupied with a case and walked ahead of R. Shemuel. When they reached the house, R. Shemuel said to Mar Ukva, "You have been involved in your case for a long time. Now involve yourself in my case." Mar Ukva realized that he had hurt R. Shemuel's feelings and apologized. (*Moed Katan* 16b)

R. Yannai sent a message to Mar Ukva, saying, "Send me some of Mar Shmuel's eye medicine." He sent him the medicine with the following instructions: "This is what Shemuel recommends: a drop of cold water in the morning and bathing the hands and feet in hot water in the evening are better than all the eye medicines in the world." (*Shabbat* 108b)

The Talmud relates that when R. Yitzhak came to Babylonia, he told them, "There was a town in Eretz Yisrael called Gofnit. In this town there were eighty pairs of brothers, all kohanim, who were married to eighty pairs of sisters, all daughters of kohanim."

The rabbis searched from Sura to Nehardea and could not find a similar case except for the daughters of R. Hisda, who were daughters of a kohen.

They were married to two brothers, Rammi b. Hama and Mar Ukva b. Hama, but their husbands were not kohanim. (*Berachot* 44a)

Mar Ukva was known for his great charity.

The Talmud relates that a poor man lived in Mar Ukva's neighborhood, and Mar Ukva would throw four zuz at his door everyday in such a way that he would not be seen. One day, the poor man wished to learn his benefactor's identity. Mar Ukva was coming home with his wife, and they threw the coins at his door. As soon as the man saw people approaching his door he went out after them. They fled and hid in a large communal oven, where Mar Ukva's feet were nearly burned. (*Ketubbot* 67b)

R. Yoseph said: "Once, I entered the baths and Mar Ukva was present, and on leaving I was offered a cup of his wine. After drinking, I experienced a terrific cooling sensation from the hair of my head to my toenails. Had I drunk another cup, I would have feared to lose some merit in the World to Come. I am told that Mar Ukva drank it every day." (*Shabbat* 140a)

Mar Zutra said, "Some say that Mar Ukva said: 'Originally the Torah was given to Israel in the Hebrew language and Hebrew letters. Later in the time of Ezra, it was also given in Assyrian square letters and in Aramaic. Finally, they chose the Assyrian script and the Hebrew language.'" (*Sanhedrin* 21b)

Mar Ukva did not hold court when there were severe winds, known as *shuta*. (*Eruvin* 65a)

The mother of Rami b. Hama gave her property in writing to Rami b. Hama in the morning, but in the evening she gave it in writing to Mar Ukva b. Hama. Rami b. Hama came to R. Sheshet, who confirmed his inheritance. Mar Ukva then went to R. Nahman, who confirmed Mar Ukva in his inheritance.

R. Sheshet thereupon went to R. Nahman and said to him: "What is the reason that you acted as you did in this matter?"

R. Nahman replied: "And what is the reason that you acted in this matter as you did?"

R. Sheshet answered, "Because the will of R. Rami was written first."

R. Nahman replied; "Do we live in Jerusalem, where the hours are recorded? We live in Babylonia, where the hours are not recorded."

R. Sheshet asked: "And why did you act the way you did?"

"I treated it as a case to be decided at the discretion of the judges," replied R. Nahman.

R. Sheshes retorted, "I also treated it as a case to be decided at the discretion of the judges."

But R. Nahman replied: "I am a judge and you are not. Furthermore, you did not say at first that you treated it as a case to be decided by a judge." (*Ketubbot* 94b)

For a glimpse of the world as it was in Mar Ukva's time, see the historical timeline from 200 to 300 C.E.

עולא
Ulla

(third century C.E.)
Amora, Eretz Yisrael

Some say that his full name was Ulla b. Yishmael.

His sons were Rabbah and Aha. (*Shabbat* 83b, *Eruvin* 21b)

Rabbi Yohanan ben Nepaha, Rabbi Eleazar ben Pedat, and Resh Lakish were his teachers. He visited Babylonia frequently. (*Hagigah* 19a, *Eruvin* 21b, *Gittin* 50b)

On one occasion, Ulla was in danger of being murdered by one of his fellow travelers. It happened during his return trip to Eretz Yisrael, when two inhabitants from Hozai joined him. During a quarrel, one of them killed the other. The murderer asked Rabbi Ulla: "Did I do well?"

"Yes," Ulla replied. When Rabbi Ulla came before Rabbi Yohanan he asked: "Did my reply perhaps give encouragement to a murderer, Heaven forbid?"

Rabbi Yohanan replied, "You saved your life." (*Nedarim* 22a)

R. Ulla once visited R. Nahman and they dined together. When they finished, R. Ulla recited the grace after meals over a cup of wine. R. Ulla passed the cup of wine to R. Nahman, who said to him, "Please pass the cup to my wife, Yalta." R. Ulla and R. Nahman then had an exchange which was uncomplimentary to women. When Yalta heard the conversation, she got up in a rage, went to the wine cellar and smashed four hundred jars of wine. R. Nahman said to R. Ulla, "Please send her another cup of wine." R. Ulla sent her a cup with the following message: "All that wine can be counted as a blessing." Yalta replied, "Peddlers spread gossip and rags produce vermin." (*Berachot* 51b)

R. Ulla once visited Pumbedita and they brought some blood for him to examine, but he refused to see it. The town was under the jurisdiction of R. Yehuda. He explained: "If R. Eleazar, who was the supreme authority in the land of Israel, refused to examine blood when he visited the town of R. Yehuda, how can I do so?"

Why was R. Eleazar described as the supreme authority in the land of Israel? Because a woman once brought R. Eleazar some blood to be examined while R. Ammi was present. R. Eleazar smelled it and said, "This is blood of lust." After she went out, R. Ammi followed to question her, and she said, "My husband was away on a trip, and I desired him." (*Niddah* 20b)

As Rabbi Ulla and Rabbi Hisda were walking past the house of R. Hana b. Hanilai, R. Hisda sighed. R. Ulla asked him, "Why do you sigh?"

R. Hisda answered, "How can I refrain from sighing? He used to have sixty cooks to cook and bake for the poor. He always had his purse ready to give charity. In time of scarcity he put the grain and barley outside at nighttime for anyone to take, since he did not want people to have to come inside and be embarrassed. Now that it is all in ruins, shall I not sigh?" (*Berachot* 58b)

R. Ulla once visited R. Menashe on a Shabbat. During the visit, he heard a knock on the door. "Who is knocking on the door on Shabbat? This is a desecration of Shabbat!" Rabbah told him that only a musical sound is prohibited. (*Eruvin* 104a)

R. Ulla said: "One who saw Resh Lakish in the house of study, engaged in debate, would get a picture of him uprooting mountains and grinding them together." (*Sanhedrin* 24a)

R. Hiyya b. Ammi said in the name of Ulla: "Since the Temple was destroyed, the most precious thing to God in this world are the four cubits of space where Halacha is studied. (*Berachot* 8a)

R. Hiyya b. Ammi said in the name of R. Ulla, "One who lives from the labor of one's own hands is greater than one who fears God." (*Berachot* 8a)

R. Hiyya b. Ammi also said in the name of R. Ulla, "One should always live in the same town as one's teacher." (*Berachot* 8a)

Rabbi Ulla died in Babylon. When Rabbi Eleazar heard the news of his death, he had his remains taken to Eretz

Yisrael for burial. R. Ulla was survived by his son, Rabbah b. Ulla. (*Shabbat* 83b)

Although R. Ulla used to visit the Land of Israel frequently, he passed away outside it. His body was brought to Israel for burial. When R. Eleazar was informed that his coffin had arrived, he remarked, "Receiving a man in his lifetime is not the same as receiving him after his death." (*Ketubbot* 111a)

For a glimpse of the world as it was in R. Ulla's time, see the historical timeline from 200 to 300 C.E.

יעקב
Yaakov

(third–fourth centuries C.E.)
Amora, Babylonia

R. Yaakov was a student of R. Yehuda and of Rabbi Hisda. He said in the name of R. Hisda, "Whoever sets out to travel on the road should recite the Traveler's Prayer." (*Berachot* 29b)

In later years when he moved to Eretz Yisrael, he studied under Rabbi Yohanan. He was an associate of Rabbi Yirmiyahu. (*Eruvin* 80a)

For a glimpse of the world as it was in R. Yaakov's time, see the historical timeline from 250 to 350 C.E.

יעקב בר אחא
Yaakov b. Aha

(third century C.E.)
Amora, Eretz Yisrael

It is likely that R. Yaakov b. Aha was a student of Rabbi Yehuda ha-Nasi. Although he was born in Eretz Yisrael, he immigrated to Babylonia.

R. Illai said in the name of R. Yaakov b. Aha, in the name of Rabbeinu, "Whoever omits to mention circumcision and Torah in the blessing over the land [in the Grace after Meals] has not fulfilled his obligation." (*Berachot* 49a)

For a glimpse of the world as it was in the time of R. Yaakov b. Aha, see the historical timeline from 200 to 300 C.E.

יעקב בר אידי
Yaakov bar Idi

(third century C.E.)
Amora, Eretz Yisrael

R. Yaakov, who studied under Rabbi Yohanan, transmitted some of his sayings. He also transmitted halachic rulings in the name of Rabbi Yehoshua b. Levi.

He was a leader in the community of Tiberias, but later on he moved to the vicinity of Tyre. (*Hullin* 98a)

Rabbi Zeira, who lived in Babylonia, asked Rabbi Yaakov, the son of Yaakov's daughter, who was making a trip to Eretz Yisrael, to make a detour to Tyre in order to visit Rabbi Yaakov ben Idi. R. Zeira wanted some clarification on some halachic matters. Rabbi Yaakov b. Idi was held in very high esteem in Babylonia. (*Eruvin* 80a)

R. Yaakov and R. Zerika said: Whenever R. Akiva and one of his colleagues disagree, Halacha goes according to R. Akiva. When R. Yosi disagrees with his colleagues, Halacha goes according to R. Yosi.

Between R. Yehuda ha-Nasi and one of his colleagues, Halacha goes according to Rebbe. What practical difference does it make? R. Assi said: General practice. R. Hiyya b. Abba said: The practical difference is that we tend in their favor. R. Yosi b. Hanina said: They are seen as acceptable views.

R. Yaakov b. Idi said in the name of R. Yohanan: Whenever there is a dispute between R. Meir and R. Yehuda, Halacha goes according to R. Yehuda. In a dispute between R. Yehuda and R. Yosi, Halacha goes according to R. Yosi. Needless to say, in a dispute between R.

Meir and R. Yosi, Halacha goes according to R. Yosi.

R. Assi said: I also learn that a dispute between R. Yosi and R. Shimon, Halacha goes according to R. Yosi.

R. Abba said in the name of R. Yohanan: In a dispute between R. Yehuda and R. Shimon, Halacha goes according to R. Yehuda. A dispute between R. Meir and R. Shimon is left unresolved. (*Eruvin* 46b)

For a glimpse of the world as it was in the time of Yaakov bar Idi, see the historical timeline from 200 to 300 C.E.

יעקב בן קרשי
Yaakov ben Korshai

(second century C.E.)
Tanna, Eretz Yisrael

R. Yaakov was a contemporary of Rabbi Shimon ben Gamliel, Rabbi Meir and Rabbi Nathan.

The Talmud relates that Rabbi Yohanan said, "The following instructions were issued in the days when Rabbi Shimon ben Gamliel was president of the Sanhedrin. Whenever the president of the Sanhedrin enters the room, everyone should rise, but when the Hacham or the president of the court enters, only a small number of the assembly should rise." Rabbi Meir was the Hacham and Rabbi Nathan was the president of the court. Rabbi Meir and Rabbi Nathan were not present when the instructions were issued. The next day, when Rabbi Meir and Rabbi Nathan entered the hall of the Sanhedrin, they noticed the lack of respect accorded to them. When they asked the reason for the change, they were told that those were the instructions of Rabbi Shimon.

Rabbi Meir and Rabbi Nathan decided to engage in a discourse in which Rabbi Shimon was not familiar. When Rabbi Yaakov ben Korshai found out what was planned, he feared that this might lead to a disgrace to the presidency of the Sanhedrin. He therefore started to study the subject just outside Rabbi Shimon's chamber, repeating it loudly, over and over. When R. Shimon heard him, he perceived that something was happening in the Sanhedrin. He concentrated on the subject and familiarized himself with it.

The next day, his two opponents approached him in order to discuss the subject. He agreed and he was able to hold his ground. When they finished, he said to them, "Had I not familiarized myself with the subject, you would have disgraced me." He issued an order to have them removed from the Sanhedrin. When they were on the outside they wrote down difficult scholastic questions on slips of paper, which they threw inside. Many of the questions could not be answered inside, and they were sent back outside unanswered. They wrote down the answer and sent it back inside. Rabbi Yosi said to the assembly, "The Torah is outside and we are sitting inside." Rabbi Shimon changed his mind and said, "We shall readmit them, but impose on them this penalty: no traditional statement shall be quoted in their names." They decided that the phrase "others say" would refer to Rabbi Meir, while the phrase "some say" would refer to Rabbi Nathan.

Rabbi Nathan was eventually reinstated.

One of Rabbi Yaakov ben Korshai's famous sayings was: "This world is like a vestibule to the world to come; prepare yourself in the vestibule that you may enter into the grand hall." (*Avot* 4:17)

For a glimpse of the world as it was in the time of R. Yaakov ben Korshai, see the historical timeline from 100 to 200 C.E.

ידוע הבבלי
Yaddua ha-Bavli

(second century C.E.)
Tanna, Eretz Yisrael

R. Yaddua, a student of Rabbi Meir, quotes Rabbi Meir in Baba Metzia. (Baba Metzia 7:9)

For a glimpse of the world as it was in the time of Yaddua ha-Bavli, see the historical timeline from 50 to 150 C.E.

יקים איש הדר
Yakim Ish Hadar

(first–second centuries C.E.)
Tanna, Eretz Yisrael

R. Yakim, a contemporary of Rabbi Yehoshua, Rabbi Tzadok and Rabbi Eliezer, is mentioned in the Mishna. (*Eduyot* 7:5)

For a glimpse of the world as it was in the time of Yakim Ish Hadar, see the historical timeline from 50 to 150 C.E.

ינאי
Yannai

(third century C.E.)
Amora, Eretz Yisrael

Some sources say that he was a descendant of Eli the high priest.

He was a student of Rabbi Hiyya, and his daughter married Rabbi Hiyya's son, Yehuda. (*Ketubbot* 62b)

He had a son by the name of Shimon.

A wealthy man, Rabbi Yannai owned orchards and vineyards. He lived in Akbara in the Upper Galilee, where he established an academy. (*Moed Katan* 12b)

It happened that Rabbi Yannai had a tree that overhung a public road. Another man also had a tree hanging over a public street. Some people who used the street objected, and the man was summoned to the court of R. Yannai. R. Yannai said to them, "Go

home and come back tomorrow."
During the night he had his workers cut
down his own tree. The next day, when
the man returned for a decision, R.
Yannai ordered him to cut down his tree.
The man objected, saying, "But sir, do
you not also have a tree that overhangs
the road?"

R. Yannai answered, "Go and see. If
mine is cut down, then cut yours down.
If mine is not, you need not cut yours
down." What was R. Yannai's thinking?
At first, he had thought that people
would be happy to sit in the tree's shade.
(*Bava Batra* 60a)

He was also a charitable person.

R. Yannai had an orchard whose
fruits ripened during the week of the
festival. His workers picked the fruit
during hol ha-mo'ed. The next year
many people waited to pick their fruits
until the festival. Realizing that the
people had been misled by his action, he
renounced the rights to the fruit of his
orchard for a year. (*Moed Katan* 12b)

Rabbi Yannai once saw a man give a
poor person a zuz in front of many
people. He told him, "It would have
been better if you had not given anything
to him at all because you embarrassed
him in public." (*Hagiga* 5a)

Some of his students were well
known, among them R. Oshaya, R.
Abba, R. Aibu, R. Yohanan and R.
Shimon ben Lakish. (*Ketubbot* 79a,
Kiddushin 19a)

He opposed reliance on miracles.

He used to say, "One should never
stand in a dangerous place and say, 'A
miracle will happen.'" (*Shabbat* 32a)

His son-in-law, R. Yehuda b. Hiyya,
spent most of his time in the house of
study, but went home every Friday
evening. Whenever he did so, R. Yannai
would see a pillar of light preceding him.
Once, R. Yehuda was so immersed in
study that he forgot to go home, and R.

Yannai, not seeing the pillar, thought
that he had died, and voiced his concern
to his associates. (*Ketubbot* 62b)

Rabbi Yannai would put on his
robes on Friday evening and call out,
"Come, O bride! Come, O bride!"
(*Shabbat* 119a)

R. Yannai said, "Tefilin require a
pure body, like that of Elisha of the
wings." He was called so because of an
incident that occurred when the Roman
government prohibited the wearing of
tefillin. Disregarding the decree, Elisha
put them on. A Roman soldier pursued
and captured him. Elisha removed the
tefillin and held them in his hand.

"What is that in your hand?" the
Roman officer demanded.

"The wings of a dove," Elisha
answered, opening his hand and showing
the wings of a dove. (*Shabbat* 49a)

For a glimpse of the world as it was in R. Yannai's
time, see the historical timeline from 200 to 300 C.E.

ינאי בר ישמעאל
Yannai bar Yishmael

(third century C.E.)
Amora, Eretz Yisrael

The Talmud quotes a statement of
his about a Halachic matter, as well as in
several other places. (*Taanit* 14a)

For a glimpse of the world as it was in the time of R.
Yannai bar Yishmael, see the historical timeline from
200 to 300 C.E.

יהודה בן בתירא
Yehuda ben Betera I

(first century C.E.)
Tanna, Eretz Yisrael and Babylonia

As a young man, Yehuda ben Betera
I lived in Jerusalem. When the Yavne
academy was first established, Rabbi
Yohanan ben Zakkai had discussions
with the Benei Betera.

The Talmud mentions him in many
places. The Mishna records that in one

instance, Halacha goes according to his decision. (*Peah* 3:6)

Rabbi Yehuda b. Betera said, "It once happened that the trough in Jerusalem had an opening in it, but it was not large enough. The school of Shammai made an opening in it of the proper size." (*Mikvaot* 4:5)

A certain non-Jewish Syrian used to go to Jerusalem to partake of the Pesah sacrifices, and boasted to Rabbi Yehuda b. Betera that he did this in spite of the prohibition against non-Jews doing so. Rabbi Yehuda asked him, "Did they give you a fat tail?"

"No," he replied.

"The next time you go up, ask for a piece of the fat tail," Rabbi Yehuda said.

The next time he went to Jerusalem, he asked for the fat tail. "The fat tail goes to the Most High," they replied, and asked him, "Who told you to say this?"

"Rabbi Yehuda ben Betera," he answered.

They investigated and learned that he was not Jewish. They then sent a message to Rabbi Yehuda, saying, "Peace be upon you! Even though you are in Nisibis, Babylonia, your net is spread as far as Jerusalem." (*Pesahim* 3b)

It happened that once, when Rosh ha-Shannah fell on Shabbat, Rabbi Yohanan ben Zakkai told the Benei Betera, "Let us blow the shofar."

They said, "Let us discuss the matter." He said, "Let us blow the shofar first and discuss it later." After they blew the shofar, they wished to discuss the matter. He replied, "The shofar has already been heard in Yavne, and what has been done is no longer open for discussion." (*Rosh ha-Shannah* 29b)

Later in life, R. Yehuda moved to Nisibis in Babylonia.

For a glimpse of the world as it was in the time of Yehuda ben Betera I, see the historical timeline from 1 to 100 C.E.

יהודה בן בתירא
Yehuda ben Betera II

(second century C.E.)
Tanna, Eretz Yisrael

Although Rabbi Yehuda was born in Rome, he studied in Eretz Yisrael in the academies of Rabbi Eliezer b. Hyrcanus and Rabbi Yoshua b. Hanania.

He often disagreed with Rabbi Akiva, who was his colleague. One controversy between them concerned the identity of Zelofhad. Later in life, he moved to Nisibis, Babylonia, where he established a yeshiva. (*Shabbat* 96b and 97a)

Our rabbis taught: "Follow the scholars to their academies: R. Eliezer to Lydda, R. Yohanan b. Zakkai to Beror Hayil, R. Yoshua to Peki'in, R. Gamliel to Yavneh, R. Akiva to Bene Berak, R. Matya to Rome, R. Hananya b. Teradyon to Sichnin, R. Yosi b. Halafta to Sepphoris, R. Yehuda b. Betera to Nisibis, R. Hanina b. Ahi Yoshua to exile, Rebbe to Bet Shearim and the Sages to the Chamber of Hewn Stone. (*Sanhedrin* 32b)

Rabbi Eliezer b. R. Yosi ha-Gelili said, "The dead whom Yehezkel revived went up to Eretz Yisrael, married wives and had sons and daughters." Rabbi Yehuda b. Betera rose and declared, "I am one of their descendants, and these are the tefillin that belonged to them. My grandfather left them to me as an heirloom." (*Sanhedrin* 92b)

For a glimpse of the world as it was in the time of R. Yehuda ben Betera II, see the historical timeline from 100 to 200 C.E.

יהודה בן בבא
Yehuda ben Bava

(second century C.E.)
Tanna, Eretz Yisrael

Rabbi Yehuda was one of the scholars from Yavne.

Rabbi Yehuda ben Bava, became a martyr when he disobeyed the decree of the Roman authorities banning rabbinical ordination. During the Hadrianic persecutions, the authorities issued a decree that anyone who ordained a rabbi or received ordination would be liable to the death penalty, the city where the ordination took place would be demolished, and the boundaries around the city uprooted.

In order to avoid the destruction of a city, Rabbi Yehuda b. Bava sat between two great mountains and between the two cities of Usha and Shefaram. Five prominent students sat before him: Rabbi Meir, Rabbi Yehuda bar Illai, Rabbi Shimon, Rabbi Yosi, and Rabbi Eleazar ben Shammua. The ceremony was held and he ordained them. Rabbi Avia adds the name of Rabbi Nehemia. As soon as the ceremony ended, they noticed the Romans approaching from a distance. Rabbi Yehuda told his students to flee. They wanted to take him with them, but he urged them to flee without him, saying, "I would cause all of you to be captured. I am too old to run. I will lie before them like a stone." It was said that the Romans stabbed him three hundred times. (*Sanhedrin* 14a)

Whenever the Talmud talks about a certain pious man, it refers to either Rabbi Yehuda ben Bava or R. Yehuda bar Illai. (*Baba Kamma* 103b)

On giving evidence about a dead person, Rabbi Yehuda felt that not all men, places and times are equal. (*Yevamot* 16:3, 121b)

Rabbi Yehuda testified regarding five opinions. One of them was that a woman may marry again on the testimony of a single witness. (*Eduyyot* 6:1)

R. Nahman said: R. Yehuda ben Bava testified about five things: that a minor girl is instructed to refuse marriage, that a woman may remarry on the evidence of a single witness, that a rooster was stoned to death in Jerusalem because it had killed a human being, that wine forty days old was poured as a libation on the altar, that the daily offering was brought at the fourth hour of the morning. (*Berachot* 27a)

For a glimpse of the world as it was in the time of Yehuda ben Bava, see the historical timeline from 100 to 200 C.E.

יהודה בן חייא
Yehuda b. Hiyya

(third century C.E.)
Amora, Eretz Yisrael

R. Yehuda was the twin brother of Rabbi Hizkiyah ben Hiyya. Together with their father, the two brothers moved from Babylonia to Eretz Yisrael.

R. Yehuda earned his living from agriculture.

R. Avin b. R. Adda quoted R. Menahem as saying, "It happened once that a child was born to the same mother three months after the first one, and both of those students were sitting in our academy. Who are these students? They are Rabbi Yehuda and Rabbi Hizkiyah, the sons of Rabbi Hiyya. But did we not learn that a woman could not conceive twice during one pregnancy? Rabbi Abbaye replied, "It was the same drop, which was split in two. The features of one were completed at the beginning of the seventh month, and the features of the other were completed at the end of the ninth month." (*Niddah* 27a)

The Talmud relates that Resh Lakish said, "In ancient times when the Torah was forgotten, Ezra came up from Babylon and established it. When it was forgotten again, Hillel the Babylonian came up and established it. When it happened yet again, Rabbi Hiyya and his sons came up and established it." (*Sukkah* 20a)

R. Yehuda once said that the Torah is a medication of life for the whole body. (*Eruvin* 54a)

He is quoted as saying that exile atones for half of Israel's sins. (*Sanhedrin* 37b)

R. Yehuda b. Hiyya, the son-in-law of R. Yannai, spent most of his time in the house of study, but went home every Friday evening. Whenever he came home on Friday evenings, R. Yannai would see a pillar of light preceding him. Once R. Yehuda was so immersed in his study that he forgot to go home, and R. Yannai, not seeing the pillar, thought that he had died, and voiced his concern to his associates. (*Ketubbot* 62b)

They studied under R. Yehuda ha-Nasi. (*Sanhedrin* 38a)

R. Yehuda and R. Hizkiyah, the sons of R. Hiyya, were having dinner with Rebbe, and their father, R. Hiyya, was also present. When the sons did not utter a word during the meal, Rebbe said: "Give the young men plenty of strong wine, so that they will open up and say something."

When the wine took effect, they started talking and said, "The son of David cannot come until the two ruling houses of Israel come to an end." To back it up, they quoted a passage from Scripture.

Rebbe became annoyed and exclaimed, "My children, you throw thorns in my eyes." R. Hiyya intervened, saying, "Rebbe, do not be angry. The numerical value of the Hebrew letters in the word 'wine' is the same as that of the word 'secret.' When wine enters, secrets come out."

For a glimpse of the world as it was in the time of Yehuda bar Hiyya, see the historical timeline from 200 to 300 C.E.

יהודה בן דוסתאי
Yehuda ben Dostai

(first century C.E.)
Tanna, Eretz Yisrael

Rabbi Yehuda is not mentioned much in the Talmud, except where he cited a ruling in the name of Rabbi Shimon ben Shetah. (*Makkot* 7a)

It was taught Rabbi Dostai b. Yehuda, or Rabbi Yehuda b. Dostai, said, "The principle of an eye for an eye, as commanded in the Torah, means only monetary compensation." (*Bava Kamma* 83b)

For a glimpse of the world as it was in the time of R. Yehuda ben Dostai, see the historical timeline from 1 to 100 C.E.

יהודה בן גרים
Yehuda ben Gerim

(second century C.E.)
Tanna, Eretz Yisrael

Rabbi Yehuda was the son of parents who were converts.

Rabbi Yonathan ben Asmai and Rabbi Yehuda b. Gerim studied under Rabbi Shimon bar Yohai. They said good-bye to Rabbi Shimon in the evening, and in the morning they said good-bye to him again. He said to them, "Didn't you say good-bye last night?" They answered him, "You taught us that a student must say good-bye again to his teacher regardless."

Rabbi Shimon said to his son, "These are men of substance. Go along with them so that they may bless you." (*Moed Katan* 9a)

The Talmud relates that Rabbi Yehuda ben Gerim inadvertently repeated the words of Rabbi Shimon bar Yohai, in which he criticized the Roman authorities in a conversation among friends. As a result, the Roman authorities found out what R. Shimon had said and sentenced him to death. He escaped and hid, together with his son, in a cave for thirteen years. (*Shabbat* 33b)

For a glimpse of the world as it was in the time of Yehuda ben Gerim, see the historical timeline from 100 to 200 C.E.

יהודה בן אלעי
Yehuda b. Illai

(second century C.E.)
Tanna, Eretz Yisrael

R. Yehuda lived for a time in Usha, a town in the Galilee, where he was born and studied under his father.

His father was a student of Rabbi Eliezer ben Hyrcanus, whom Rabbi Yehuda often quoted and whose halachot he transmitted. When the Talmud attaches no other name to the name Yehuda, it refers to Rabbi Yehuda bar Illai. (*Menachot* 18a)

While a young man he studied in Lydda at Rabbi Tarfon, and he also studied at Rabbi Akiva and Rabbi Yehuda ben Bava. He was one of the last five students who received ordination from Rabbi Yehuda ben Bava.

During the Hadrianic persecutions, the authorities issued a decree that anyone who ordained a rabbi or received ordination would be liable to the death penalty, the city where the ordination took place would be demolished, and the boundaries around the city uprooted.

In order to avoid the destruction of a city, Rabbi Yehuda b. Bava sat between two great mountains and between the two cities of Usha and Shefaram. Five prominent students sat before him: Rabbi Meir, Rabbi Yehuda bar Illai,

Rabbi Shimon, Rabbi Yosi, and Rabbi Eleazar ben Shammua. The ceremony was held and he ordained them. Rabbi Avia adds the name of Rabbi Nehemia. As soon as the ceremony ended, they noticed the Romans approaching from a distance. Rabbi Yehuda told his students to flee. They wanted to take him with them, but he urged them to flee without him, saying, "I would cause all of you to be captured. I am too old to run. I will lie before them like a stone." It was said that the Romans stabbed him three hundred times. (*Sanhedrin* 14a)

The students fled, meeting again only after Hadrian's death. Seven of the students assembled in the valley of Rimmon to intercalate the year. They were Rabbi Meir, Rabbi Yehuda, Rabbi Yosi, Rabbi Shimon, Rabbi Nehemia, Rabbi Eliezer ben Yaakov and Rabbi Yohanan ha-Sandlar. Rabbi Yehuda participated in the conventions of the scholars at Usha.

On one occasion, Rabbi Yehuda, Rabbi Shimon and Rabbi Yosi were making remarks to an audience. Rabbi Yehuda b. Illai remarked on how fine the works of the Romans were, citing their markets, bridges and bathhouses. Rabbi Yosi ben Halafta was silent, but Rabbi Shimon ben Yohai commented, "Whatever they built, they did for themselves. They built markets to place prostitutes in them, bridges to levy tolls on them, and bathhouses to indulge their bodies." Someone carried his words to the Romans. They decreed that Rabbi Yehuda should be rewarded, Rabbi Yosi exiled to Sepphoris and Rabbi Shimon executed. Rabbi Shimon and his son Rabbi Eleazar went and hid in a cave. Miraculously, a carob tree grew nearby and they found a well in the cave. To conserve wear and tear on their clothing, they sat naked in the sand during the day as they studied Torah. Twelve years later, when the emperor Hadrian died, they left the cave, but due to some circumstances they returned for one more year. Because R. Yehuda spoke well of the Roman government, he was promoted to be the foremost spokesman for the scholars. (*Shabbat* 33b)

It is stated that Rabbi Akiva had twelve thousand pairs of students, all of whom died at the same time because they did not treat each other with respect. A tanna taught that all of them died between Pesah and Shavuot. The remaining students of Rabbi Akiva who revived the Torah at that time were Rabbi Meir, Rabbi Yehuda bar Illai, Rabbi Yosi ben Halafta, Rabbi Shimon bar Yohai and Rabbi Eleazar ben Shammua. (*Yevamot* 62b)

R. Yehuda said in Rav's name: "This was the practice of Rabbi Yehuda bar Illai: on Friday afternoon, they put before him a basin of hot water. He washed his face, hands and feet and wrapped himself in a fringed linen robe, and he looked like an angel of God." (*Shabbat* 25b)

The most renowned student of R. Yehuda bar Illai was Rabbi Yehuda ha-Nasi.

For most of his life, R. Yehuda was very poor.

The Talmud refers to that period as the generation of Rabbi Yehuda bar Illai. It was said that poverty was so great on account of the Hadrian persecution that six students had to cover themselves with one garment, but nevertheless they studied Torah. The son of Rabbi Yehuda b. Illai, Rabbi Yosi, was also a great and respected scholar. (*Sanhedrin* 20a)

It is related that after Rabbi Meir passed away, Rabbi Yehuda bar Illai told his students: "Do not allow the students of Rabbi Meir to enter our academy, since they come only for disputations and in order to overwhelm me with citations from traditions, but not to learn Torah."

Rabbi Sumchos forced his way into the academy. He quoted Rabbi Meir on an important halachic issue. Rabbi Yehuda became very angry and told his students: "Didn't I instruct you not to admit any of Rabbi Meir's students?"

Rabbi Yosi responded, "People will say, 'Rabbi Meir is dead, Rabbi Yehuda is angry and Rabbi Yosi is silent.'" (*Nazir* 49b, *Kiddushin* 52b)

Whenever the Talmud talks about a certain pious man it refers to either Rabbi Yehuda ben Bava or R. Yehuda bar Illai. (*Bava Kamma* 103b)

It was recorded: R. Yehuda b. Illai used to suspend Torah study in order to escort a corpse to the cemetery. He also suspended Torah study in order to escort a bride to the canopy on her wedding day. (*Megillah* 29a)

What did Yehuda the son of Jacob do that he merited a special blessing from Yaakov? R. Meir used to say, "We have learned that when the Israelites stood at the Red Sea, the tribes argued about who would jump into the sea first. The men of the tribe of Benjamin jumped in first, and the princes of Yehuda hurled stones at them because they wanted to be first."

R. Yehuda said to R. Meir, "That is not the story I heard. This is what happened. The tribes were not willing to jump into the sea, but Nahshon ben Amminadav, who was a prince from the tribe of Yehuda, came forward and jumped in first. At that time, Moshe was busy praying to God, Who said to him, "My children are drowning and you utter a lengthy prayer?"

"What should I do?" Moshe asked.

God answered him, "Lift up your staff, stretch it over the sea and go forward."

As they marched into the water, the sea split. As a reward, the kings of Israel belong to the tribe of Yehuda. (*Sotah* 36b, 37a)

R. Yehuda stated: "We were once sitting in the presence of R. Akiva; and that day was the ninth of the month of Av that occurred on a Friday. They brought him a lightly roasted egg and he ate it without salt. He did this not because he had an appetite for it, but to show the students what the halacha was." (*Eruvin* 41a)

R. Yaakov and R. Zerika said: Whenever R. Akiva and one of his colleagues disagree, Halacha goes according to R. Akiva. When R. Yosi disagrees with his colleagues, Halacha goes according to R. Yosi.

In a dispute between R. Yehuda ha-Nasi and one of his colleagues, Halacha goes according to Rebbe. What practical difference does it make? R. Assi said: General practice. R. Hiyya b. Abba said: The practical difference is that we tend in their favor. R. Yosi b. Hanina said: They are seen as acceptable views.

R. Yaakov b. Idi said in the name of R. Yohanan: Whenever there is a dispute between R. Meir and R. Yehuda, Halacha goes according to R. Yehuda. In a dispute between R. Yehuda and R. Yosi, Halacha goes according to R. Yosi. Needless to say, in a dispute between R. Meir and R. Yosi, Halacha goes according to R. Yosi.

R. Assi said: I also learn that a dispute between R. Yosi and R. Shimon, Halacha goes according to R. Yosi.

R. Abba said in the name of R. Yohanan: In a dispute between R. Yehuda and R. Shimon, Halacha goes according to R. Yehuda. A dispute between R. Meir and R. Shimon is left unresolved. (*Eruvin* 46b)

For a glimpse of the world as it was in the time of Yehuda bar Illai, see the historical timeline from 100 to 200 C.E.

יהודה בר נחמני
Yehuda bar Nahmeni

(third century C.E.)
Amora, Eretz Yisrael

R. Yehuda was the interpreter for Rabbi Shimon ben Lakish. It happened once that the office of the Nasi appointed an unqualified person to lecture at the academy. They asked Rabbi Yehuda to stand near him and interpret. Rabbi Yehuda bent down to listen what the lecturer had to say, but made no attempt to say anything. Thereupon, Rabbi Yehuda delivered his own lecture. He said, "Woe into him who talks to wood or to a dumb stone. Though it be overlaid with gold and silver, there is no breath in it." (*Sanhedrin* 7b)

For a glimpse of the world as it was in the time of Yehuda bar Nahmeni, see the historical timeline from 200 to 300 C.E.

יהודה בן שמוע
Yehuda ben Shammua

(second century C.E.)
Tanna, Eretz Yisrael

Rabbi Yehuda ben Shammua was a student of Rabbi Meir in the yeshiva at Tiberias. (*Rosh ha-Shannah* 19a)

He is credited with successfully interceding with the Roman authorities to nullify the decree forbidding the study of Torah. The Roman authorities had issued a decree against Torah study, circumcision and Sabbath observance. Rabbi Yehuda ben Shammua consulted a Roman matron who had many influential Roman friends. She advised him on how to get the decree annulled. (*Rosh ha-Shannah* 19a)

For a glimpse of the world as it was in the time of R. Yehuda ben Shammua, see the historical timeline from 100 to 200 C.E.

יהודה בר סימון
Yehuda bar Simon

(third–fourth centuries C.E.)
Amora, Eretz Yisrael

R. Yehuda, who was a member of the priestly family, was a grandson of R. Pazzi. (*Sanhedrin* 100a)

R. Yehuda bar Simon said, "Any person whose face becomes black on account of hard toil studying Torah in this world will be rewarded with a bright face in the future world."

For a glimpse of the world as it was in the time of Yehuda bar Simon, see the historical timeline from 250 to 350 C.E.

יהודה בן טבאי
Yehuda ben Tabbai

(first century B.C.E.)
Tanna, Eretz Yisrael

Rabbi Yehuda was one of the zugot, or study partners of the Talmud, together with his colleague, Shimon ben Shetah.

He was a student of Rabbi Yoshua ben Perahia and Nittai ha-Arbeli. At one time, he was the Nasi of the Sanhedrin, and at another time he was the head of the rabbinical court. He left Jerusalem and moved to Alexandria.

The Talmud quotes him saying: "Act not the part of an advocate when you are a judge, and when the parties stand before you consider them in your eyes as guilty, and when they leave regard both of them as innocent." (*Avot* 1:8)

For a glimpse of the world as it was in the time of R. Yehuda ben Tabbai, see the historical timeline from 100 to 1 B.C.E.

יהודה בן תימא
Yehuda ben Tema

(second century C.E.)
Tanna, Eretz Yisrael

Rabbi Yehuda is quoted as saying: "Be strong as a leopard, light as an eagle, swift as a deer and powerful as a lion to do the will of your Creator." (*Avot* 5:20)

The Talmud refers to Rabbi Yehuda ben Tema and his colleagues as the masters of the Mishna. (*Hagigah* 14a)

For a glimpse of the world as it was in the time of R. Yehuda ben Tema, see the historical timeline from 100 to 200 C.E.

יהודה בר יחזקאל
Yehuda bar Yehezkel

(third century C.E.)
Amora, Babylonia
Head of the Academy in Pumbedita

R. Yehuda was the founder of the academy at Pumbedita. His father was Rabbi Yehezkel, the well-known wonder-worker and amora, and his brother was Rabbi Rammi b. Yehezkel.

He studied at the academy of Rav in Sura, under Rabbi Assi in Huzal and under Rabbi Shemuel in Nehardea.

R. Shemuel called him "Shinena," an affectionate nickname. (*Berachot* 36a)

R. Yehuda's contemporaries included Rabbi Huna, Rabbi Nahman, Rabbi Eleazar and Rabbi Ulla. Among his prominent students were Rabbi Kahana, Rabbi Yoseph, Rabbi Zeira and Rabbi Abba.

Rabbi Yehuda did not approve of leaving Babylonia in order to return to Eretz Yisrael on the grounds that one should return only when the Messiah arrived.

It is related that Rabbi Zeira evaded Rabbi Yehuda because he wanted to make aliyah to Eretz Yisrael. He disagreed with the opinion of his teacher

R. Yehuda, that whoever left Babylonia for Eretz Yisrael violated a commandment, and interpreted the relevant scriptural passages differently. (*Ketubbot* 110b)

R. Yehuda's contemporaries considered him a saint and believed that he could work miracles.

R. Yehuda said in Rav's name, "This was the practice of Rabbi Yehuda bar Illai. On Friday afternoon, they would put a basin of hot water before him. He would wash his face, hands and feet and wrap himself in a fringed linen robe, and he looked like an angel of God."

It was stated that Rabbi Yehuda had only to remove his shoes and a pouring rain would start to fall. Rabbi Yitzhak b. Yehuda was his son. (*Berachot* 20a)

The Talmud states: The day R. Akiva died, Rebbe was born. When Rebbe died, Rav Yehuda was born. When Rav Yehuda died, Rava was born, and when Rava died, R. Ashi was born. (*Kiddushin* 72b)

R. Haviva said, "The Elders of Pumbedita issued one additional ruling. Rava had said that they ruled on two matters and R. Haviva added one more because Rav Yehuda said in R. Shmuel's name that one may light a fire on Shabbat for a woman in childbirth." (*Eruvin* 79b)

Rav Yehuda said in Rav's name, "Once, when Queen Shel Zion (Salome Alexandra) made a banquet for her son, all her utensils became defiled. She ordered (probably on the advice of her brother R. Shimon b. Shetah) all her golden dishes melted down and new ones made of the molten gold." (*Shabbat* 16b)

R. Yehuda established the academy in Pumbedita at a time when Nehardea was already a town with a sizable Jewish population. The seat of the Exilarch (the leader of the Jewish community in Babylonia) was in Nehardea. When the town of Nehardea was destroyed by Papa b. Nasser, the commander in chief of Palmyra, in 259 C.E., the academy at Nehardea ceased to exist. After the destruction many of the students went to Pumbedita. The main focus of his studies was *nezikin* (damages).

R. Papa said to Abbaye: "How is it that miracles were performed for past generations but not for us? It could not be because of their study, because in the time of R. Yehuda their entire study was confined to *nezikin*, while in our generation we study all six orders." (*Berachot* 20a)

R. Ulla once visited Pumbedita and they brought some blood for him to examine, but he refused to see it. The town was under the jurisdiction of R. Yehuda. He explained, "If R. Eleazar, who was the supreme authority in the Land of Israel, refused to examine blood when he visited the town of R. Yehuda, how could I do so?"

Why was R. Eleazar described as the supreme authority in the land of Israel? Because a woman once brought to R. Eleazar some blood to be examined while R. Ammi was present. R. Eleazar smelled it and declared, "This is blood of lust."

After the woman left, R. Ammi followed her in order to question her. She admitted, "My husband was away on a trip and I desired him." (*Niddah* 20b)

Rav Yehuda said in the name of Rav: "Every day a bat kol issues forth from Mount Horev and proclaims, 'The whole world is fed for the sake of my son Hanina – and yet my son Hanina is satisfied with a small measure of carobs from one Friday to the next." (*Berachot* 17b)

In the Talmud, Rav Yehuda said in the name of R. Shemuel: "Sumchos ruled that money claimed by two parties whose ownership is in doubt must be shared by both parties. However, the rabbis say that it is a fundamental principle that if one has possession of the money and the other makes a claim, the claimant has to bring proof." (*Bava Kamma* 46a)

Rav Yehuda said in the name of Rabbi Shemuel, quoting Rabbi Shimon ben Gamliel: "There were a thousand students in my father's house. Five hundred of them studied Torah, while the other five hundred studied Greek wisdom. Of these, only I and the son of my uncle in Assia were left." (*Sotah* 49b)

R. Yehuda said in the name of R. Shemuel, "When King Shlomo ordained the laws of *eruv* and the washing of hands. a bat kol proclaimed, "My son has a wise heart." (*Eruvin* 21b)

R. Yehuda says in the name of R. Shemuel, "Scholars must have marital relations every Friday night." (*Ketubbot* 62b)

R. Yehuda believed that it was a good thing to enjoy the wonderful things that God created in this world. R. Shemuel said to Rav Yehuda, Hurry and eat and drink, because the world from which we must depart is like a wedding feast. (*Eruvin* 54a)

R. Eliezer b. Yaakov disagreed with his colleagues about an *eruv* where Jews lived with non-Jews in one courtyard. Further on in the same tractate Abbaye said to R. Yoseph, "We have a tradition that R. Eliezer b. Yaakov's teachings are few in quantity but well sifted." Also, Rav Yehuda said in the name of R. Shemuel that Halacha accords with R. Eliezer b. Yaakov. (*Eruvin* 61b, 62b)

The Talmud tells us R. Yehuda said in the name of Rav:

When Moshe ascended on high in order to receive the Torah, he found the Almighty busy placing coronets over the letters of the Torah.

Moshe said to God, "Is anything holding back your hand? Is anything missing from the Torah? Are those additions necessary?"

God answered, "In future years there will be a man by the name of Akiva ben Yoseph who will expound on this and derive something from each point, sign or elevation."

Moshe said, "Lord of the Universe, permit me to see this man."

God replied, "Turn around!"

Moshe turned around and found himself in the academy of Rabbi Akiva. He sat down behind the eight rows of students. As he listened to the discussion, he could not follow what the students were arguing about and felt ill at ease. When the class came to a certain subject, one of the students asked, "Whence do we know all this?"

Rabbi Akiva replied, "It is the law that was given to Moshe on Mount Sinai."

When Moshe heard this, he was comforted. He asked God, "You have such a great man and yet you wish to give the Torah through me?"

God replied, "Be silent. Do not question me, for that is my decree." (*Menahot* 29b)

Rav Yehuda said in the name of Rabbi Shemuel in the name of Rabbi Meir: When I was a student at Rabbi Akiva I used to put kankantum into the ink and he didn't object to it. But when I came to study at Rabbi Yishmael he asked me, "What is your profession?"

I answered him, "I am a scribe."

Rabbi Yishmael then said to me, "Be meticulous in your work, for your work is sacred to Heaven. Should you omit or add one letter, you could cause a situation in which a world is destroyed." (Rashi comments that by adding a single letter to a word, one might change that word from singular to plural – and when speaking of God, that would be blasphemous.)

I told him that I put kankantum in the ink, which makes the ink permanent immediately. (*Eruvin* 13a)

R. Yehuda said: "One should never pray for things in Aramaic. R. Yohanan said that when one petitions for one's needs in Aramaic, the ministering angels do not understand." (*Shabbat* 12b)

A man who found a sum of money tied in a kerchief in the river Biran came to R. Yehuda to ask what to do with the money. R. Yehuda told the man to announce his find. The man asked, "Is this not similar to retrieving it from the sea?" R. Yehuda answered him that the river Biran is different because people do not regard objects lost there as lost forever. (*Bava Metzia* 24b)

There was a man who died in the neighborhood where R. Yehuda lived, but there were no one to mourn for him. R. Yehuda assembled ten men who sat shiva for him. After seven days, the spirit of the deceased appeared to R. Yehuda in a dream and told him, "Your mind will be at peace because you have set my mind at peace." (*Shabbat* 152a and b)

R. Yehuda said in the name of Rav: "It is forbidden to eat before feeding your own animals." (*Berachot* 40a)

On one occasion R. Yehuda and Rabbah went to visit Rabbah Bar b. Hana at his home while he was sick. They were having a pleasant visit, discussing a halachic matter, when some fanatical fire-worshipping Persian gangs invaded his home. The gangs caused havoc and removed the lamps from the house. When Rabbah bar b. Hana prayed for relief, he mentioned that it was hard to believe that the Persians were worse than the Romans. (*Gittin* 16b, 17a)

According to some sources, Pumbedita had a Jewish settlement as early as the Second Temple Era. It took on extra importance in 259 C.E., when Nehardea and its academy were destroyed by Papa b. Nasser, the commander-in-chief of Palmyra. The scholars from Nehardea fled and established an academy in Pumbedita, under the leadership of Rabbi Yehuda b. Yehezkel. That academy remained the central religious authority for Babylonian Jewry for many centuries. (*Gittin* 60b, *Yoma* 77b)

When R. Akiva died, Rebbe was born. When Rebbe died, Rav Yehuda was born. When Rav Yehuda died, Rava was born, and when Rava died, R. Ashi was born. (*Kiddushin* 72b)

Rav Yehuda related in the name of Rav: The rabbis granted the daughter of Nakdimon b. Gurion, whose husband had died, an allowance of four hundred gold coins for her perfume basket. She said to them, "May you grant such allowances to your own daughters." They answered her, "Amen." (*Ketubbot* 66b)

There was a man who used to say, "Happy is a person who hears himself abused and ignores it, for hundreds of evils pass him by." R. Shemuel remarked on this to R. Yehuda, "It is hinted in a verse in Scripture." (*Sanhedrin* 7a)

R. Yehuda said in the name of Rav, "Forty days before the embryo is formed, a heavenly voice calls out, saying, "The daughter of So-and-so shall wed So-and-so." (*Sanhedrin* 22a)

We have learned that R. Yehuda said, "Heaven forbid that we should think that R. Akavia was excommunicated. That was a mistake. The doors of the Temple hall never held any man in Israel who was the equal of Rabbi Akavia ben Mahalalel in wisdom, purity and fear of God. What happened was that they excommunicated Eleazar ben Hanoch, who raised doubts about washing the hands." (*Berachot* 19a)

For a glimpse of the world as it was in the time of R. Yehuda bar Yehezkel, see the historical timeline from 200 to 300 C.E.

יהודה הכהן
Yehuda ha-Kohen

(second century C.E.)
Tanna, Eretz Yisrael

Some believe that Yehuda ha-Kohen, a contemporary of Rabbi Yehuda ben Bava and Rabbi Akiva, was the son of Rabbi Yohanan ben Zakkai.

For a glimpse of the world as it was in the time of Yehuda ha-Kohen, see the historical timeline from 100 to 200 C.E.

יהודה הנשיא
Yehuda ha-Nasi

(second–third centuries C.E.)
Tanna, Eretz Yisrael

Rabbi Yehuda, who was the son of Rabbi Shimon ben Gamliel, is referred to as the Patriarch of Judea and redactor of the Mishna. The Talmud also refers to him as Rebbe. The great-grandson of Rabbi Hillel, he could trace his lineage to King David.

Some of his students, such as Rabbi Hanina ben Hama, Rabbi Yannai ha-Kohen, Levi and Rav, became the leading amoraim of the next generation. Due to Rabbi Yehuda's redaction of the Mishna, in which he set everything down in proper order, later generations were able to create the Gemara.

In the Gemara, the various halachic principles are debated, checked and double-checked against each other, and contradictions resolved. Thus, Rabbi Yehuda ha-Nasi laid the foundation for The Talmud, as we know it today.

The Talmud says: When Rabbi Akiva died, Rebbe was born. When Rebbe died, Rav Yehuda was born. When Rav Yehuda died, Rava was born, and when Rava died, R. Ashi was born. (*Kiddushin* 72b)

Rabbi Yehuda ha-Nasi was a student of his father and of Rabbi Yehuda b. Illai, Rabbi Shimon ben Yohai, Rabbi Hiyya, Rabbi Eleazar ben Shammua, Rabbi Yaakov ben Korshai and Rabbi Meir.

It was taught Rebbe said. When we studied Torah under Rabbi Shimon b. Yohai in Tekoa, we would carry oil and towels up from the courtyard to the roof and from the roof to an enclosure until we came to the spring where we bathed. (*Shabbat* 147b)

When R. Shimon b. Gamliel and R. Yoshua b. Korha were teaching in the academy they sat on couches, while R. Eleazar b. Shimon b. Yohai and Rebbe sat in front of them on the ground asking questions and raising objections. (*Bava Metzia* 84b)

The students objected; they said: "We are drinking from their water, but they are sitting on the ground. Let seats be placed for them." They placed seats for them.

R. Shimon b. Gamliel objected, "I have a pigeon among you and you want to destroy it?" So Rebbe was made to sit on the ground again.

R. Yoshua b. Korha was displeased and said, "Shall one who has a father live, while the one who has no father dies?" Thereupon R. Eleazar was also made to sit upon the ground.

R. Eleazar was hurt and said, "You have made him equal to me."

Until this incident whenever Rebbe made a statement R. Eleazar supported him, but after this day when Rebbe spoke R. Eleazar said: "Your statement has no substance." Humiliated, Rebbe complained to R. Shimon b. Gamliel, his father.

"Do not let it bother you," said his father. "He is a lion and the son of a lion, while you are a lion and the son of a fox."

R. Eleazar was the son of R. Shimon ben Yohai. Rebbe later on became Rabbi Yehuda ha-Nasi.

On one occasion when Rav was still very young, he and R. Hiyya were having dinner at Rabbi Yehuda ha-Nasi's table.

Rebbe said to Rav, "Get up and wash your hands." R. Hiyya saw that Rav was trembling. He said to him: "Son of princes, he is telling you to prepare yourself to lead in the blessings after the meal." (*Berachot* 43a)

Yehuda ha-Nasi, who was wealthy, lived in Beis Shearim, where he established his great yeshiva. He used his wealth for the common good, assisting many students with his generosity. His friends included Rabbi Shimon ben Menashye and Rabbi Yosi ben Meshullam. (*Sanhedrin* 32b)

R. Yehuda and R. Hizkiya, the sons of R. Hiyya, were having dinner with Rebbe. Their father, R. Hiyya, was also present. When the sons did not utter a word during the meal, Rebbe said, "Give the young men plenty of strong wine so that they will open up and say something."

As the wine took effect, they started talking and said, "The son of David cannot come until the two ruling houses of Israel come to an end." To support this assertion, they quoted a passage from scripture. Rebbe became annoyed and exclaimed, "My children, you are throwing thorns in my eyes." R. Hiyya intervened, saying, "Rebbe, please do not be angry. The numerical value of the Hebrew letters for the word 'wine' is the same as for the word 'secret.' When wine goes in, secrets come out." (*Sanhedrin* 38a)

In a year of scarcity, Rabbi Yehuda ha-Nasi opened his storehouse and proclaimed, "Let those who have studied Scripture, Mishna and Halacha enter to receive food for free. But the ignorant shall not be admitted."

R. Yonathan b. Amram entered and asked for food. They asked him, "Have you learned the Torah?"

He answered, "No."

"Have you learned Mishna?"

He answered, "No."

He was refused food.

"Feed me as a dog or as a raven," he said. Thereupon, he was given some food. After he left, Rebbe was upset and regretted that he had fed a man who did not take the time or trouble to learn. When Rebbe's son Shimon saw his father so distressed, he told him, "Don't be upset. That man was your student, Rabbi Yonathan, who has made it his principle not to derive benefit from his Torah study."

After this incident, Rebbe changed his rules and declared, "Everyone may enter and receive food without payment." (*Bava Batra* 8a)

Rabbi Yehuda ha-Nasi lived in splendor. The Roman authorities placed guards at his residence. (*Berachot* 16b)

Rabbi Yehuda Hanasi preferred the Hebrew language. He declared: "What has the Syrian language have to do with Eretz Yisrael?"

"Why use the Syrian language in the Land of Israel? One should use either the holy tongue or Greek." (*Bava Kamma* 82b, 83a, *Sotah* 49b)

Rabbi Hiyya once saw the waning moon early in the morning on the twenty-ninth day of the month. Speaking to himself in an undertone, he said, "Tonight we want to sanctify the new month, and you are still here? Go and hide yourself." Rabbi, who must have overheard him, said, "Go to Ein Tov and sanctify the month and send me the following watchword: 'David, King of Israel, is alive and enduring.'" (*Rosh ha-Shannah* 25a)

Rebbe showed respect to wealthy people, as did R. Akiva. (*Eruvin* 86a)

Rebbe asked R. Shimon b. Halafta: "Why were we not permitted to receive you on the festival, as my ancestors used to receive your ancestors?"

Rabbi Shimon b. Halafta answered: "The rocks have grown tall, the near has become far, the two have turned into three and the peacemaker of my house is gone." (*Shabbat* 152a)

It happened once when Rabbi Yehuda was delivering a lecture, he noticed a smell of garlic in the room. He told his students, "Let the person who ate garlic leave the room." R. Hiyya rose and left the room, and all the students followed. The next morning, Rabbi Hiyya was asked by R. Shimon, the son of Rebbe, "Was it you who caused annoyance to my father? Heaven forbid that such a thing should happen in Israel!" (*Sanhedrin* 11a)

Rabbi Yehuda was on good terms with the Roman emperors. During the reign of Emperor Antonius, he once said to Rebbe: "I would like my son to become emperor after me, and I would like Tiberias to be declared a free colony. But I am concerned that if I ask the Senate for one request it will be granted, while if I ask for both, they will be denied."

Rebbe gave him advice by way of a demonstration. He brought in two men, one riding on the other's shoulders. He put a dove into the hand of the man riding on the other's shoulders and told the man upon whose shoulders he was riding to order his fellow to release the dove. Antonius perceived that he should ask the Senate to appoint his son to succeed him, and to tell his son to make Tiberias a free colony.

On another occasion, Antonius mentioned to Rebbe that some prominent Romans were annoying him.

Once again, Rebbe used a demonstration to advise him. He took him into his garden, and in his presence he picked radishes, one at a time. The emperor concluded that his advice was to get rid of them one at a time, but not all at once. (*Avodah Zarah* 10a)

Emperor Antoninus had a discussion with Rebbe. (*Sanhedrin* 91a–b)

The Emperor asked, "The body and soul have a good argument to escape punishment. The body can plead: 'The soul has sinned, and the proof of it is that when the soul leaves me, I lie in the grave like a stone.' On the other hand, the soul can plead: 'The body has sinned, and the proof of it is that once I leave the body, I fly in the air without committing sins.' Rebbe replied, "This is comparable to two watchmen, one blind and one lame. The lame man told the blind man, 'I see beautiful figs in the orchard. Take me on your shoulders and I will pick some for us to eat.' The blind man carried the lame man, and they ate the figs. Some time later, the owner of the orchard asked his watchmen. "Where are those beautiful figs you were supposed to guard in my orchard?" The lame watchman replied, "Do I have feet to walk with?" The blind man asked, "Do I have eyes to see with?" The owner of the orchard told the lame one to ride on the shoulders of the blind one and judged them together.

The Talmud relates an incident that occurred in the academy of Rabbi Yehuda ha-Nasi. As the students were involved in a discussion, Rabbi Yishmael came over to ask them what subject they were discussing. They told him, "Prayer." While this was occurring, Rabbi Yehuda entered the academy. All the students rushed to their seats, but since Rabbi Yishmael, who was heavy-set, could not move that quickly to his seat, he squeezed himself through, climbing over several students. Rabbi Avdan inquired who was climbing over the heads of the holy people.

"I am Yishmael the son of Rabbi Yosi, and have come to learn Torah from Rebbe," Yishmael answered.

"Are you really fit to learn Torah from Rebbe?" asked Rabbi Avdan.

"Was Moshe fit to learn Torah from the lips of God?" retorted Rabbi Yishmael.

"Are you Moshe?" asked Rabbi Avdan.

"Is Rebbe God?" asked Rabbi Yishmael.

In the meantime a woman came to the academy to inquire about a matter, and R. Yehuda sent R. Avdan to attend to it. After Avdan left, Rabbi Yishmael gave the answer to Rebbe in the name of his father, Rabbi Yosi ben Halafta.

Rebbe called after Avdan, "Come back! We have already the answer."

When Avdan came back, he pushed himself through the students. Rabbi Yishmael said to him, "He who is needed by the holy people may stride over their heads, but how dare he stride over the heads of the holy people?" Rebbe told Rabbi Avdan, "Sit where you are." (*Yevamot* 105b)

When R. Yishmael ben Yosi fell ill, Rebbe sent him a message requesting, "Tell us two or three things that you heard from your father, Rabbi Yosi ben Halafta." Rabbi Yishmael sent back a few of his father's sayings. (Pesahim 118b)

On another occasion, Rabbi Yehuda ha-Nasi was expounding a halachic decision to his students when Rabbi Yishmael b. R. Yosi was present. He said: "My father ruled differently."

To this R. Yehuda replied, "In that case, if the old man already issued a ruling, then mine is retracted."

R. Pappa observed, "Come and see how much they loved each other. Had R Yosi been alive, he would have sat before R. Yehuda with respect, but now that his son occupied his father's place and sat before R. Yehuda with utmost respect, R. Yehuda said, 'Because your father already decided, my ruling is retracted.'" (*Shabbat* 51a)

Rabbah quoted R. Hiyya as saying, "R. Yehuda ha-Nasi once went to a certain place to teach there on Shabbat, but the room was too small. He therefore went outside in order to teach in the open field. However, the field was not suitable since it was full of sheaves. He removed the sheaves in order to make room." R. Yoseph related a similar story about R. Hiyya in the name of R. Oshaya. (*Shabbat* 127a)

R. Yehuda ha-Nasi visited the town of R. Eleazar b. Shimon b. Yohai. He inquired, "Did that tzadik leave a son?"

"Yes," they replied, "and every harlot whose hire is two zuz is willing to hire him for herself for eight zuz."

R. Yehuda summoned him, ordained him as a rabbi in order to bestow respect on him and entrusted him to be educated by R. Shimon b. Issi b. Lakonia, his maternal uncle.

Every day, the young man would say: "I am going back to my town." The teacher would reply, "They made you a sage and spread a gold-trimmed cape over you. They call you rabbi, and still you say, 'I am going back to my town'?"

The young man answered his teacher, "I swear that I am cured, that I have put aside my desires."

Some years later, when he became a great scholar, he went to Rebbe's academy and participated in the discussions. Upon hearing his voice, Rebbe observed, "His voice is similar to that of R. Eleazar b. Shimon."

"He is the son of R. Eleazar," said the students of the academy.

Very pleased, Rebbe cited a scriptural verse in praise. He also complimented R. Shimon b. Issi b. Lakonia on having accomplished his mission. When R. Yosi b. Elazar b. Shimon died, they buried him next to his father. (*Bava Metzia* 85a)

Rebbe's son-in-law was Ben Eleasa. Rebbe was asked: "What kind of a haircut did the High Priest wear?" Rebbe answered; "Go and look at the haircut of my son-in-law Eleasa." It has been taught that while R. Eleasa was no spendthrift, he spent money to learn the style of haircut the Kohen Gadol used to have. He did this in order to display and teach the style of haircut the High Priest had. (*Sanhedrin* 22b)

(Bava Metzia 85b) Shemuel Yarchinah was Rebbe's physician. When Rebbe contracted an eye disease, R. Shemuel offered to treat it with bathing the eye in a lotion, but Rebbe said: "I cannot bear it."

R. Shemuel then suggested treating it with an ointment. "I cannot bear that, either."

Thereupon R. Shemuel placed a small bottle of medication under his pillow, and he was cured.

Rebbe was upset over not having had the opportunity to ordain R. Shemuel. But R. Shemuel told him, "Do not be upset. I have seen the book of Adam, in which is written that Shemuel Yarchinah will be called a sage but not a rabbi, and Rebbe's cure will come through him."

R. Yaakov and R. Zerika said: whenever R. Akiva and one of his colleagues are in disagreement the Halacha is in accordance to R. Akiva. When R. Yosi is in disagreement with his colleagues the Halacha is with R. Yosi. (*Eruvin* 46b)

In a dispute between R. Yehuda ha-Nasi and one of his colleagues, Halacha goes according to Rebbe.

It is stated that Rabbi Yehuda lived in Beit Shearim, but when he fell ill, he was brought to Sepphoris because it was situated on higher ground and fresher air. He died in 219 C.E. (*Ketubbot* 103b)

Before Rabbi Yehuda ha-Nasi died, he left instructions that his son Rabbi Gamliel and his student Rabbi Hanina ben Hama succeed him as Nasi, and that his son Shimon be Hacham.

He had two sons: Rabbi Gamliel, who succeeded him as Patriarch, and Rabbi Shimon, who was appointed Hacham.

"When Rabbi Yehuda Hanasi died humility and the fear of sin ceased." (*Sotah* 9:15, 49a)

R. Yehuda ha-Nasi and R. Nathan concluded the Mishna, while R. Ashi and Ravina concluded the Horaah (Gemara). (*Bava Metzia* 86a)

The town of Sepphoris – called Tzippori in Hebrew – is an ancient Jewish city, located in the Galilee, east of Haifa and north of Afula. The seat of the Sanhedrin under Rabbi Yehuda ha-Nasi was located there. Some of the priestly families settled there after the destruction of the Temple. The city, which had a large Jewish population, was the center of several revolts against foreign occupiers.

It was stated: When R. Akiva died, Rebbe was born. When Rebbe died, Rav Yehuda was born. When Rav Yehuda died, Rava was born, and when Rava died, R. Ashi was born. (*Kiddushin* 72b)

When R. Levi attended the wedding feast of R. Shimon, the son of Rebbe, he recited five benedictions. (*Ketubbot* 8a)

Our rabbis taught: When Rebbe was about to die, he said, "I would like to have my sons present." When they came, he instructed them, "Take care to show respect to your mother. The light shall continue to burn in its usual place, the table shall be set in its usual place and my bed shall be made up in its usual place. Yoseph of Haifa and Shimon of Efrat, who attended to me in my lifetime, shall attend on me when I am dead." (*Ketubbot* 103a)

Rebbe then said, "I would like to speak to the sages of Israel." When they entered, he told them, "Do not lament for me in the smaller towns, and reassemble the academy after thirty days. My son Shimon is to be the Hacham, my son Gamliel shall be the Nasi and Hanina b. Hama shall be Rosh Yeshiva."

On the day Rebbe died, a bat kol announced, "Whoever was present at the death of Rebbe shall enjoy the life of the World to Come."

Although Rebbe had designated R. Hanina as Rosh Yeshiva, R. Hanina did not accept because R. Afes was two and a half years older than he. Therefore, R. Afes presided.

R. Hanina sat and studied outside the academy, and R. Levi joined him. When R. Afes passed away, R. Hanina succeeded him as president and R. Levi moved to Babylonia.

Rebbe said, "I would like to speak to my younger son." When R. Shimon entered, Rebbe instructed him on being a Hacham.

Rebbe then said, "I wish to see my elder son." When R. Gamliel entered, he instructed him in the traditions and regulations of the Patriarchate. "My son," he said, "run your patriarchate with men of high caliber and keep strong discipline among your students." (*Ketubbot* 103b)

On the day Rebbe died, the rabbis decreed a public fast. (*Ketubbot* 104a)

R. Yehuda ha-Nasi said, "Which path is the proper one to choose? Whatever is honorable to you and earns

you the esteem of your fellowmen. Be as scrupulous in performing a minor good deed as a major one, for one does not know which has the greater reward. Consider three things and you will avoid sinning. Know what is above you – an eye that sees, an ear that hears, and all your deeds are recorded in a book." (*Avot* 2:1)

For a glimpse of the world as it was in the time of R. Yehuda ha-Nasi, see the historical timeline from 150 to 250 C.E.

יהודה נשיאה
Yehuda Nesiah

(third century C.E.)
Amora, Eretz Yisrael

R. Yehuda was a grandson of Rabbi Yehuda ha-Nasi and the son of Gamliel III. (*Avodah Zarah* 36a)

His bet din permitted the use of oil produced by non-Jews.

Rabbi Shimon ben Lakish said in the name of Rabbi Yehuda Nesiah, "The world endures only for the sake of the breath of schoolchildren." (*Shabbat* 119b)

Resh Lakish also said in the name of R. Yehuda Nesiah, "Schoolchildren must not be allowed to neglect their studies even for the building of the Temple." Resh Lakish also said to R. Yehuda Nesiah: I have the following tradition from my fathers – others say from your fathers: "Every town in which there are no schoolchildren deserves to be destroyed."

Rabbi Shimon ben Lakish also criticized Rabbi Yehuda when the latter imposed a tax on the rabbis in order to build a wall. He said, "Rabbis need no wall to protect them. Torah is their protection." (*Bava Batra* 7b)

Once a man went out on Shabbat wearing an item of jewelry. When he noticed R. Yehuda Nesiah, he tried to hide it from view. (*Eruvin* 69a)

For a glimpse of the world as it was in the time of R. Yehuda Nesiah, see the historical timeline from 200 to 300 C.E.

יהודה נשיאה
Yehuda Nesiah III
(third–fourth centuries C.E.)
Amora, Eretz Yisrael

(*Rosh ha-Shannah* 20a) R. Yehuda Nesiah III, who was a close friend of Rabbi Ammi and Rabbi Assi, was a student of Rabbi Yohanan.

A grandson of Rabbi Yehuda Nesiah and the son of Gamliel IV, he was Nasi of the Sanhedrin in Tiberias from 290 to 320 C.E.

For a glimpse of the world as it was in the time of Yehuda Nesiah III, see the historical timeline from 250 to 350 C.E.

ירמיה בר אבא
Yirmiyahu b. Abba
(fourth century C.E.)
Amora, Eretz Yisrael and Babylonia
Head of academy in Tiberias

Yirmiyahu b. Abba moved to Eretz Yisrael while still a young man.

Rabbi Hiyya bar Abba was his teacher. He also studied under Rabbi Zeira in Eretz Yisrael. (*Megilah* 4a, *Moed Katan* 4a)

He became head of the academy in Tiberias when Rabbi Ammi and Rabbi Assi passed away.

R. Hamnuna held that the times for prayer and for Torah study are distinct from each other. It happened once, when Rabbi Yermiyahu was studying with R. Zeira, it was getting late for the prayer service. Rabbi Yirmiyahu asked R. Zeira to interrupt the study so he could pray. (*Shabbat* 10a)

R. YIrmiyahu said – and some say that R. Hiyya b. Abba said, "The Targum on the Torah was written by Onkelos the proselyte under the guidance of R. Eliezer and R. Yoshua." (*Megillah* 3a)

It has been taught, that Sumchos said, "Whoever prolongs the word 'ehad' [while reciting the shema] will have his days prolonged." (*Berachot* 13b)

R. Abba b. Yaakov said that the stress is on the daled. Once, when R. Yirmiyahu sat before R. Hiyya b. Abba, R. Hiyya noticed that R. Yirmiyahu prolonged the word "ehad" a great deal. He taught him how long to prolong the word and counseled him not to overdo it.

R. Yirmiyahu said in the name of R. Eleazar, "When two scholars sharpen each other in Halacha, God grants them success and they even ascend to greatness."

R. Yirmiyahu also said in the name of Resh Lakish: "When two scholars are agreeable to each other, God listens to them." (*Shabbat* 63a)

(*Shabbat* 121a–b) Rav Yehuda, R. Yirmiyahu b. Abba and R. Hanan b. Rava visited the home of Avin Deman Neshikya. They brought seats for the guests but not for R. Hanan b. Rava, and found the host teaching his son laws with which R. Hanan disagreed. He said to him, "Avin the fool teaches nonsense to his son."

When the Talmud states, "They said in the west," it refers to Rabbi Yirmiyahu. (*Sanhedrin* 17b)

R. Yirmiyahu had a dispute with R. Abba and R. Abba felt insulted. R. Yirmiyahu went to R. Abba's home and sat down at his door. While he sat there, the maid poured waste water outside, and some of it fell upon R. Yermiyahu's head. He remarked, "They have made a dung heap of me."

R. Abba heard what happened and came out apologizing. He said to R. Yirmiyahu: "Now I think that you are the injured party, and I must ask your forgiveness." (*Yoma* 87a)

For a glimpse of the world as it was in the time of R. Yirmiyahu b. Abba, see the historical timeline from 300 to 400 C.E.

ישבב
Yeshevav

(first century C.E.)
Tanna, Eretz Yisrael

Sometimes R. Yeshevav is referred to as "Yeshevav the Scribe." (*Hullin* 2:4, 32a) He was a contemporary of Rabbi Hutzpit, Rabbi Akiva and Rabbi Yehoshua. The sages list him as one of the Ten Martyrs.

For a glimpse of the world as it was in Yeshevav's time, see the historical timeline from 1 to 100 C.E.

ישמעאל
Yishmael

(first–second centuries C.E.)
Tanna, Eretz Yisrael

Rabbi Yishmael ben Elisha, who was still a child when the Temple was destroyed, was taken captive to Rome among the other Jewish captives.

The Talmud relates that when Rabbi Yoshua ben Hananya visited Rome, he was told that in prison there was a beautiful Jewish child with beautiful eyes. Rabbi Yoshua stood at the prison gate and asked in Hebrew: "Who gave Jacob up for plunder and Israel to robbers?"

The child responded, "We sinned against God and did not follow His way." Rabbi Yoshua said, "I will not budge from here until I ransom this boy, whatever price may be demanded." It is reported that he paid a very high price to ransom him. The boy became Rabbi Yoshua's student, with whom he studied for many years, and became one of the great scholars of his time. He also studied under Rabbi Nehunya ben ha-Kana. (*Gittin* 58a)

Rabbi Meir was one of his outstanding students.

Rabbi Yohanan stated that Rabbi Yishmael served and studied under Rabbi Nehunya b. ha-Kana, who expounded the Torah according to the principles of generalization and specification, and he also expounded by the same principles. R. Akiva, who served R. Nahum Ish Gam Zu – who expounded the whole Torah on the principle of amplification and limitation – also expounded the Torah by the same principles. (*Shevuot* 26a)

Rabbi Yishmael, a kohen, lived in Kefar Aziz, near Hevron.

It happened that Rabbi Yehoshua went to R. Yishmael at Kefar Aziz and he showed him a vine that was trained and twisted around a fig tree. They discussed whether it is permitted. (*Kilayim* 6:4)

R. Yishmael, who was one of the chief spokesmen in the Yavne yeshiva, was present when Rabbi Gamliel was deposed as Nasi and Rabbi Eleazar was appointed in his place.

On the day that Rabbi Gamliel was deposed, the Mishna states that Rabbi Yishmael told his colleague R. Eleazar b. Azaryah, "If you wish to be more strict, then you must be the one to produce evidence."

Rabbi Akiva was a close friend of his. Rabbi Yishmael is the author of the thirteen hermeneutical rules in the baraita entitled "Bi-shlosh esreh middot ha-Torah nidreshet."

Rabbi Yishmael felt that the Torah demands that people should both pursue a livelihood and study Torah. Rabbi Shimon bar Yohai held the opposite view. Yet when his nephew asked him whether he might study Greek philosophy, he pointed out the injunction, "The Torah shall not cease from your mouth." (*Berachot* 35b)

Rabbi Yishmael founded the school that was known as Tanna de-Bei Rabbi Yishmael.

Rav Yehuda related in the name of Rav: The son and the daughter of Rabbi Yishmael ben Elisha were carried off and sold as slaves to two masters. Some time later, the two masters met and discussed their two slaves and their exceptional good looks. One suggested marrying them to each other and sharing their children. Accordingly, one night they placed them together in one room. The boy sat in one corner and the girl in another. The boy said to himself, "I am a descendant of high priests. How could I marry a slave-girl?"

The girl said to herself, "I am a descendant of high priests. How could I marry a slave?"

They passed that night in tears. In the morning, when they recognized each other, they fell upon each other's necks and wept until they died. (*Gittin* 58a)

Once, a man vowed not to marry his sister's daughter. He had no other prospects and the family was in favor of their marriage. They brought the girl to Rabbi Yishmael, who instructed his household to dress her in fine clothing and adorn her. Rabbi Yishmael then asked the prospective groom, "Is this the woman whom you vowed not to marry?" He answered, "No."

Rabbi Yishmael annulled his vow. Then he wept and said, "The daughters of Israel are beautiful, but poverty makes them uncomely." (*Nedarim* 9:10, 66a)

R. Yishmael's school taught, "One should always use clean language." (*Pesahim* 3a)

Another saying of his was, "Why is the entire ear made of hard tissue and the lobe of soft tissue? It is so that if one hears unworthy language, he may stop his ears." (*Ketubbot* 5b)

Rabbi Yoshua ben Levi said, "Whenever you find a statement in the Talmud that says, 'A student said it in the name of Rabbi Yishmael in the presence of Rabbi Akiva,' it refers to Rabbi Meir, who was an attendant to both Rabbi Akiva and R. Yishmael." (*Eruvin* 13a)

The Talmud teaches that Rabbi Meir said, "When I was with Rabbi Yishmael, I used to put a chemical called kankantum into the ink, and he never told me not to do it. But when I was with Rabbi Akiva and I tried to do the same thing, he forbade it."

A similar story was related by Rav Yehuda in the name of Rabbi Shemuel in the name of Rabbi Meir: "When I was a student of Rabbi Akiva's, I used to put kankantum into the ink and he never told me not to do it. But when I came to study under Rabbi Yishmael, he asked me: "What is your profession?"

I said, "I am a scribe."

Rabbi Yishmael then said to me, "Be meticulous in your work because your work is sacred to heaven. Should you omit or add one letter, you could cause a situation in which a world is destroyed." (Rashi comments that by adding one letter to a word, one might change that word from singular to plural, and when speaking of G-d that would be blasphemous.) I told him I put kankantum in the ink, which makes the ink permanent immediately.

R. Abbaye said: R. Shimon b. Gamliel, R. Shimon, R. Yishmael and R. Akiva maintain that all Israelites are princes.

We have learned that if one was in debt for a thousand zuz and wore a robe costing a hundred maneh, he is stripped of that robe and dressed in a less expensive one. R. Yishmael and R. Akiva disagreed because all Israel are worthy of that robe. (*Bava Metzia* 113b)

R. Yishmael said: "If one desires to become wise from learning, then one should study Halacha on monetary judgment, since no subject in the Torah surpasses this. It is like a perpetual fountain." (*Berachot* 63b)

Rabbi Yishmael said: "Show esteem toward a great person, and receive all people cheerfully." (*Avot* 3:12)

For a glimpse of the world as it was in R. Yishmael's time, see the historical timeline from 50 to 150 C.E.

ישמעאל בנו של רבי יוחנן בן ברוקא
Yishmael ben Yohanan ben Beroka

(second century C.E.)
Tanna, Eretz Yisrael

R. Yishmael, a contemporary of Rabbi Shimon ben Gamliel, was present at Usha when the rabbis met there.

He often disagreed with Rabbi Shimon ben Gamliel on halachic issues and with the other rabbis regarding the case of a father kidnapping his own son. (*Sanhedrin* 11:1, 85b)

He was known for saying, "He who learns in order to teach will be granted the means to learn and teach. He who learns in order to practice will be granted the opportunity to learn, teach, practice and observe." (*Avot* 4:5)

For a glimpse of the world as it was in the time of Yishmael ben Yohanan ben Beroka, see the historical timeline from 100 to 200 C.E.

ישמעאל בן יוסי בן חלפתא
Yishmael ben Yosi ben Halafta

(second–third centuries C.E.)
Tanna, Eretz Yisrael

R. Yishmael, who succeeded his father in the leadership of Sepphoris, was highly esteemed there. (*Eruvin* 86b)

As a student of Rabbi Yehuda Hanasi he was also a member of his halachic council. Rabbi Yehuda consulted Rabbi Yishmael on various halachic issues. (*Shabbat* 113b)

The Talmud relates an incident that occurred in the academy of Rabbi Yehuda ha-Nasi. As the students were involved in a discussion, Rabbi Yishmael came over to ask them what subject they were discussing. They told him, "Prayer." While this was occurring, Rabbi Yehuda entered the academy. All the students rushed to their seats, but since Rabbi Yishmael, who was heavy-set, could not move that quickly to his seat, he squeezed himself through, climbing over several students. Rabbi Avdan inquired who was climbing over the heads of the holy people.

"I am Yishmael the son of Rabbi Yosi, and have come to learn Torah from Rebbe," Yishmael answered.

"Are you really fit to learn Torah from Rebbe?" asked Rabbi Avdan.

"Was Moshe fit to learn Torah from the lips of God?" retorted Rabbi Yishmael.

"Are you Moshe?" asked Rabbi Avdan.

"Is Rebbe God?" asked Rabbi Yishmael.

In the meantime a woman came to the academy to inquire about a matter, and R. Yehuda sent R. Avdan to attend to it. After Avdan left, Rabbi Yishmael gave the answer to Rebbe in the name of his father, Rabbi Yosi ben Halafta.

Rebbe called after Avdan, "Come back! We have already the answer."

When Avdan came back, he pushed himself through the students. Rabbi Yishmael said to him, "He who is needed by the holy people may stride over their heads, but how dare he stride over the heads of the holy people?" Rebbe told Rabbi Avdan, "Sit where you are." (*Yevamot* 105b)

Rav Kahana said: When R. Yishmael b. R. Yosi b. Halafta became sick, the rabbis sent him a request: Tell us two or three things that you heard from your father.

He replied; "One hundred and eighty years before the Temple was destroyed, Eretz Yisrael was occupied by the wicked government. Eighty years before the Temple was destroyed, a rabbinical prohibition of ritual impurity was enacted against certain vessels and people. Forty years before the Temple was destroyed, the Sanhedrin went into exile and moved to the commercial zone of the Temple."

During this period, the heads of the Sanhedrin were R. Yosi b. Yoezer, R. Yosi b. Yohanan, R. Hillel, R. Shimon, R. Gamliel and R. Shimon. The Talmud further states that Hillel and his descendants Shimon, Gamliel and Shimon were the leaders of the Sanhedrin for one hundred years during the Temple's existence. (BT *Shabbat* 15a)

When R. Yishmael ben Yosi fell ill, Rebbe sent him a message, saying, "Tell us two or three things that you heard from your father, R. Yosi ben Halafta." Rabbi Yishmael sent him several of his father's sayings. (*Pesahim* 118b)

R. Yishmael stated: "The older the scholars get the more wisdom they acquire, but the reverse is true of the ignorant. The older they get, the more foolish they become." (*Shabbat* 152a)

He is quoted as saying: "Judge not alone, for none may judge alone save for One." (*Avot* 4:8)

Rabbi Yehuda ha-Nasi was once expounding a halachic decision to his students when Rabbi Yishmael b. R. Yosi was present. He said: "My father ruled differently."

To this R. Yehuda replied, "In that case, if the old man already issued a ruling, then mine is retracted."

R. Pappa observed, "Come and see how much they loved each other. Had R Yosi been alive, he would have sat before R. Yehuda with respect, but now that his son occupied his father's place and sat before R. Yehuda with utmost respect, R. Yehuda said, 'Because your father already decided, my ruling is retracted.'" (*Shabbat* 51a)

R. Yishmael said: "One who avoids judging people removes from himself hatred, robbery and unnecessary oaths, but one who is too self-confident in judging others is a fool, wicked and arrogant." (*Avot* 4:7)

For a glimpse of the world as it was in the time of Yishmael b. Yosi b. Halafta, see the historical timeline from 150 to 250 C.E.

יצחק
Yitzhak

(second century C.E.)
Tanna, Eretz Yisrael and Babylonia

Although Rabbi Yitzhak was originally from Babylonia, he settled in Eretz Yisrael.

Rabbi Yitzhak debated halachic matters with Rabbi Shimon ben Yohai, Rabbi Yehuda ha-Nasi and others. (*Berachot* 48b)

On one occasion, he disagreed with Rebbe about divorces. (*Gittin* 27b)

Rabbi Yitzchak also delved into the mystical, and debated about it with Rebbe. (*Hagiga* 13a)

Rabbi Yitzchak said: "A worm's bite is as painful to a corpse as a needle is to the living." (*Shabbat* 152a)

After the destruction of the Temple, the rabbis wanted the Jewish people to avoid ostentation. They ruled that during a lavish banquet, one item should be omitted. R. Pappa said that it should be the hors d'oeuvre.

R. Yitzhak said: At a wedding, ashes should be put on the bridegroom's head as a reminder of the destruction of the Temple. R. Pappa asked R. Abbaye: "Where on the head should the ashes be placed?" R. Abbaye answered, "On the spot where the tefilin are usually worn." (*Bava Batra* 60b)

R. Avin b. Adda said in the name of R. Yitzhak, "The reason why there is no fruit called *ginossar* in Jerusalem is so that it should not be said that the pilgrims went to Jerusalem during the festivals solely to eat from the fruit of Ginossar." (*Pesahim* 8b)

Rabbi Yitzchak said: "If one recites the shema before going to sleep, demons keep away from him." (*Berachot* 5a)

R. Avin b. Rav Adda said in the name of R. Yitzhak, "How do we know that God puts on tefillin? We know it from a passage in Yeshaya [62:8]." (*Berachot* 6a)

R. Avin b. Rav Ahava said in the name of R. Yitzhak: "If a man is accustomed to attend the synagogue daily and is absent one day, God asks for him." (*Berachot* 6b)

For a glimpse of the world as it was in R. Yitzhak's time, see the historical timeline from 100 to 200 C.E.

יצחק בר יהודה
Yitzhak bar Rav Yehuda

(third–fourth centuries C.E.)
Amora, Babylonia

R. Yitzchak was the son of Rabbi Yehuda b. Yehezkel, the head of the academy in Pumbedita. (*Shabbat* 35b)

When Ulla visited Pumbedita, R. Yehuda said to his son, R. Yitzhak, "Go and offer him a basket of fruit and observe how he recites havdalah."

Although R. Yitzhak studied at his father's academy, he also studied under Rabbi Huna and Rabbah bar Nahmeni. (*Shabbat* 35b, *Shevuot* 36b)

Rabbi Yitzhak did not marry young because he was searching for a wife from a good family and could not find one to his satisfaction.

When Rabbi Ulla visited Rabbi Yehuda in Pumbedita, he asked him,

"Why have you not taken a wife for your son?" They discussed the matter. Eventually, R. Yitzhak married and had children. (*Pesahim* 104b, *Kiddushin* 71b)

His granddaughter Hama, the daughter of Issi, was married to Abbaye. (*Yevamot* 64b)

For a glimpse of the world as it was in the time of Yitzhak b. Rav Yehuda, see the historical timeline from 250 to 350 C.E.

יצחק בר אבדימי
Yitzhak bar Avdimi

(third–fourth centuries C.E.)
Amora, Babylonia

The Talmud relates that when R. Yitzhak came from Eretz Yisrael to Babylonia he said, "There was a town in Eretz Yisrael by the name of Gofnit in which eighty pairs of brothers, all priests, married eighty pairs of sisters, all from priestly families. The rabbis searched from Sura to Nehardea and could not find a similar case except for the daughters of R. Hisda, who were married to Rami b. Hama and to Mar Ukva b. Hama. While the daughters of R. Hisda were descended from kohanim, their husbands were not kohanim. (*Berachot* 44a)

For a glimpse of the world as it was in the time of Yitzhak bar Avdimi, see the historical timeline from 250 to 350 C.E.

יצחק בן אלעזר
Yitzhak ben Eleazar

(fourth century C.E.)
Amora, Eretz Yisrael

It was said of R. Eleazar b. Pedat that he studied Torah in the lower market of Sepphoris, but left his coat in the town's upper market.

R. Yitzhak b. Eleazar related, "Once, when a man wanted to take the coat for himself, he found a venomous serpent inside." (*Eruvin* 54b)

For a glimpse of the world as it was in the time of Yitzhak ben Eleazar, see the historical timeline from 300 to 400 C.E.

יצחק בר שמואל
Yitzhak bar Shemuel

(third century C.E.)
Amora, Babylonia

R. Yitzhak was a student of Rav.

R. Yitzhak said in the name of Rav, "The night has three watches. At each watch, the Holy One sits and roars like a lion, lamenting: 'Woe for my children! On account of their sins I have destroyed My house, burnt My Temple, and exiled them among the nations of the world.'" (*Berachot* 3a)

R. Berona said in the name of Rav: "If one washed his hands for bread, he should not make Kiddush over wine." R. Yitzhak b. Shemuel b. Matha said to them, "Rav is barely dead, and we have already forgotten his ruling? I attended upon Rav many times. Sometimes he chose to make Kiddush over bread, while at other times he chose to make Kiddush over wine." (*Pesahim* 106a–b)

For a glimpse of the world as it was in the time of Yitzhak bar Shemuel, see the historical timeline from 200 to 300 C.E.

יצחק נפחא
Yitzhak Nepaha

(third century C.E.)
Amora, Eretz Yisrael

R. Yitzhak Nepaha, who was a student of R. Yohanan in Tiberias, was an older colleague of R. Ammi and R. Assi.

The Talmud relates that when R. Ammi and R. Assi sat before R. Yitzhak Nepaha, one of them asked him, "Would you please teach us some halacha?" The other requested, "Would you please relate some agadata?"

When he began speaking on agadata, one of them was unhappy, and when he started instruction on halacha, the other was unhappy. Noticing this, he stopped and said. "I will tell you a story. A man had two wives, one younger and one older. The younger one used to pluck out his white hair, while the older one used to pluck out his black hair. At the end he was left completely bald. Therefore I will tell you something that will be of interest to both of you." (*Bava Kamma* 60b)

Rabbi Yitzhak was a guest of Rabbi Nahman. When he was about to leave, R. Nahman asked, "Please bless me."

Rabbi Yitzhak replied: "Let me tell you to what your request may be compared. A traveler crossing the desert was hungry, weary and thirsty, but he had no more food and he longed for a little shade. All of a sudden, he came upon a fruit tree. He ate from the fruit, which was sweet. He rested in its shade and drank from the stream of water flowing beneath the tree. When he was about to continue on his journey, he said: "O tree, with what should I bless you? Your fruit is sweet, your shade is already pleasant and the stream of water is already flowing beneath you. Therefore I bless you with this: May it be God's will that all the shoots taken from you should also be like you." The same is with you. Shall I bless you with Torah knowledge? You are already blessed with Torah knowledge. Shall I bless you with riches? You have riches already. Shall I bless you with children? You have children already. Therefore, may it be God's will that your offspring be like you." (*Taanit* 5b)

R. Yohanan interpreted a passage in the Torah, and R. Yitzhak the smith offered a different interpretation. When Resh Lakish heard it, he said, "I like the interpretation of the smith better than that of the smith's son." (*Sanhedrin* 96a)

R. Yitzhak served as a judge in Tiberias and Caesarea together with his colleagues, R. Abbahu and R. Hanina b. Papi. (*Bava Kamma* 117b)

R. Yitzhak said: "If you see a wicked man on whom fortune is smiling, do not contend with him." (*Berachot* 7b)

R. Yitzhak said: "One should always divide his wealth into three parts: one third invested in land, one third in merchandise and one third in ready cash." (*Bava Metzia* 42a)

R. Yitzhak said: "If a man tells you, 'I have worked hard but have not achieved results,' do not believe him. If he says, 'I have not worked, yet I have achieved results,' do not believe him. If he says, 'I have worked hard and I have achieved results,' you may believe him." (*Megillah* 6b)

A certain man declared, "I come from Shot-Mishot in Babylonia." When R. Yitzhak Nepaha heard this, he rose and said, "Shot-Mishot lies between the rivers." (*Kiddushin* 72a)

For a glimpse of the world as it was in R. Yitzhak Nepaha's time, see the historical timeline from 200 to 300 C.E.

יוחנן בן ברוקא
Yohanan ben Beroka

(second century C.E.)
Tanna, Eretz Yisrael

Rabbi Yohanan ben Beroka was a student of Rabbi Yoshua ben Hananya and of Rabbi Yohanan ben Nuri. His closest associate was Rabbi Eleazar Hisma. He is quoted in many Mishnayot in the Talmud.

R. Yohanan said, "He who profanes the name Heaven in secret will suffer the consequences in public." (*Avot* 4:4)

R. Yohanan said, "A woman or a child may testify in certain cases." (*Bava Kamma* 10:2)

R. Yohanan determined the amount of food required to prepare an eruv. (*Eruvin* 8:2, 82b)

For a glimpse of the world as it was in the time of Yohanan ben Beroka, see the historical timeline from 100 to 200 C.E.

יוחנן בן גודגדא
Yohanan ben Gudgeda

(first–second centuries)
Tanna, Eretz Yisrael

Rabbi Yohanan ben Gudgeda served in the Temple as a Levite in charge of opening and closing the gates. He is quoted often in the Talmud. His close associate was Rabbi Yoshua ben Hanania.

Once, when Rabbi Yehoshua went to help R. Yohanan ben Gudgeda close the Temple doors, Rabbi Yohanan said, "Go back. You are a member of the choir, not one of the doorkeepers." (*Arachin* 11b)

He was very careful about the purity of foods. (*Hagiga* 2:7, 18b)

There were two men in Rebbe's neighborhood who were unable to speak. Some say that they were the sons of R. Yohanan b. Gudgeda's daughter, while others say that they were his sister's sons. They sat in Rebbe's academy and nodded their heads and moved their lips. Rebbe prayed for them and they were cured. They were found to be well versed in Halacha and proficient in the entire Talmud. (*Hagiga* 3a)

In a case where a father had given a deaf daughter in marriage, Rabbi Yohanan Gudgeda testified that she could be given a *get*. (*Gittin* 5:5, 55a)

For a glimpse of the world as it was in the time of R. Yohanan Gudgeda, see the historical timeline from 50 to 150 C.E.

יוחנן בן ההורני
Yohanan ben ha-Horani

(first century C.E.)
Tanna from Eretz Yisrael

Rabbi Yohanan was a contemporary of Rabbi Hillel and Rabbi Shammai. Although the Talmud does not quote him often, he is generally regarded as a follower of Rabbi Shammai.

When the elders of Beit Shammai and Beit Hillel went to visit Rabbi Yohanan, they found him eating in the sukkah, but his table was inside his house. This was according to the view of Rabbi Hillel. (*Sukkah* 2:7, *Sukkah* 28a)

For a glimpse of the world as it was in the time of Yohanan ben ha-Horani, see the historical timeline from 1 to 100 C.E.

יוחנן בן מתיא
Yohanan ben Mathya

(second century C.E.)
Tanna, Eretz Yisrael

The Talmud relates that Rabbi Yohanan ben Mathya told his son to hire laborers to work for them. He did as his father asked, and promised to provide food for them. When his father heard what he had done, he told him, "Son, even if you should prepare them a banquet like King Solomon did, you would not meet your obligation towards them. Before they begin work, tell them that they may work only on condition that you feed them bread and pulses." (*Bava Metzia* 83a)

For a glimpse of the world as it was in the time of Yohanan ben Mathya, see the historical timeline from 100 to 200 C.E.

יוחנן בן נפחא
Yohanan ben Nepaha

(third century C.E.)
Amora, Eretz Yisrael
Head of the academy in Tiberias

R. Yohanan ben Nepaha, who was born in Sepphoris, had a difficult start in life.

His father died on the day that he was conceived, and his mother died in childbirth on the day he was born. He inherited fields and vineyards from his parents and used the income for his livelihood, which allowed him free time to study Torah. (*Kiddushin* 31b)

He was raised by his grandfather and he studied in the academy of Rabbi Yehuda ha-Nasi.

Rebbe himself predicted that Rabbi Yohanan would be a great teacher in Israel. His other teachers were Rabbi Yannai, Rabbi Hanina b. Hama and Rabbi Oshaya Rabbah. He was familiar with science, medicine, astronomy and mathematics. (*Pesahim* 3b)

Ten of Rabbi Yohanan's sons died in his lifetime. Several daughters survived. (*Berachot* 5b)

Rabbi Yohanan must have thought highly of R. Zeiri because he offered him his daughter in marriage. However, R. Zeiri did not accept the offer for reasons of his own. One day, Rabbi Yohanan and Rabbi Zeiri were traveling on the road. They came to a pool of water, whereupon Rabbi Zeiri carried Rabbi Yohanan on his shoulder. Rabbi Yohanan remarked: "It seems that our learning is good enough, but our daughters are not good enough for you." (*Kiddushin* 71b)

At first, R. Yohanan taught in the academy of Rabbi Banah in Sepphoris, but later he opened his own academy in Tiberias. Some of his distinguished students became the leading scholars in Eretz Yisrael. Among them were Rabbi Abbahu, Rabbi Ammi, Rabbi Assi, Rabbi Eleazar b. Pedat, Rabbi Hiyya b. Abba, Rabbi Yosi b. Hanina and Rabbi Shimon b. Abba.

R. Yohanan stated: when we studied under R. Oshaya, eight of us sat cramped together in an area of one cubit. (*Eruvin* 53a)

R. Yohanan also said, "R. Oshaya in his generation was like R. Meir in his generation. His colleagues could not fathom the depth of his knowledge." (*Eruvin* 53a)

The Talmud relates: Rabbi Issi came from Babylonia to Eretz Yisrael and met Rabbi Yohanan. Rabbi Yohanan asked him, "Who is the head of the academy in Babylon?"

Rabbi Issi replied, "It is Abba Aricha." Rabbi Yohanan remarked: "You simply call him Abba Aricha? I remember when I was sitting before Rabbi Yehuda ha-Nasi, seventeen rows behind Rav, and I saw sparks flying from the mouth of Rav into the mouth of Rebbe and in turn from the mouth of Rebbe into the mouth of Rav, and I could not even understand what they were saying – and you simply call him Abba Aricha?" (*Hullin* 137b)

Rabbi Yohanan was a very handsome man. One day, as he was bathing in the Jordan River, Resh Lakish also happened to be there. He jumped into the river. R. Yohanan said, "Your strength should be used for learning Torah." Resh Lakish returned the compliment by saying; "Your beauty should be saved for women." Rabbi Yohanan said. "I have a sister who is more beautiful than I am. If you repent I will give her to you in marriage." (*Bava Metzia* 84a)

He undertook to repent and Rabbi Yohanan taught him the Torah and

Mishna. Subsequently Resh Lakish became a great scholar.

Resh Lakish, who was very diligent student, prepared himself well before studying with Rabbi Yohanan. He systematically went over the text forty times before he came for his lecture. (*Taanit* 8a)

He married R. Yohanan's sister, and they had a son who also became a great scholar. (*Taanit* 9a)

Resh Lakish had halachic disagreements with Rabbi Yohanan and other scholars. (*Ketubbot* 84b)

Rabbi Kahana had to flee Babylonia because of the following incident. A man who planned to denounce another Jew to the Persian authorities and show them where he was hiding his straw was brought before Rav. Rav ordered the man not to do so, but the man insisted. "I will." Rabbi Kahana, who was present during this incident, became enraged that the man was defying Rav, and during the argument he struck him, killing him accidentally. Rav advised Rabbi Kahana to move to Eretz Yisrael and to study under Rabbi Yohanan, but made him promise that for seven years he would not give Rabbi Yohanan a hard time with his sharp questions.

When Kahana arrived, he found Resh Lakish going over the lecture with the young rabbis. When he sat down to listen, he pointed out the difficult points in the lecture and also provided some of the answers.

Resh Lakish went to R. Yohanan and told him, "A lion has come up from Babylonia. Be well prepared for tomorrow's lecture." The next day, R. Kahana was seated in the first row because Resh Lakish thought him a scholar. But he kept quiet for a long while, as he had promised Rav. Consequently, the scholars of the academy demoted him, seating him in the seventh row.

R. Yohanan said to Resh Lakish, "It looks like the lion is a fox."

Rabbi Kahana prayed that the humiliation that he had suffered in having been demoted to the seventh row be considered equivalent to the seven years during which he had promised Rav not to ask R. Yohanan difficult questions. The next day, when Rabbi Yohanan lectured, he threw out one question after another, quoting sources in contradiction. After this, the academy's scholars seated him in the first row once more. (*Bava Kamma* 117a)

It is related in the Talmud that Rabbi Yohanan was very anxious to ordain Rabbi Hanina and Rabbi Hoshia, but somehow it never came about because he could not get a quorum of three qualified rabbis to do it. When Rabbi Hanina saw how distressed Rabbi Yohanan was on account of it, he said to him, "Master, do not grieve, for we are descended from Eli the High Priest, and because of that we are destined not to be ordained." (*Sanhedrin* 14a)

R. Keruspedai said in the name of R. Yohanan, "If an ox was condemned to be stoned and the witnesses were proved to be false witnesses, then whoever takes possession of the ox is the legal owner." (*Keritot* 24a)

R. Keruspedai said in the name of R. Yohanan: "Three books are opened in heaven on Rosh ha-Shannah: one for the completely wicked, one for the completely righteous and one for those in between. The completely righteous are immediately inscribed for life, the completely wicked are immediately inscribed for death and the fate of those in between is suspended from Rosh ha-Shannah till Yom Kippur. If they are worthy, they are inscribed for life. If not,

they are inscribed for death. (*Rosh ha-Shannah* 16b)

R. Hiyya b. Abba fell ill and R. Yohanan went to visit him. He asked him, "Do you desire your suffering?"

He answered, "I desire neither the suffering nor its reward."

R. Yohanan said to him, "Give me your hand," and he did. Afterwards, he felt cured. (*Berachot* 5b)

When R. Yohanan fell ill, R. Hanina went to visit him. He asked him, "Do you desire your suffering?"

He answered, "I desire neither the suffering nor its reward." R. Hanina told him, "Give me your hand." He gave him his hand and he cured him. The question was asked: If R. Yohanan could cure others, why was he unable to cure himself? The rabbis replied, "A prisoner cannot set himself free." (*Berachot* 5b)

Once, Rabbi Yohanan inadvertently insulted Resh Lakish when he referred to the latter's past during a discussion about the ritual purity of a sword, saying, "A robber knows his trade." One word led to another and they hurt one another's feelings.

Shortly afterwards, Resh Lakish fell ill. His wife came to her brother, R. Yohanan, and pleaded, "Forgive my husband for the sake of my son." (*Bava Metzia* 84a)

Resh Lakish died, and R. Yohanan was plunged into a deep depression. The rabbis sent R. Eleazar b. Pedat to comfort him. He went and sat before him and they learned together. R. Eleazar supported R. Yohanan's every dictum by saying, "There is a baraita that supports you."

"You are no replacement for Resh Lakish," R. Yohanan complained. "When I stated a law, Resh Lakish raised twenty-four objections, to which I gave twenty-four answers. This led to a fuller understanding of the law. You tell me that a baraita supports me. Do I not know myself that what I said is correct?"

R. Yohanan rent his garments and wept, "Where are you, Resh Lakish? Where are you, Resh Lakish?" Shortly afterwards, he died of grief. (*Bava Metzia* 84a)

Rabbah said in the name of R. Yohanan: "In the future world, God will give a banquet for the righteous, and they will be served the flesh of the Leviathan." (*Bava Batra* 75a)

Rabbah also said in the name of R. Yohanan: "In the future world, God will make a tabernacle for the righteous from the skin of the Leviathan."

R. Yohanan said, "Three kinds of people earn special approval from God: a bachelor who lives in a large city and does not sin, a poor man who returns lost property to its owner, and a wealthy man who tithes his produce in secret."

When R. Safra, who was a bachelor living in a large city, heard this statement, his face lit up. Rava told him, "Rabbi Yohanan did not have someone like you in mind, but rather persons like R. Hanina and R. Hoshia. They are sandal makers in Eretz Yisrael who live in a neighborhood of prostitutes. They make sandals for them, and when they deal with them they do not lift their eyes to look at them. When the prostitutes take an oath, they do so 'by the life of the holy rabbis of Eretz Yisrael.'" (*Pesahim* 113 a–b)

Rabbi Yohanan was very considerate, even to apostates. He preached that God does not rejoice in the downfall of the wicked. (*Megillah* 10b)

He set down the rules as follows: "Wherever R. Shimon b. Gamliel teaches his view in the Mishna, Halacha follows his view, except in three cases." (*Sanhedrin* 31a)

He also established that Halacha is always as an anonymous Mishna. (*Shabbat* 46a)

He stated that whenever God comes to a synagogue and does not find ten people praying, He becomes angry. (*Berachot* 6b)

R. Hiyya b. Abba said in the name of R. Yohanan: "It is a disgrace for a Torah scholar to go to the market place in patched shoes." (*Shabbat* 114a)

R. Yohanan also said: "All their lives, Torah scholars are engaged in improving the world."

R. Yohanan composed one of the blessings over Torah study. (*Berachot* 11b)

R. Yohanan said three things in the name of the men of Jerusalem. One was, "When one goes into battle, one should be among the last one to leave in order to be among the first to return." (*Pesahim* 113a)

R. Yohanan was ascending a staircase, as R. Ammi and R. Assi supported him, when the staircase suddenly collapsed beneath them. R. Yohanan rose up and carried both R. Ammi and R. Assi to the top. The rabbis asked him, "Since you still have all your strength, why do you need to be supported?" He answered them: "If I use up all my strength now, what will I have for my old age?" (*Ketubbot* 62a)

Relatives of R. Yohanan seized a cow that belonged to orphans. They were brought before R. Yohanan, who ruled the seizure lawful, but when they appealed to Resh Lakish, he ruled that they must return the cow. They appealed again to R. Yohanan, who told them, "What can I do when one of equal authority differs from me?" (*Ketubbot* 84b)

R. Yohanan said: "The men appointed to the Sanhedrin must be men of stature, wisdom, good appearance, mature age, with knowledge of sorcery and knowledge of seventy languages so that there will be no need for an interpreter." (*Sanhedrin* 17a)

According to R. Yohanan, the destruction of Jerusalem came about because of two men named Kamza and Bar Kamza. A certain man in Jerusalem had a friend Kamza and an enemy named Bar Kamza. He invited many guests to a party and told his servant to invite Kamza. But the servant invited Bar Kamza instead of Kamza. When the host saw Bar Kamza in his house, he said to him, "What are you doing here? Get out."

Bar Kamza said to him, "Since I am here already, let me stay and I will pay the cost of half the party."

"No," said the host. "I don't want you here."

"Let me pay for the cost of the whole party," said Bar Kamza.

The host would not consent, and he seized Bar Kamza by the hand and took him outside.

Bar Kamza said, "Since the rabbis were sitting there and did not stop him, he must have acted with their consent." He went to the authorities and denounced his fellow Jews, saying, "The Jews are rebelling against you."

When the authorities asked for proof, Bar Kamza advised them to send an offering for the altar and see whether it was accepted. They sent a fine calf back with him as an offering. On the way, he made a small blemish in the calf's upper lip. The rabbis wanted to offer it in order not to offend the government, but R. Zechariah b. Avkulos opposed doing so. He reasoned that people would say that it was permitted to offer blemished animals on the altar.

R. Yohanan remarked: "Through the scrupulousness of R. Zechariah our home was destroyed, our Temple burnt and we were exiled from our land." (*Gittin* 55b)

Rabbi Abbahu stated in the name of Rabbi Yohanan: "Rabbi Meir had a student, Sumchos, who was able to supply forty-eight reasons to support every ruling of ritual impurity." (*Eruvin* 13b)

It is related that after Rabbi Meir passed away, Rabbi Yehuda told his students: "Do not allow the students of Rabbi Meir to enter our academy. They come only for disputations and in order to overwhelm me with citations from traditions, but not to learn Torah."

Rabbi Sumchos forced his way into the academy and quoted Rabbi Meir on an important halachic issue. Rabbi Yehuda became very angry and told his students, "Didn't I tell you not to admit any of Rabbi Meir's students?" Rabbi Yosi responded, "People will say, 'Rabbi Meir is dead, Rabbi Yehuda is angry and Rabbi Yosi is silent.'" (*Nazir* 49b)

R. Hanina said, "The planets influence wisdom and wealth, and Israel is also under planetary influences." R. Yohanan maintained that Israel was immune to planetary influences. (*Shabbat* 156a)

R. Yehuda b. Shila said in the name of R. Assi in the name of R Yohanan: "There are six good deeds from which one can derive benefit in this world and still receive reward in the World to Come: hospitality to guests, visiting the sick, concentration during prayer, rising early for prayer, bringing up a son with Torah study and judging everyone favorably." (*Shabbat* 127a)

R. Yohanan said, "The letter nun is omitted from Ashrei because it bodes misfortune. The word *nafal* [fell] begins with the letter nun." (*Berachot* 4b)

Rabbi Yohanan said in the name of Rabbi Yosi: "Do not attempt to placate a man when he is angry." (*Berachot* 7a)

R, Yohanan stated, "The hearts of the ancient rabbis was like the door of the *ulam,* but the last generation was like the *hechal* and our generation's heart is like the eye of a needle." (*Eruvin* 53a)

R. Akiva is among the ancients, and R. Eleazar b. Shammua among the last generation. Others say that R. Oshaya is among the last generation.

Rabbi Yohanan said that Rabbi Yishmael expounded the Torah on the principle of generalization and specification, just as his teacher Rabbi Nehunya b. Hakoneh had. Rabbi Akiva expounded the Torah on the principle of amplification and limitation, as his teacher Rabbi Nachum Ish Gam Zu taught him. (*Shevuot* 26a)

R. Yohanan said in the name of R. Shimon b. Yehotzedek: "A community should not appoint an administrator over its affairs unless he carries a basket of reptiles on his back. If he becomes arrogant the community can tell him, 'Turn around.'" (*Yoma* 22b)

Rabbi Yohanan said in the name of Rabbi Shimon ben Yochai, "If Israel were to keep two Shabbats according to the laws, they would be redeemed immediately." (*Shabbat* 118b)

Tiberias (Hebrew: Teveryah) is a city in Eretz Yisrael on the western shore of the Sea of Galilee. Herod Antipas, the son of King Herod, established Tiberias in the first century C.E. Built on steep slopes spread over a wide area, the city rises from below sea level to approximately eight hundred feet above. Tiberias is famous for its hot springs, whose temperature reaches the boiling point. Rabbi Shimon bar Yohai lived there briefly, and the sages of the time established the seat of the Sanhedrin there. Tiberias was also the seat of the famous rabbinical academy in Eretz Yisrael.

The graves of several great sages are in Tiberias, among them Rabbi Yohanan ben Zakkai, Rabbi Meir Ba'al ha-Nes, Rabbi Akiva, Rabbi Ammi and Rabbi Assi.

R. Yohanan said in the name of R. Shimon b. Yohai: "Where do we find in scripture that God will resurrect the dead and knows the future?" "Behold, you shall sleep with thy fathers and rise again" [Deut. 31:16]. (*Sanhedrin* 90b)

Rabbah bar b. Hana said in the name of R. Yohanan: "To pair up a couple for marriage is as difficult as splitting the Red Sea." (*Sanhedrin* 22a)

R. Hiyya b. Abba said in the name of R. Yohanan: It is a mitzvah to pray with the first and last appearance of the sun. (*Berachot* 29b)

For a glimpse of the world as it was in the time of Yohanan ben Nepaha, see the historical timeline from 200 to 300 C.E.

יוחנן בן נורי
Yohanan ben Nuri

(second century C.E.)
Tanna, Eretz Yisrael

During his life, Rabbi Yohanan ben Nuri resided in Beit Shearim, Sepphoris and Nagninar. His poverty was so great that he had to go to the fields to gather the leftover produce that farmers were required to leave for the poor. He was a student of Rabbi Eliezer ben Hyrcanus and Rabbi Halafta.

Rabbi Yohanan gave a ruling concerning marriages among kohanim. (*Ketubbot* 1:10, 14b)

Rabbi Gamliel and Rabbi Yehoshua once traveled on board a ship. Rabbi Gamliel's food supply ran out and he had to rely on the food that Rabbi Yehoshua had brought with him. "Did you know that we would be delayed so long that you brought additional food with you?" asked Rabbi Gamliel.

"I calculated that a certain star that appears every seventy years is due to appear," answered Rabbi Yehoshua. "It leads sailors to miscalculate their position."

"You posses so much knowledge," Rabbi Gamliel told him, "and yet you travel on board a ship."

"Don't marvel at me. Rather be surprised at two of your students who live on land, Rabbi Eleazar Hisma and Rabbi Yohanan ben Gudgeda (perhaps it was R. Yohanan b. Nuri), who can calculate how many drops of water there are in the sea, and yet they have neither bread to eat nor clothes to wear."

Rabbi Gamliel decided to appoint them as supervisors, and when he landed he sent for them to offer them those positions. Reluctant to accept the positions on account of their humility, they did not show up, but Rabbi Gamliel sent for them again, saying, "Do you imagine that I offer you rulership? It is servitude that I offer you." (*Horayot* 10a)

Rabbi Yohanan was a close friend of Rabbi Akiva.

For a glimpse of the world as it was in the time of R. Yohanan ben Nuri, see the historical timeline from 100 to 200 C.E.

יוחנן בן תורתא
Yohanan ben Torta

(second century C.E.)
Tanna, Eretz Yisrael

Rabbi Yohanan ben Torta, who was a contemporary of Rabbi Akiva, opposed him concerning the acceptance of Bar Kochva as the Messiah.

R. Yohanan b. Torta said: "Why was the Tabernacle at Shiloh destroyed? It was destroyed on account of two sins: immorality and contemptuous treatment of sacred objects." (*Yoma* 9a)

יוחנן בן יהושע
Yohanan b. Yehoshua

(second century C.E.)
Tanna, Eretz Yisrael

R. Yohanan was a nephew of Rabbi Akiva. As they discussed the sanctity of the various biblical books, he recalled what he remembered. (*Yadayim* 3:5)

יוחנן בן זכאי
Yohanan ben Zakkai

(first century C.E.)
Tanna from Eretz Yisrael

It is said that he lived to the age of one hundred twenty years. He spent forty years in business, forty in study and taught for forty. (*Rosh ha-Shannah* 31b)

R. Yohanan lived through the Temple's destruction in 70 C.E.

Although his residence was in Jerusalem, he spent eighteen years in Arav in the lower Galilee. (*Shabbat* 16:7, 121a)

It happened that on one occasion, Rabbi Hanina ben Dosa went to study with Rabbi Yohanan ben Zakkai in Arav. While he was there, Rabbi Yohanan's child fell gravely ill. He said to him, "Hanina, pray for my son that he may live."

Rabbi Hanina put his head between his knees and prayed for the child's recovery. The child recovered. R. Yohanan ben Zakkai said, "If ben Zakkai had stuck his head between his knees all day long, it would have gone unnoticed. His wife said to him, "Is Hanina greater than you are?"

"No, but he is like a servant before the king, who has permission to enter at any time, while I am like a nobleman before a king." (*Berachot* 34b)

It was said of Rabbi Yohanan ben Zakkai that throughout his life, he never uttered a profane word or walked four amot without studying Torah or wearing tefillin. No one arrived at the academy before him, nor did he leave the academy before everyone else had gone. He never dozed off in the academy, nor did he think of sacred matters in any place that was not clean. He always sat at his study, and he opened the door for his students. He always quoted his teacher, and never did he say, "It is time to stop learning," except on Pesah eve and Yom Kippur eve. (*Sukkah* 28a)

(*Ketubbot* 66b) The Talmud relates that Rabbi Yohanan ben Zakkai once left Jerusalem riding on a donkey while his students followed him. They saw a young woman picking barley grains from the dung of Arab cattle. When she saw R. Yohanan, she approached and said. "Master, feed me."

"Who are you?" he asked her.

"I am the daughter of Nakdimon ben Gurion," she said.

"My daughter," he asked, "what happened to your father's wealth?"

"It is gone."

"What about the wealth of your father-in-law?"

"One came and destroyed the other."

She asked him, "Do you remember when you signed my ketubbah?"

"I remember," he said. "Your ketubbah contained one million dinarii from your father's house, in addition to another million from your father-in-law."

Afterwards, Rabbi Yohanan wept and said, "How fortunate are the people of Israel! When they obey God's will, no nation on earth has any power over them. But when they defy God's will, they are delivered into the hands of a base people."

It was related that no one was able to greet Rabbi Yohanan ben Zakkai first because he always greeted everyone first, even non-Jews. (*Berachot* 17a)

Our rabbis taught: "Rabbi Hillel had eighty students, the greatest of whom was Yonathan ben Uzziel, and the least of whom was R. Yohanan ben Zakkai."

There was a family in Jerusalem whose members died at the age of eighteen. When Rabbi Yohanan was told of it, he suggested that they might be descended from Eli the high priest, whose offspring were cursed. He advised, "Go and study Torah, and you will live." They did so and survived. That family was known as Yohanan ben Zakkai's family, even though they were not. (*Rosh ha-Shannah* 18a)

R. Yohanan, a leader of the Pharisees, engaged frequently in debate with the Sadducees. As one of the leaders of the peace party in Jerusalem, he advised his people not to engage in resistance against the Romans. He felt that it would be futile and bring only death and destruction upon the Jewish people.

The Talmud relates that Abba Sikra, the head of the Jewish guards, was a nephew of Rabbi Yohanan. During Vespasian's siege of Jerusalem, R. Yohanan sent for his nephew to visit him in secret. During their meeting, he asked Abba Sikra, "How long are you going to starve the people to death?"

He answered, "What can I do? If I say a word, they will kill me."

Rabbi Yohanan said to him, "Devise a plan so that I may escape from the city. Perhaps something can still be saved."

His nephew advised him, "Pretend to be ill so that people will come to visit you. Then put something with a terrible odor next to you so that people will say that you have died. Let your students carry you out in a coffin, but no one else, because people will notice you are lighter than a corpse." He took his nephew's advice and faked his death. His students carried the coffin, Rabbi Eliezer on one side and Rabbi Yehoshua on the other, and smuggled him out of Jerusalem. Abba Sikra himself also accompanied the coffin. When the gatekeepers wanted to pierce the coffin, Abba Sikra prevented them from doing so, saying, "Shall it be said that they pierced their own teacher?"

Once Rabbi Yohanan had left Jerusalem, he met with Vespasian, who was the commander, and addressed him as Emperor. When Vespasian corrected him, Rabbi Yohanan told him that according to Scripture, only a king could conquer Jerusalem. Shortly after that a messenger arrived with the news from Rome that the Emperor had died and that that the Senate wished him to be the next Emperor of Rome.

As Rabbi Yohanan spoke with Vespasian, the latter realized that he was speaking to a very wise person. Finally, Vespasian told Rabbi Yohanan, "I must leave now, but make a request of me and I will grant it to you."

Rabbi Yohanan said, "Give me Yavne and its sages to be allowed to teach, allow the family chain of R. Gamliel to continue and send a physician to heal Rabbi Tzadok."

His wish was granted, and the academy at Yavne was established.

After the destruction of the Temple, Rabbi Yohanan did much to reconstruct Jewish life in Judea. He was the head of the yeshiva in Yavne, which he founded. (*Gittin* 56a)

Among his many students, the following ones are frequently mentioned by name: Rabbi Yoshua ben Hananya, Rabbi Eliezer ben Hyrcanus, Rabbi Yosi ha-Kohen, Rabbi Shimon ben Nathaniel, and Rabbi Eliezer ben Arach. Rabbi Akiva was also his student. (*Avot* 2:8)

Later on in the last years of his life he also established a yeshiva in Beror Hayil, where he died. (*Sanhedrin* 32b)

It was taught that Rabbi Yohanan ben Zakkai said, "Just as the sin offering makes atonement for Israel, so charitable acts make atonement for the nations of the world." (*Bava Batra* 10b)

When R. Yohanan b. Zakkai fell ill, his students went to visit him. When he saw them, he began to weep. The students said to him: "Light of Israel, pillar of righteousness, strong hammer, why do you weep?"

He answered them, "If I were to be taken before a human king, whose power is limited, I would weep. How much more should I do so now that I am being taken before the supreme King of Kings, who lives forever and whose powers are unlimited? I certainly should cry."

They said to him, "Please bless us."

He answered, "May it be God's will that the fear of heaven be upon you like the fear of flesh and blood."

The students asked him, "Is that all?"

He answered, "If you can attain that, you have achieved a great deal, because when a person does something wrong he fears most that another person will see him committing the wrong." (*Berachot* 28b)

R. Yohanan b. Zakkai had five outstanding students. He said to them: "Go and discern the proper way that one should choose."

R. Eliezer said: "A good eye."

R. Yoshua said: "A good friend."

R. Yosi said: "A good neighbor."

R. Shimon said: "One who considers the outcome of his actions."

R. Eleazar said: "A good heart."

R. Yohanan b. Zakkai answered, "I prefer the words of R. Eleazar b. Arach, because all your words are included in his." (*Avot* 2:9)

The Talmud states that when Rabbi Yohanan ben Zakkai died, the glory of wisdom ceased.

For a glimpse of the world as it was in the time of Yohanan ben Zakkai, see the historical timeline from 1 to 100 C.E.

יוחנן הסנדלר
Yohanan ha-Sandlar

(second century C.E.)
Tanna, Eretz Yisrael

Originally from Alexandria, Rabbi Yohanan ha-Sandlar, who became a great scholar, was one of the last students of Rabbi Akiva. When Rabbi Akiva was imprisoned after the Bar Kochva revolt, Rabbi Yohanan was sent to visit him in order to ask him some halachic questions. Disguised as a peddler, he was able to pass the prison guards.

It is stated Rabbi Yohanan ha-Sandlar, the disciple of Rabbi Akiva, mentioned a halachic ruling in the name of Rabbi Akiva about a person who was ritually impure. (*Berachot* 22a)

He used to say, "Every assembly that is for the sake of heaven will endure in the end, but that which is not for the sake of heaven will not endure." (*Avot* 4:11)

For a glimpse of the world as it was in the time of R. Yohanan ha-Sandlar, see the historical timeline from 100 to 200 C.E.

יוחנן כהן גדול
Yohanan Kohen Gadol

(second century B.C.E.)
King of Judea

Yohanan Kohen Gadol was the king of Judea from 135 to 105 B.C.E.

A son of Simon the Hasmonean and a grandson of Matityahu, who began the revolt against Antiochus Epiphanes, he was also known as John Hyrcanus, king of Judea.

He lived to a very old age, and according to the Talmud, he served as high priest for eighty years. King Yohanan enlarged the kingdom by subduing the Edomites and the Samaritans and spent many years at war, freeing the country from many of its enemies. (*Berachot* 29a)

He is mentioned in *Parah* 3:5, *Yadayim* 4:6, and in *Maaser Sheni* 5:15.

The Talmud mentions that he did away with certain practices that he deemed to be irreverent, and he instituted several new regulations. (*Sotah* 9:10, 47a–b)

For a glimpse of the world as it was in the time of Yohanan Kohen Gadol, see the historical timeline from 200 to 100 B.C.E.

יונה
Yonah

(fourth century C.E.)
Amora, Eretz Yisrael
Head of the academy in Tiberias

R. Yonah, who studied under Rabbis Illai and Zeira, was considered one of the saintly people of Eretz Yisrael. He lived in Tiberias, where he was the head of the Beit Vaad. He was the father of Rabbi Mani and a close friend of Rabbi Yosi.

The Talmud relates that Rabbi Yonah would go out in time of severe drought and pray for rain until rain came. (*Taanit* 23b)

R. Zerika said to R. Safra: Come and see the difference in approach between the good men of Eretz Yisrael and the pious men of Babylonia. When the world was in need of rain, the pious men of Babylonia, R. Huna and R. Hisda said, "Let us pray. Perhaps the Almighty will be appeased and send us rain." But the great men of Eretz Yisrael, like R. Yonah, the father of R. Mani, would go into his house and tell his family, "Get me my sacks so that I can go and buy grain for a zuz." He was so humble that he did not want his family to know that he was the one praying for rain. He then went to a low area, put on sackcloth and prayed for rain, and rain came. When he returned home, his family asked him, "Have you brought grain?" He would answer, "Now that rain has come, the world will feel relieved." (*Taanit* 23b)

He was also a very charitable man. When a person of a good family became impoverished, Rabbi Yonah told him: "I heard that you have been left an inheritance. Take this money and you can pay me back when you receive it." After the man accepted the money, he said, "I changed my mind. Let it be a gift to you."

His son Rabbi Mani succeeded him as head of the Vaad of the Tiberias community.

For a glimpse of the world as it was in the time of R. Yonah, see the historical timeline from 300 to 400 C.E.

יונתן
Yonathan

(second century C.E.)
Tanna, Eretz Yisrael

Rabbi Yonathan was a student of Rabbi Yishmael ben Elisha.

The Mishna quotes him as saying, "He who observes the Torah while poor will observe it in affluence. Whoever neglects the Torah amidst affluence will live to neglect it in poverty." (*Avot* 4:9)

Rabbi Yonathan derived from the Torah that saving a life supersedes Shabbat. (*Yoma* 85b)

During the Hadrianic persecution, he wanted to leave Eretz Yisrael. He set out to leave, but changed his mind in the middle of the journey. He could not bring himself to leave the Holy Land.

R. Hiyya and R. Yonathan were visiting a cemetery when R. Hiyya noticed that R. Yonathan's blue fringes

were trailing on the ground. R. Hiyya said to him, "Lift your fringes so that the dead will not say, 'Tomorrow they are coming to join us, and today they are insulting us.'" (*Berachot* 18a)

R. Shemuel b. Nachmeni said in the name of R. Yonathan: "A man is shown in a dream only what is suggested by his own thoughts."

Rava said, "This is proven by the fact that no one dreams of a golden palm tree or an elephant going through the eye of a needle." (*Berachot* 55b)

R. Shemuel b. Nahmeni said in the name of R. Yonathan: "When one teaches Torah to the son of his neighbor, it is as if he had given him birth." (*Sanhedrin* 19b)

For a glimpse of the world as it was in the time of R. Yonathan, see the historical timeline from 100 to 200 C.E.

יונתן בן עמרם
Yonathan b. Amram

(second–third centuries C.E.)
Tanna, Eretz Yisrael

R. Yonathan was a student of Rabbi Yehuda ha-Nasi.

In a year of scarcity Rabbi Yehuda ha-Nasi opened his storehouse and proclaimed, "Let those who studied scripture, Mishna and Halacha enter and receive food for free – but the unlearned will not be admitted." R. Yonathan entered and asked for food. They asked him, "Have you learned the Torah?"

He answered, "No."

"Have you studied Mishna?"

He answered, "No."

He was refused food.

"Feed me as you would a dog or a raven," he said, and Rebbe gave him some food. After he left, Rebbe was upset, and regretted that he fed a man who took no trouble to learn. When Rebbe's son Shimon saw his father so upset, he told him, "Do not be upset.

That man was your student, Rabbi Yonathan, who has made it his principle never to derive benefit from his Torah study."

After that incident, Rebbe changed his mind and announced that everyone could receive free food from him. (*Bava Batra* 8a)

For a glimpse of the world as it was in the time of R. Yonathan b. Amram, see the historical timeline from 150 to 250 C.E.

יונתן בן אלעזר
Yonathan ben Eleazar

(third century C.E.)
Amora, Babylonia

R. Yonathan moved to Eretz Yisrael while a young man. He settled in Sepphoris, where he was a highly respected member of the community.

A student of Rabbi Shimon ben Yosi, he was a colleague of Rabbi Yohanan and of Rabbi Hanina ben Hama. (*Gittin* 78b)

Rabbi Shemuel bar Nahmeni, one of his students, said in the name of Rabbi Yonathan, "Anyone who asserts that David sinned is in error, because it is written [1 Samuel 18:14]: 'God was with him.'" (*Shabbat* 56a)

For a glimpse of the world as it was in the time of R. Yonathan ben Eleazar, see the historical timeline from 200 to 300 C.E.

יונתן בן עוזיאל
Yonathan b. Uzziel

(first century B.C.E.–first century C.E.)
Tanna, Eretz Yisrael

R. Yonathan b. Uzziel was a student of Rabbi Hillel.

It is stated that Rabbi Hillel had eighty disciples, and the greatest of them was Rabbi Yonathan b. Uzziel. (*Bava Batra* 134a)

It is also related that a certain person who disapproved of his children's

conduct left his estate to Rabbi Yonathan b. Uzziel. Rabbi Yonathan divided the estate into three parts. He sold one, consecrated another, and gave the third to the sons of the deceased. (*Bava Batra* 133b)

Rabbi Shammai objected, since he felt that the father did not want his children to benefit from his estate. Rabbi Yonathan told him, "If you can get back what I consecrated and what I sold, then you can also get back what I gave to his sons." Rabbi Shammai admitted, "The son of Uzziel has confounded me. The son of Uzziel has confounded me."

The Talmud states: "The Targum on the Prophets was authored by R. Yonathan b. Uzziel under the guidance of Haggai, Zechariah and Malachi. After the Targum was finished, there was an earthquake in the Land of Israel over an area of four hundred by four hundred parasangs, and a bat kol issued forth, calling out: "Who is responsible for revealing my secrets to humankind?"

R. Yonathan b. Uzziel rose and declared: "It is I who revealed the secret to humankind. It is fully known to you, O God, that I did not do it for my honor or for the honor of my father's house, but for Your honor, that dissension not increase among Jews." R. Yonathan b. Uzziel also wished to reveal the inner meaning of the portion of Scripture known as Ketuvim, but a bat kol issued forth, calling, "Enough!" Why? Because the date of Mashiah's arrival would have been revealed. (*Megillah* 3a)

For a glimpse of the world as it was in the time of R. Yonathan b. Uzziel, see the historical timeline from 50 B.C.E. to 50 C.E.

יוסף בר חייא
Yoseph b. Hiyya
(third–fourth centuries C.E.)
Amora, Babylonia
Head of the Academy in Pumbedita

R. Yoseph, who was a student of Rabbi Yehuda b. Yehezkel, became head of the academy in Pumbedita after Rabbah passed away and served in that position for two and a half years.

The Talmud relates that when a leader was about to be chosen for the yeshiva in Pumbedita; the choice was between Rabbah and R. Yoseph. The elders of Pumbedita sent a query to Eretz Yisrael asking which one to choose, explaining, "One, R. Yoseph, is Sinai, while the other, Rabbah, is an uprooter of mountains."

The answer came from Eretz Yisrael that Sinai is preferable because everyone is in need of the knowledge of Sinai. However, R. Yoseph declined because the astrologers told him that he would serve as head of the yeshiva for only two years. Rabbah took the position and served for twenty-two years. Afterwards, R. Yoseph served for two and a half years. During Rabbah's term as head of the academy, R. Yoseph did not summon anyone to his house, but went to the person himself. (*Berachot* 64a)

R. Yoseph used to chop wood on Friday in order to prepare for Shabbas. He did so because he wanted to engage in a physical activity in order to welcome Shabbat. (*Shabbat* 119a)

The Talmud relates that when a woman died and left a child to be nursed, her husband, who could not afford to pay for a wet nurse, was miraculously given the ability to nurse the child himself. Rabbi Yoseph commented: "How great this man must be that such a miracle befell him."

Rabbi Nahman observed, "The proof is that miracles do happen, but food is rarely created miraculously." (*Shabbat* 53b)

The Talmud states that when the majority of the rabbis departed from the academy of Rav in Sura, twelve hundred students remained. When the students left R. Huna's academy, eight hundred students remained. (*Ketubbot* 106a)

When R. Huna delivered a lecture, thirteen interpreters assisted him.

When the students left the academy of Rabbah and R. Yoseph in Pumbedita, four hundred students remained, and they described themselves as orphans. When the students left the academy of R. Abbaye – others say the academy of R. Pappa, and still others say from the academy of R. Ashi – two hundred rabbis remained, and they described themselves as orphans of the orphans.

R. Eliezer b. Yaakov was in disagreement with his colleagues about an eruv where Jews lived with non-Jews in a single courtyard. Abbaye said to R. Yoseph, "We have a tradition that the teachings of R. Eliezer b. Yaakov are few in quantity but well sifted." Also, Rav Yehuda said in the name of R. Shemuel that Halacha accords with R. Eliezer b. Yaakov. (*Eruvin* 62b)

The sister of R. Rami b. Hama was married to R. Avia, but her ketubbah was lost. The couple came to R. Yoseph for a ruling as to whether they could continue to live together without a ketubbah. He told them that the matter was a point of disagreement between R. Meir and the sages. According to the sages, in such a case, a man may live with his wife for two to three years without a ketubbah. When R. Abbaye objected, R. Yoseph replied, "In that case, go and write her a new ketubbah." (*Ketubbot* 56b, 57a)

R. Yoseph was very ill most of his life and became blind in his later years. He was so ill that he forgot much of his learning. His student, Rabbi Abbaye, had to relearn with him everything that he had forgotten. (*Nedarim* 41a)

After the destruction of the Temple, the rabbis were concerned about ostentation on the part of Jews, including living in ornate dwellings. They declared that while a house may be plastered, one should leave a small area bare. How large should the area be? R. Yoseph said, "It should be a cubit square."

R. Hisda said, "It should be near the entrance." (*Bava Batra* 60b)

When the Talmud states, "The amoraim from Pumbedita," it refers to Rabbah and Rabbi Yoseph. (*Sanhedrin* 17b)

R. Yoseph said: "Once, when I entered the baths, Mar Ukva was present, and on leaving I was offered a cup of his wine. After I drank it, I experienced a terrific cooling sensation from the hair of my head to my toenails. Had I drunk another goblet, I would have feared that I might lose some of my merit in the World to Come. I am told that Mar Ukva drank it every day." (*Shabbat* 140a)

Rabbah and R. Yoseph were traveling together on a Friday evening, but it was getting close to Shabbat. Rabbah said to R. Yoseph, "Let our Shabbat resting place be under that particular palm tree, which is leaning on another tree."

"I do not know that tree," said R. Yoseph.

"Rely on me and make me your messenger, and I will declare our Shabbat resting place." (*Eruvin* 51a)

Pumbedita, whose academy he headed, is a town in Babylonia that is located northwest of Baghdad. It is situated on the bank of the Euphrates River near the Shanvatha canal (*Gittin* 60b) and near the Papa canal (*Yoma* 77b). According to some, the town had already a Jewish settlement in Second Temple times. It took on extra importance in the year 259 C.E., when Nehardea and its academy were destroyed by Papa b. Nasser, the commander-in-chief of Palmyra. The scholars of Nehardea fled and established an academy in Pumbedita under the leadership of Rabbi Yehuda b. Yehezkel. This academy was the central religious authority for Babylonian Jewry for many centuries.

For a glimpse of the world as it was in the time of R. Yoseph b. Hiyya, see the historical timeline from 250 to 350 C.E.

יאשיה רבה
Yoshaya Rabbah
(second century C.E.)
Tanna, Babylonia

R. Yoshaya lived in Huzal, a town in Babylonia. (*Gittin* 61a)

Later in his life, he moved to Eretz Yisrael, where he studied under Rabbi Yishmael. (*Menahot* 57b)

He had halachic disagreements with his colleague, Rabbi Yonathan, about how to interpret Scripture. (*Yoma* 57b)

R. Menashye b. Avas said, "I asked R. Oshaya Rabbah a question in the graveyard of Huzal, and he told me that ten people are required for a condolence row, not counting the mourners." (*Sanhedrin* 19a)

For a glimpse of the world as it was in the time of Yoshaya Rabbah, see the historical timeline from 100 to 200 C.E.

אושעיא
Oshaya

(second century C.E.)
Amora, Eretz Yisrael

R. Yoshaya studied under Bar Kappara and R. Hiyya. (*Moed Katan* 24a)

The Talmud tells us that Rabbi Hama left his home and spent twelve years at a house of study. When he returned home, he stopped at the local academy before going home. A young man entered the academy, sat down next to him and asked him a question on the subject of study. When R. Hama saw the great knowledge that this young man possessed, he became depressed, thinking, "Had I been here, I also could have had such a son." After he finally went home, the young man followed him and knocked on the door. Believing that he had come to ask him another question, he rose before him as he entered the house. His wife broke out in laughter, saying, "What kind of father rises before his son?" The young man who had followed him turned out to be Rabbi Oshaya, his own son. It was said of them, "A threefold cord is not quickly broken." (*Ketubbot* 62b)

R. Oshaya was a member of the rabbinical court in Sepphoris under R. Yehuda ha-Nasi. Later, he founded his own academy in Caesarea. He organized and collected many baraitot.

R. Zeira replied to an argument by another rabbi, "Have I not told you that every baraita that was not taught in the school of R. Hiyya and R. Oshaya are not authentic?" (*Hullin* 141 a–b)

There was a dispute between R. Hama and his son, R. Oshaya. R. Hama ruled one way and R. Oshaya ruled differently. They went to ask R. Hama's father and R. Oshaya's grandfather, R. Bisa, who decided in favor of R. Oshaya.

Rami b. Hama applied to them the verse: "A threefold cord is not easily broken." (*Bava Batra* 59a)

R. Yohanan stated, "When we studied under R. Oshaya, eight of us sat cramped together in one square cubit." (*Eruvin* 53a)

R. Yohanan also said, "R. Oshaya in his generation was like R. Meir was in his generation. His colleagues could not fathom the depth of his knowledge." (*Eruvin* 53a)

R. Yohanan stated: "The hearts of the ancient rabbis was like the door of the ulam, but the last generation was like the hechal, and our generation's heart is like the eye of a needle. R. Akiva is among the ancients, R. Eleazar b. Shammua among the last generation. Others say that R. Oshaya is among the last generation." (*Eruvin* 53a)

For a glimpse of the world as it was in the time of R. Yoshaya Rabbah, see the historical timeline from 100 to 200 C.E.

יהושע בן עקיבא
Yoshua ben Akiva

(second century C.E.)
Tanna, Eretz Yisrael

The Talmud relates that Rabbi Akiva charged his son Yoshua with seven instructions:

Do not sit to study Torah at the highest point of the city.

Do not live in a town where the leaders of the town are scholars, because they will neglect the needs of the town.

Do not enter your own house suddenly. This applies even more strongly to your neighbor's house.

Do not walk without shoes.

Arise early in the summer on account of the heat and in the winter on account of the cold.

Treat your Shabbat like a weekday rather than be dependent on others.

Be on good terms with the person on whom the hour smiles. (*Pesahim* 112a)

Rabbi Akiva lost two sons, both of them were bridegrooms, and people came from all over Israel to lament for them. Rabbi Akiva stood on a podium and addressed the people. "Even though these two sons were bridegrooms, I am consoled on account of the honor you have done to them." (*Moed Katan* 21b)

For a glimpse of the world as it was in the time of Yoshua ben Akiva, see the historical timeline from 100 to 200 C.E.

יהושע בן חנניא
Yoshua ben Hanania

(first–second century C.E.)
Tanna, Eretz Yisrael

Rabbi Yoshua was one of the principal students of Rabbi Yohanan ben Zakkai. Since he was already a mature young man before the Temple was destroyed, he had vivid memories of the water-drawing festivities at the Temple, and gave a full account of them.

R. Yehoshua stated: "When we made merry at the Water-Drawing, our eyes saw no sleep. In the first hour, we offered the morning sacrifice. Then we recited the prayers, offered the Musaf sacrifice, recited its accompanying prayers, and went to the house of study. Then came eating and drinking, the afternoon prayers, the evening sacrifice and, afterwards, the rejoicing at the Water-Drawing." (*Sukkot* 53a)

A Levite, he was one of the singers in the Temple. It happened that once, when he went to assist R. Yohanan ben Gudgeda to fasten the Temple doors, and Rabbi Yohanan told him, "Go back. You are a member of the choir, not one of the doorkeepers." (*Arachin* 11b)

Rabbi Yoshua was one of the students who hid and carried Rabbi Yohanan ben Zakkai out of Jerusalem in a coffin during the siege.

Although he was a great scholar, Rabbi Yoshua had to earn a living as a blacksmith. (*Berachot* 28a)

The Talmud relates that Rabbi Yoshua had a halachic dispute with Rabbi Gamliel about the day on which to fix the calendar for the new month. As head of the academy, Rabbi Gamliel fixed the date and ordered Rabbi Yoshua to appear before him with his staff and money on Yom Kippur, according to R. Yoshua's calculation. Rabbi Yoshua did as he was ordered, winning praise from Rabbi Gamliel. (*Rosh ha-Shannah* 2:9, 25a)

It is related that a certain student asked Rabbi Yehoshua a question as to whether the evening prayer was compulsory or optional. Rabbi Yehoshua replied that it was optional. When the same student asked Rabbi Gamliel, he replied that it is compulsory.

The student replied, "Rabbi Yehoshua told me it is optional."

Rabbi Gamliel told the student to wait until the beginning of the session. When the question was asked, Rabbi Gamliel said that it was compulsory. He then asked the Sages, "Does anyone here disagree?"

"No," replied Rabbi Yehoshua.

"Did they not report to me that you said it is optional? Rise now, and let them testify against you."

Rabbi Yehoshua stood up, while Rabbi Gamliel remained sitting and expounding for a long time. Rabbi Yehoshua was still standing until all the scholars in the assembly began to shout at Hutzpit the interpreter, "Stop!"

The interpreter stopped. They said, "How long will Rabbi Gamliel go on insulting R. Yehoshua? Last Rosh ha-Shanah he insulted him, in the matter of R. Tzadok regarding the first-born he insulted him, and now he insults him again. Come, let us depose Rabbi Gamliel."

"Whom shall we appoint in his place? We can hardly appoint R. Yehoshua, because he is a party to the dispute. Nor can we appoint R. Akiva because he has no ancestral merit."

"Let us appoint Rabbi Eleazar ben Azaryah, who is wise, wealthy and a descendant of Ezra. He is wise, for he gives the proper answer to a question. Since he is wealthy, he can pay if money is needed to appease the government. As a descendant of Ezra, he has great ancestral merit."

They asked him, "Would you honor us by becoming the head of the academy?"

He replied, "I will consult the members of my family."

When he consulted his wife, she said, "Maybe they will also depose you."

He answered: "Let one use a cup of honor for one day, even if it be broken on the morrow." She said to him, "You have no white hair." He was eighteen years old that day, and a miracle occurred: eighteen rows of his hair turned white. That is why R. Eleazar b. Azaryah said: I am like a seventy-year-old man. He accepted the position.

It was learned that on that day the doors were opened for all the disciples to enter the assembly. Rabbi Gamliel had previously issued an injunction to the assembly that those students whose interior did not match their exterior appearance were not permitted entrance.

During R. Eleazar's presidency, the doors of the yeshiva were opened for everyone who wished to study. They added hundreds of benches to accommodate the students. This had not been the case under R. Gamliel.

It was taught that testimonies were formulated on that day, and whenever the phrase "on that day" is mentioned, it refers to this particular day.

Rabbi Gamliel also did not absent himself from the assembly, even for one hour, after he was deposed. (*Berachot* 27b)

Another halachic dispute between Rabbi Gamliel and Rabbi Yehoshua concerned whether Ammonites may be accepted into the Jewish community. Rabbi Yehoshua was in favor and Rabbi Gamliel was opposed. The Sanhedrin sided with Rabbi Yehoshua. When Rabbi Gamliel saw the great respect that the Sanhedrin accorded to Rabbi Yehoshua, he decided to go to him to apologize. When he reached his house he saw that the walls were black from charcoal. He said to him, "I can tell by your walls that you are a blacksmith."

Rabbi Yehoshua replied, "Woe to the generation of which you are the leader! You know nothing of the problems, struggles and difficulties that the scholars face in order to sustain themselves."

Rabbi Gamliel said, "I apologize. Forgive me," but Rabbi Yoshua ignored him.

"Do it out of respect for my father," Rabbi Gamliel persisted.

Rabbi Yehoshua agreed, and they were reconciled. (*Berachot* 28a)

The next time Rabbi Yoshua came to the Sanhedrin, Rabbi Gamliel rose from his seat and kissed him on his head, calling him "My teacher and my colleague." Later on, Rabbi Gamliel was restored to his office. However, the presidency was rotated between him and Rabbi Eleazar ben Azaryah. It was Rabbi Yoshua who advocated the reinstatement of Rabbi Gamliel. (*Rosh ha-Shannah* 2:9, 25a)

Rabbi Eliezer had halachic differences with the rabbis. Although he brought forth every argument to prove his point, the rabbis refused to accept them. He declared: "If Halacha agrees with me, let this carob tree prove it." The carob tree uprooted itself. The rabbis retorted: "The carob tree cannot prove the argument."

He then said to them: "If I am right, then let the stream of water prove it." Thereupon the stream of water started flowing in the opposite direction. The rabbis retorted: "The stream of water couldn't prove anything in this matter." Rabbi Eliezer then said: "If I am right, then let the walls of this school prove it." Thereupon the walls began to incline. Rabbi Yehoshua spoke up and rebuked the walls. "When scholars are disputing sacred matters, what business do the walls have to interfere?" The walls stopped to incline, but did not straighten out either.

Rabbi Eliezer said: "If I am right, let the heavens prove it." Thereupon a heavenly voice came forth, saying, "The halacha goes according to Rabbi Eliezer." Rabbi Yoshua spoke up and said: "The Torah is not in heaven." Rabbi Yirmiyahu arose and declared: "The Torah was already given on Mount Sinai. It belongs here on earth, and we do not pay attention to heavenly voices." He added, "It has been written in the Torah that the majority decides."

Later on, Rabbi Natan encountered Elijah the Prophet and asked him, "What did God do during that time?" Elijah answered, "He rejoiced, laughing, 'My sons have defeated me! My sons have defeated me!'" (*Bava Metzia* 59b)

The Talmud relates during one Sukkot festival, when R. Gamliel, R. Yoshua, R. Eleazar b. Azaryah and R. Akiva were traveling together on a ship, the only one among them who owned a lulav was R. Gamliel, who had bought it for one thousand zuz. R. Gamliel performed the mitzvah of waving the lulav. When he finished, he gave the lulav to R. Yoshua as a gift. R. Yoshua

performed the mitzva of waving it, and then gave it as a gift to R. Eleazar b. Azaryah, who did likewise and then gave it as a gift to R. Akiva. R. Akiva performed the mitzvah and then returned the lulav to R. Gamliel. (*Sukkah* 41b)

Abba Sikra was the son of Rabbi Yohanan ben Zakkai's sister. He was the head of the rebels fighting against the Romans in Jerusalem during the siege of the city.

The Jewish people had two parties. One wanted peace and the other wanted to continue to resist the Romans. Rabbi Yohanan ben Zakkai sent word to his nephew, Abba Sikra, to come to visit him in secret. When Abba Sikra arrived, R. Yohanan asked him, "How long are you going to starve the people to death?"

He answered, "What can I do? If I say a word, they will kill me."

Rabbi Yohanan said to him, "Devise a plan so that I may escape from the city. Perhaps something can still be saved."

His nephew advised him, "Pretend to be ill so that people will come to visit you. Then put something with a terrible odor next to you so that people will say that you have died. Let your students carry you out in a coffin, but no one else, because people will notice you are lighter than a corpse." He listened to his advice and faked his death. His students carried the coffin, Rabbi Eliezer on one side and Rabbi Yehoshua on the other, and smuggled him out of Jerusalem. Abba Sikra himself also accompanied the coffin. When the gatekeepers wanted to pierce the coffin, Abba Sikra prevented them from doing so, saying, "Shall it be said that they pierced their own teacher?" Once Rabbi Yohanan had left Jerusalem, he met with Vespasian, who was the commander, and addressed him as Emperor. When Vespasian corrected him, Rabbi Yohanan told him that according to Scripture, only a king could conquer Jerusalem. Shortly after that a messenger arrived with the news from Rome that the Emperor had died and that that the Senate wished him to be the next Emperor of Rome.

As Rabbi Yohanan spoke with Vespasian, the latter realized that he was speaking to a very wise person. Finally, Vespasian told Rabbi Yohanan, "I must leave now, but make a request of me and I will grant it to you."

Rabbi Yohanan said, "Give me Yavne and its sages to be allowed to teach, allow the family chain of R. Gamliel to continue and send a physician to heal Rabbi Tzadok."

His wish was granted, and the academy at Yavne was established. (*Gittin* 56a)

Our rabbis taught: when R. Eliezer fell ill, four sages went to visit him: R. Tarfon, R. Yoshua, R. Eleazar b. Azaryah and R. Akiva.

R. Tarfon said to him: "You are more valuable to Israel than rain, for rain is precious in this world, but you are precious in this world and the next."

R. Yoshua said: "You are more valuable to Israel than the disc of the sun, for the sun's disc is only in this world, while you are for this and the next world."

R. Eleazar b. Azaryah said: "You are better to Israel than a father and mother, they are only for this world, but you are for this and the next world."

But R. Akiva remarked: "Suffering is precious." R. Eliezer liked R. Akiva's remark best. (*Sanhedrin* 101a)

The Talmud describes a conversation between the Emperor of Rome and Rabbi Yehoshua. The emperor said that he wished to see the Jewish God. Rabbi Yehoshua told him, "That is impossible."

When the emperor insisted, Rabbi Yehoshua told the emperor to look at the sun during the summer solstice. The Emperor said, "I cannot."

"Well then," said Rabbi Yehoshua, "if you cannot look at one of the servants of God, how do you expect to be able to look at God Himself?" (*Hullin* 59b, 60a)

The emperor said to Rabbi Yoshua b. Hanania, "Why does your Shabbat dish have such a wonderful aroma?"

"We use a special seasoning called Shabbat," Rabbi Yoshua replied.

"I would like to have some of that wonderful seasoning," the emperor said.

"Only those who observe Shabbat can benefit from it," the rabbi answered. (*Shabbat* 119a)

The emperor asked R. Yoshua ben Hanania, "Why didn't you come to the *avidan*" [a debating club between sectarians]?

R. Yoshua answered: "The mountain is snowy, it is surrounded by ice, the dog does not bark and the grinders do not grind." He spoke poetically, meaning, I am too old. (*Shabbat* 152a)

R. Yoshua b. Hananya was having a discussion with the emperor (most likely Trajan), who asked him a question. "Since you are very clever, can you tell me what I will dream about?"

R. Yoshua answered him, "You will see the Persians forcing you to work at hard labor for them and making you feed rodents with a golden stick." The emperor thought about that all day, and at night that is what he dreamed. (*Berachot* 56a)

The Talmud relates that when Rabbi Yoshua ben Hananya visited Rome, he was told that in prison there was a beautiful Jewish child with beautiful eyes. Rabbi Yoshua stood at the prison gate and asked in Hebrew: "Who gave Jacob up for plunder and Israel to robbers?"

The child responded, "We sinned against God and did not follow His way." Rabbi Yoshua said, "I will not budge from here until I ransom this boy, whatever price may be demanded." It is reported that he paid a very high price to ransom him. The boy, who was the future R. Yishmael, became Rabbi Yoshua's student. He studied with him for many years and became one of the great scholars of his time. (*Gittin* 58a)

Rabbi Yehoshua traveled to Alexandria, Egypt, where the Jewish community received him with great honor. They put before him twelve questions: Three were of a scientific nature, three were matters of aggadah, three were silly questions and three were matters of human conduct. (*Niddah* 69b)

R. Yehoshua b. Hanania remarked: "No one has ever had the better of me except a woman, a little boy and a little girl."

What was the incident with the little girl?

"I was once walking on the road, and I saw a path through a field. I started walking across the field when a little girl called out to me: 'Master, isn't it part of the field where you are walking?'

"'No, I answered. 'This is a trodden path.'

"'Yes,' replied the girl. 'Robbers like you have trodden it down.'"

What was the incident with the little boy?

"I was once walking on the road, when I noticed a little boy sitting at a crossroads. I asked him, 'Which road leads to the town?'

"He replied: 'This road is short but long, and that road is long but short.'

"I took the short and long road. When I got to the town, I discovered that gardens and orchards fenced the town in. I returned to where the boy was

sitting and said to him, 'My son, didn't you tell me that this road was short?'

"'Yes,' he answered, 'but didn't I also tell me that it is also long?'"

I kissed him on his forehead and said, "Fortunate are you, nation of Israel! All of you are wise, both young and old."

Rabbi Yehoshua was fluent in Greek and an expert in mathematics and astronomy. He successfully predicted the appearance of a comet.

Rabbi Gamliel and Rabbi Yehoshua once traveled on board a ship. Rabbi Gamliel's food supply ran out and he had to rely on the food that Rabbi Yehoshua had brought with him. "Did you know that we would be delayed so long that you brought additional food with you?" asked Rabbi Gamliel.

"I calculated that a certain star that appears every seventy years is due to appear," answered Rabbi Yehoshua. "It leads sailors to miscalculate their position."

"You posses so much knowledge," Rabbi Gamliel told him, "and yet you travel on board a ship."

"Don't marvel at me. Rather be surprised at two of your students who live on land, Rabbi Eleazar Hisma and Rabbi Yohanan ben Gudgeda (perhaps it was R. Yohanan b. Nuri), who can calculate how many drops of water there are in the sea, and yet they have neither bread to eat nor clothes to wear."

Rabbi Gamliel decided to appoint them as supervisors, and when he landed he sent for them to offer them those positions. Reluctant to accept the positions on account of their humility, they did not show up, but Rabbi Gamliel sent for them again, saying, "Do you imagine that I offer you rulership? It is servitude that I offer you." (*Horayot* 10a)

Rabbi Yoshua had scientific and philosophical discussions with the

Roman emperor and the wise men of Athens. (*Bechorot* 8b)

Later on, he was appointed the head of the rabbinical court in the academy of Yavne. (*Bava Kamma* 74b)

Our rabbis taught: When the second Temple was destroyed, many people in Eretz Yisrael wished to bind themselves by oath to abstain from eating meat or drinking wine. R. Yoshua spoke to them, asking, "Why don't you eat meat or drink wine?"

They answered, "How can we eat meat, which was brought on the Temple altar? How can we drink wine, which was used for libations on the Temple altar?"

He answered them, "In that case you should not eat bread either, because it was used for a meal offering on the Temple altar." They were ready to abstain from bread as well, but he pointed out that water was also used in the Temple. They were silent.

He said to them: "My children, listen to me. Not to mourn at all is impossible, because the decree is so very harsh, but to mourn excessively is also impossible, because we do not impose a hardship on the community that the majority cannot bear." (*Bava Batra* 60b)

After the destruction of the Temple, he established a yeshiva in Pekiin, a small town near Yavne. (*Sanhedrin* 32b)

R. Yirmiyahu said – some say that R. Hiyya b. Abba said – "The Targum on the Torah was written by Onkelos the proselyte under the guidance of R. Eliezer and R. Yoshua." (*Megillah* 3a)

When Rabbi Yehoshua died, goodness ceased to exist in this world. (*Sotah* 9:15)

He used to say, "An evil eye, the evil inclination, and hatred of one's fellow-creatures remove one from his world." (*Avot* 2:11)

R. Yohanan b. Zakkai had five outstanding students. He said to them, "Go find the proper way that a person should follow."

R. Eliezer said, "A good eye."

R. Yoshua said, "A good friend."

R. Yosi said, "A good neighbor."

R. Shimon said, "One who considers the outcome of his actions."

R. Eleazar said, "A good heart."

On this, R. Yohanan b. Zakkai remarked: "I prefer the words of R. Eleazar b. Arach, because all your words are included in his words."

For a glimpse of the world as it was in the time of Yoshua ben Hanania, see the historical timeline from 50 to 150 C.E.

יהושע בן גמלא
Yoshua ben Gamla
(first century C.E.)
High Priest, Jerusalem

R. Yehoshua was married to Martha the daughter of Boethus, the wealthiest person in Jerusalem. It once happened with Yoshua b. Gamla that he betrothed Martha the daughter of Boethus, and the king appointed him high priest. The marriage was nevertheless consummated in spite of the fact that she was a widow. (*Yevamot* 61a)

It is related Rabbi Assi said. "Martha, the daughter of Boethus, gave King Yannai a basket of dinars to nominate Yoshua ben Gamla as high priest." R. Yoshua is credited with perpetuating Jewish studies in Eretz Yisrael. (*Yoma* 18a)

He introduced a universal system of education, which was adopted and took root in the country. Rav Yehuda said in the name of Rav, "The name of Rabbi Yoshua ben Gamla should be blessed, because if not for his efforts the Torah would have been forgotten from Israel." Before the ordinance of Yoshua b. Gamla the system was that if a child had a father, his father taught him, and if he had no father he did not learn at all. Then they made an ordinance that teachers should be appointed and teach in Jerusalem. If a child had a father, the father would take him to attend the school in Jerusalem. If he had no father, he would not learn. They changed the ordinance and appointed teachers and schools in each district. Boys entered school at the age of sixteen or seventeen. When the teachers punished the students, they would rebel and leave school. Finally, Yoshua b. Gamla came and ordained that schools and teachers should be appointed in each town and that children should enter school at the age of six or seven. (*Bava Batra* 21a)

The two he-goats [used for the service on Yom Kippur] waited with an urn containing two lots. They were made of box-wood, but ben Gamla donated gold urns to replace the wooden ones. For this he was praised.

King Monobaz of Adiabene had all the vessels used on Yom Kippur made of gold. His mother, Helene, donated a golden candlestick for the door of the hechal. She also donated a golden tablet that was inscribed with the oath that a suspected adulteress must take. (*Yoma* 37a)

For a glimpse of the world as it was in the time of Yoshua b. Gamla, see the historical timeline from 1 to 100 C.E.

יהושע בן הורקנוס
Yoshua ben Hyrcanus

(second century C.E.)
Tanna, Eretz Yisrael

A member of the Sanhedrin, Rabbi Yehoshua was present when they installed Rabbi Eleazar ben Azaryah as Nasi of the Sanhedrin in Yavne.

The Talmud says that on that day Rabbi Yehoshua ben Hyrcanus was

delivering a discourse on an important subject. (*Sotah* 5:5, 27b)

For a glimpse of the world as it was in the time of Yoshua b. Hyrcanus, see the historical timeline from 100 to 200 C.E.

יהושע בן קרחה
Yoshua ben Korha

(second century C.E.)
Tanna, Eretz Yisrael

As a young man, R. Yoshua b. Korha studied under Rabbi Yohanan ben Nuri and Rabbi Eleazar ben Azaryah.

In scholarship he was considered equal to Rabbi Shimon ben Gamliel, the Nasi of the Sanhedrin, and both of them taught Rabbi Yehuda ha-Nasi, Rabbi Shimon's son. (*Bava Metzia* 84b)

He was blessed to live to a very old age. (*Megillah* 28a)

Rabbi Yehuda ha-Nasi once asked him, "To what do you attribute your long life?"

He replied, "Do you begrudge me my long life?"

Rabbi answered him, "Heaven forbid! Rather, it is a question of Torah. I need to learn from it."

Rabbi Yehoshua answered, "Never in my life have I looked a wicked man in the face."

Rabbi Yehuda said to him, "Give me a blessing."

His blessing was, "May it be God's will that you should live to half my age."

He was very much against the sectarians, and spoke out forcefully against them. He was also very much opposed to cooperating with the Romans, as in the case of Rabbi Eleazar b. Shimon, who was appointed to arrest thieves.

R. Eleazar once met a Roman officer who was sent to arrest thieves. R. Eleazar asked him: "How can you tell which one is a thief? Perhaps you are arresting the innocent and the guilty are walking free."

The officer replied, "What can I do? I am commanded by the king."

R. Eleazar advised the officer to go to the tavern and talk to the people and find out their occupations. If they did not have a trade or a satisfactory answer regarding how they made a living then they were thieves. When the report of this conversation was brought to the authorities, the order was issued: "Let the adviser become the enforcer." They sent for R. Eleazar b. Shimon and ordered him to go out and arrest the thieves. R. Eleazar had to obey.

R. Yoshua b. Korha sent a reproving message: "Vinegar son of wine, how long will you deliver the people of our God to slaughter?"

R. Eleazar sent a reply: "I weed out thorns from the vineyard." R. Yoshua retorted, "Let the owner of the vineyard come and weed out the thorns." (*Bava Metzia* 83b)

When R. Shimon b. Gamliel and R. Yoshua b. Korha were learning in the academy they sat on couches, while R. Eleazar b. Shimon and Rebbe sat in front of them on the ground asking questions and raising objections. When the other students objected, they said: "We are drinking from their water, but they are sitting on the ground. Let seats be placed for them."

They placed seats for them. R. Shimon b. Gamliel objected: "I have a pigeon amongst you and you want to destroy it?" So Rebbe was put down again. R. Yoshua b. Korha was displeased and said, "Shall he who has a father live, while he who has no father dies?" Thereupon R. Eleazar was also put on the ground. R. Eleazar was hurt and expressed himself by saying: "You have made him equal to me."

Until this incident, whenever Rebbe made a statement R. Eleazar supported him, but after this day when Rebbe spoke, R. Eleazar said, "Your statement lacks substance." Humiliated, Rebbe complained to R. Shimon b. Gamliel, his father, who replied, "Let it not bother you. He is a lion and the son of a lion, whereas you are a lion and the son of a fox." (*Bava Metzia* 84b)

R. Eleazar was the son of R. Shimon bar Yohai. Rebbe later on became Rabbi Yehuda ha-Nasi.

For a glimpse of the world as it was in the time of Yoshua b. Korha, see the historical timeline from 100 to 200 C.E.

יהושע בן לוי
Yoshua ben Levi
(third century C.E.)
Amora, Eretz Yisrael
Head of the academy in Lydda

A native of Lydda, R. Yoshua was a student of Rabbi Eleazar ha-Kappar and Rabbi Yehuda b. Pedayah. His close associate was Rabbi Hanina b. Hama. (*Zevahim* 88b)

R. Yoshua was an active communal leader who went on missions to Rome on the community's behalf. He spoke out strongly against slander.

He had a son, R. Yoseph, and a grandson, Meyasha. (*Berachot* 24b, *Pesahim* 50a)

It was recorded in R. Yoshua b. Levi's notebook that a man's fate is determined by the day of the week on which he was born. R. Hanina said to his people, "Go and tell the son of Levi that it is not the mazal of the day but the mazal of the hour that influences one's fate.

"A person born under the influence of the sun will distinguish himself. He will eat and drink what he himself has earned, and his secrets will be revealed.

If he becomes a thief, he will not succeed.

"A person born under Venus will be wealthy and immoral.

"A person born under Mercury will have a retentive memory and be wise.

"A person born under the moon will suffer. He will build and demolish, eat and drink that which is not his own, and his secrets will remain hidden. If he chooses to be a thief, he will be successful.

"A person born under Saturn will have his plans frustrated." (*Shabbat* 156a)

R. Yoseph, the son of R. Yoshua b. Levi, fell ill and lost consciousness. When he regained consciousness, his father asked him, "What did you see?"

"I saw an upside-down world. The upper class occupied an inferior position, and those who are ignored in this world were on top."

"My son," said R. Yehoshua, "you saw a clear world." (*Pesahim* 50a)

The Talmud says that R. Yoshua b. Levi had a conversation with the Angel of Death, who gave him the following advice: "Do not take your shirt from your attendant when dressing in the morning. Do not take water from one who did not wash his own hands, and do not stand in the way when women return from the presence of a dead person." (*Berachot* 51a)

R. Yoshua b. Levi met Eliyahu standing at the entrance to the tomb of Rabbi Shimon ben Yohai. He asked him, "When will Mashiah come?"

Eliyahu answered, "Go and ask him yourself."

"Where will I find him?"

"He is sitting at the entrance to the city of Rome."

"How will I recognize him?" asked R. Yoshua.

"He is sitting among the poor lepers. All the lepers untie their bandages all at once and treat their wounds all at once, but the one who unties his bandages one at a time and treats his wounds one at a time is Mashiah. He does it that way because if he should be called to appear as Mashiah, he wants to be ready and not cause a delay."

R. Yoshua went over to him and greeted him, saying, "Peace to you, my Rebbe and Master." Mashiah replied, "Peace to you, son of Levi."

He asked Mashiah, "When will you come?"

Mashiah replied, "I am coming today." When R. Yoshua returned to Eliyahu, he asked R. Yoshua, "What did he tell you?"

"He said, 'Peace be upon you, son of Levi.'"

Eliyahu said to R. Yoshua: "In this answer he assured you that your father and you are assured of a place in the World to Come."

But R. Yoshua was not happy. He said, "He lied to me. He told me that he would come today, and he did not."

Eliyahu answered, "His promise was conditional: if the people of Israel would listen to His voice." (*Sanhedrin* 98a)

R. Yoshua b. Levi said: "When Moshe ascended to receive the Torah the angels said to God, "What business has one born of woman among us?"

"He has come to receive the Torah," came the answer. The angels asked in wonderment, "This great, secret treasure that you kept hidden for nine hundred seventy-four generations before the world was created You now wish to give to human beings of flesh and blood?"

God said to Moshe, "Answer them."

Moshe said to the angels, "It is written in the Torah, 'I am the Lord your God, Who brought you out of the land of Egypt.' Did you go down to Egypt? Were you enslaved by Pharaoh?"

Moshe also said, "It is written in the Torah: 'Honor your father and mother.' Do you have fathers and mothers?" Moshe asked them other questions. Finally, the angels were convinced and conceded to Moshe. After this encounter, they became his friends. (*Shabbat* 88b)

R. Shimon ben Pazzi said in the name of Rabbi Yoshua ben Levi in the name of Bar Kappara, "If one knows how to calculate the cycles of the planetary courses and does not do it, that person has no regard for God's work." (*Shabbat* 75a)

Rabbi Yoshua ben Levi said, "Whenever you find a statement in the Talmud, 'A student said this in the name of Rabbi Yishmael, in front of Rabbi Akiva,' it refers to Rabbi Meir, who was an attendant to both Rabbi Akiva and Rabbi Yishmael." (*Eruvin* 13a)

Rabbi Meir said: "When I was with Rabbi Yishmael, I used to put a chemical called kankantum into the ink and he never told me not to do it. But when I was with Rabbi Akiva and I tried to do the same thing, he forbade it."

Rabbi Zerika said in the names of Rabbi Ami and Rabbi Yehoshua ben Levi: "In the presence of the deceased, do not speak about anything other than himself." (*Berachot* 3b)

R. Yoshua b. Levi said: "If a person teaches his son Torah, it is as if he had received it at Mount Horeb." (*Berachot* 21b)

For a glimpse of the world as it was in the time of R. Yoshua ben Levi, see the historical timeline from 200 to 300 C.E.

יהושע בן מתיא
Yoshua ben Mathya

(second century C.E.)
Tanna, Eretz Yisrael

Rabbi Yoshua, a student of Rabbi Yishmael, was a contemporary of Rabbi Akiva. (*Eduyot* 2:5)

For a glimpse of the world as it was in the time of Yoshua ben Mathya, see the historical timeline from 100 to 200 C.E.

יהושע בן פרחיא
Yoshua ben Perahia

(second–first centuries B.C.E.)
Tanna, Yerushalayim

R. Yoshua and his colleague, Rabbi Nittai ha-Arbeli, made up one of the zugot, or sets of study partners, mentioned in the Talmud.

Rabbis Yosi ben Yoezer and Yosi ben Yohanan were his teachers. Although he was the Nasi of the Sanhedrin, he had to flee to Alexandria when Yohanan Hyrcanus began persecuting the Pharisees.

The Talmud quotes him as saying, "Acquire a teacher and a colleague to learn, and judge everyone favorably." (*Avot* 1:6)

For a glimpse of the world as it was in the time of Yoshua ben Perahia, see the historical timeline from 200 to 100 B.C.E.

יהושע הגרסי
Yoshua ha-Garsi

(second century C.E.)
Tanna, Eretz Yisrael

R. Yoshua, a student of Rabbi Akiva, was his devoted and loyal friend.

R. Akiva was imprisoned for having disobeyed the Roman edict forbidding the teaching of Torah in public. R. Yoshua the Garsi, who attended Rabbi Akiva in prison, brought him a certain quantity of water every day. One day, the warden said to him, "Today you have too much water. Do you perhaps want to use it in order to dig beneath the prison?"

The warden spilled half the water and allowed R. Yoshua to take the remainder inside. When Rabbi Akiva saw how little water he had brought, he said to him. "Yoshua, don't you know that I am an old man and my life depends on you?" Rabbi Yoshua told him what happened.

Rabbi Akiva said to him. "Give me some water to wash my hands before I eat bread." The other hesitated. "It will not even suffice for drinking, let alone for washing hands." Rabbi Akiva answered him, "What can I do, seeing that one who disobeys the rabbis' rulings deserves to die?"

He refused to taste any food until R. Yoshua had brought him water to wash his hands first. (*Eruvin* 21b)

For a glimpse of the world as it was in the time of R. Yoshua ha-Garsi, see the historical timeline from 100 to 200 C.E.

יוסי
Yosi

(fourth century C.E.)
Amora, Eretz Yisrael
Head of the academy in Tiberias

According to some sources, he is the same Rabbi Yosi as the man who is known as Rabbi Yosi bar Zevida. He was a contemporary and a close associate of R. Yonah. (*Menahot* 70b)

After Rabbi Ammi moved to Caesarea, he and Rabbi Yonah became the heads of the academy in Tiberias. He had a son, Eleazar.

R. Benyamin b. Yafeth said, "R. Yosi asked R. Yohanan in Sidon a question about making havdala, but some say that it was R. Shimon b. Yaakov from Tyre who asked the question." (*Berachot* 33a)

For a glimpse of the world as it was in R. Yosi's time, see the historical timeline from 300 to 400 C.E.

יוסי בן עקביא
Yosi ben Akavia

(second century C.E.)
Tanna, Babylonia

Rabbi Yosi is sometimes called Rabbi Issi ben Akavia and at other times is called Rabbi Issi bar Yehuda. The Talmud quotes him often.

Once, when he failed to attend the academy of Rabbi Yosi ben Halafta for three days; Wardimus, Rabbi Yosi ben Halafta's son, happened to meet him outside and asked, "Why have you not shown up at the academy for the past three days?" He answered, "I did not receive a proper explanation from your father for the rulings that he issued." (*Nedarim* 81a)

Rabbi Issi was of the opinion that honoring a father takes precedence over performing another mitzvah, provided that someone else fulfill it in his stead. Rabbi Masna agreed with him.

Rabbi Issi must have kept secret scrolls of traditions, because the Talmud mentions that Rabbi Hiyya found some of the scrolls. (*Shabbat* 6b)

For a glimpse of the world as it was in the time of R. Yosi b. Akavia, see the historical timeline from 100 to 200 C.E.

יוסי בן חלפתא
Yosi ben Halafta

(second century C.E.)
Tanna, Eretz Yisrael

Rabbi Yosi ben Halafta was born in Sepphoris, where his father's family lived. He studied under his father, but he also studied with other rabbis. He went to Galilee to study under Rabbi Yohanan ben Nuri, and later he studied under Rabbi Tarfon in Judea. However, he received most of his teachings from Rabbi Akiva, whom he often quoted.

Rabbi Yosi was one of the few remaining students of Rabbi Akiva.

It is stated Rabbi Akiva had twelve thousand pairs of students. All of them died at the same time because they did not treat each other with respect. A tanna taught that all of them died between Pesah and Shavuot. The remaining students of Rabbi Akiva who revived the Torah at that time were Rabbi Meir, Rabbi Yehuda bar Illai, Rabbi Yosi ben Halafta, Rabbi Shimon bar Yohai and Rabbi Eleazar ben Shammua. (*Yevamot* 62b)

R. Yosi was ordained by Rabbi Yehuda ben Bava, whose defiance of the Roman decree against ordination resulted in his death. (*Sanhedrin* 14a)

The decree, which the authorities issued during the Hadrianic persecution, stipulated that anyone who ordained a rabbi or received rabbinic ordination would be put to death, the city where the ordination had taken place demolished, and the boundaries around it uprooted. In order to avoid the destruction of a city, Rabbi Yehuda ben Bava sat between two mountains between the two cities of Usha and Shefaram. Five prominent students sat before him: Rabbi Meir, Rabbi Yehuda bar Illai, Rabbi Shimon, Rabbi Yosi ben Halafta, and Rabbi Eleazar ben Shammua. The ceremony was held and he ordained them. Rabbi Avia adds the name of Rabbi Nehemia to the list.

As soon as the ceremony was completed, they noticed the Romans approaching. Rabbi Yehuda told his students to flee. They wanted to take him with them, but he urged them to go on without him, saying, "I would cause all of you to be captured. I am too old to run. I will lie before them like a stone." It was said that the Romans stabbed him three hundred times.

The students fled their separate ways, meeting again only after Hadrian's death. Seven of the students assembled in the valley of Rimmon in order to intercalate the year. They were Rabbi Meir, Rabbi Yehuda, Rabbi Yosi, Rabbi Shimon, Rabbi Nehemia, Rabbi Eliezer ben Yaakov and Rabbi Yohanan ha-Sandlar. R. Yosi participated in the conventions of the scholars at Usha.

Among the assembled at Usha was Rabbi Yehuda, who spoke well of the Romans. On one occasion Rabbi Yehuda bar Illai, Rabbi Shimon bar Yohai and Rabbi Yosi ben Halafta were making remarks to an audience. Rabbi Yehuda remarked on how fine the works of the Romans were, citing their markets, bridges and bathhouses as examples. Rabbi Yosi was silent, but Rabbi Shimon ben Yohai remarked, "Whatever they built, they built for themselves. They constructed markets in order to put prostitutes there, bridges in order to levy tolls, and bathhouses in order to indulge their bodies."

Someone carried his words to the Romans. They decreed that Rabbi Yehuda should be rewarded, Rabbi Yosi exiled to Sepphoris and Rabbi Shimon put to death. Rabbi Shimon and his son, Rabbi Eleazar, hid in a cave. For his silence, Rabbi Yosi was banished from Usha to his community of Sepphoris. Later, when the decree was annulled, he returned to Usha and persuaded Rabbi Shimon ben Gamliel to recall Rabbi Meir and Rabbi Nathan from their exclusion. (*Shabbat* 33b)

Like his father, he settled in Sepphoris, became the head of the beit din there, and introduced takkanot. He once endangered his life in order to perform the mitzvah of circumcision in spite of the decree against it. He had to flee to Asia to avoid arrest. (*Sanhedrin* 19a)

Rabbi Yosi's beit din was considered one of the most outstanding in Eretz Yisrael, and most of the Talmud's tractates mention him frequently. (*Shabbat* 49a–b)

He made a living as a tanner, as the Talmud relates. Rabbi Yishmael, the son of Rabbi Yosi, said, "My father was a hide worker, and he would ask me to fetch a hide for him so that he could sit on it."

R. Yosi married his deceased brother's wife, with whom he had five sons, Rabbi Yishmael and Rabbi Eleazar among them.

Rabbi Abbahu stated in the name of Rabbi Yohanan: Rabbi Meir had a student by the name of Sumchos who was able to supply forty-eight reasons to support every ruling of ritual impurity. (*Eruvin* 13b, *Nazir* 49b)

It is related that after Rabbi Meir passed away, Rabbi Yehuda told his students, "Do not allow the students of Rabbi Meir to enter our academy. They come only for disputations and to overwhelm me with citations from traditions, but not to learn Torah." Rabbi Sumchos forced his way into the academy and quoted Rabbi Meir on an important halachic issue. Rabbi Yehuda became angry and told his students, "Did I not tell you not to admit any of Rabbi Meir's students?" Rabbi Yosi answered, "People will say: 'Rabbi Meir is dead, Rabbi Yehuda is angry and Rabbi Yosi is silent.'"

R. Yaakov and R. Zerika said, "Whenever R. Akiva and one of his colleagues disagree, Halacha accords with R. Akiva. When R. Yosi disagrees with his colleagues, Halacha accords with R. Yosi. (*Eruvin* 46b)

R. Yaakov b. Idi said in the name of R. Yohanan: in a dispute between R. Meir and R. Yehuda, Halacha goes according to R. Yehuda. In a dispute between R. Yehuda and R. Yosi, Halacha goes according to R. Yosi. Needless to say, that a dispute between R. Meir and R. Yosi, Halacha goes according to R. Yosi.

R. Assi said: I also learn that in a dispute between R. Yosi and R. Shimon, Halacha goes according to R. Yosi.

R. Yosi said: "As I was traveling on the road, I once entered a ruin in Jerusalem in order to pray. Eliyahu of blessed memory appeared and guarded me until I finished praying. After I finished, he said to me: "Peace be upon you, my Rebbe."

I replied to him, "Peace be upon you, my Rebbe and teacher."

He said to me, "My son, why did you enter this ruin?"

I answered him, "I went inside to pray."

He said, "You should have prayed on the road."

I said to him, "I feared to be interrupted by passersby."

Eliyahu told me, "You should have recited an abbreviated prayer."

From this I learned three things: one should not enter a ruin, one may pray on the road, and prayer on the road should be brief. (*Berachot* 3a)

Rabbi Yohanan said in the name of Rabbi Yosi: "Do not placate a man when he is angry." (*Berachot* 7a)

R. Yosi said: Whoever honors the Torah is honored by people and whoever disgraces the Torah is himself disgraced by people. (*Avot* 4:6)

For a glimpse of the world as it was in the time of R. Yosi ben Halafta, see the historical timeline from 100 to 200 C.E.

יוסי בר חנינא
Yosi bar Hanina

(third century C.E.)
Amora, Eretz Yisrael

R. Yosi was a student of Rabbi Yohanan.

Rabbi Yosi bar Hanina, who was a wealthy landowner in Tiberias, served as a judge and was a member of the academy. (*Bava Batra* 90b)

Rabbi Assi called him a great man, one who penetrates the innermost intention of the law. (*Bava Kama* 42b)

To his sorrow, his children died in his lifetime. (*Taanit* 13b)

Rabbi Yosi said in the name of Rabbi Eliezer ben Yaakov, "Being host to a scholar is equal to making an offering on the altar." (*Berachot* 10b)

R. Yosi b. Hanina also said in the name of R. Eliezer b. Yaakov, "When you pray, stand in a low area." (*Berachot* 10b)

He also said in the name of R. Eliezer b. Yaakov: "One should not eat before one has prayed."

He said further in the name of R. Eliezer b. Yaakov: "One should pray with feet next to each other, standing erect."

R. Yosi b. Hanina said, "A woman recognizes a guest's character better than a man does." (*Berachot* 10b)

R. Kahana escorted R. Shimi b. Ashi from Pum Nahara to Bei Zenitha of Babylonia. When they arrived, he asked him, "Do people really say that these palm trees date back to Adam's time?"

He answered, "Your question reminds me of a saying by R. Yosi b. Hanina: 'Any land that was decreed by Adam to be inhabited became inhabited, and any land that Adam decreed to be uninhabited is still uninhabited.'" (*Berachot* 31a)

Rabbi Zeira relates that R. Yosi bar Hanina appeared to him in a dream after his death. R. Zeira asked him, "Next to whom are you seated in the Heavenly Academy?" He answered, "Next to Rabbi Yohanan." (*Bava Metzia* 85b)

For a glimpse of the world as it was in the time of Yosi bar Hanina, see the historical timeline from 200 to 300 C.E.

יוסי בר דורמסקית
Yosi ben Dormaskit

(first–second centuries C.E.)
Tanna, Eretz Yisrael

Rabbi Yosi ben Dormaskit, who was born in Damascus, studied in Yavne and in Lydda under Rabbi Eliezer ben Hyrcanus. Although the Talmud mentions his name in connection with Rabbi Yosi ha-Gelili, he was mainly a student of R. Eliezer b. Hyrcanus.

It is related that when Rabbi Yosi came to Rabbi Eliezer in Lod, Rabbi Eliezer asked him, "What new subject have you learned in the house of study today?" He answered him, "They counted the votes and the majority decided that the residents of Ammon and Moab must give the poor man's tithe during the sabbatical year." (*Yadayim* 4:3)

For a glimpse of the world as it was in the time of R. Yosi b. Dormaskit, see the historical timeline from 50 to 150 C.E.

יוסי בן כיפר
Yosi ben Kippar

(second century C.E.)
Tanna, Eretz Yisrael

Although Rabbi Yosi ben Kippar is not mentioned in the regular Mishna, he is quoted in the baraita.

R. Safra said: R. Abbahu used to tell this story: When R. Hananya b. Ahi Yoshua left for Babylonia, he began to intercalate the years and to fix the new months outside Israel. The bet din of Israel sent two scholars to stop him from doing so: R. Yosi b. Kippar and the grandson of R. Zechariah b. Kavutal. When R. Hananya saw them, he asked them, "Why have you come?" They answered, "We have come to learn Torah from you." When he heard that, he proclaimed to the community: These men are the great scholars of our generation. They and their ancestors have served in the Temple. As we have learned, Zechariah b. Kavutal said: Many times have I read from the book of Daniel.

Shortly afterwards, they issued rulings against his declarations. Everything that he said was impure they declared pure, and permitted what he had forbidden. R. Hananya became upset and announced to the community: "These men are false and worthless."

They said to him, "You have already built our reputation and you cannot destroy it. You have already made fences and you cannot break them down." He asked them, "Why do you declare pure that which I declared to be impure?"

They answered him, "Because you intercalate years and fix the new moon outside Israel." He retorted, "Did not R. Akiva b. Yoseph intercalate years and fix the new month outside of Israel?" They answered him; "Do not cite R. Akiva, who had no equal in Israel." He retorted; "I also left no equal in the land of Israel." They said to him, "The kids that you left behind in Israel have become goats with horns, and they sent us to speak to you in their name. If you listen, well and good, but if you do not, you will be excommunicated. They also empowered us to tell the community here in Babylonia: If you heed us, well and good. But if you do not, then let them go up the mountain, let Ahia build an altar, and Hananya play the harp. All

of you will become deniers and will have no portion in the God of Israel." When the community heard this, they started to weep and declared: Heaven forbid. (*Berachot* 63a)

The rabbis of Eretz Yisrael also asked R. Yosi to travel to Babylon in order to raise funds for the scholars in the yeshiva in Eretz Yisrael. He and Rabbi Dostai ben Yannai undertook the mission and traveled together.

For a glimpse of the world as it was in the time of R. Yosi ben Kippar, see the historical timeline from 100 to 200 C.E.

יוסי בן קיסמא
Yosi ben Kisma

(second century C.E.)
Tanna, Eretz Yisrael

Rabbi Yosi, who lived briefly in Tiberias and in Caesarea, was a contemporary and a colleague of Rabbi Hanania ben Teradion.

The Mishna quotes him as saying. "One day, I was on the road and I met a person who greeted me with 'Shalom.' He asked me, "Where are you from?' I answered, 'I come from a large city, where they have many sages and scribes.'

"He said to me, 'I would like you to come and live in our town. I will give you thousands and thousands of golden dinars.'

"I answered him, 'You can't give me enough money to move away from the place where I live. I will only live in a place where I can learn Torah. Furthermore; when a person departs from this world, no silver, gold, precious jewels or pearls will accompany him. He will be accompanied only by his reputation, his learning and his good deeds." (*Avot* 6:9)

Our rabbis taught when Rabbi Yosi b. Kisma was ill, R. Hanania b. Teradion went to visit him. R. Yosi said to him. "Don't you know that Heaven has ordained that the Romans will destroy our Temple and rule over us? I heard that you are defying them by teaching Torah in public."

R. Hanania answered. "Heaven will show mercy."

R. Yosi said to him, "I am telling you plain facts and you tell me Heaven will show mercy? I would not be surprised if they were to burn you and the scroll of Torah in the same fire."

R. Hanania asked R. Yosi, "How do I stand in the future world?"

"Is there any particular act that you are concerned about?"

"Yes. Once I inadvertently mixed up the Purim money with the ordinary charity."

Rabbi Yosi replied, "I wish your lot were mine."

R. Yosi b. Kisma died several days later. All the great men of Rome came to his funeral and eulogized him. On their return, they came upon R. Hanania b. Teradion sitting and teaching Torah in public. They took him together with his Torah scroll, wrapped the scroll around his body, placed bundles of wood about him and set them on fire. They soaked tufts of wool in water and placed them over his heart in order to prolong his agony. When his daughter saw him, she exclaimed, "Father, woe is me to see you in this state!"

He told her, "If it were only myself being burned it would be hard to bear, but since the Torah scroll is being burned together with me, the Power that will avenge the offense against the Torah will also avenge the offense against me."

His students asked him, "Rabbi, what do you see?"

He answered. "I see the parchment burning, but the letters are soaring high."

His students advised him, "Open your mouth so that the fire will enter and put an end to your sufferings." But

Hanania replied, "It is best that He Who gave the soul should also take it away. No one may hasten his death."

Impressed by Rabbi Hanania's fortitude, the executioner asked him, "Rabbi, if I remove the wool from your heart, will you take me with you into the life of the World to Come?"

The rabbi answered, "Yes."

The executioner removed the wool and fanned the fire, hastening Rabbi Hanania's death. He then threw himself into the flames. (*Avodah Zarah* 18a)

For a glimpse of the world as it was in the time of R. Yosi ben Kisma, see the historical timeline from 100 to 200 C.E.

יוסי בן המשולם
Yosi ben ha-Meshullam (Yosi ben Meshullam)

(second–third centuries C.E.)
Tanna, Eretz Yisrael

Rabbi Shimon ben Menashye and Rabbi Yosi Meshullam were close colleagues. It was said of them that they divided the waking hours of the day into three parts: one-third for Torah study, one third for prayer and one third for work.

Rabbi Yosi associated with Abba Yosi ben Dostai, Shimon ben Menashye and Shimon ben Eleazar. He was a frequent visitor in the home of Rabbi Yehuda ha-Nasi. He also belonged to a circle of several rabbis who ate only food that was ritually pure. He was an expert on Temple sacrifices. (*Bechorot* 3:3, 24b)

For a glimpse of the world as it was in the time of R. Yosi ben ha-Meshullam, see the historical timeline from 150 to 250 C.E.

יוסי בן יהודה
Yosi ben Yehuda

(second–third centuries C.E.)
Tanna, Eretz Yisrael

Rabbi Yosi was the son of Rabbi Yehuda bar Illai, at whose academy he studied together with Rabbi Yehuda ha-Nasi.

R. Yosi b. Yehuda gave three instructions to his colleague, Rebbe: "Do not go out alone at night, do not stand naked in front of a lamp, and do not enter a new bath-house, lest it crack." (*Pesahim* 112b)

R. Yehuda ha-Nasi and R. Yosi b. Yehuda engaged in halachic disputes and traveled together throughout Eretz Yisrael. When they arrived in a particular place, Rebbe ate the figs, but R. Yosi did not. The owner came in and asked, "Why do the rabbis not eat? Most of the knives have been folded." Rabbi Yosi thought that the owner was speaking sarcastically. The Talmud quotes him frequently. (*Shabbat* 18a, *Nedarim* 62a)

Rabbi Yosi b. Yehuda used to say, "Two ministering angels accompany a person Friday evening from the synagogue to his home." (*Shabbat* 119b)

R. Yosi b. Yehuda said, "When you say yes it should be justifiable, and when you say no it should be justifiable." (*Bava Metzia* 49a)

For a glimpse of the world as it was in the time of R. Yosi b. Yehuda, see the historical timeline from 150 to 250 C.E.

יוסי בן יהודה איש כפר הבבלי
Yosi b. Yehuda Ish Kefar ha-Bavli

(second century C.E.)
Tanna, Eretz Yisrael

R. Yosi said: "One who learns from the young and immature is likened to one who eats unripe grapes or drinks new wine from his vat. But one who

learns from an older, mature person is likened to one who eats ripe grapes or drinks aged wine." (*Avot* 4:20)

For a glimpse of the world as it was in the time of Yosi ben Yehuda, see the historical timeline from 100 to 200 C.E.

יוסי בן יוחנן
Yosi ben Yohanan

(second century B.C.E.)
Tanna, Eretz Yisrael

Yosi ben Yohanan and his colleague, Rabbi Yosi ben Yoezer, constituted one of the zugot, or study partners, mentioned in the Talmud.

Often referred to as Rabbi Yosi ben Yohanan ha-Tanna of Jerusalem, and he was the head of the Sanhedrin's rabbinical court. Both he and R. Yosi ben Yoezer were disciples of Antigonus Ish Socho. He lived during the time of the Hasmonean revolution.

The Talmud quotes him as saying, "Let your house be wide open, and let the needy be guests in your house." (*Avot* 1:5)

The Talmud states that when R. Yosi b. Yoezer and R. Yosi b. Yohanan died, the renowned scholars ceased to exist. (*Sotah* 9:9, 47a)

R. Kahana said: When R. Yishmael ben R. Yosi b. Halafta became ill, the rabbis sent him a message with the following request: "Tell us two or three things which you heard from your father."

He replied; "One hundred and eighty years before the Temple was destroyed, Eretz Yisrael was occupied by the wicked government. Eighty years before the Temple was destroyed, a rabbinical prohibition of ritual impurity was enacted against certain vessels and people. Forty years before the Temple was destroyed, the Sanhedrin went into exile and moved to the commercial zone of the Temple."

During this period, the heads of the Sanhedrin were R. Yosi b. Yoezer, R. Yosi b. Yohanan, R. Hillel, R. Shimon, R. Gamliel and R. Shimon. (*Shabbat* 15a)

For a glimpse of the world as it was in the time of Yosi ben Yohanan, see the historical timeline from 100 to 200 B.C.E.

יוסי בן יועזר
Yosi ben Yoezer

(second century B.C.E.)
Tanna, Eretz Yisrael

Rabbi Yosi ben Yoezer and his colleague, Yosi ben Yohanan, constituted one of the zugot, or study partners, mentioned in the Talmud.

Rabbi Yosi ben Yoezer was the Nasi of the Sanhedrin, while Yosi ben Yohanan was the head of the court. Both were disciples of Antigonus Ish Socho. His place of origin was Zereda in Samaria. It was the time of the Hasmonean revolution. The Syrians appointed Alchimus, who was Rabbi Yosi's nephew, as High Priest, in opposition to Judah Maccabee. Eventually, Alchimus sentenced Rabbi Yosi to death, and he and all the scholars were murdered. It is related that his wicked nephew, Yakum (Alchimus) encountered him on his way execution and taunted him.

The Talmud relates that Rabbi Yosi gave all his property to the Temple, leaving nothing to his son because he considered him unworthy. (*Bava Batra* 133b)

R. Yosi b. Yoezer said: "Let your house be a meeting place for the wise. Sit in the dust of their feet and drink in their words thirstily." (*Avot* 1:4)

The Talmud states that when R. Yosi b. Yoezer and R. Yosi b. Yohanan died, the renowned scholars ceased to exist. (*Sotah* 9:9, 47a)

During this period, the heads of the Sanhedrin were R. Yosi b. Yoezer, R. Yosi b. Yohanan, R. Hillel, R. Shimon, R. Gamliel and R. Shimon.

For a glimpse of the world as it was in the time of R. Yosi ben Yoezer, see the historical timeline from 200 to 100 B.C.E.

יוסי בן זימרא
Yosi ben Zimra

(second century C.E.)
Tanna, Eretz Yisrael

The Talmud mentions that he was a Kohen. (*Yoma* 78a)

His daughter was married to the son of Rabbi Yehuda ha-Nasi. (*Ketubbot* 62b)

Rabbi Yohanan and Rabbi Eleazar b. Pedat quoted his sayings in the Talmud.

Rabbi Yohanan said in the name of R. Yosi b. Zimra: "The tongue is guarded by two walls, one of bone and one of flesh, in order to guard it from speaking evil." He also said, "One who bears evil tales is almost as bad as one who denies the foundation of faith." (*Arachin* 15b)

For a glimpse of the world as it was in the time of Yosi ben Zimra, see the historical timeline from 100 to 200 C.E.

יוסי חלי קופרי
Yosi Hali Kofri

(first century C.E.)
Tanna, Eretz Yisrael

R. Yosi was a contemporary of Rabbi Yohanan ben Zakkai, and one of his students. He is quoted in the Talmud. (*Machshirin* 1:3)

For a glimpse of the world as it was in the time of R. Yosi Hali Kofri, see the historical timeline from 1 to 100 C.E.

יוסי הגלילי
Yosi ha-Gelili

(second century C.E.)
Tanna, Eretz Yisrael

Although he lived in the Galilee in his younger years, he later joined the scholars in Yavne. He was a close colleague of Rabbi Tarfon and Rabbi Akiva. At one point in his life, he studied in Tiberias with Rabbi Shimon ben Hanina. He had three sons: Eliezer, Hanina and a third who died young.

Many regarded Rabbi Yosi as a wonder-worker. His prayers for rain were particularly effective. The Talmud quotes him very often.

R. Yosi ha-Gelili was once traveling when he met Beruria, the wife of Rabbi Meir. He asked her, "Which road does one take to get to Lydda?" She replied, "Foolish Galilean, did the rabbis not teach that you should not engage in much conversation with a woman? You should have asked, 'Which way to Lydda?'" (*Eruvin* 53b)

The sages were assembled in the vineyard of Yavne. Rabbi Tarfon and Rabbi Akiva among others were there. A certain disciple by the name of R. Yosi ha-Gelili was there for the first time. He raised several questions. (*Zevahim* 57a)

R. Yosi ha-Gelili said: "One who is occupied with the performance of a mitzvah is exempt from the performance of other religious duties." (*Sukkah* 26a)

For a glimpse of the world as it was in the time of R. Yosi ha-Gelili, see the historical timeline from 100 to 200 C.E.

יוסי הכהן
Yosi ha-Kohen

(first–second centuries)
Tanna, Eretz Yisrael

Rabbi Yosi was a student of Rabbi Yohanan ben Zakkai.

It is related that R. Yosi ha-Kohen never sent a letter with a non-Jew for fear that he might deliver it on Shabbat. (*Shabbat* 19a)

It is related that R. Yehoshua and R. Yosi ha-Kohen discussed the Work of the Chariot as they traveled together. (*Hagigah* 14b)

R. Yohanan b. Zakkai had five outstanding students. He said to them, "Go and discern the proper path that a person should follow."

R. Eliezer said, "A good eye."

R. Yoshua said, "A good friend."

R. Yosi said, "A good neighbor."

R. Shimon said, "One who considers the outcome of his actions."

R. Eleazar said, "A good heart."

R. Yohanan b. Zakkai remarked, "I prefer the words of R. Eleazar b. Arach because all your words are included in his words." (*Avot* 2:13)

What is important in human relations? Rabbi Yosi ha-Kohen listed his preference: "A good neighbor." (*Avot* 2:9)

He also used to say, "Let the money of your fellow human beings be as valuable to you as your own." (*Avot* 2:12)

For a glimpse of the world as it was in the time of R. Yosi ha-Kohen, see the historical timeline from 50 to 150 C.E.

צדוק
Zadok

(first century B.C.E.–first century C.E.)
Tanna, Eretz Yisrael

R. Zadok, who came from a priestly family, officiated in the Temple while it still stood. Since he foresaw the destruction of the Temple, he prayed and fasted for forty years in an attempt to prevent the tragedy. As a result, his stomach shrank and his health declined. When Rabbi Yohanan ben Zakkai went to see the Roman general Vespasian to seek relief for Jerusalem, he also spoke on behalf of Rabbi Zadok.

The Talmud relates that when the interview was over Vespasian told Rabbi Yohanan, "I am leaving now for Rome, and someone else will take my place here. However, you can make a request of me and I will grant it to you." Rabbi Yohanan answered: "Give me Yavne and its scholars and the dynasty of Rabbi Gamliel, and also a physician to heal Rabbi Zadok."

Rabbi Yohanan's request was granted. It further states that the physicians healed Rabbi Zadok by means of diet. On the first day, they gave him bran soaked in water. The next day, they gave him a little more of the same, only coarser. The day after that, they gave him water with flour, so that his stomach expanded a little more every day until he was able to digest regular food. (*Gittin* 56b)

Although R. Zadok was a student of Rabbi Shammai, in practice he always followed the school of Rabbi Hillel. (*Yevamot* 15b)

The Talmud relates that R. Eliezer, R. Yoshua and R. Zadok were attending a banquet at the home of Rabbi Gamliel's son, and R. Gamliel served them drinks. R. Eliezer did not accept, but R. Yoshua did. "R. Eliezer said to R. Yoshua, 'What is this? We are sitting while R. Gamliel stands and serves us?"

"R. Zadok replied, 'If we allow the Almighty to do so, we can allow Rabbi Gamliel to do so. God causes the winds to blow, the rain to fall, the earth to yield its fruit, and sets the table before everyone – and we shall not permit R. Gamliel to serve us drinks?" (*Kiddushin* 32b)

R. Zadok, who was a member of the assembly at Yavne, had a close relationship with R. Gamliel.

It once happened that two priests ran up the altar ramp in order to perform part of the Temple service, and one of them reached the altar first. The other seized a knife and stabbed him. Rabbi Zadok ha-Kohen mounted the platform and addressed the priests as follows: "On whose behalf shall we offer the heifer whose neck is to be broken – on behalf of the city or on behalf of the

Temple court?" All the people burst out weeping. (*Yoma* 23a)

In R. Zadok's father's time, they made certain that measurements were checked. (*Shabbat* 157a)

R. Zadok said: "Do not separate yourself from the community. When you are appointed as judge, do not act as a lawyer. Do not use the Torah as a crown for self-glorification, nor should you use the Torah as a spade with which to dig." (*Avot* 4:7)

For a glimpse of the world as it was in R. Zadok's time, see the historical timeline from 50 B.C.E. to 50 C.E.

צדיק
Zadok II

(second century C.E.)
Tanna, Eretz Yisrael

R. Zadok, the son of R. Eliezer and a grandson of R. Zadok, was taken captive and sold to a wealthy family in Rome.

A Roman woman, who was politically powerful, made an immoral proposition to R. Zadok. To reject her would have put him in danger. He told her, "I am hungry," and she offered him non-kosher meat. He said to her, "What is the meaning of this – that he who commits one immoral act may commit other forbidden acts?"

As the woman lit the fire and began to cook the meat, Zadok climbed into the fire. She said to him, "Had I known that it was so heinous to you, I would not have tormented you." (*Kiddushin* 40a)

For a glimpse of the world as it was in the time of Zadok II, see the historical timeline from 100 to 200 C.E.

זכריה בן אבקולוס
Zechariah ben Avkulos

(first century C.E.)
Tanna, Eretz Yisrael

A certain man in Jerusalem had a friend Kamza and an enemy named Bar Kamza. He invited many guests to a party and told his servant to invite Kamza. But the servant invited Bar Kamza instead of Kamza. When the host saw Bar Kamza in his house, he said to him, "I hear that you tell tales about me. What are you doing here? Get out!"

Bar Kamza said to him, "Since I am here already, let me stay and I will pay the cost of half the party."

"No," said the host. "I don't want you here."

"Let me pay for the cost of the whole party," said Bar Kamza.

The host would not consent, and he seized Bar Kamza by the hand and took him outside.

Bar Kamza said, "Since the rabbis were sitting there and did not stop him, he must have acted with their consent." He went to the authorities and denounced his fellow Jews, saying, "The Jews are rebelling against you."

When the authorities asked for proof, Bar Kamza advised them to send an offering for the altar and see whether it was accepted. They sent a fine calf back with him as an offering. On the way, he made a small blemish in the calf's upper lip. The rabbis wanted to offer it in order not to offend the government, but R. Zechariah b. Avkulos opposed doing so. He reasoned that people would say that it was permitted to offer blemished animals on the altar.

R. Yohanan remarked: "Through the scrupulousness of R. Zechariah, our

home was destroyed, our Temple was burnt and we were exiled from our land." (*Gittin* 55b–56a)

For a glimpse of the world as it was in the time of R. Zechariah ben Avkulos, see the historical timeline from 1 to 100 C.E.

זכריה בן הקצב
Zechariah ben ha-Ketzav

(first century C.E.)
Tanna, Eretz Yisrael

The Temple still stood when he was a young man, and he witnessed its destruction.

Rabbi Yehoshua, who was one of his students, quoted him in the Mishna. (*Sotah* 5:1)

For a glimpse of the world as it was in the time of R. Zechariah ben ha-Ketzav, see the historical timeline from 1 to 100 C.E.

זכריה בן קבוטל
Zechariah ben Kavutal

(first century C.E.)
Tanna, Eretz Yisrael

R. Zechariah was a Kohen. He relates that on Yom Kippur, he read for the high priest from the book of Daniel. (*Yoma* 1:6, 18b)

R. Safra said: R. Abbahu used to tell this story: When R. Hananya b. Ahi Yoshua left for Babylonia, he began to intercalate the years and to fix the new months outside Israel. The bet din of Israel sent two scholars to stop him from doing so: R. Yosi b. Kippar and the grandson of R. Zechariah b. Kavutal. When R. Hananya saw them, he asked them, "Why have you come?" They answered, "We have come to learn Torah from you." When he heard that, he proclaimed to the community: These men are the great scholars of our generation. They and their ancestors have served in the Temple. As we have learned, Zechariah b. Kavutal said: Many times have I read from the book of Daniel.

Shortly afterwards, they issued rulings against his declarations. Everything that he said was impure they declared pure, and permitted what he had forbidden. R. Hananya became upset and announced to the community: "These men are false and worthless."

They said to him, "You have already built our reputation and you cannot destroy it. You have already made fences and you cannot break them down." He asked them, "Why do you declare pure that which I declared to be impure?"

They answered him, "Because you intercalate years and fix the new moon outside Israel." He retorted, "Did not R. Akiva b. Yoseph intercalate years and fix the new month outside of Israel?" They answered him; "Do not cite R. Akiva, who had no equal in Israel." He retorted; "I also left no equal in the land of Israel." They said to him, "The kids that you left behind in Israel have become goats with horns, and they sent us to speak to you in their name. If you listen, well and good, but if you do not, you will be excommunicated. They also empowered us to tell the community here in Babylonia: If you heed us, well and good. But if you do not, then let them go up the mountain, let Ahia build an altar, and Hananya play the harp. All of you will become deniers and will have no portion in the God of Israel." When the community heard this, they started to weep and declared: Heaven forbid. (*Berachot* 63a)

For a glimpse of the world as it was in the time of R. Zechariah ben Kavutal, see the historical timeline from 1 to 100 C.E.

זְעֵירָא
Zeira

(third–fourth centuries C.E.)
Amora, Babylonia

R. Zeira was a student of Rabbi Huna at the Sura academy and of Rabbi Yehuda b. Yehezkel at the Pumbedita academy. (*Berachot* 39a)

He was very eager to move to Eretz Yisrael, but since he knew that his teacher Rabbi Yehuda disapproved, he left without telling him. (*Ketubbot* 110b)

The Talmud relates that when Rabbi Zeira still lived in Babylonia, he avoided his teacher, Rabbi Yehuda bar Yehezkel, because he wanted to move to Eretz Yisrael against R. Yehuda's wishes. Rabbi Yehuda had said that anyone who left Babylonia in order to move to Eretz Yisrael violated a commandment. (*Shabbat* 41a)

When Rabbi Zeira reached the Jordan River and could not find a ferry, he crossed the river on a rope bridge. (*Ketubbot* 112a)

In Eretz Yisrael, he studied under Rabbi Yohanan, Rabbi Ammi, Rabbi Assi and Rabbi Eleazar. He was respectful of everyone and showed friendship even to some lawless men. (*Kiddushin* 52a)

Rabbi Zeira settled in Caesarea.

When Rava and R. Zeira visited the Exilarch, they were served an abundant meal. After the trays were removed, a basket of fruit, a gift from the Exilarch, was brought in. Rava ate from the fruit, but R. Zeira did not. R. Zeira asked Rava, "Don't you hold that if the food has been removed, one may not eat?"

Rava replied, "We can rely on the fact that the Exilarch usually sends a gift." (*Berachot* 42a)

Rabbah sat engaged in a halachic discussion with R. Zeira and Rabbah b.

R. Hanan. R. Abbaye sat beside them. During the discussion, R. Zeira and R. Abbaye disagreed with each other, and each cited proof to make his point. Then Rabbah b. Hanan also argued with R. Abbaye. In the meantime, Rava heard about the argument and sent word to them with R. Shemaya b. Zeira. The debate was lively. (*Eruvin* 92a)

Lawless men lived in R. Zeira's neighborhood. Although he was on friendly terms with them in the hope that they would repent, the rabbis were annoyed with him on account of it. When R. Zeira passed away, the lawless men mourned for him, saying, "Until now, the man with the burned short leg prayed for us. Who will pray for us now?" Feeling remorse, they repented. (*Sanhedrin* 37a)

R. Zeira acquired that nickname after an incident. When he moved to Eretz Yisrael, he performed one hundred fasts in order to forget the method of study in Babylonia. He performed another hundred fasts for R. Eleazar to stay alive and that the burden of the community should not fall on his shoulders. He performed yet another hundred in order to render the fires of Gehinnom powerless against him. Every thirty days, he would heat an oven and test the power of fire over his body. He never suffered injury until one day when the rabbis cast an envious eye upon him and his legs were singed. From that day on, he was nicknamed "The one with the short, burned leg." (*Bava Metzia* 85a)

When Rabbi Zeira was tired from study, he would sit at the door of Rabbi Yehuda ben Ammi's school and rise every time the rabbis passed by. One day, when a child emerged, R. Zeira asked him, "What did your teacher teach you?" The child answered, "I was taught how to make a blessing over a vegetable." (*Eruvin* 28b)

The students asked Rabbi Zera, "To what do you attribute your old age?" He replied. "Never have I been harsh with my household, never have I stepped in front of one greater than I, never have I studied Torah in a dirty place, never have I rejoiced in the misfortune of others and never have I called people by their nicknames." (*Megillah* 28a)

Rabbi Yaakov was the son of Yaakov's daughter. When Rabbi Zeira was in Babylonia, he asked Rabbi Yaakov, the son of Yaakov's daughter – who was making a trip to Eretz Yisrael – to make a detour to Tyre in order to visit Rabbi Yaakov ben Idi, who was held in very high esteem in Babylonia. He wanted to get some clarification on some halachic matters. (*Eruvin* 80a)

R. Hiyya b. Abba said in the name of R. Yohanan: "The blessing over boiled vegetables is *peri adama.*" However, R. Binyamin b. Yafet said in the name of R. Yohanan: "The blessing over boiled vegetables is *she-ha-kol.*" R. Nahman b. Yitzhak said: "Ulla made an error in accepting the word of R. Benyamin b. Yafet."

R. Zeira expressed astonishment. "How can you compare R. Binyamin b. Yafet to R. Hiyya b. Abba? R. Hiyya b. Abba was very particular to get the exact teachings of R. Yohanan, while R. Binyamin b. Yafet was not so careful. Furthermore, R. Hiyya b. Abba used to go over his learning with R. Yohanan every thirty days, while R. Binyamin did not." (*Berachot* 38b)

When R. Zeira was ill, R. Abbahu went to visit him. R. Abbahu made a vow, saying: "If the little one with burned legs recovers, I will make a Yom Tov meal for the rabbis." R. Zeira recovered and R. Abbahu made a feast in his honor. When the time came to begin the meal, R. Abbahu said to R. Zeira,

"Would you please make the blessing and begin?"

But R. Zeira said to him: "Don't you accept R. Yohanan's ruling that the host begins the meal?" R. Abbahu began the meal with the blessing. When it came to reciting the blessings after the meal, R. Abbahu said to R. Zeira: "Would you lead us in the blessings?"

R. Zeira said to him: "Don't you accept the ruling of R. Huna from Babylon that the person who recites the blessings before the meal also recites the blessing after the meal?" (*Berachot* 46a)

R. Zeira said to R. Hisda; "Teach us about the blessings after the meal."

R. Hisda replied, "I do not know them myself. How could I teach them to others?"

"What do you mean?" asked R. Zera.

"I was once in the house of the Resh Gelutha. When I recited the blessings after the meal, R. Sheshet stretched out his neck at me like a serpent because I left out some passages."

R. Zeira said in the name of R. Yirmiyahu b. Abba: "In the time just before the coming of Mashiah, the scholars of the generation will be persecuted. When I repeated this statement in front of R. Shemuel, he said, 'There will also be test after test.'" (*Ketubbot* 112b)

R. Zera used to hide to avoid ordination, because R. Eleazar said: "Always remain unknown and you will live with peace of mind."

However, when he heard R. Eleazar say, 'One does not obtain greatness unless all his sins are forgiven,' he himself strove to obtain ordination. (*Sanhedrin* 14a)

R. Zeira's father served as a tax collector for thirteen years. When the head of the tax collectors came to town to impose an additional tax on the town,

he would ask the Torah scholars to hide in his house so that the town's population would appear smaller. When he saw the other inhabitants of the town, he would say to them: "The chief tax collector is coming to town, and he will slaughter the father in the presence of the son and the son in the presence of the father." All the inhabitants hid themselves, and the head tax collector rebuked the father of R. Zeira for failing in his duty. (*Sanhedrin* 25b)

R. Zeira said in the name of Rava b. Zimuna: "If we say that the scholars were the offspring of angels, then we are offspring of human beings. If the earlier scholars were the offspring of human beings, then we are like donkeys – and not even like the kind of donkey that belonged to R. Hanina b. Dosa or R. Pinhas b. Yair, but like common donkeys." (*Shabbat* 112b)

R. Pinhas b. Yair arrived at an inn, where they put food in front of his donkey, but the donkey would not eat. They asked R. Pinchas why his donkey would not eat. He told them, "Perhaps the grain was not tithed." They immediately tithed the grain, and the donkey ate it. (*Hullin* 7a)

For a glimpse of the world as it was in R. Zeira's time, see the historical timeline from 250 to 350 C.E.

זעירי
Zeiri

(third century C.E.)
Amora, Babylonia

Although R. Zeiri was born in Babylonia, he studied in the academies of Eretz Yisrael. His main teacher was Rabbi Yohanan, whose teachings he frequently transmitted, though he also studied under Rabbi Hanina ben Hama. Rabbi Zeiri is quoted as saying in the name of Rabbi Hanina that the son of David – that is, the Messiah – will not come until there are no conceited men in Eretz Yisrael. (*Sanhedrin* 98a)

Rabbi Yohanan must have thought him very worthy, because he offered him his daughter in marriage. For his own reasons, he did not accept the offer, but evaded R. Yohanan. One day, when Rabbi Yohanan and Rabbi Zeiri were traveling on the road, they came to a pool of water; whereupon Rabbi Zeiri carried Rabbi Yohanan on his shoulder. Rabbi Yohanan said to him, "It seems that our learning together is appropriate for you – but my daughter is not?" (*Kiddushin* 71b)

R. Zeiri deposited some money with his landlady while he went away to study under Rav. In the meantime, she died. He went to the cemetery where she was buried and asked her spirit, "Where is my money?" She replied, "Go and dig beneath the doorpost at such and such a place and you will find it. While you are there, tell my mother to send me my comb and my eye paint with So-and-so, who is coming here tomorrow."

While visiting Eretz Yisrael, Rabbi Zeiri was kidnapped by bandits. Rabbi Ammi and Rabbi Shemuel tried to negotiate his release, but there were other disturbances in the land. In the confusion, Rabbi Zeiri managed to escape. (*Berachot* 18b)

He returned to Babylonia and taught in the academy of Nehardea. Rabbi Hiyya ben Ashi was one of his closest students. Other rabbis who transmitted his teachings included Rabbi Hisda, Rabbah, Rabbi Yoseph, Rabbi Yehuda, Rabbi Nahman and Rabbi Giddal. (*Hullin* 56a)

Rava said, "Every text that R. Yitzhak b. Avdimi did not explain, and every baraita that R. Zeiri did not explain are not really explained." (*Zevahim* 43b)

For a glimpse of the world as it was in R. Zeiri's time, see the historical timeline from 200 to 300 C.E.

זריקא
Zerika

(fourth century C.E.)
Amora, Babylonia

R. Zerika said to R. Safra, "Come and see the difference in style between the good men of Eretz Yisrael and the pious men of Babylonia. When the world was in need of rain, the pious men of Babylonia, R. Huna and R. Hisda, would say: 'Let us pray. Perhaps the Almighty will be appeased and send us rain.' But the great men of Eretz Yisrael, such as R. Yonah the father of R. Mani, would dress in sackcloth, stand in a low spot and pray for rain." (*Taanit* 23b)

Rabbi Zerika said in the names of R. Ami and R. Yehoshua ben Levi, "In front of a deceased person, speak of no other matters but the deceased." (*Berachot* 3b)

R. Yaakov and R. Zerika said: "Whenever R. Akiva and one of his colleagues disagree, Halacha goes according to R. Akiva." (*Eruvin* 46b)

For a glimpse of the world as it was in R. Zerika's time, see the historical timeline from 300 to 400 C.E.

זביד
Zevid

(fourth century C.E.)
Amora, Babylonia

R. Zevid was a contemporary of R. Kahana.

Rabbi Kahana's son was very wealthy. Once, R. Zevid told R. Kahana that his daughter-in-law threw gold around as if it were worthless. (*Meilah* 19a)

For a glimpse of the world as it was in R. Zevid's time, see the historical timeline from 300 to 400 C.E.

זוטרא בר טוביה
Zutra b. Toveya

(third century C.E.)
Amora, Babylonia

R. Zutra was a student of Rav.

R. Zutra b. Toveya said in the name of Rav – according to others, R. Hana b. Bizna said in the name of R. Shimon Hasida, and according to others, R. Yohanan said in the name of R. Shimon b. Yohai – that it is better to be thrown into a fiery furnace than to shame another in public. (*Berachot* 43b)

R. Zutra b. Toveya said in the name of Rav: A blessing should be recited over fragrances.

R. Zutra b. Toveya also said in the name of Rav: A torch is as good as two, and moonlight is as good as three.

For a glimpse of the world as it was in the time of Zutra b. Toveya, see the historical timeline from 200 to 300 C.E.

מר זוטרא
Zutra, Mar

(fourth–fifth centuries C.E.)
Amora and Exilarch in Babylonia

The Aramaic term for the Exilarch – the leader of the Babylonian Jewish community in exile – was Resh Gelutha. It was a hereditary office that was usually held by descendants of King David. The Exilarch's office had the recognition of the king, the court and secular authorities. He was the chief tax collector among the Jews, who were autonomous during that time, and he held an honored place on the king's council. The Exilarch lived in royal fashion, appointed judges, and exercised criminal jurisdiction over the Jews.

Mar Zutra I, who was a great scholar, was a student of Rabbi Papa and a contemporary of Rabbi Ashi.

Rabbi Hisda spoke of him as Mar Zutra the Pious. (*Bava Kama* 81b)

Whenever he had to put a colleague in herem, he would put himself in herem first. (*Moed Katan* 17a)

The Talmud relates that Rabbi Amemar, Mar Zutra and Rabbi Ashi were sitting at the gate of the Persian king Yezdegerd when the king's steward passed them by. R. Ashi observed that Mar Zutra turned pale, dipped his finger into the dish that the steward was carrying, and put his finger in the mouth of Mar Zutra. The officers asked him, "Why did you do that? You have rendered the meal unsuitable for the king."

R. Ashi answered them, "I saw a piece of contaminated meat in the dish." They examined the dish but found nothing contaminated. He pointed with his finger to a part of the dish, and asked, "Did you examine this part?"

They examined it and found it contaminated. The rabbis asked him, "Why did you rely on a miracle?" He answered them, "I saw a sickness hovering over Mar Zutra." (*Ketubbot* 61a–b)

When Amemar, Mar Zutra and R. Ashi dined together, they were served dates and pomegranates. Mar Zutra took some and threw them in front of R. Ashi. R. Ashi said to Mar Zutra, "Does not your honor agree with what was taught – that one should not throw food?" (*Berachot* 50b)

When Amemar, Mar Zutra and R. Ashi sat together, they said, "Let each one of us say something that the others never heard before."

One of them said, "If a person had a dream and does not know its meaning, he should say the prayer for dreams, which starts with the phrase 'Ruler of the World.' It is recited when the Kohanim bless the congregation in the synagogue." The others also said something new. (*Berachot* 55b)

Mar Zutra – some say Mar Ukva – said, "Originally the Torah was given to Israel in the Hebrew language and Hebrew letters. Later on, in the time of Ezra, it was also given in Assyrian square letters and in Aramaic. Finally, they chose the Assyrian script and the Hebrew language." (*Sanhedrin* 21b)

R. Shimon b. Eleazar said in the name of R. Eliezer b. Parta, who said it in the name of R. Eleazar ha-Modai: "The style of the Torah script was never changed." (*Sanhedrin* 22a)

For a glimpse of the world as it was in Mar Zutra's time, see the historical timeline from 350 to 450 C.E.

מר זוטרא
Zutra, Mar II

(fifth–sixth centuries C.E.)
Exilarch, Babylonia

The father of Mar Zutra II was Mar Huna, who was killed by King Firuz of Persia. Mar Zutra defeated the Persians and established an independent Jewish state that lasted for seven years. He and his grandfather, Hanina, were taken prisoner and killed.

For a glimpse of the world as it was in the time of Mar Zutra II, see the historical timeline from 450 to 550 C.E.

LIST OF SIGNIFICANT PLACES
NAMED IN THE TALMUD

Acco

Acco (also called Acre), a coastal city in northern Israel, is located fourteen miles north of Haifa. Already an important town in the fifteenth century B.C.E., it was best known for producing glass.

R. Abba (third–fourth centuries C.E.), who lived in Acco, was the head of the academy there.

Bet She'arim

Bet She'arim, an ancient city in the lower Galilee region of Israel, was located fairly close to Kiryat Tivon and Haifa. **Rabbi Yehuda ha-Nasi** (second–third centuries C.E.), who took up residence in Bet She'arim in 170, moved his academy there. Consequently, Bet She'arim was the seat of the Sanhedrin during his tenure. It is also his burial place.

Hundreds of students attended the academy of Rabbi Yehuda ha-Nasi, who redacted the Mishnah, upon which the whole Gemara is based. He did most of that work in Bet She'arim. The great amoraim of Babylonia, including Rav, studied in Rabbi Yehuda ha-Nasi's academy. Rav eventually established his own academy in Sura, Babylonia.

Excavations of the area revealed burial caves and the remains of large buildings.

Bene Berak

The city of Bene Berak is located in Israel, near Jaffa and Tel Aviv.

During the second century C.E., the tannaitic era, Benai Berak became a center of Jewish learning. **Rabbi Akiva ben Yoseph** (first–second centuries C.E.) established his academy there.

The Hagadah mentions that R. Eliezer, R. Yoshua, R. Eleazar b. Azaryah and R. Tarfon visited R. Akiva in Bene Berak. Such luminaries as Rabbi Meir, Rabbi Shimon ben Yohai and Rabbi Yehuda bar Illai studied in Rabbi Akiva's academy (BT *Sanhedrin* 32b).

Beror Hayil

Beror Hayil, a small community in southern Israel, was located eight miles southeast of Ashkelon.

When **R. Yohanan b. Zakkai** (first century C.E.) moved to Beror Hayil in his later years, many students followed him there (BT *Sanhedrin* 32b).

Caesarea

Caesarea, an ancient city on the Mediterranean coast of Israel, is located between Tel Aviv and Haifa. In Hebrew the city was called Kisri. In 96 B.C.E., King Alexander Yannai captured the city during the Hasmonean wars, and it remained a Jewish city for many years afterwards.

Marcus Antonius gave Caesarea to Cleopatra of Egypt as a gift, but the Emperor Augustus later gave it to Herod, who in turn enlarged it, surrounded it with a wall, and built a deep-sea harbor. When Judea became a Roman province, Caesarea became its capital. The disputes between the Jewish and gentile inhabitants were one of the causes of the war with Rome in 66–70 C.E. Vespasian made Caesarea a Roman colony.

Rabbi Abbahu (third–fourth centuries C.E.), who lived in Caesarea, had a small academy there. He was the people's representative to the Roman governor (BT *Ketubbot* 17a).

Many well-known Talmudic rabbis lived in Caesarea, including R. Abba, R. Adda, R. Hanina, R. Assi, R. Hoshaya, R. Hezkiya, R. Abbahu, R. Ahava, R. Yannai and R. Zeira (BT *Eruvin* 76b).

Jerusalem

Jerusalem was the seat of the Sanhedrin and the academy of learning for many years.

The following people were the heads of the academy in Jerusalem: Shemaya (first century B.C.E.); Avtalyon (first century B.C.E.), Hillel ha-Zaken (first century B.C.E.–first century C.E.); Menachem (first century B.C.E.–first century C.E.); Shammai (first century B.C.E.–first century C.E.); Gamliel ha-Zaken (first century C.E.); and Shimon ben Gamliel (first century C.E.).

Lydda

Lydda (also known as Lod), a town in Israel, is located south of Tel Aviv and Jaffa. During Talmudic times, it was briefly the seat of the Sanhedrin. **Yehoshua b. Levy** (third century C.E.)

was the head of the academy there. Other great Talmudic scholars who taught in Lydda include R. Tarfon, R. Eliezer Hyrcanus, R. Akiva, R. Eleazar b. Kappara and R. Hanina b. Hama.

Demetrius II gave the city to King Yonatan the Hasmonean, and later on Julius Caesar granted some privileges to the Jews of Lydda.

There was a time when the city was detached from Judea due to the fortunes of war. Cestius Gallus, the Roman proconsul, burned Lydda in 351 C.E. on his way to Jerusalem.

The Roman emperor Septimus Severus changed the name of the city during his reign.

Mata Mehasya

Mata Mehasya, a town in Babylonia near Sura, is located on the banks of the Euphrates River. Rabbi Ashi (fourth–fifth centuries C.E.) was the head of the academy there.

Mehoza

Mehoza, a town in Babylonia, is located on the banks of the Tigris River (BT *Berachot* 59b). It is also next to the Malka canal, which connects the Euphrates River with the Tigris. There were many Jewish farmers in Mehoza who owned orchards and fields, raised cattle and traded in grain. In Talmudic times, the town was located on a central trading route through which many caravans passed.

When Odenath and Papa ben Nasser, the commander-in-chief of Palmyra, destroyed the Nehardean academy, Mehoza became a place of learning. It gained prominence after Rabbi Abbaye passed away. Rava, who lived in Mehoza, directed the academy for fourteen years. The large Jewish community in Mehoza constituted a majority of the town's population. When Rabbi Abbaye visited there, he was surprised to find no *mezuzah* on the town's gateposts (BT *Yoma* 11a). Although Emperor Julian destroyed the city in 363, it was later rebuilt.

The Exilarch Mar Zutra II led a successful revolt against the Persians in 513 C.E. He established an independent Jewish state in the area with Mehoza as its capital. The heads of the academy in Mehoza were **Rabbah bar Avuha** (third century C.E.) **Rava** (third–fourth centuries C.E.), and **Amemar** (fourth–fifth centuries C.E.).

Nehardea

The town of Nehardea is located southwest of Baghdad on the Euphrates River, at its junction with the Malka River. It is a fortified city surrounded by walls and protected on one side by the Euphrates River. The Jewish presence in the town dates back to before the destruction of the Temple. According to tradition, the first settlers came when they were exiled from Eretz Yisrael in the sixth century B.C.E., during the time of King Yehoyachim of Judah. According to tradition, they constructed a synagogue with stones and earth brought from Jerusalem and named it Shaf Yativ.

Nehardea, which was the seat of the Exilarch and his bet din, was well known in the Jewish world because of its great academy. Its influence was widespread, particularly during the period when **Rabbi Shemuel** (third century C.E.) was the head of the academy (BT *Ketubbot* 54a).

Many great amoraic scholars lived in Nehardea, including R. Karna, R. Sheila, and Abba b. Abba, who was R.

Shmuel's father. **R. Amemar** lived there in the fourth century C.E.

When Odenath, a rich citizen of Palmyra, led a revolt against King Shapur of Persia, he made incursions into Syria and Palestine. He destroyed the city of Nehardea and the Jewish population of that city.

The amoraim who lived in Nehardea fled to Mehoza and other cities. The daughters of Rabbi Shemuel were taken captive and brought to Sepphoris, where they were held for ransom.

When Odenath was assassinated in 266 C.E., his wife Zenobia succeeded him.

Naresh

Naresh, a town in Babylonia on the banks of the Euphrates, is located south of the old city of Babylon and of Sura. It was situated in a hilly district and spread over a wide area (BT *Eruvin* 56a).

The Jews of Naresh were farmers. Among the best-known products made there were thick felt cloth and blankets (BT *Yoma* 69a).

Naresh was well known in Talmudic circles because **Rabbi Pappa** (fourth century C.E.) established a successful academy there to which students flocked. **R. Huna b. Yoshua** was the head of the Kalla.

Nitzivin

Nitzivin (Nisibis) was a community in North-eastern Mesopotamia. **R. Yehuda b. Betera** (BT *Sanhedrin* 32b; second century C.E.) established an academy there.

Pekiin

Pekiin, a village in Israel's upper Galilee region, is the place where, according to tradition, Rabbi Shimon bar Yohai and his son, Rabbi Eleazar, hid in a cave for thirteen years during the Hadrianic persecutions (BT *Sanhedrin* 32b). After the destruction of the Temple, **Rabbi Yehoshua ben Hananya** (first–second century C.E.) settled in Pekiin and established a yeshiva there, which he headed. The grave of Rabbi Yosi of Pekiin is located in the village.

Pumbedita

Pumbedita, a town in Babylonia located northwest of Baghdad, is situated on the bank of the Euphrates River, near the canals of Shunya-Shumvatha (BT *Gittin* 60b) and Papa (BT *Yoma* 77b).

According to some sources, Jewish settlement in Pumbedita dated back to the time of the second Temple. In 259 C.E., Nehardea and its academy were destroyed by Odenath and Papa ben Nasser. When the scholars from Nehardea fled, they established an academy in Pumbedita under the leadership of Rabbi Yehuda b. Yehezkel. The academy of Pumbedita was the central religious authority for the Babylonian Jewry for many centuries.

The heads of the academy in Pumbedita were **Yehuda bar Yechezkel** (third century C.E.); **Rabbah** (third–fourth centuries C.E.); **Yoseph b. Hiyya** (third–fourth centuries C.E.), **Abbaye** (third–fourth centuries C.E.), **Bibi bar Abbaye** (third–fourth centuries C.E.); **Nahman b. Yitzhak** (third–fourth centuries C.E.); **Hama** (fourth century C.E.);

Dimi of Nehardea (fourth century C.E.); **Rafram b. Papa** (fourth–fifth centuries C.E.); **Rehumei II** (fifth century C.E.).

Pum Nahara

Pum Nahara (also called Pur Nahara) is mentioned in BT *Berachot* 31a. R. Kahana escorted R. Shimi b. Ashi from Pum Nahara to Bei Tzenitha in Babylonia. When they arrived, he asked him: "Do people really say that these palm trees are from the time of Adam?"

R. Kahana V (fourth century C.E.) was the head of the academy in Pum Nahara.

Sepphoris

Sepphoris (Zippori), an ancient city in Israel, is located in the Galilee, north of Caesarea and south of Acco. During King Alexander Yannai's reign, it had many inhabitants and was the administrative capital of the Galilee. It became the seat of the Patriarchate and of the Sanhedrin under Rabbi Yehuda ha-Nasi. When the Talmud advises scholars to follow their teachers to their locations, it mentions to follow Rabbi Yosi ben Halafta to Sepphoris (BT *Sanhedrin* 32b).

Elsewhere (BT *Shabbat* 33b) it is mentioned that that Rabbi Yosi was exiled to his hometown of Sepphoris.

The following were the heads of the academy in Sepphoris: **Yehuda ha-Nasi** (second–third century C.E.); **Hanina bar Hama** (third century C.E.); **Mani** (fourth century C.E.).

Sichnin

Sichnin (or Sikhnin) in the Galilee, was located three miles from Arabah.

The Talmud advises scholars to follow their teachers to their locations and mentions following **Rabbi Hananya ben Teradyon** (BT *Sanhedrin* 32b, second century C.E.) to Sikhnin.

Sura

Sura, a town in Babylonia south of Baghdad, is situated on the banks of the Euphrates River, where the river divides into two branches. An important Torah center for several centuries, it was also an important agricultural area, where the rabbis of the Talmud were active in farming, planting vineyards, producing wine, raising cattle and engaging in trade.

Sura became a famous center of learning in 219, when Rav moved there and established his famous yeshiva, which attracted hundreds of students and scholars.

When Rav passed away in 247, the academy lost its preeminence to Nehardea for seven years. However, when Rabbi Shemuel of Nehardea passed away in 254, Sura regained its role under the leadership of Rabbi Huna.

The following people were the heads of the academy in Sura: **Rav** (third century C.E.); **Huna** (third century C.E.); **Hisda** (third–fourth centuries C.E.); **Rabbah bar Huna** (third–fourth centuries C.E.); **Meremar** (fourth–fifth centuries C.E.); **Ashi** (fourth–fifth centuries C.E.); **Rova Tosfaah** (fifth century C.E.); **Mar b. R. Ashi** (fifth century C.E.), and **Ravina** (fifth century C.E.).

Tekoa

Tekoa, a small town in Judea, Israel; is located south of Jerusalem and Bethlehem. It is the birthplace of the prophet Amos.

R. Shimon b. Yohai (second century C.E.) established an academy in Tekoa, at which R. Yehuda Hanasi studied.

Tiberias

Tiberias (Hebrew: Teveryah) is a city in Israel on the western shore of the Sea of Galilee. Herod Antipas, the son of Herod, founded the city in the first century C.E. Built on steep slopes spread over a wide area, the city rises from below sea level to approximately eight hundred feet above. It is famous for its hot springs, in which the water temperature reaches the boiling point. Rabbi Shimon ben Yohai lived there briefly, and the sages of the time established the seat of the Sanhedrin there. Tiberias was also the seat of the famous rabbinical academy in Eretz Yisrael.

The graves of several great sages, including Rabbi Yohanan ben Zakkai, Rabbi Meir Ba'al ha-Nes, Rabbi Akiva, Rabbi Ammi and Rabbi Assi, are located in Tiberias. Several of the great amoraim taught there, including R. Yohanan, R. Shimon b. Lakish, R. Eleazar b. Pedat, R. Ammi b. Nathan and R. Assi.

The following were the heads of the academy in Tiberias: **Yohanan ben Nepaha** (third century C.E.); **Eleazar ben Pedat** (third century C.E.); **Yehuda Nesia** (third century C.E.); **Ammi bar Nathan** (third–fourth centuries C.E.); **Assi** (third–fourth centuries C.E.); **Yehuda Nesia III** (third–fourth centuries C.E.); **Hillel II** (fourth century C.E.); **Yirmiyahu b. Abba** (fourth century C.E.); **Yonah** (fourth century C.E.); **Yosi** (fourth century C.E.).

Usha

Usha, a town in Israel, is located south of Acco and west of Tiberias. **R. Yehuda b. Illai** lived there. After the suppression of the Bar Kochva revolt, the rabbis of the time convened a meeting at Usha. They enacted far-reaching legislation that the defeated Jewish people needed urgently (see BT *Ketubbot* 49b and 50a). Those present at the meeting included Rabbi Yehuda bar Illai, R. Nehemia, R. Meir, R. Yosi ben Halafta, R. Shimon bar Yohai, R. Eliezer b. Yosi ha-Gelili and R. Eliezer b. Yaakov. Rabbi Shimon b. Gamliel (head of the Sanhedrin, second century C.E.) was still in hiding.

Yavne

Yavne, an ancient biblical city in Israel, is located south of Jaffa and north of Ashdod. During the Hasmonean period, it had its share of conflict. Yonathan the Hasmonean fought one of the decisive battles nearby. Shimon the Hasmonean also fought nearby and captured Yavne. After the fall of Jerusalem, the Sanhedrin moved its location there from Jerusalem. Although at first, the Sanhedrin was under the leadership of Rabbi Yohanan ben Zakkai, later on Rabbi Gamliel II became Nasi.

The academy in Yavne was called the Sanhedrin. As a legislative institution, it served not only as an academy of learning, but also as the highest court in the land. Because the Sanhedrin met on the upper floor of a house that was located in a vineyard, was called the Kerem be-Yavne (the Vineyard at Yavne).

At one time, Yavne was a thriving city with its own markets for cattle and wheat. It was a center for Torah study even before the destruction of the second Temple. At that time, it had a bet din of twenty-three members that decided capital cases (BT *Sanhedrin* 11:4).

The following were the heads of the academy in Yavne: **R. Yohanan b. Zakkai** (first century C.E.); **Gamliel ben Shimon de-Yavne** (first–second centuries C.E.); and **Eleazar ben Azaryah** (first–second centuries C.E.)

WORLD AND JEWISH HISTORY
DURING THE TALMUDIC PERIOD

THE PURPOSE of this historical overview is not to provide a detailed history of the periods under examination, but to highlight some of the events that occurred during the Talmudic era. It highlights the people and events that influenced Jewish life at the time.

We begin with the first Jewish exile to Babylonia, which corresponds more or less to the period of the authorship of the Talmud.

600–550 B.C.E.

King Amon, the son of King Menashe, reigned for only two years before he was assassinated. His son, Yoshiyahu, succeeded to the throne of Judea at the age of eight. A God-fearing man and a good king, he destroyed all the idols and banned idol worship.

In 608 B.C.E., Necho, king of Egypt, went to war against the powers of the Euphrates. In order to reach his enemies, he had to pass through Judea and Israel. Yoshiyahu, who decided to oppose him, was defeated and killed in the battle against Necho at Megiddo (Kings 23:29, 30).

That same year, the people anointed Yehoahaz, Yoshiyahu's second son, king of Judea. Necho, who did not approve, removed him and imprisoned him in Egypt, installing Elyakim, Yoshiyahu's eldest son, on the throne in 607 B.C.E. (Kings 23:31–33). Elyakim reigned until 576 B.C.E. (Kings 23:34–36).

Unlike his father Yoshiyahu, who had been loyal to God, Elyakim reverted to the idolatrous ways of past kings such as Omri and Ahab. Although the prophet Jeremiah warned the people of God's anger, they refused to listen and sought to kill him. Several princes who believed Yirmiyahu's prophecies rescued him.

The prophets Nahum and Zephaniah prophesied the fall of Assyria. Indeed, the Chaldean general Nabopolassar seized the Babylonian throne, conquered the Assyrian empire and took over its capital, Nineveh. Judea was thus thrown into the sphere of the Babylonian empire.

In 605 B.C.E., Nabopolassar's son, Nebuchadnezzar, succeeded his father as king of Babylonia. When Necho of Egypt decided to go to war against the young king, thinking that he would be easy to defeat, Nebuchadnezzar, who despite his age was an experienced warrior, defeated the Egyptians at Carchemish in 603 B.C.E. Yirmiyahu's prophecy of Egypt's defeat – which freed Judea temporarily from Egyptian domination – was thus confirmed. Jeremiah also predicted that Babylonia would become a great power once more.

Nebuchadnezzar, who wished to conquer Egypt, started a campaign of conquest. Syria surrendered without resistance, as did Ithobal, king of Phoenicia. With Judea between Egypt and his army, Nebuchadnezzar offered Elyakim a choice between subjugation and annihilation.

At first, Elyakim agreed to the terms and made peace with Nebuchadnezzar, but when he later changed his mind and formed an alliance with Egypt and Phoenicia, he refused to pay the required tribute to him (II Kings 24:1).

In 597 B.C.E., Elyakim died. His son Yehoyachin, who succeeded him, was king for only three months (II Kings 24:8).

That same year, Nebuchadnezzar advanced towards Jerusalem. He captured Yehoyachin and exiled him and his family to Babylonia. He placed Tzidkiyahu, Yoshiyahu's youngest son, on the throne, and plundered the Temple and the country, taking many artisans and thousands of citizens to Babylonia (II Kings 24:17).

In approximately 590 B.C.E., the prophet Yehezkel appeared on the scene. He was carried away to Babylonia with King Yehoyachin and the other exiles.

In 587 B.C.E., on the tenth day of the tenth month, Nebuchadnezzar and his army began the siege of Jerusalem (II Kings 25:1), which lasted for more than a year. Egypt had promised to help, but hesitated. When King Apries of Egypt finally sent a strong army against Nebuchadnezzar, the siege of Jerusalem was lifted temporarily. But in 586 B.C.E., Nebuchadnezzar's army routed the Egyptians, leaving Judea to fend for itself.

The siege resumed, and the city's inhabitants suffered terribly from starvation. Children died in their mothers' arms. Many people fled the city, some even going over to the Babylonians.

The Babylonians entered the city of Jerusalem and plundered it, massacring the priests and desecrating the Temple. Tzidkiyahu managed to escape the city with some of his officers, but they were captured before they could cross the Jordan.

Tzidkiyahu and his family were taken before Nebuchadnezzar, who ordered his sons killed before his eyes and Tzidkiyahu blinded. He then had Tzidkiyahu sent to Babylonia in chains (II Kings 25:7).

On the ninth of Av, 586 BCE, the walls of Jerusalem were razed to the ground, the Temple and the palaces were burned and all the holy vessels were broken to pieces or carried away.

Nebuchadnezzar then appointed Gedalyah as governor of the territories. He wanted a peaceful Judea because he needed an open highway that would allow him to reach Egypt, which he wished to conquer. Gedalyah made Mitzpah the governor's residence, and many of the farmers and working people who were allowed to remain in Judea were content to have him as their governor.

In 582 B.C.E., a Judean prince by the name of Yishmael assassinated Gedalyah at a banquet (II Kings 25:25). Afterwards, many of the people who still lived in Judea, including Jeremiah the prophet, fled to Egypt. Judea subsequently became depopulated, and that same year, its last 745 inhabitants were taken to Babylonia.

Many of the Judean captives were taken to the city of Babylon. Nebuchadnezzar enlarged the city, assigning districts to the captives of various nationalities, including the Jews, and their families.

In 561 B.C.E., after having reigned for forty-three years, Nebuchadnezzar died. He was succeeded by his son Evilmerodach, who released Yehoyachin after thirty-seven years' imprisonment (II Kings 25:27). However, in 560 B.C.E., Evilmerodach was assassinated by his brother-in-law Neriglissar who, in turn, was overthrown by Nabonad, a Chaldean nobleman, who became king in 555 B.C.E.

Cyrus, a Persian warrior, overthrew his father-in-law, the Median king Styages, and took the Median throne.

550–500 B.C.E.

In his prophecy, Yeshayahu predicted that Cyrus would conquer Babylonia (Yeshayah 44 and 45). Cyrus entered the city of Babylonia in 539 B.C.E. after a war that lasted two years. With the conquest of Babylonia, Cyrus was king not only of Persia but also of all the territories that had been in its possession, including Judea.

In 537 B.C.E., Cyrus allowed the Judean exiles to return to Jerusalem and rebuild the Temple. A written proclamation was issued throughout the empire. Mithradat, the royal treasurer, was commanded to hand over the holy vessels from the Temple that Nebuchadnezzar had stolen (Ezra 1:7–11 and Divrei ha-Yamim 36:22–23).

Cyrus appointed Zerubavel, a grandson of Yehoyachin, the last king of Judea, governor of the Judean territory. Zerubavel formed a council of twelve leaders that included Yoshua, the grandson of Sherayah, the last high priest in Jerusalem.

In approximately 537 B.C.E., 42,360 men, women and children joined the expedition to return to Jerusalem (Ezra 2:64).

Upon Cyrus's death in 529 B.C.E., his son Cambyses became king of Persia.

The new arrivals started building the Temple, but the foreigners who settled the land during the absence of the Jews, particularly the Samaritans, wanted to take part in building the Temple. Zerubavel rejected their offer because he did not consider them to be Jews.

When Cambyses died in 521 B.C.E., Darius succeeded to the throne, reigning until 485 B.C.E.

The prophet Haggai encouraged the people to build the Temple, and Zecharyah the Prophet spoke to the people in order to awaken their love for Zion.

The foreigners of the land caused problems, sending letters to the king in which they wrote that the Jews were planning a rebellion (Ezra 4:1–24). The building of the Temple was stalled for fifteen years due to unfavorable conditions in the land. Once construction resumed in 519, it took four years. The rebuilt Temple was dedicated before Pesah of 516 B.C.E.

In approximately 600 B.C.E., when Judea was an independent kingdom and the Temple was at the height of its splendor, Rome was one of many city-states on the Italian peninsula. In ancient Rome, the people were divided into an upper class, a middle class and a lower class. In 508 B.C.E. Rome established itself as a republic, which lasted until 49 B.C.E. The power rested in the Senate and in the assembly.

500–450 B.C.E.

Between 496 and 272 B.C.E. there were many wars between Rome and the various city states of Italy. Rome finally won.

In 494 B.C.E., a large group of the lower class seceded from Rome, withdrawing to a mountain near the Anio River, three miles from Rome, a place that they held to be sacred. They were protesting the treatment they received from the upper classes, and they demanded cancellation of their debts.

In 451 B.C.E., Rome adopted new laws. They were written on twelve tablets and displayed for all to see. For nine hundred years, these twelve tablets were the basic law of Rome.

Darius of Persia died in 485 B.C.E. He was succeeded by Xerxes (who is identified with Ahashverosh), whose reign lasted until 465 B.C.E., when he was assassinated. Xerxes was succeeded by Artaxerxes, who reigned from 465 to 424 B.C.E.

450–400 B.C.E.

In 458 BCE Ezra ben Seraya the Sofer (scribe) went up from Babylon to Jerusalem with 1600 men, together with their wives and children. He brought with him a letter from King Artaxerxes (Ezra 7:1–8), who sent costly gifts for the sanctuary.

Ezra was a descendant of the high priests. When he arrived in Judea, he found that many of the Jewish people in Judea had intermarried with the local non-Jewish population, who had been settled there by the occupying powers while the Jews were in exile. Many Jews in Judea intermarried and no longer lived by the Torah. Those who remained observant complained to Ezra as soon as he arrived, telling him about the intermarriages. On hearing these reports, Ezra became distressed, rent his garments and began a fast (Ezra 9:4). Shechanya, one of the old residents, suggested that all the marriages be dissolved (Ezra 10:2).

Ezra accepted the suggestion. He gathered all the people and made them promise to dissolve their marriages and to swear to uphold the laws of the Torah. Many people, including prominent leaders of the community, refused to divorce their wives. The terrible friction between those who favored intermarriage and those who opposed it lasted from 457 to 444 B.C.E.

The Samaritans, who were also belligerent, went to war against the Jews. Their leader, Sanballat, led an army and made an open attack on Jerusalem.

A delegation of Judeans from Jerusalem went to Persia in 445 B.C.E. to ask for help. They spoke to Nehemia, a prominent Jew who was Artaxerxes's cup-bearer. Hanani, a relative of Nehemia, was a member of the delegation (Nehemia 1:2).

Nehemia decided to go to Jerusalem, but waited for the right moment to ask the king's permission. The opportunity presented itself and the king gave him his blessing, even sending soldiers to protect him and appointing him governor (Nehemia 2:1–8).

Nehemia arrived in Jerusalem in 444 B.C.E. In addition to being the king's cupbearer, he was also independently wealthy (Nehemia 2:11). Upon his arrival, he did not reveal himself to the people, but first inspected the fortifications, where he found breaches in the wall (Nehemia 2:13).

After inspecting the walls he introduced himself to the elders of the city and told them that he came in the name of the king. He gave order to rebuild the walls.

Sanballat, the leader of the Samaritans, tried to undermine everything that Nehemia tried to build. Although his troops attacked, they were repulsed (Nehemia 4:1–17).

Nehemia lectured the people about observing God's commandments. In 444 B.C.E., he began a project to repopulate the city of Jerusalem and erected a citadel to protect the Temple. He placed Persian soldiers in the Birah. Ezra, who had remained in the background for some time, came forth to teach the people and to read to them from the Torah. The institution of the *Anshei knesseth ha-gedola* was born approximately during this time.

Nehemia encouraged people to move into the city of Jerusalem, even constructing homes at his own expense for those who could not afford to do so. He was governor from 444 to 432 B.C.E.

Menashe, a member of the high priestly family, married Nicaso, the daughter of Sanballat. This upset Nehemia very much. Although he later returned to Persia, in his absence the people in Judea returned to their old ways, and intermarriages resumed as before.

With the permission of King Artaxerxes, Nehemia returned to Jerusalem a second time, from approximately 430 to 425 B.C.E. (Nehemia13:6).

Another impropriety occurred at this time when Elyashiv, the high priest, gave a home on Temple property to Toviya, an Ammonite. In addition, when a grandson of Elyashiv married another daughter of Sanballat and refused to divorce her, Nehemia removed Elyashiv from the priesthood.

Nehemia urged the people to observe Shabbat and lectured them about its importance (Nehemia 13:15–22). He locked the gates of the city on that day in order to keep the vendors out.

Sanballat built a temple on top of Mount Gerizim for the Samaritans. This temple competed with the Temple in Jerusalem.

On the urging of Ezra and Nehemia, a seventy-one member court was instituted in Jerusalem. Most of its members were scholars, and the Nasi presided. This court, which explained and interpreted the Torah as it applied to new situations, laid the foundation for the Talmud.

400–350 B.C.E.

Artaxerxes II reigned in Persia from 404 to 362 B.C.E. He was succeeded by Artaxerxes III, who reigned from 361 to 338 B.C.E.

When Yoyada, the high priest, died, his younger son Yoshua bribed Bagoas, a eunuch in the court of Artaxerxes III and a commander of the troops in Syria, to appoint him high priest. Angry at having been passed over, Yoshua's older brother, Yohanan, killed his younger brother. When Bagoas heard what had happened, he came to Jerusalem and forced the country to pay him a huge sum of money, otherwise he would not permit the daily sacrifices. This state of affairs continued for seven years.

350–300 B.C.E.

When Philip of Macedonia was assassinated in Aegae in 336 B.C.E., he was succeeded by Alexander the Great, who ruled until 323 B.C.E.

Alexander the Great conquered Tyre and Jerusalem in 332 B.C.E. and appointed the first governor over Coele-Syria, which included Jerusalem. He defeated Darius at Gaugamela in 331 B.C.E.

The Samaritans, who occupied an area that had formerly belonged to Israel, rebelled against Alexander and killed Andromachus, the Macedonian governor of Samaria.

Alexander avenged the assassination by killing the perpetrators and by appointing Memnon as the new governor. Knowing that the Samaritans hated the Judeans, he showed favor to Judeans by freeing Judea from all taxes during the Sabbatical year, 331 B.C.E., and giving Judea a stretch of territory that was claimed by both the Samaritans and Judea.

When Alexander died in 323 B.C.E., leaving no successor who was able to lead a great empire, his empire split. Ptolemy reigned over Egypt and after a successful war he took over Coele-Syria and Judaea.

In 312 B.C.E., General Antigonus and his son Demetrius fought against Ptolemy I, who emerged the victor in the war over Alexander's empire that took place in Gaza. However, in a subsequent battle, Ptolemy was forced to retreat to Egypt. Antigonus was killed in battle in 301 B.C.E., leaving the empire to be divided among the four generals Ptolemy, Lysimachus, Cassander and Seleucus. Judea became part of the Ptolemaic kingdom in 301 B.C.E.

The descendants of Seleucus, the general who won the war for Ptolemy I, became heirs to part of Alexander's empire. Judea, Babylonia and some Persian cities formed part of the Seleucid kingdom.

300–250 B.C.E.

Shimon ha-Zaddik (Simon the Just, son of Onias I) flourished from approximately 300 to 270 B.C.E. The High Priest, he was also the nation's political leader. He rebuilt and fortified the walls of Jerusalem and made many improvements to the Temple, which was in great disrepair. He also built a reservoir underneath the Temple and connected it to the fresh-water well of Etam via a subterranean canal.

In the third century B.C.E., Carthage – a Semitic city on the African continent near Tunis, with a language that was similar to Hebrew – possessed what was probably the most powerful navy of its time and reached its zenith. In 264 B.C.E., following Carthage's successful conquest of Sicily, Rome went to war against Carthage in what would be the first of the three Punic wars. The Roman soldiers were led by Regulus and the Carthaginians by Hamilcar.

Carthage and Rome fought a great sea battle in 256 B.C.E. Although the Romans were victorious, after landing in Africa the Roman fleet was destroyed and their general, Regulus, was taken into captivity, where he died five years later.

250–200 B.C.E.

When Rome and Carthage fought again in 241 B.C.E., Rome landed in Sicily and retook the part of it that had been occupied by Carthage. Hamilcar invaded Spain and captured several cities there, but died in battle in 229 B.C.E.

In 221 BCE Hamilcar's son Hannibal succeeded him at the age of twenty-six.

In Judea, a man named Tobias married the daughter of Shimon ha-Zaddik. Tobias's son, Joseph, was appointed ambassador to Egypt in order to negotiate and to settle a dispute. Joseph became the tax-collector for the Egyptians in Syria, Phoenicia and Judea, the territories that Egypt controlled, outbidding all other bidders for the job. Egypt provided him with two thousand mercenaries to enforce the tax collection.

He served in this capacity for twenty-two years. At this time, Judea was under Egyptian rule.

When Ptolemy III, ruler of Egypt, died in 222 B.C.E., Ptolemy IV became king of Egypt, reigning until 206 B.C.E.

Antiochus fought Egypt for control of Coele-Syria and won, also capturing Samaria. Ptolemy IV counterattacked and won a decisive victory against Antiochus at Raphia. Because Joseph remained loyal to Egypt, Judea was left in peace.

In 218 B.C.E. Hannibal crossed the Ebro with fifty thousand infantry and thousands of cavalry. Although he crossed the Alps in seventeen days, he sustained heavy losses due to landslides, ice and freezing.

In 217 B.C.E., Carthage and the Roman army fought again. The Roman forces suffered a humiliating defeat, which lasted on and off for over a year.

Phillip V of Macedonia allied himself with Hannibal against Rome in 214 B.C.E.

In 202 B.C.E., Hannibal returned to Carthage after a long absence. At the age of forty-five, he was half-blind, having lost one eye to some unknown illness. He engaged the Romans but was defeated, and Carthage sued for peace.

When Joseph died in 208 B.C.E. in Judea, his youngest son Hyrcan by his second wife inherited the tax collecting job. Joseph had seven sons from his first wife. Dissention and hatred broke out between Hyrcan and his brothers.

When Hyrcan was openly attacked by his brothers, he fled to Egypt. He was counting on Egypt to help him, but in 206 B.C.E. Ptolemy IV died. In addition, both Antiochus of Syria and Philip of Macedonia went to war against Egypt.

In Judea, Hyrcan's brothers sided with Antiochus, and opened the gates of Jerusalem to him. In 202 B.C.E., Egypt had to give up Jerusalem to Antiochus and the Seleucids.

In 201 B.C.E., Egypt sent a mercenary army under the command of General Scopas to make war on Antiochus. This army conquered Jerusalem, causing much destruction and killing many of the residents. In the next battle, which took place near Mount Hermon, Judea became a battleground and Egypt was defeated.

Rome sent Scipio Africanus to liberate Spain from occupation by Hannibal. In 205 B.C.E. he captured most of the Spanish cities and Spain became a Roman province.

Rome then asked Scipio to invade Carthage, putting an army at his disposal. Hannibal was still tied down with his army in Italy. Carthage sent an urgent appeal to Hannibal, asking him to return in order to save his homeland.

Hannibal had to flee several times due to plots against his life. He fled to Antioch, which became his ally against Rome. In 184 B.C.E. he lost the war against Rome and, rather than face capture, committed suicide by poison.

200–150 B.C.E.

In 200 B.C.E., Rome sent a fleet against Macedonia under a thirty-year-old commander, Quintius Flaminius, who overwhelmed and defeated Phillip in 197 B.C.E.

Antiochus III of Syria took Judea from Egypt in 198 B.C.E.

The Roman Senate sent Scipio Africanus with a Roman army to Asia in 189 B.C.E. to fight against Antiochus III. Scipio was victorious. In that same year, Parthia absorbed Persia and Mesopotamia into its dominion. Antiochus III died approximately two years later, in 187 B.C.E.

About this time a party known as the Hasidim was formed in Judea. Among its members were two outstanding teachers: Yosi ben Yoezer of Zereda and Yosi ben Yohanan from Jerusalem. Between them, they directed two academies.

The high priest, Onias III, the son of Simon II, was also the country's political leader at this time. A pious man, he had no tolerance for wrongdoing. He was also a friend of Hyrcan the tax collector, who was still hated by his brothers, but was a favorite of the Egyptian king Ptolemy V Epiphanes. Consequently, Hyrcan's brothers were enemies of the high priest.

Seleucus IV became king of Coele-Syria, to which Judea was subject, in 187 B.C.E. He was assassinated in 175 B.C.E. by a palace courtier and succeeded by his brother, Antiochus Epiphanes.

There was great strife in Judea between Onias and the Hellenists, who tried to undermine him at every opportunity. In 174 B.C.E. Onias's brother, Joshua, who was also called Jason, offered Antiochus a large sum of money to appoint him to the high priesthood. Antiochus accepted, and Joshua subsequently became high priest.

Joshua encouraged Hellenization and Jewish participation in the Olympic Games, sending a delegation to the Olympic Games in 172 B.C.E., which took place in Tyre. Nevertheless, he was also a traditionalist and a strong nationalist.

Menelaus, one of the sons of Joseph, offered Antiochus a bigger annual bribe to be appointed high priest. Antiochus accepted it, and in 172 B.C.E. he appointed Menelaus as high priest. But Menelaus, a Benjaminite, was not a descendent of the priestly family. Moreover, he did not have the money that he had promised Antiochus. Therefore, he took many of the sacred vessels from the Temple and sold them in order to raise the sum.

Onias was about to accuse Menelaus of robbing the Temple, but Menelaus bribed Antiochus's representative, Andronicus, to assassinate Onias. The assassination caused an uprising among the population, and Antiochus was compelled to sentence Andronicus to death.

The people of Judaea sent three elders to Antiochus to accuse Menelaus of having robbed the Temple. However, Menelaus bribed a high official who influenced Antiochus. As a result, he was acquitted and his accusers condemned to death.

Perseus, king of Macedonia, went to war against Rome in 171 B.C.E. He was defeated and taken in captivity to Rome.

Cleopatra, the wife of Ptolemy IV, was the sister of Antiochus. When Ptolemy died, he was survived by two young sons, Philometor, the designated heir, and Physcon. Both had guardians.

Antiochus Epiphanes wanted to conquer Egypt. On the pretext that he needed to protect his nephew Philometor from his guardians, he invaded Egypt in 170 B.C.E. On his way to Egypt, he plundered Jerusalem, massacring the population.

When Antiochus Epiphanes undertook another war against Egypt, Rome intervened, giving Antiochus an ultimatum. He decided to leave Egypt.

In 168 B.C.E., Antiochus Epiphanes issued a decree that all Judeans must cease to obey the laws of the Torah and offer sacrifices to the Greek gods only. Observance of the Sabbath and the dietary laws and the practice of circumcision were outlawed.

Antiochus sent his representatives and troops to Jerusalem in 168 B.C.E. in order to enforce the new decrees. On the seventeenth of Tammuz, his representatives forced the people to dedicate the Temple to the Olympian god Zeus, offering a pig on the altar. Its flesh was cooked, and Menelaus the High Priest and other Judeans were forced to partake of it.

Matisyahu the Hasmonean of the town of Modiin and his five sons – Yohanan, Shimon, Yehuda, Eleazar and Yonatan – decided to fight back. When Apelles, the Syrian official, came to Modiin to enforce the laws and one of the Judeans was about to offer a sacrifice to Zeus; Matisyahu killed him with his dagger. His sons killed the Syrian troops, starting the Maccabean revolution.

Many Judeans joined in the fighting. Hiding in caves at first, when they came across a small contingent of Syrian troops they destroyed them. When Matisyahu died in 167 B.C.E., his son Yehuda, surnamed the Maccabee (hammer), became the commander of the revolution.

In the first open battle between the Syrian forces under the command of Apollonius in 166 B.C.E., Yehuda was victorious, and Apollonius was killed in battle. The Syrians came back with a stronger army and under a new commander, Horon. Yehuda and his small army defeated the larger Syrian forces. Many of them were killed and the rest fled to the mountains.

Antiochus sent a much larger force under the command of Gorgias. The battle was fought at Emmaus in 166 B.C.E., and the Judeans under the command of Yehuda was victorious again.

Lysias, the foremost general of Antiochus's army, led a large force against Judea once again. The battle was fought at Beth Tzur in the autumn of 165 B.C.E., and once more the Judeans were victorious. On the twenty fifth of Kislev 165 B.C.E., the Temple was consecrated to Jewish service once again.

Antiochus Epiphanes died in 164 B.C.E. in a fit of insanity. Before his death, he appointed Philippus as regent and guardian of his young son, Antiochus V Eupator.

After Antiochus died, Lysias besieged Jerusalem until the situation in the city became desperate. Suddenly Lysias had to retreat because Philippus, who was making a bid for the throne, marched against him. Thus the siege on Jerusalem was lifted and its inhabitants saved from certain death. Yet before Lysias left, he executed the high priest Menelaus, who had been the cause of so much misery.

Since Onias III, the son of the former high priest, was living in Egypt, Yehuda the Maccabee was appointed to that high office. Prince Demetrius, who was a hostage in Rome, managed to flee, and removed Eupator and Lysias from the Syrian throne.

Two Judean dissidents, Yakim and Alchimus, both Hellenists, took advantage of the new situation and brought complaints against Yehuda Maccabee to Demetrius, the new king of Syria. When Alchimus bribed the king with expensive gifts, he removed Yehuda Maccabee from the high priesthood, replacing him with Alchimus who, as the newly-appointed high priest, came to Jerusalem accompanied by a Syrian army under the command of Bacchides.

Suspecting that there might be trouble, Yehuda the Maccabee fled to the mountains. The scholars and the Hasidim were deceived into trusting Alchimus, and the Great Assembly welcomed both him and Bacchides. But the suspicions of Yehuda the Maccabee proved true. As soon as Alchimus took possession of the city in 161 B.C.E., he ordered Bacchides to execute sixty scholars of the Great Assembly. Among the condemned was his own uncle, Rabbi Yosi ben Yoezer. In the wake of the murders, the people revolted, joining Yehuda the Maccabee in order to fight against the Hellenists and the Syrians.

King Demetrius of Syria sent his general, Nicanor, to suppress the revolt. Yehuda was victorious and Nicanor was killed in battle. On hearing of Nicanor's defeat, Demetrius sent a larger force to suppress the Judeans. Yehuda was compelled to flee to the south. In 160 B.C.E., the Syrians defeated the much smaller Judaean army, and Yehuda the Maccabee was killed.

After Yehuda's death, his brother Yonatan became the leader of the Hasmoneans. He changed the Judean army's tactics, using guerrilla warfare rather than open battle.

Alchimus, the high priest, was struck with paralysis in 159 B.C.E. and died soon afterwards. Onias, the legitimate heir to the high priesthood, remained in Egypt. In 153 B.C.E., he built a Temple to the God of Israel in the Egyptian town of Leontopolis. Although the exterior did not look like the Temple in Jerusalem, the interior had many vessels that resembled those that were used there. Priests offered sacrifices in this temple.

King Philometor behaved kindly toward his Jewish subjects, providing for the maintenance of the temple in Leontopolis. At about this time, in approximately 153 B.C.E., the Torah was translated into Greek.

150–100 B.C.E.

A rival to King Demetrius of Syria, by the name of Alexander, came upon the scene. Both sought the alliance of Yonatan the Maccabee, allowing him to return to Jerusalem and to raise an army. In the course of Yonatan's government; from 160 to 144 B.C.E., he made many improvements in order to enhance the welfare of the country.

Yonatan made an alliance with Alexander Balas of Syria. He ignored Demetrius's promises, remaining loyal to Alexander, who finally vanquished Demetrius. Alexander reigned in Syria from 152 to 146 B.C.E.

King Philometor of Egypt was succeeded by his brother, Ptolemy VII Physcon. Cleopatra, the mother of the former king and who ran the government in the interim, was an opponent of Ptolemy. When Physcon and Cleopatra quarreled, a compromise was reached. Physcon married his sister in 145 B.C.E. and they reigned jointly.

Tryphon, the commander-in-chief of the Syrian army, was the regent for the young king Antiochus V, who inherited the throne of Syria from his father Alexander Balas. Tryphon removed the young king and put the crown on his own head, but Yonathan from Judea remained loyal to the young king.

Nevertheless, Tryphon turned against Yonatan and broke all treaties and promises. He wanted to remove Yonatan from the Judean throne and was prepared to use treachery in order to do so. He invited Yonatan to turn the city of Acco over to him. When Yonatan arrived, he was arrested, and Tryphon's troops butchered his guards.

Yonatan's brother Simon, an old man by this time, took up arms. He acted with vigor and was assisted by four sons. All records for Simon's kingship were dated from that year – 142 B.C.E. – and coins were minted. In 143 B.C.E., Simon raised an army and went against Tryphon, who ordered the execution of Yonatan.

The king of Syria was bitter at the defeat he suffered at the hands of Simon's forces. He conspired with Simon's son-in-law, Ptolemy ben Habib, who was governor of Jericho. Ptolemy's ambition was to become ruler of Judea. In 135 B.C.E. he invited Simon for a feast in his honor, and in the midst of the festivities, his band fell upon Simon and his two sons and murdered them.

Yohanan, Simon's oldest son, did not attend the party in Jericho. Before Ptolemy and the Syrian forces could reach him, he was warned in advance and was ready for them. In the subsequent fight, Yohanan won. His brother-in-law, Ptolemy, locked himself in his castle. Yohanan became king of Judea in 135 B.C.E. Yohanan Hyrcanus extended the boundaries of his country. His brother-in-law fled the land across the Jordan.

In 134 B.C.E., Antiochus Sidetes of Syria invaded the country again. There was a long siege of Jerusalem. A peace was negotiated and a large sum of money paid for the enemy to go away.

In 152 B.C.E. Rome went to war again against Carthage. After three years of fighting, Carthage was defeated and the city burned to the ground.

In 146 B.C.E., Rome invaded and conquered Greece which, together with Macedonia, became a Roman province.

Yohanan Hyrcanus of Judea sent ambassadors to Rome in 133 B.C.E. to complain against Antiochus Sidetes. Rome ordered him to restore all fortresses to Judea.

In 133 B.C.E. Tiberius Gracchus passed an agrarian reform law in Rome, by which the land was distributed to the landless. Tiberius was killed by his opponents at the instigation of the Senate.

After Syria suffered defeats from wars with its neighbors in 123 B.C.E., Yohanan felt free to go to war against his enemies. Judea was surrounded on three sides by the Idumeans to the south, the Samaritans to the north and the Greeks to the east, across the Jordan.

Hiring mercenaries, Yohanan conquered several cities across the Jordan to the east. Turning north against the Samaritans, he conquered their capital, Shechem. He then turned south, toward the Idumeans. After conquering their major cities, Yohanan gave them a choice: expulsion or conversion to Judaism. They chose conversion.

Pontus was a mountainous country in Asia Minor that was rich in timber and minerals. Mithridates VI, who was eleven years old, became the heir to the throne upon his father's death. His guardians plotted to assassinate him. Learning of the plot, he fled to the forest, where he survived. When he was old and strong enough, he and his loyal friends deposed his mother and took the throne in 115 B.C.E. When the Romans invaded his country, he defended it successfully. He conquered Armenia and all the Greek cities.

Germanic tribes descended upon Rome in 113 B.C.E. The Roman general Marius fought against them.

Cleopatra of Egypt had two Jewish generals who were brothers, Chilkiah and Ananias, who were sons of Onias IV. Cleopatra did not get along with her son, Ptolemy Lathyrus. Upon his expulsion from Egypt in 108 B.C.E., he fled to Cyprus.

In approximately 108 B.C.E., a new Jewish movement known as the Essenes emerged. A group split away from them and became known as the Perushim, or Pharisees. Still another party was formed who were known as the Zedukim, or Sadducees.

Yohanan Hyrcanus died in 106 B.C.E. at the age of sixty. He left five sons: Aristobulus, Antigonus, Alexander, Absalom, and one other. Before his death, he appointed his wife as queen and regent. He also appointed Aristobulus (Judas) as high priest.

Aristobulus removed his mother as queen and assumed the title of king, keeping the title of high priest. He imprisoned his three brothers and his mother, who died in prison. In 105 B.C.E., he died of illness. His brother Antigonus was assassinated.

Jonathan, who was also called Alexander or Yannai, succeeded Aristobulus as king. He married Salome, the sister of Shimon ben Shetach. Salome changed her name to Alexandra.

Shimon ben Shetach, who was a Pharisee, had an influence on his brother-in-law King Yannai, who favored the Pharisees during the first years of his reign.

100–50 B.C.E.

Julius Caesar was born in 100 B.C.E.

Alexander Yannai (reigned 105–79 B.C.E.), who conducted many wars against the enemies of Judea, employed mercenaries as soldiers. He wanted to take possession of Acco, which had declared its independence. When the city's rulers asked the Egyptian king, Ptolemy Lathyrus, for help, he sent thirty thousand soldiers, who defeated the Judean army on Shabbat.

As we will remember, Cleopatra, the mother of Ptolemy Lathyrus, was at war with her son. She sent an army under the command of two Judean generals, Hilkiah and Ananias, both sons of Onias. When Hilkiah died in battle, his brother took command.

Cleopatra formed a defensive alliance with Alexander Yannai in 98 B.C.E.

At first, Yannai was friendly towards the Pharisees, but changed his attitude toward them in 96 B.C.E. On one occasion, when he officiated in the Temple as high priest on the festival of Sukkot, he poured the ritual water libation in front of his feet instead of upon the altar. The people were so outraged that they threw their etrogs (citrons) at him and denounced him as unworthy of the priestly office.

In response, Yannai's mercenaries fell upon the people, killing six thousand men in the Temple. Six years of bloody riots followed, from 94 to 89 B.C.E. Fifty thousand men perished during this period, including eight hundred Pharisees who were killed in a single day.

In 88 B.C.E., Pontus, a small country in Asia Minor, was invaded by a neighboring country with the help of the Romans. The army of Mithridates defeated the Romans and the other invaders.

When Cinna was chosen as consul in 86 B.C.E., he changed Rome from a republic into a dictatorship.

The Romans invaded Pontus again, this time successfully, under General Sulla in 83 B.C.E. That same year, Sulla became the dictator of Rome.

Valerius Flaccus contended with Sulla for the leadership. Fimbria killed Flaccus, and when Sulla was about to defeat him, Fimbria committed suicide in 81 B.C.E. Sulla resigned his position and retired the following year.

Alexandra became queen of Judea in 79 B.C.E. after her husband died. She reigned for nine years and appointed her oldest son Hyrcan as high priest.

Shimon ben Shetach, the brother of Alexandra, had great influence on the queen. She released all the Pharisees who had been imprisoned by her husband Yannai. Shimon ben Shetach later became joint president of the Sanhedrin together with Yehuda ben Tabbai, who was recalled from Egypt, where he had fled.

Corruption was rampant in Rome during the years 77–60 B.C.E. There was hardly a single politician who was honest.

In 75 B.C.E. the Romans attempted once more to conquer Pontus under the leadership of Lucullus and Pompey. Although Mithridates fought hard, he lost and fled to Crimea.

Rome took slaves from the countries that it conquered. In 73 B.C.E., several hundred slaves revolted under the leadership of Spartacus, a Thracian general. Soon thousands more joined in the revolt.

Rome appointed Crassus to lead an army against Spartacus. The forces under Pompey joined Crassus, and in 71 B.C.E., Spartacus was killed in battle.

Marcus Licinus Crassus became the wealthiest man in Rome through corrupt practices. Because of his wealth he became governor of Syria, which put him also in charge of Judea. He was assassinated in 53 B.C.E.

Queen Alexandra of Judea died in 69 B.C.E. When her two sons, Hyrcan and Aristobulus, fought over the crown, civil war broke out. Before her death, Queen Alexandra turned the crown over to the older brother, Hyrcan II, but his brother Aristobulus II challenged her decision and went to war against Hyrcan, defeating him. A compromise was reached whereby Hyrcan would become high priest and Aristobulus king. Aristobulus succeeded to the throne in 69 B.C.E.

Antipater was governor of Idumea under Alexander and Alexandra. Hyrcan II cultivated Antipater's friendship.

Hyrcan II, who wished to regain the crown, invited Aretas, king of the Nabateans, to help him against his brother Aristobulus. Aretas marched on Judea with an army of fifty thousand and defeated Aristobulus.

Aretas and Hyrcan laid siege to Jerusalem. The siege, which lasted for many months, caused a famine. Eventually there were no more animals for sacrifices.

Passover was approaching and the besiegers agreed to sell lambs, which were offered as sacrifices for the holiday and later eaten. The inhabitants of the city lowered baskets filled with money from the wall and drew up lambs in return. One time when they lowered the basket with money, Hyrcan's partisans placed a pig in the basket.

A holy man in Judea named Onias (probably Honi ha-Maagel) was known for his successful prayers for rain. Soldiers from Hyrcan's camp asked him to curse Aristobulus and his camp. When Onias refused, they murdered him.

Julius Caesar was appointed as commander in Spain and was later chosen as Quaestor.

In 67 B.C.E. the assembly granted Pompey limitless authority to act against the pirates. Pompey proceeded and within three months had captured the pirate ships.

In 66 B.C.E., Pompey was authorized to take command of the armies in Asia in order to conquer Cappadocia, Syria and Judea. He sent Scaurus to Judea as his representative. Both Hyrcan and Aristobulus sent expensive gifts to appease him. Since Aristobulus's gift was larger, the Romans sided with Aristobulus and ordered Aretas to lift the siege on Jerusalem. Aretas obeyed and withdrew.

Hyrcan II and Aristobulus continued to fight for the crown, but Antipater manipulated the situation and bribed Pompey on Hyrcan's behalf. Pompey ordered both brothers to appear before him. Although each presented his case, Pompey sided with Hyrcan and Aristobulus surrendered. However, the patriots withdrew into the Temple Mount.

Pompey marched on Jerusalem in 63 B.C.E. He besieged Jerusalem and attacked the Temple deliberately on Shabbat. When he breached the wall, his troops slaughtered twelve thousand Jews. Pompey's attack ended Judean independence. Hyrcanus was made high priest.

Pompey entered the Holy of Holies in order to find out whether it contained the image of a god. Since Antiochus had spread rumors that the Jews worshipped a donkey or other animal, Pompey was surprised to find no such images. He did not touch the Temple treasury, which was substantial.

In 62 B.C.E., Pompey returned to Rome from his campaigns in triumph. He had cleansed the Mediterranean of pirates, conquered Syria, and meddled in the affairs of Judea. Although he was given a triumph, the Senate refused his requests and rejected the agreements he had made with the countries in the East.

In 60 B.C.E., Julius Caesar wanted to become a consul. In order to accomplish this, he needed the support of Pompey and Crassus. He formed a triumvirate with them and was elected consul in 59 B.C.E. The other elected consul was Bibulus.

Julius Caesar gave his daughter Julia as a wife to Pompey to strengthen his alliance with him in the triumvirate.

In 59 B.C.E., Cicero, a well-known orator but also an anti-Semite, represented the Roman Praetor Flaccus, who had stolen the money sent by the Jews to Jerusalem. During the trial he made terrible accusations against the Jews. For reasons that had nothing to do with his hatred of the Jews, Cicero was banished from Rome one year later and his house razed to the ground.

In approximately 57 B.C.E. Alexander II, the oldest son of Aristobulus, escaped Roman captivity. He formed an army of ten thousand infantry and fifteen hundred cavalry and marched on Jerusalem. Hyrcan and Antipater fled the city.

Aulus Gabinius, who was the governor of Syria at the time, was one of the cruelest governors and strongly anti-Judean. He banished Alexander II to Rome once again and divided the land of Judea into five districts, each with its own capital and separate administrations. Five district capitals were created: Jerusalem, Gazara, Emmaus, Jericho, and the Galilee, which had Sepphoris as its capital.

Soon after the partition, Gabinius ended his term as governor of Syria, but the separation of Judea from the rest of the land did not last.

Julius became governor of northern Italy and southern France in 58 B.C.E. He declared war against the German and Swiss tribes, fought against them and won. He also fought various tribes in Gaul, where he was governor.

Upon the deaths of Shimon ben Shetach and Yehuda ben Tabbai, Shemaya and Avtalyon became presidents of the Sanhedrin. Their term lasted for twenty-five years.

Aristobulus and his son Antigonus escaped from Rome and arrived in Judea. They formed an army with Pitholaus as its general. The Romans defeated them in 56 B.C.E. and banished him to Rome a second time.

Alexander, Aristobulus' son, was released by Pompey and returned to Judea. He subsequently formed an army and fought the Romans, and was defeated at Mount Tabor in 55 B.C.E.

In 55 B.C.E., Julius invaded Britain.

Julius, Pompey and Crassus formed a triumvirate in 54 BCE. They divided the empire into three districts. Crassus received Syria, of which Judea was a part.

Crassus marched against the Parthians in 54 B.C.E. On his way, he detoured to Jerusalem in order to rob the Temple of the treasure that Pompey had left intact. The treasurer, Eleazar, tried to bribe him with a golden bar weighing about four hundred pounds. Crassus swore that once he received the golden bar he would not touch the Temple treasury, but broke his oath, taking the treasure, the golden bar and the golden Temple vessels.

In 53 B.C.E. Crassus sailed to Syria with a large army in order to fight the Parthians. He was defeated and slain, and his son was also killed in the battle.

Attempting to take advantage of Crassus's defeat, the Judeans went to war with a large army. They were defeated, and thirty thousand Judean soldiers were sold as slaves in 52 B.C.E.

When the Parthians, governed they permitted the Jews to practice their religion.

In 52 B.C.E., a battle took place in the city of Alesia, in present-day France. The enemy leader, Vercingetorix, surrendered and was taken in chains to Rome. This, the last battle that the Romans fought on the European continent, made lasting changes in the future map of Europe.

That same year, the Roman Senate empowered Pompey to become sole consul.

50–0 B.C.E.

Julius Caesar had many enemies, especially in the Senate. In 50 B.C.E., the senate declared him a public enemy. There was a fierce struggle between Julius Caesar and Pompey for supremacy.

Julius freed Aristobulus and gave him two Roman legions to support him in the struggle against Pompey in Judea and Syria. Pompey's men poisoned Aristobulus in 49 B.C.E. His friends preserved his body in honey and later took it to Jerusalem.

Pompey ordered Aristobulus's son, Alexander, beheaded in 49 B.C.E.

Antipater, who supported Pompey, sent Judean troops into battle alongside the Roman troops. When he realized that Julius was gaining the upper hand, he switched sides, providing him with provisions and with three thousand Judean troops. Upon his victory, Julius rewarded him with full Roman citizenship and exemption from taxes.

Julius acknowledged Hyrcan as high priest as a favor to Antipater and made him Ethnarch in 47 B.C.E.

Julius Caesar also gave some relief to Judea, granting permission to restore the walls of Jerusalem and exempting Judea from paying the burdensome taxes of the war.

The Senate confirmed a public declaration in favor of the Judeans that stated: "The Judeans are friends and allies of Rome, and Hyrcan is recognized as the Ethnarch and high priest of Judea."

In 49 B.C.E., the Senate voted to give Pompey dictatorial powers.

The rivalry between Pompey and Julius continued. Each had legions at his command. In 49 B.C.E., Julius led one legion across the River Rubicon without the consent of the Senate. This was the beginning of his challenge to the Senate and eventually led to his becoming dictator of Rome.

Pompey, who was in Rome as Julius's forces advanced on the city, fled. Julius entered the city unarmed, leaving his troops in nearby towns. In 49 B.C.E., Julius Caesar was declared dictator of Rome. The Jews supported him.

The decisive battle between Pompey and Julius took place at Pharsalia in 48 B.C.E. Although Julius had half as many troops as Pompey did, Julius defeated him. Pompey fled to Egypt, where he was assassinated by Ponthius, an advisor to King Ptolemy XII of Egypt.

Antipater, who was procurator of Judea in 47 B.C.E., appointed his oldest son, Phasael, as governor of Jerusalem and his second son, Herod, who was twenty-five years old, as governor of Galilee.

Julius also confirmed the Jews of Alexandria as citizens of Rome. They were not to be summoned to court on the Sabbath, and he bestowed other privileges upon them.

In 47 B.C.E., there were plots in Egypt against Julius, but he survived them. Julius had an affair with Queen Cleopatra of Egypt. She gave birth to a son, Caesarion, whom he acknowledged as his.

From the remnant of Aristobulus's army a man named Hezekiah organized a band of armed men to fight the Roman occupiers. Herod undertook to go after Hezekiah and his men. He captured them and had them beheaded.

The patriots who were followers of Hezekiah were angry with Herod. They complained to Hyrcan, and in spite of his close friendship with Herod's family, Hyrcan granted the Sanhedrin permission to summon Herod. In the year 46 B.C.E., Herod came to the court with armed men. At first, the judges were intimidated, but Shemaya encouraged the judges to treat him the same way as everyone else. Hyrcan postponed the trial and Herod fled to Damascus.

In 46 B.C.E., Julius returned from Egypt to Rome, where revolt was brewing. His enemies – Metellus, Scipio, Cato and Labienus – organized against him. King Juba I of Numidia joined them. Julius won, and Juba I and Cato committed suicide. Scipio fled.

In 45 B.C.E. Julius left for Spain to face the remnants of the Pompeian army, which he defeated. That same year, he devised a new calendar consisting of 365 days, which was not the case prior to this time. The Romans named one month after him, and the Senate declared him dictator for life in 45 B.C.E.

On the Ides of March (March 15), 44 B.C.E., Julius was assassinated as he entered the Senate, which was meeting in the Pompey theatre. Among his attackers was Brutus, whom he had supposed his friend.

Julius Caesar's funeral took place later that month. Mark Antony delivered the eulogy. The crowd built a fire upon which veterans cast their weapons and members of the crowd threw their personal valuables. Many Jews of Rome stayed at the site of the funeral for three days in order to pray.

After the assassination, the republicans came into power. Cassius Longinus, a republican, arrived in Syria and demanded a large sum of money for his legions. When the Judeans were slow to deliver the amount that he demanded, he sold the inhabitants of four cities into slavery.

Hyrcan finally realized that he could not trust Herod and his family, who were looking out for their own interests and worked against the interests of the Judeans.

Marcus Antonius, who had been a friend of Julius Caesar, convened the Senate after the assassination. He secured Caesar's will, private papers and funds. Although Julius had named his adopted son Caius Octavian, a grandson of his sister Julia, as his heir, Marcus Antonius wished to succeed Julius himself. The Senate was not inclined to do so. The Senators had not liked Julius because he chipped away at their authority, and Marcus Antonius intended to adopt the same policies. Julius had expanded the Senate to nine hundred members, many of whom were not even Romans.

When Antony assumed power, the Senate became alarmed. They invited Caius Octavian to come to Rome in 44 BCE, when he was eighteen years old. Caius Octavian was frail and sickly, and suffered from indigestion. The Senate named him consul, and a quarrel broke out between him and Marcus Antonius. Octavian joined the two legions under him with those of Hirtius and Pansa. They marched against Marcus Antonius, who was defeated and fled.

The Senate had granted amnesty to all the conspirators who assassinated Julius. Octavian – who later took the title Augustus, and whom the Jews eventually supported – compelled the Senate to repeal the amnesty. Many of conspirators were then condemned to death.

In Judea, Hyrcan had a confidant by the name of Malich, who found out that Antipater was planning to dethrone Hyrcan and place Herod on the throne. At a banquet given by Hyrcan in 43 B.C.E., he placed poison in Antipater's plate, killing him. He in turn was killed in 43 B.C.E. by Roman troops at Herod's command. Wishing to gain Herod's friendship, Hyrcan gave his granddaughter Mariamne to him as a wife.

When Octavian discovered that he had many enemies in the Senate, he formed a triumvirate with Marcus Antonius and Lepidus. Their combined legions marched into Rome and the senators fled.

The triumvirate condemned three hundred senators and two thousand patricians to death. The orator Cicero was beheaded and his right hand severed. In 43 B.C.E., Crassus was killed. When the news reached Jerusalem, the Jews tried to reclaim the country, but the new governor, Longinus, suppressed the revolt and sold thirty thousand Jews into slavery.

In 43 B.C.E., the Parthians defeated the Romans and they put Antigonus, son of Aristobulus, on the throne of Judea. However, the Romans were not out of the picture. Marcus Antonius and Octavian countered by placing Herod on the throne.

In 42 B.C.E., Marcus Antonius and Octavian led their legions across the Adriatic to fight the remnants of the republican army under Brutus and Cassius, who needed funds to finance the war. Cassius ordered many cities to give him the funds on pain of death. In Judea, Cassius demanded a large sum of money and sold the inhabitants of four towns into slavery.

In 42 B.C.E., the opposing armies fought at Philippi, and Marcus Antonius and Octavian won. Cassius and Brutus committed suicide. The Triumvirate divided the Empire between them. Lepidus was given Africa, Octavian took the West and Marcus Antonius took Greece, Egypt, and the East. He went to live in Egypt.

Marcus Antonius was not very friendly towards Hyrcan and the Judeans. He appointed Herod and his brother Phasael as governors of Judea, giving them the title of Tetrarch.

While Marcus Antonius was in Egypt, he fell deeply in love with Cleopatra. He gave her, as gifts, the areas of Phoenicia, Syria, Judea and Cyprus.

Parthia, a region in Persia ruled by Prince Pacorus, made an incursion into Syria. In 40 B.C.E. the Parthians marched on Jerusalem in alliance with Antigonus, the son of Aristobulus II. They aimed to dethrone Hyrcan and place Antigonus on the throne.

The Parthians imprisoned Hyrcan and mutilated his ears in order to disqualify him from priestly service. Herod's brother Phasael committed suicide, but Herod fled to Egypt, where Cleopatra offered him a generalship in her army. He declined and sailed to Rome.

Antigonus ascended the throne in 40 B.C.E. and reigned for three years only, to 37 B.C.E.

In 40 B.C.E., Marcus Antonius's wife, Fulvia, and brother sent an army against Octavian in order to overthrow him. Marcus Antonius crossed the sea with an army, but a peace was arranged between them.

Traveling to Rome after he escaped, Herod succeeded in convincing Marcus Antonius and Octavian that Antigonus was Rome's enemy and that he, Herod, should be put on the throne of Judea. He was also able to convince the Roman senate to recognize him as king of Judea. The Senate also declared Antigonus as the enemy of Rome in 40 B.C.E.

In 37 B.C.E., Herod laid siege to Jerusalem with the aid of the Roman legions. Unable to resist this overwhelming force, Jerusalem fell.

Herod drove out the Parthians in 37 B.C.E. and slew all the Jewish leaders who supported Antigonus. He then sent Antigonus as a captive to Marcus Antonius, with a request that Antonius have him beheaded. The request was granted.

One of the first things Herod did when he became king was to kill all the members of the Sanhedrin except for Shemaya and Avtalyon. He also killed the most prominent men of Jerusalem and confiscated their property.

Herod appointed Hananel as High-Priest in 37 B.C.E.

When Shemaya and Avtalyon died, Herod appointed the Benei Beteira to the presidency of the Sanhedrin. Octavian gave Herod all the cities that had been part of Judea during the Hasmonean period.

Herod surrounded himself with Greek scholars and named a Greek man, Nicolas of Damascus, his counselor. He built monuments to Augustus, beautified Jerusalem, built himself a magnificent palace and enlarged the Temple.

Hyrcan, who was being held captive in Parthia, was freed in 36 B.C.E. Herod invited him to come to Judea. In 35 B.C.E., Herod appointed Aristobulus III, who was seventeen years old, as high priest. Since he was worried that Aristobulus III might claim the throne for himself; he invited him to his palace in Jericho, where he ordered his servants to drown him. The grandson of Aristobulus II, he was the last Hasmonean high priest.

Alexandra, the mother of Aristobulus, denounced Herod to Cleopatra, who in turn denounced Herod to Antonius. She disliked him in any case, and now had a good excuse to make him look bad. In 34 B.C.E., Antonius summoned Herod before him to explain his actions. Herod brought precious gifts to Antonius and succeeded in appeasing him. Antonius merely took Jericho and added it to his domain, then gave it to Cleopatra as a gift.

In 32 B.C.E. Antony divorced his wife Octavia and married Cleopatra. That same year, Octavian declared war against Cleopatra.

War broke out between Octavian, who ruled the western Roman Empire, and Antonius, who ruled the eastern empire. In 31 B.C.E., Octavian crossed the Adriatic Sea with four hundred ships, and a battle ensued at Actium in the gulf of Ambracian. Marcus Agrippa was the general who conducted the engagement for Augustus. Antonius and Cleopatra were defeated, and Antonius committed suicide.

When Cleopatra realized that Antonius had been defeated, she followed him in death. The Jews of Alexandria sided with Octavian, since Cleopatra had expressed a wish to kill all the Judeans of Alexandria with her own hands.

Herod, who had sided with Antonius, now had to explain himself to Octavian. He had to travel to Rhodes in 30 B.C.E. to meet with Octavian and explain himself. During that meeting, he pledged his loyalty to Octavian.

Hillel, who traced his descent on his maternal side to King David, was appointed President of the Sanhedrin in 30 B.C.E. Originally from Babylonia, he was a disciple of Shemaya and Avtalyon. His brother Shebna, who was wealthy, provided him with partial support.

Herod appointed Menahem, an Essene who had predicted that Herod would become king, vice-president of the Sanhedrin. However, he did not hold the position for long because he was uncomfortable in it, and withdrew to the solitude of his order. He was succeeded by Shammai.

Herod's wife, Mariamne, was one of the most beautiful women in Judea. He was very jealous of her, and many people plotted against her, including Herod's sister Salome. Mariamne was executed in 29 B.C.E. on a trumped-up charge of infidelity.

Herod accused the eighty-year-old Hyrcan of conspiring against him. He was found guilty by Herod's court and executed. Alexandra, Mariamne's mother, was executed in 28 B.C.E., as were the judges who condemned Mariamne. Alexandra was accused of plotting against Herod.

The Roman poet Virgil (b. 70 B.C.E.) was introduced to Augustus by a wealthy Roman businessman. Horace, another Roman poet, and Livy, a historian who was active for forty years, also lived during the era of Augustus.

After Augustus had dealt with his adversaries, he undertook great public works and forgave property taxes. The Senate conferred upon him the title Augustus. He treated his client kings with courtesy and invited their children to come to Rome in order to receive a Roman education at his palaces. One of his loyal friends was Marcus Agrippa, who became his son-in-law. Augustus was worshipped as a god, and his name was included in the Roman pantheon. He banned the exercise of Egyptian and Asiatic religions, but made an exception for Jews.

In 21 B.C.E., Herod built a harbor city on the Mediterranean, naming it Caesarea in honor of the Roman emperor. It took nine years to build and began to rival Jerusalem in importance.

Herod appointed Joshua as high priest, then removed him and appointed Shimon, of the house of Boethus, who was the father of a woman he wanted to marry. Her name was also Mariamne.

In the year 20 B.C.E., Herod ordered the people to take an oath of fealty to him.

Herod spent large sums of money on urban beautification in Syria and in other foreign countries in order to please the Roman emperor. Augustus expressed satisfaction, declaring, "Herod was worthy of the crowns of Syria and Egypt."

In the year 19 B.C.E., Herod ordered construction to begin on the Temple.

Augustus Octavian was favorably inclined towards the Jews. In 15 B.C.E., he issued a decree that the Jews of the Roman Empire were not to be molested or summoned to the courts on the Sabbath, and that their donations to the Temple not be seized. These orders were to be engraved on bronze tablets.

Herod had two sons by Mariamne, Alexander and Aristobulus. Alexander married Glaphyra, daughter of Archelaus, king of Cappadocia, and Aristobulus married Berenice, Salome's daughter.

Before his marriage to Mariamne, Herod had been married to a woman named Doris. Their son was Antipater who, together with Herod's sister Salome and Herod's brother Pherora, conspired against Mariamne's children and accused them of plotting against Herod.

Alexander and Aristobulus, Herod's children by Mariamne, were taken before Herod's court of one hundred and fifty judges and condemned to death. The order was executed hastily in 7 B.C.E. on Herod's orders.

It was later revealed that Antipater had been the true conspirator against Herod. In 4 B.C.E., a court sentenced him to death. Herod asked Augustus to confirm the verdict. Antipater was briefly kept in jail and then put to death on Herod's orders.

In 15 B.C.E., Marcus Agrippa, the son-in-law of Augustus and a close friend of Herod, visited Jerusalem.

Shimon ben Boethus, whom Herod had appointed high priest, was removed. Matisyahu, son of Theophilus, was appointed high priest in 4 B.C.E. He too was removed, and Herod appointed Yoezer ben Shimon as high priest.

1–50 C.E.

Herod died in the year 4 B.C.E., four days after he had his son Antipater executed. He was seventy-nine years old, and reigned thirty-three years.

Herod was survived by six sons and several daughters borne to him by his ten wives. He divided the country among three of his sons. To Archelaus he gave Judea and Samaria, to Herod Antipas he gave Galilee and Peraea, and to Philip he gave several districts east of the Jordan. Herod's will was subject to Augustus's approval – and although Augustus approved it, he did not bestow the title of king on Archelaus. Instead, he gave him the title of Ethnarch.

Archelaus addressed the people of Jerusalem, promising to be a good ruler. But the people demanded action. On Pesah, a large crowd came to Jerusalem and demanded immediate relief. When Archelaus ordered his troops to disperse the people, they fell upon the throngs. Three thousand people died that day.

Archelaus removed Yoezer from the high priesthood in 4 B.C.E. and appointed his brother Eleazar. He did not last long, and was replaced with Joshua as high priest in 5 C.E.

Yoshua was also removed in 5 C.E. and Yoezer was reappointed as High Priest.

When Archelaus married Glaphyra, the widow of his executed brother Alexander, the people were outraged.

In 6 C.E., during Archelaus's reign, a delegation of Jewish leaders went to Rome to petition Augustus to abolish the kingdom. Augustus removed Archelaus and made Judea a Roman province. He appointed a procurator over Judea, who was responsible to the Syrian governor.

Augustus banished Archelaus to Gaul. In all, Archelaus had reigned as Ethnarch from 4 B.C.E. to 6 C.E.

Octavian's daughter, Julia, had affairs with many men. Her father banished her to an island in 2 B.C.E. on account of her indiscretions. In 2 B.C.E. Augustus recalled Tiberius, the son of his wife Livia, to Rome, adopted him as a son and made him co-regent.

As a consequence to the unrest in Judea, Varus, the governor of Syria, entered Judea with twenty thousand troops. He defeated the rebels and sold thirty thousand Jews into slavery.

After Archelaus was removed, Judea became subjugated completely to Rome. Rome appointed a procurator who ruled Judea from Caesarea, where he resided.

The Procurator's job was to maintain order in the land and to collect taxes. He also had the authority to impose capital punishment, overrule the Sanhedrin and appoint the High Priest. The Romans kept the high priestly vestments locked, releasing them only for the Jewish festivals.

Coponius was the first procurator in 6 C.E. and Quirinius was the Syrian pro-consul. Coponius directed the daily affairs of Judea, removing Yoezer as high priest and appointing Anan from the family of Seth in his stead.

Hillel's successor as head of the Sanhedrin was his son Shimon I.

Augustus's reign as Emperor of Rome lasted from 31 B.C.E. to his death in 14 C.E. He was succeeded by Tiberius, who reigned for twenty-three years, until 37 C.E. He appointed as procurator Valerius Gratus, who administered Judea for eleven years, from 15 to 26 C.E.

Sejanus, who was Tiberius's chief minister in Rome, persuaded Tiberius to exile the Jews from Rome in 19 C.E.

In Judea, the procurator Gratus interfered in the internal affairs of the country. During his administration, he removed five high priests. Only one high priest, Joseph Caiphas, served for a long time, from 19 to 36 C.E.

Germanicus, a nephew of Tiberius, was transferred to the East to be commander of the troops in 19 C.E. He died that same year.

The Emperor Tiberius was strongly influenced by his mother, Livia, and communicated through Sejanus, his chief minister. Sejanus, who disliked the Jews, constantly influenced Tiberius against them.

In 26 C.E., when Tiberius realized that Sejanus had misled him, he allowed the Jews to return to Rome.

In 31 C.E., when Tiberius informed Sejanus that Caius Caligula would succeed him, Sejanus plotted to assassinate Tiberius. When Tiberius received warning of the plot, he took precautions, replacing the commander of the guards. Sejanus was accused in the Senate and condemned to death.

Herod Antipas, Herod's son, who was the Tetrarch of Galilee, moved his capital from Sepphoris to a new site that he constructed at the Sea of Galilee which he named Tiberias, in honor of his king. He took up his residence there in 24 C.E.

Antipas's brother Philip, who served as Tetrarch for the districts east of the Jordan, reigned for thirty-seven years, from 4 B.C.E. to 33 C.E.

Pontius Pilate, who succeeded Gratus as procurator in 26 C.E., administered Judea from 26 to 36 C.E.

When Tiberias was assassinated by strangling in 37 C.E., Caius Caligula succeeded him on the throne.

Agrippas I (c. 10 B.C.E.–44 C.E.) was the son of Aristobulus and Berenice and a grandson of Herod and Mariamne. He developed a friendship first with Drusus, the son of Tiberius, and also with Caligula before he became emperor. After Caligula became emperor, he showed favor to Agrippas I and conferred upon him the title of king.

Caligula gave Agrippas the principality of Philippi, making him a praetor in 37 C.E. In 39, Caligula also gave Agrippas the area of Galilee. In 41, Claudius, who was then emperor, gave him Samaria and Judea. Thus, from 41 to 44, Agrippas was king over the entire land of Israel.

In 38 C.E., King Agrippas appeared in Jerusalem.

Caligula was a ruthless dictator who, among other terrible deeds, committed incest with his sisters. He was assassinated in 41 C.E., at the age of twenty-nine, by an officer of the guard.

Flaccus, a proconsul of Egypt in the time of Caligula's reign, was very anti-Jewish. The Greeks of Alexandria also envied and hated the Jews. Flaccus took Roman citizenship from the Jews of Egypt. In 38 C.E., encouraged by Flaccus, a mob attacked the Jews of Alexandria. Driven from their homes, the Jews crowded into the Delta quarter of Alexandria. Although Flaccus was later recalled in order to account to Caligula and put to death, the damage had been done.

Apion, an arch enemy of the Judeans, published a letter in approximately 38 C.E. that was full of slander and incitement against the Jews.

Caligula declared himself a god, ordering that his statue be displayed in the Temple in Jerusalem. In 40 C.E., he ordered that the Temple in Jerusalem be dedicated to the worship of Caligula. Petronius, the pro-consul of Syria, received an order in 40 C.E. to proceed with his legions to Jerusalem to enforce the order.

The people of Judea revolted. Petronius marched on Jerusalem with two legions, but before he could carry out the order, Caligula was assassinated by the praetorian tribune Chaerea. Caligula's decree was annulled.

Claudius succeeded Caligula as emperor in 41 C.E. King Agrippas had a hand in Claudius's accession by mediating with the reluctant Senators.

Claudius made Agrippas king over all of Judea, Samaria, Galilee and Peraea in 41 C.E. Herod II was given the rank of praetor and he was made king of Chalcis in the Lebanon region.

Agrippas appointed Simon the Just as high priest. Rabban Gamliel, the grandson of R. Hillel, was the head of the Sanhedrin during Agrippas's reign.

In 41 C.E., the Greeks and Syrians attacked the Jews of Babylonia and Parthia. Thousands were killed.

In the Mishna (*Sotah* 7:8), it is stated that Agrippas stood while reading the Torah and that the rabbis praised him for it, because as king he was allowed to read while sitting. When he came to the sentence "You may not put a foreigner as king over you," tears streamed from his eyes because he was not from pure stock. Those present reassured him that he was their brother nevertheless. The Mishna also mentions (*Bikkurim* 3:4) that even King Agrippas carried his basket on his shoulder until he reached the Temple.

Berenice, the oldest daughter of Agrippas, married Herod II, Agrippas's brother. His second daughter, Mariamne, married Julius Archelaus, the son of Hilkiah. His youngest daughter married a non-Jew who had to undergo circumcision and embrace Judaism.

The philosopher Philo (10 B.C.E.–60 C.E.), a brother of Arabarch Alexander Lysimachus, was a contemporary of Agrippas and of Claudius.

In approximately 30 C.E., two Jewish youths in the community of Nehardea, Babylonia, established a Jewish state near Nehardea that existed for fifteen years. It was defeated by Mithridates, the son-in-law of the Parthian king.

Adiabene, a small state on the banks of the Tigris River, was ruled by King Monobaz and Queen Helene. Their son Izates and his wife Samash converted to Judaism, as so did Queen Helene. When Monobaz died, his son Izates became king in 22 C.E.

Queen Helene yearned to see Jerusalem. She and her son Izates, together with five of his sons, traveled there in 43 C.E.

That same year, Claudius sent his legions to invade Britain.

Agrippas died of a mysterious intestinal ailment in 44 C.E. at the age of fifty-four. He had reigned from 41 to 44 C.E., and prior to that he had been Tetrarch from 37 to

41 C.E. After his death, Judea was placed again under Roman procurators, the first of whom was Cuspius Fadus.

The procurators – Felix, Festus, and Albinus and others – were corrupt, making life intolerable with their plundering and high taxation.

By order of Claudius, Herod II – the grandson of Herod I and the son of Aristobulus – was given the power to appoint the high priest. At first, he removed the high priest Elionai and replaced him with Joseph, but soon afterwards replaced Joseph with Ananias ben Nebedai. Although the Sanhedrin had gained some power under Agrippas, it lost it again under the procurators.

When the procurator Fadus was recalled in 46 C.E., Tiberius Julius Alexander, a nephew of Philo the philosopher, was appointed procurator.

A great number of Jews settled in foreign countries. There were many Jews in Alexandria, Rome, Damascus, and the Parthian countries.

London was founded in 43 C.E.

50–100 C.E.

In 48 C.E., Claudius married Agrippina the Younger, who was already the mother of the future emperor, Nero, from her first marriage.

Cumanus was procurator from 48–52, succeeding Tiberius Alexander.

Felix was appointed procurator by Claudius in 53 C.E. at the request of Agrippa II and Agrippina the Younger. He succeeded Cumanus, but was even worse for Judea. His term lasted until 59 C.E. Felix and Cumanus were bitter enemies.

In 48 C.E., there was a great famine in Judea. Queen Helene, the mother of King Izates of Adiabene, brought shiploads of grain from Egypt to feed the starving population of Jerusalem.

In an ongoing dispute between the Samaritans and Judea, Claudius decided in favor of Judea.

Agrippas II (27–92), was only seventeen years old when his father died, spent his youth in Rome in the courts of the emperor. He ascended the throne of an area called Chalcis in the Lebanon region in 49 C.E., when his uncle Herod II died. Claudius gave him the title of king of Judea, but without any powers except the authority to appoint the high priest. He took up residence in Jerusalem in approximately 59 C.E.

Agrippina murdered Claudius by feeding him poisoned mushrooms. Her son Nero became emperor in 54 C.E. at the age of seventeen. His reign lasted until 68 CE.

When Izates, king of Adiabene, died in 55 C.E., his brother Monobaz II, who was also a convert to Judaism, succeeded him. The bodies of both Queen Helene and King Izates were sent to Jerusalem for burial.

Monobaz, who had a palace in Jerusalem, he presented the Temple with a set of golden vessels to be used during the Yom Kippur service.

Seneca the philosopher, who was Nero's teacher, ran the government for Nero. Parthia signed a peace treaty with Rome that lasted fifty years.

Felix was recalled in 59 C.E.

Festus succeeded Felix as procurator in 59 C.E., serving until 61 C.E.

Poppaea Sabina, the Emperor Nero's mistress, was very influential. Nero wanted to divorce his wife Octavia, the daughter of his predecessor, the Emperor Claudius, in order to marry her. When Agrippina the Younger, his mother, opposed the match, Nero had her murdered.

In 62 C.E., Nero divorced Octavia and married Poppaea. Octavia was later murdered on Nero's orders at the age of twenty-two.

Poppaea Sabina was friendly towards the Jews. In 63, she asked Nero to free two Judeans who had been sent to Rome as criminals. They were so observant that they ate only fruit while in prison.

Albinus succeeded Festus as procurator in 61 to 64 C.E.

Anan, a Sadducee who was the high priest at this time, had serious disagreements with R. Yohanan ben Zakkai. He was removed from his position by Albinus the procurator. Yoshua ben Domnai became the high priest in 61 and served until 63 C.E.

Yoshua ben Gamliel was appointed high priest in 63 and served until 65 C.E. He married Martha, a wealthy widow, although according to the Torah, a high priest may not marry a widow. However, he made many improvements to the education system, establishing schools for boys from the age of five in every city.

Jews lived in Rome as far back as 140 B.C.E., and more Jews were brought to Rome by Pompey as war captives during the war of 63 B.C.E. There were many synagogues in Rome, and some Jews served in the Assemblies.

Florus was appointed procurator in 64 and served until 66 C.E. He was one of the worst.

Eleazar ben Ananias, a descendant of the high-priestly family, was the leader of the revolutionary party, also called the Zealots. A follower of the school of Shammai, he was a scholar himself.

The peace party consisted of those following the school of Hillel. Agrippas II also urged the people to obey the Romans.

Gessius Florus was appointed procurator from 64 to 66 C.E. In approximately 64 C.E., Cestius Gallus was prefect for the Romans and he was stationed in Syria.

Nero declared himself a god and had a temple built for his worship. In July 64 C.E., a fire broke out in Rome and spread quickly, destroying most of the city. Nero raised funds and ordered the city be rebuilt.

Poppaea, Nero's wife, died in 64 C.E. After her death, Nero neglected Judea.

Yoshua Ben Gamliel was removed and Matityahu ben Theophilus was appointed high priest in 65 C.E.

Shimon ben Gamliel, a member of the Zealot party, fought the Roman occupation with fervor. In approximately 66 C.E., he also became the head of the Sanhedrin.

Nero's spies informed him that Seneca and other senators were conspiring to depose him. Nero ordered Seneca and the senators put to death.

Cestius Gallus, the prefect of Syria, marched on Jerusalem at the head of the Roman armies in 66 C.E. The zealots confronted and defeated them.

The Romans were under the command of Castius and Florus. Joseph Matthias, better known as Flavius Josephus, was commander of the Judean troops. Many of the Judeans opposed him because they considered him a traitor.

There was bad blood in Caesarea between the Greek and Jewish population. Things came to a head in 66 C.E.

In Jerusalem, the procurator Florus demanded a great sum of money from the Temple treasury. His soldiers plundered and murdered three thousand men, women and children, and humiliated the Judean leaders. Florus and his soldiers proceeded to march on the Temple as the people threw stones at them.

The Jewish people were divided. Rabbi Yohanan ben Zakkai, who was highly respected and influential, belonged to the peace party, as did Agrippa II. Opposing them were the zealots. In 66 C.E., there was a meeting in the house of Eleazar ben Hizkiya. The Shammaites, who were in the majority, enacted eighteen enactments.

Eleazar ben Yair was commander of Masada.

In 66 C.E., Nero traveled to Greece to compete in the Olympic Games. When, in the middle of his tour, he was informed that a revolt had broken out in Judea, he appointed Flavius Vespasian to deal with the insurrection. Vespasian took command in 67.

The Zealots party removed the high priest, Matisyahu ben Theophilus, because they suspected him of favoring surrender to Vespasian, and appointed Pinhas ben Shemuel in his place.

Agrippa II put his troops at the disposal of Vespasian, who had fifty thousand troops and fought fiercely.

The leaders of the revolution were Shimon ben Giora and Yohanan ben Levi. Josephus was commander of the troops near Jerusalem and Galilee. The Sanhedrin appointed Yoezer and Yudah to help Josephus.

In 67 C.E. Josephus surrendered to Vespasian, who treated him well.

Gaul declared its independence from Rome in 68 C.E.

Galba, the Roman commander, was in Spain with his troops when he decided to revolt and march on Rome.

Eventually, the Senate declared Nero a public enemy. Although Nero managed to escape from Rome, he committed suicide on June 9, 68 C.E.

Although Galba became ruler in 68 C.E., his reign did not last long. He was deposed by Senator Marcus Otho and assassinated on June 17, 69. Two rival emperors were then proclaimed: Otho in Rome and Vitellius in Germany. The two fought each other while Vespasian was in Judea, ready to attack Jerusalem, but waiting.

Vespasian saw an opportunity to become emperor. His son, Titus, was campaigning for him among the powerful generals in the provinces. In 69 the legions in Egypt swore allegiance to Vespasian, followed by the legions in Judea and Syria.

Vitellius invaded Italy in 68 C.E. When Otho killed himself after 95 days in office, Vitellius became emperor.

A list of the Roman emperors whose reigns were brief:

Galba: June 68–January 69

Otho: January–April 69

Vitellius: January–December 69

Vespasian, who was in Judea besieging Jerusalem, sent General Antonius to Italy to challenge Vitellius, who was defeated and killed in 69 C.E. Vespasian became emperor, reigning until 79 C.E.

In 68 C.E., during the civil war in Jerusalem between the moderates and the zealots, the Idumeans sided with the zealots, whose leader was John Gischala (Yohanan mi-Gush Halav).

As the inhabitants of Jerusalem waited for Vespasian to attack in 67–69 C.E., there was civil war in the city. The storehouses of food were burned to the ground, and the zealots gained the upper hand.

In 70, Titus returned to Jerusalem, determined to conquer the city. He had the aid of three prominent leaders: Tiberius Alexander from Egypt, King Agrippa, and Josephus.

Titus began the siege of Jerusalem around Pesah of 70 C.E. He conquered Jerusalem and returned to Rome in triumph.

Machaerus, a fortress east of the Jordan, held out for a while under the leadership of Eleazar. It was stormed by the Romans under General Bassus.

Herodium, a fortress south of Jerusalem, surrendered without resistance.

Masada, a mountain fortress near the Dead Sea, held out under the leadership of Eleazar ben Yair. In 73 C.E., on the first day of Passover, its inhabitants took their own lives rather than surrender to the Romans.

The Temple was destroyed for the second time on the ninth of Av, 70 C.E.

Titus committed many atrocities. He enslaved thousands of people and murdered many more.

When Titus's triumph over Jerusalem was celebrated in Rome, John of Gischala and Shimon bar Giora, together with seven hundred of the finest youth, were dragged in chains through the streets of Rome.

Titus captured and sold seventy thousand Jews into slavery. According to Josephus, 1,200,000 Jews were killed during the siege in 70 C.E., during which there were about seven million Jews in the Roman Empire.

Titus also brought with him Berenice, the Jewish princess, whom he made his mistress. It was said that he wanted to marry her, but his father Vespasian opposed it.

Vespasian sent General Agricola to Britain in 70 C.E.

He ordered the half-shekel, which the Jews normally contributed to the Temple, to be given to rebuild Rome, which had been burned down during Nero's reign.

Vespasian rewarded the Jewish traitors, including Josephus, with honors and wealth. Agrippas was given additional territory. Tiberius Alexander received a high rank among the Roman nobles, and Josephus was also rewarded for his treachery.

Vespasian ordered the Temple in Egypt, which had been in existence for 243 years, closed in 73 C.E. The sacred vessels were transferred to Rome.

Vespasian imposed a special tax on all the Jews of the Roman Empire. Agrippas II remained king of the Galilee as a puppet and subject of Rome.

In approximately 73 C.E., the wealthiest man in Jerusalem was Kalba Savua. His daughter Rachel married his shepherd, Akiva, who subsequently became a great scholar and Jewish leader.

Josephus wrote a book of his experiences and the wars the Judeans fought against Rome. When he submitted his book to the emperors, Titus gave him permission to publish it sometime between 75–79 C.E.

Justus of Tiberias, one of the leaders of the Zealots, also wrote a history of the wars a few years before Josephus.

There was hatred for Jews in many places of the Roman Empire. In Alexandria lived a fiery anti-Semite by the name of Apion who wrote scurrilous attacks against the Jews in 75 C.E. Josephus answered Apion in a pamphlet, which he distributed. Josephus rejoiced when he learned that Apion had to be circumcised for health reasons.

Josephus accompanied Titus to Rome. Vespasian gave Josephus Roman citizenship and showed him favor.

Vespasian died in 79 C.E. at the age of sixty-nine, while visiting Reate.

Titus became emperor of Rome in 79 C.E. and reigned until 81.

In 79 C.E. a fire broke out in Rome that lasted three days and destroyed many of Rome's buildings. In that same year, Mount Vesuvius erupted, burying Pompeii, together with its inhabitants, in rock and ash.

Gamliel de-Yavne, the son of R. Shimon ben Gamliel, became the head of the Sanhedrin.

Titus died in 81 C.E. of a fever. That same year, the Arch of Titus was erected in Rome.

Domitian, the brother of Titus and the younger son of Vespasian, became emperor in 81. He was assassinated in 96 C.E.

Domitian ordered Agricola to withdraw from Britain.

In 86 C.E., Domitian declared himself a god and ordered his subjects to worship his godhead. The Jews refused.

Josephus completed his work of twenty books in 93 C.E. A history of the Jewish people, he gave it the title *Antiquities*. It was written during the reign of Emperor Domitian and his empress, Domitia.

Josephus also wrote an essay entitled "Reply to the Greeks," in which he extols the religious and moral superiority of the Jewish people and accuses the Greeks of slandering them.

The tannaim of this period, 93–117, were Rabbi Gamliel de-Yavne, Rabbi Yehoshua ben Hananya, Rabbi Eliezer ben Hyrcanus and R. Eleazar ben Azaryah.

R. Yehoshua established an academy in Bekiin and R. Eliezer ben Hyrcanus established a school in Lydda.

R. Akiva also lived during this time – 50–135.

In 94 C.E., Domitian banished the Jews from Rome to the valley of Egeria.

Rabbi Akiva and Rabbi Gamliel traveled to Rome in 95 C.E., together with Rabbi Yehoshua and Rabbi Eleazar ben Azaryah, to make an appeal to Emperor Domitian. However, while they were in Rome, Domitian was assassinated. He was forty-five years old and had reigned for fifteen years, from 81 to 96 C.E.

Domitian was succeeded by Nerva, who granted their request. Nerva reigned from 96 until 98 C.E.

In 96 C.E., Nerva annulled the banishment of the Jews and allowed them back into Rome with full civil rights. Nerva was sixty-six years old when he became emperor of Rome. He also abolished the tax which Vespasian imposed on the Jews.

Ulpius Trajan, a Spaniard by birth, became emperor in 98 and reigned until 116 C.E. Trajan was in Cologne, Germany when he was informed that he had become emperor, and waited for several years before returning to Rome. He returned in 102 C.E. after conquering Dacia (Romania). He was forty years old.

100–150 C.E.

In 105, Trajan had to return to Dacia in order to put down a rebelion. He did so with a great deal of gold and silver from the Transylvanian mines.

Trajan conquered Armenia, and Parthia and Mesopotamia. After his return to Rome, revolts broke out in Parthia, Mesopotamia, Judea and Egypt. In 114 C.E., Trajan sent Marcius Turba to suppress the Jews in Africa and sent his nephew Hadrian to Syria.

Although Nisibis had a large Jewish population which resisted the Romans, the city fell to them in 114 C.E.

Mebarsapes, King of Adiabene, whose ancestors converted to Judaism and whose king was Jewish, fought against Trajan's forces, but was overwhelmed in 114 C.E.

Pappus and Julian, who were also called Shemaya and Shimon, were the leaders of an uprising in Alexandria (which was only one of the many uprisings that took place in all the territories of the Roman occupation). It lasted from 114 until 117 and beyond. As the Jews of Cyrenaica and in many countries in the Euphrates region fought against the Romans, Trajan sent Lucius Quietus, a Moorish prince and a cruel general, to suppress the revolt in 115.

In 116, the great synagogue of Alexandria was destroyed. That same year, the Jews of Cyprus were annihilated by the Roman general Marius Turbo. That same year, Lucius Quietus suppressed a revolt in Babylonia, killing thousands of Babylonian Jews. He subsequently became Prefect of Judea.

Although Trajan wanted Quietus to succeed him, his wife Plotina told the army that Trajan had adopted Aelius Hadrian as his son and heir. Consequently Hadrian became emperor in 117, and his reign lasted until 138.

Hadrian traveled to Gaul in 121 and fought against the Moors in Africa in 123.

Lucius Quietus was very harsh with the Jews of Judea. When he was about to condemn the two Jewish leaders; Julian and Pappus, to death, Hadrian removed him from office, saving their lives.

Although Hadrian had granted permission to rebuild the Temple, the Christians agitated against it.

Hadrian changed his mind and avoided fulfilling his promise by declaring that the Jews could build the Temple anywhere but in Jerusalem. The Jews became very angry and gathered in the valley of Jezrael to demonstrate. Fearing the worst, the Jewish leaders asked Rabbi Yehoshua, a revered leader, to calm the people. He was able to convince the people to go home in peace. Hadrian thought everything was under control in Judea because on the surface everything was quiet; he was not aware that trouble was brewing. Although the people came out to greet him when he visited Judea, they secretly prepared for war, building tunnels, acquiring arms and practicing warfare.

When Hadrian traveled to Judea in 130 and found Jerusalem in ruins, he ordered that it be rebuilt as a Roman city, giving it the name Aelia Capitolina. That same year, Hadrian declared his intention to build a shrine to himself on the Temple site.

Wishing to extinguish all forms of Jewish religious life; he appointed Tinnius Rufus as procurator and imposed severe restrictions on all Jewish observances. He forbade the Jews to practice circumcision and study the Torah.

When R. Yehoshua died in around 125, R. Akiva became the religious leader of the Jewish people.

There was an earthquake in approximately 126, which destroyed Caesarea and Emmaus.

In 132, Bar Kochva led a revolution against the Romans with between 400,000 and 580,000 armed men. They fought successfully, defeating the Romans in many battles. Tinnius Rufus, the governor of Judea under Hadrian, lost fifty strongholds.

Hadrian ordered the revolt put down without mercy. When Tinnius Rufus asked Rome for help, Hadrian sent reinforcements from Phoenicia, Egypt and Arabia. He also sent his ablest generals, Publius Marcellus and Lollius Urbicius.

The Romans destroyed 985 towns, and after three years, the revolt faltered. Hadrian sent his greatest general, Julius Severus, who besieged Betar for an entire year. Bethar fell in 135.

In 135, Hadrian was struck with a painful illness. Suspecting a conspiracy to assassinate him by poison, he ordered several of his friends executed. He bestowed the title of Caesar on Antonius.

R. Eleazar of Modiin was killed during the Bar Kochva revolt.

The revolt ended in 135 with the total defeat of Judea. Five hundred eighty thousand men died in the revolt, in addition to thousands of women and children who died of starvation and more who were sold as slaves. Hadrian became even more cruel, forbidding the observance of the Sabbath and Jewish holidays. The Sanhedrin was dissolved in 135. Rabbi Akiva, who supported the revolt and disobeyed the edict against teaching Torah, was imprisoned for three years and then executed.

Hadrian removed the Jewish population from Jerusalem, replacing it with Syrians and Phoenicians. He rebuilt Jerusalem in approximately 136, but north of its former location. He erected statues of himself and of Jupiter and called the city Aelia Capitolina.

When R. Yehuda ben Bava wished to ordain his students in approximately 136, there was a decree against it that was enforced by Tinnius Rufus, who was procurator of Judea at that time. R. Yehuda took his students to a place between Usha and Shefaram and ordained them. Afterwards, he was seized and killed by the Romans.

When Hadrian died in 138, Antonius Pius became emperor. He reigned from 138 until 161, when he was succeeded by his adopted sons Marcus Aurelius and Lucius Aurelius Verus.

After Hadrian's death, R. Yehuda ben Shammua petitioned Rufus the procurator to ask the new emperor, Antonius, to revoke the edicts against religious observances. Although the edicts were revoked in 139, the Jews were not permitted to enter Jerusalem.

In 139, the students of R. Akiva assembled at Usha to reinstitute the Sanhedrin. Among those assembled were R. Meir, R. Yehuda b. Illai, R. Yosi b. Halafta and R. Shimon b. Yochai. They elected R. Gamliel de-Yavne as president. R. Nathan became vice president and R. Meir became Hacham.

R. Meir's real name was Miasa or Moise. His wife, Beruriah, was the daughter of R. Hanania b. Teradyon.

Rabbi Yosi ben Halafta wrote a historical book entitled *Seder Olam,* which begins with the Creation and ends with the Bar Kochva revolt.

R. Shimon bar Yochai had his academy in Tekoa in the Galilee.

There was an attempt to establish a Sanhedrin in Babylonia in the town of Nehar-Pakod. R. Hanania, the nephew of R. Yehoshua, tried to organize it. When R. Shimon b.Gamliel sent a delegation to discourage him, it was disbanded.

150–200 C.E.

In 161, the last year of Antonius's reign, the Jews revolted against Rome once more, this time with help from the Parthians.

Marcus Aurelius and Lucius Aurelius Verus became co-emperors in 161. In retaliation for the revolt, Verus renewed the Hadrian edicts, in particular prohibiting circumcision, observance of the Sabbath and the use of the ritual bath for women.

In 162, Britain revolted against Rome. That same year, the Parthian king Vologaeses declared war against Rome. Marcus Aurelius sent Lucius Verus to fight Vologaeses, but he failed. Marcus Aurelius sent another general, Avidius Cassius, with a battle plan. He drove Vologaeses back.

In 166, a mysterious plague ravaged the entire region. Although it began in Asia, it spread quickly as the Roman legions took it with them to Egypt, Greece, Gaul, Italy and Rome.

German tribes invaded many of Rome's colonies in 167. Marcus Aurelius went to war against them and drove them back.

When Verus died in 169, R. Shimon ben Yohai and R. Eleazar ben Yosi traveled to Rome to petition Marcus Aurelius to rescind the edicts. Marcus Aurelius granted R. Shimon ben Yochai's request.

In 169, Marcus Aurelius had to fight new invasions by the Moors and the German tribes. Although he was at war on all fronts, he was victorious. While he was at war, Avidius Cassius declared himself emperor. A centurion killed him.

In 175, Marcus Aurelius visited the city of Caesarea in Judea. Upon his return to Rome in 176, he was awarded a triumph. In 178, he set out with his son Commodus on a campaign to defeat the German tribes, but fell ill.

In 180, the Romans were defeated in Scotland and retired to Hadrian's Wall.

That same year, Marcus Aurelius died of the plague that swept Europe at that time.

In 178, before his death, he made his son Commodus his successor. Commodus was fifteen years old.

In 193, Commodus was assassinated and Julianus became emperor. Julianus was assassinated the same year and Septimus succeeded him.

Septimus was emperor from 193–211. His wife, Julia Domna, was the daughter of a wealthy Syrian priest. Julia gave birth to two sons, Carracalla and Geta. Septimus conquered Byzantium and invaded Parthia and Mesopotamia.

In 193–194 there was civil war between Septimus Severus and Pescennius Niger, both of whom were fighting to become emperor of Rome. The Jews sided with Severus, while the Samaritans sided with Pescennius Niger. Severus was victorious and rewarded the Jews for their loyalty, restoring many of the privileges that they had enjoyed before.

Rabbi Shimon ben Gamliel died during the reign of Marcus Aurelius in approximately 175. His son, Rabbi Yehuda, succeeded him.

Rabbi Yehuda ha-Nasi was born c. 136. He died in c. 205–210.

200–250 C.E.

The Sanhedrin of R. Yehuda ha-Nasi, which was located first in Beit Shearim, later moved to Sepphoris. R. Yehuda was able to command complete authority on all religious matters in Israel. He appointed all officials and judges.

During Rabbi Yehuda ha-Nasi's time, in approximately 200, King Vologaeses of the Parthians asked the Judaeans to join him in a revolt against Rome. The revolt failed, and in 201 they were defeated by Severus. The Jewish people were divided. Some sided with the Romans, including Rabbi Eleazar ben Shimon ben Yohai and Rabbi Yishmael ben Yosi.

Rabbi Yehoshua ben Korha was also an opponent of Rome.

Vologaeses IV died in 209, survived by two sons, Vologaeses V and Artabanus IV. The two brothers fought for the throne. Artabanus won, and then fought against the Romans and defeated the Romans at Nisibis.

When R. Yehuda ha-Nasi passed away in approximately 210, his son, R. Gamliel III, succeeded him.

Emperor Septimus fought in Scotland and in Britain. He died in 211 in York, Britain. He left his empire to his two sons, Carracalla and Geta.

Carracalla ordered the assassination of his brother Geta in 212, and made his mother Julia Domna run the internal affairs of the empire.

In 217, while on a campaign against Parthia, Carracalla was killed by his own soldiers. Marcinus, the perfect of the guards, claimed the crown for himself. Julia Domna was banished to Antioch, where she died.

Artabanus, king of Parthia, reigned from 216–226.

Rav opened his academy in Sura in approximately 219.

The Parthian kings gave the Jews full freedom in Babylonia. King Artabanus was a friend of Rav's.

R. Shemuel lived in approximately 180–257. In addition of being a great scholar in Jewish law he was also familiar in the sciences of medicine and astronomy. He had a close relationship with Ablaat, a non-Jewish Persian astronomer.

Elagabalus became Emperor of Rome in 219 after Carracalla was murdered. The son of Soamia, of Syrian descent, he was only sixteen years old. The Syrian legions proclaimed him Emperor. He was favorably inclined towards Jews.

Before, he had been a high priest in a Syrian cult. The Romans assassinated Elagabalus in 222. He was succeeded by his cousin, Marcus Aurelius Alexander Severus, a boy of fourteen.

Alexander Severus was friendly towards Jews and often quoted the Bible. He had the following quotation engraved on the walls of his palace: "What you do not wish a man to do to you, don't do to him." Alexander Severus chose sixteen senators as his close advisors. He gave an estate to Rabbi Yehuda ha-Nasi II as a gift. The estate was located east of the Jordan River. He also restored all the rights to the Jewish people.

R. Yehuda Hanasi II became Patriarch in 225.

Artaxerxes, a descendant of the ancient Persian kings, fought a battle against Artabanus in 226 and defeated him. He founded the Sassanid dynasty and called himself King of Kings. He restored the Zoroastrian religion and the worship of fire.

The Jews in Persia did not fare well under Artaxerxes. On the Persian holidays when Persians worshipped fire, the Jews were not permitted to light fires in their homes. Jews were not permitted to bury their dead in the ground or bathe in spring water because the Persians considered earth and water sacred.

Ardashir of Persia invaded Mesopotamia in 230. Alexander Severus warned him to withdraw and then went to war against him. Ardashir withdrew.

Some of the provinces in Europe wanted to become independent of Rome. Although Alexander Severus went to war against them, his soldiers disliked him. They assassinated both him and his mother in 235.

Maximinus was emperor of Rome from 235 to 238. He was assassinated by his troops.

He was succeeded by Gordian I, Gordian II, Balbinus, Pupienus and Gordian III.

R. Yehuda ha-Nasi II was a grandson of R. Yehuda I. He lived during difficult times, during which the Roman government was unstable and the emperors were assassinated one after another. Because economic conditions in Israel were extremely difficult, R. Yehuda had to send messengers to the Jewish communities abroad to ask for financial support.

R. Yehoshua ben Levi, an eminent amora, traveled to Rome to ask for contributions from wealthy Jews abroad. They responded generously.

In Babylonia, which was the home of a great many Jews after the fall of Jerusalem, were many prominent Jewish centers. The Parthian kings allowed the Jews to conduct their own affairs. Between 240 and 300 they had well established communal organizations. The cities that stand out as Jewish centers were: Nehardea, Sura, Pumbedita, Mechuza and Mata Mechasya. The Jews made a living from agriculture, business, crafts, raising cattle and shipping.

The Exilarch (*Resh Galuta*) – the leader of the Jewish community – was appointed by the Persian king. In rank he was the fourth highest in the country. The Exilarch was also the Chief Judge for the Jewish people in Babylonia, and he appointed the other judges.

Rav also known as Abba Aricha lived around 175–247 CE, he returned to Babylonia from the academy of Rabbi Yehuda Hanasi. R. Shila was the head of the academy in Nehardea when Rav arrived there.

When Shapur ascended the throne of Persia in 241 CE a new age of tolerance began. Shapur reigned from 241 to 272. He was an intimate friend of Rabbi Shemuel

Gordian III was killed in 244 while fighting the Persians. Philip the Arabian was emperor of Rome from 244 to 249. Although Emperor Decius followed him in 249, he was assassinated in 251.

250–300 C.E.

Gallus became emperor in 251 and was assassinated in 253. He was succeeded by Valerian, who was sixty years old. He made his son Gallienus emperor of the West, keeping the East for himself.

Several countries invaded Italy and other Roman provinces in 257. The Allemani invaded Italy, but they were defeated by Gallienus.

Valerian attempted to recover the territories lost to King Shapur of Persia, but was captured by Shapur in 259 and held captive until his death ten years later, in 269.

Valerian's son Gallienus reigned from 260 to 268. He was co-emperor with his father, but when his father was captured he became sole emperor. Forced to relinquish Gaul in the west and Palmyra in the east, he was assassinated by his own troops in 268.

Emperor Claudius II reigned from 268–270.

In 260, Shapur I invaded Syria, Antioch and Cappadocia.

Odenath, a wealthy citizen of Palmyra, led a revolt against Shapur and made incursions into Syria and Palestine. He destroyed the city of Nehardea, killing the Jewish population of that city.

The amoraim from Nehardea fled to Mehoza and to other cities. The daughters of Rabbi Shemuel were taken captive and brought to Sepphoris, where they were held for ransom.

When Odenath was assassinated in 266, he was succeeded by his wife, Zenobia, who reigned from 267 to 273. She went to war and conquered Cappadocia, Egypt and Alexandria.

Aurelian became Roman emperor in 270. In 272, he attacked Zenobia, retaking Egypt and the Balkans. Zenobia was captured and brought in chains to Rome.

In 274, Aurelian recaptured Gaul, Spain and Britain. He reconquered most of the territories that had been lost during the reign of the previous emperors. He had Palmyra razed to the ground and the city of Tadmor buried in sand.

Aurelian was assassinated in 275.

In approximately 270, R. Gamliel IV, son of R. Yehuda ha-Nasi II, was the patriarch.

Rabbi Yohanan and Rabbi Shimon ben Lakish were the leading rabbis in approximately 270. They attracted many students from Babylonia to their academy in Tiberias. Rabbi Yohanan's most prominent students were R. Eleazar b. Pedat, R. Ammi and R. Assi, R. Shimon b. Abba and R. Hiyya b. Abba.

Rabbi Huna was the head of the academy in Sura, Babylonia, having succeeded Rav. When Nehardea was destroyed, Rabbi Yehuda ben Yehezkel (c. 225–299) founded the academy in Pumbedita in northern Babylonia.

Jewish academic life was reorganized under Rabbi Huna. The academies were called *metivta* and the head of the academy was called *resh metivta*. The head teachers were called *resh kalla*. The judges were also rabbis who had been appointed by the Exilarch and were known as *dayyanim*. Rabbi Huna remained the director of the Sura academy in southern Babylonia for forty years. He died in 247 at the age of eighty.

Tacitus became emperor when Aurelian was assassinated. He died six months later, in 276.

Probus, who became emperor in 276, was assassinated in 282.

Diocletian became emperor in 284 after defeating Carinus. On the day Diocletian was crowned as emperor, Rabbi Ammi of Tiberias had a dream that his successor would be the last Roman emperor.

Diocletian's reign lasted until 305.

Rabbi Yehuda III, the son of Rabbi Gamliel, was patriarch during Diocletian's reign. R. Ammi and R. Assi were the directors of the academy in Tiberias, and R. Abbahu and R. Hiyya b. Abba also lived during this period.

During the latter part of the third century Carus, Carinus and Carausius ruled Rome for brief periods. Although their successor, Diocletian, was intolerant towards the Christians, he was fairly tolerant towards the Jews.

R. Yehuda Nasia III paid a great deal of attention to the communities of Judea. From his academy in Tiberias, he sent teachers on a circuit of the cities of Judea to examine the educational institutions. They found some communities without teachers for children or for adults.

Emperor Diocletian summoned R. Yehuda Nasia III to appear before him to answer complaints by his enemies that he had spoken contemptuously of the emperor. R. Yehuda's reply must have satisfied him because he treated the Jews kindly.

R. Abbahu of Caesarea, who was active during Diocletian's reign, was influential with the Roman authorities and spoke fluent Greek. A maker of women's veils by profession, he became a wealthy man. He was vociferous in his attacks against the Christian sects.

R. Hillel II was the son of R. Yehuda Nasia III. During Diocletian's reign, the patriarchate was elevated to a distinguished position. An imperial edict declared, "Whoever dares to offend the illustrious patriarch in public will be subject to a heavy penalty."

300–350 C.E.

Constantine became both Rome's sole emperor and its first Christian ruler when his father Constantius died in York in 306.

In 325, several hundred bishops led by Constantine attended the first meeting of the council of Christian churches in Nicea. Constantine renewed Hadrian's edict forbidding Jews to enter Jerusalem.

The seat of the Roman Empire moved to Constantinople in 331.

Rabbi Hillel II lived approximately from 310–362.

Rabbah bar Nahmeini (270–330) was the head of the academy in Pumbedita. His two outstanding students were Rava and Abbaye.

King Shapur II of Persia was friendly towards the Jews. His mother, Queen Ifra-Ormuzd, leaned towards Judaism. She sent a purse full of golden coins to R. Yoseph, who used it to ransom Jewish captives.

When Rabbah died, R. Yoseph (270–333) succeeded him as head of the academy in Pumbedita. He was a wealthy man and owned fields, palm trees and vineyards, but lost his eyesight and his memory in his later years. When R. Yoseph passed away, Abbaye succeeded him as head of the academy in Pumbedita.

A Persian army was quartered in Mehoza in approximately 334, and the Jews of Mehoza were forced to maintain them at their own expense.

Rava was the head of the academy in Mehoza. On one occasion, as president of the academy, he ordered a Jewish man flogged for having had illicit relations with a Persian woman. The man died of injuries sustained during the flogging. King Shapur sent his troops to arrest Rava, but he had escaped. The troops plundered his home. When the queen mother, Ifra, interceded on his behalf, he was spared punishment. Queen Ifra sent four hundred golden dinars to Rava, which he distributed among the Jewish and the non-Jewish poor.

During Constantius's reign, the two Roman generals who were active in Judea, Gallus and Ursicinus, did not respect the Jewish religion at all. They demanded that the Jews supply them with fresh bread on the Sabbath and with leavened bread on Passover. Constantius forbade the observance of Yom Kippur.

Constantius II did not permit the patriarch to declare a leap year, which would have postponed Passover by another month. The Greek Orthodox and the Christians of the east celebrated Easter according to the Jewish calendar, while Rome did not. Had they postponed Passover, the Christians of Rome would have been embarrassed to celebrate their Easter on a different day, and there was jealousy between the two Christian groups.

350–400 C.E.

Gallus, who ruled over Judea and all the eastern provinces from 351 to 354, held the title of Caesar. During this time there was a Jewish revolt led by Natrona. Gallus suppressed the revolt, killing thousands of Jews. Sepphoris was razed to the ground and Tiberias, Lydda and other cities suffered terrible destruction. Gallus was put to death by Constantius in 354.

Rava died in approximately 352.

Rabbi Ashi (352–427) the son of Simlai, was active in Sura for fifty-two years. He was a contemporary of two Exilarchs, Mar Kahana and Mar Zutra. Sura was again the outstanding academy, but the academies of Pumbedita and Nehardea were also active.

Yezdegerd I, the Sassanid king of Persia who ruled from 399 to 420, was friendly towards the Jews.

The Jewish plight did not diminish with the death of Gallus. In the court of Constantinople, where Emperor Constantius II lived, Jews were considered atheists. There was some relief during Julian's reign.

In approximately 355, Rabbi Hillel II established a perpetual fixed Jewish calendar.

Julian, who had been co-emperor with Constantius II, became sole emperor in 361 when Constantius II died. He was favorably disposed towards the Jews and admired their charitableness. Rabbi Hillel II had correspondence with him, and Julian addressed a letter to the Jewish community in which he informed them that he intended to rebuild the Temple at his own expense. Soon afterwards he appointed his best friend,

Alypius of Antioch as superintendent in charge of the project. The officials of Syria and Palestine were ordered to provide the materials and labor. A Christian soldier assassinated him in 363.

In 362, workers began to clear the rubbish that accumulated on the Temple site. During this operation, flames arose from subterranean passages due to the combustion of compressed air, and work was halted.

When Persia tried to win its independence from Rome in 363, Julian went to war against it with all the Roman forces. Shapur II had a large army at his disposal. The war took place in Babylonia, an area which was predominantly settled by Jews. Although Julian had initial successes, at length he was struck down by an arrow. The Jews thus lost the opportunity to rebuild the Temple.

Jovian succeeded Julian, but died in 364.

Once again, Rome had two emperors. In 364, the brothers Valentinian and Valens became emperors of the West and of the East, respectively.

The Roman Empire began gradually to unravel. After Julian died the Christian influence dominated both Rome and Constantinople, the two capitals of the Roman Empire, and the empire reverted to persecution of the Jews.

From 370 onward there were several Patriarchs: R. Hillel II, R. Yehuda IV, and R. Gamliel V.

Theodosius I became Roman emperor of the east in 379. In 388 he became sole emperor. He died in 395. His empire was divided between his two sons, Honorius and Arcadius.

During his reign, R. Gamliel V was the Patriarch.

In approximately 379, there were two notorious anti-Semites by the names of Ambrose of Milan and John Chrysostom, who thundered and agitated from their pulpits against Jews.

Theodosius issued an edict confirming the rights of the Patriarchs and ordered the secular authorities not to meddle in Jewish affairs.

Many Jews lived in the city of Antioch, and the Christians of that city were attracted to Judaism. Many Christians attended the synagogue on the Sabbath and on Jewish festivals.

In 395, Rome's two emperors were Honorius, who ruled the West, and Arcadius, who ruled the East. Arcadius, whose reign lasted until 408, ordered strong measures against attacks on synagogues. His two chamberlains were Rufinus and Eutropius, who were all-powerful and favorably disposed towards Jews. The royal court was now a Byzantine, arbitrary court.

Sura became the center of the Babylonian Jewry. The Exilarchs went there for special ceremonies and public assemblies.

On royal festivals, three representatives of the Babylonian Jews came to the court of King Yezdegerd I of Persia, who was favorably disposed toward the Jews. R. Ashi for Sura, Mar Zutra for Pumbedita and R. Amemar for Nehardea took their places among the other Persian noblemen.

In approximately 400, Rav Ashi began to write down the Babylonian Talmud as we know it today.

400–450 C.E.

The Visigoths invaded Italy in 401.

Alaric, the Gothic leader, sacked Rome in 410. The Roman legions withdrew from Britain in 410.

Gaiseric was king of the Vandals in 428–477.

Theodosius II (reigned 408–450) was dominated by monks in his court. He issued edicts forbidding Jews to build new synagogues or to possess Christian slaves, and forbade Jewish judges to preside when one party was Christian. In 415, Theodosius divested R. Gamliel of some of his titles, and in 425, when the last R. Gamliel died, he abolished the Patriarchate altogether. Theodosius was succeeded by Mercian.

In the fifth century C.E. the Vandals, a Teutonic tribe, established itself in Carthage, Africa (Will Durant, *The Age of Faith*, 41).

450–500 C.E.

In 455, the Vandals under their leader Gaiseric sacked Rome, carrying off the Empress Eudocia and her two daughters. They also carried off the golden tables, the seven-branched golden Menorah, and other sacred vessels of the Jerusalem Temple, which had been plundered by Titus four centuries before.

Attila became the ruler of the Huns in 433 and died in 453.

Zeno was the emperor of the eastern Roman empire from 474 to 491.

Yezdegerd II was not friendly towards the Jews and his son Firuz (reigned 474–484), was even worse. Firuz demanded that all Jews convert to his religion, and during his reign, Jewish children were abducted and forcefully converted. During the reign of King Firuz many prominent Jews were martyred, including Exilarch Huna Mari, Amemar bar Mar Yanka and Mesharshia bar Pakod. The persecutions stopped only upon King Firuz's death.

The academies opened again in 488 and R. Ravina headed the academy in Sura and R. Yosi in Pumbedita.

There were fifteen Patriarchs during a span of about 350 years. Starting with Hillel the Elder, there were two Hillels, three Shimons, four Yehudas and six Gamliels.

During the reigns of the co-emperors Theodosius II and Honorius, the Jews from Alexandria were expelled by the Bishop Cyril, who incited the Christian mob to plunder their homes and synagogues. He converted the synagogues into churches and drove the Jewish population out from the city half-naked. The Jews had lived in Alexandria for over a thousand years.

Orestes, the prefect of Alexandria, was powerless against the mob. When he lodged a complaint against Cyril to the emperor, the bishop incited the mob against Orestes and they almost stoned him to death.

In the city of Antioch, the Christians fell upon the Jews and took the synagogue by force and destroyed it. The prefect of the city complained to Theodosius. At first he ordered the city to restore the synagogue, but later changed his mind.

500–550 CE

Justin I was Byzantine Emperor from 500 to 527. He was followed by Justinian, who reigned from 527 to 565 and was very anti-Jewish.

Cavad was king of Persia from 488 to 531. During his reign a man named Mazdak preached a new religion called Zend. King Cavad became a follower of Mazdak and issued a decree that all inhabitants of the land must accept Zend as their religion. Under this religion there was no private property and no one could claim his wife as his own.

Henceforth there was neither private property nor exclusive relationships. The Jews organized a rebellion, which was led by Mar Zutra II, the Exilarch (whose term lasted from 496 to 520). He and four hundred armed men expelled the Zendists and declared independence from Persia. The Jews formed an independent Jewish state with Mehoza as its capital. After seven years, the new state was overthrown by the Persian army. Mar Zutra and his grandfather, Mar Hanina, were executed in 520.

Ravina was the director of the Sura academy from 488 to 499. R. Yosi was the director of the Pumbedita academy from 471 to 520.

SELECTED BIBLIOGRAPHY

The Babylonian Talmud. Vilna edition. Israel: 1988.

Blackman, Philip. *Mishnayot: Six Volumes of the Babylonian Talmud.* New York: The Judaica Press, Inc., 1964.

The Babylonian Talmud, bilingual edition. Translated into English by Dr. E.W Kirzner, Maurice Simon and Rabbi I. Epstein. Traditional Press, New York, and Soncino Press: London, 1938.

Babylonian Talmud. Artscroll Series, Schottenstein edition, Mesorah Publications. Brooklyn, NY, 1990.

Babylonian Talmud. Rabbi Adin Steinsaltz edition, Israel Institute for Talmudic Publications, Jerusalem: 1974.

Durant, Will. *The Story of Civilization.* Simon & Schuster. New York: 1954.

Graetz, H. *The History of the Jews.* Translated by Rabbi A.B. Rhine. Hebrew Publishing Company, USA: 1949.

Jastrow, Marcus, ed. Talmudic Dictionary. Pardes Publishing House. New York: 1903.

The Encyclopaedia Judaica, Jerusalem: Keter, 1982–1992.

Roth, Cecil, and Geoffrey Wigoder, eds. The New Standard Jewish Encyclopedia. Doubleday & Company. Garden City, NY: 1970.

ABOUT THE AUTHOR

MORDECHAI JUDOVITS is a long time student of the Talmud, a retired businessman and a Holocaust survivor. He is the grandson of Rabbi Moshe Paneth, the rabbi of Dej, and a great-grandson of Yechezkel Paneth, the author of *Sefer Mareh Yechezkel* and former chief Rabbi of Transylvania.

Mordechai Judovits attended the *yeshivot* headed by his cousins, first at the yeshiva of Rabbi Elisha Horowitz and later at the yeshiva of Rabbi Yaakov Meilach Paneth, who was also the chief rabbi of Dej.

The author, along with his parents, brothers and sister were carried away to Auschwitz in 1944. He was liberated in 1945 and in 1947 he immigrated to the USA, where he married and raised a family. He and his wife Helen have two sons, one daughter, seven grandchildren and one great-grandchild. Since retiring he has devoted his time to studying and writing, and has been active in many Jewish organizations, in particular the Boca Raton Synagogue.